by
NAOKI URASAWA
STORY by
HOKUSEI KATSUSHIKA, NAOKI URASAWA

MASTER KEATON

9

by
NAOKI URASAWA
STORY by
HOKUSEI KATSUSHIKA, NAOKI URASAWA

MASTER KEATON

CONTENTS

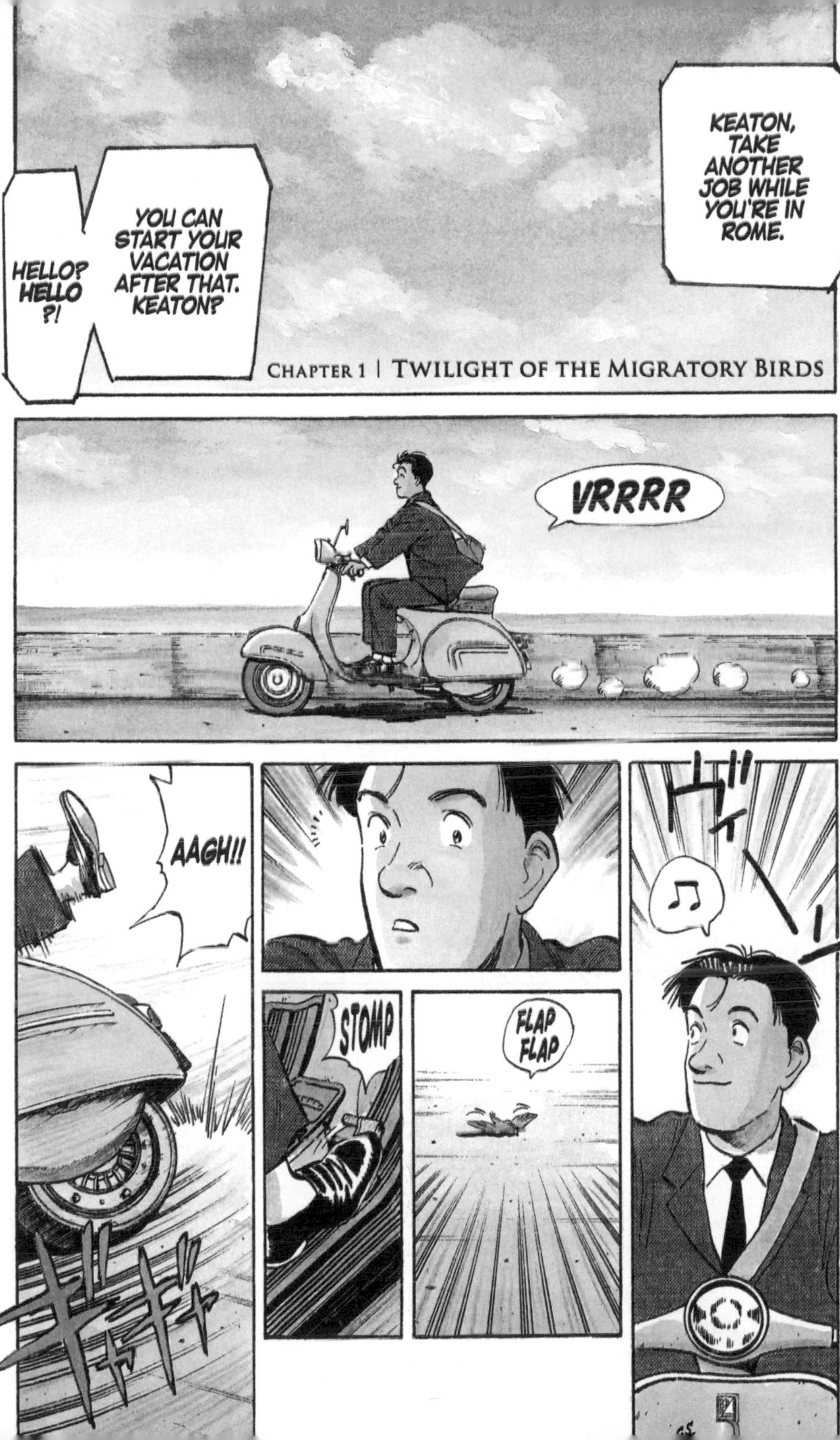
KEATON, TAKE ANOTHER JOB WHILE YOU'RE IN ROME.
YOU CAN START YOUR VACATION AFTER THAT. KEATON?
HELLO? HELLO ?!
Chapter 1 | Twilight of the Migratory Birds
VRRRR
♫
AAGH!!
STOMP
FLAP FLAP

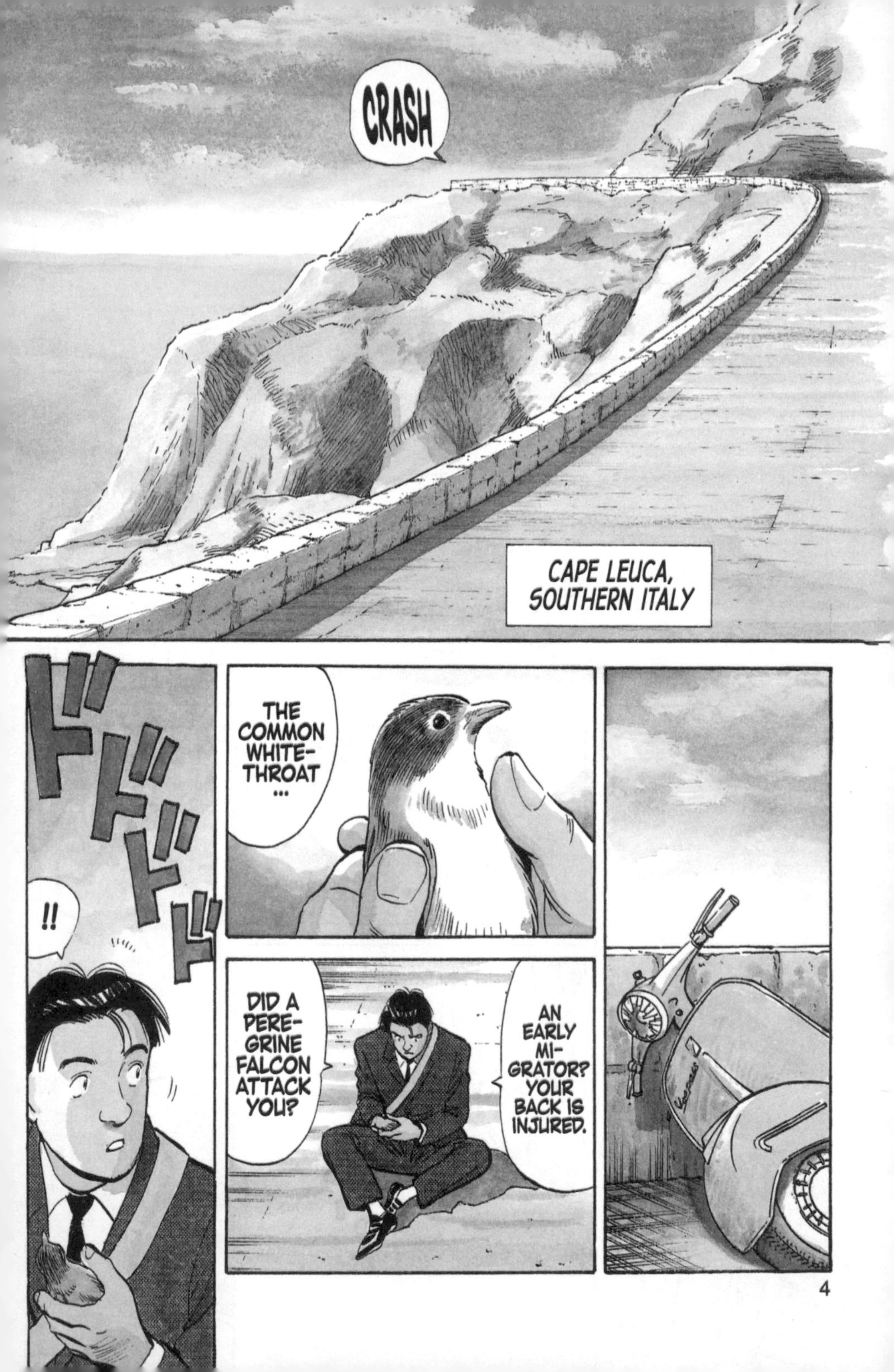
CRASH
CAPE LEUCA, SOUTHERN ITALY
THE COMMON WHITE-THROAT ...
AN EARLY MI-GRATOR? YOUR BACK IS INJURED.
DID A PERE-GRINE FALCON ATTACK YOU?
ドドドドド
!!

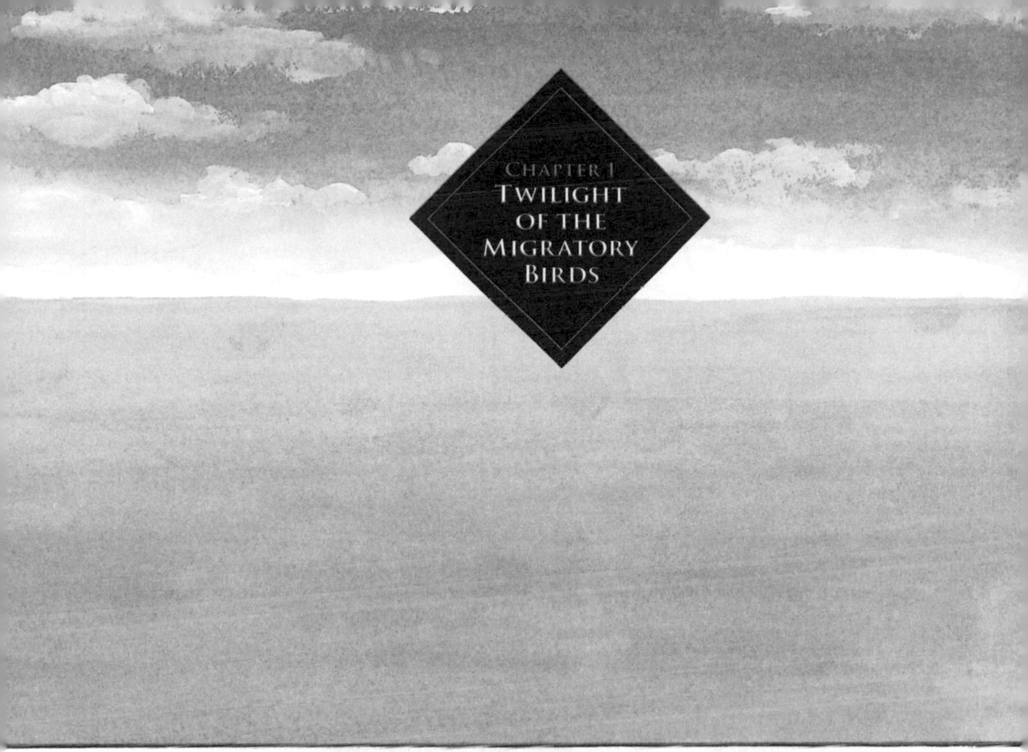

Chapter 1
Twilight of the Migratory Birds

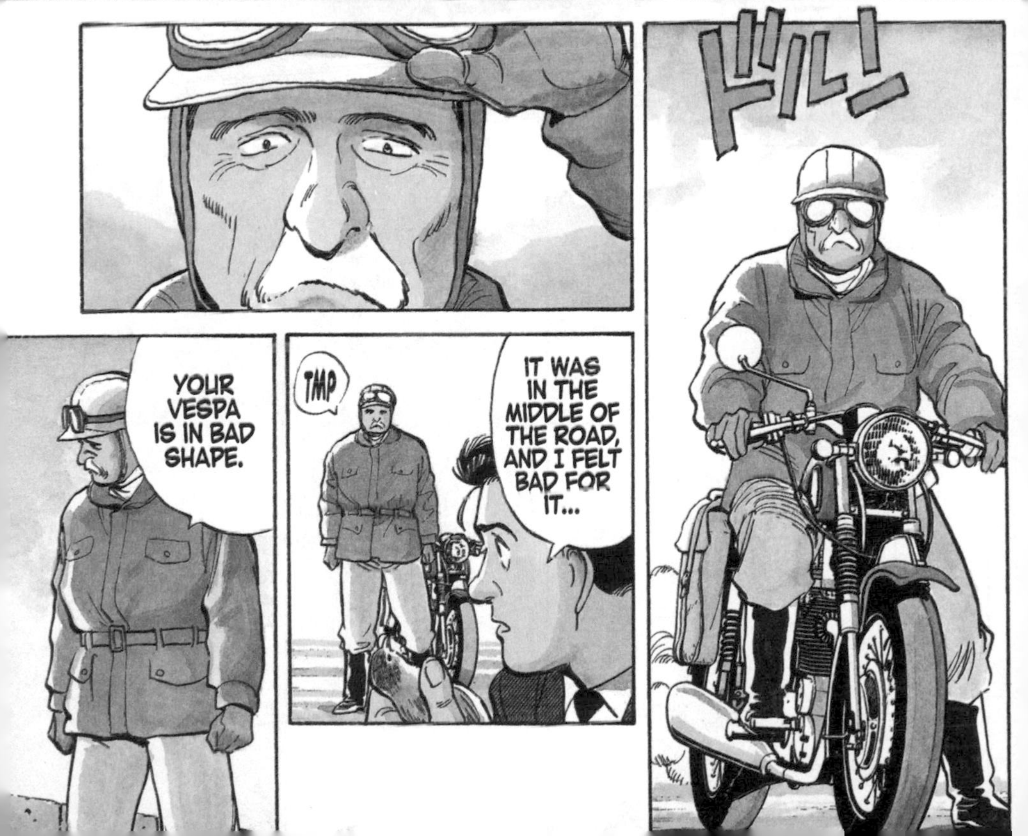
TMP
IT WAS IN THE MIDDLE OF THE ROAD, AND I FELT BAD FOR IT...
YOUR VESPA IS IN BAD SHAPE.

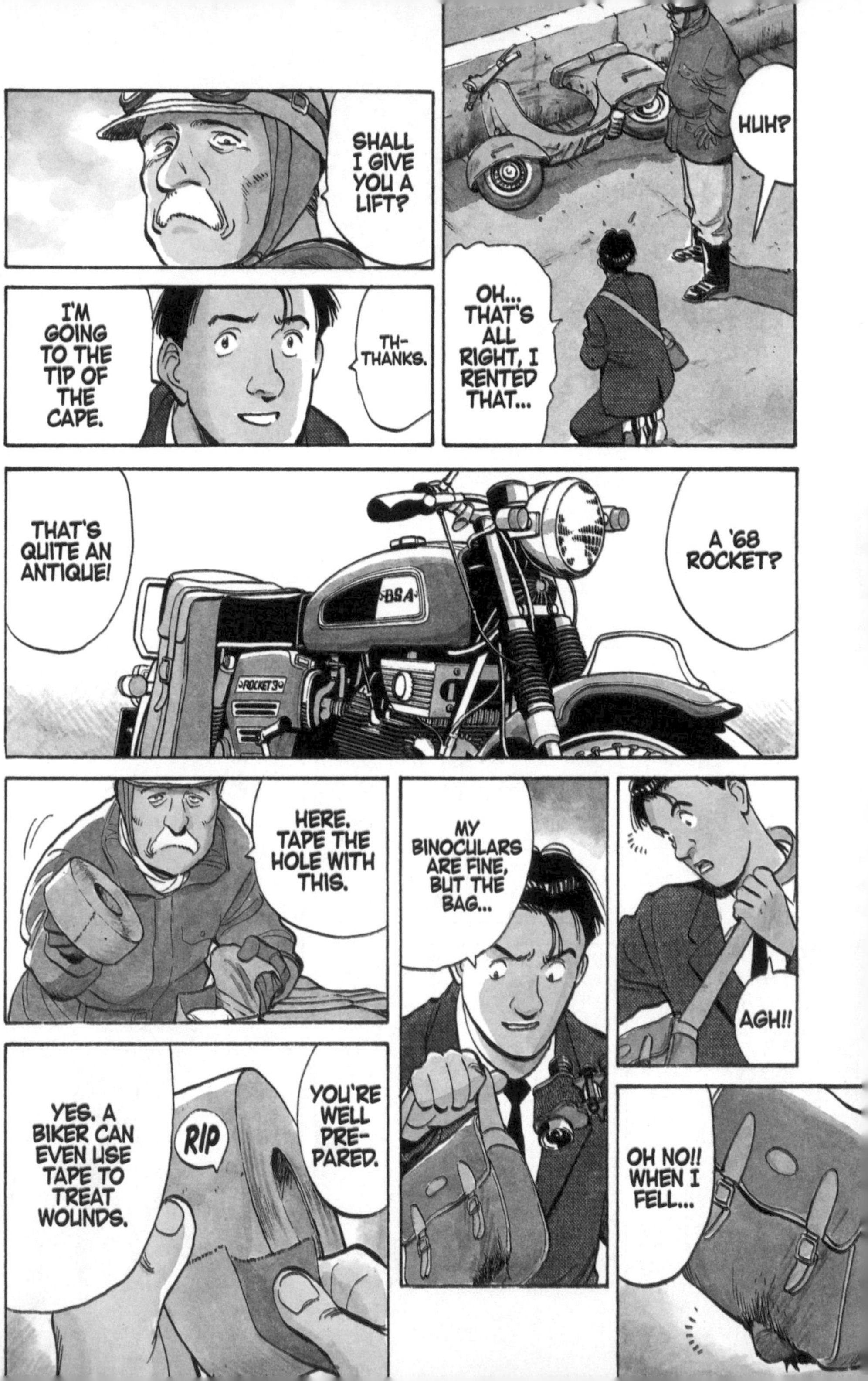
HUH?
OH... THAT'S ALL RIGHT, I RENTED THAT...
SHALL I GIVE YOU A LIFT?
TH-THANKS.
I'M GOING TO THE TIP OF THE CAPE.
A '68 ROCKET?
BSA
ROCKET 3
THAT'S QUITE AN ANTIQUE!
AGH!!
OH NO!! WHEN I FELL...
MY BINOCULARS ARE FINE, BUT THE BAG...
HERE. TAPE THE HOLE WITH THIS.
YOU'RE WELL PRE-PARED.
RIP
YES. A BIKER CAN EVEN USE TAPE TO TREAT WOUNDS.

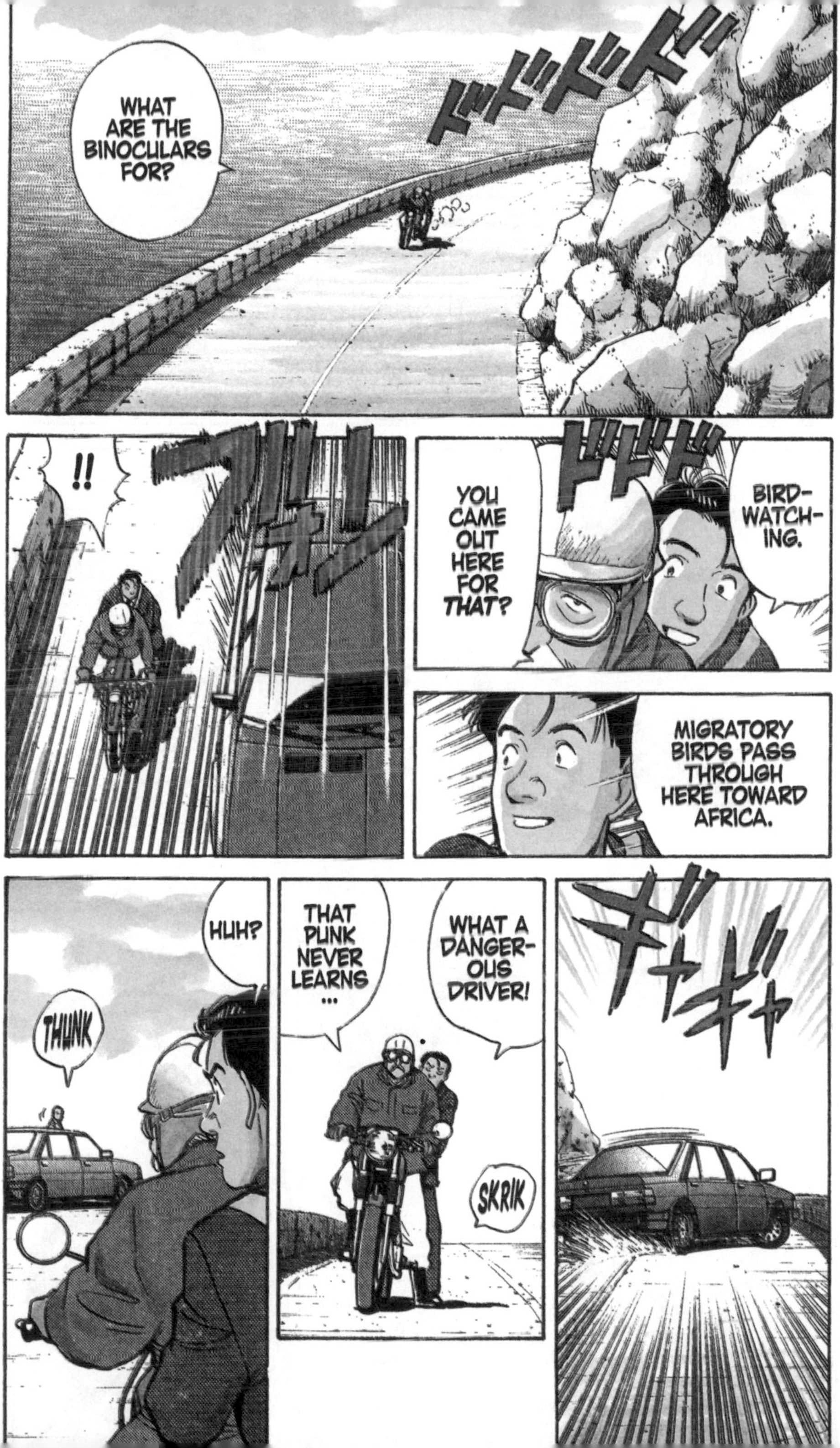
WHAT ARE THE BINOCULARS FOR?
BIRD-WATCHING.
YOU CAME OUT HERE FOR *THAT*?
MIGRATORY BIRDS PASS THROUGH HERE TOWARD AFRICA.
!!
WHAT A DANGEROUS DRIVER!
THAT PUNK NEVER LEARNS...
SKRIK
HUH?
THUNK

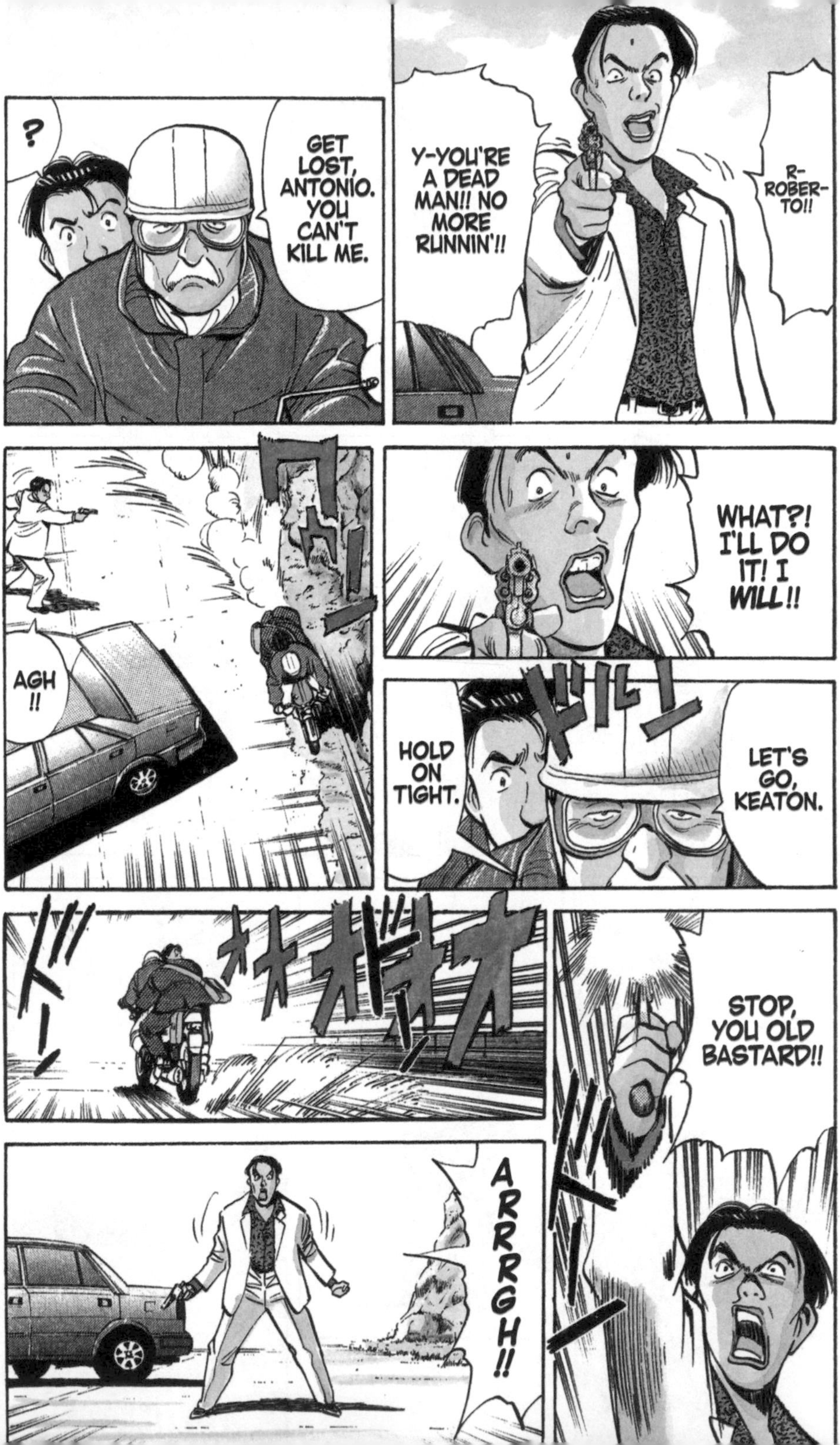
R-ROBERTO!!
Y-YOU'RE A DEAD MAN!! NO MORE RUNNIN'!!
GET LOST, ANTONIO. YOU CAN'T KILL ME.
?
WHAT?! I'LL DO IT! I *WILL*!!
LET'S GO, KEATON.
HOLD ON TIGHT.
AGH!!
STOP, YOU OLD BASTARD!!
ARRRGH!!

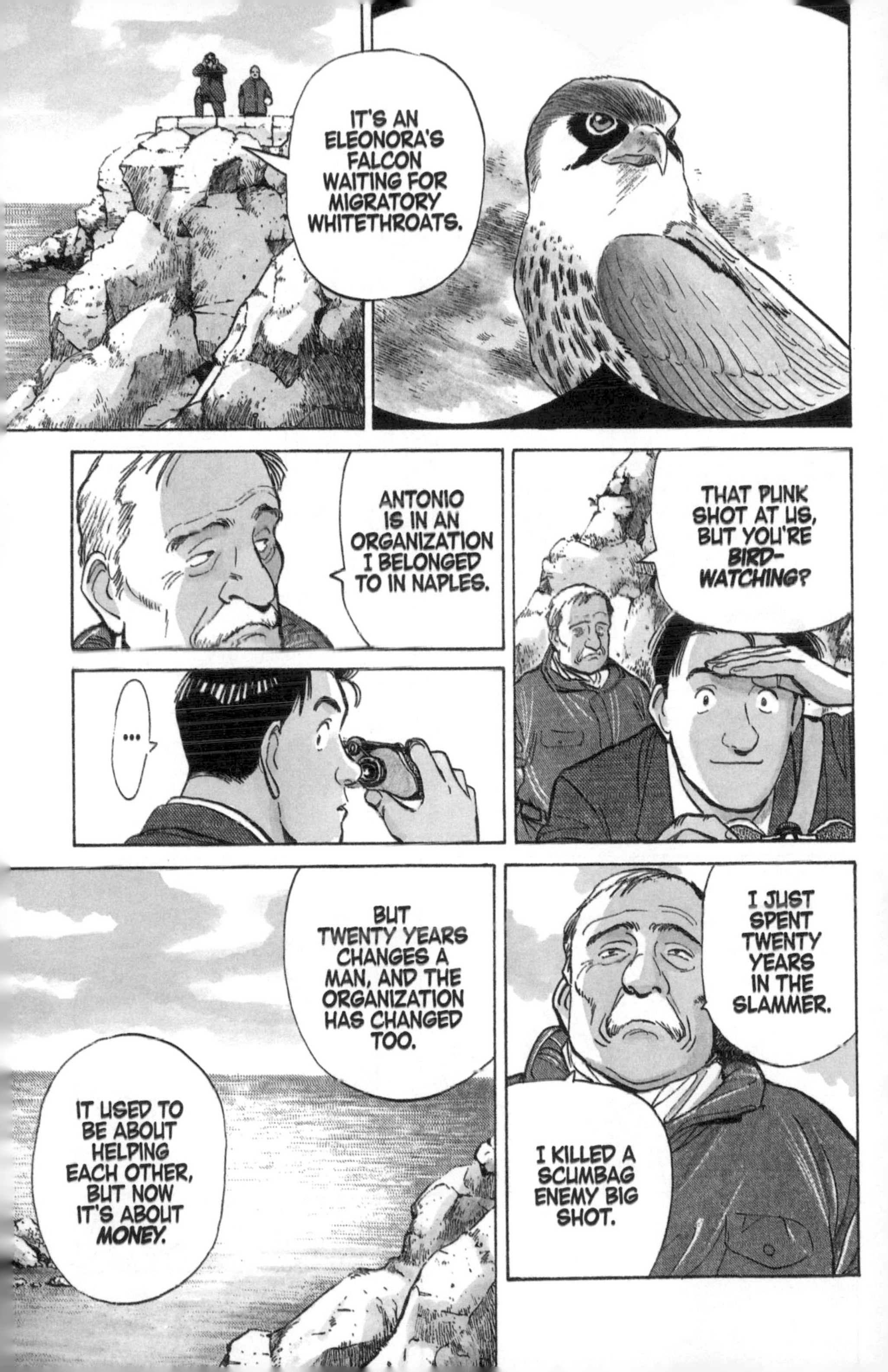
IT'S AN ELEONORA'S FALCON WAITING FOR MIGRATORY WHITETHROATS.
THAT PUNK SHOT AT US, BUT YOU'RE *BIRD-WATCHING?*
ANTONIO IS IN AN ORGANIZATION I BELONGED TO IN NAPLES.
...
I JUST SPENT TWENTY YEARS IN THE SLAMMER.
I KILLED A SCUMBAG ENEMY BIG SHOT.
BUT TWENTY YEARS CHANGES A MAN, AND THE ORGANIZATION HAS CHANGED TOO.
IT USED TO BE ABOUT HELPING EACH OTHER, BUT NOW IT'S ABOUT *MONEY.*

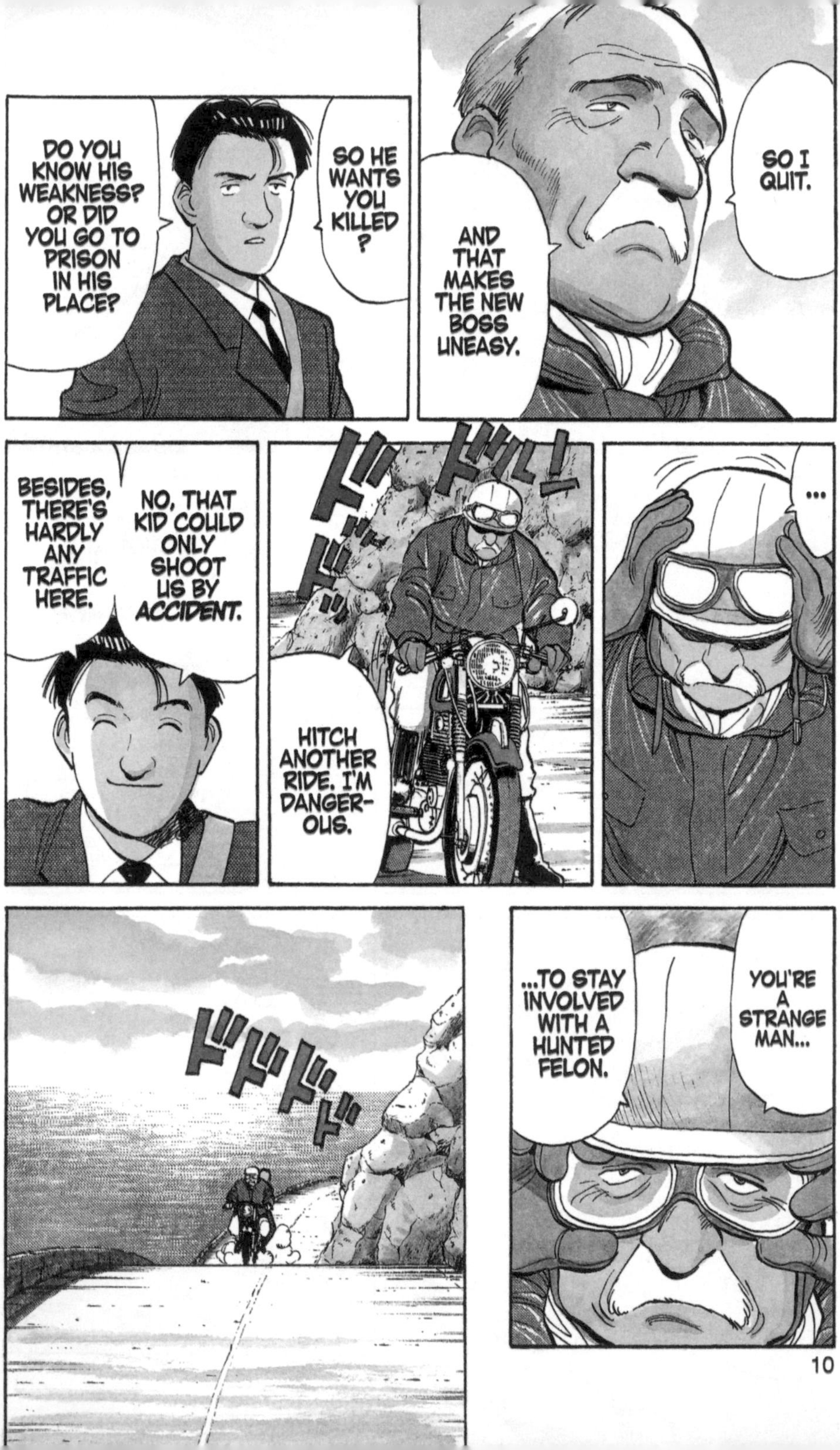
SO I QUIT.
AND THAT MAKES THE NEW BOSS UNEASY.
SO HE WANTS YOU KILLED?
DO YOU KNOW HIS WEAKNESS? OR DID YOU GO TO PRISON IN HIS PLACE?
...
HITCH ANOTHER RIDE. I'M DANGER-OUS.
NO, THAT KID COULD ONLY SHOOT US BY ACCIDENT.
BESIDES, THERE'S HARDLY ANY TRAFFIC HERE.
YOU'RE A STRANGE MAN...
...TO STAY INVOLVED WITH A HUNTED FELON.

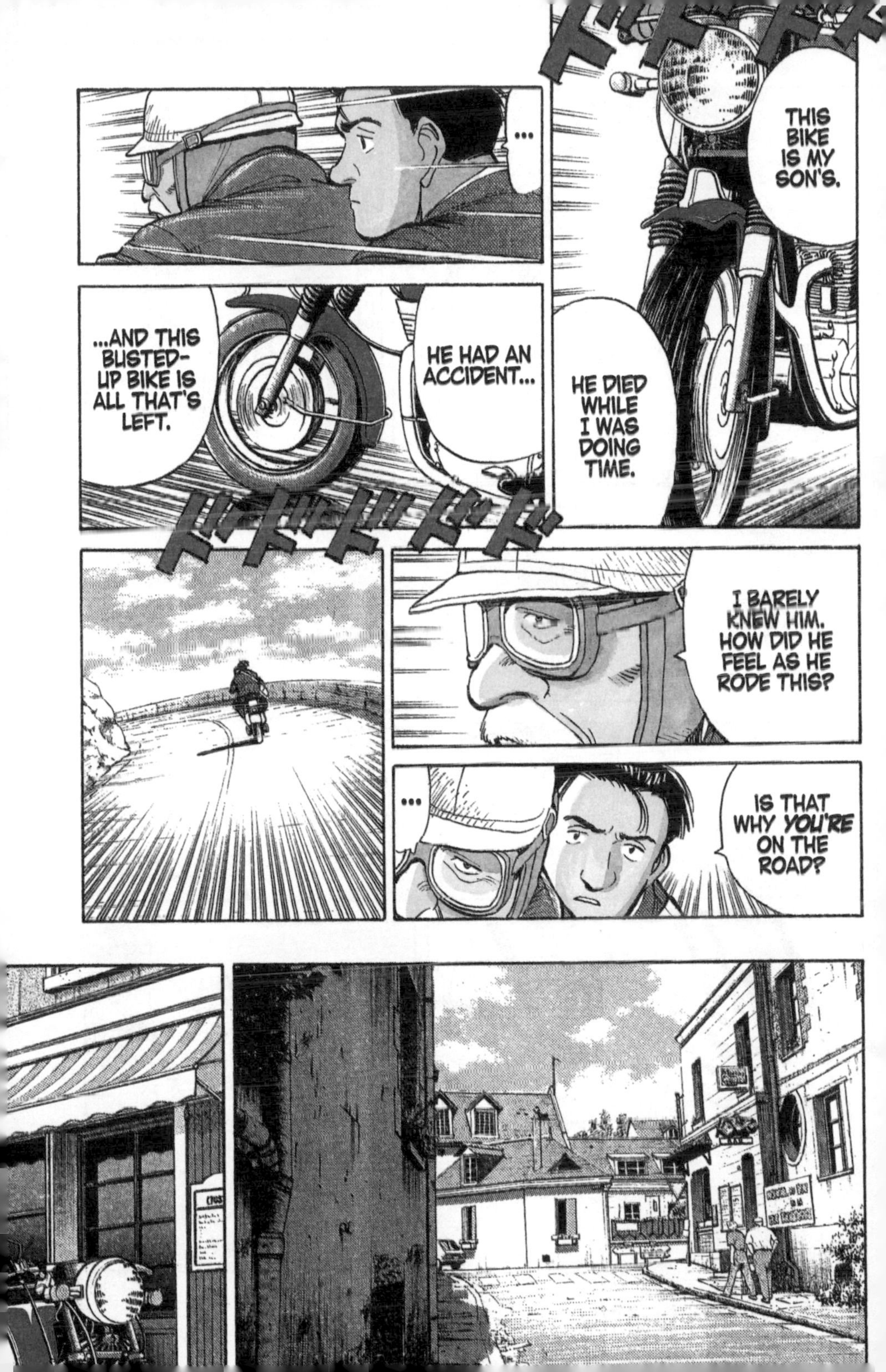
THIS BIKE IS MY SON'S.
HE DIED WHILE I WAS DOING TIME.
...
HE HAD AN ACCIDENT...
...AND THIS BUSTED-UP BIKE IS ALL THAT'S LEFT.
I BARELY KNEW HIM. HOW DID HE FEEL AS HE RODE THIS?
IS THAT WHY *YOU'RE* ON THE ROAD?
...

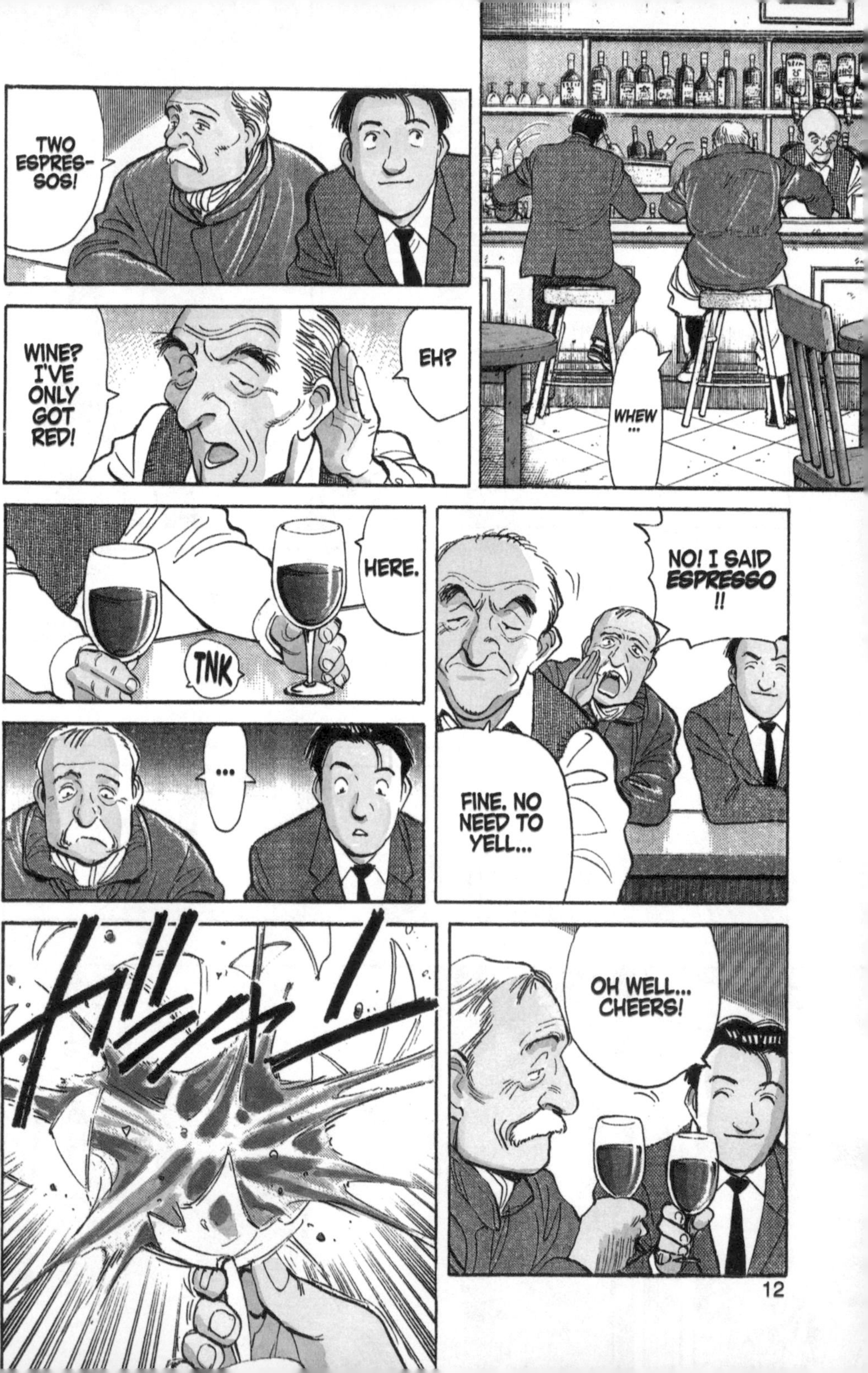
WHEW
...
TWO ESPRES-SOS!
EH?
WINE? I'VE ONLY GOT RED!
NO! I SAID ESPRESSO !!
FINE. NO NEED TO YELL...
HERE.
TNK
...
OH WELL... CHEERS!

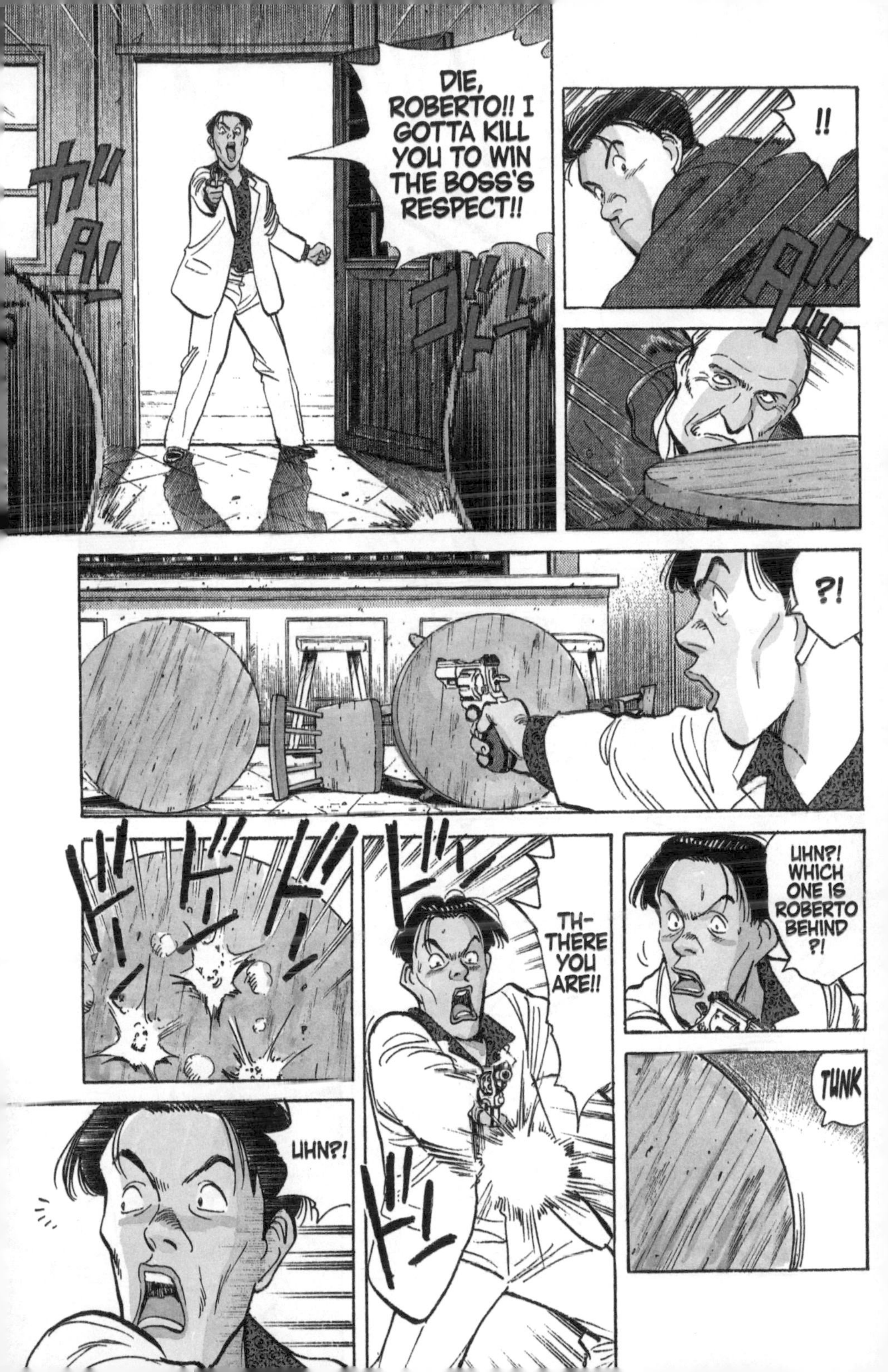
!!
DIE, ROBERTO!! I GOTTA KILL YOU TO WIN THE BOSS'S RESPECT!!
?!
UHN?! WHICH ONE IS ROBERTO BEHIND ?!
TUNK
TH- THERE YOU ARE!!
UHN?!

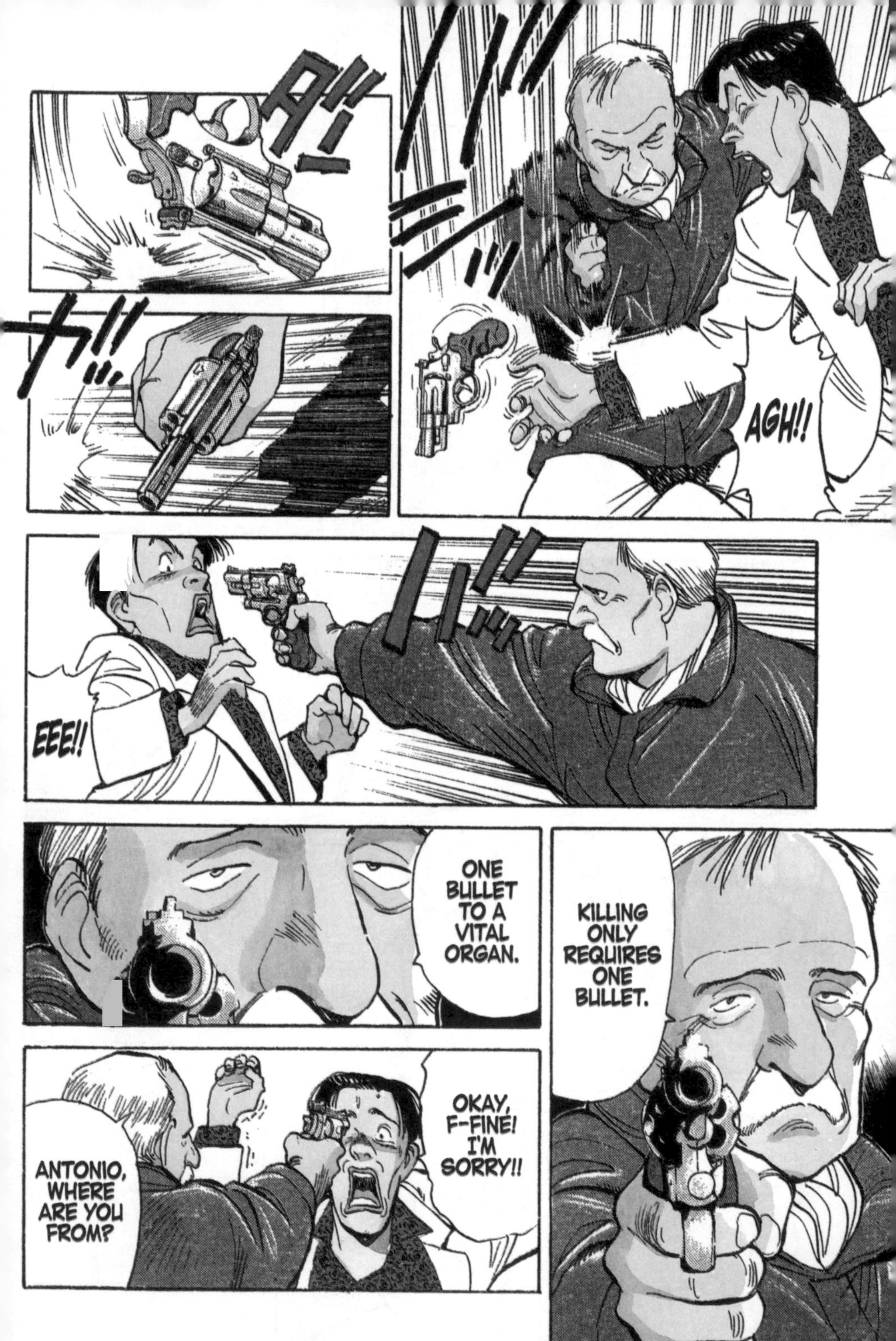
AGH!!
EEE!!
KILLING ONLY REQUIRES ONE BULLET.
ONE BULLET TO A VITAL ORGAN.
OKAY, F-FINE! I'M SORRY!!
ANTONIO, WHERE ARE YOU FROM?

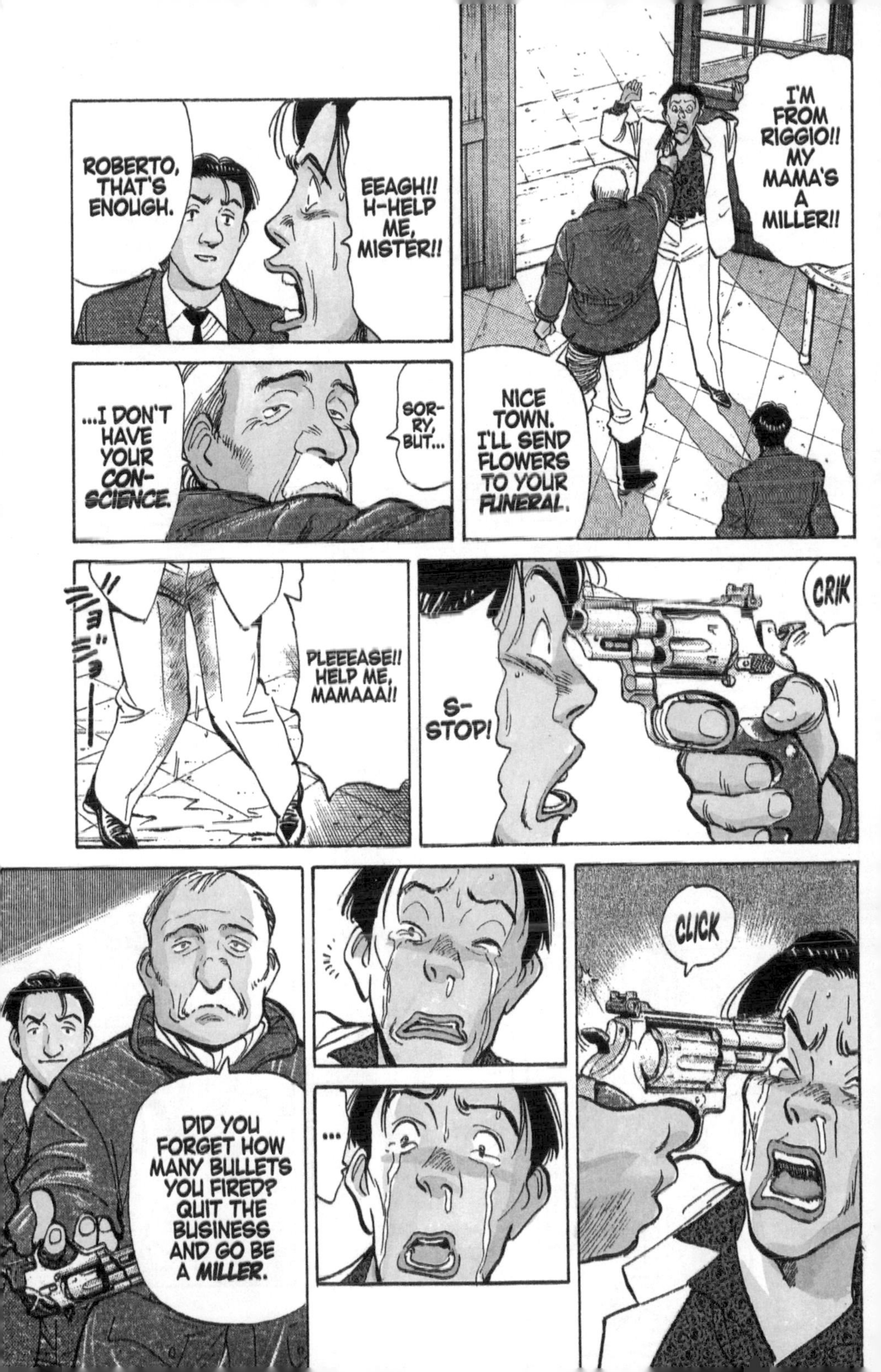
I'M FROM RIGGIO!! MY MAMA'S A MILLER!!
NICE TOWN. I'LL SEND FLOWERS TO YOUR FUNERAL.
EEAGH!! H-HELP ME, MISTER!!
ROBERTO, THAT'S ENOUGH.
SORRY, BUT...
...I DON'T HAVE YOUR CON-SCIENCE.
CRIK
S-STOP!
PLEEEASE!! HELP ME, MAMAAA!!
CLICK
...
DID YOU FORGET HOW MANY BULLETS YOU FIRED? QUIT THE BUSINESS AND GO BE A MILLER.

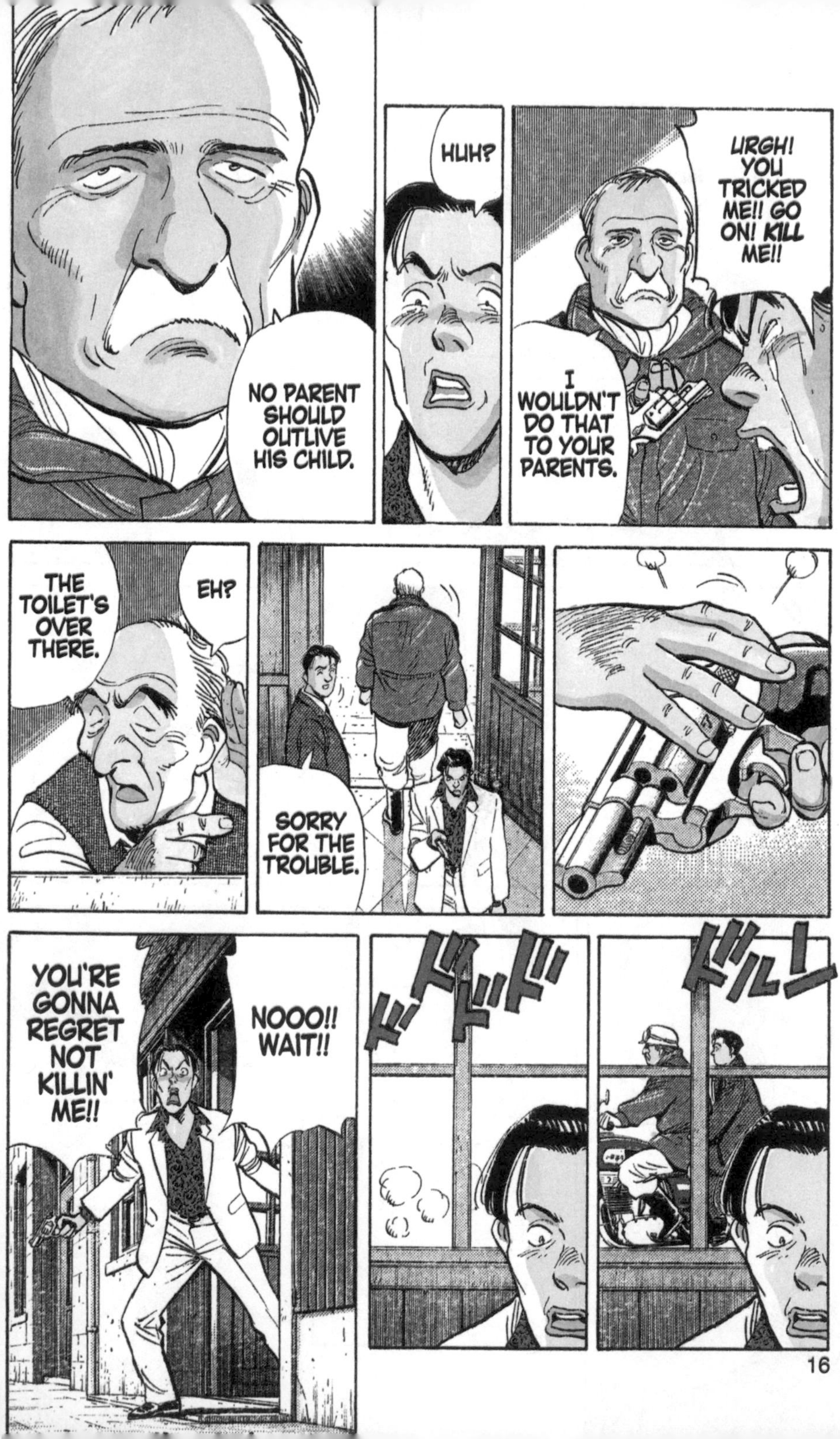
URGH! YOU TRICKED ME!! GO ON! KILL ME!!
I WOULDN'T DO THAT TO YOUR PARENTS.
HUH?
NO PARENT SHOULD OUTLIVE HIS CHILD.
SORRY FOR THE TROUBLE.
EH?
THE TOILET'S OVER THERE.
ドルルン
ドドッドド
NOOO!! WAIT!!
YOU'RE GONNA REGRET NOT KILLIN' ME!!

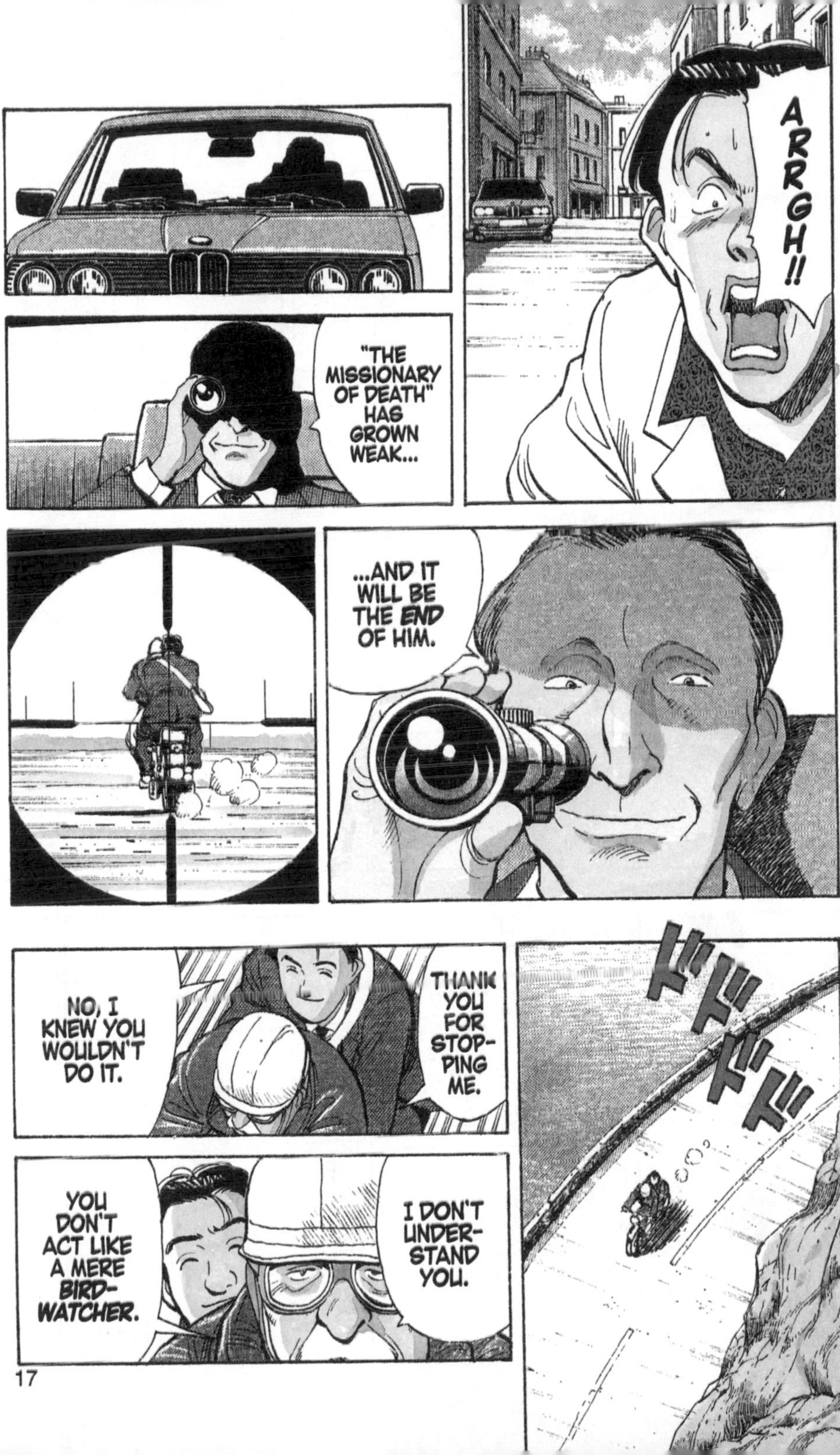
ARRGH!!
"THE MISSIONARY OF DEATH" HAS GROWN WEAK...
...AND IT WILL BE THE END OF HIM.
ドドドド
THANK YOU FOR STOPPING ME.
NO, I KNEW YOU WOULDN'T DO IT.
I DON'T UNDERSTAND YOU.
YOU DON'T ACT LIKE A MERE BIRD-WATCHER.

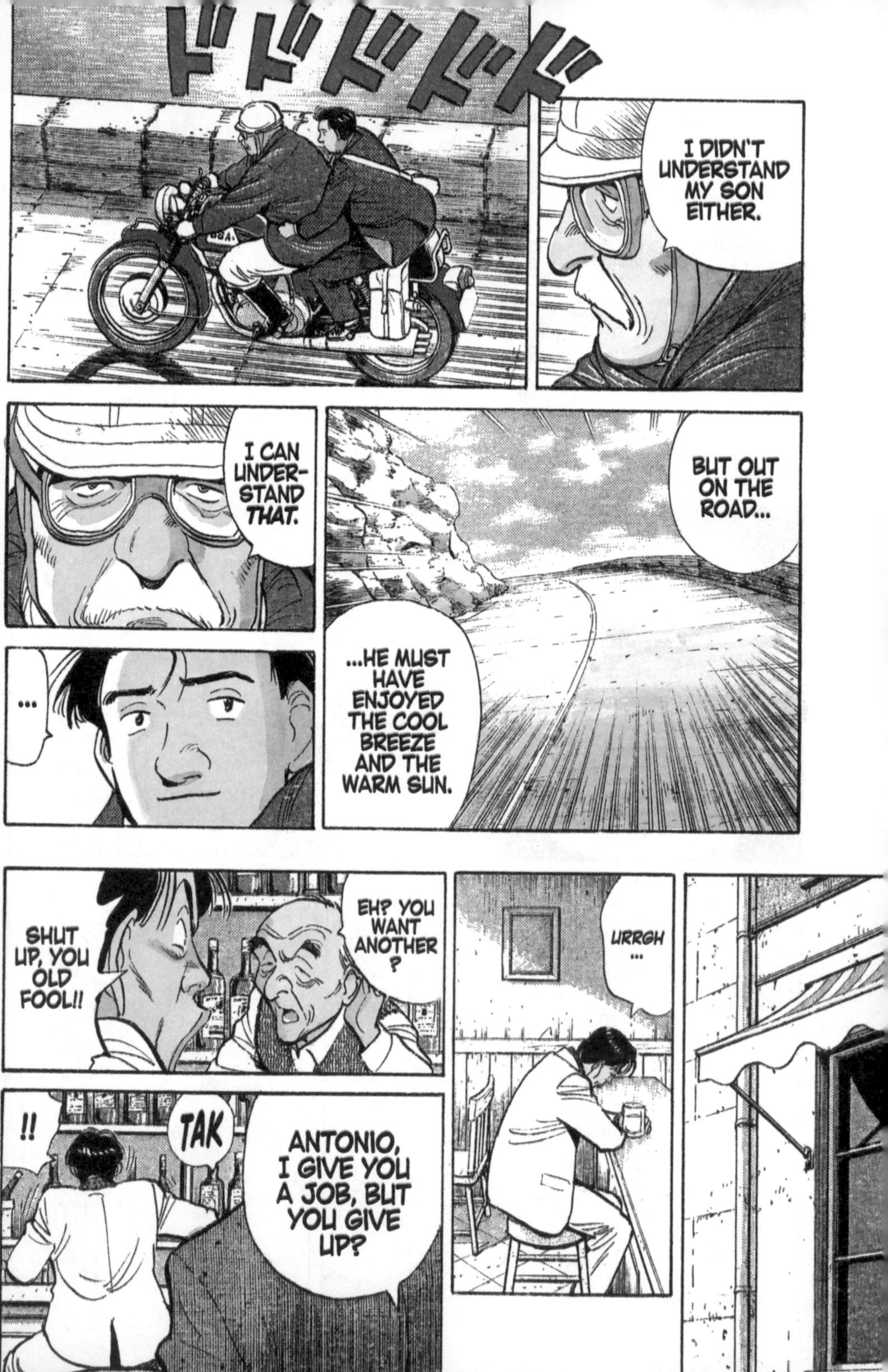
I DIDN'T UNDERSTAND MY SON EITHER.
ドドドドド
BUT OUT ON THE ROAD...
...HE MUST HAVE ENJOYED THE COOL BREEZE AND THE WARM SUN.
I CAN UNDER-STAND THAT.
...
URRGH ...
EH? YOU WANT ANOTHER ?
SHUT UP, YOU OLD FOOL!!
ANTONIO, I GIVE YOU A JOB, BUT YOU GIVE UP?
TAK
!!

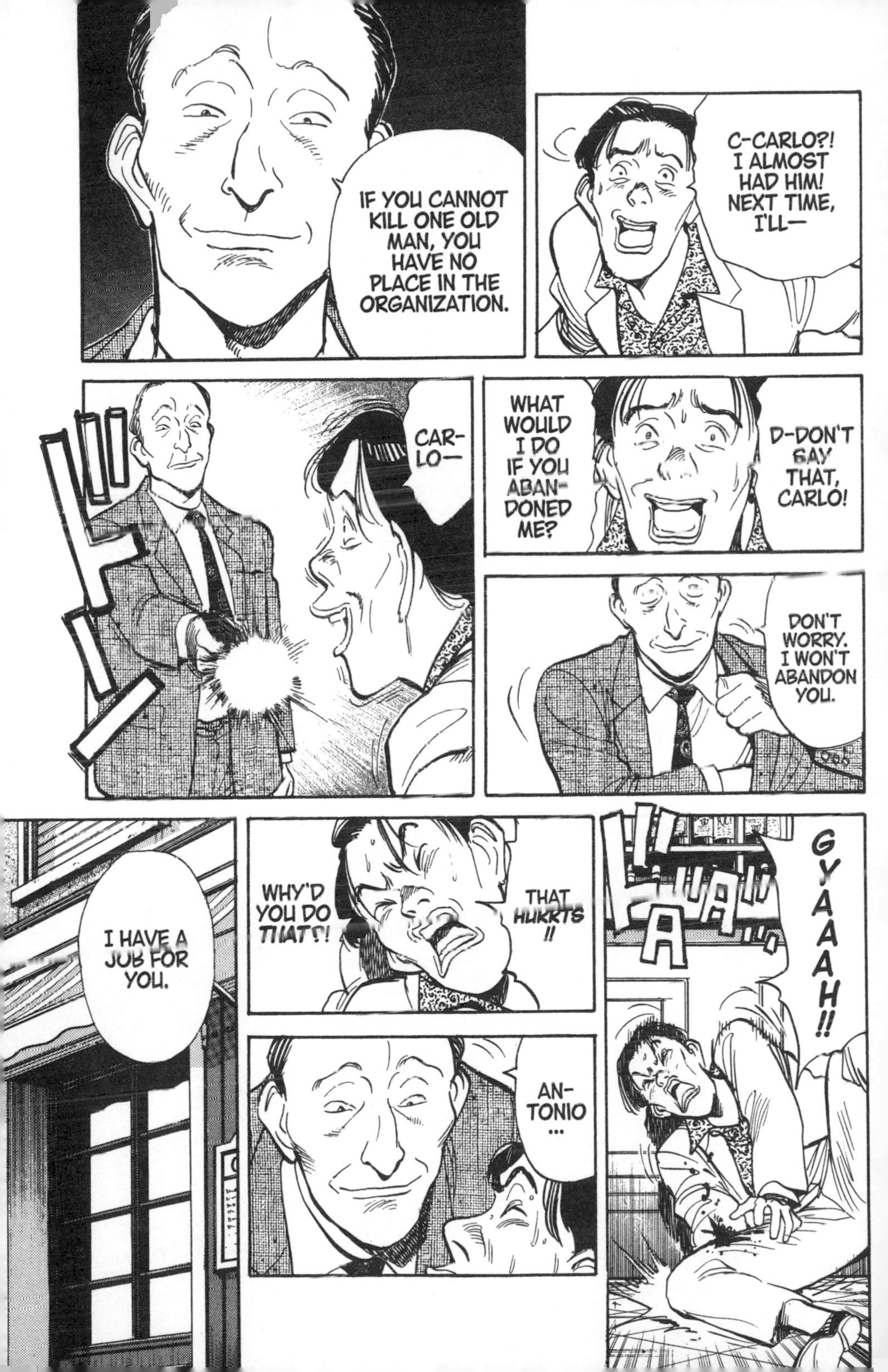
C-CARLO?! I ALMOST HAD HIM! NEXT TIME, I'LL—
IF YOU CANNOT KILL ONE OLD MAN, YOU HAVE NO PLACE IN THE ORGANIZATION.
D-DON'T SAY THAT, CARLO!
WHAT WOULD I DO IF YOU ABANDONED ME?
DON'T WORRY. I WON'T ABANDON YOU.
CARLO—
GYAAAAH!!
THAT HURTS!!
WHY'D YOU DO THAT?!
ANTONIO...
I HAVE A JOB FOR YOU.

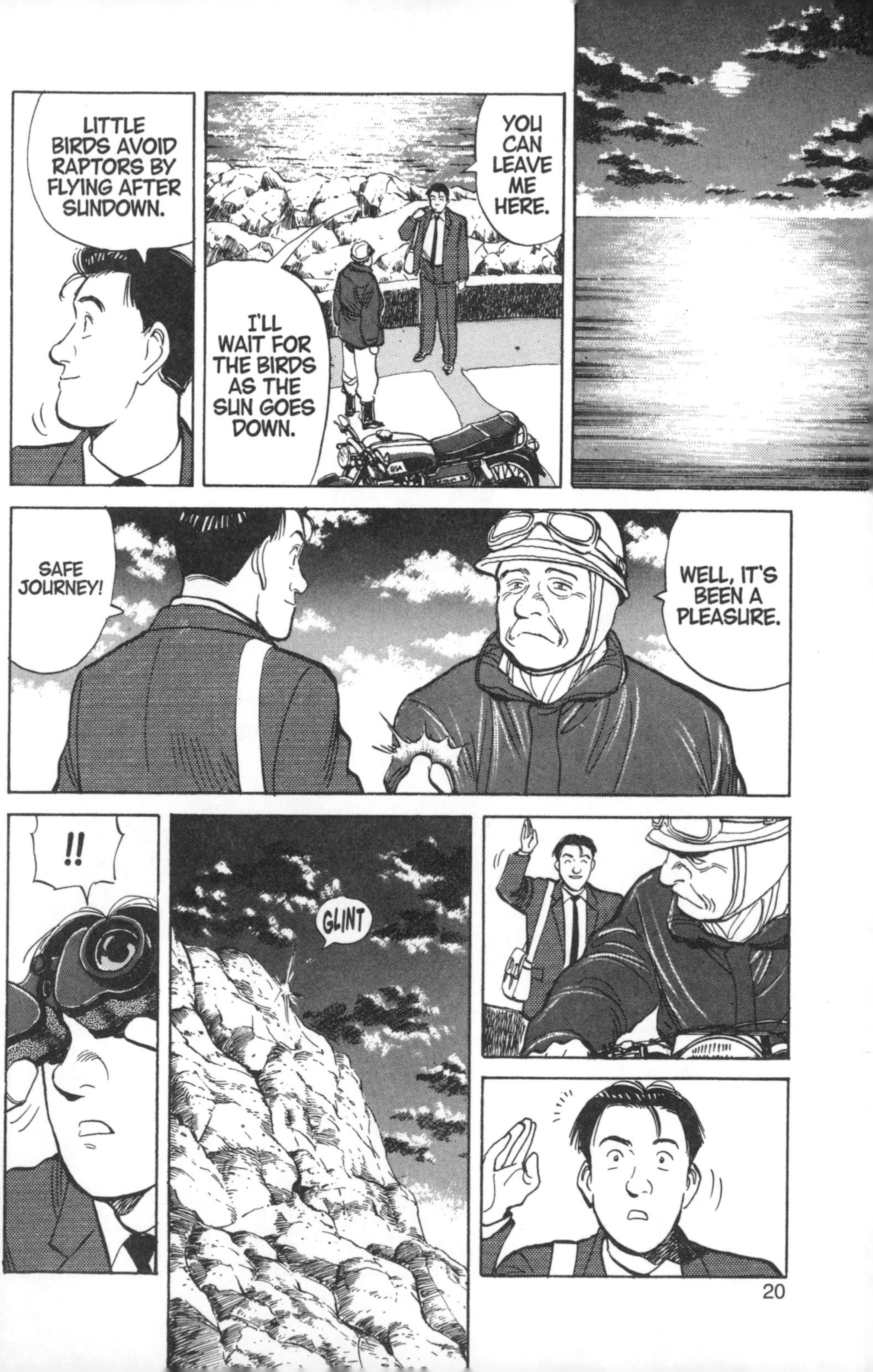
YOU CAN LEAVE ME HERE.
I'LL WAIT FOR THE BIRDS AS THE SUN GOES DOWN.
LITTLE BIRDS AVOID RAPTORS BY FLYING AFTER SUNDOWN.
WELL, IT'S BEEN A PLEASURE.
SAFE JOURNEY!
GLINT
!!

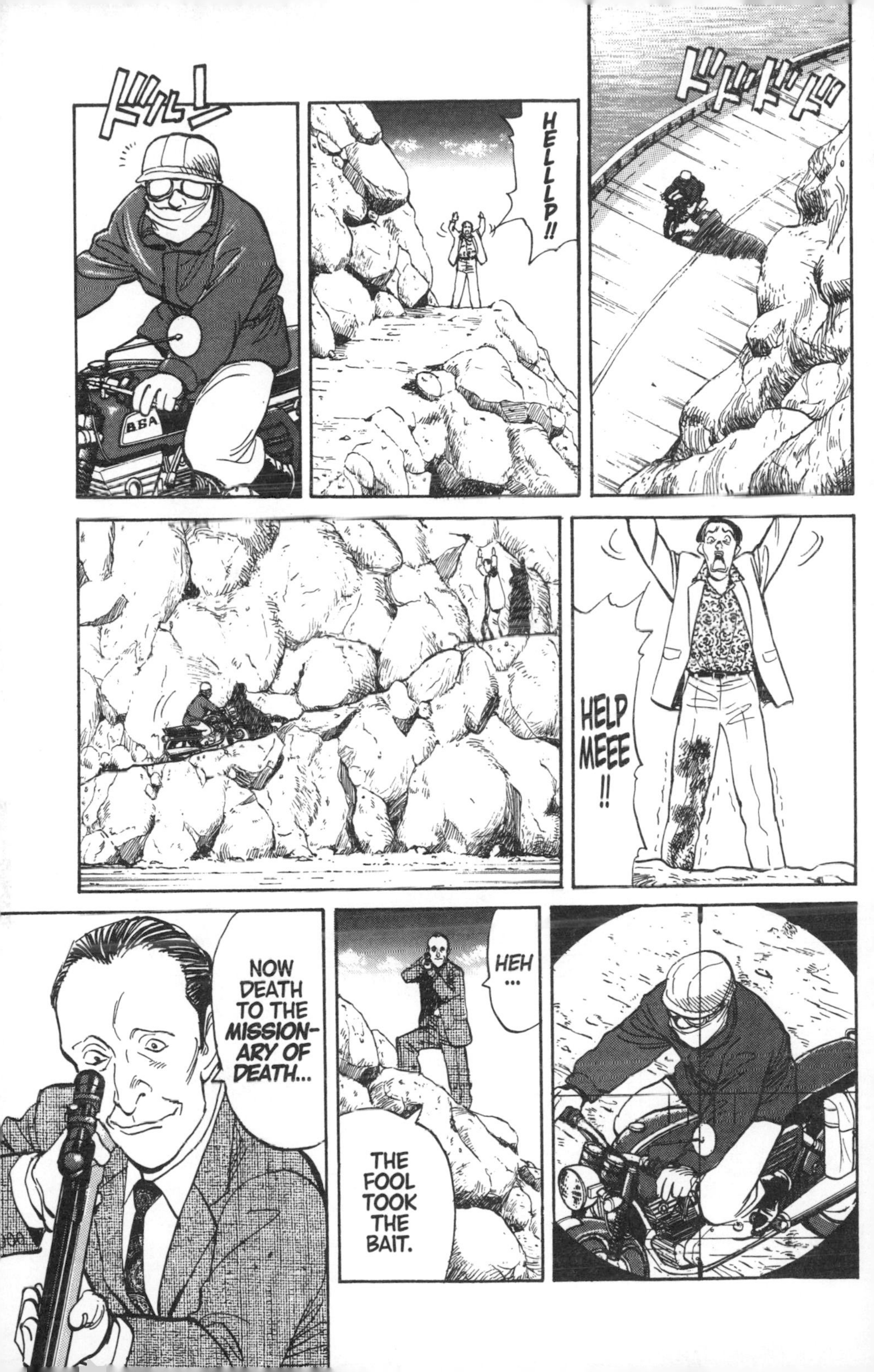
ドドドドド
HELLLP!!
ドルン
HELP MEEE !!
HEH ...
THE FOOL TOOK THE BAIT.
NOW DEATH TO THE MISSIONARY OF DEATH...

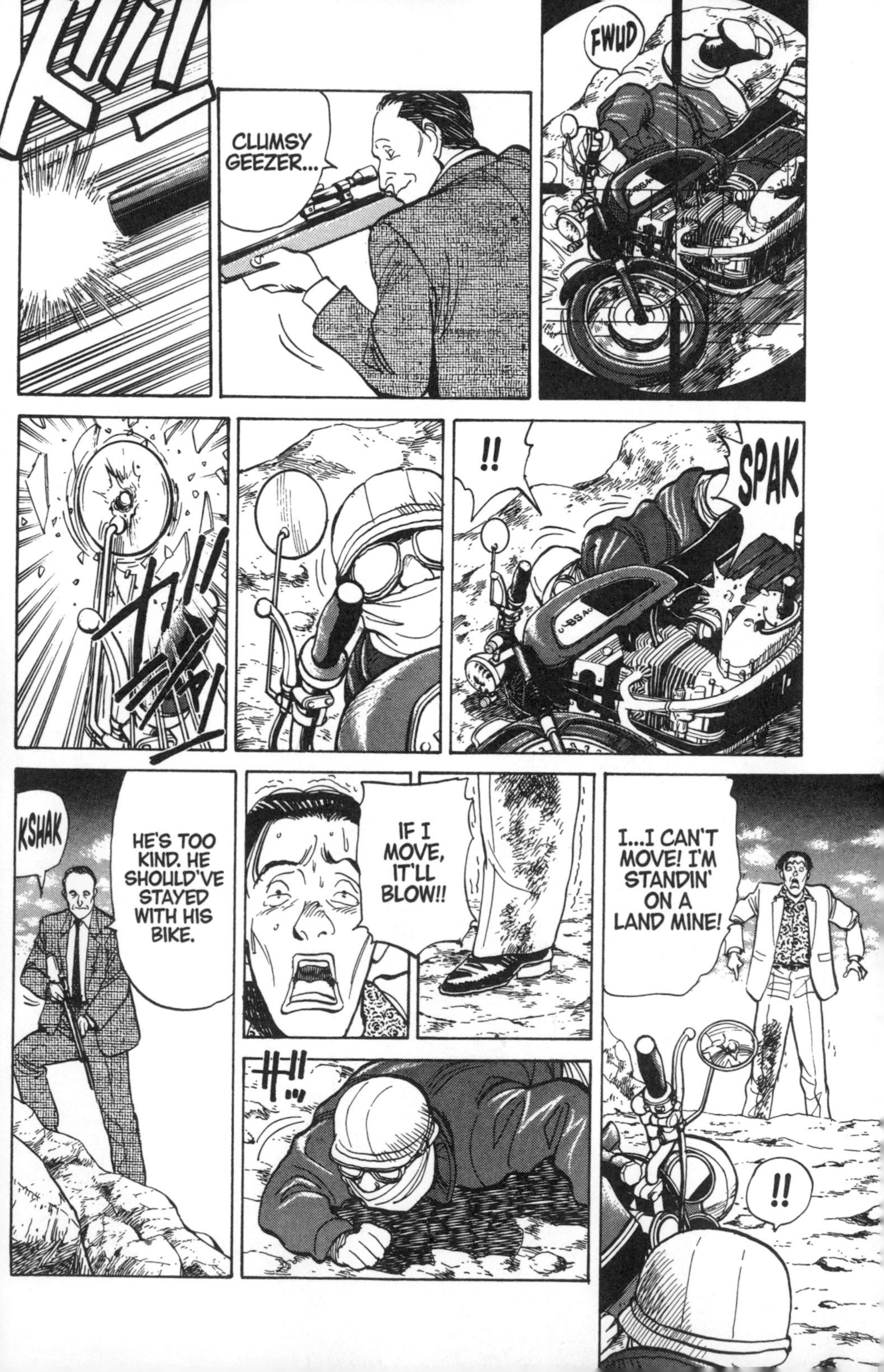
FWUD
CLUMSY GEEZER...
SPAK
!!
I...I CAN'T MOVE! I'M STANDIN' ON A LAND MINE!
!!
IF I MOVE, IT'LL BLOW!!
HE'S TOO KIND. HE SHOULD'VE STAYED WITH HIS BIKE.
KSHAK

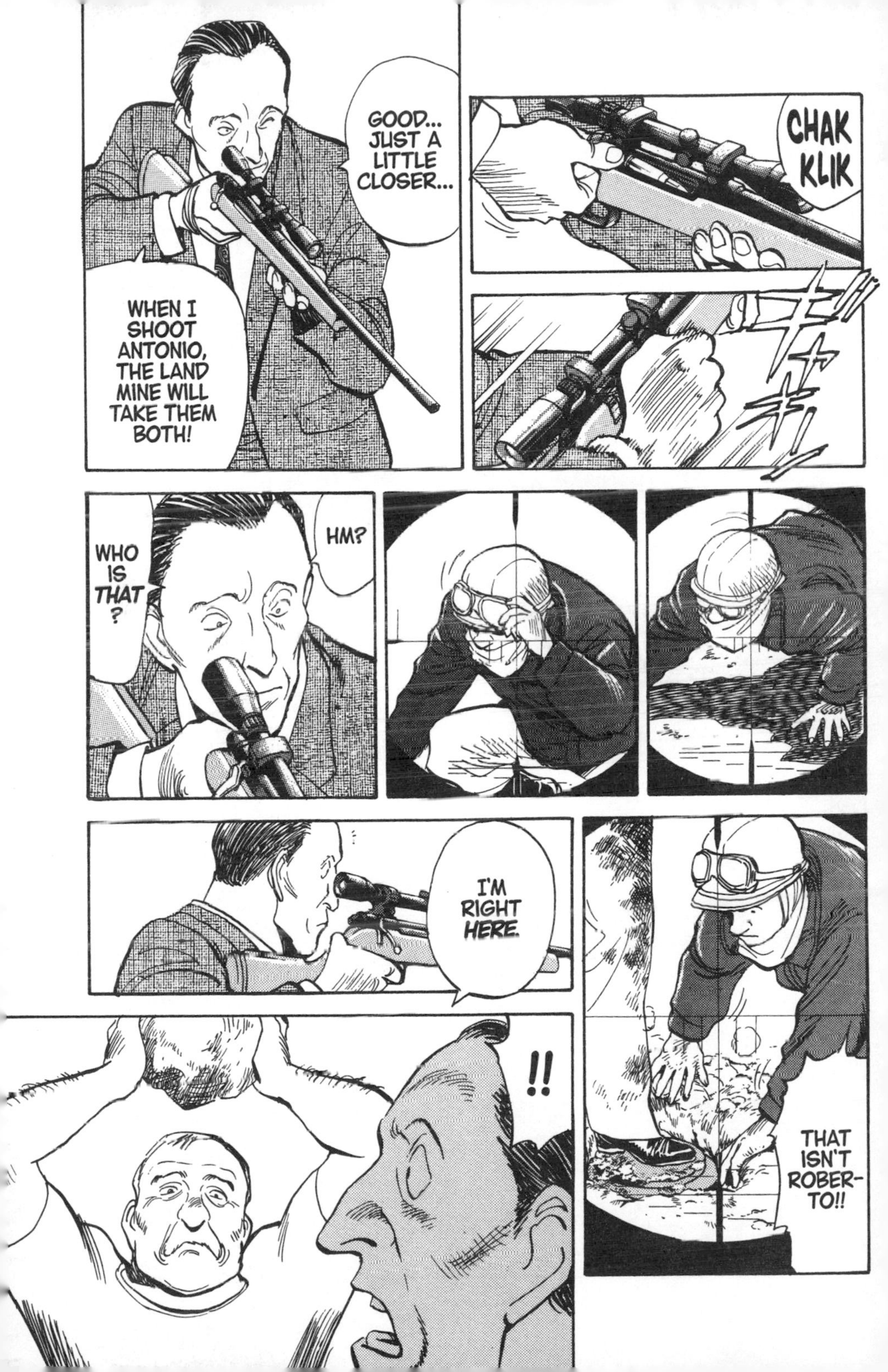
CHAK KLIK
GOOD... JUST A LITTLE CLOSER...
WHEN I SHOOT ANTONIO, THE LAND MINE WILL TAKE THEM BOTH!
HM?
WHO IS THAT?
THAT ISN'T ROBER-TO!!
I'M RIGHT HERE.
!!

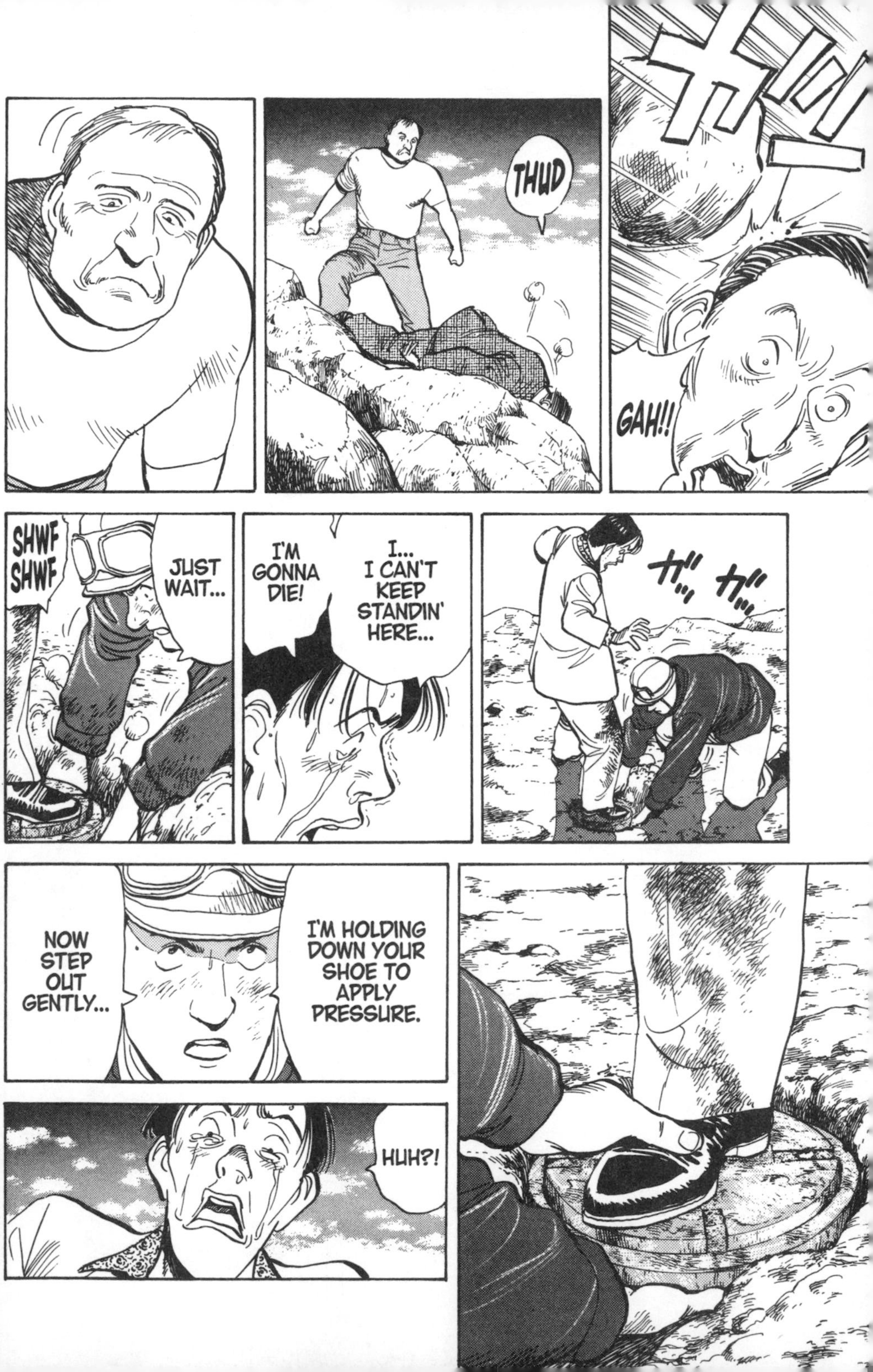
GAH!!
THUD
I... I CAN'T KEEP STANDIN' HERE...
I'M GONNA DIE!
JUST WAIT...
SHWF SHWF
I'M HOLDING DOWN YOUR SHOE TO APPLY PRESSURE.
NOW STEP OUT GENTLY...
HUH?!

YOU S-SAVED ME!!
SHK SHK
BUT NOW WHAT'RE YOU GONNA DO?!
UM...
I HADN'T THOUGHT THAT FAR.
KEATON, YOU REALLY ARE UNUSUAL. YOU RISKED YOUR LIFE FOR ME AND THAT PUNK.
...
RUSTLE

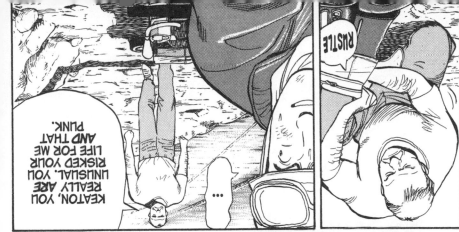

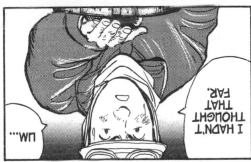

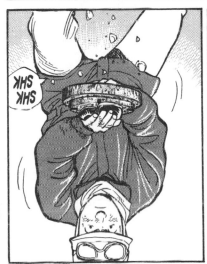

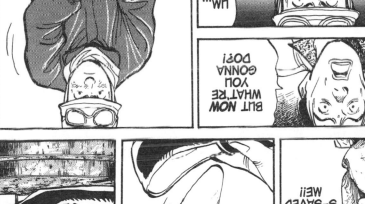

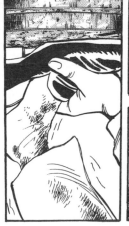

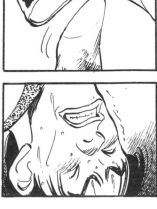

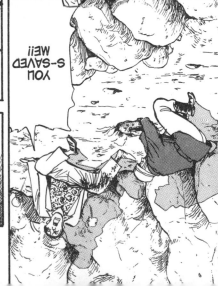

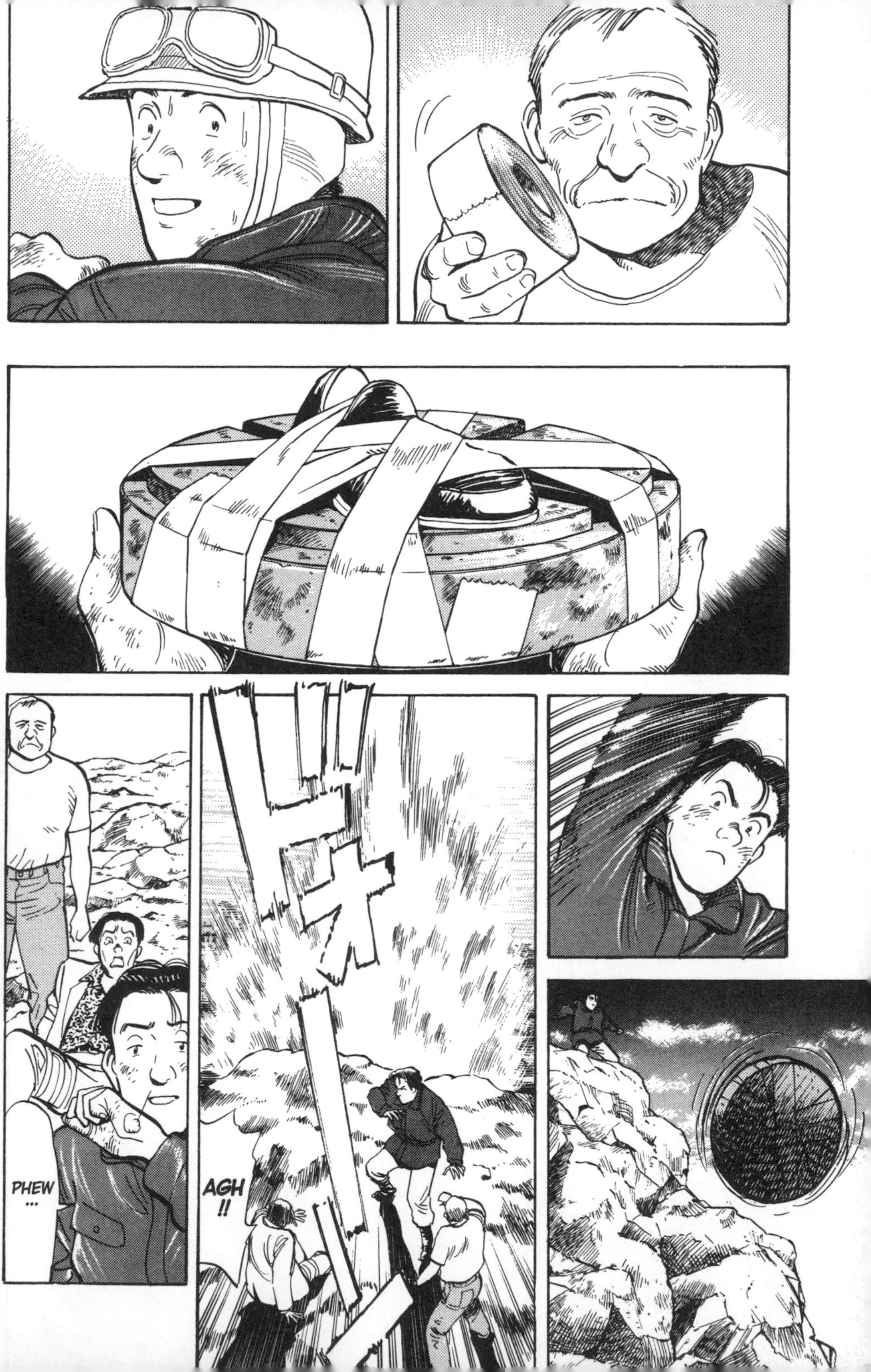
AGH !!
PHEW ...

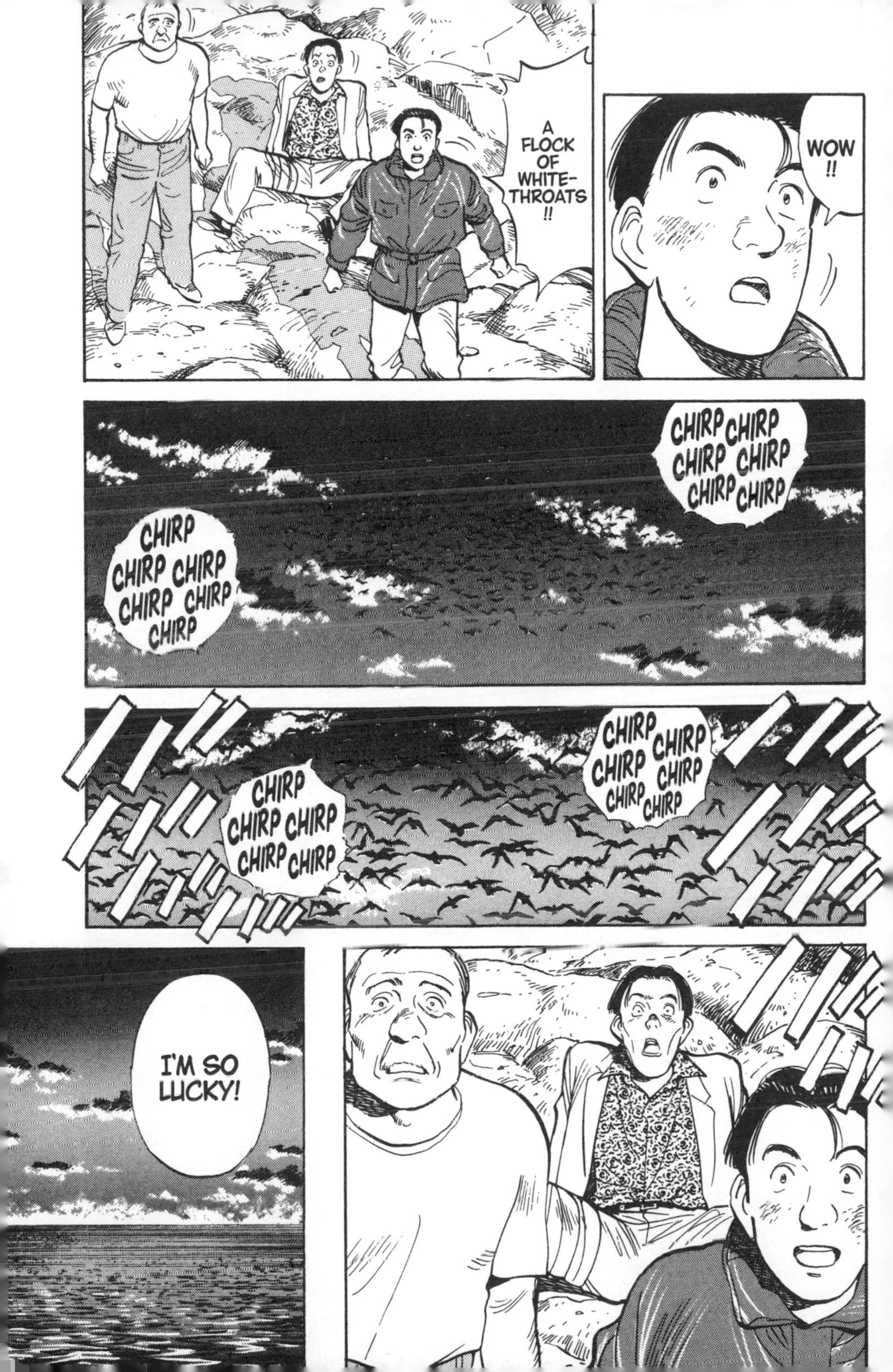
WOW !!
A FLOCK OF WHITE-THROATS !!
CHIRP CHIRP CHIRP CHIRP CHIRP CHIRP
CHIRP CHIRP CHIRP CHIRP CHIRP CHIRP
CHIRP CHIRP CHIRP CHIRP CHIRP CHIRP
CHIRP CHIRP CHIRP CHIRP CHIRP
I'M SO LUCKY!

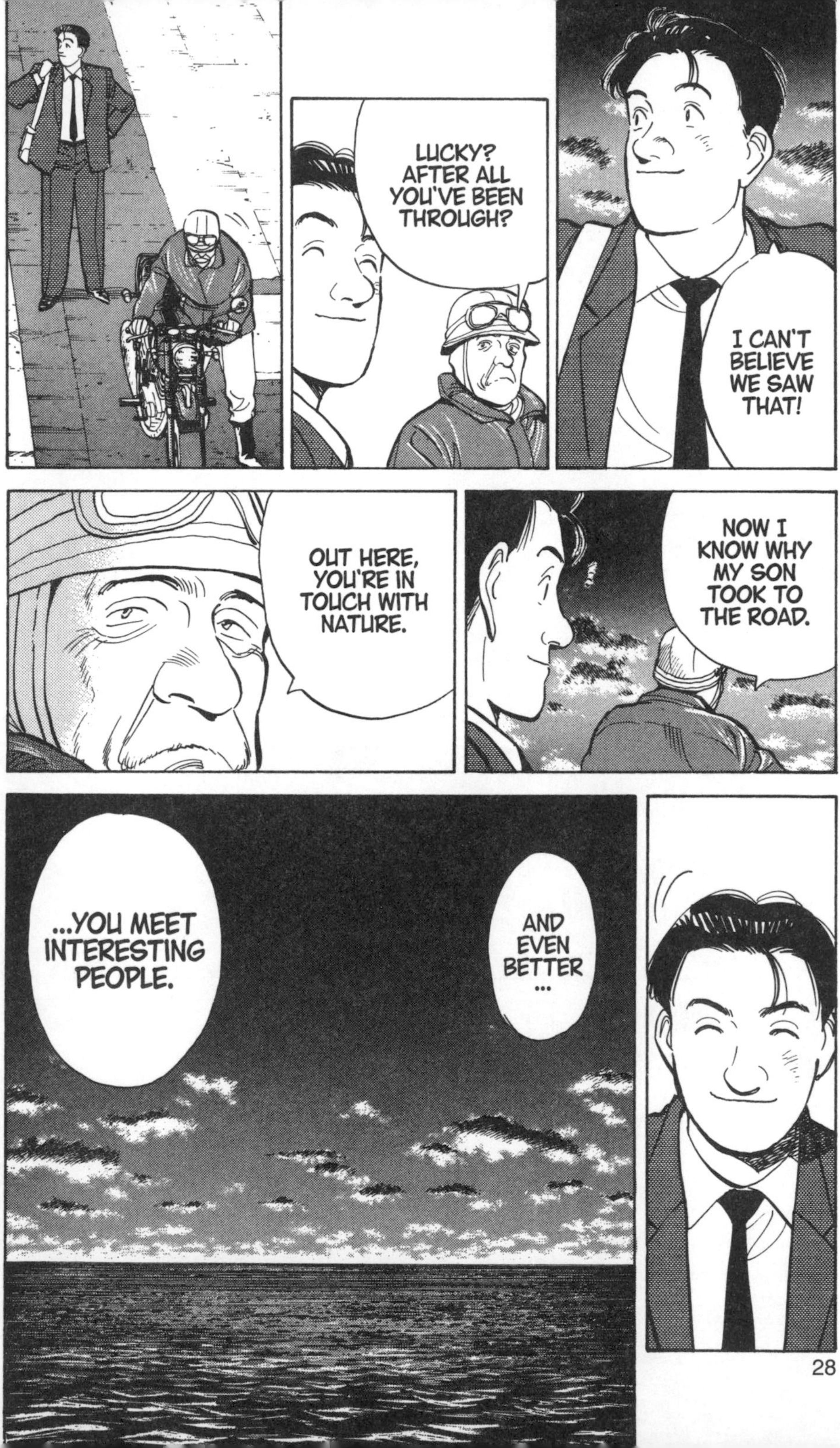
I CAN'T BELIEVE WE SAW THAT!
LUCKY? AFTER ALL YOU'VE BEEN THROUGH?
NOW I KNOW WHY MY SON TOOK TO THE ROAD.
OUT HERE, YOU'RE IN TOUCH WITH NATURE.
AND EVEN BETTER ...
...YOU MEET INTERESTING PEOPLE.

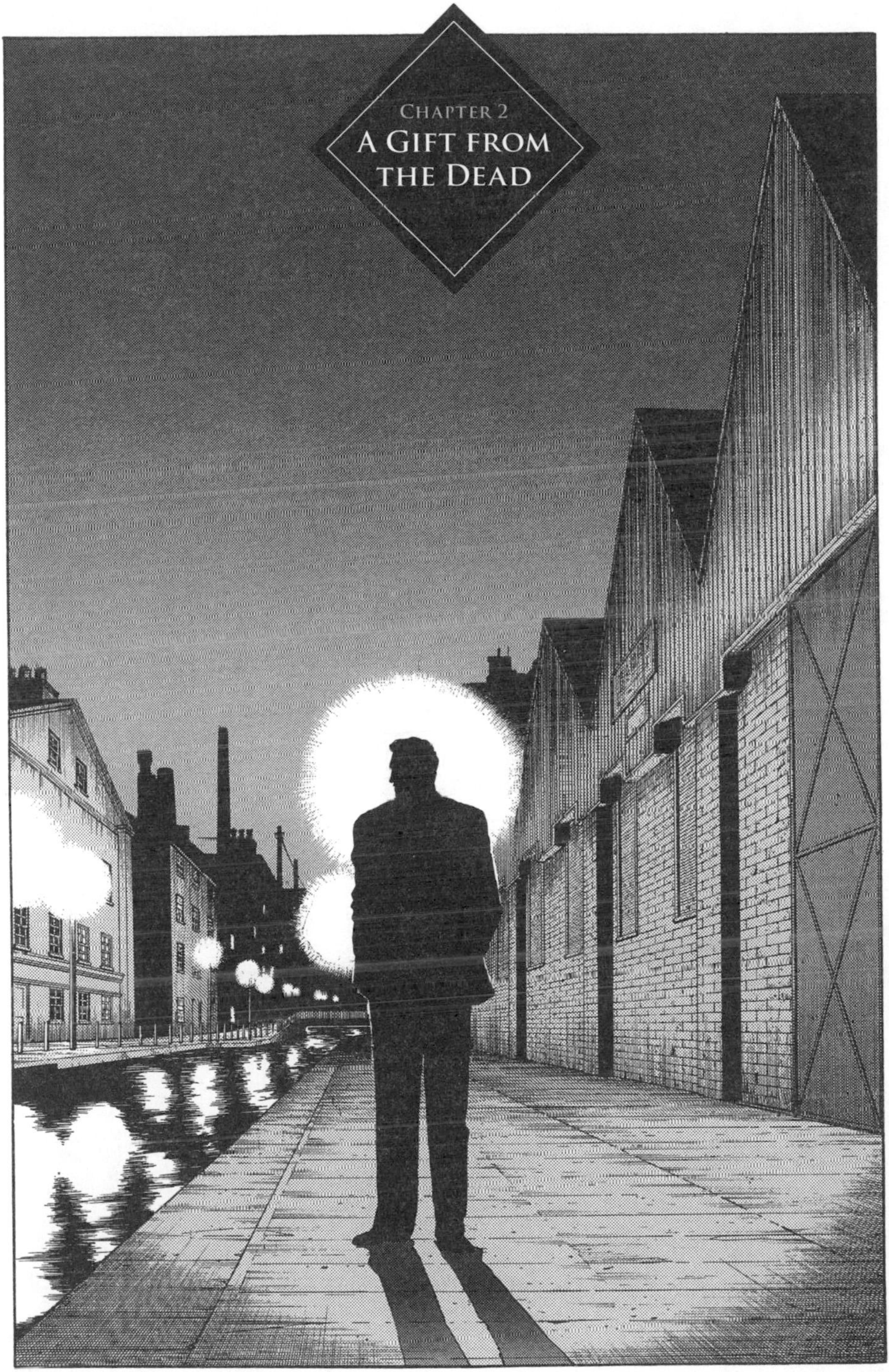
Chapter 2
A Gift from the Dead

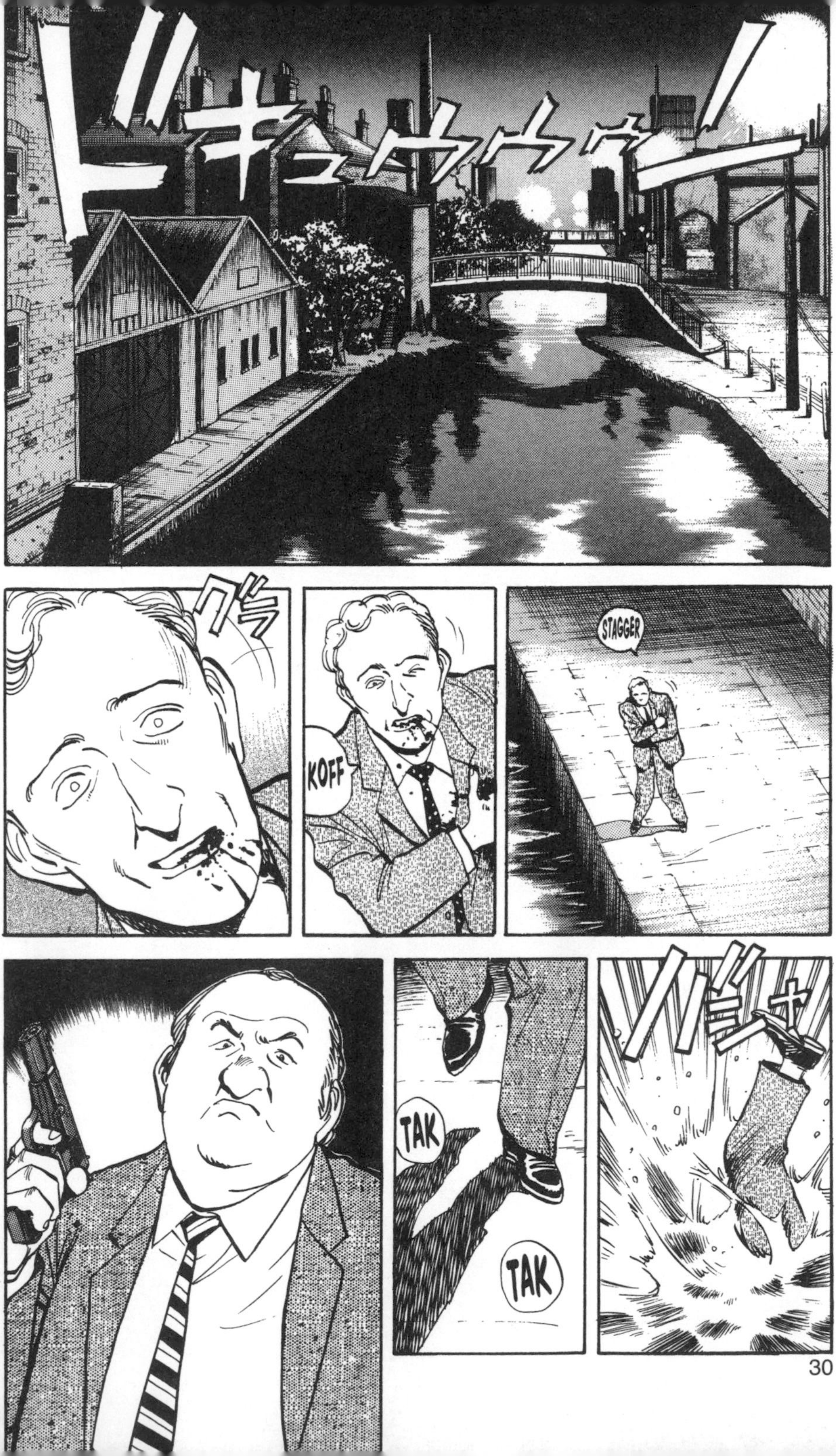
STAGGER
KOFF
TAK
TAK

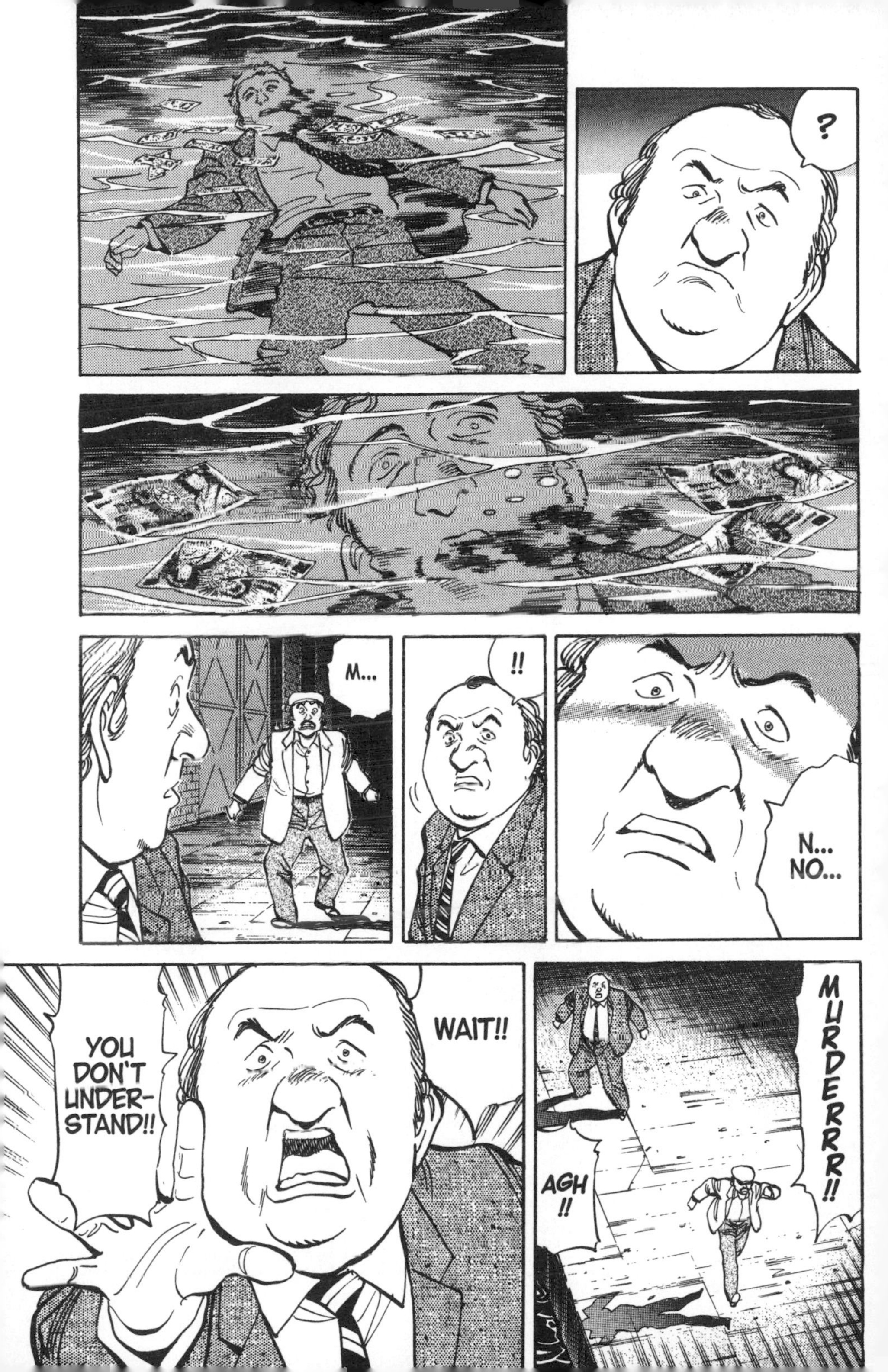
?
N... NO...
!!
M...
MURDERRR!!
AGH !!
WAIT!!
YOU DON'T UNDER-STAND!!

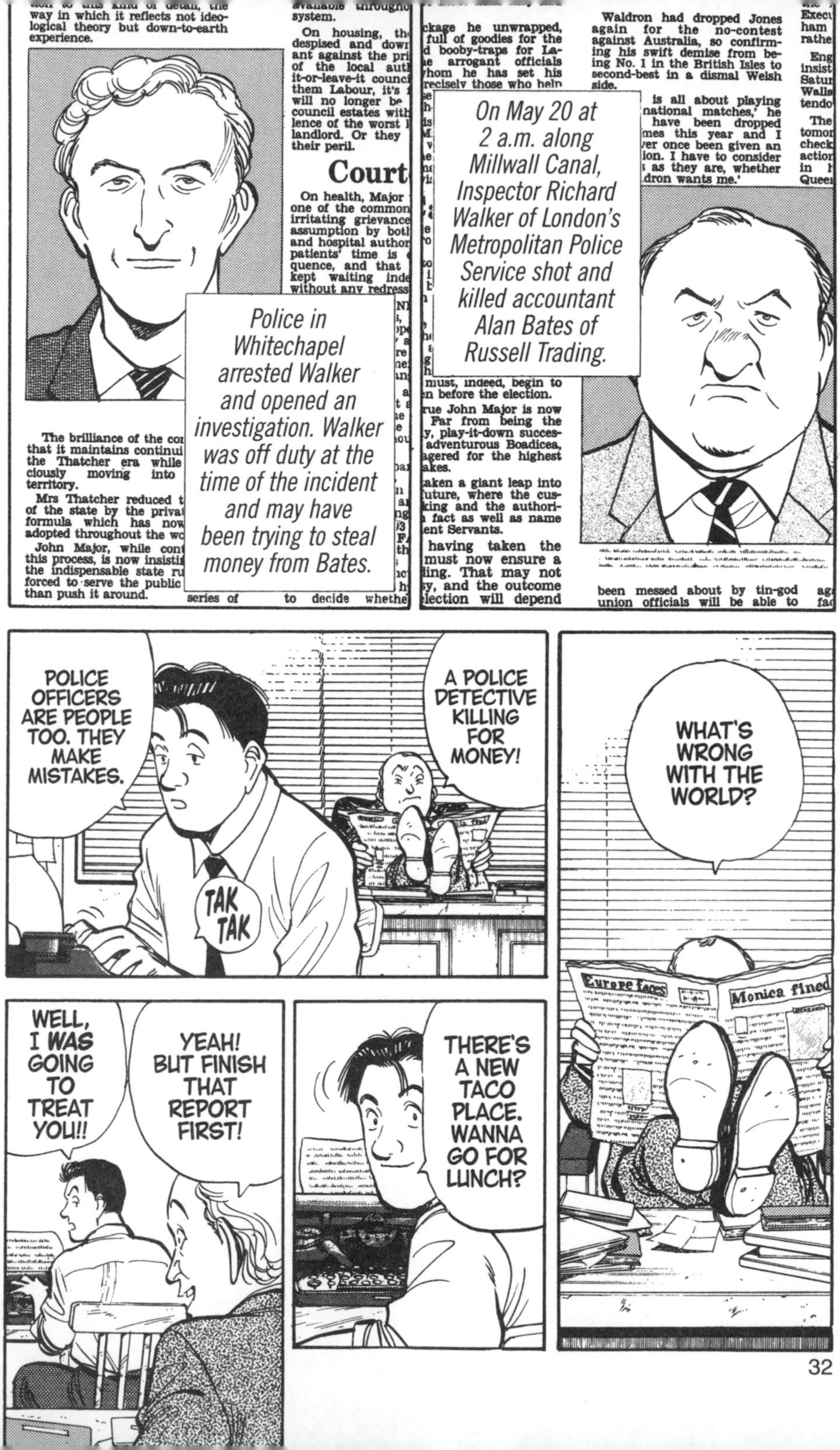
On May 20 at 2 a.m. along Millwall Canal, Inspector Richard Walker of London's Metropolitan Police Service shot and killed accountant Alan Bates of Russell Trading.
Police in Whitechapel arrested Walker and opened an investigation. Walker was off duty at the time of the incident and may have been trying to steal money from Bates.
Court
WHAT'S WRONG WITH THE WORLD?
Europe faces
Monica fined
A POLICE DETECTIVE KILLING FOR MONEY!
POLICE OFFICERS ARE PEOPLE TOO. THEY MAKE MISTAKES.
TAK TAK
THERE'S A NEW TACO PLACE. WANNA GO FOR LUNCH?
YEAH! BUT FINISH THAT REPORT FIRST!
WELL, I WAS GOING TO TREAT YOU!!

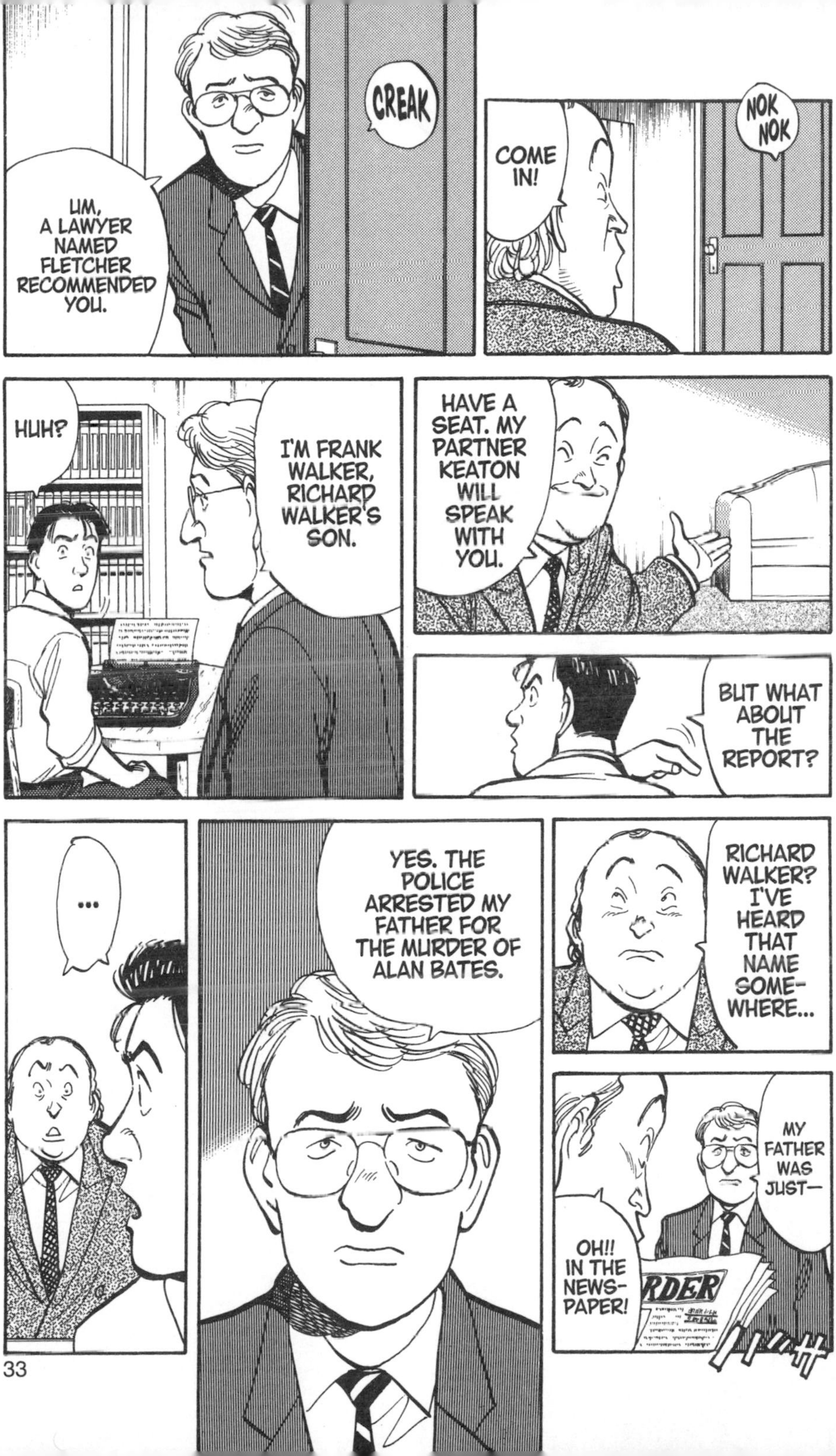
NOK NOK
COME IN!
CREAK
UM, A LAWYER NAMED FLETCHER RECOMMENDED YOU.
HAVE A SEAT. MY PARTNER KEATON WILL SPEAK WITH YOU.
BUT WHAT ABOUT THE REPORT?
I'M FRANK WALKER, RICHARD WALKER'S SON.
HUH?
RICHARD WALKER? I'VE HEARD THAT NAME SOME-WHERE...
MY FATHER WAS JUST—
OH!! IN THE NEWS-PAPER!
YES. THE POLICE ARRESTED MY FATHER FOR THE MURDER OF ALAN BATES.
...

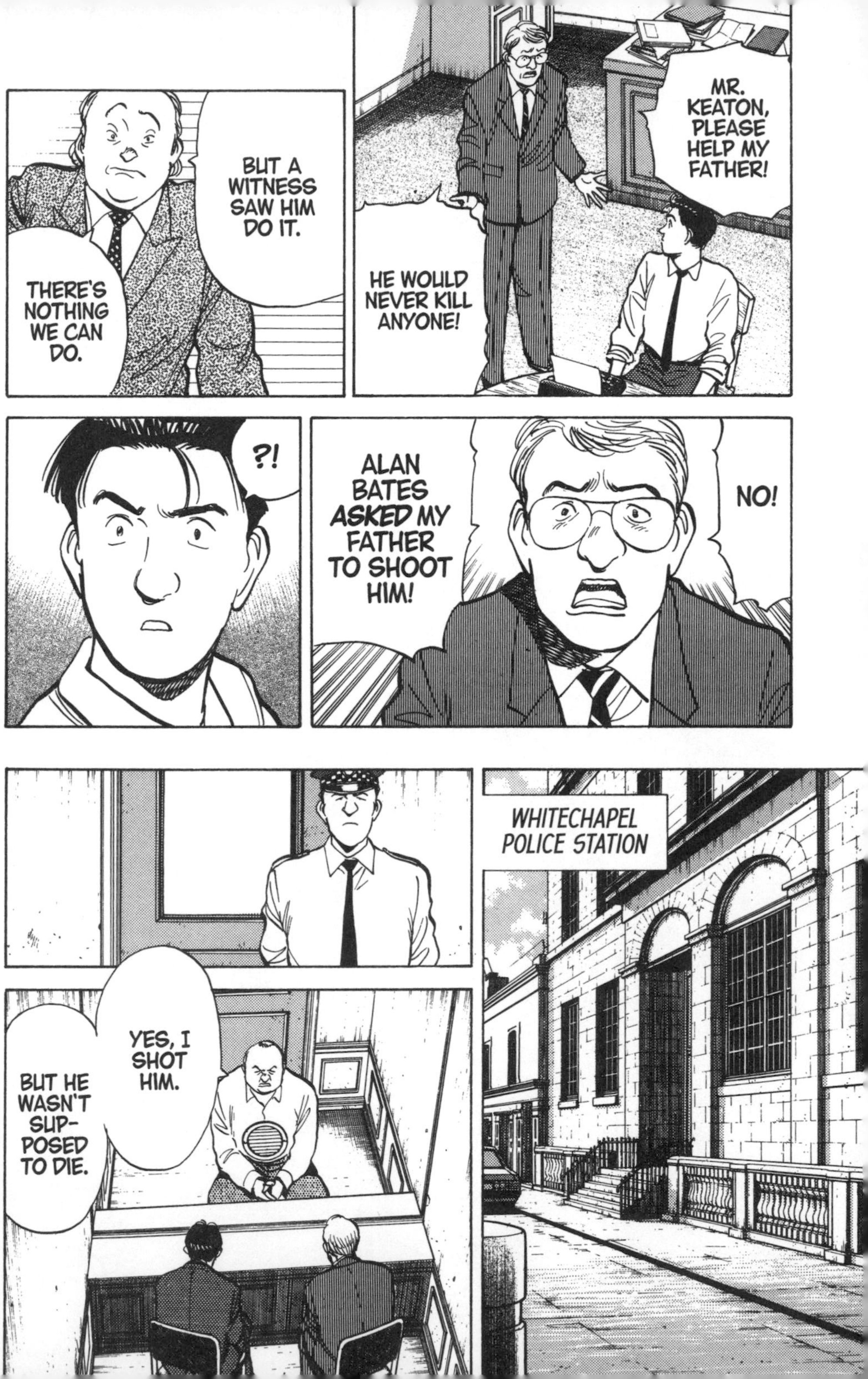
MR. KEATON, PLEASE HELP MY FATHER!
HE WOULD NEVER KILL ANYONE!
BUT A WITNESS SAW HIM DO IT.
THERE'S NOTHING WE CAN DO.
NO!
ALAN BATES ***ASKED*** MY FATHER TO SHOOT HIM!
?!
WHITECHAPEL POLICE STATION
YES, I SHOT HIM.
BUT HE WASN'T SUP-POSED TO DIE.

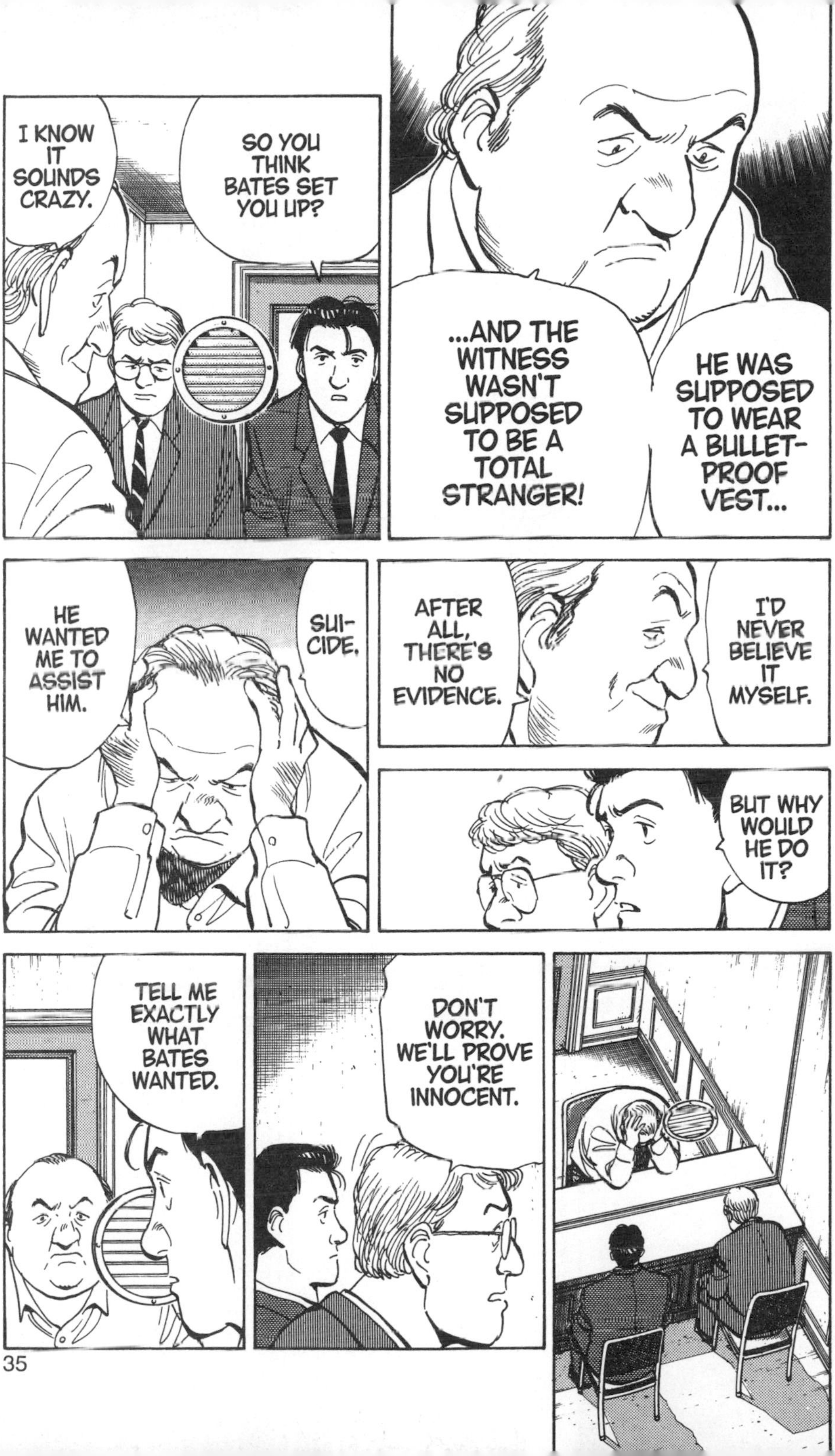
HE WAS SUPPOSED TO WEAR A BULLET-PROOF VEST...
...AND THE WITNESS WASN'T SUPPOSED TO BE A TOTAL STRANGER!
SO YOU THINK BATES SET YOU UP?
I KNOW IT SOUNDS CRAZY.
I'D NEVER BELIEVE IT MYSELF.
AFTER ALL, THERE'S NO EVIDENCE.
BUT WHY WOULD HE DO IT?
SUI-CIDE.
HE WANTED ME TO ASSIST HIM.
DON'T WORRY. WE'LL PROVE YOU'RE INNOCENT.
TELL ME EXACTLY WHAT BATES WANTED.

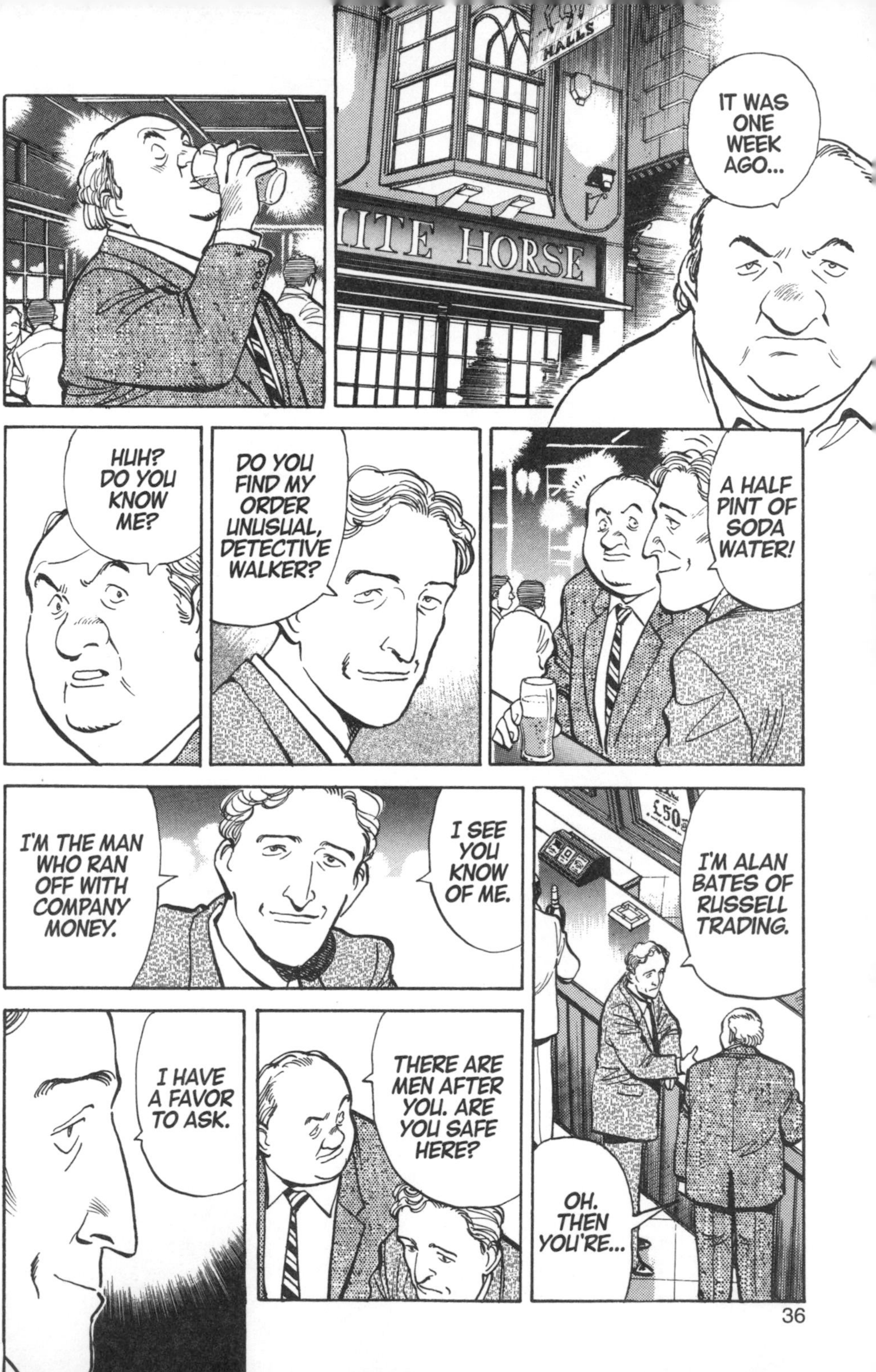
IT WAS ONE WEEK AGO...
HALLS
ITE HORSE
A HALF PINT OF SODA WATER!
DO YOU FIND MY ORDER UNUSUAL, DETECTIVE WALKER?
HUH? DO YOU KNOW ME?
I'M ALAN BATES OF RUSSELL TRADING.
£50
OH. THEN YOU'RE...
I SEE YOU KNOW OF ME.
I'M THE MAN WHO RAN OFF WITH COMPANY MONEY.
THERE ARE MEN AFTER YOU. ARE YOU SAFE HERE?
I HAVE A FAVOR TO ASK.

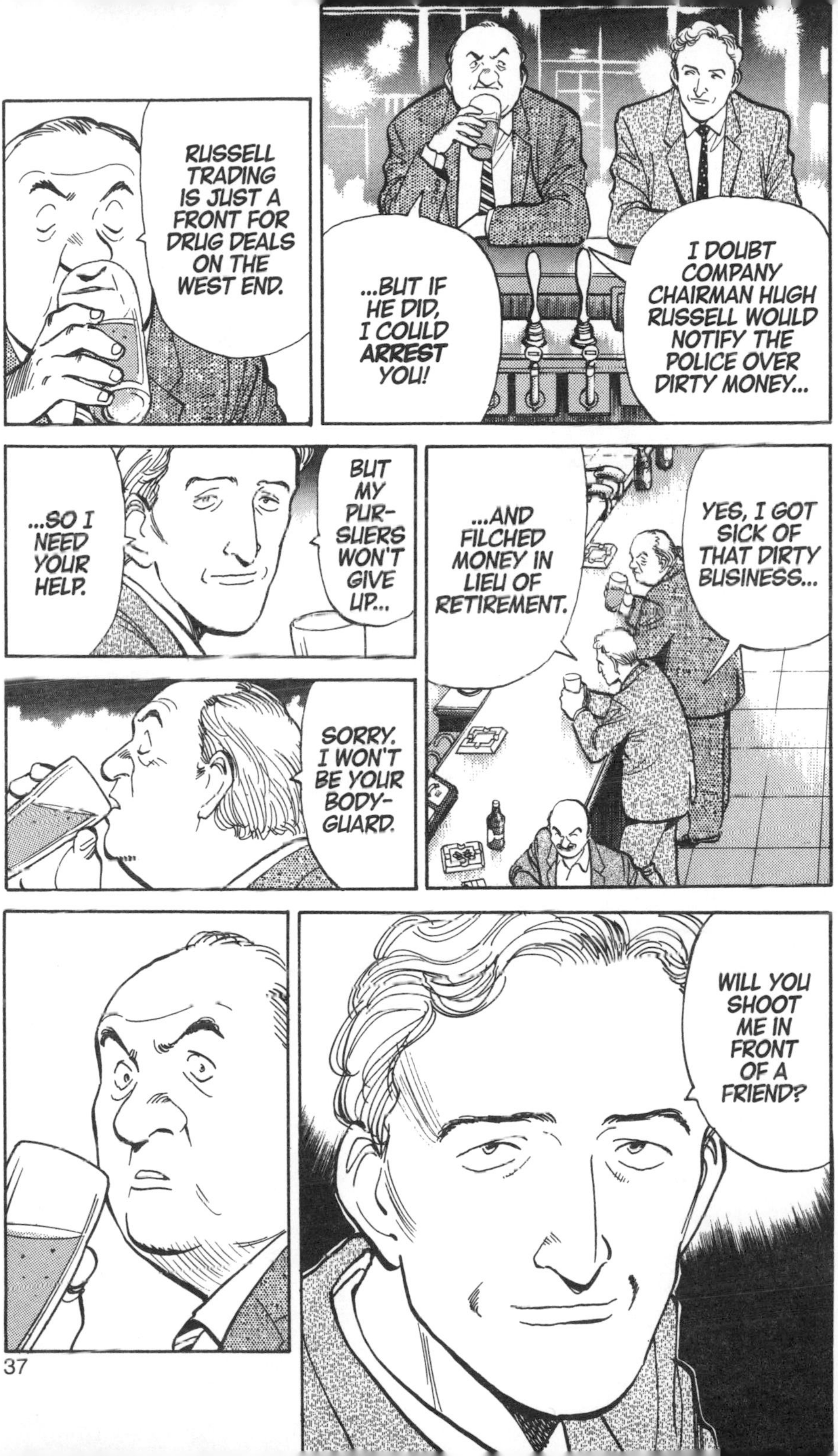
I DOUBT COMPANY CHAIRMAN HUGH RUSSELL WOULD NOTIFY THE POLICE OVER DIRTY MONEY...
...BUT IF HE DID, I COULD ARREST YOU!
RUSSELL TRADING IS JUST A FRONT FOR DRUG DEALS ON THE WEST END.
YES, I GOT SICK OF THAT DIRTY BUSINESS...
...AND FILCHED MONEY IN LIEU OF RETIREMENT.
BUT MY PURSUERS WON'T GIVE UP...
...SO I NEED YOUR HELP.
SORRY. I WON'T BE YOUR BODYGUARD.
WILL YOU SHOOT ME IN FRONT OF A FRIEND?

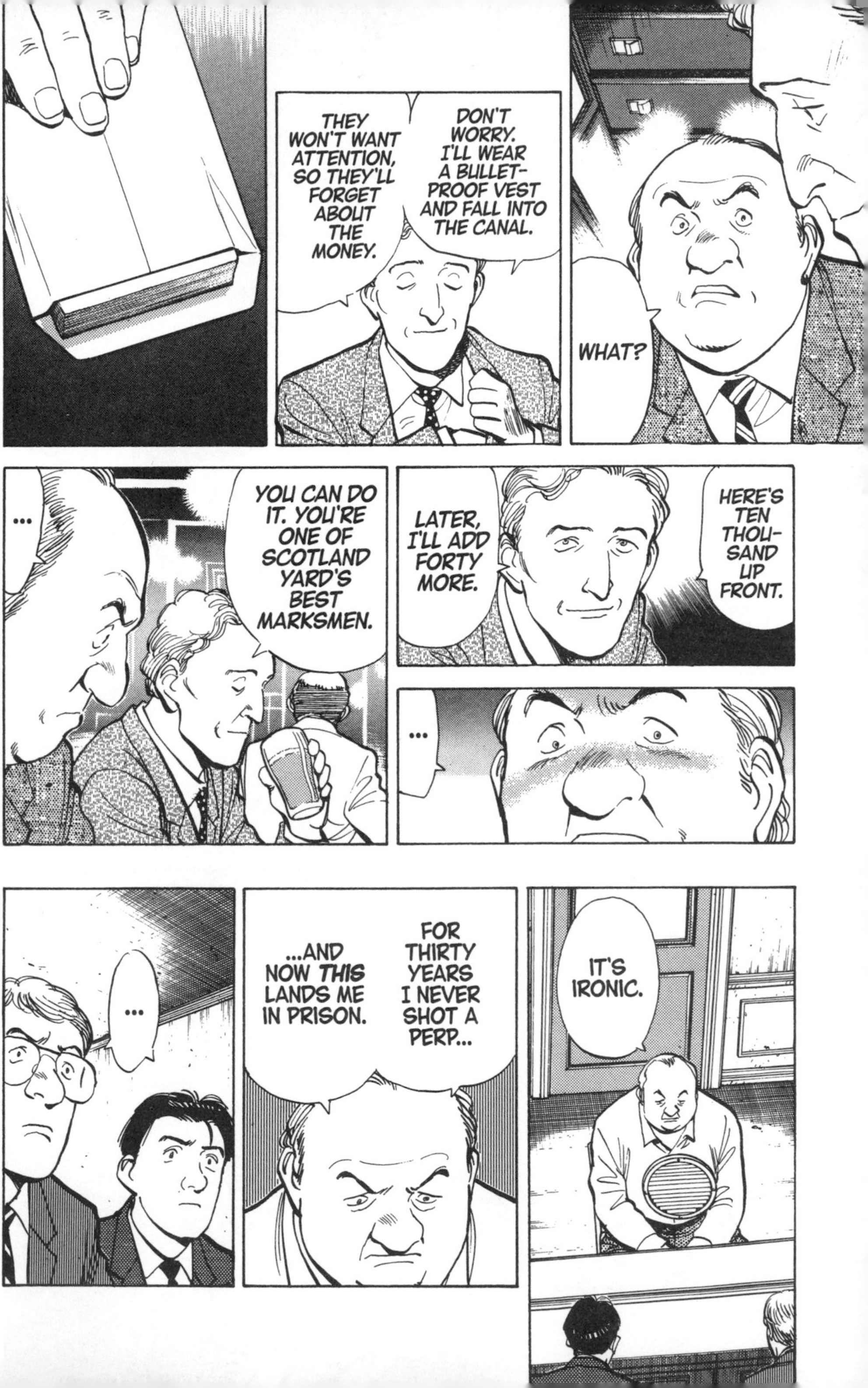
WHAT?
DON'T WORRY. I'LL WEAR A BULLET-PROOF VEST AND FALL INTO THE CANAL.
THEY WON'T WANT ATTENTION, SO THEY'LL FORGET ABOUT THE MONEY.
HERE'S TEN THOU-SAND UP FRONT.
LATER, I'LL ADD FORTY MORE.
...
YOU CAN DO IT. YOU'RE ONE OF SCOTLAND YARD'S BEST MARKSMEN.
...
IT'S IRONIC.
FOR THIRTY YEARS I NEVER SHOT A PERP...
...AND NOW *THIS* LANDS ME IN PRISON.
...

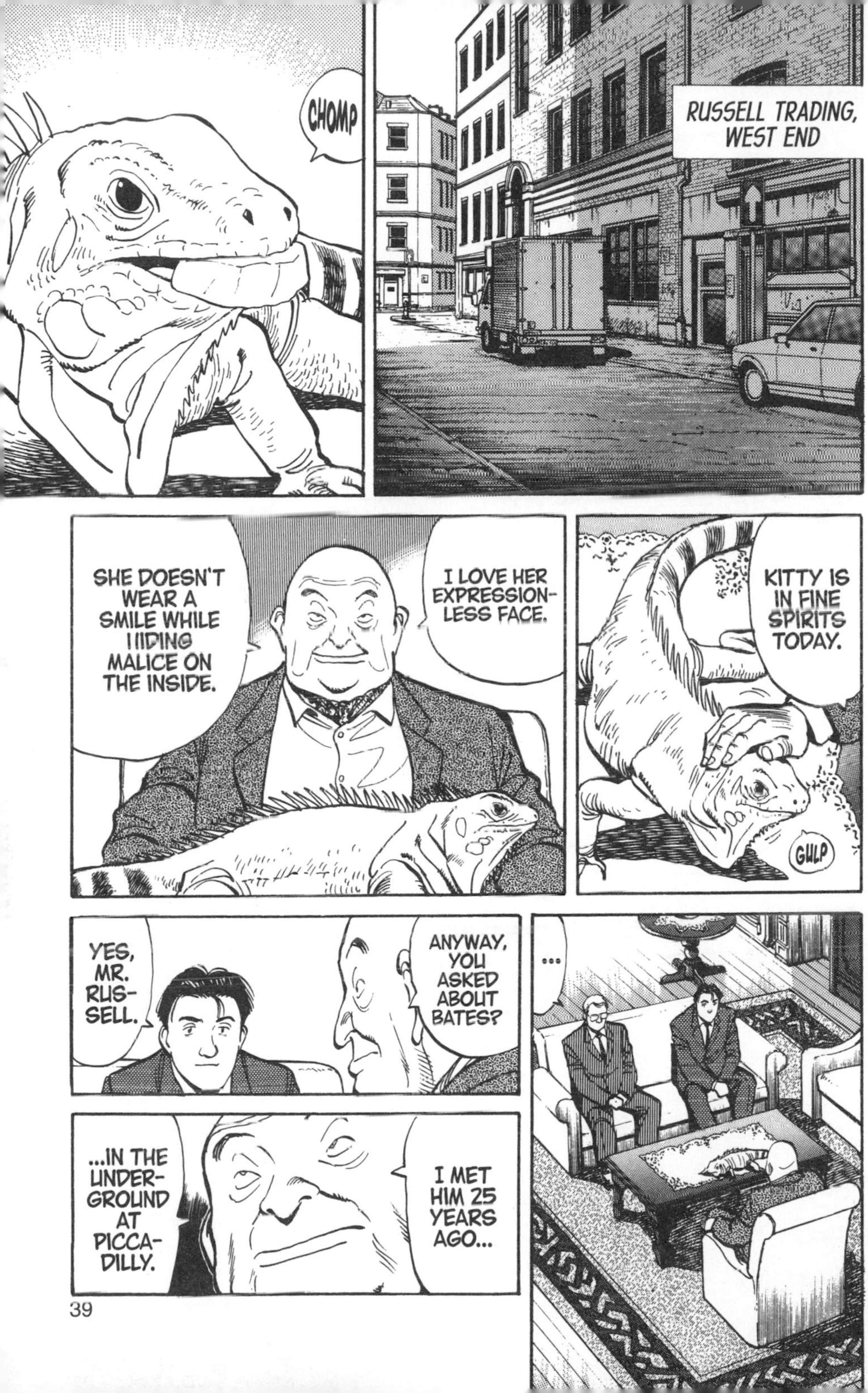
RUSSELL TRADING,
WEST END
CHOMP
KITTY IS IN FINE SPIRITS TODAY.
GULP
I LOVE HER EXPRESSIONLESS FACE.
SHE DOESN'T WEAR A SMILE WHILE HIDING MALICE ON THE INSIDE.
...
ANYWAY, YOU ASKED ABOUT BATES?
YES, MR. RUSSELL.
I MET HIM 25 YEARS AGO...
...IN THE UNDERGROUND AT PICCADILLY.

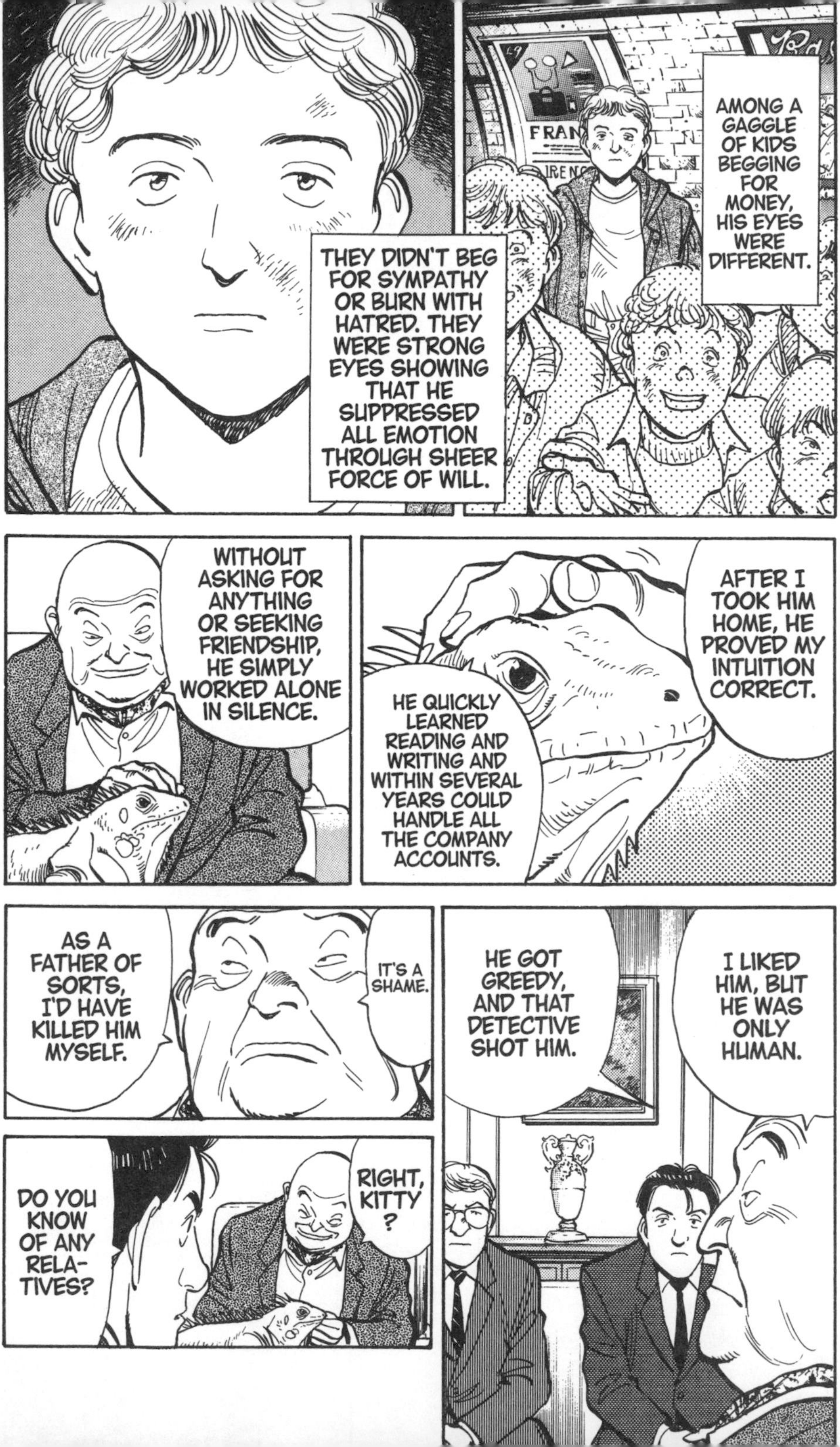
AMONG A GAGGLE OF KIDS BEGGING FOR MONEY, HIS EYES WERE DIFFERENT.
THEY DIDN'T BEG FOR SYMPATHY OR BURN WITH HATRED. THEY WERE STRONG EYES SHOWING THAT HE SUPPRESSED ALL EMOTION THROUGH SHEER FORCE OF WILL.
AFTER I TOOK HIM HOME, HE PROVED MY INTUITION CORRECT.
HE QUICKLY LEARNED READING AND WRITING AND WITHIN SEVERAL YEARS COULD HANDLE ALL THE COMPANY ACCOUNTS.
WITHOUT ASKING FOR ANYTHING OR SEEKING FRIENDSHIP, HE SIMPLY WORKED ALONE IN SILENCE.
I LIKED HIM, BUT HE WAS ONLY HUMAN.
HE GOT GREEDY, AND THAT DETECTIVE SHOT HIM.
IT'S A SHAME.
AS A FATHER OF SORTS, I'D HAVE KILLED HIM MYSELF.
RIGHT, KITTY?
DO YOU KNOW OF ANY RELA-TIVES?

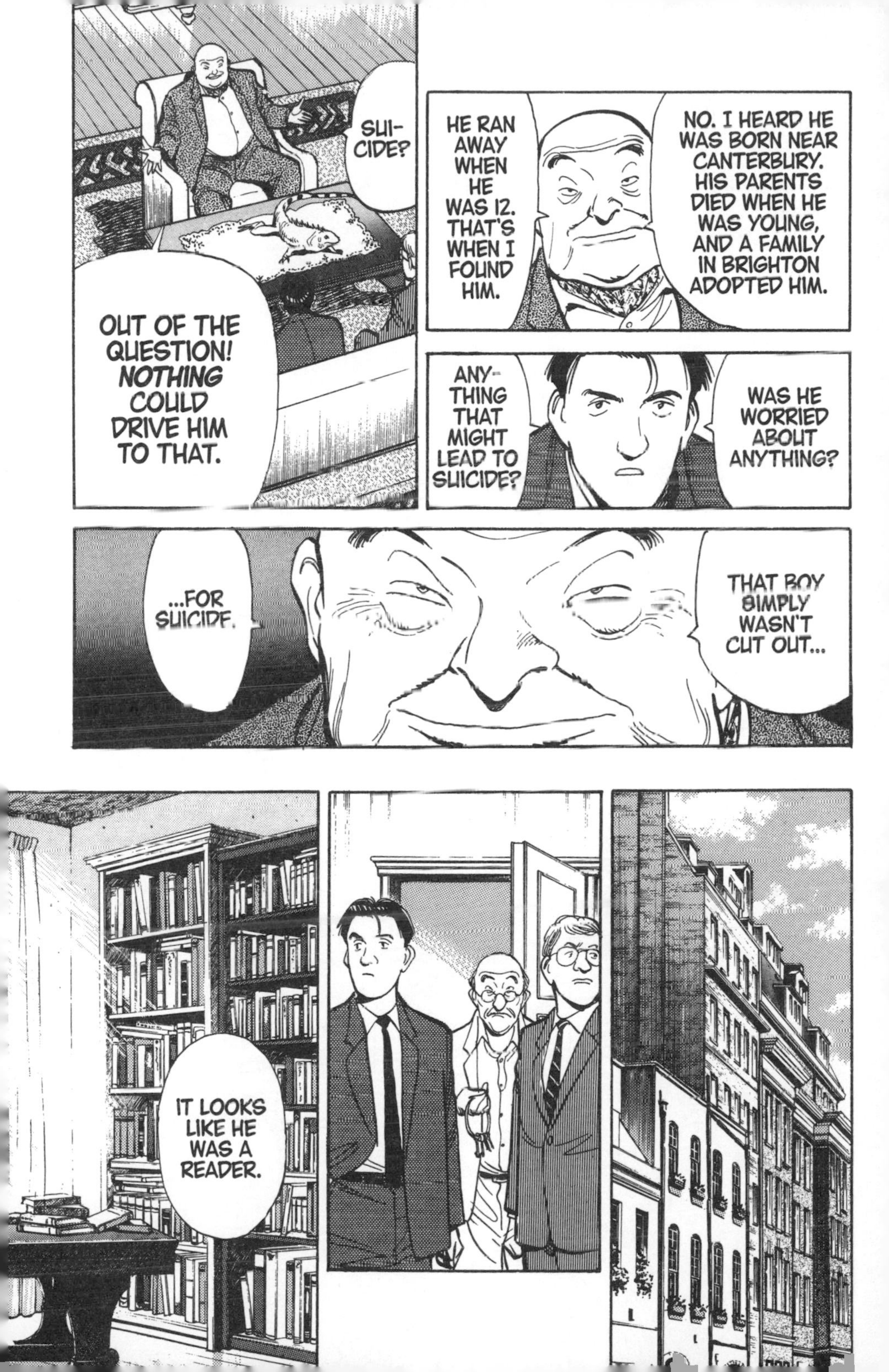
NO. I HEARD HE WAS BORN NEAR CANTERBURY. HIS PARENTS DIED WHEN HE WAS YOUNG, AND A FAMILY IN BRIGHTON ADOPTED HIM.
HE RAN AWAY WHEN HE WAS 12. THAT'S WHEN I FOUND HIM.
WAS HE WORRIED ABOUT ANYTHING?
ANY-THING THAT MIGHT LEAD TO SUICIDE?
SUI-CIDE?
OUT OF THE QUESTION! NOTHING COULD DRIVE HIM TO THAT.
THAT BOY SIMPLY WASN'T CUT OUT...
...FOR SUICIDE.
IT LOOKS LIKE HE WAS A READER.

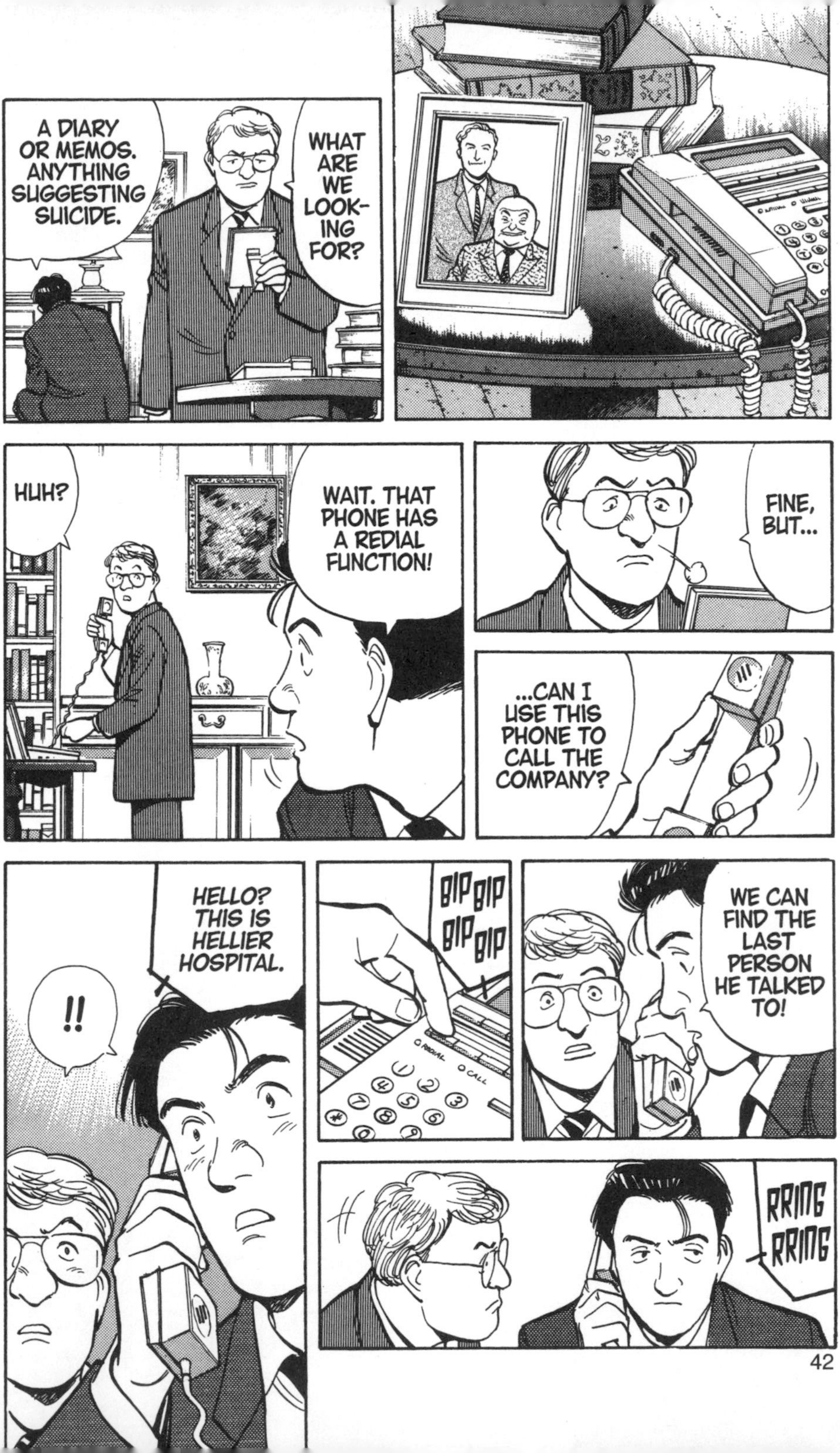
WHAT ARE WE LOOKING FOR?
A DIARY OR MEMOS. ANYTHING SUGGESTING SUICIDE.
FINE, BUT...
...CAN I USE THIS PHONE TO CALL THE COMPANY?
WAIT. THAT PHONE HAS A REDIAL FUNCTION!
HUH?
WE CAN FIND THE LAST PERSON HE TALKED TO!
BIP BIP BIP BIP
RRING RRING
HELLO? THIS IS HELLIER HOSPITAL.
!!

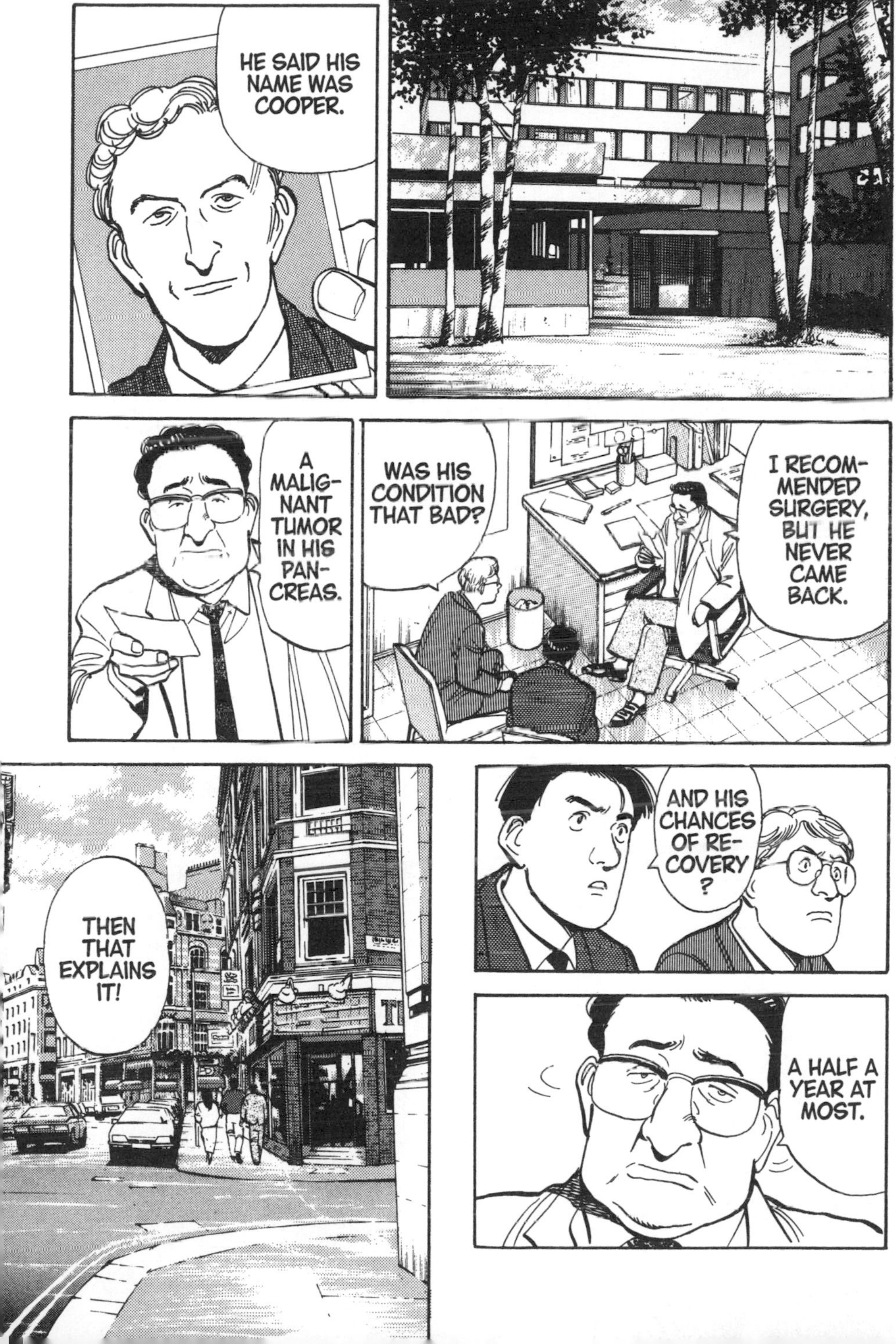
HE SAID HIS NAME WAS COOPER.
I RECOMMENDED SURGERY, BUT HE NEVER CAME BACK.
WAS HIS CONDITION THAT BAD?
A MALIGNANT TUMOR IN HIS PANCREAS.
AND HIS CHANCES OF RECOVERY?
A HALF A YEAR AT MOST.
THEN THAT EXPLAINS IT!

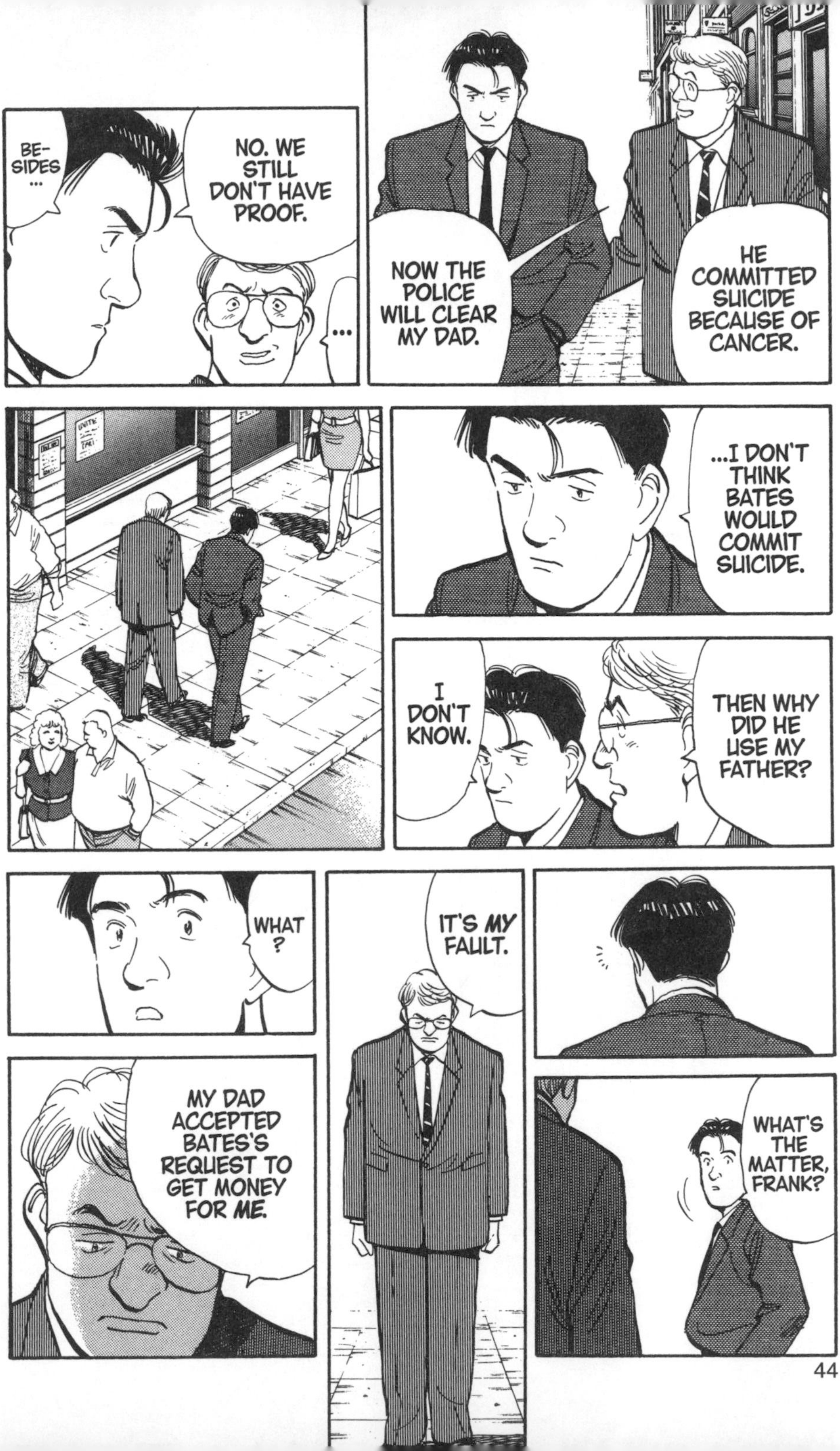
HE COMMITTED SUICIDE BECAUSE OF CANCER.
NOW THE POLICE WILL CLEAR MY DAD.
NO. WE STILL DON'T HAVE PROOF.
...
BE-SIDES...
...I DON'T THINK BATES WOULD COMMIT SUICIDE.
THEN WHY DID HE USE MY FATHER?
I DON'T KNOW.
WHAT'S THE MATTER, FRANK?
IT'S MY FAULT.
WHAT?
MY DAD ACCEPTED BATES'S REQUEST TO GET MONEY FOR ME.

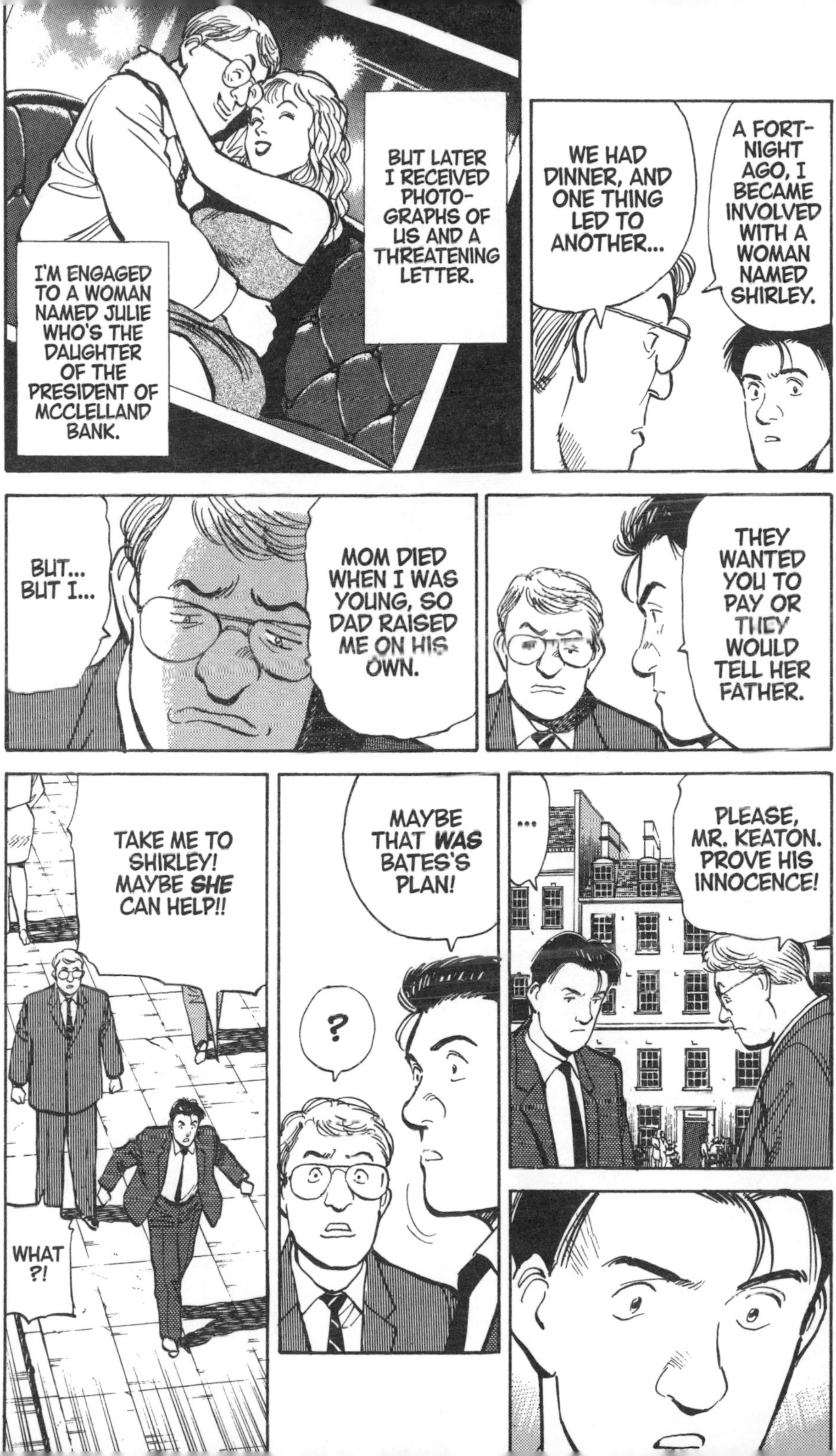
A FORTNIGHT AGO, I BECAME INVOLVED WITH A WOMAN NAMED SHIRLEY.
WE HAD DINNER, AND ONE THING LED TO ANOTHER...
BUT LATER I RECEIVED PHOTOGRAPHS OF US AND A THREATENING LETTER.
I'M ENGAGED TO A WOMAN NAMED JULIE WHO'S THE DAUGHTER OF THE PRESIDENT OF MCCLELLAND BANK.
THEY WANTED YOU TO PAY OR THEY WOULD TELL HER FATHER.
MOM DIED WHEN I WAS YOUNG, SO DAD RAISED ME ON HIS OWN.
BUT... BUT I...
PLEASE, MR. KEATON. PROVE HIS INNOCENCE!
...
MAYBE THAT WAS BATES'S PLAN!
?
TAKE ME TO SHIRLEY! MAYBE SHE CAN HELP!!
WHAT ?!

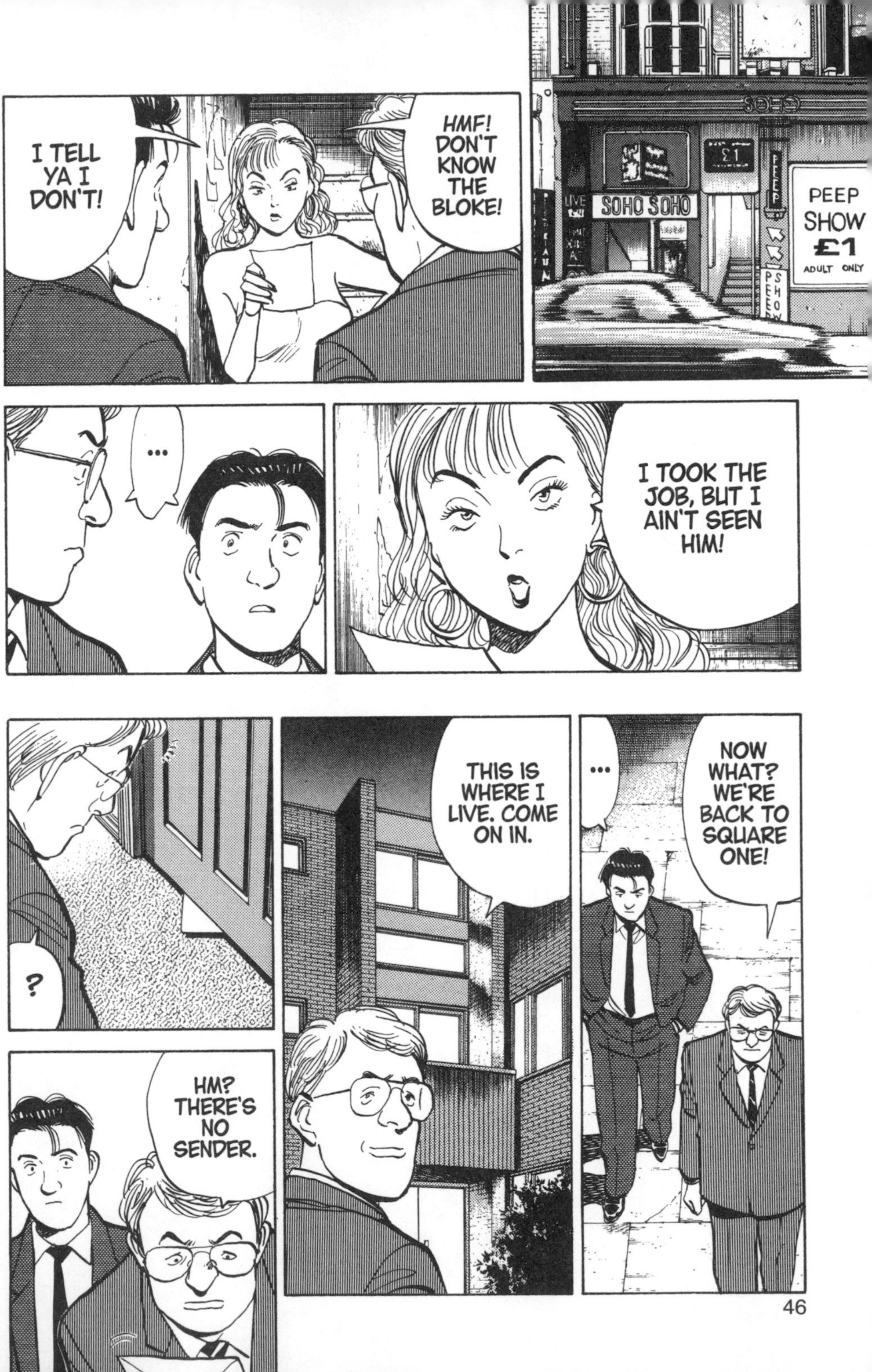
PEEP SHOW £1 ADULT ONLY
PEEP SHOW
SOHO SOHO
LIVE
£1
HMF! DON'T KNOW THE BLOKE!
I TELL YA I DON'T!
I TOOK THE JOB, BUT I AIN'T SEEN HIM!
...
NOW WHAT? WE'RE BACK TO SQUARE ONE!
...
THIS IS WHERE I LIVE. COME ON IN.
?
HM? THERE'S NO SENDER.

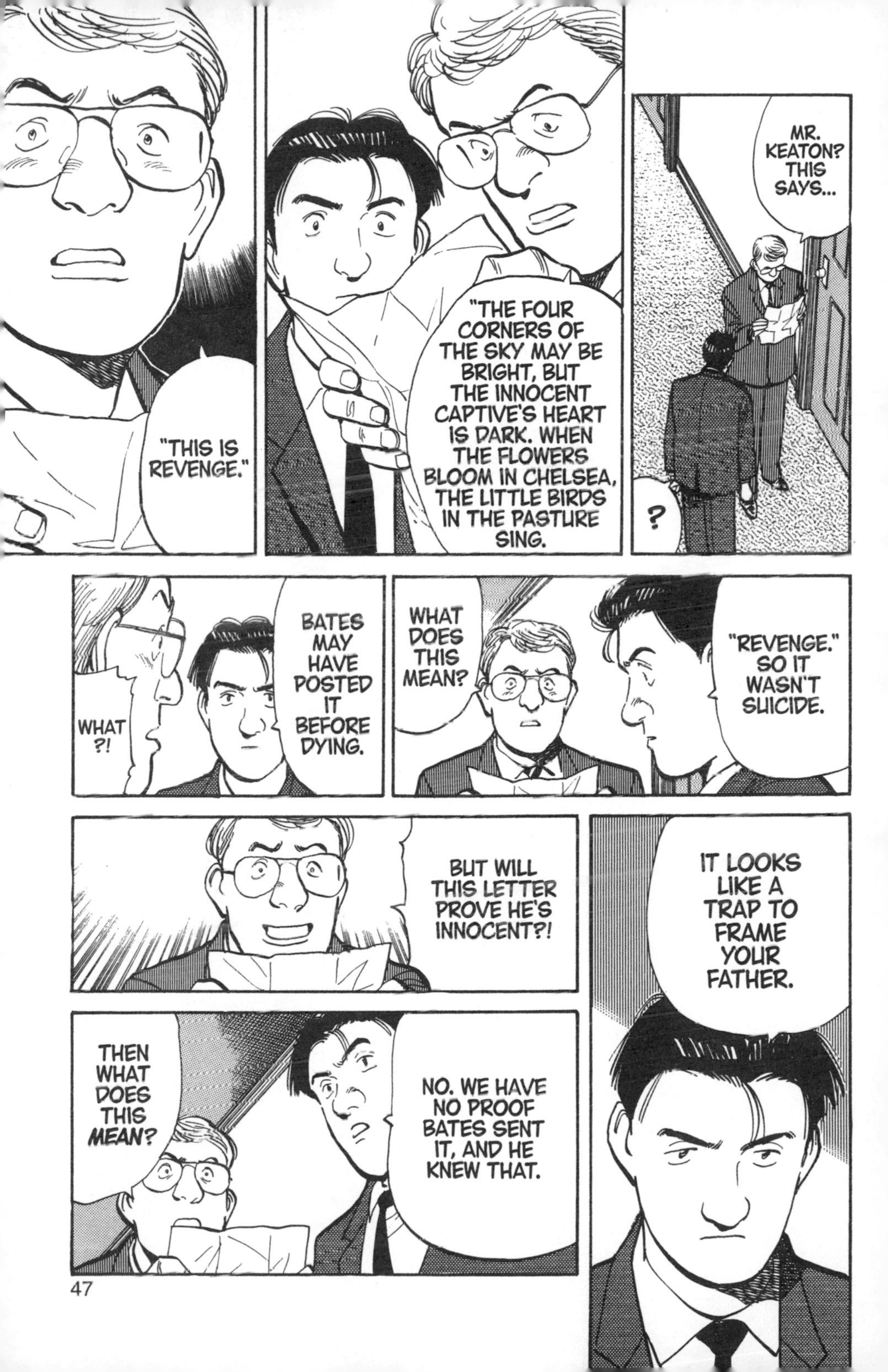
MR. KEATON? THIS SAYS...
?
"THE FOUR CORNERS OF THE SKY MAY BE BRIGHT, BUT THE INNOCENT CAPTIVE'S HEART IS DARK. WHEN THE FLOWERS BLOOM IN CHELSEA, THE LITTLE BIRDS IN THE PASTURE SING.
"THIS IS REVENGE."
"REVENGE." SO IT WASN'T SUICIDE.
WHAT DOES THIS MEAN?
BATES MAY HAVE POSTED IT BEFORE DYING.
WHAT ?!
IT LOOKS LIKE A TRAP TO FRAME YOUR FATHER.
BUT WILL THIS LETTER PROVE HE'S INNOCENT?!
NO. WE HAVE NO PROOF BATES SENT IT, AND HE KNEW THAT.
THEN WHAT DOES THIS *MEAN*?

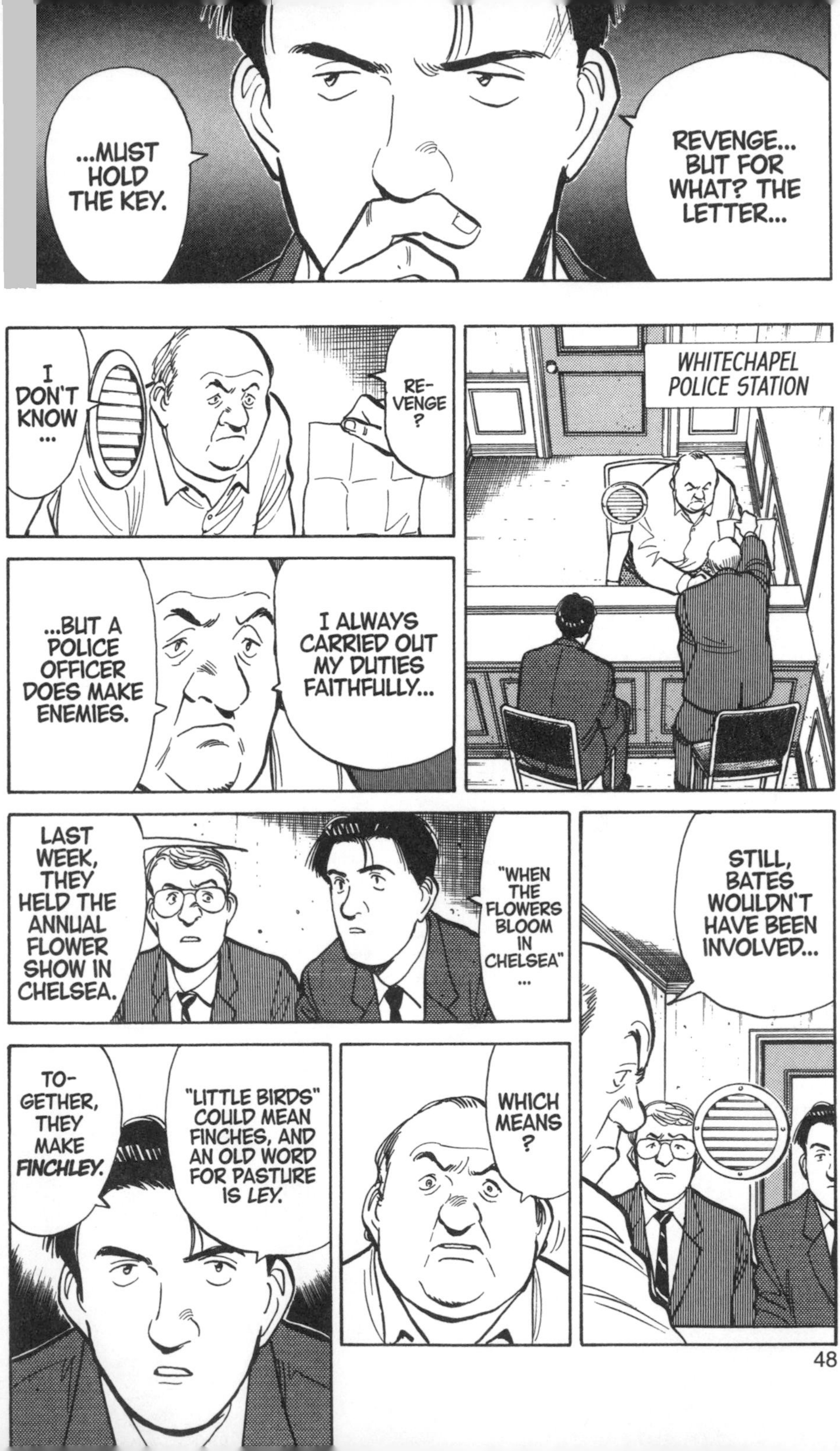
REVENGE... BUT FOR WHAT? THE LETTER...
...MUST HOLD THE KEY.
WHITECHAPEL POLICE STATION
RE-VENGE?
I DON'T KNOW...
I ALWAYS CARRIED OUT MY DUTIES FAITHFULLY...
...BUT A POLICE OFFICER DOES MAKE ENEMIES.
STILL, BATES WOULDN'T HAVE BEEN INVOLVED...
"WHEN THE FLOWERS BLOOM IN CHELSEA"...
LAST WEEK, THEY HELD THE ANNUAL FLOWER SHOW IN CHELSEA.
WHICH MEANS?
"LITTLE BIRDS" COULD MEAN FINCHES, AND AN OLD WORD FOR PASTURE IS LEY.
TO-GETHER, THEY MAKE FINCHLEY.

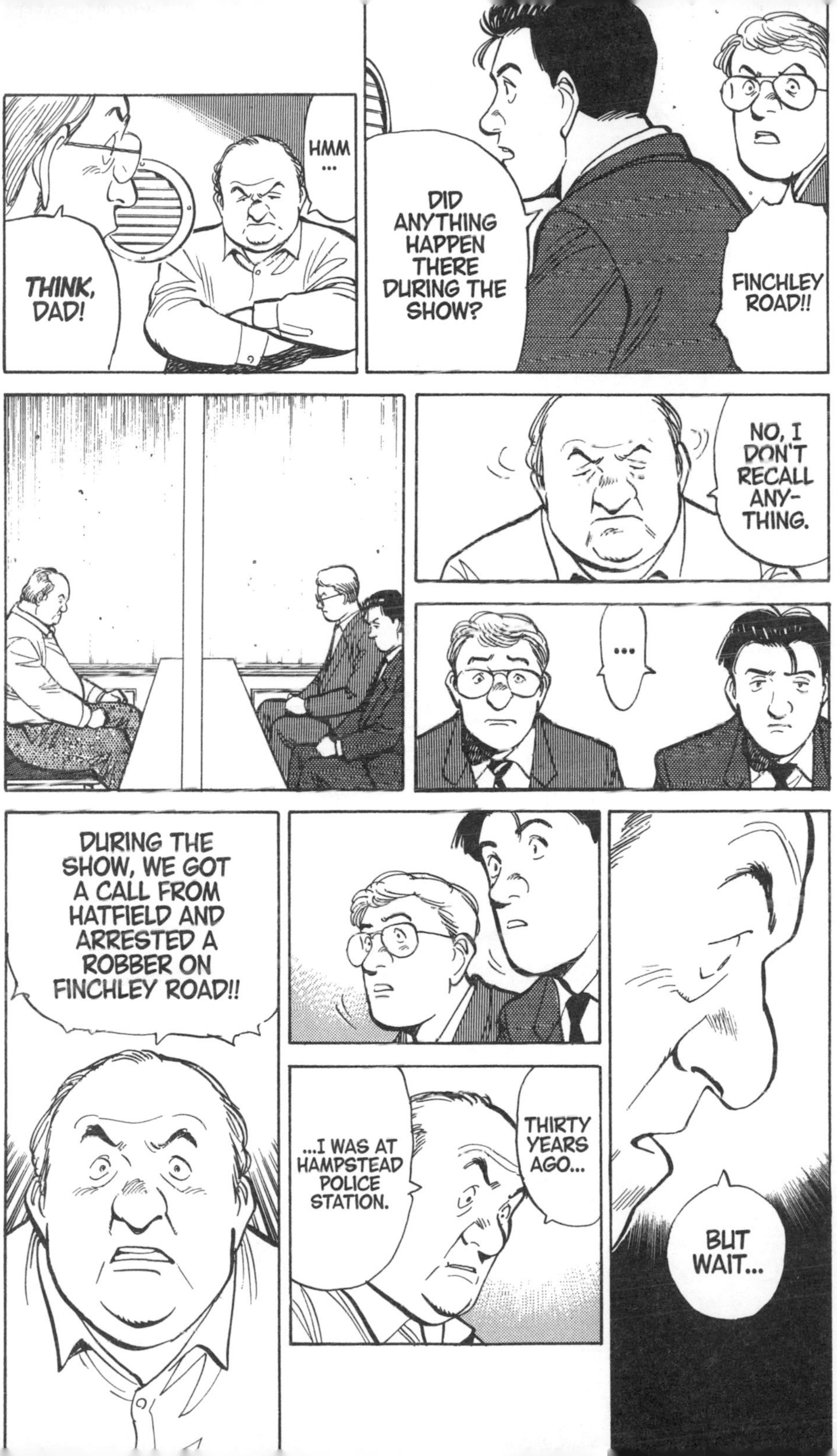
FINCHLEY ROAD!!
DID ANYTHING HAPPEN THERE DURING THE SHOW?
HMM...
THINK, DAD!
NO, I DON'T RECALL ANY-THING.
...
BUT WAIT...
THIRTY YEARS AGO...
...I WAS AT HAMPSTEAD POLICE STATION.
DURING THE SHOW, WE GOT A CALL FROM HATFIELD AND ARRESTED A ROBBER ON FINCHLEY ROAD!!

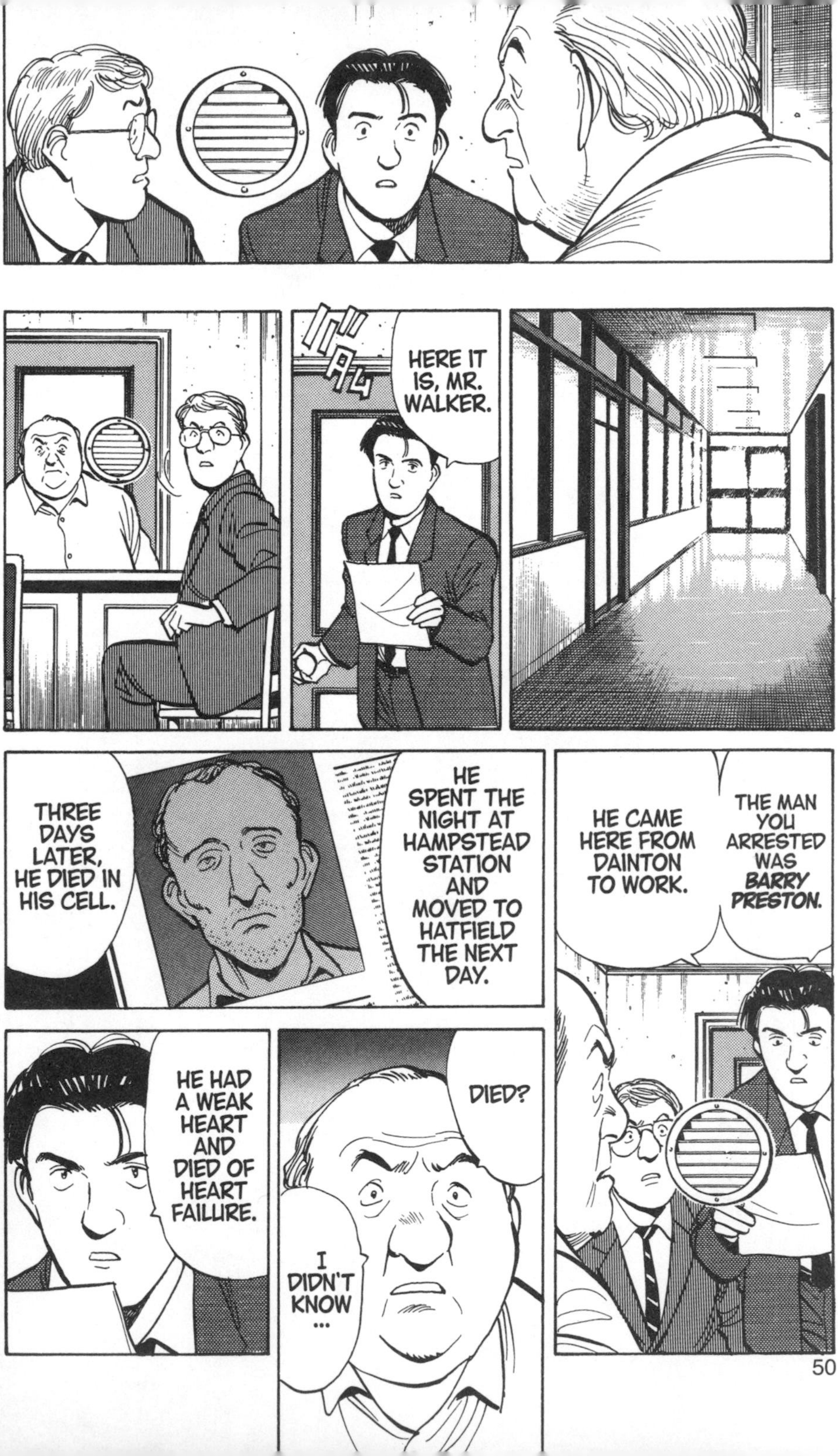
HERE IT IS, MR. WALKER.
THE MAN YOU ARRESTED WAS BARRY PRESTON.
HE CAME HERE FROM DAINTON TO WORK.
HE SPENT THE NIGHT AT HAMPSTEAD STATION AND MOVED TO HATFIELD THE NEXT DAY.
THREE DAYS LATER, HE DIED IN HIS CELL.
DIED?
I DIDN'T KNOW ...
HE HAD A WEAK HEART AND DIED OF HEART FAILURE.

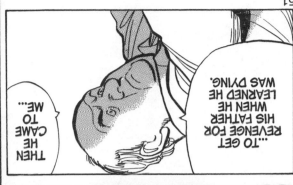

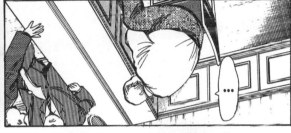

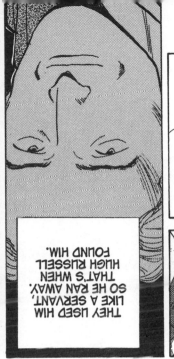

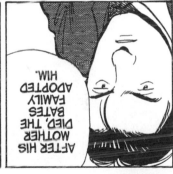

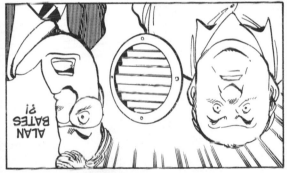

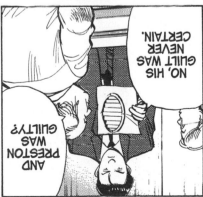

AND PRESTON WAS GUILTY?
NO, HIS GUILT WAS NEVER CERTAIN.
THEN MAYBE HE WAS INNOCENT.
HIS SON IS ALAN PRESTON, THE MAN WHO FRAMED YOU.
ALAN BATES ?!
AFTER HIS MOTHER DIED, THE BATES FAMILY ADOPTED HIM.
THEY USED HIM LIKE A SERVANT, SO HE RAN AWAY. THAT'S WHEN HUGH RUSSELL FOUND HIM.
...
THEN HE CAME TO ME...
...TO GET REVENGE FOR HIS FATHER WHEN HE LEARNED HE WAS DYING.

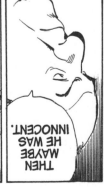

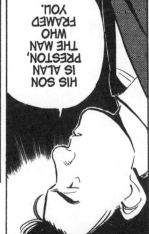

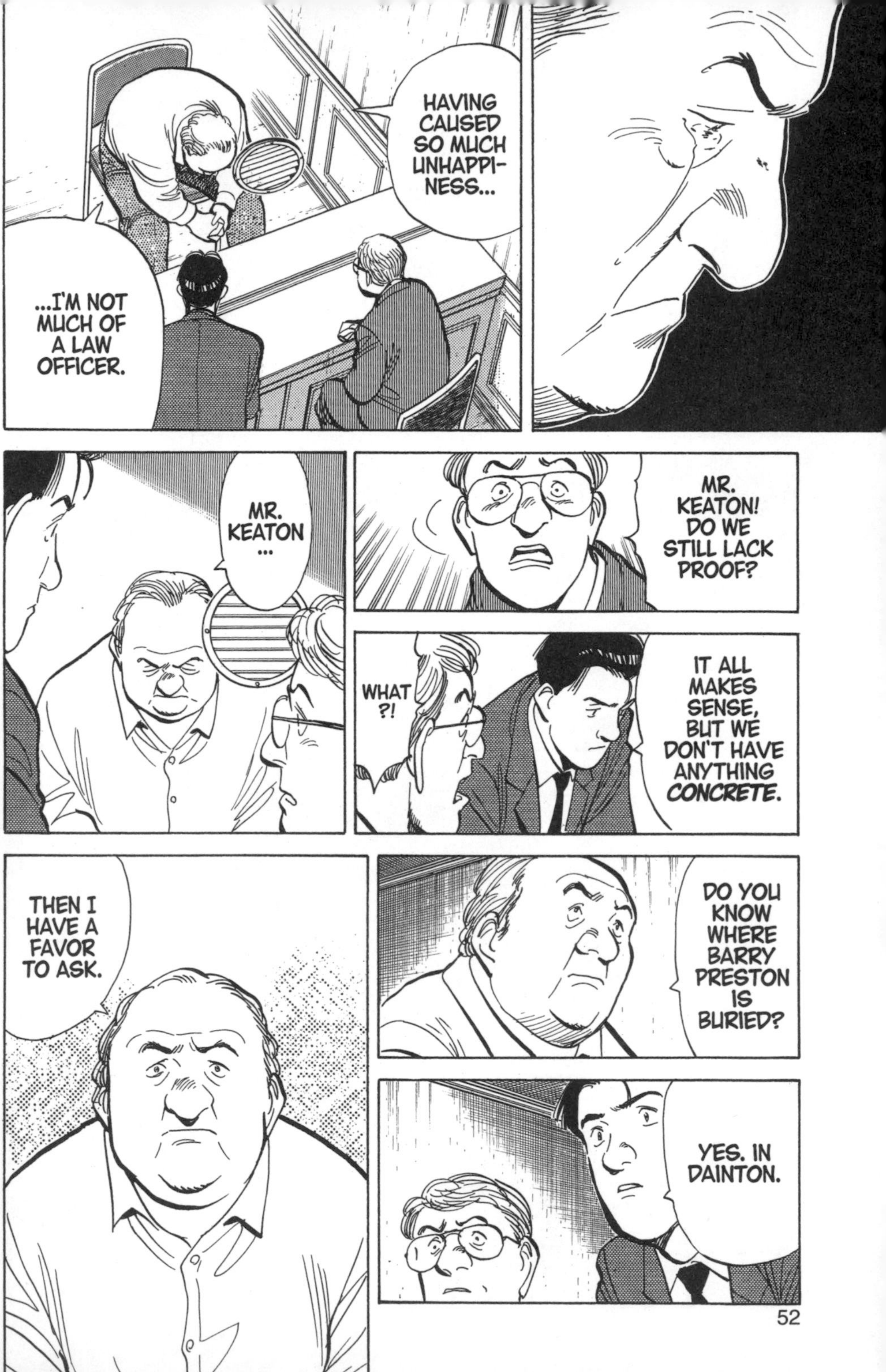
HAVING CAUSED SO MUCH UNHAPPINESS...
...I'M NOT MUCH OF A LAW OFFICER.
MR. KEATON! DO WE STILL LACK PROOF?
IT ALL MAKES SENSE, BUT WE DON'T HAVE ANYTHING *CONCRETE*.
WHAT?!
MR. KEATON...
DO YOU KNOW WHERE BARRY PRESTON IS BURIED?
YES. IN DAINTON.
THEN I HAVE A FAVOR TO ASK.

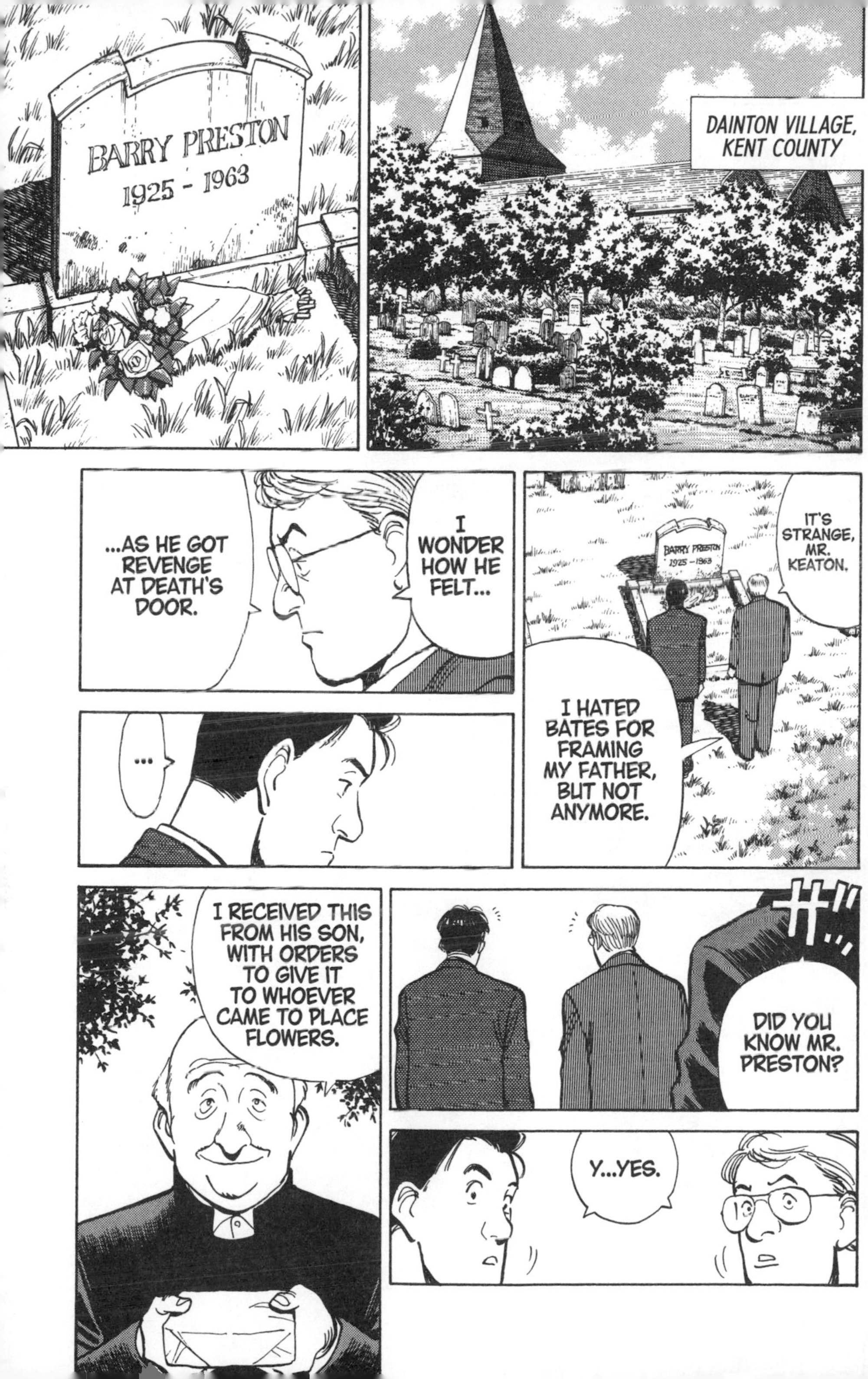
DAINTON VILLAGE, KENT COUNTY
BARRY PRESTON 1925 - 1963
IT'S STRANGE, MR. KEATON.
I HATED BATES FOR FRAMING MY FATHER, BUT NOT ANYMORE.
I WONDER HOW HE FELT...
...AS HE GOT REVENGE AT DEATH'S DOOR.
...
DID YOU KNOW MR. PRESTON?
Y...YES.
I RECEIVED THIS FROM HIS SON, WITH ORDERS TO GIVE IT TO WHOEVER CAME TO PLACE FLOWERS.

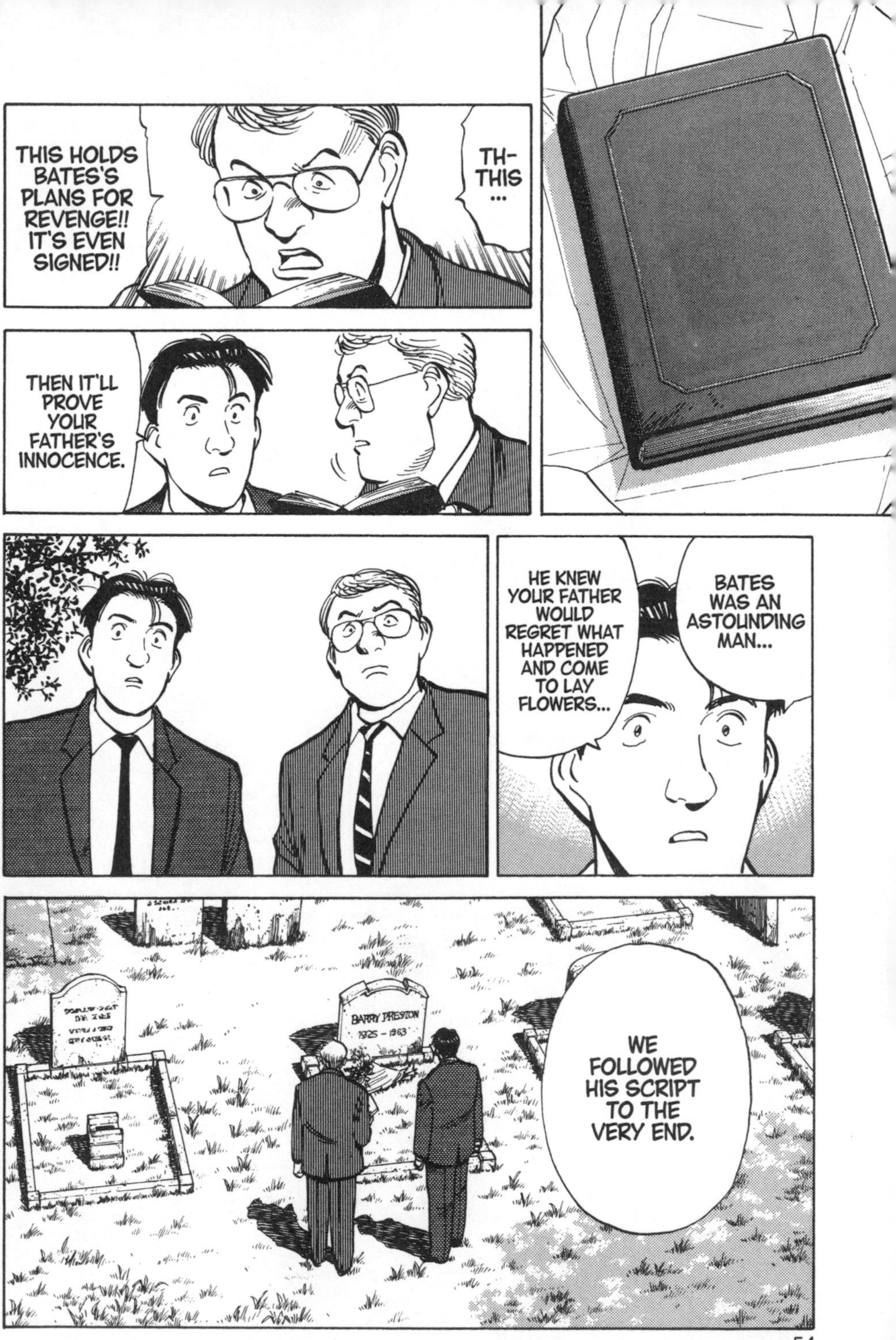
TH-
THIS
...
THIS HOLDS BATES'S PLANS FOR REVENGE!! IT'S EVEN SIGNED!!
THEN IT'LL PROVE YOUR FATHER'S INNOCENCE.
BATES WAS AN ASTOUNDING MAN...
HE KNEW YOUR FATHER WOULD REGRET WHAT HAPPENED AND COME TO LAY FLOWERS...
BARRY PRESTON
1925 - 1963
WE FOLLOWED HIS SCRIPT TO THE VERY END.

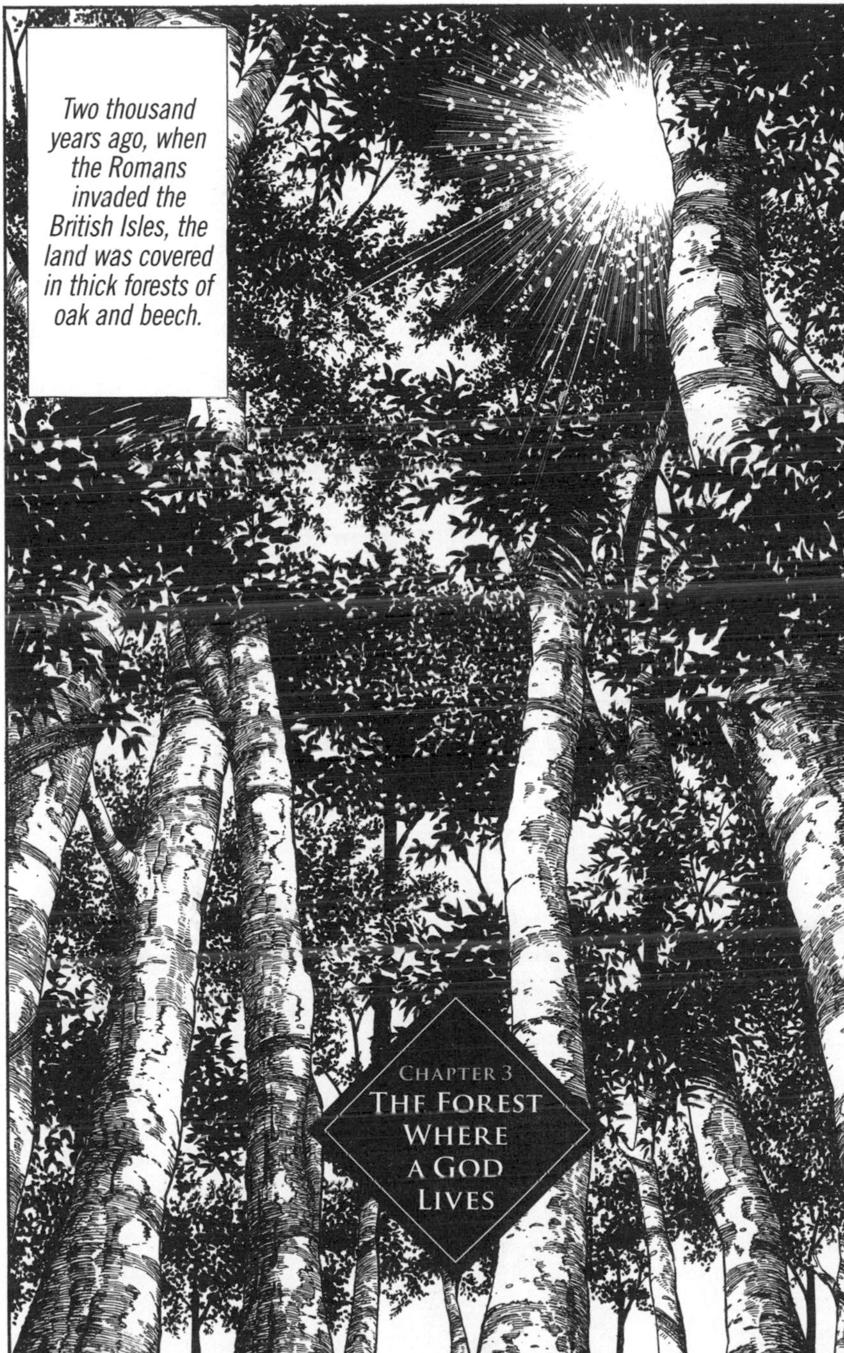
Two thousand years ago, when the Romans invaded the British Isles, the land was covered in thick forests of oak and beech.
CHAPTER 3 THE FOREST WHERE A GOD LIVES

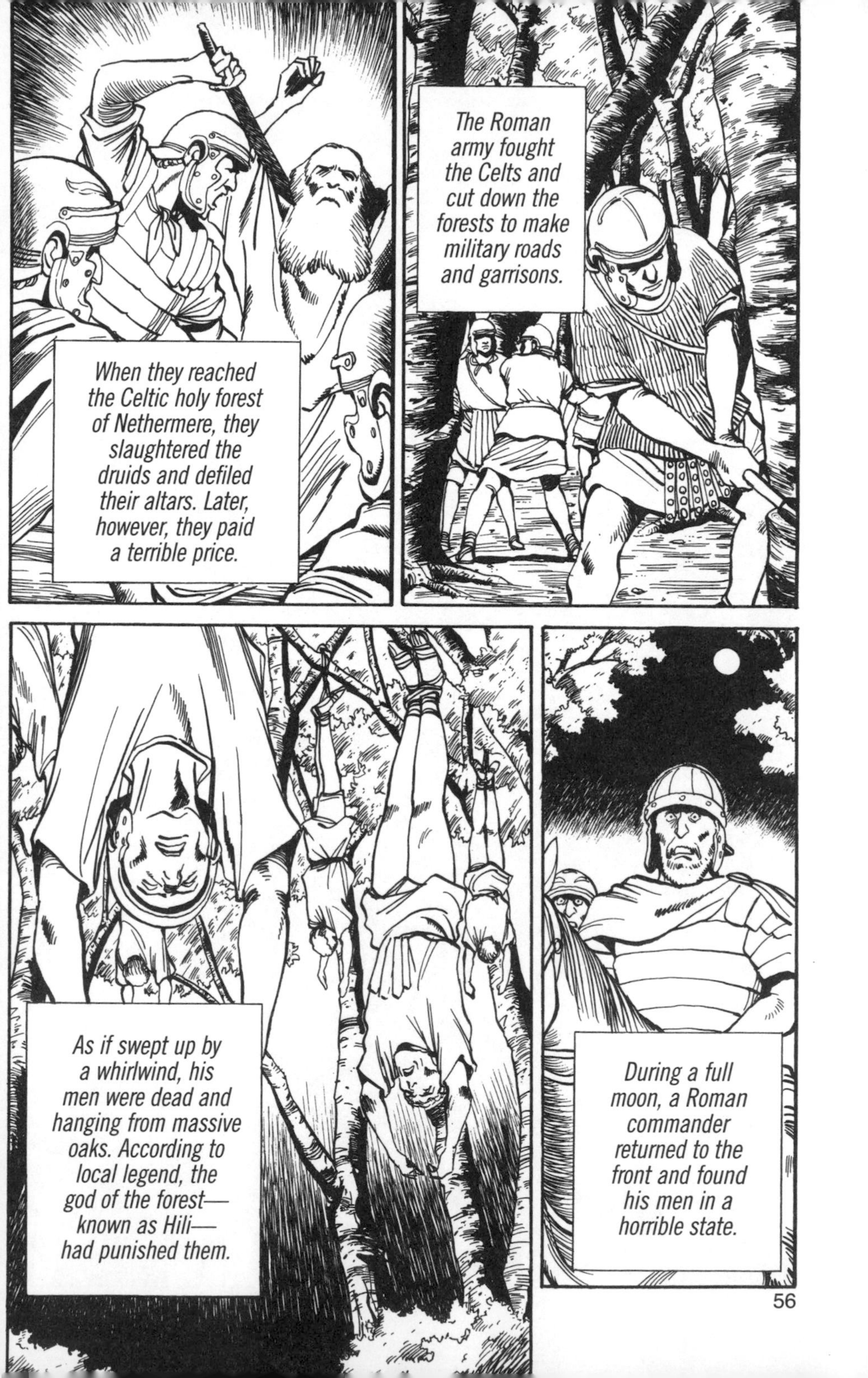
The Roman army fought the Celts and cut down the forests to make military roads and garrisons.
When they reached the Celtic holy forest of Nethermere, they slaughtered the druids and defiled their altars. Later, however, they paid a terrible price.
During a full moon, a Roman commander returned to the front and found his men in a horrible state.
As if swept up by a whirlwind, his men were dead and hanging from massive oaks. According to local legend, the god of the forest—known as Hili—had punished them.

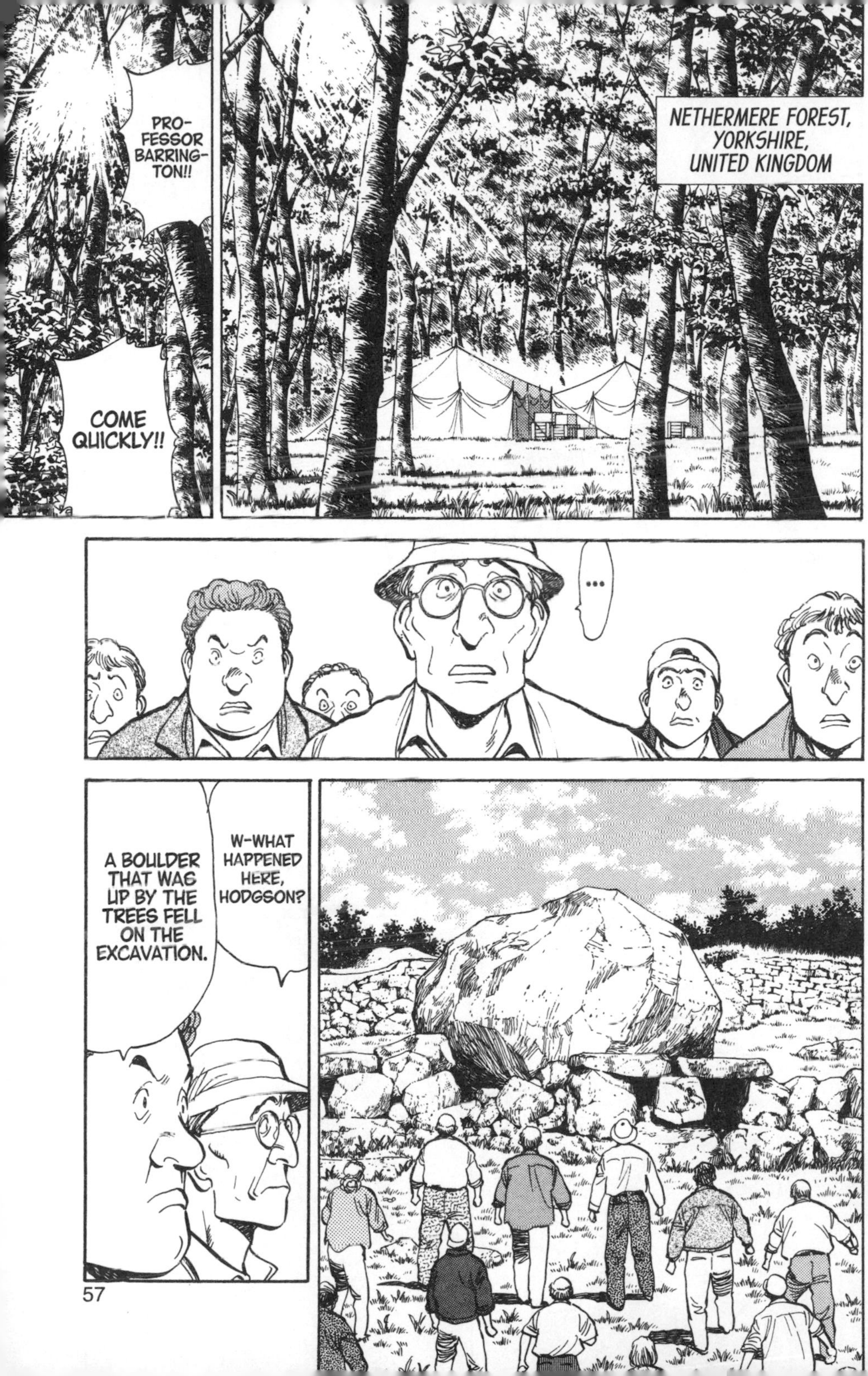
NETHERMERE FOREST, YORKSHIRE, UNITED KINGDOM
PRO-FESSOR BARRING-TON!!
COME QUICKLY!!
...
W-WHAT HAPPENED HERE, HODGSON?
A BOULDER THAT WAS UP BY THE TREES FELL ON THE EXCAVATION.

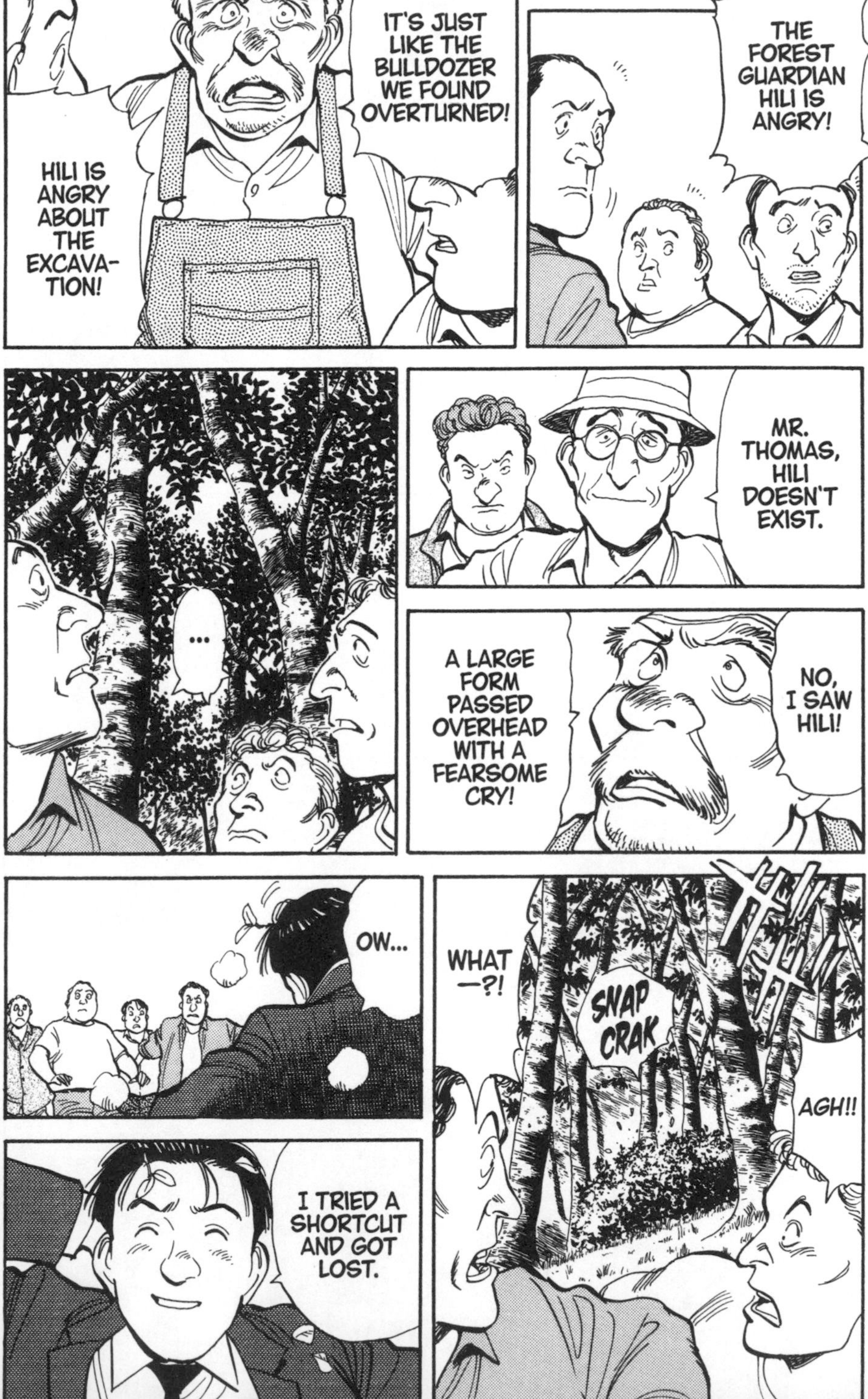
THE FOREST GUARDIAN HILI IS ANGRY!
IT'S JUST LIKE THE BULLDOZER WE FOUND OVERTURNED!
HILI IS ANGRY ABOUT THE EXCAVATION!
MR. THOMAS, HILI DOESN'T EXIST.
NO, I SAW HILI!
A LARGE FORM PASSED OVERHEAD WITH A FEARSOME CRY!
...
WHAT—?!
SNAP CRAK
AGH!!
OW...
I TRIED A SHORTCUT AND GOT LOST.

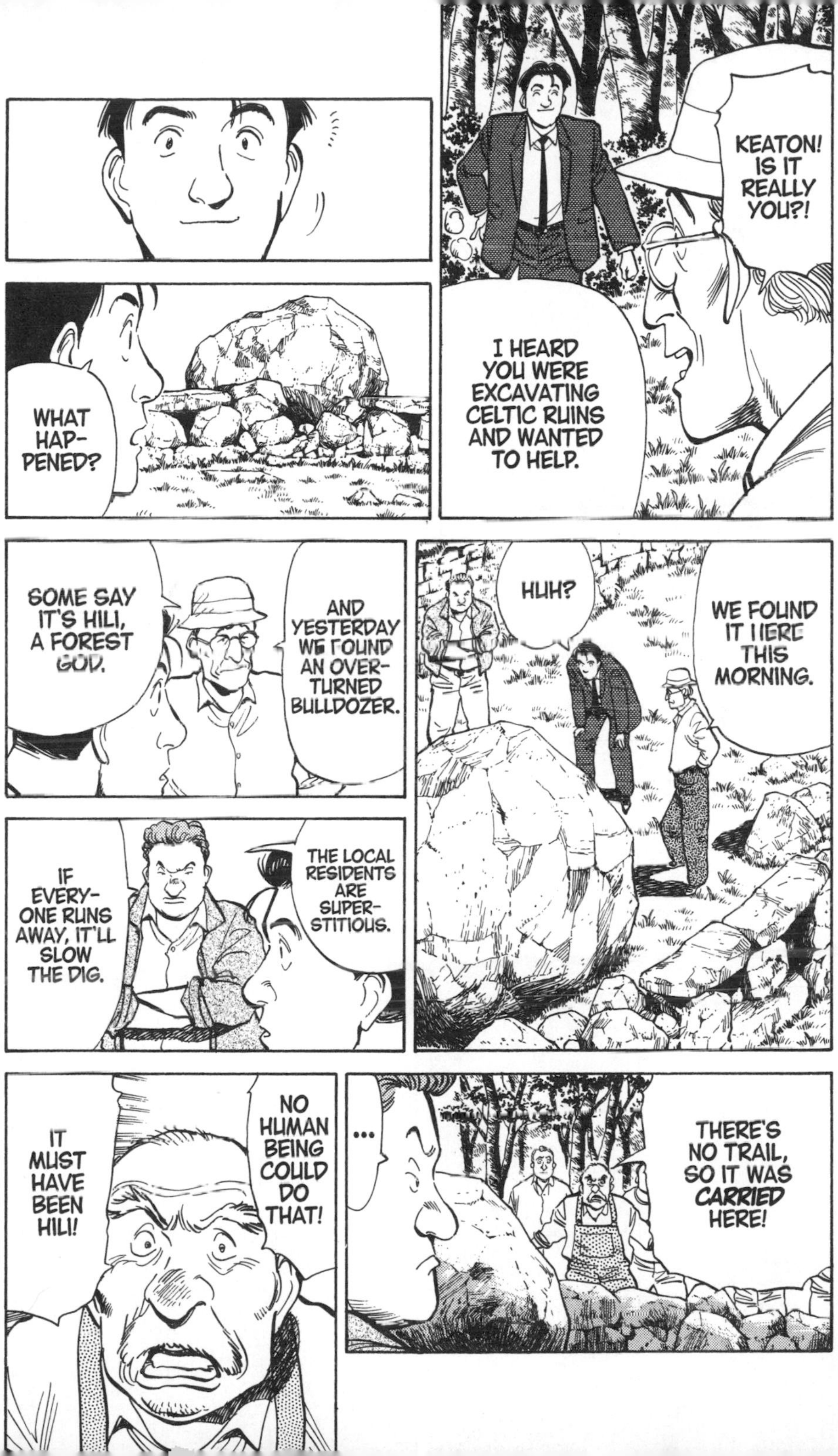
KEATON! IS IT REALLY YOU?!
I HEARD YOU WERE EXCAVATING CELTIC RUINS AND WANTED TO HELP.
WHAT HAP-PENED?
WE FOUND IT HERE THIS MORNING.
HUH?
AND YESTERDAY WE FOUND AN OVER-TURNED BULLDOZER.
SOME SAY IT'S HILI, A FOREST GOD.
THE LOCAL RESIDENTS ARE SUPER-STITIOUS.
IF EVERY-ONE RUNS AWAY, IT'LL SLOW THE DIG.
THERE'S NO TRAIL, SO IT WAS CARRIED HERE!
...
NO HUMAN BEING COULD DO THAT!
IT MUST HAVE BEEN HILI!

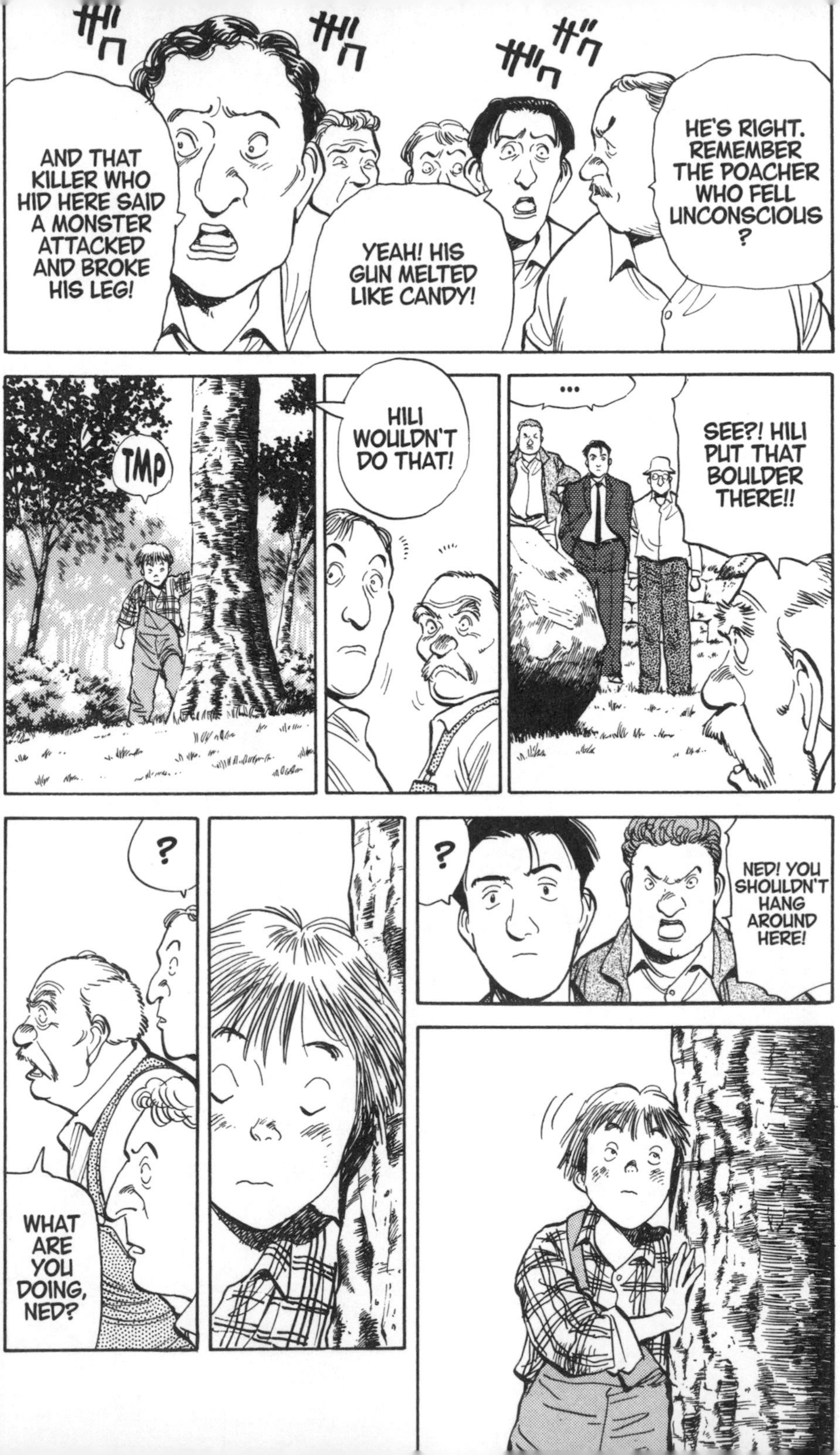
HE'S RIGHT. REMEMBER THE POACHER WHO FELL UNCONSCIOUS?
YEAH! HIS GUN MELTED LIKE CANDY!
AND THAT KILLER WHO HID HERE SAID A MONSTER ATTACKED AND BROKE HIS LEG!
SEE?! HILI PUT THAT BOULDER THERE!!
...
HILI WOULDN'T DO THAT!
TMP
NED! YOU SHOULDN'T HANG AROUND HERE!
?
?
WHAT ARE YOU DOING, NED?

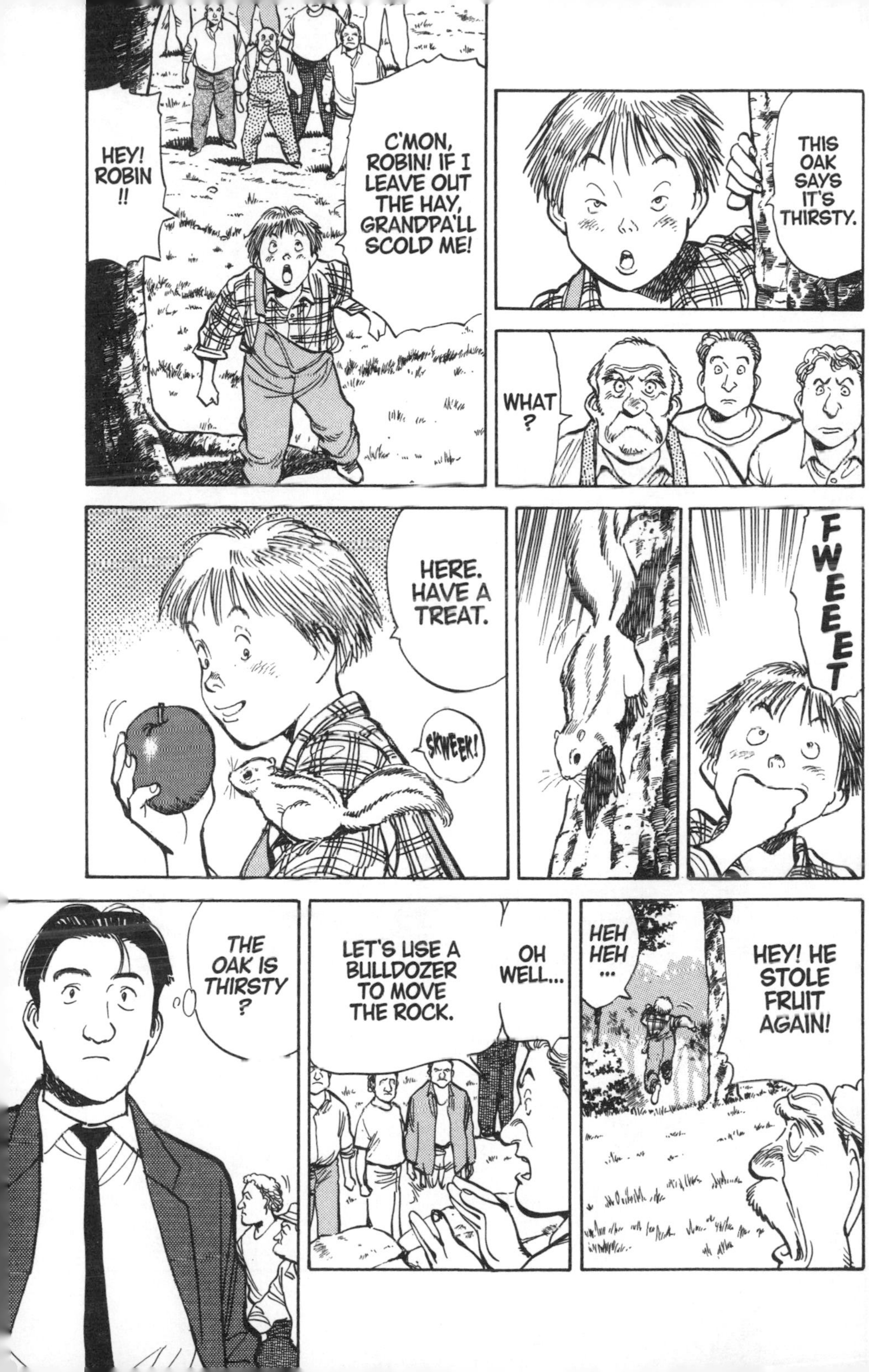
THIS OAK SAYS IT'S THIRSTY.
WHAT?
C'MON, ROBIN! IF I LEAVE OUT THE HAY, GRANDPA'LL SCOLD ME!
HEY! ROBIN!!
FWEEET
HERE. HAVE A TREAT.
SKWEEK!
HEY! HE STOLE FRUIT AGAIN!
HEH HEH...
OH WELL...
LET'S USE A BULLDOZER TO MOVE THE ROCK.
THE OAK IS THIRSTY?

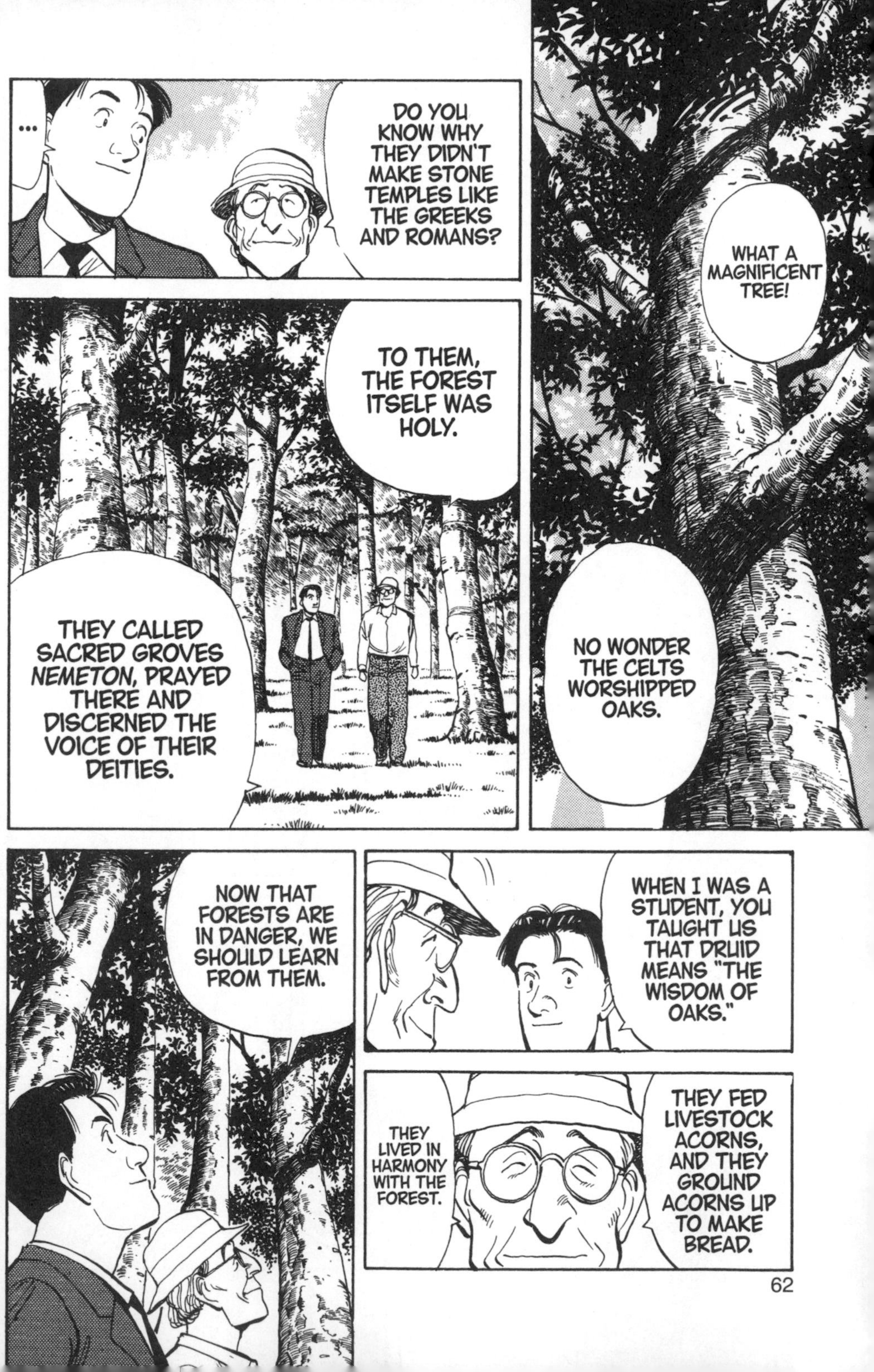
WHAT A MAGNIFICENT TREE!
NO WONDER THE CELTS WORSHIPPED OAKS.
...
DO YOU KNOW WHY THEY DIDN'T MAKE STONE TEMPLES LIKE THE GREEKS AND ROMANS?
TO THEM, THE FOREST ITSELF WAS HOLY.
THEY CALLED SACRED GROVES NEMETON, PRAYED THERE AND DISCERNED THE VOICE OF THEIR DEITIES.
WHEN I WAS A STUDENT, YOU TAUGHT US THAT DRUID MEANS "THE WISDOM OF OAKS."
THEY FED LIVESTOCK ACORNS, AND THEY GROUND ACORNS UP TO MAKE BREAD.
THEY LIVED IN HARMONY WITH THE FOREST.
NOW THAT FORESTS ARE IN DANGER, WE SHOULD LEARN FROM THEM.

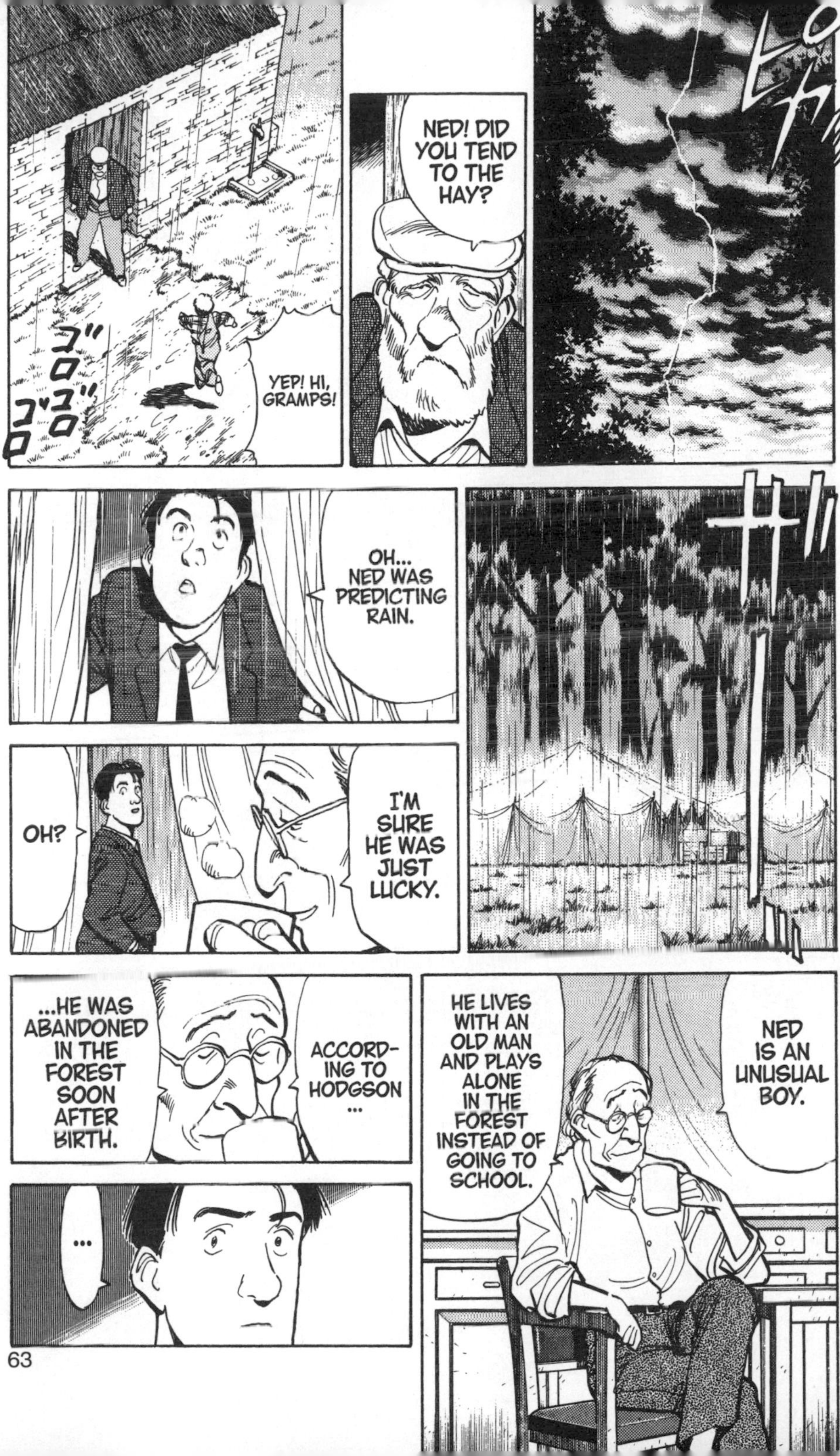
ピカ
NED! DID YOU TEND TO THE HAY?
YEP! HI, GRAMPS!
ゴロゴロゴロ
ザー
OH... NED WAS PREDICTING RAIN.
I'M SURE HE WAS JUST LUCKY.
OH?
NED IS AN UNUSUAL BOY.
HE LIVES WITH AN OLD MAN AND PLAYS ALONE IN THE FOREST INSTEAD OF GOING TO SCHOOL.
ACCORD-ING TO HODGSON ...
...HE WAS ABANDONED IN THE FOREST SOON AFTER BIRTH.
...

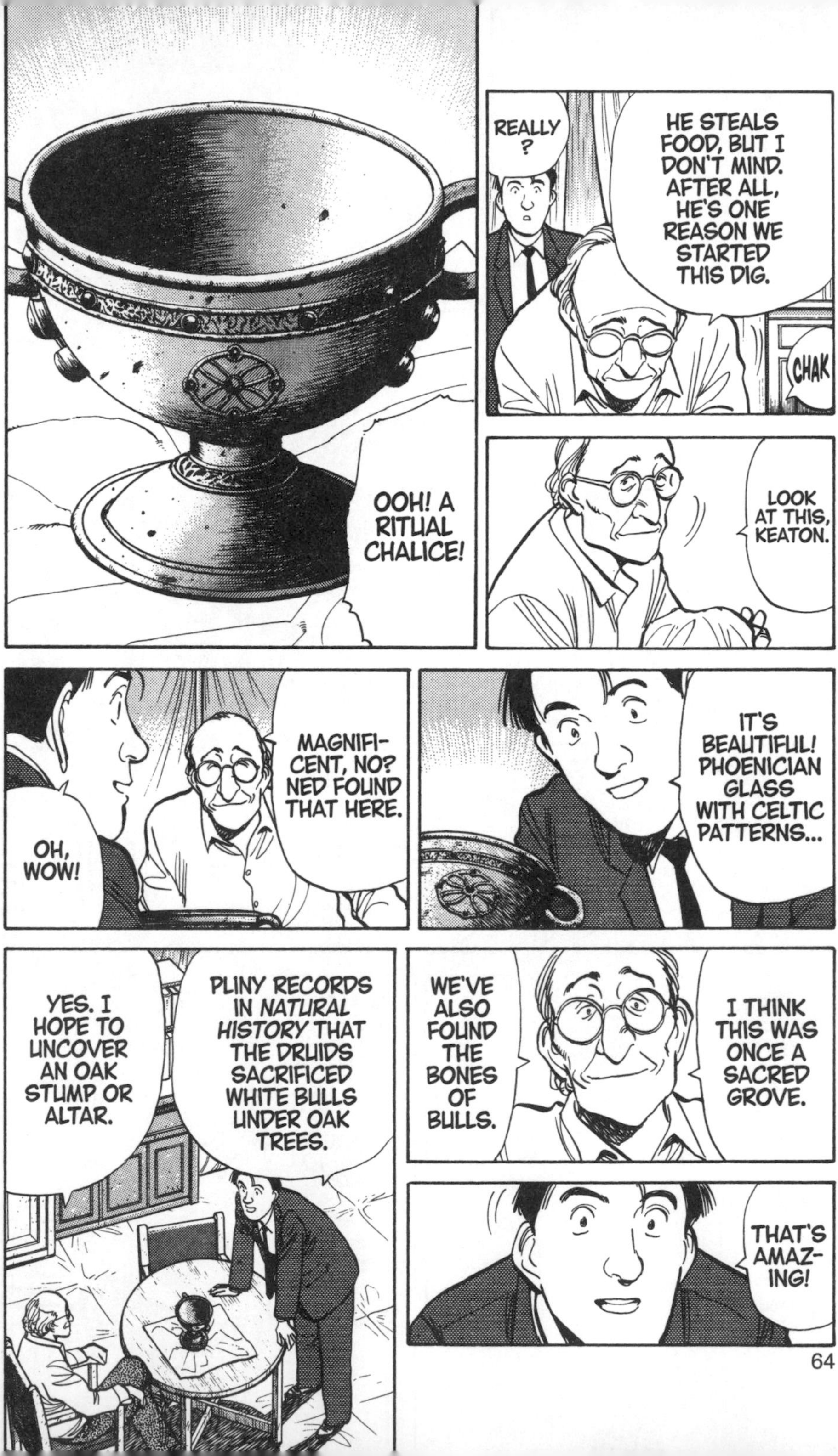
HE STEALS FOOD, BUT I DON'T MIND. AFTER ALL, HE'S ONE REASON WE STARTED THIS DIG.
REALLY ?
CHAK
LOOK AT THIS, KEATON.
OOH! A RITUAL CHALICE!
IT'S BEAUTIFUL! PHOENICIAN GLASS WITH CELTIC PATTERNS...
MAGNIFI-CENT, NO? NED FOUND THAT HERE.
OH, WOW!
I THINK THIS WAS ONCE A SACRED GROVE.
WE'VE ALSO FOUND THE BONES OF BULLS.
THAT'S AMAZ-ING!
PLINY RECORDS IN *NATURAL HISTORY* THAT THE DRUIDS SACRIFICED WHITE BULLS UNDER OAK TREES.
YES. I HOPE TO UNCOVER AN OAK STUMP OR ALTAR.

WOW! HOPEFULLY, I'LL BE THERE WHEN YOU DO!
HOWEVER, IT WON'T BE EASY BECAUSE OF THE ACCIDENTS.
ARE THE VILLAGERS OPPOSED TO THE DIG?
NO, THEY'VE BEEN COOPERATIVE BECAUSE IT PROVIDES JOBS.
THEN WHO'S INTER-FERING?
I SUSPECT BRITISH LAND, A REAL ESTATE COMPANY THAT WANTS TO DEVELOP AN INDUSTRIAL SITE HERE.
IF WE FOUND ANYTHING OF VALUE, IT WOULD LIMIT THEIR PLANS.
...
RUSTLE

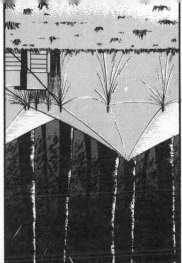

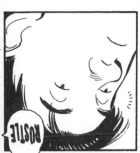

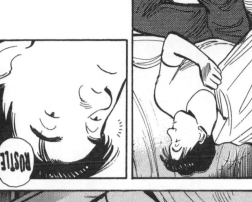

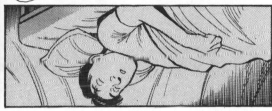

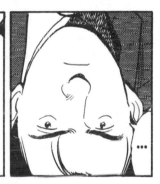

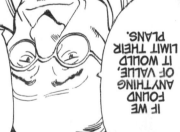

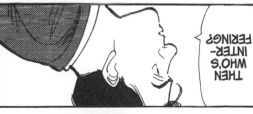

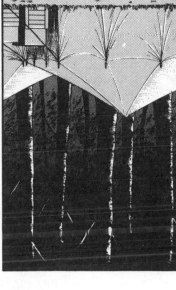

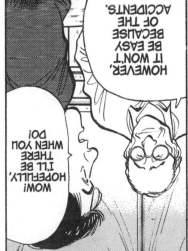

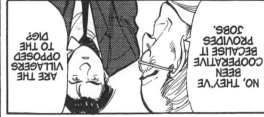

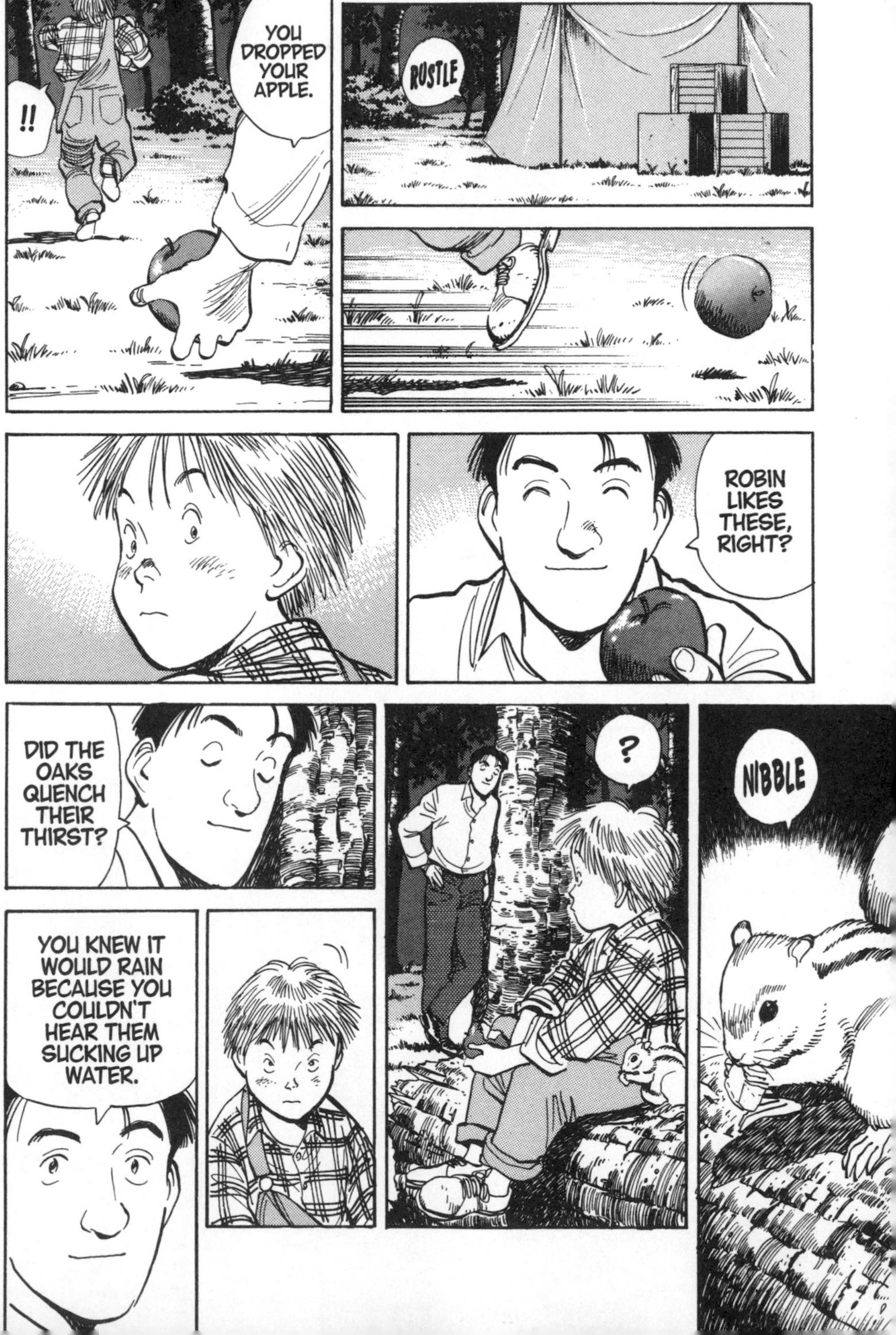
RUSTLE
YOU DROPPED YOUR APPLE.
!!
ROBIN LIKES THESE, RIGHT?
NIBBLE
?
DID THE OAKS QUENCH THEIR THIRST?
YOU KNEW IT WOULD RAIN BECAUSE YOU COULDN'T HEAR THEM SUCKING UP WATER.

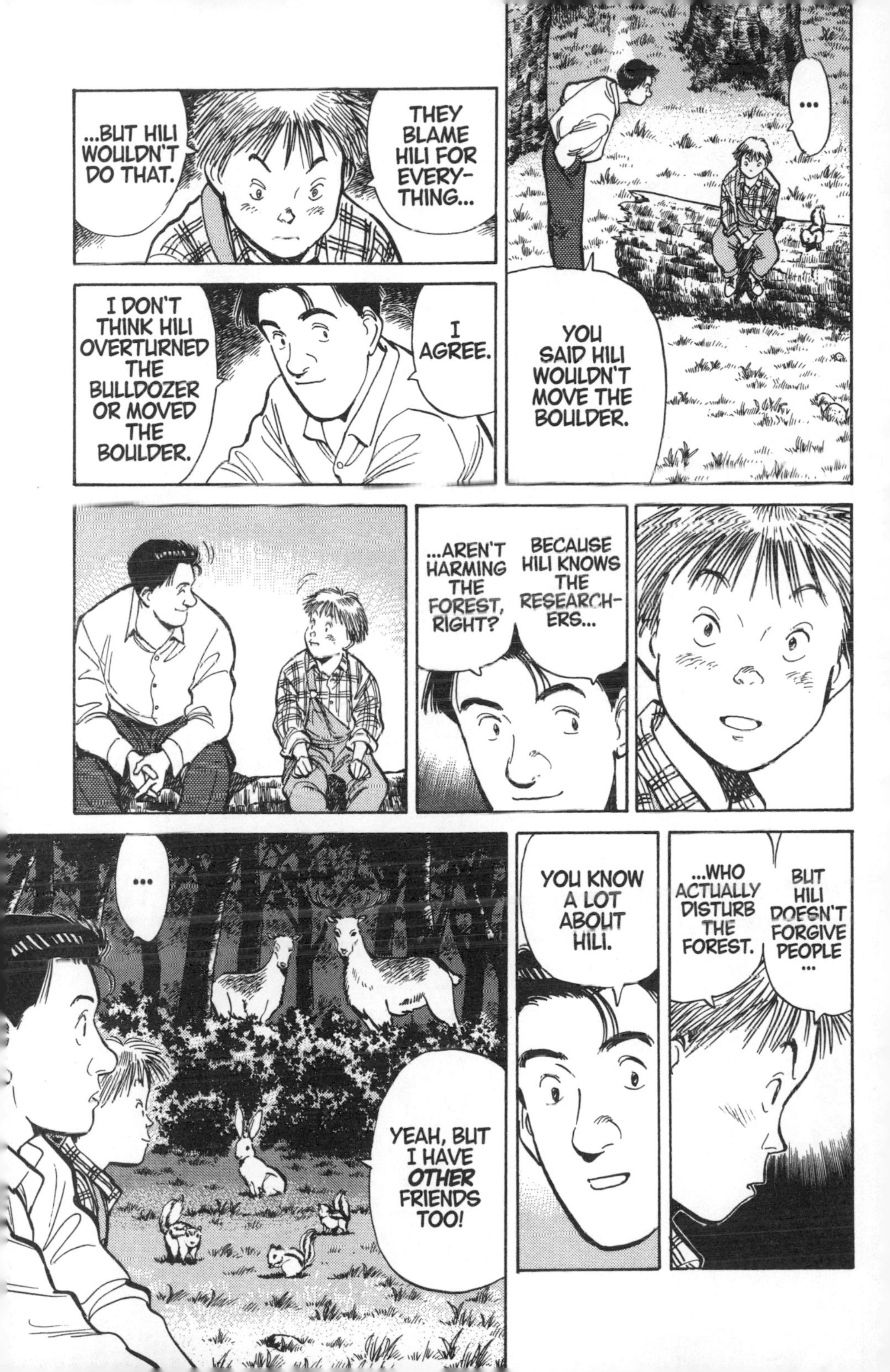
...
YOU SAID HILI WOULDN'T MOVE THE BOULDER.
THEY BLAME HILI FOR EVERY-THING...
...BUT HILI WOULDN'T DO THAT.
I AGREE.
I DON'T THINK HILI OVERTURNED THE BULLDOZER OR MOVED THE BOULDER.
BECAUSE HILI KNOWS THE RESEARCH-ERS...
...AREN'T HARMING THE FOREST, RIGHT?
BUT HILI DOESN'T FORGIVE PEOPLE ...
...WHO ACTUALLY DISTURB THE FOREST.
YOU KNOW A LOT ABOUT HILI.
...
YEAH, BUT I HAVE *OTHER* FRIENDS TOO!

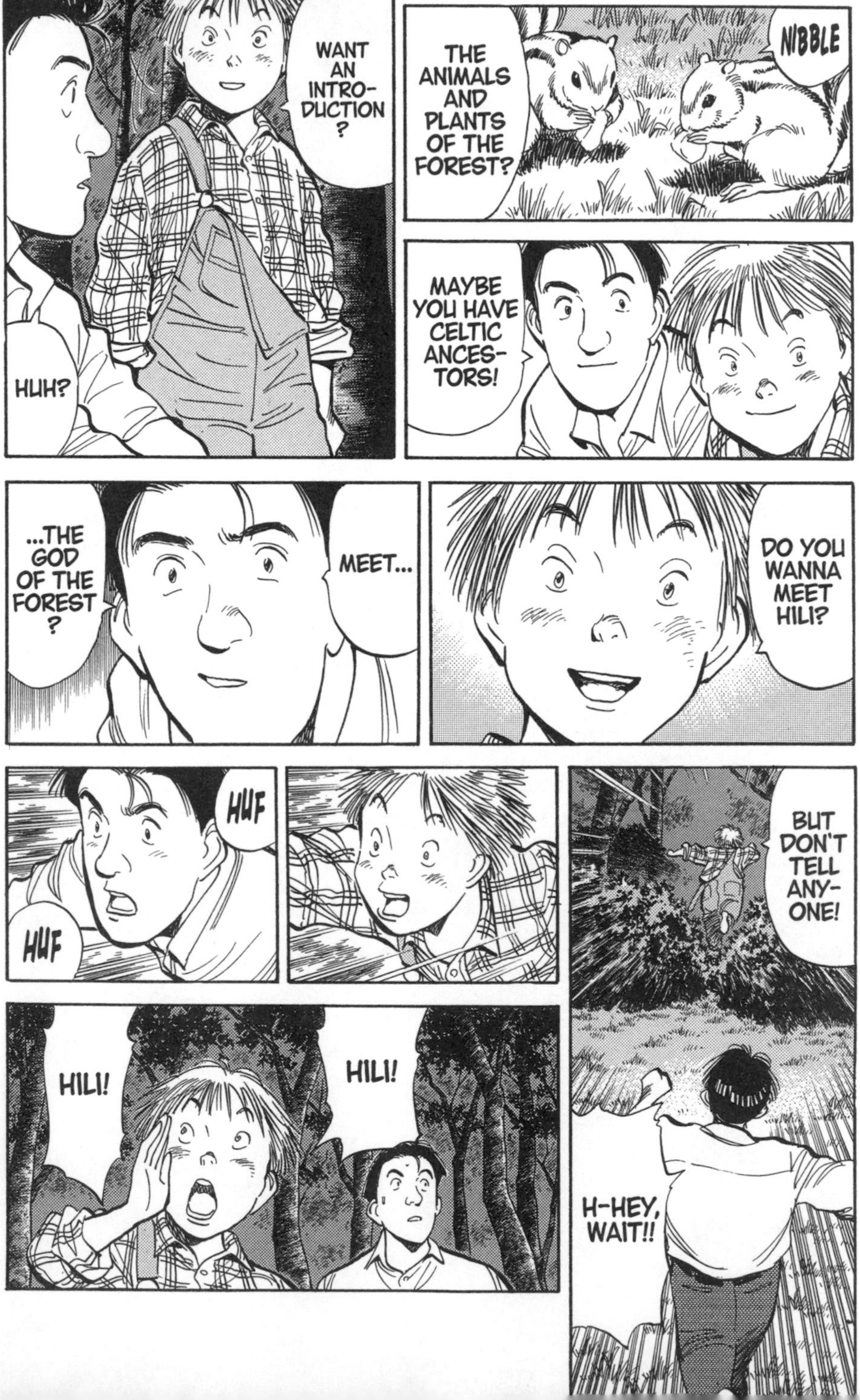
NIBBLE
THE ANIMALS AND PLANTS OF THE FOREST?
MAYBE YOU HAVE CELTIC ANCES-TORS!
WANT AN INTRO-DUCTION ?
HUH?
DO YOU WANNA MEET HILI?
MEET...
...THE GOD OF THE FOREST ?
BUT DON'T TELL ANY-ONE!
H-HEY, WAIT!!
HUF
HUF
HILI!
HILI!

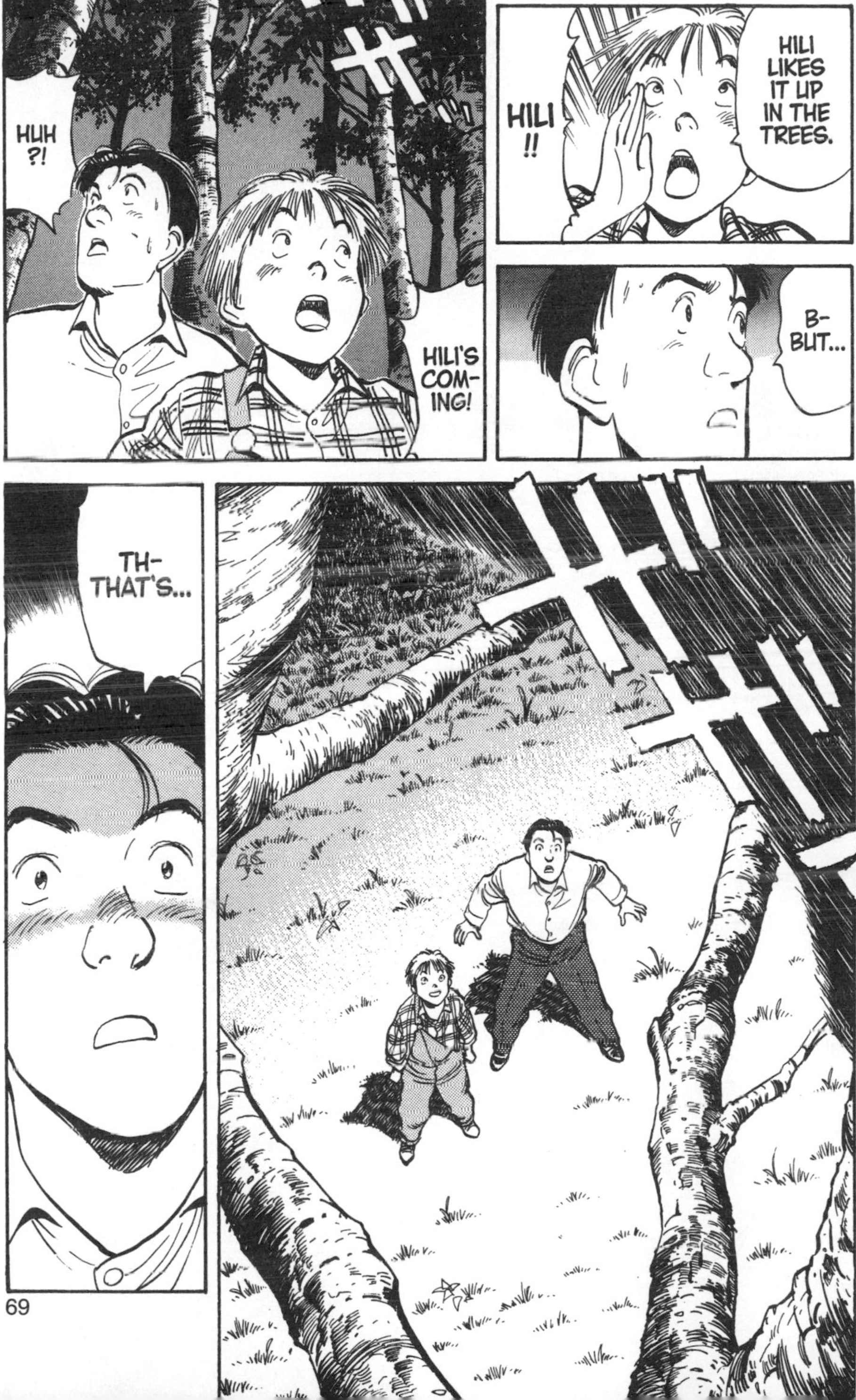
HILI LIKES IT UP IN THE TREES.
HILI !!
B-BUT...
HILI'S COM-ING!
HUH ?!
TH-THAT'S...

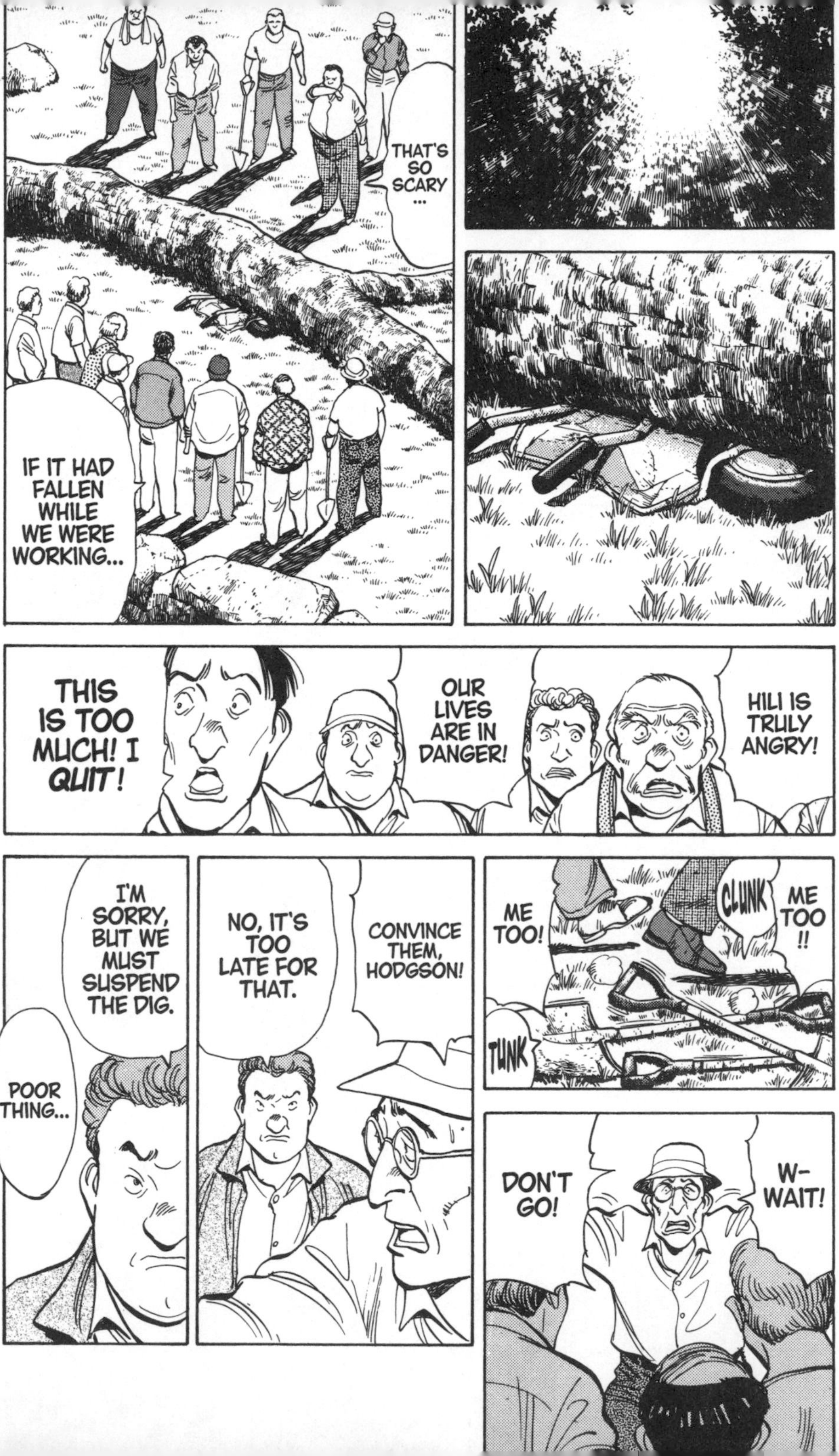
THAT'S SO SCARY...
IF IT HAD FALLEN WHILE WE WERE WORKING...
HILI IS TRULY ANGRY!
OUR LIVES ARE IN DANGER!
THIS IS TOO MUCH! I QUIT!
ME TOO !!
CLUNK
ME TOO!
TUNK
W- WAIT!
DON'T GO!
CONVINCE THEM, HODGSON!
NO, IT'S TOO LATE FOR THAT.
I'M SORRY, BUT WE MUST SUSPEND THE DIG.
POOR THING...

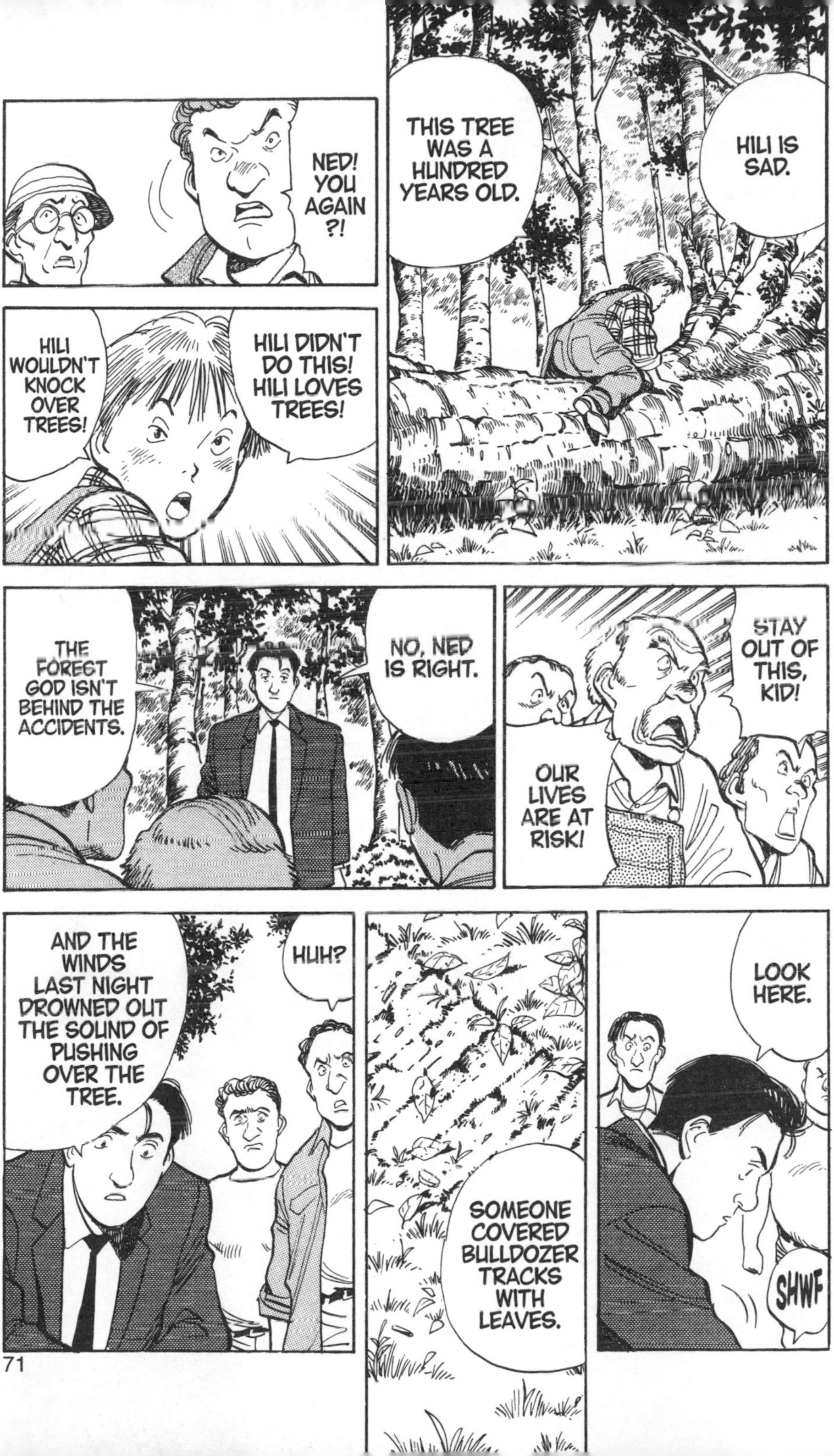
HILI IS SAD.
THIS TREE WAS A HUNDRED YEARS OLD.
NED! YOU AGAIN ?!
HILI DIDN'T DO THIS! HILI LOVES TREES!
HILI WOULDN'T KNOCK OVER TREES!
STAY OUT OF THIS, KID!
OUR LIVES ARE AT RISK!
NO, NED IS RIGHT.
THE FOREST GOD ISN'T BEHIND THE ACCIDENTS.
LOOK HERE.
SHWF
SOMEONE COVERED BULLDOZER TRACKS WITH LEAVES.
HUH?
AND THE WINDS LAST NIGHT DROWNED OUT THE SOUND OF PUSHING OVER THE TREE.

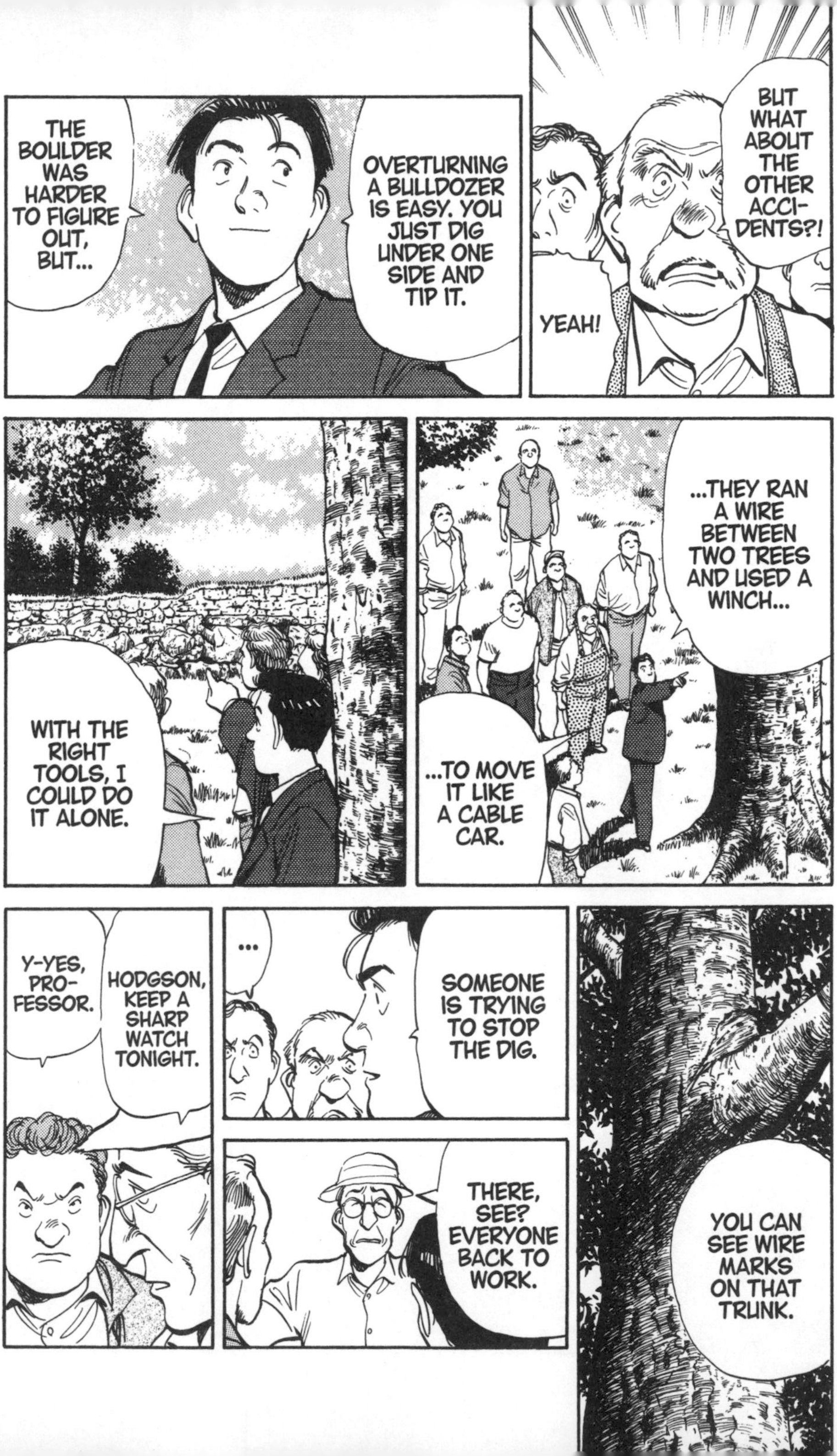
BUT WHAT ABOUT THE OTHER ACCI-DENTS?!
YEAH!
OVERTURNING A BULLDOZER IS EASY. YOU JUST DIG UNDER ONE SIDE AND TIP IT.
THE BOULDER WAS HARDER TO FIGURE OUT, BUT...
...THEY RAN A WIRE BETWEEN TWO TREES AND USED A WINCH...
...TO MOVE IT LIKE A CABLE CAR.
WITH THE RIGHT TOOLS, I COULD DO IT ALONE.
YOU CAN SEE WIRE MARKS ON THAT TRUNK.
SOMEONE IS TRYING TO STOP THE DIG.
...
THERE, SEE? EVERYONE BACK TO WORK.
HODGSON, KEEP A SHARP WATCH TONIGHT.
Y-YES, PRO-FESSOR.

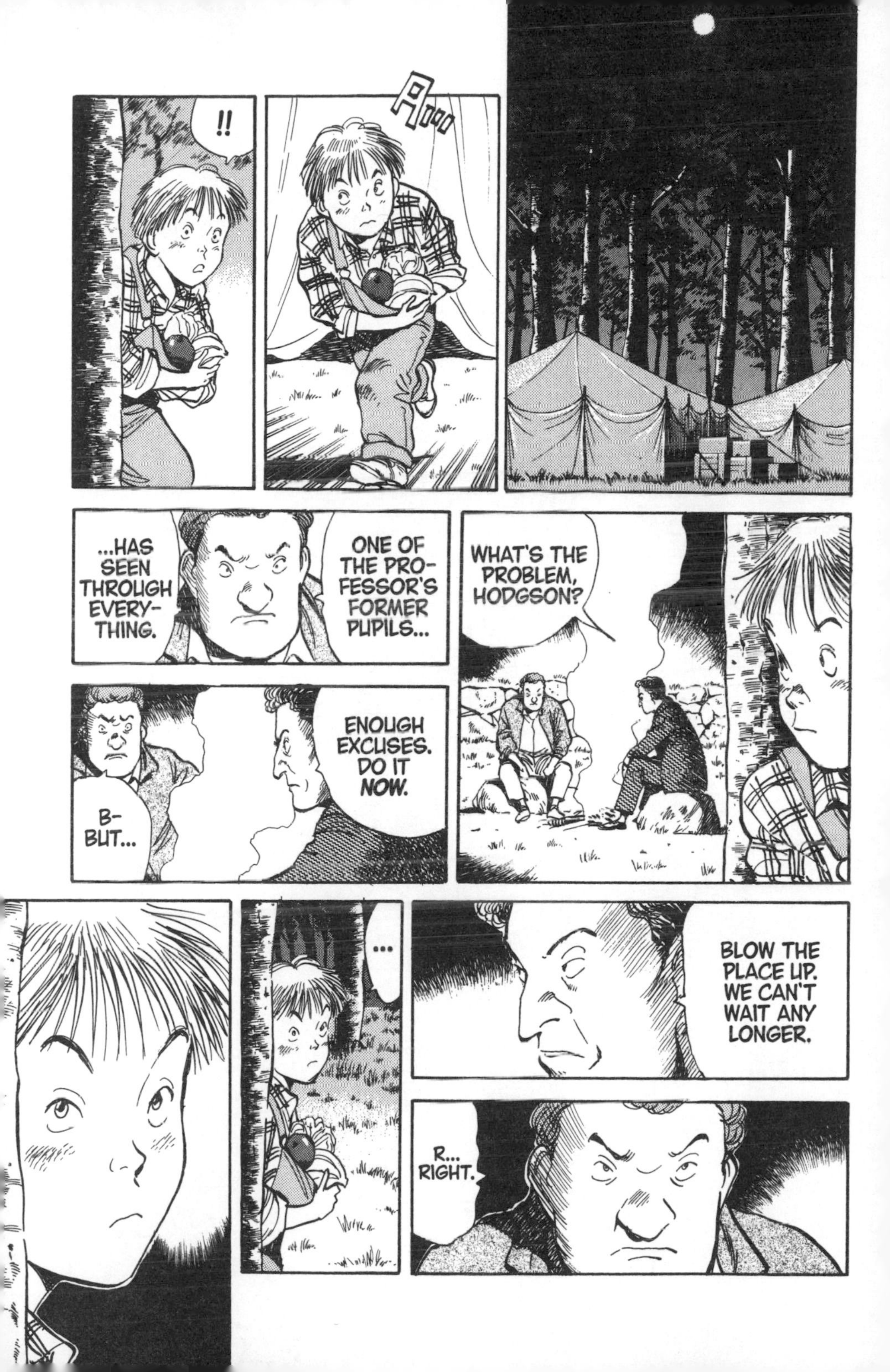
!!
WHAT'S THE PROBLEM, HODGSON?
ONE OF THE PRO- FESSOR'S FORMER PUPILS...
...HAS SEEN THROUGH EVERY- THING.
ENOUGH EXCUSES. DO IT NOW.
B- BUT...
BLOW THE PLACE UP. WE CAN'T WAIT ANY LONGER.
R... RIGHT.
...

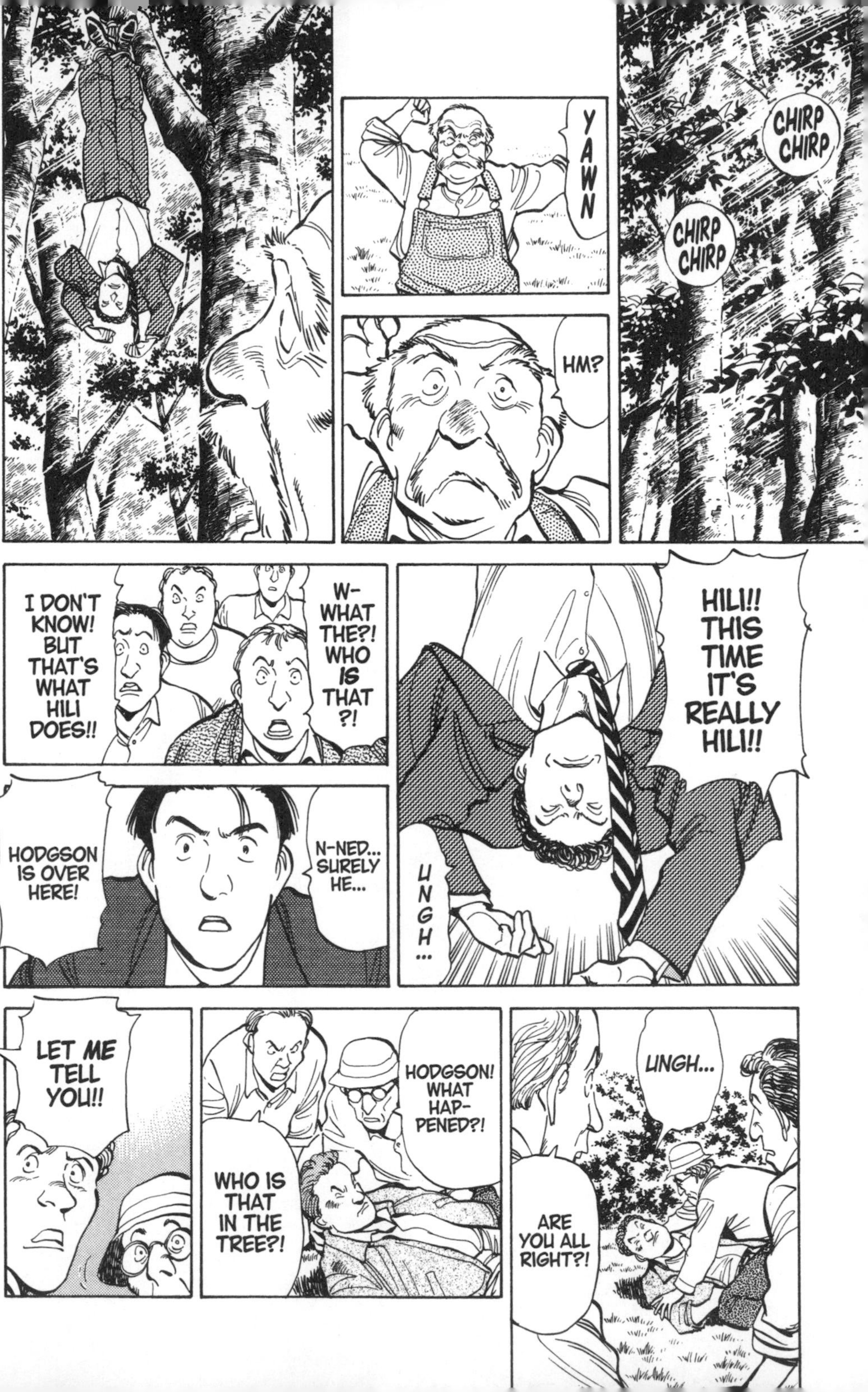
CHIRP CHIRP
CHIRP CHIRP
YAWN
HM?
W-WHAT THE?! WHO IS THAT ?!
I DON'T KNOW! BUT THAT'S WHAT HILI DOES!!
N-NED... SURELY HE...
HODGSON IS OVER HERE!
HILI!! THIS TIME IT'S REALLY HILI!!
UNGH...
UNGH...
ARE YOU ALL RIGHT?!
HODGSON! WHAT HAP-PENED?!
WHO IS THAT IN THE TREE?!
LET ME TELL YOU!!

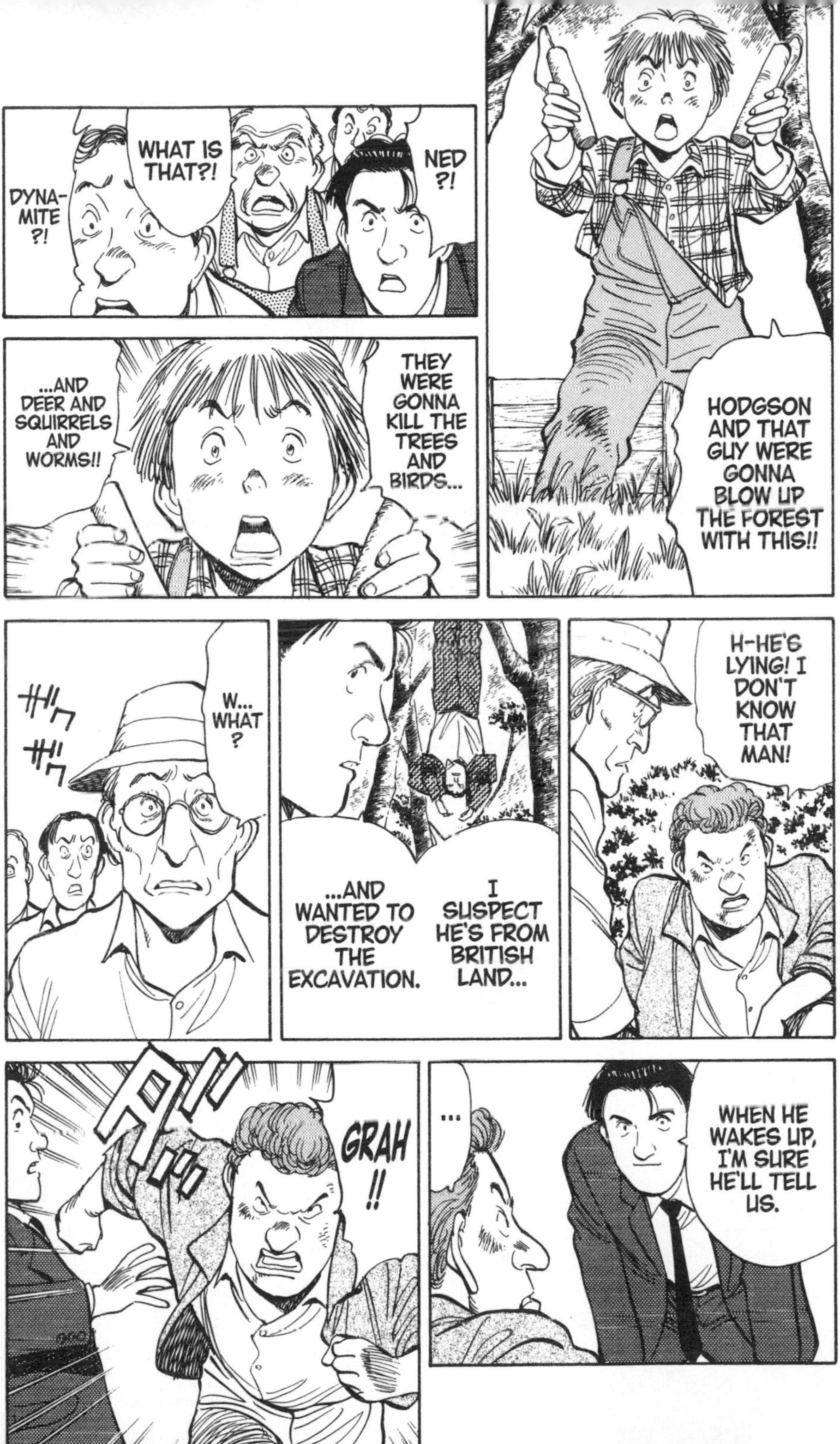
HODGSON AND THAT GUY WERE GONNA BLOW UP THE FOREST WITH THIS!!
NED ?!
WHAT IS THAT?!
DYNA-MITE ?!
THEY WERE GONNA KILL THE TREES AND BIRDS...
...AND DEER AND SQUIRRELS AND WORMS!!
H-HE'S LYING! I DON'T KNOW THAT MAN!
I SUSPECT HE'S FROM BRITISH LAND...
...AND WANTED TO DESTROY THE EXCAVATION.
W... WHAT ?
WHEN HE WAKES UP, I'M SURE HE'LL TELL US.
...
GRAH !!

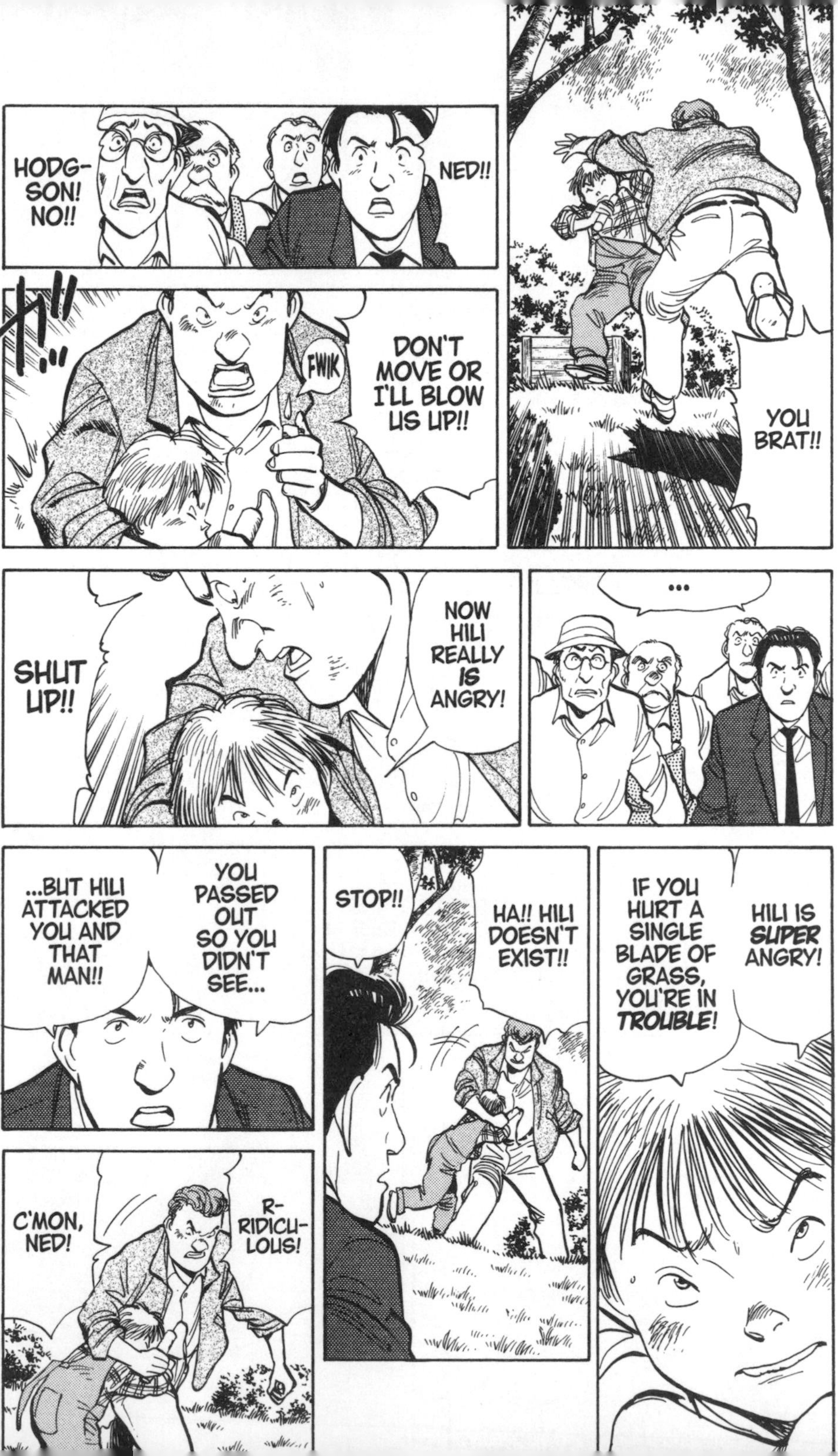
YOU BRAT!!
NED!!
HODG-SON! NO!!
DON'T MOVE OR I'LL BLOW US UP!!
FWIK
ガッ!!
...
NOW HILI REALLY IS ANGRY!
SHUT UP!!
HILI IS SUPER ANGRY!
IF YOU HURT A SINGLE BLADE OF GRASS, YOU'RE IN TROUBLE!
HA!! HILI DOESN'T EXIST!!
STOP!!
YOU PASSED OUT SO YOU DIDN'T SEE...
...BUT HILI ATTACKED YOU AND THAT MAN!!
R-RIDICULOUS!
C'MON, NED!

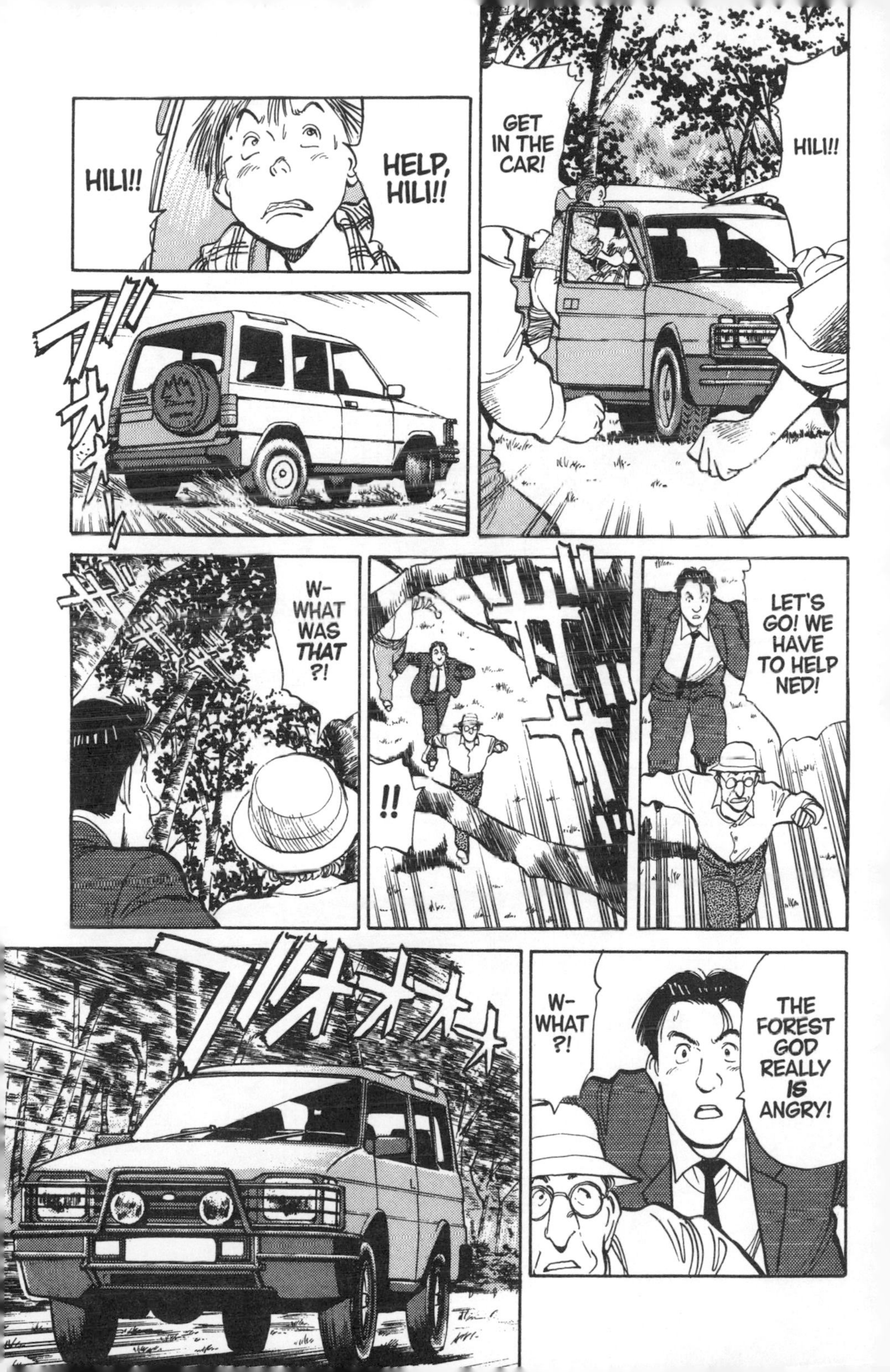
GET IN THE CAR!
HILI!!
HELP, HILI!!
HILI!!
LET'S GO! WE HAVE TO HELP NED!
!!
W-WHAT WAS THAT?!
THE FOREST GOD REALLY IS ANGRY!
W-WHAT?!

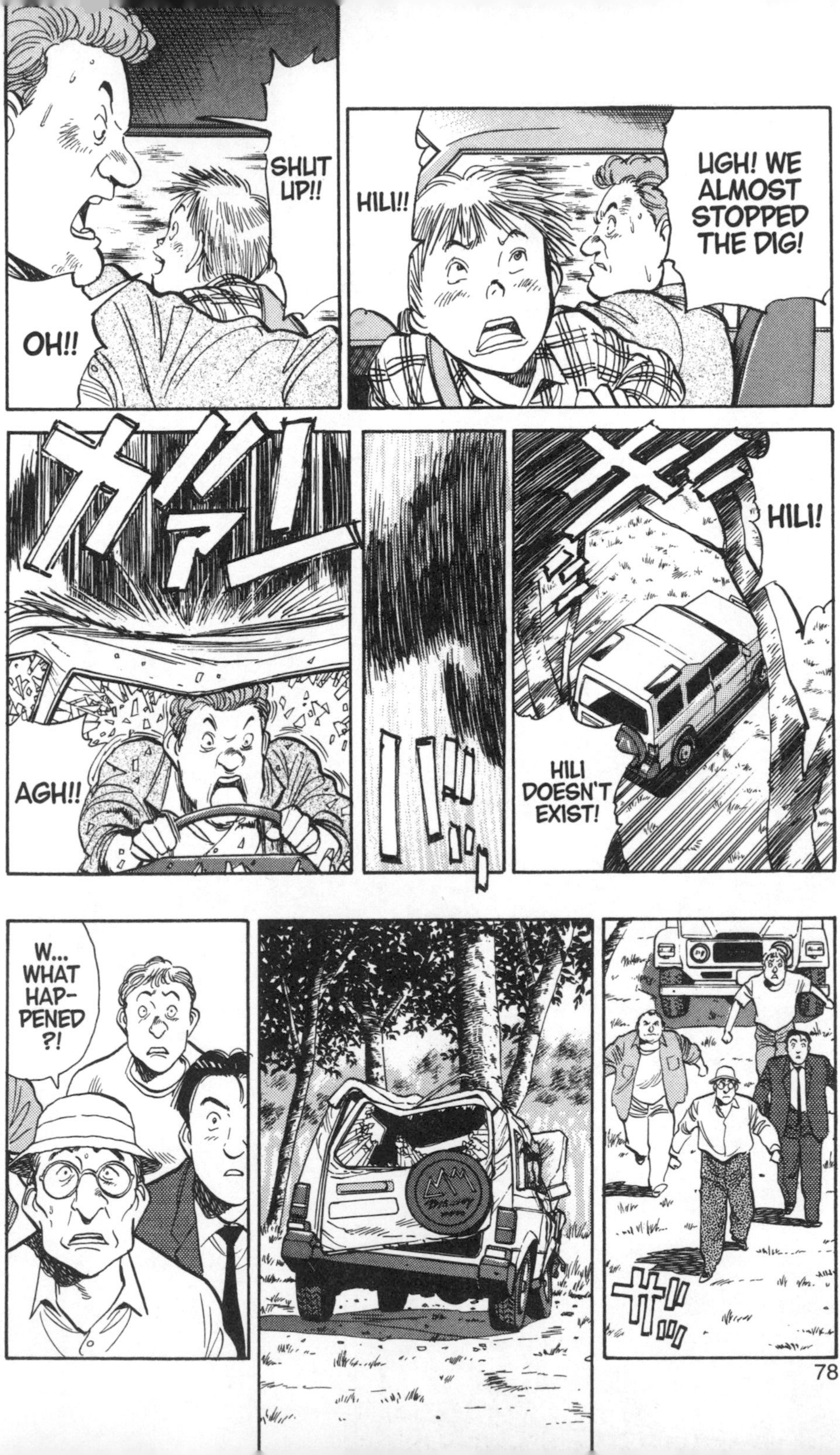
UGH! WE ALMOST STOPPED THE DIG!
HILI!!
SHUT UP!!
OH!!
HILI!
HILI DOESN'T EXIST!
AGH!!
W... WHAT HAP-PENED ?!

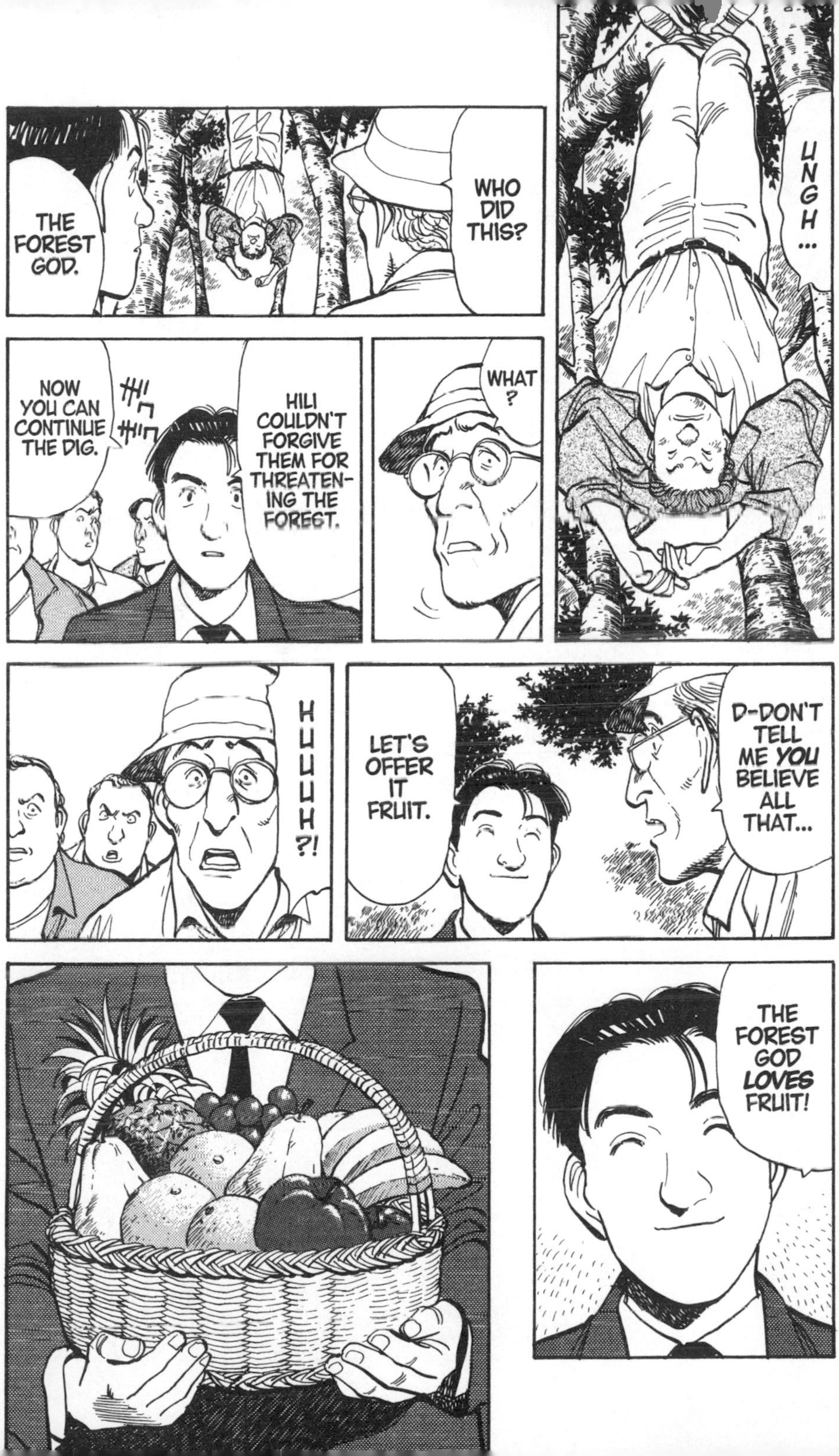
UNGH...
WHO DID THIS?
THE FOREST GOD.
WHAT?
HILI COULDN'T FORGIVE THEM FOR THREATEN-ING THE FOREST.
NOW YOU CAN CONTINUE THE DIG.
D-DON'T TELL ME *YOU* BELIEVE ALL THAT...
LET'S OFFER IT FRUIT.
HUUUUH?!
THE FOREST GOD *LOVES* FRUIT!

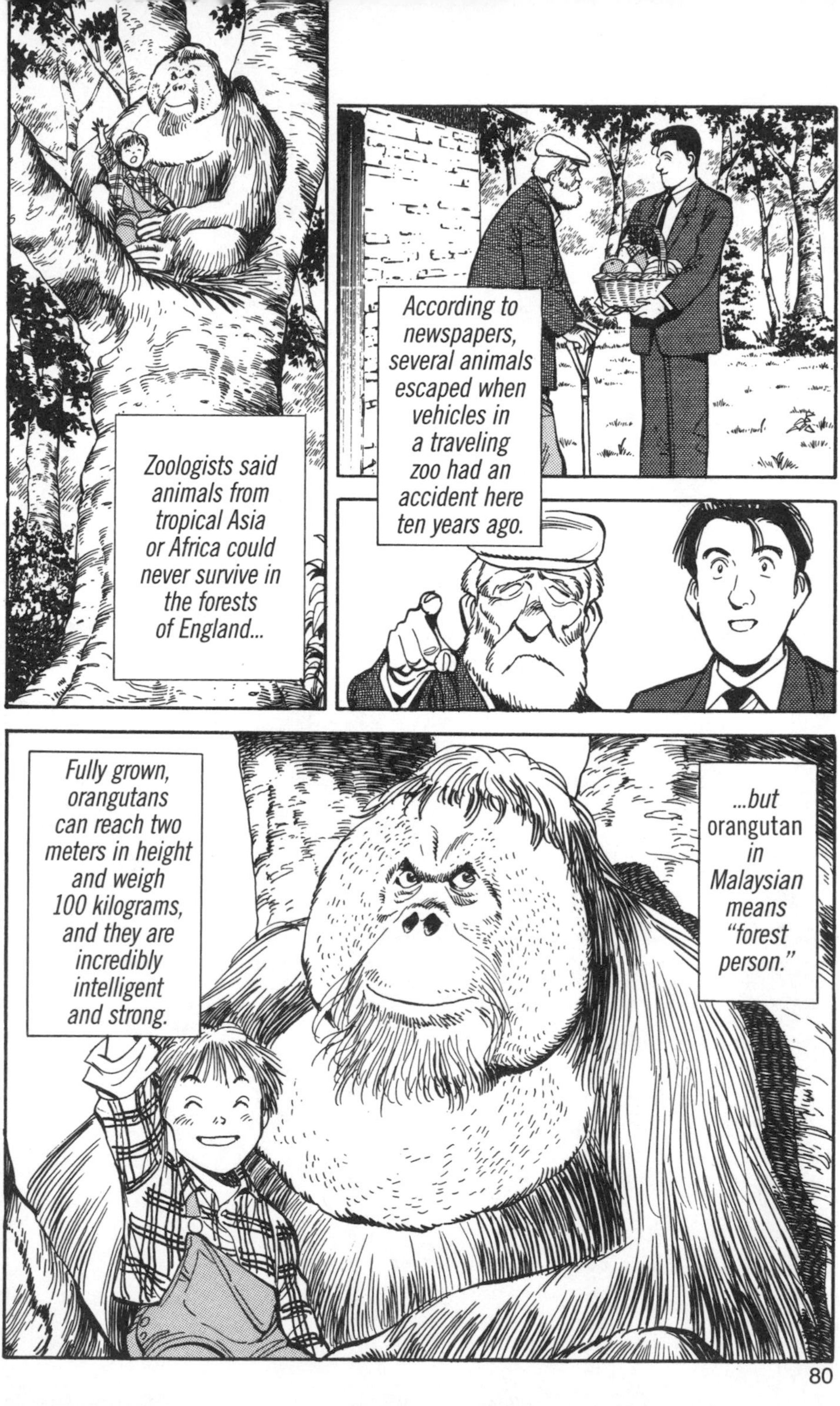
According to newspapers, several animals escaped when vehicles in a traveling zoo had an accident here ten years ago.
Zoologists said animals from tropical Asia or Africa could never survive in the forests of England...
...but orangutan in Malaysian means "forest person."
Fully grown, orangutans can reach two meters in height and weigh 100 kilograms, and they are incredibly intelligent and strong.

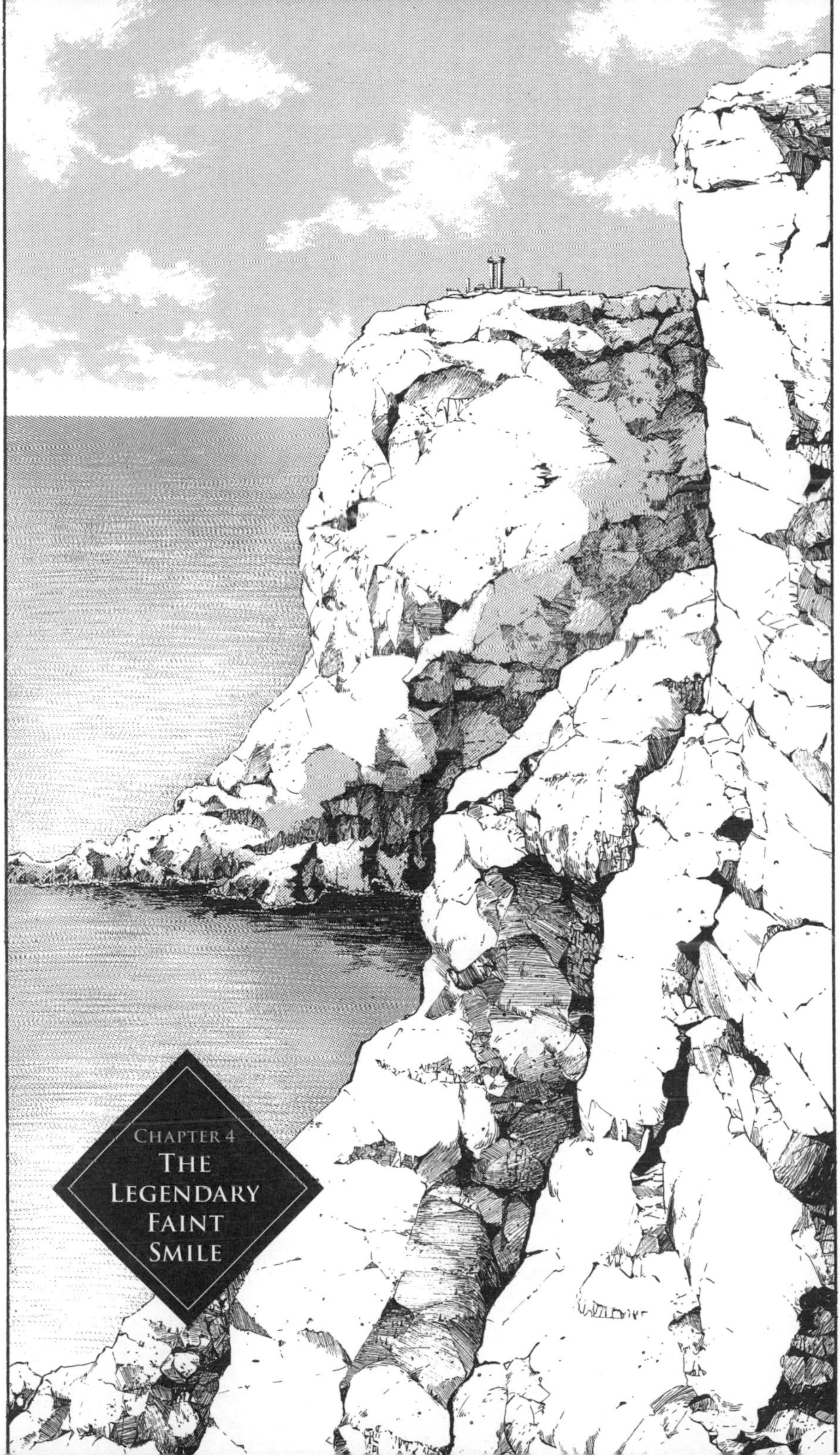
Chapter 4
The Legendary Faint Smile

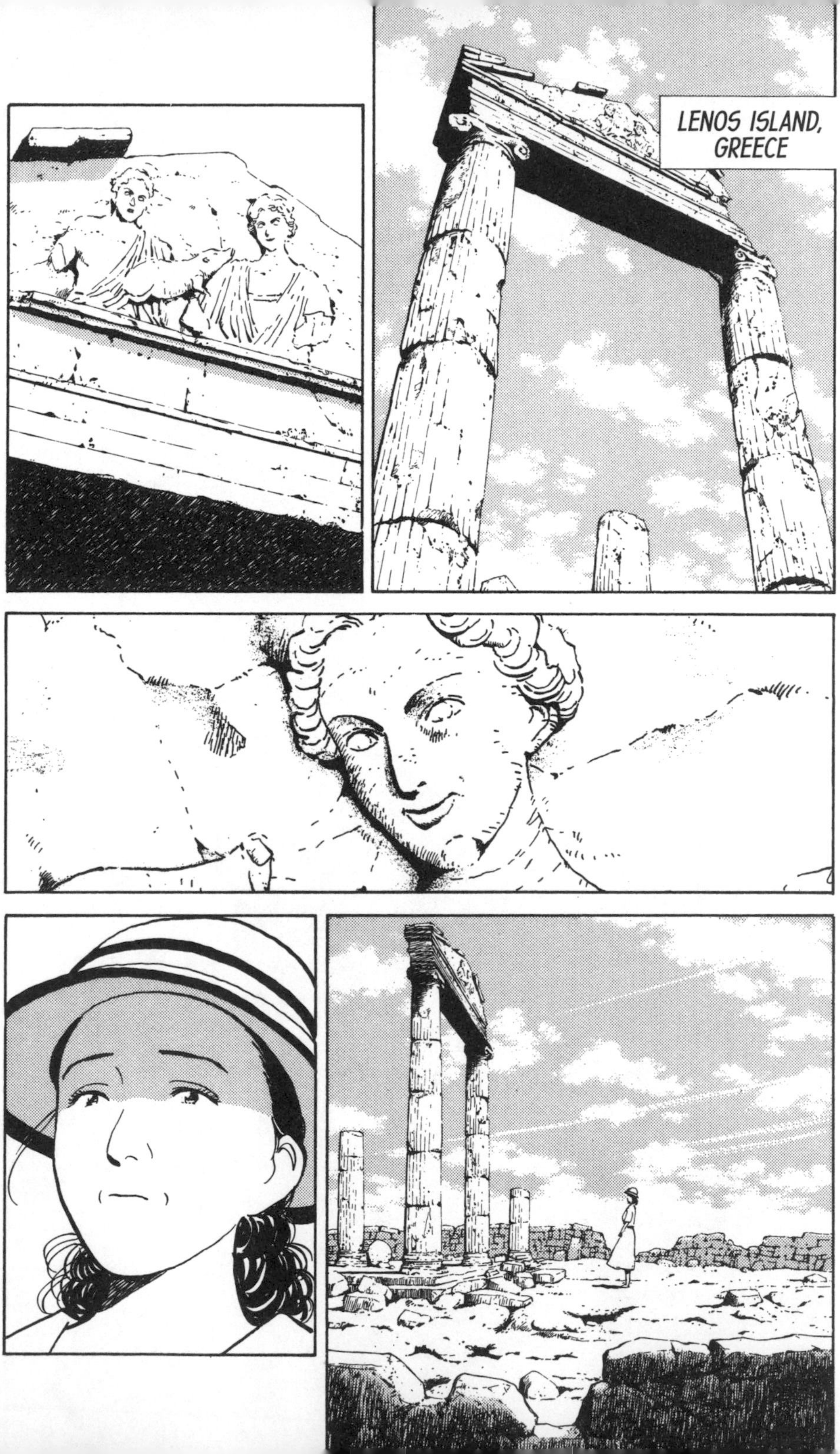
LENOS ISLAND, GREECE

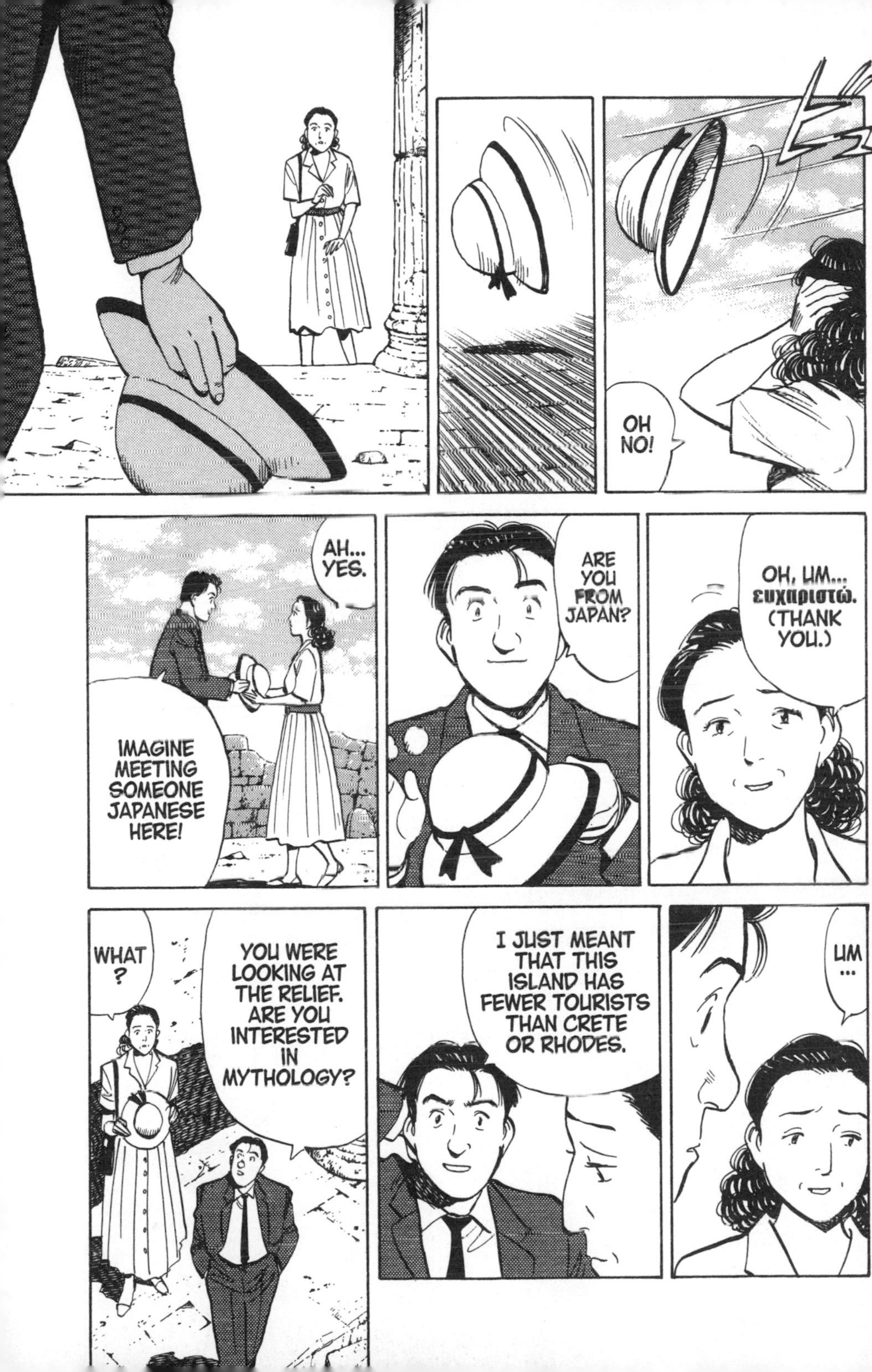
OH NO!
OH, UM... ευχαριστώ. (THANK YOU.)
ARE YOU FROM JAPAN?
AH... YES.
IMAGINE MEETING SOMEONE JAPANESE HERE!
UM...
I JUST MEANT THAT THIS ISLAND HAS FEWER TOURISTS THAN CRETE OR RHODES.
WHAT?
YOU WERE LOOKING AT THE RELIEF. ARE YOU INTERESTED IN MYTHOLOGY?

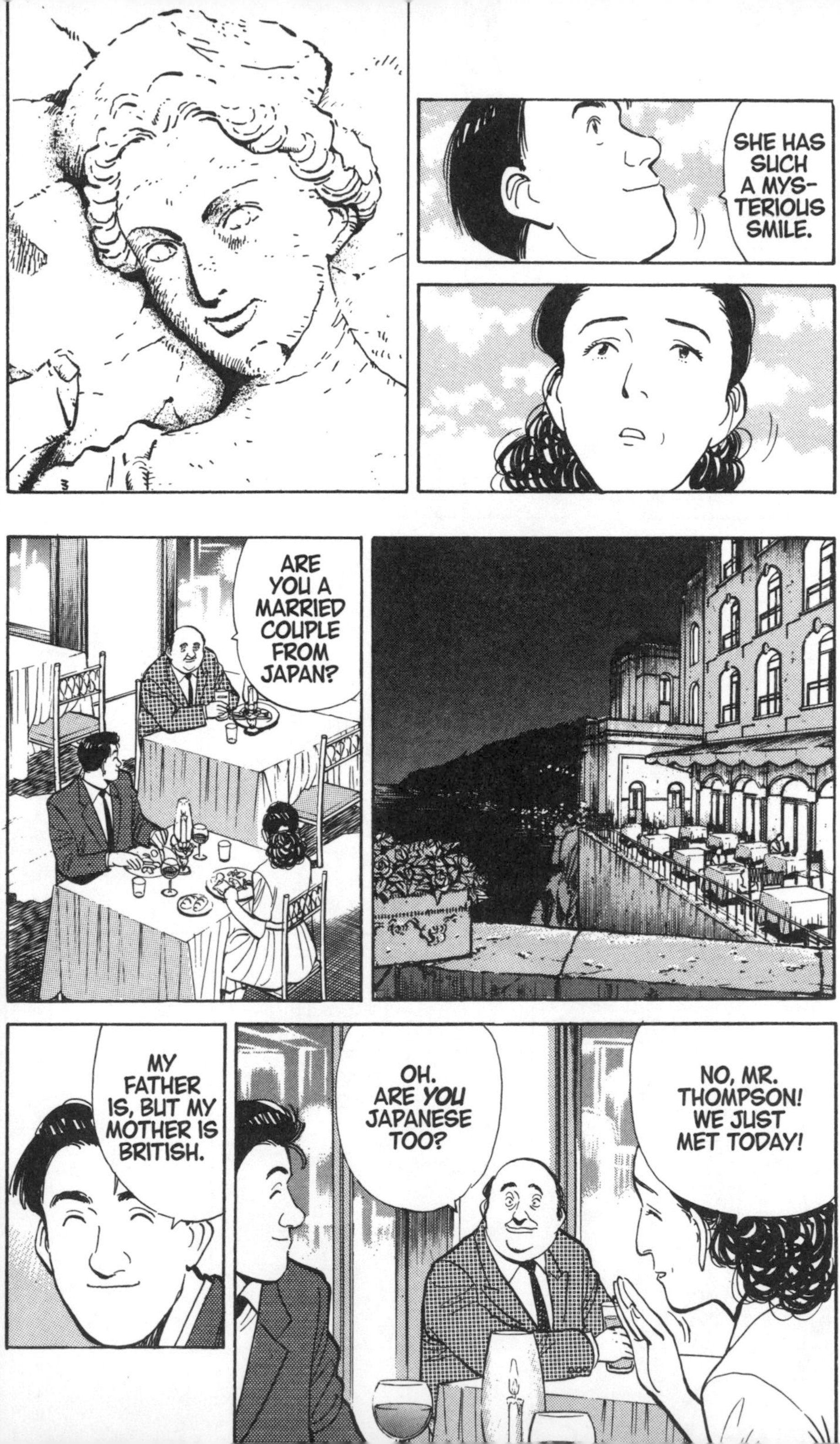
SHE HAS SUCH A MYSTERIOUS SMILE.
ARE YOU A MARRIED COUPLE FROM JAPAN?
NO, MR. THOMPSON! WE JUST MET TODAY!
OH. ARE *YOU* JAPANESE TOO?
MY FATHER IS, BUT MY MOTHER IS BRITISH.

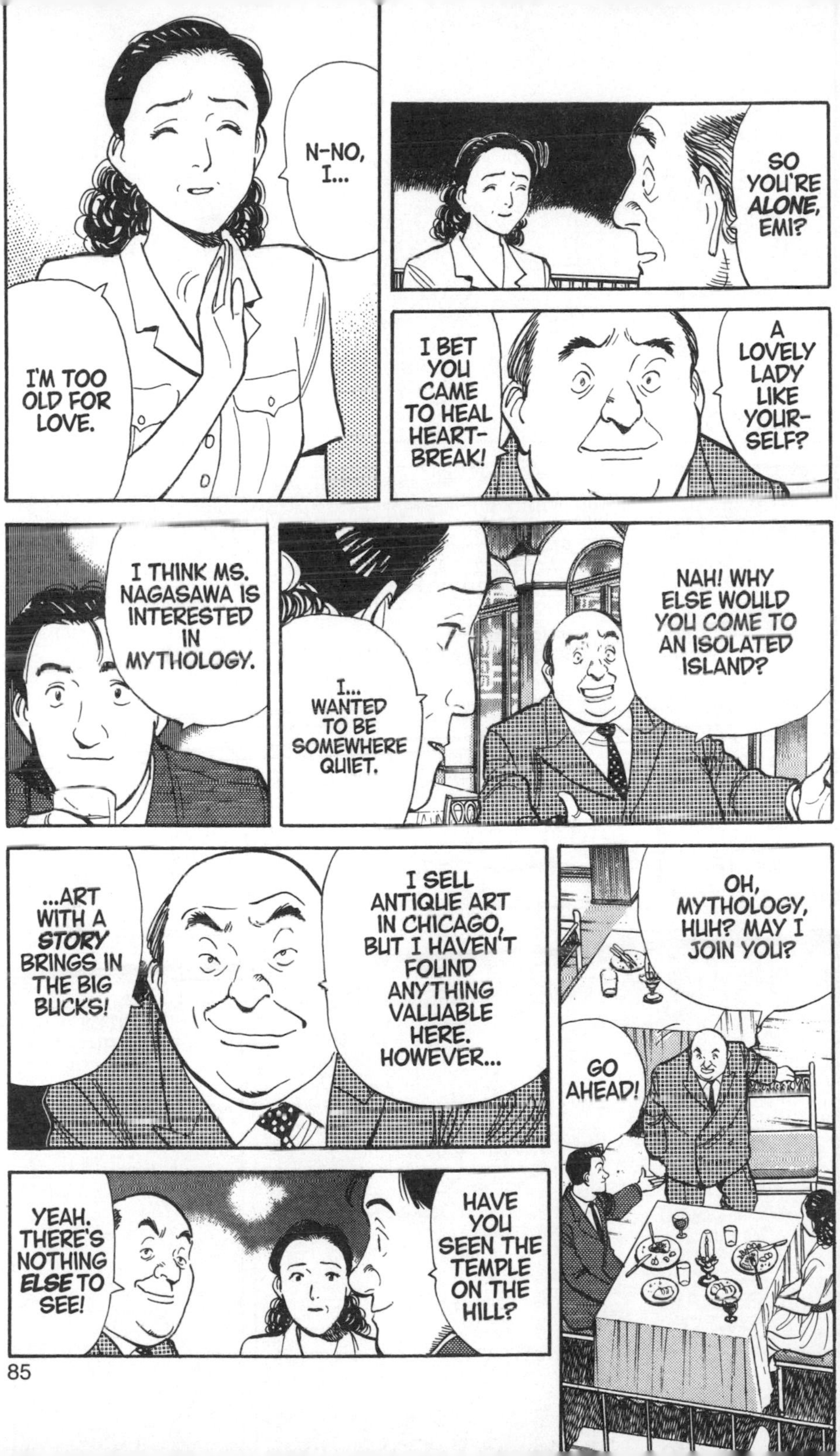
SO YOU'RE ALONE, EMI?
A LOVELY LADY LIKE YOURSELF?
I BET YOU CAME TO HEAL HEART-BREAK!
N-NO, I...
I'M TOO OLD FOR LOVE.
NAH! WHY ELSE WOULD YOU COME TO AN ISOLATED ISLAND?
I... WANTED TO BE SOMEWHERE QUIET.
I THINK MS. NAGASAWA IS INTERESTED IN MYTHOLOGY.
OH, MYTHOLOGY, HUH? MAY I JOIN YOU?
GO AHEAD!
I SELL ANTIQUE ART IN CHICAGO, BUT I HAVEN'T FOUND ANYTHING VALUABLE HERE. HOWEVER...
...ART WITH A STORY BRINGS IN THE BIG BUCKS!
HAVE YOU SEEN THE TEMPLE ON THE HILL?
YEAH. THERE'S NOTHING ELSE TO SEE!

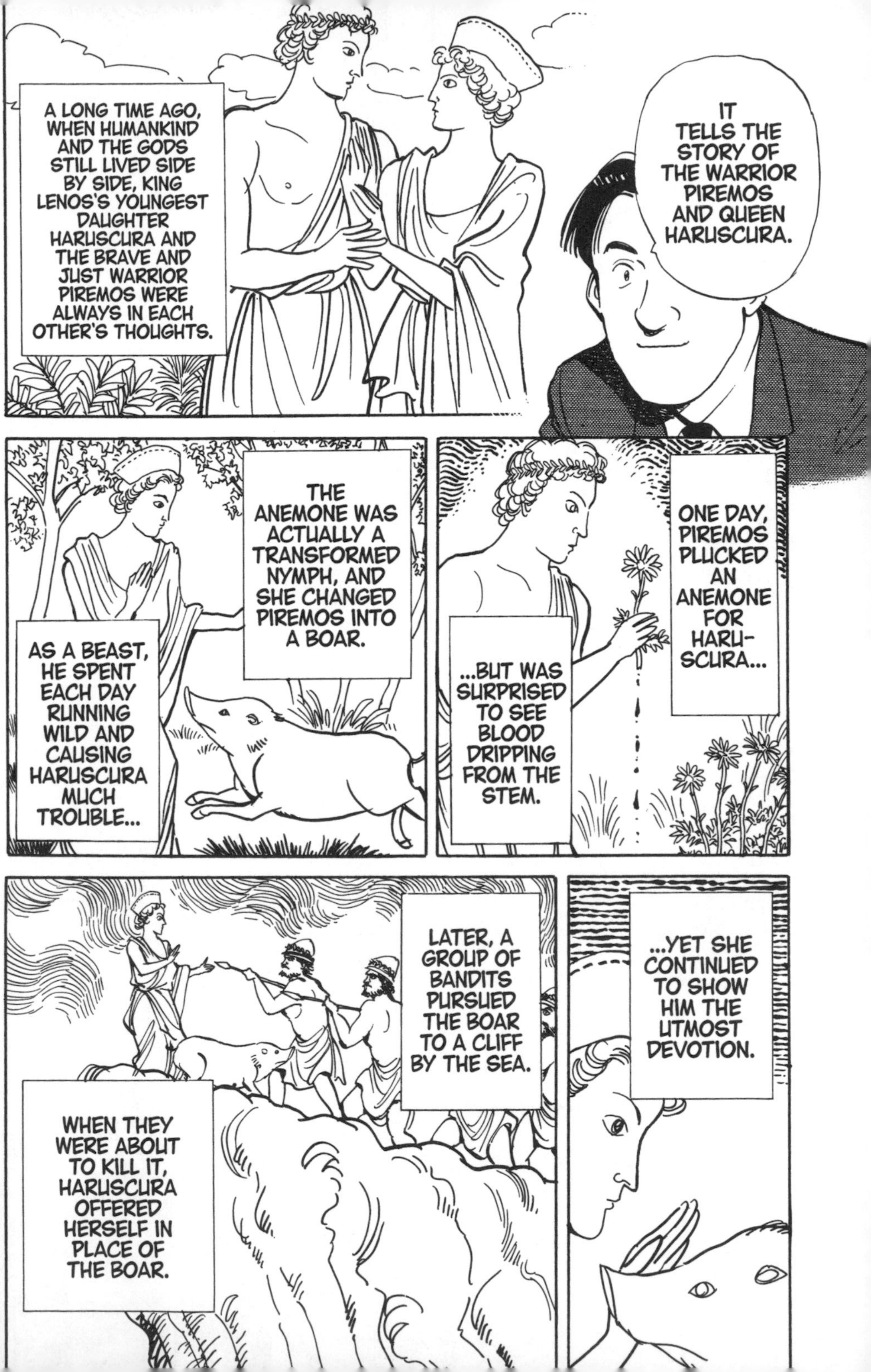
IT TELLS THE STORY OF THE WARRIOR PIREMOS AND QUEEN HARUSCURA.
A LONG TIME AGO, WHEN HUMANKIND AND THE GODS STILL LIVED SIDE BY SIDE, KING LENOS'S YOUNGEST DAUGHTER HARUSCURA AND THE BRAVE AND JUST WARRIOR PIREMOS WERE ALWAYS IN EACH OTHER'S THOUGHTS.
ONE DAY, PIREMOS PLUCKED AN ANEMONE FOR HARU-SCURA...
...BUT WAS SURPRISED TO SEE BLOOD DRIPPING FROM THE STEM.
THE ANEMONE WAS ACTUALLY A TRANSFORMED NYMPH, AND SHE CHANGED PIREMOS INTO A BOAR.
AS A BEAST, HE SPENT EACH DAY RUNNING WILD AND CAUSING HARUSCURA MUCH TROUBLE...
...YET SHE CONTINUED TO SHOW HIM THE UTMOST DEVOTION.
LATER, A GROUP OF BANDITS PURSUED THE BOAR TO A CLIFF BY THE SEA.
WHEN THEY WERE ABOUT TO KILL IT, HARUSCURA OFFERED HERSELF IN PLACE OF THE BOAR.

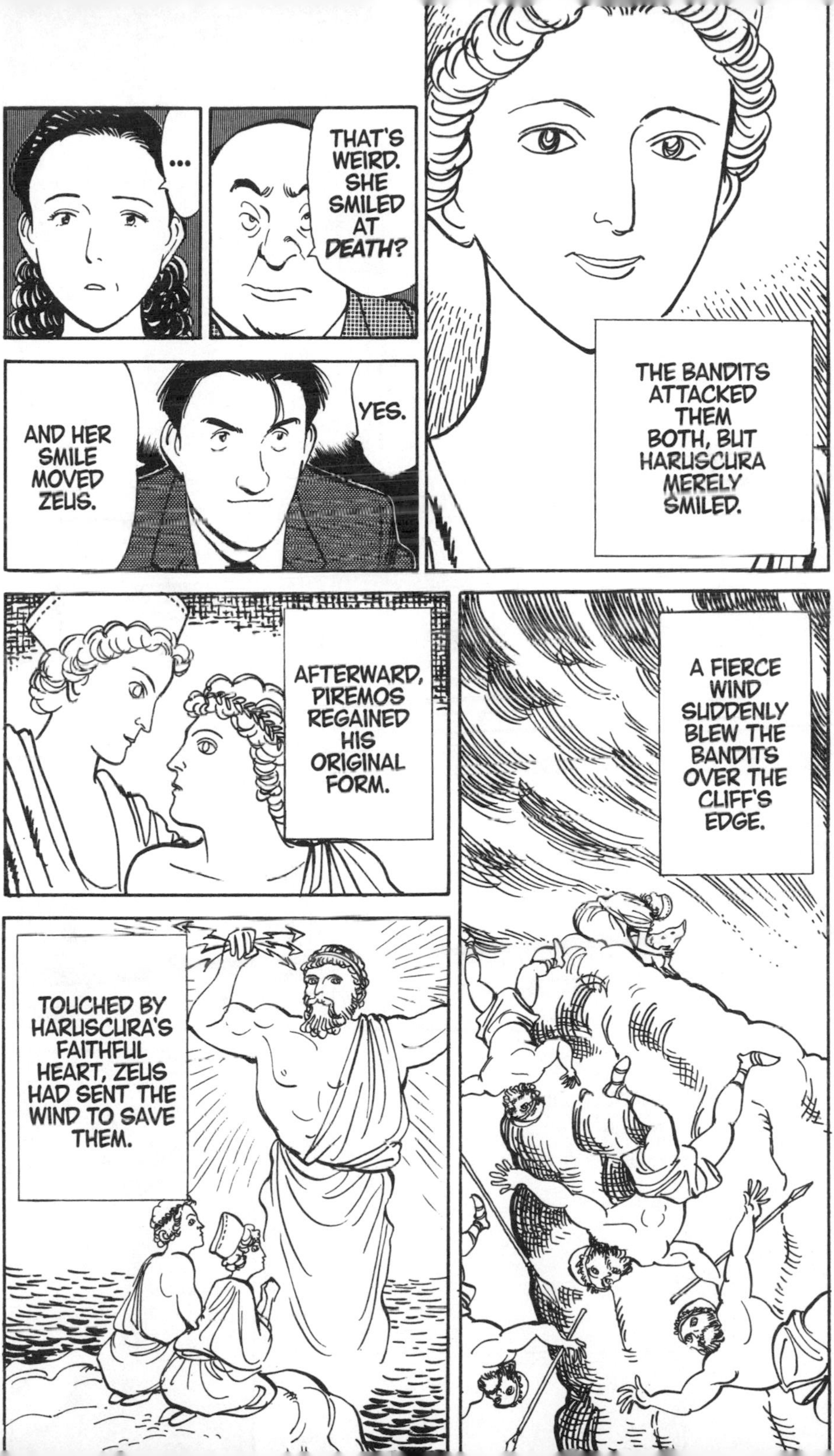
THE BANDITS ATTACKED THEM BOTH, BUT HARUSCURA MERELY SMILED.
THAT'S WEIRD. SHE SMILED AT DEATH?
...
YES.
AND HER SMILE MOVED ZEUS.
A FIERCE WIND SUDDENLY BLEW THE BANDITS OVER THE CLIFF'S EDGE.
AFTERWARD, PIREMOS REGAINED HIS ORIGINAL FORM.
TOUCHED BY HARUSCURA'S FAITHFUL HEART, ZEUS HAD SENT THE WIND TO SAVE THEM.

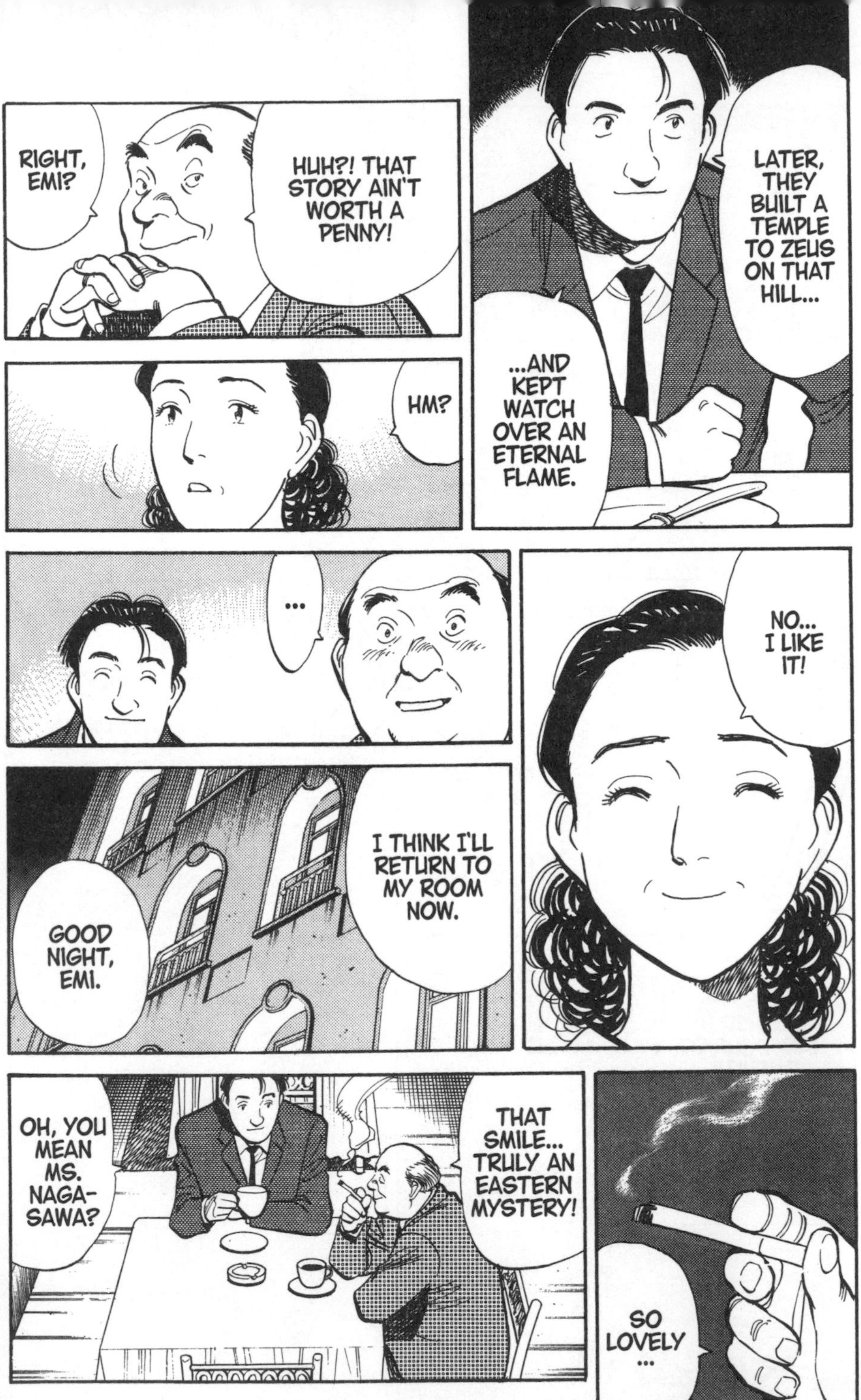
LATER, THEY BUILT A TEMPLE TO ZEUS ON THAT HILL...
...AND KEPT WATCH OVER AN ETERNAL FLAME.
HUH?! THAT STORY AIN'T WORTH A PENNY!
RIGHT, EMI?
HM?
NO... I LIKE IT!
...
I THINK I'LL RETURN TO MY ROOM NOW.
GOOD NIGHT, EMI.
SO LOVELY ...
THAT SMILE... TRULY AN EASTERN MYSTERY!
OH, YOU MEAN MS. NAGA-SAWA?

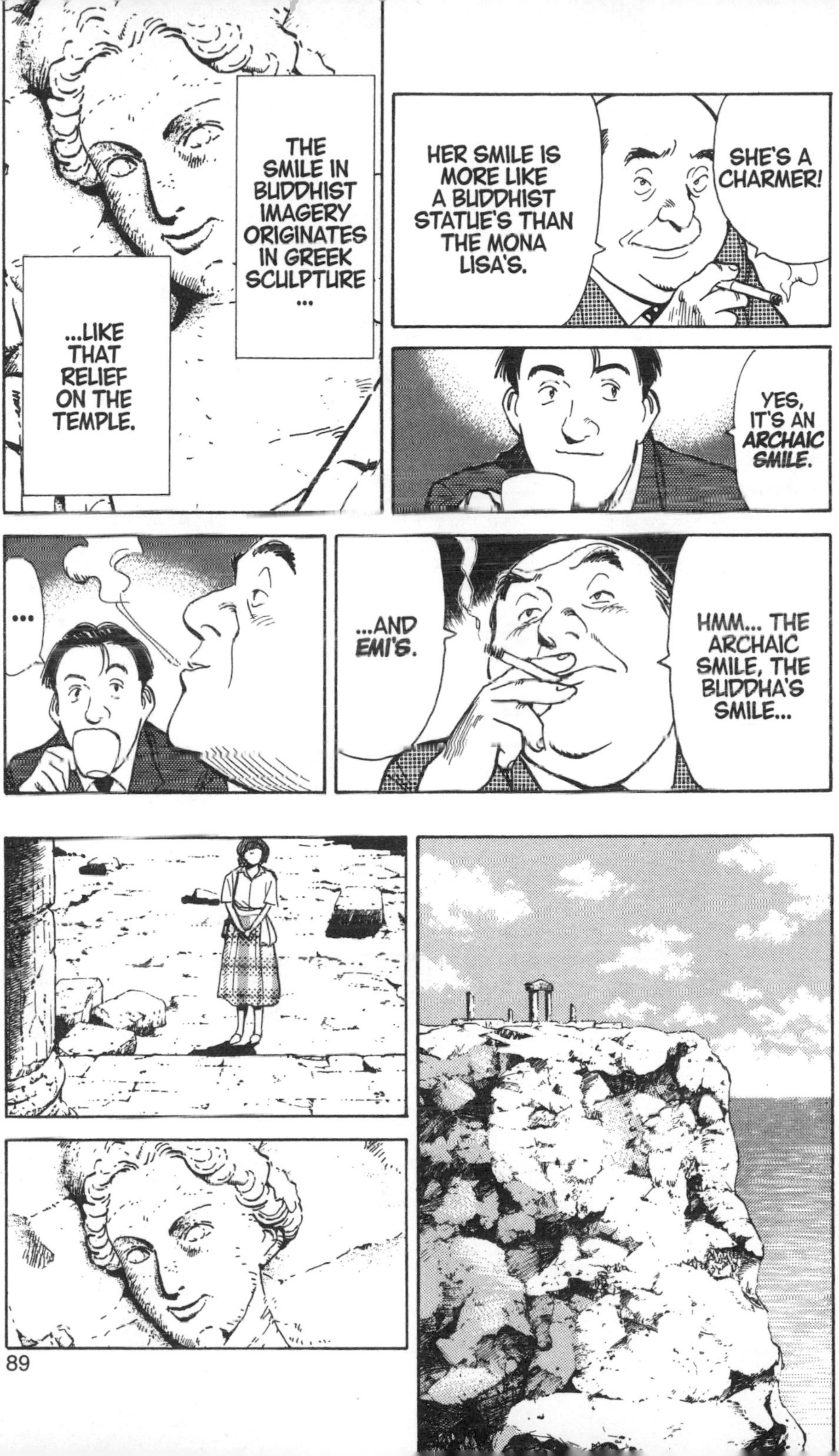
SHE'S A CHARMER!
HER SMILE IS MORE LIKE A BUDDHIST STATUE'S THAN THE MONA LISA'S.
YES, IT'S AN ARCHAIC SMILE.
THE SMILE IN BUDDHIST IMAGERY ORIGINATES IN GREEK SCULPTURE ...
...LIKE THAT RELIEF ON THE TEMPLE.
HMM... THE ARCHAIC SMILE, THE BUDDHA'S SMILE...
...AND EMI'S.
...

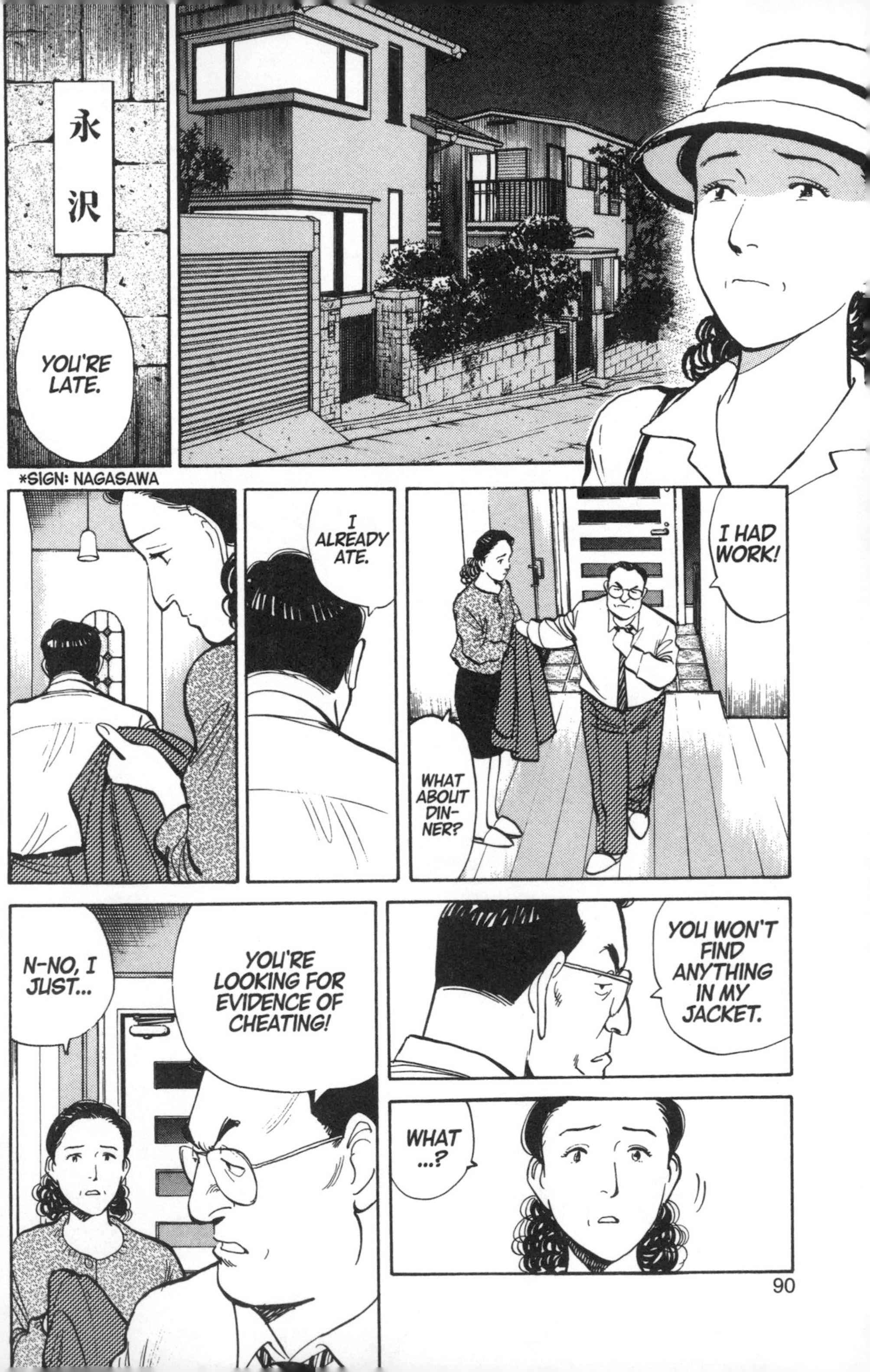

永沢
YOU'RE LATE.
*SIGN: NAGASAWA
I HAD WORK!
WHAT ABOUT DIN-NER?
I ALREADY ATE.
YOU WON'T FIND ANYTHING IN MY JACKET.
WHAT ...?
YOU'RE LOOKING FOR EVIDENCE OF CHEATING!
N-NO, I JUST...

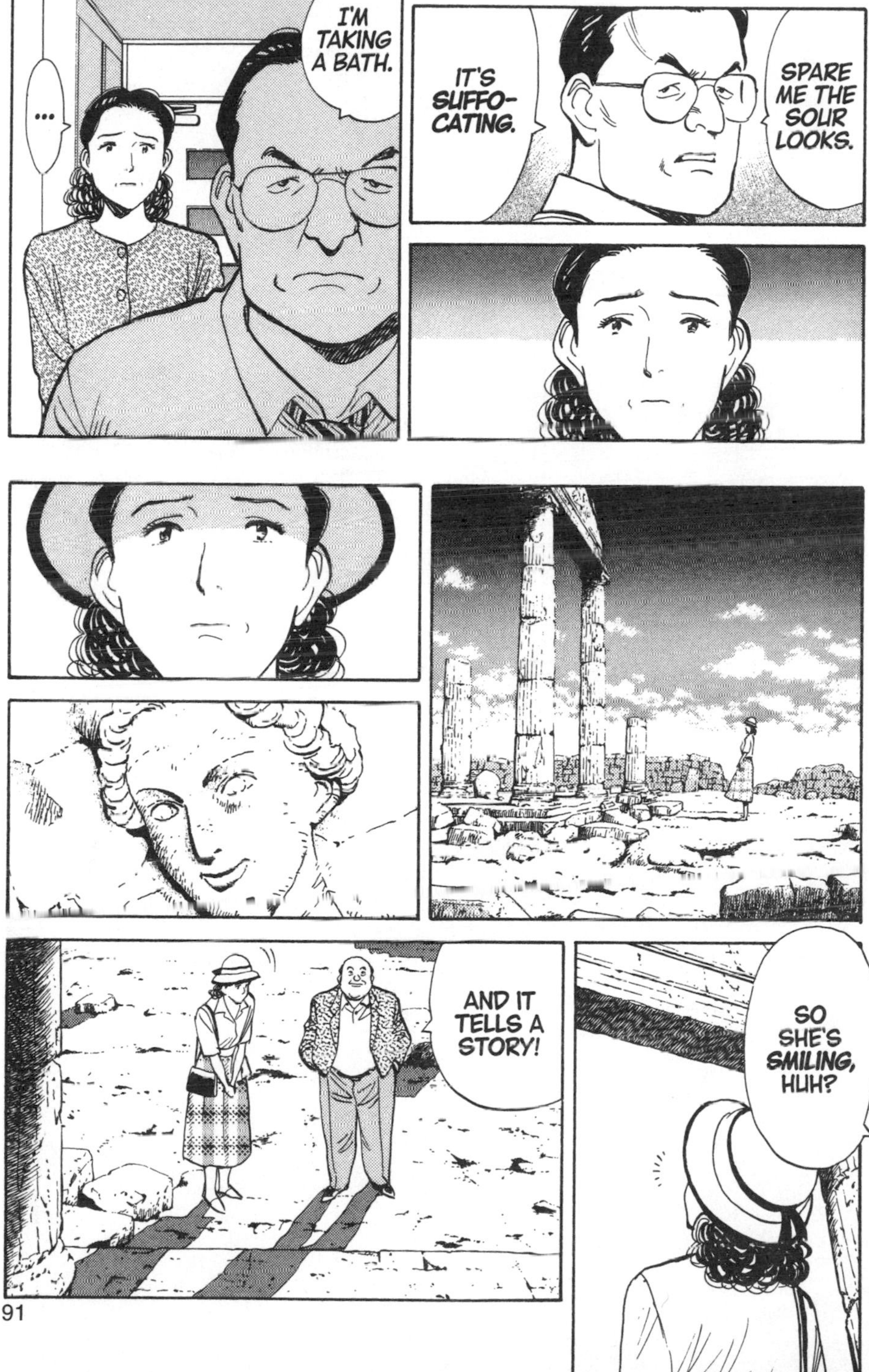
SPARE ME THE SOUR LOOKS.
IT'S SUFFO-CATING.
I'M TAKING A BATH.
...
SO SHE'S SMILING, HUH?
AND IT TELLS A STORY!

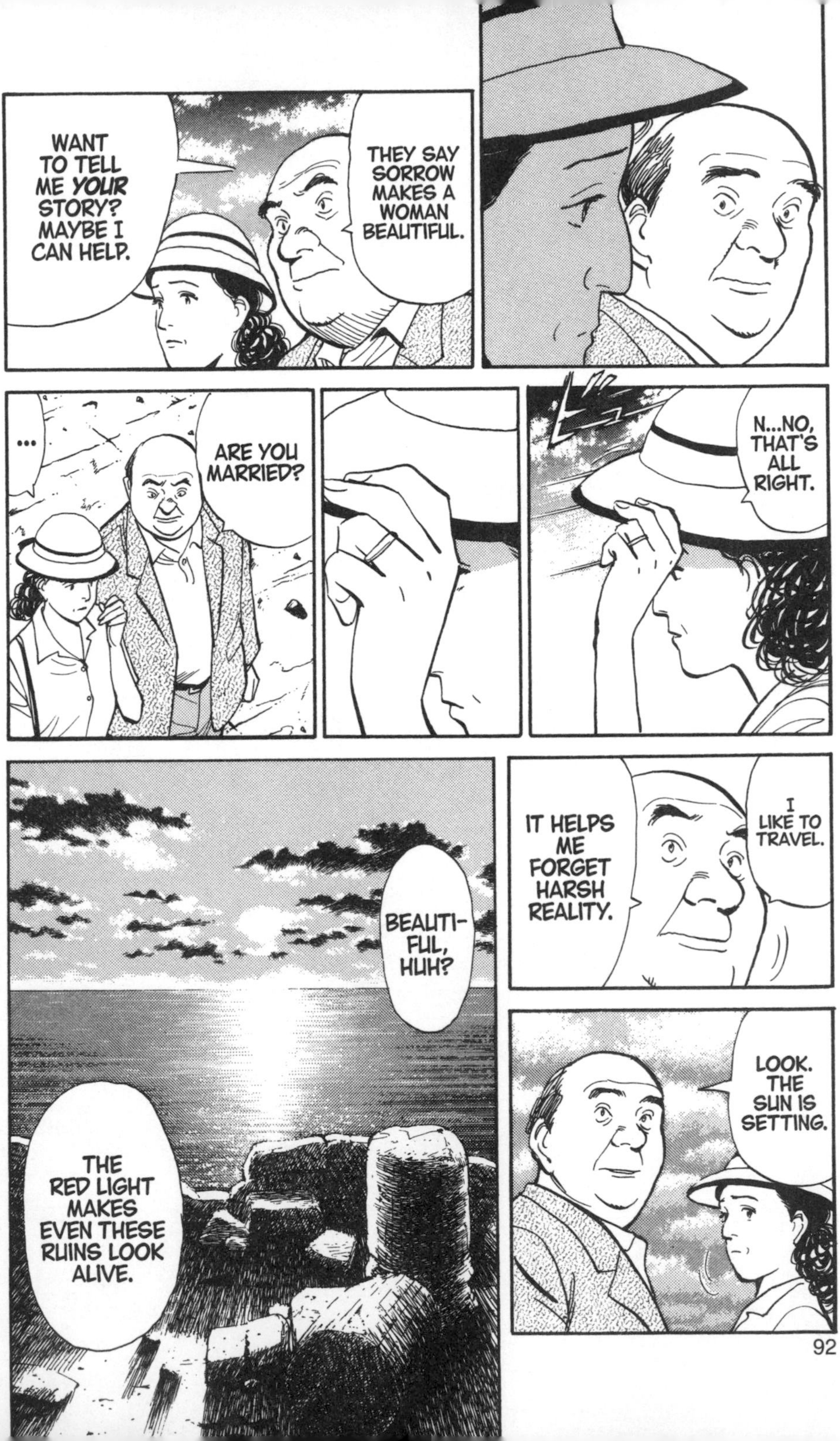
THEY SAY SORROW MAKES A WOMAN BEAUTIFUL.
WANT TO TELL ME *YOUR* STORY? MAYBE I CAN HELP.
N...NO, THAT'S ALL RIGHT.
ARE YOU MARRIED?
...
I LIKE TO TRAVEL.
IT HELPS ME FORGET HARSH REALITY.
LOOK. THE SUN IS SETTING.
BEAUTIFUL, HUH?
THE RED LIGHT MAKES EVEN THESE RUINS LOOK ALIVE.

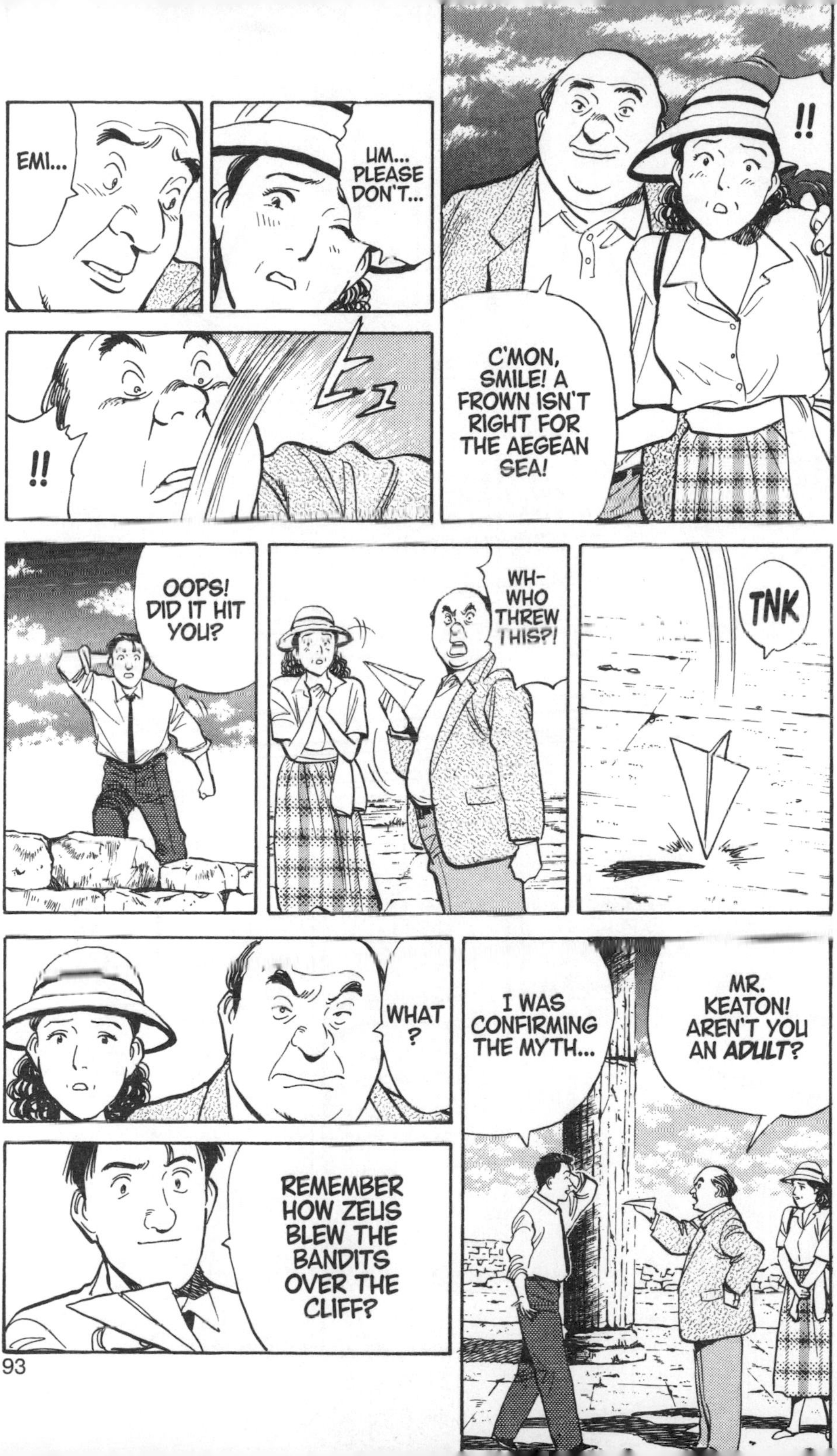

!!
C'MON, SMILE! A FROWN ISN'T RIGHT FOR THE AEGEAN SEA!
UM... PLEASE DON'T...
EMI...
!!
TNK
WH- WHO THREW THIS?!
OOPS! DID IT HIT YOU?
MR. KEATON! AREN'T YOU AN *ADULT*?
I WAS CONFIRMING THE MYTH...
WHAT?
REMEMBER HOW ZEUS BLEW THE BANDITS OVER THE CLIFF?

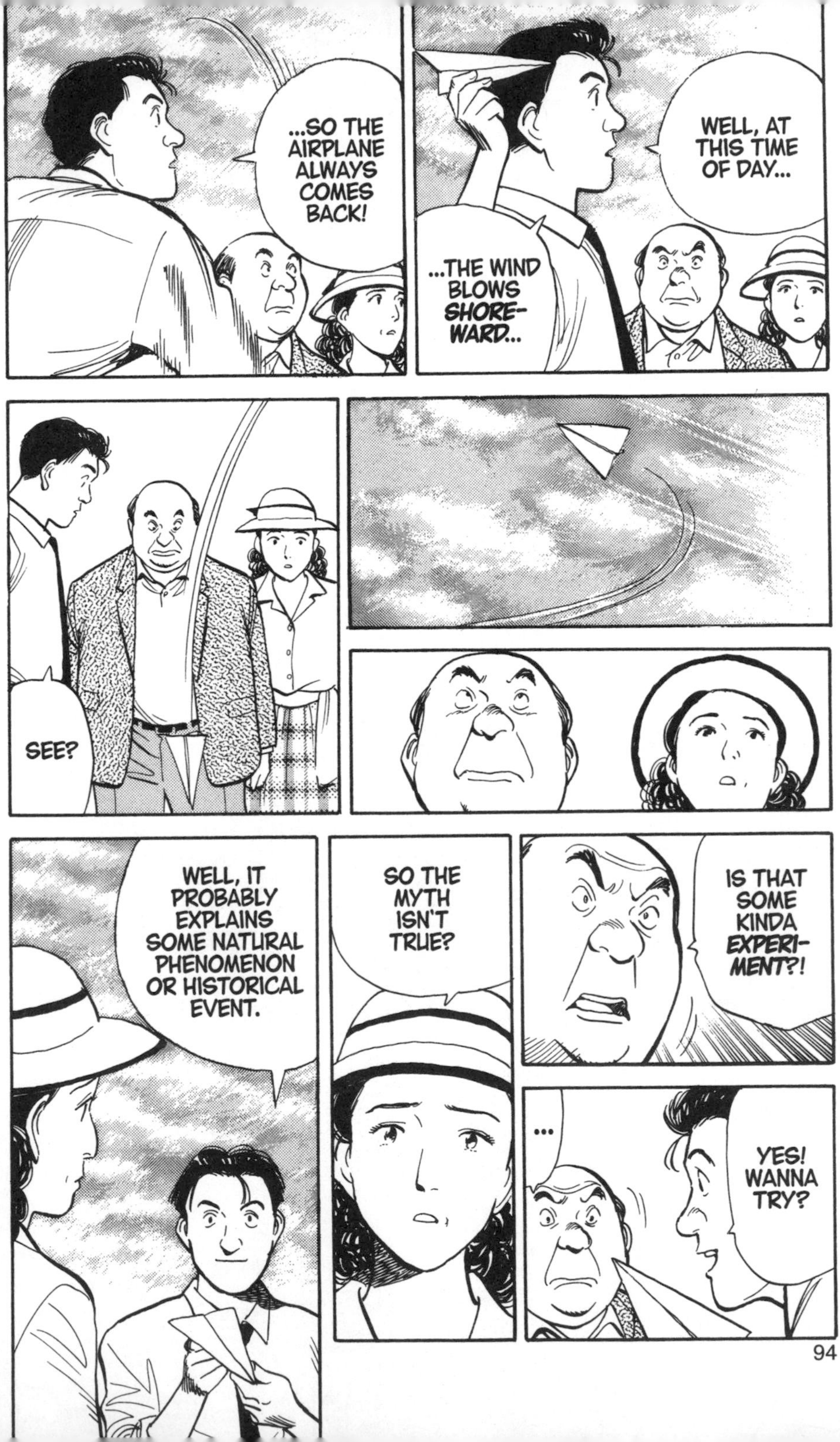
WELL, AT THIS TIME OF DAY...
...THE WIND BLOWS SHOREWARD...
...SO THE AIRPLANE ALWAYS COMES BACK!
SEE?
IS THAT SOME KINDA EXPERIMENT?!
...
YES! WANNA TRY?
SO THE MYTH ISN'T TRUE?
WELL, IT PROBABLY EXPLAINS SOME NATURAL PHENOMENON OR HISTORICAL EVENT.

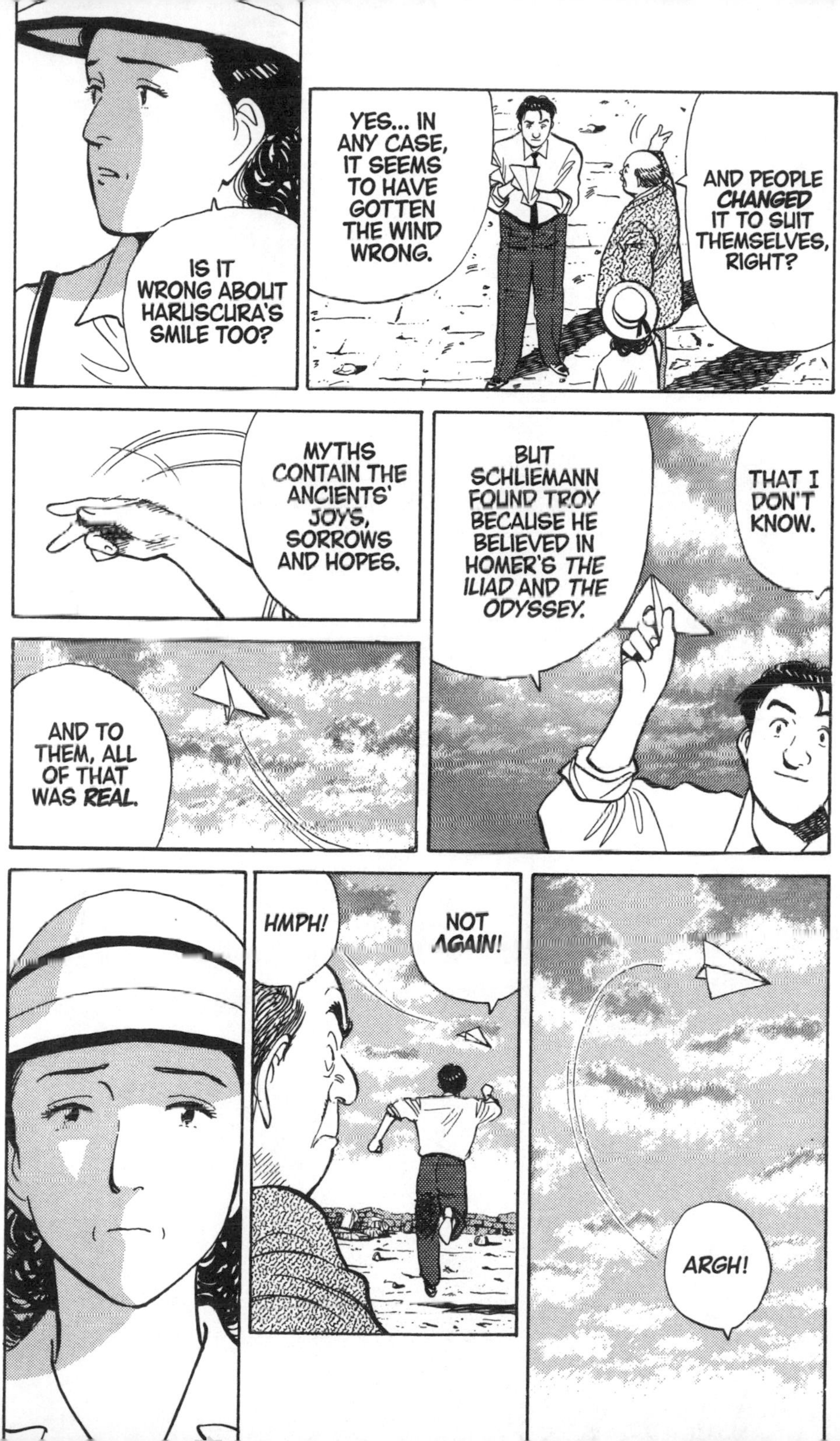
AND PEOPLE CHANGED IT TO SUIT THEMSELVES, RIGHT?
YES... IN ANY CASE, IT SEEMS TO HAVE GOTTEN THE WIND WRONG.
IS IT WRONG ABOUT HARUSCURA'S SMILE TOO?
THAT I DON'T KNOW.
BUT SCHLIEMANN FOUND TROY BECAUSE HE BELIEVED IN HOMER'S THE ILIAD AND THE ODYSSEY.
MYTHS CONTAIN THE ANCIENTS' JOYS, SORROWS AND HOPES.
AND TO THEM, ALL OF THAT WAS REAL.
ARGH!
NOT AGAIN!
HMPH!

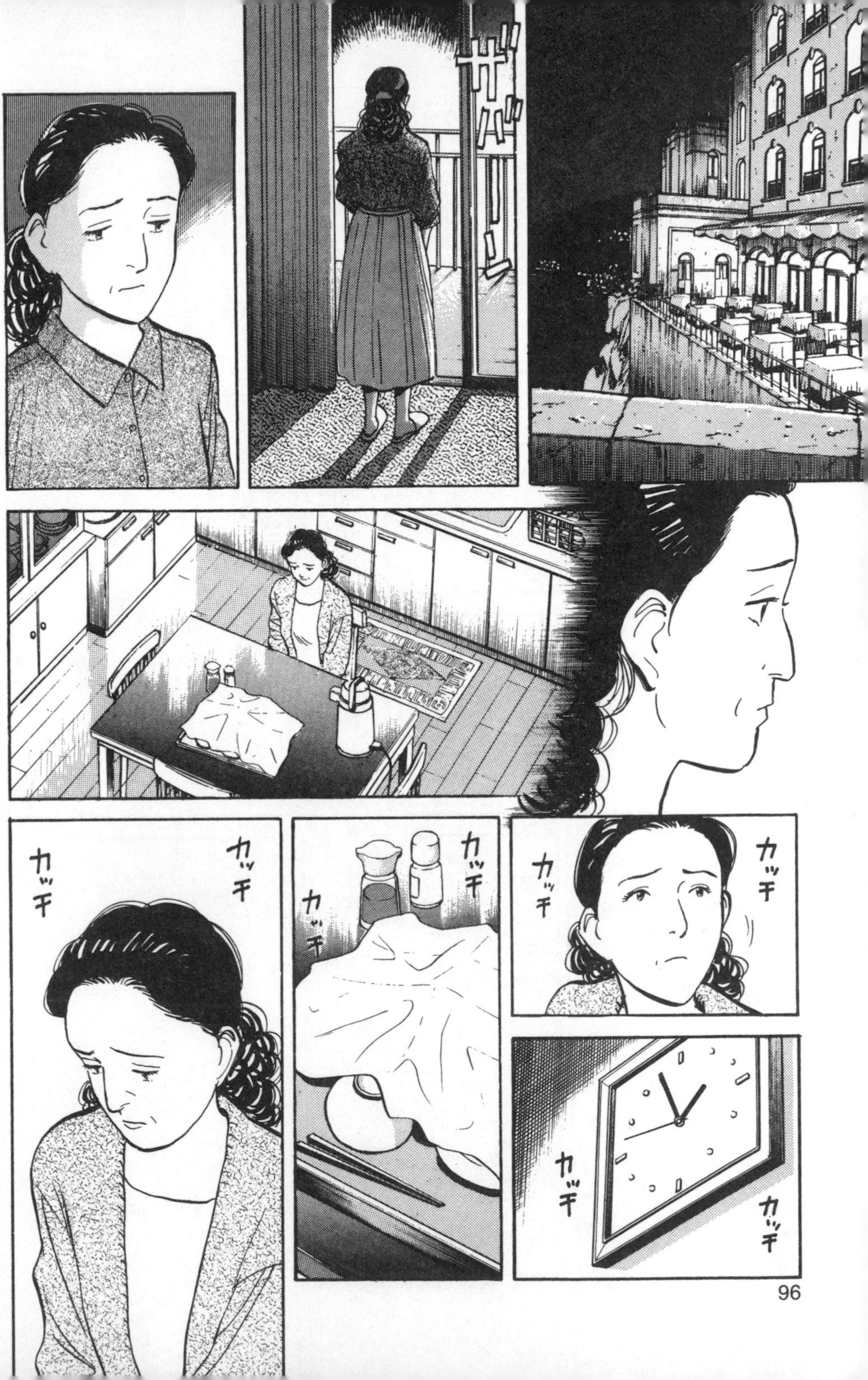
ザバーン
カッチ
カッチ
カッチ
カッチ
カッチ
カッチ
カッチ
カッチ

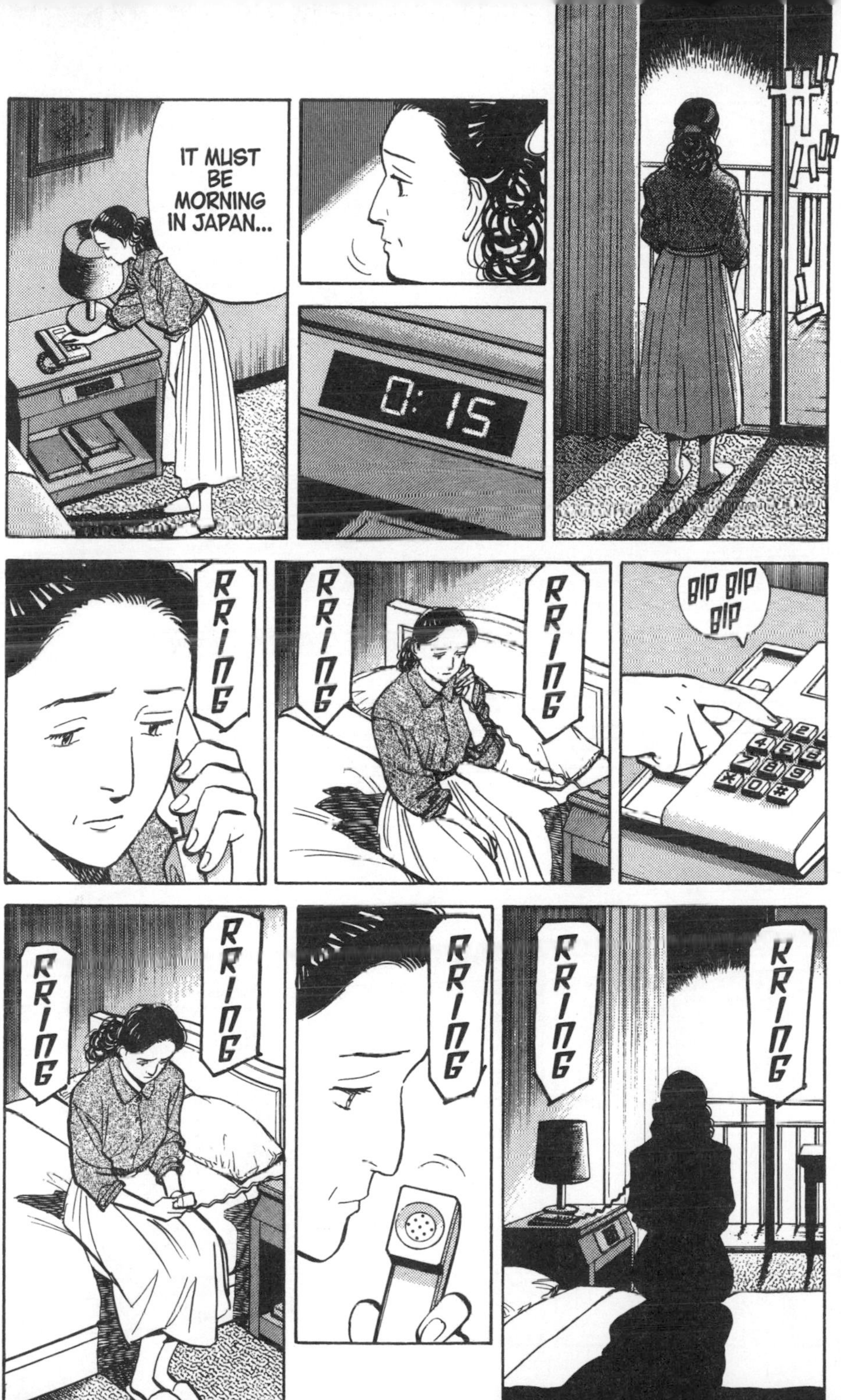
0: 15
IT MUST BE MORNING IN JAPAN...
BIP BIP BIP
RRING
RRING
RRING
RRING
RRING
RRING
RRING

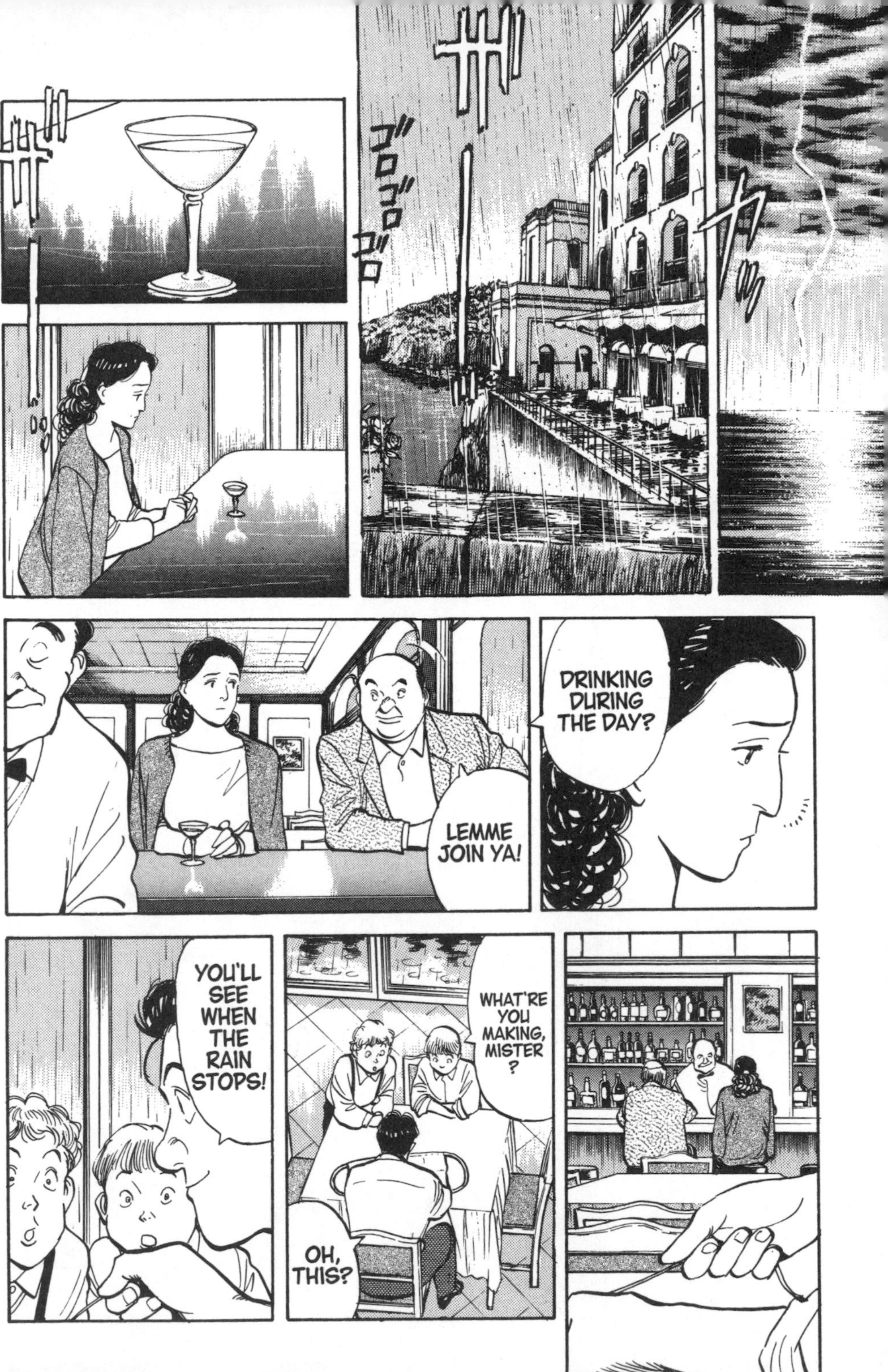
ゴロゴロゴロ
DRINKING DURING THE DAY?
LEMME JOIN YA!
WHAT'RE YOU MAKING, MISTER?
OH, THIS?
YOU'LL SEE WHEN THE RAIN STOPS!

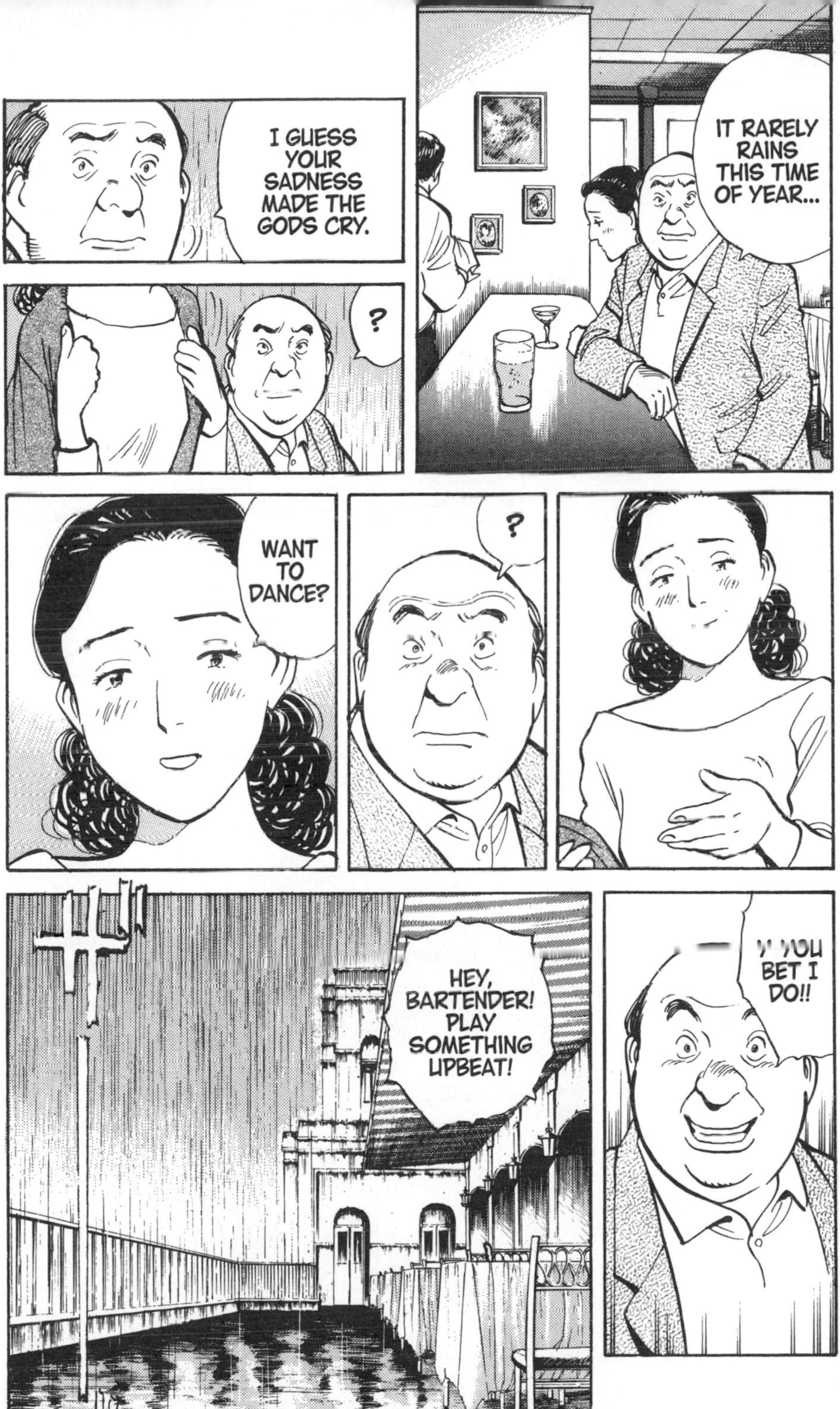
IT RARELY RAINS THIS TIME OF YEAR...
I GUESS YOUR SADNESS MADE THE GODS CRY.
?
?
WANT TO DANCE?
Y-YOU BET I DO!!
HEY, BARTENDER! PLAY SOMETHING UPBEAT!

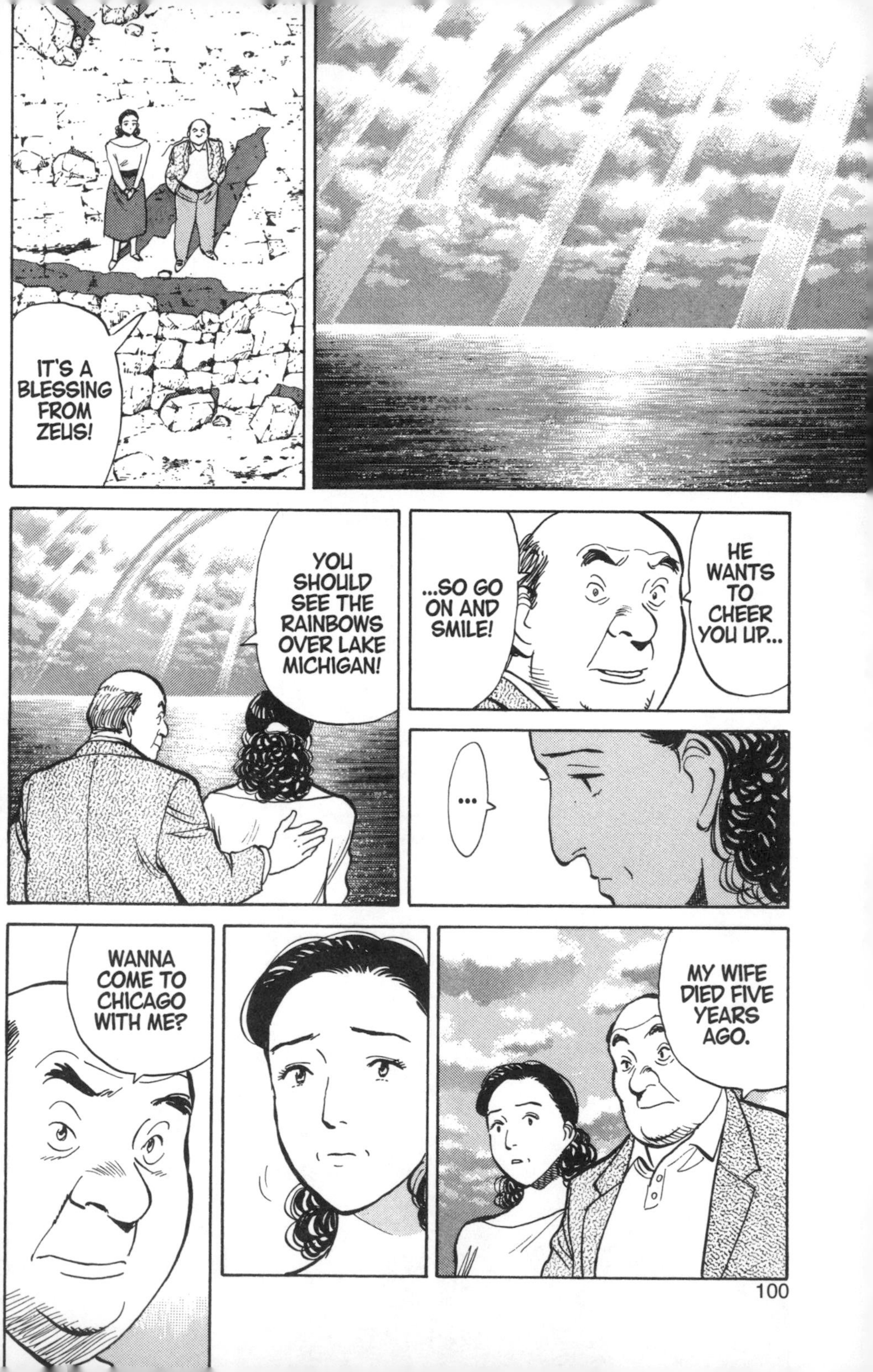
IT'S A BLESSING FROM ZEUS!
HE WANTS TO CHEER YOU UP...
...SO GO ON AND SMILE!
...
YOU SHOULD SEE THE RAINBOWS OVER LAKE MICHIGAN!
MY WIFE DIED FIVE YEARS AGO.
WANNA COME TO CHICAGO WITH ME?

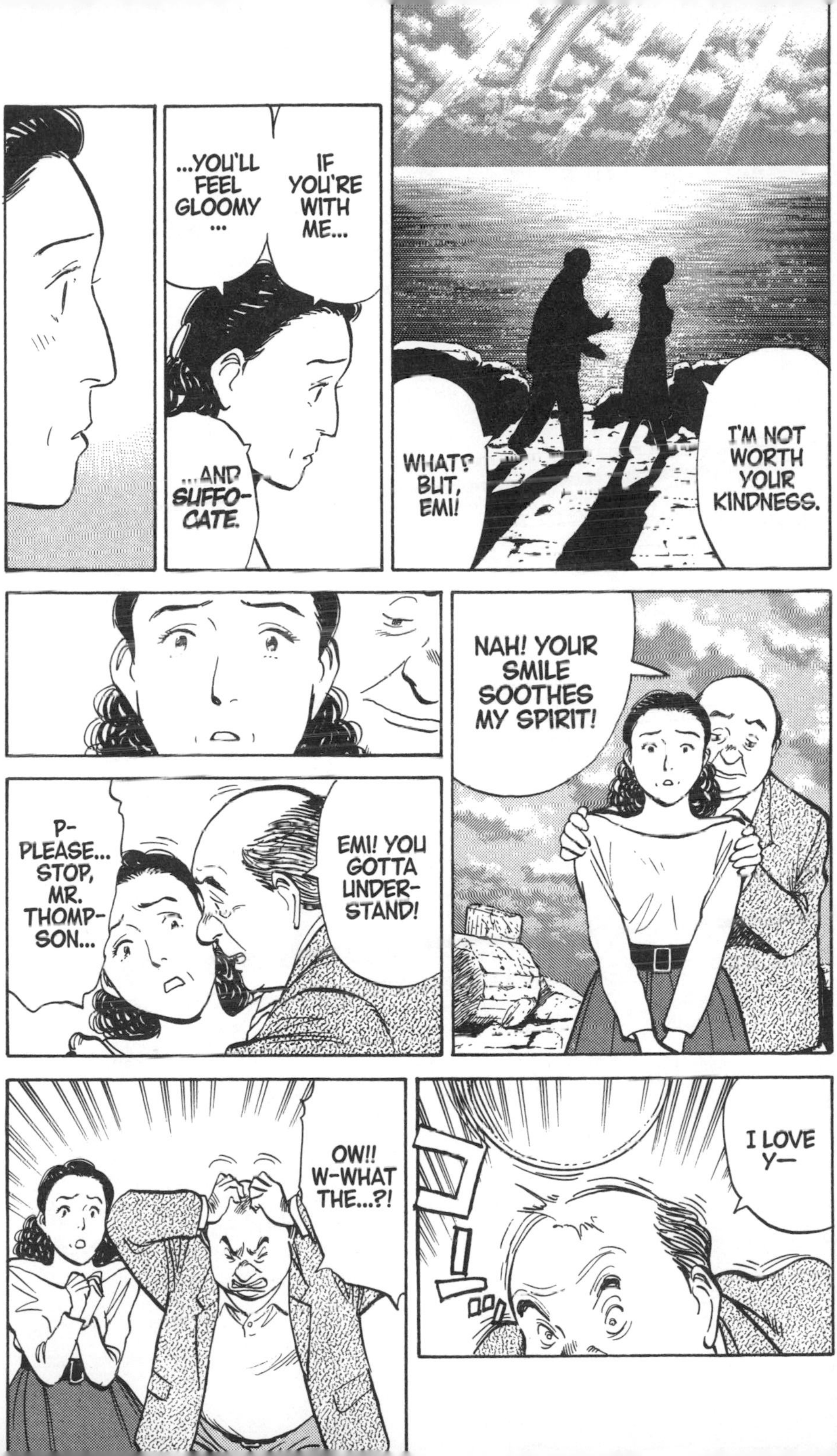
I'M NOT WORTH YOUR KINDNESS.
WHAT? BUT, EMI!
IF YOU'RE WITH ME...
...YOU'LL FEEL GLOOMY ...
...AND SUFFOCATE.
NAH! YOUR SMILE SOOTHES MY SPIRIT!
EMI! YOU GOTTA UNDERSTAND!
P-PLEASE... STOP, MR. THOMPSON...
I LOVE Y—
OW!! W-WHAT THE...?!

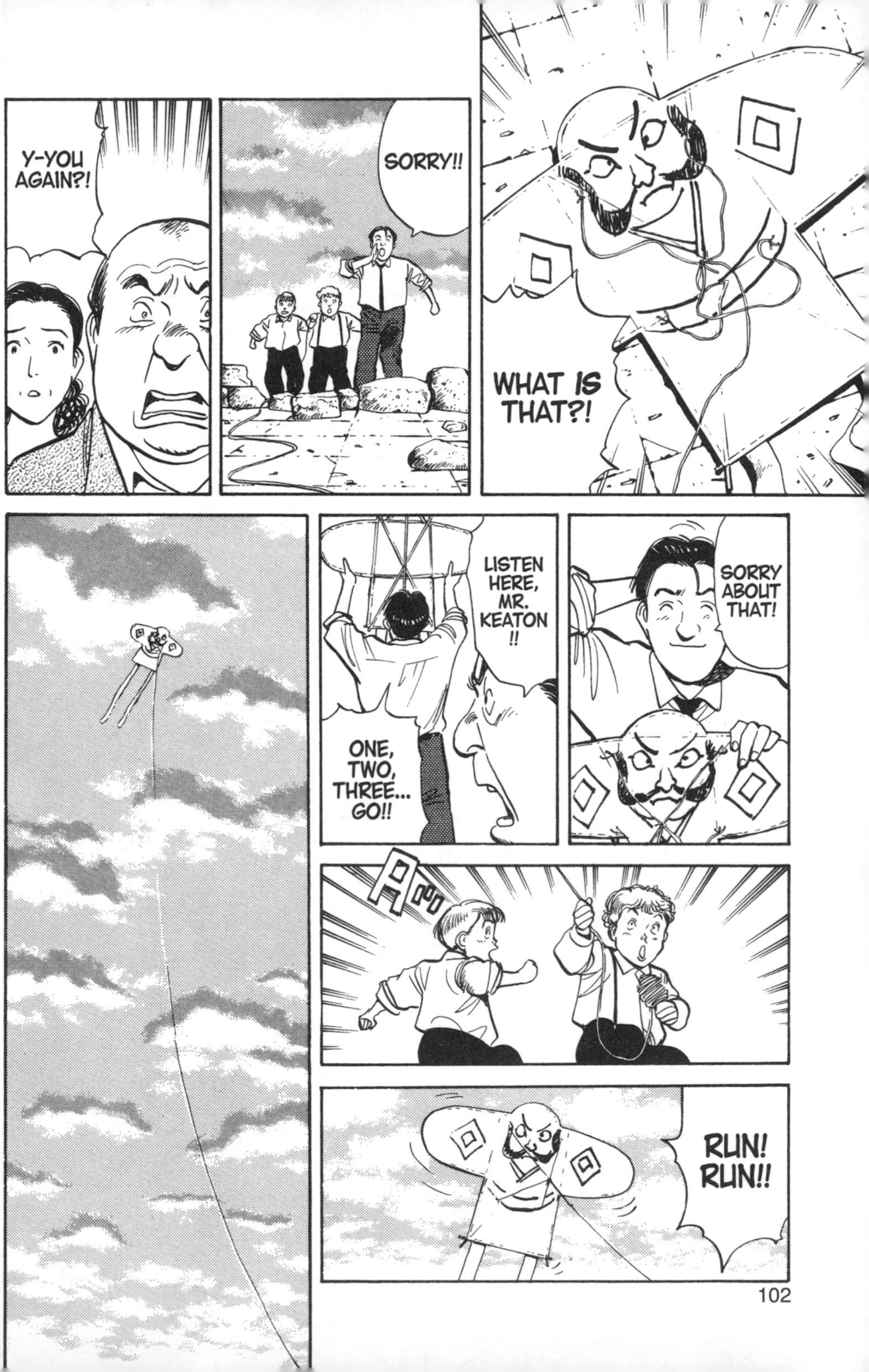
WHAT IS THAT?!
SORRY!!
Y-YOU AGAIN?!
SORRY ABOUT THAT!
LISTEN HERE, MR. KEATON !!
ONE, TWO, THREE... GO!!
RUN! RUN!!

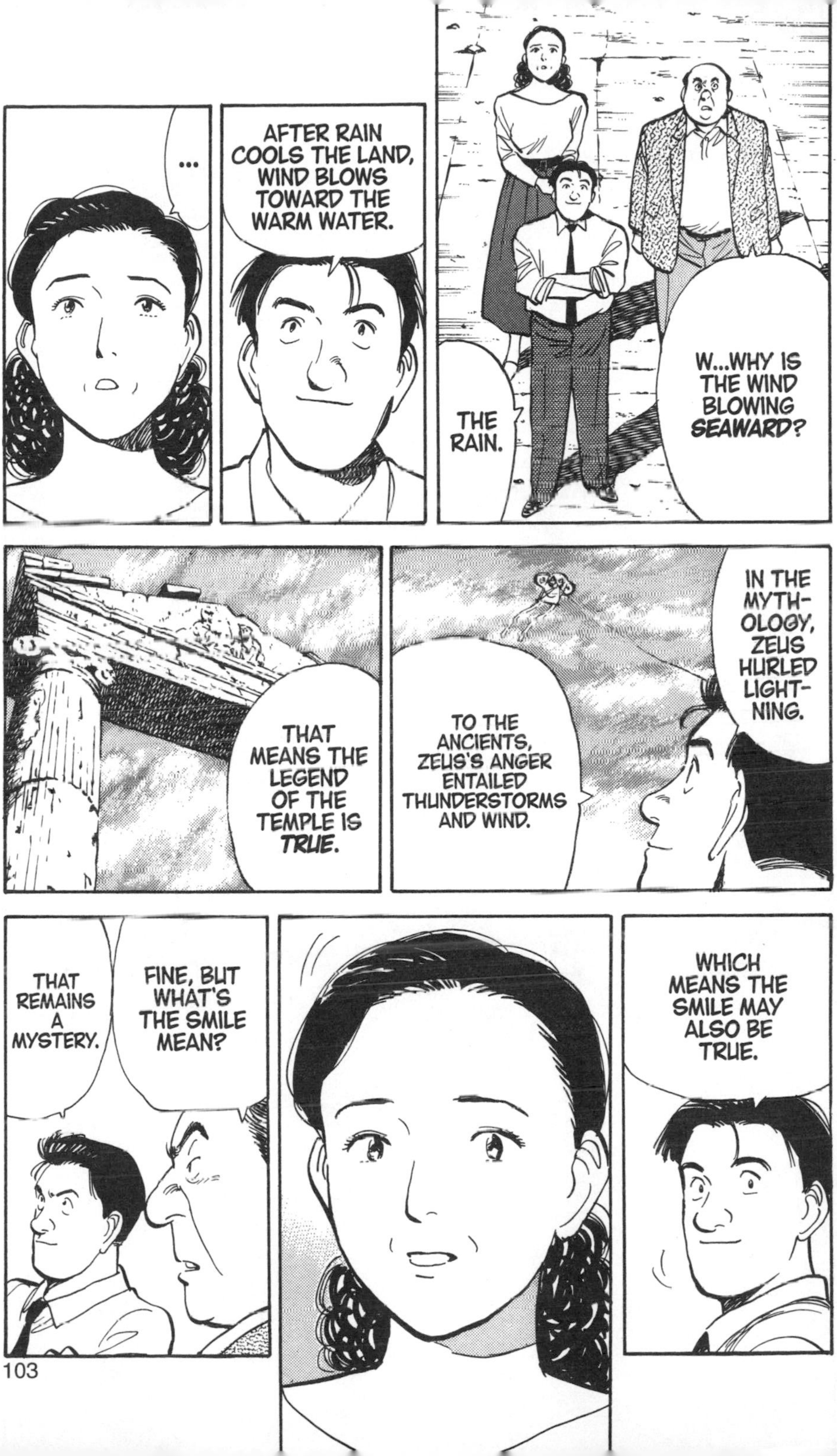
W...WHY IS THE WIND BLOWING SEAWARD?
THE RAIN.
AFTER RAIN COOLS THE LAND, WIND BLOWS TOWARD THE WARM WATER.
...
IN THE MYTHOLOGY, ZEUS HURLED LIGHTNING.
TO THE ANCIENTS, ZEUS'S ANGER ENTAILED THUNDERSTORMS AND WIND.
THAT MEANS THE LEGEND OF THE TEMPLE IS TRUE.
WHICH MEANS THE SMILE MAY ALSO BE TRUE.
FINE, BUT WHAT'S THE SMILE MEAN?
THAT REMAINS A MYSTERY.

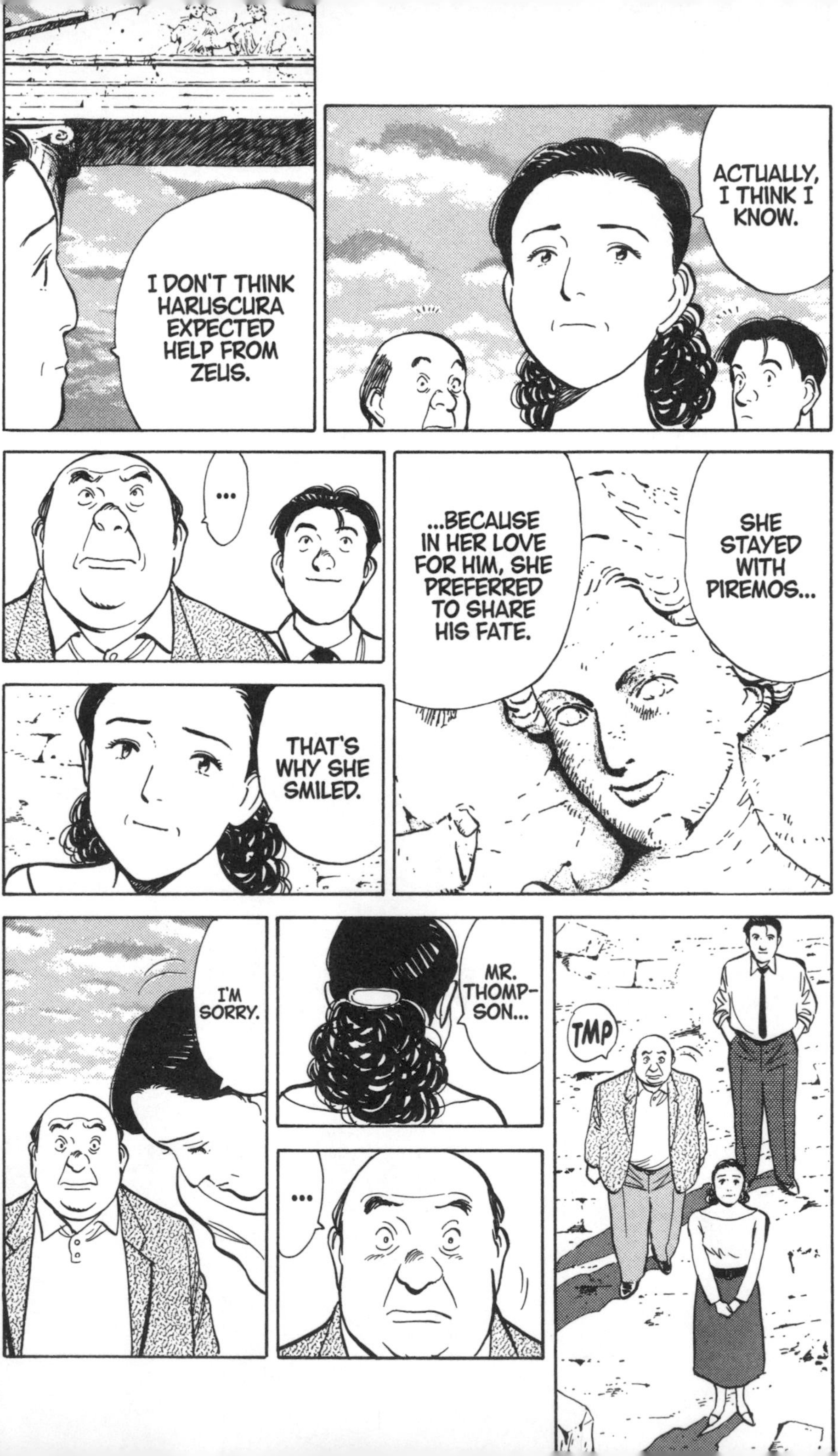
ACTUALLY, I THINK I KNOW.
I DON'T THINK HARUSCURA EXPECTED HELP FROM ZEUS.
SHE STAYED WITH PIREMOS...
...BECAUSE IN HER LOVE FOR HIM, SHE PREFERRED TO SHARE HIS FATE.
...
THAT'S WHY SHE SMILED.
TMP
MR. THOMPSON...
...
I'M SORRY.

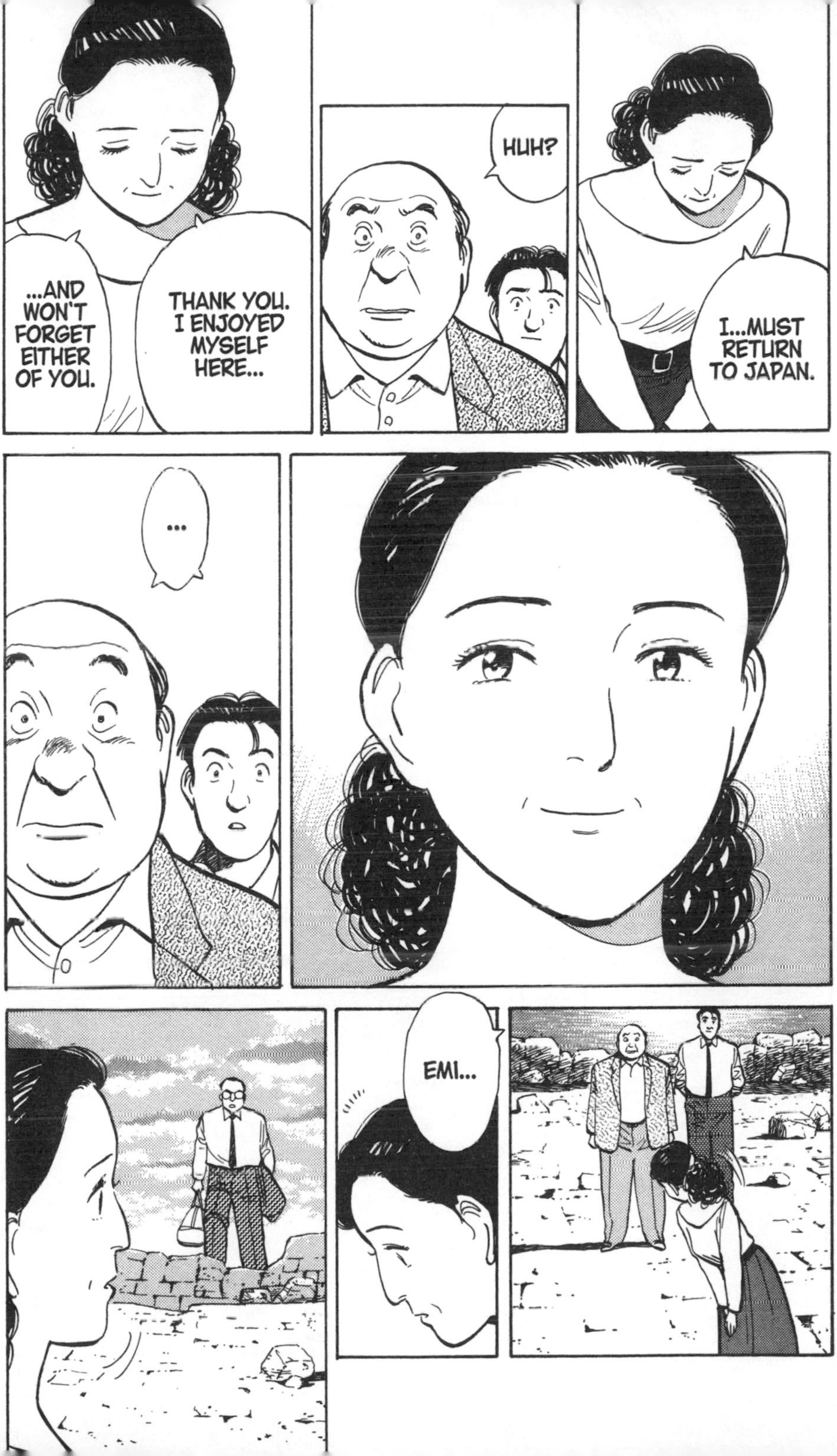
I...MUST RETURN TO JAPAN.
HUH?
THANK YOU. I ENJOYED MYSELF HERE...
...AND WON'T FORGET EITHER OF YOU.
...
EMI...

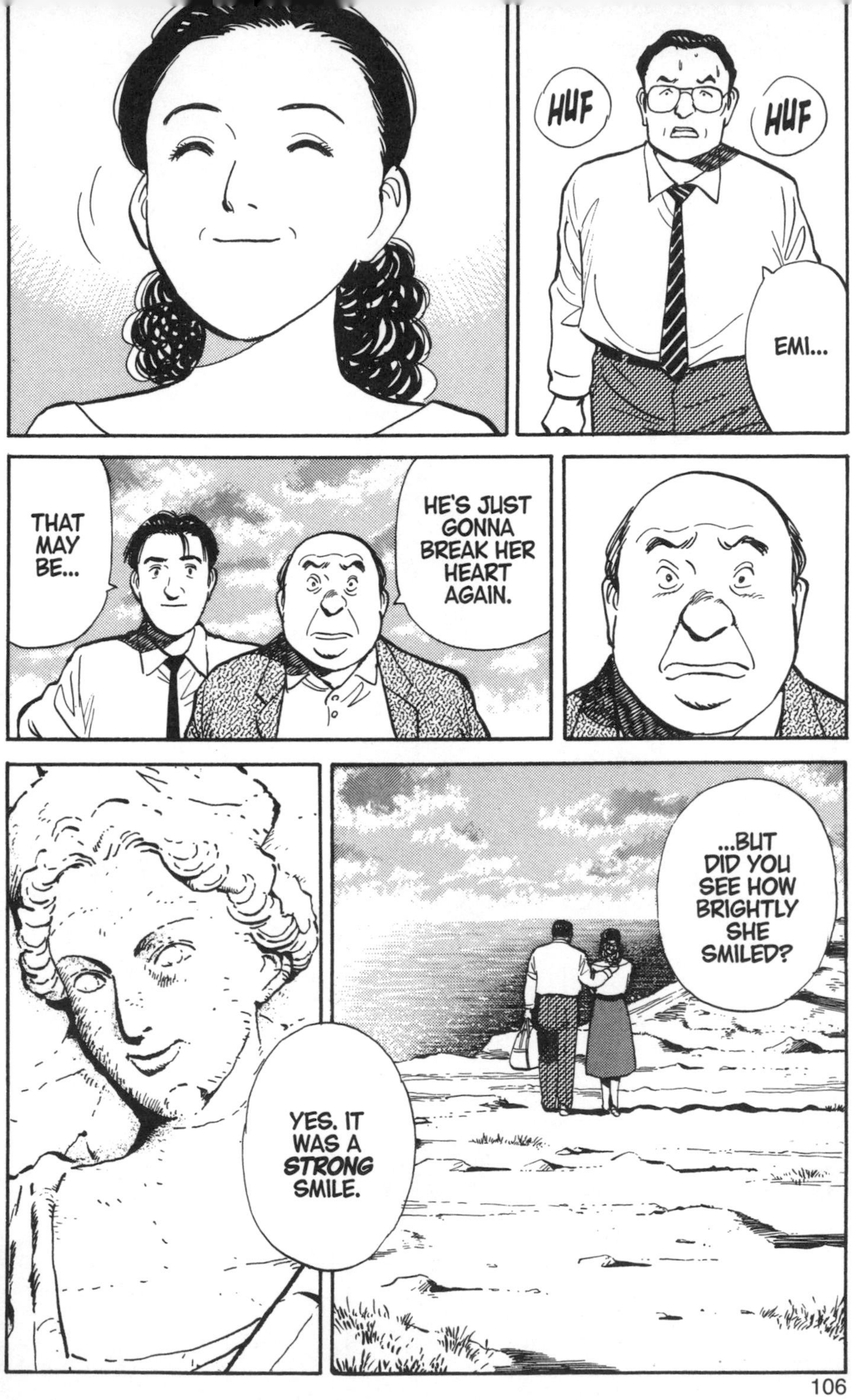
HUF
HUF
EMI...
HE'S JUST GONNA BREAK HER HEART AGAIN.
THAT MAY BE...
...BUT DID YOU SEE HOW BRIGHTLY SHE SMILED?
YES. IT WAS A STRONG SMILE.

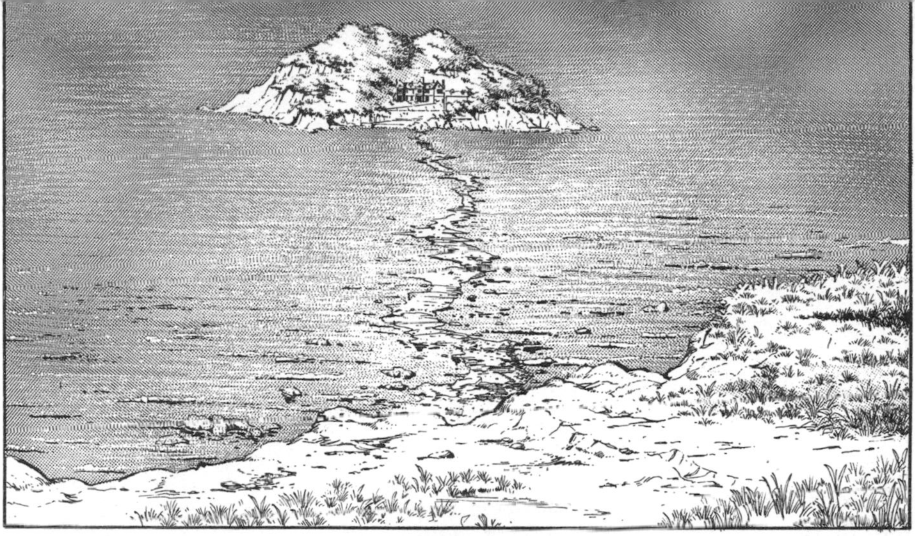

Chapter 5
Island of the Coward

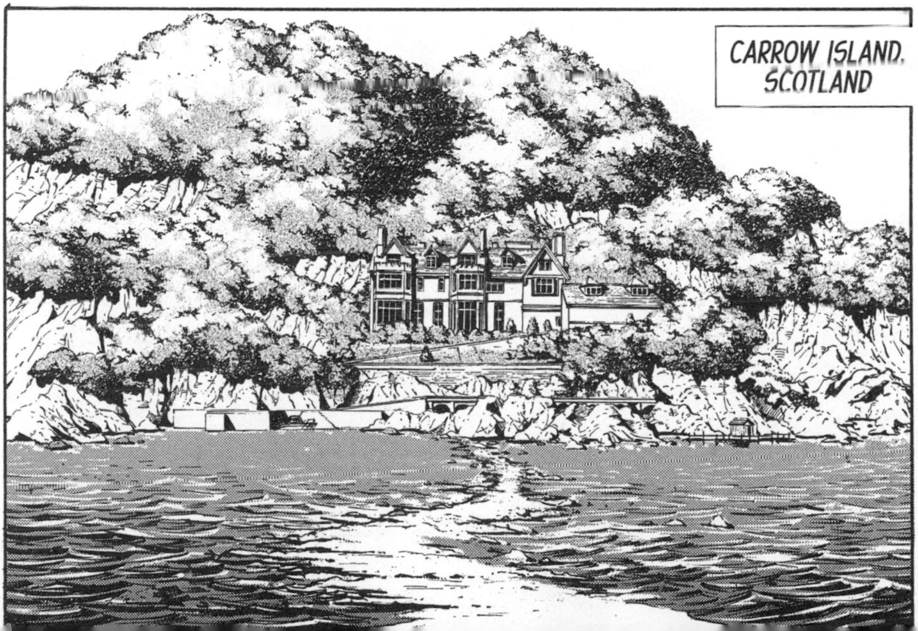
CARROW ISLAND, SCOTLAND

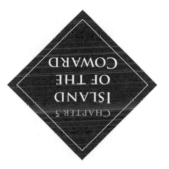

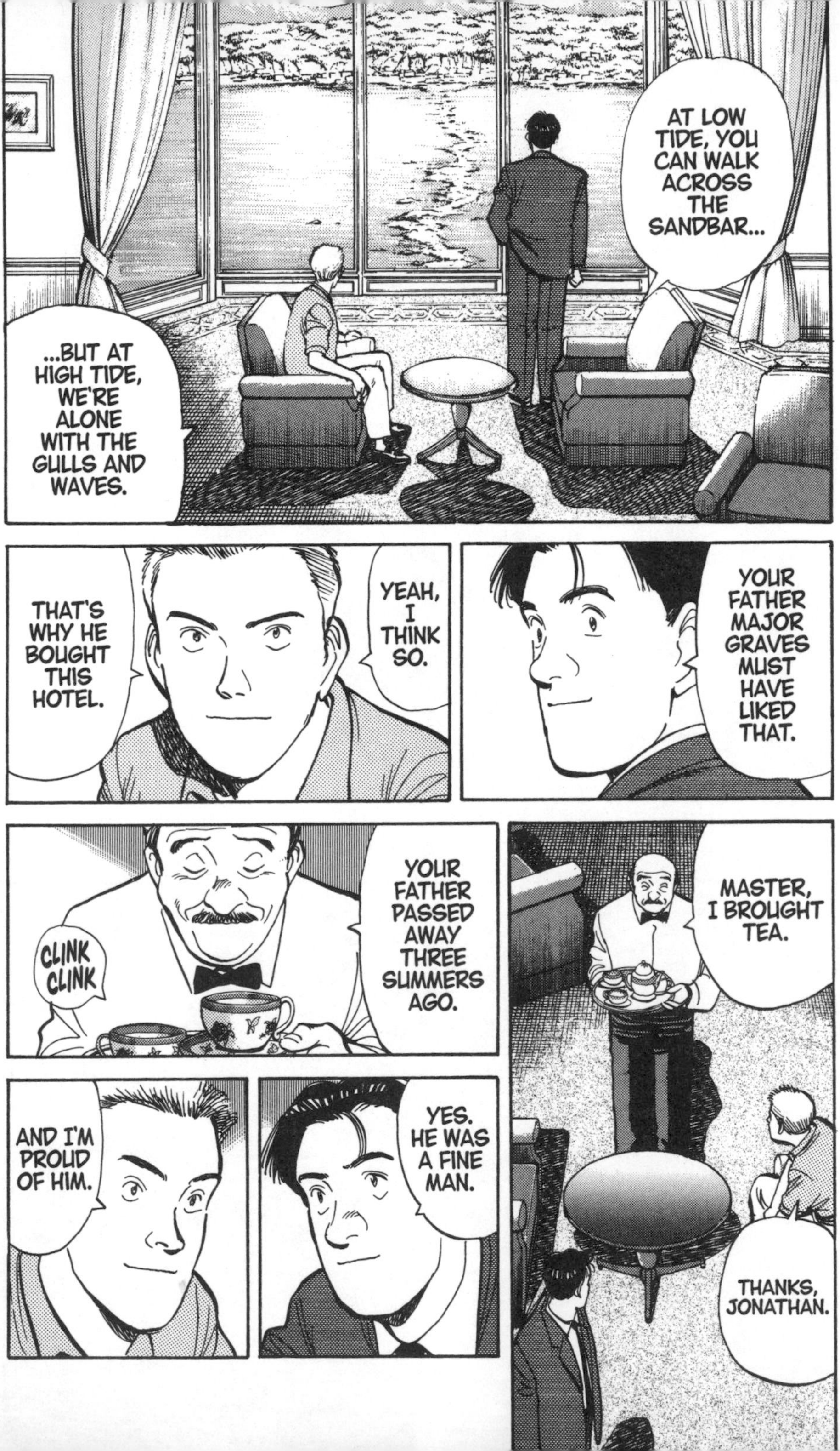
AT LOW TIDE, YOU CAN WALK ACROSS THE SANDBAR...
...BUT AT HIGH TIDE, WE'RE ALONE WITH THE GULLS AND WAVES.
YOUR FATHER MAJOR GRAVES MUST HAVE LIKED THAT.
YEAH, I THINK SO.
THAT'S WHY HE BOUGHT THIS HOTEL.
MASTER, I BROUGHT TEA.
THANKS, JONATHAN.
YOUR FATHER PASSED AWAY THREE SUMMERS AGO.
CLINK CLINK
YES. HE WAS A FINE MAN.
AND I'M PROUD OF HIM.

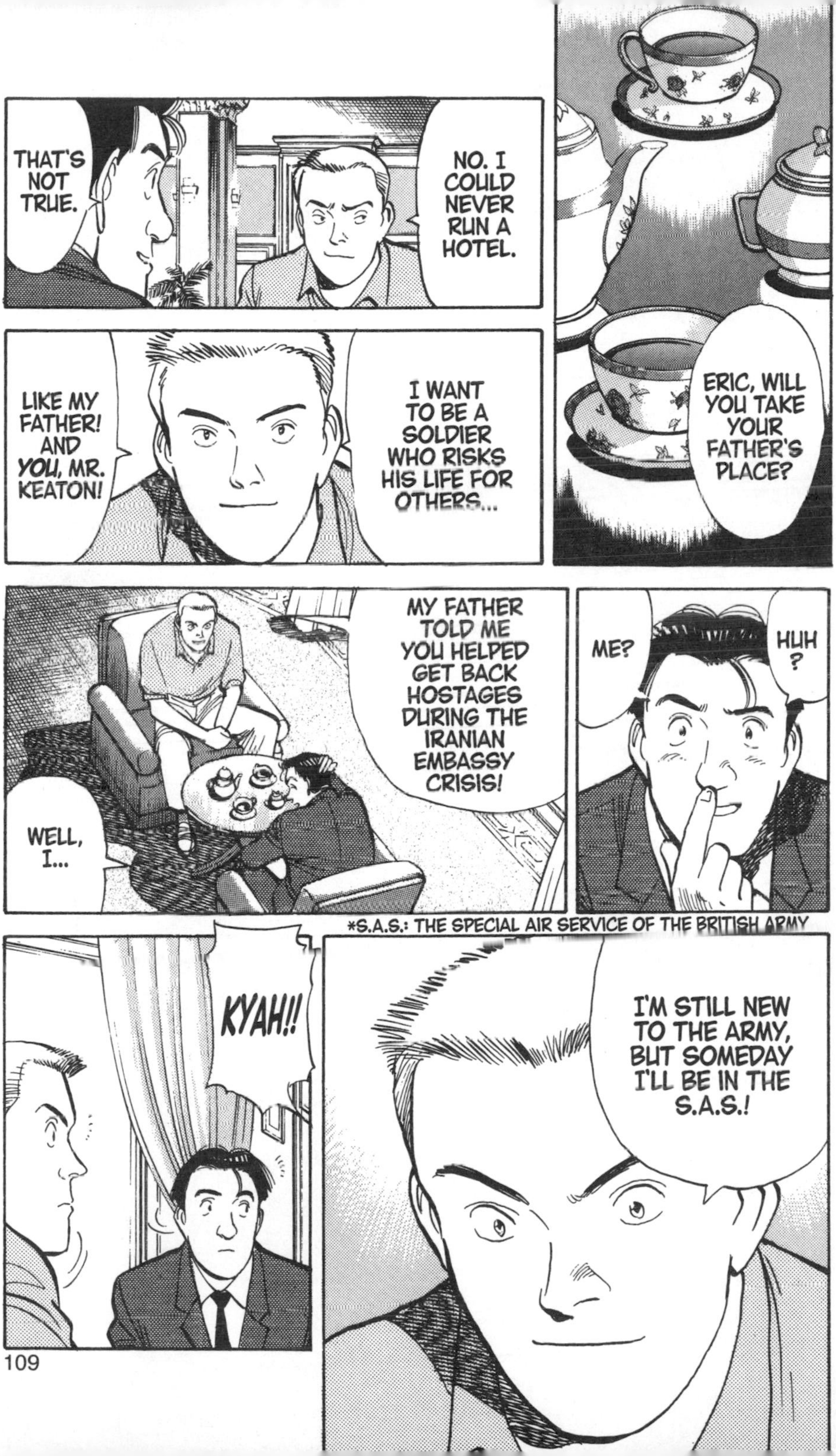
ERIC, WILL YOU TAKE YOUR FATHER'S PLACE?
NO. I COULD NEVER RUN A HOTEL.
THAT'S NOT TRUE.
I WANT TO BE A SOLDIER WHO RISKS HIS LIFE FOR OTHERS...
LIKE MY FATHER! AND *YOU*, MR. KEATON!
HUH ?
ME?
MY FATHER TOLD ME YOU HELPED GET BACK HOSTAGES DURING THE IRANIAN EMBASSY CRISIS!
WELL, I...
*S.A.S.: THE SPECIAL AIR SERVICE OF THE BRITISH ARMY
I'M STILL NEW TO THE ARMY, BUT SOMEDAY I'LL BE IN THE S.A.S.!
KYAH!!

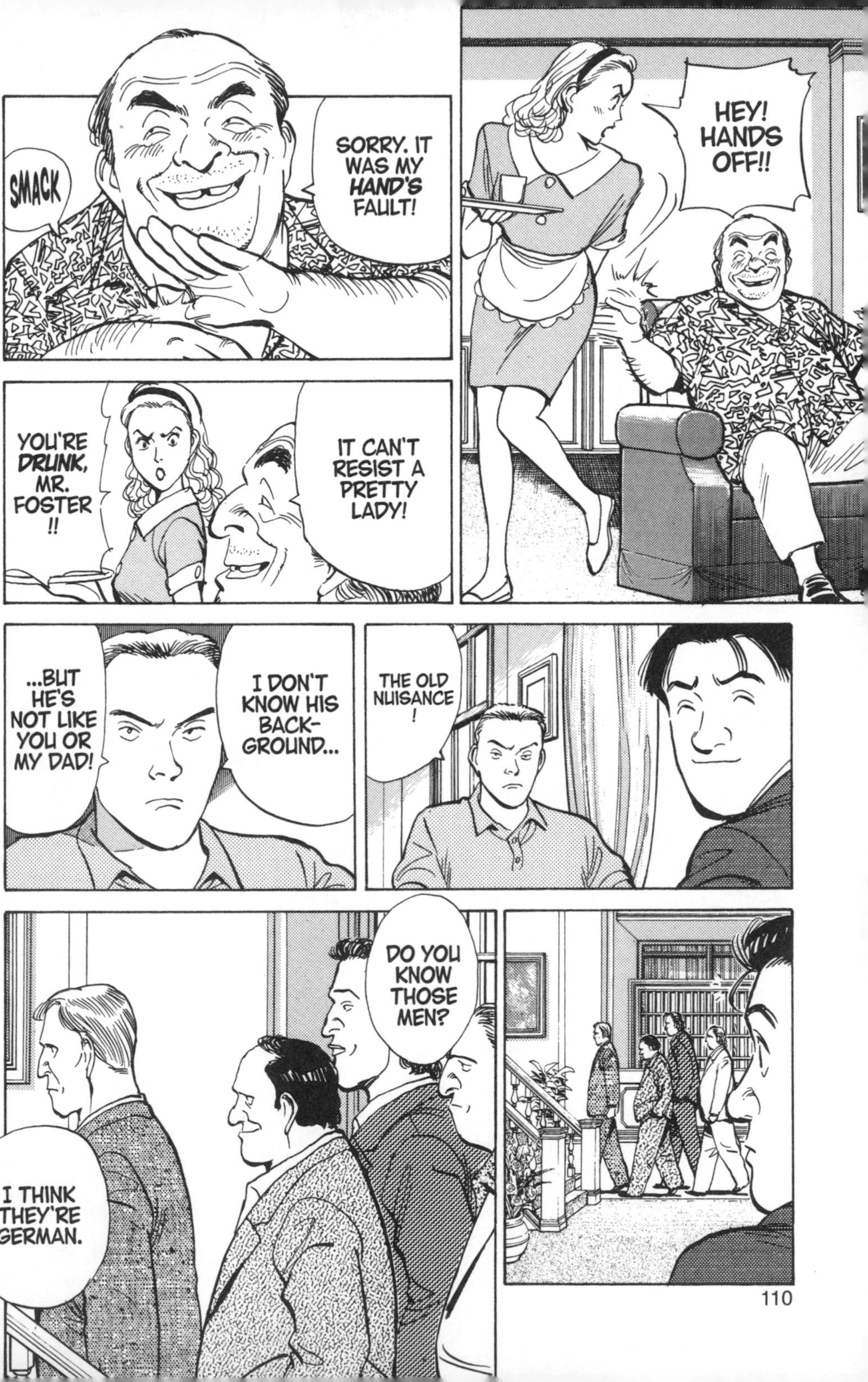
HEY! HANDS OFF!!
SORRY. IT WAS MY HAND'S FAULT!
SMACK
IT CAN'T RESIST A PRETTY LADY!
YOU'RE DRUNK, MR. FOSTER !!
THE OLD NUISANCE !
I DON'T KNOW HIS BACK-GROUND...
...BUT HE'S NOT LIKE YOU OR MY DAD!
DO YOU KNOW THOSE MEN?
I THINK THEY'RE GERMAN.

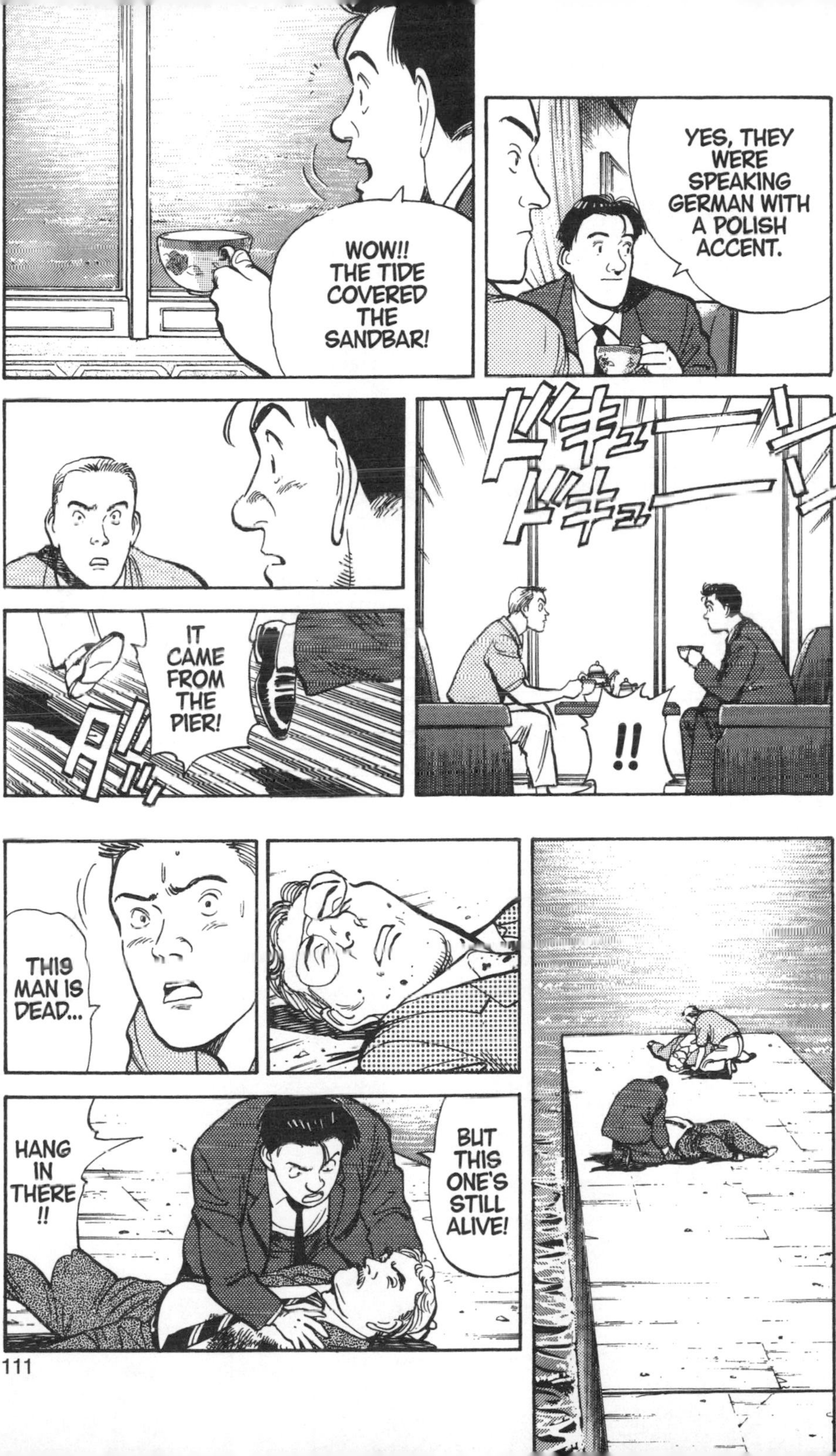

YES, THEY WERE SPEAKING GERMAN WITH A POLISH ACCENT.
WOW!! THE TIDE COVERED THE SANDBAR!
ドキューーン
ドキュー
!!
IT CAME FROM THE PIER!
ダッ
THIS MAN IS DEAD...
BUT THIS ONE'S STILL ALIVE!
HANG IN THERE!!

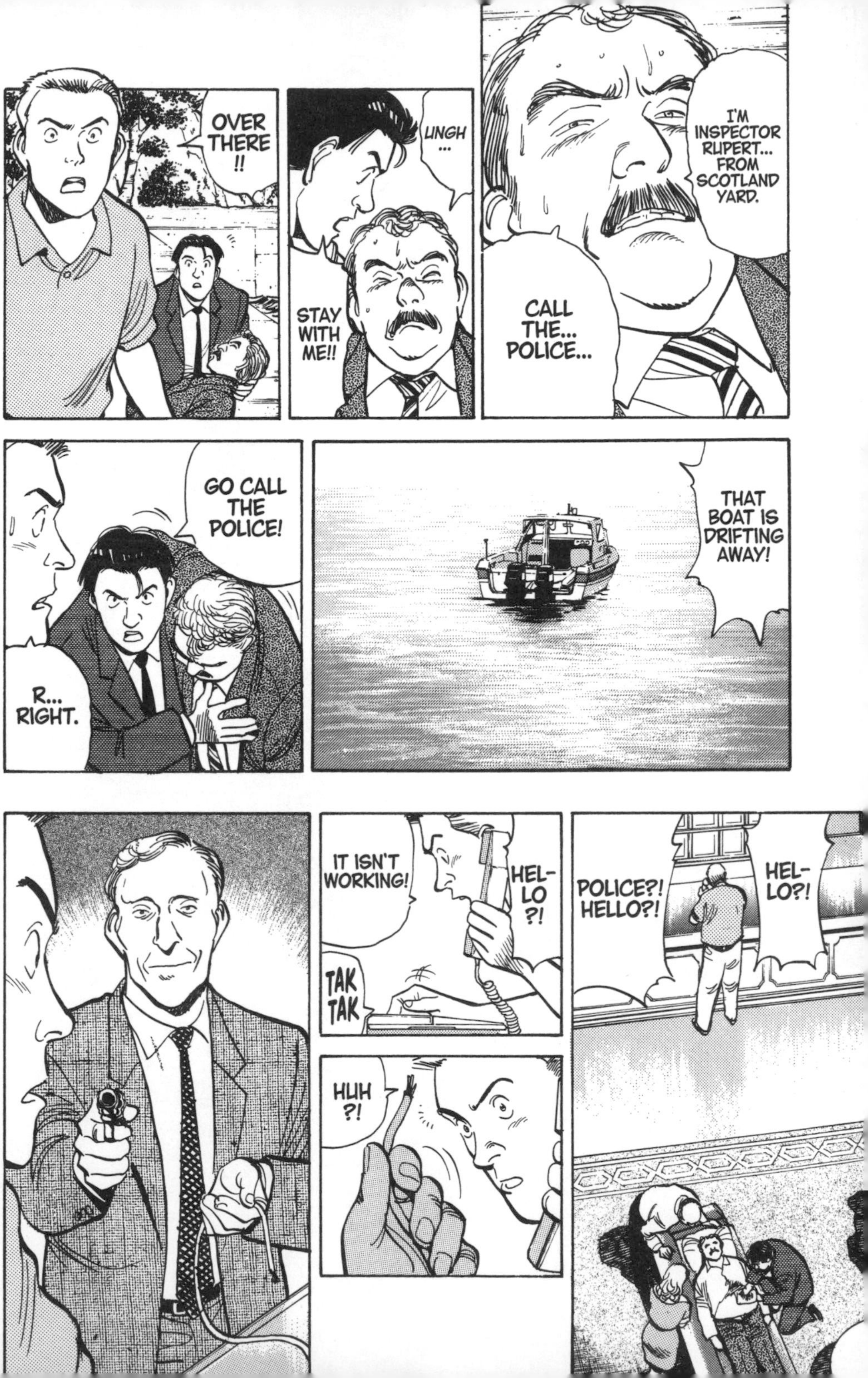
I'M INSPECTOR RUPERT... FROM SCOTLAND YARD.
CALL THE... POLICE...
UNGH ...
STAY WITH ME!!
OVER THERE !!
THAT BOAT IS DRIFTING AWAY!
GO CALL THE POLICE!
R... RIGHT.
HEL-LO?!
POLICE?! HELLO?!
HEL-LO ?!
IT ISN'T WORKING!
TAK TAK
HUH ?!

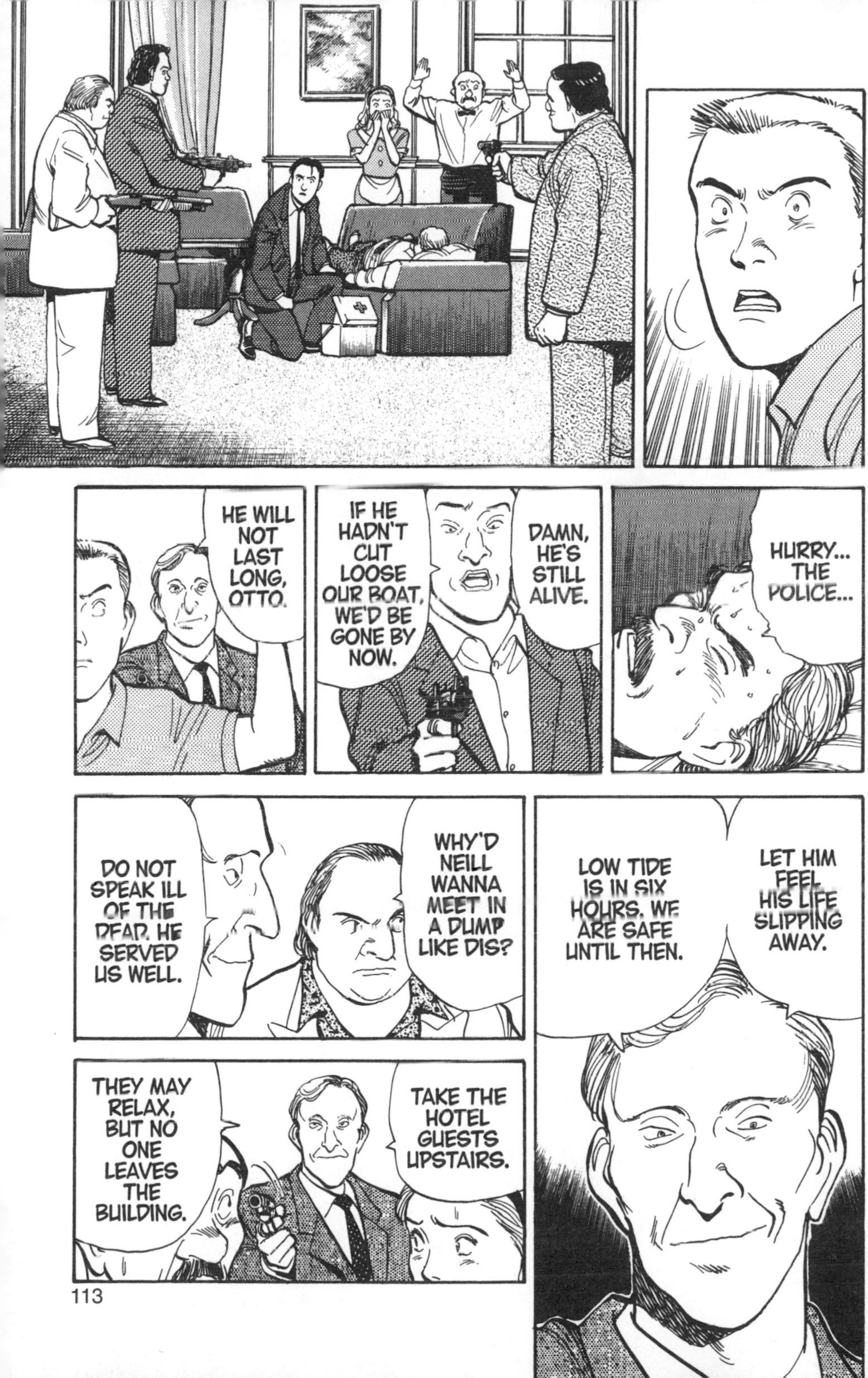
HURRY... THE POLICE...
DAMN, HE'S STILL ALIVE.
IF HE HADN'T CUT LOOSE OUR BOAT, WE'D BE GONE BY NOW.
HE WILL NOT LAST LONG, OTTO.
LET HIM FEEL HIS LIFE SLIPPING AWAY.
LOW TIDE IS IN SIX HOURS. WE ARE SAFE UNTIL THEN.
WHY'D NEILL WANNA MEET IN A DUMP LIKE DIS?
DO NOT SPEAK ILL OF THE DEAD. HE SERVED US WELL.
TAKE THE HOTEL GUESTS UPSTAIRS.
THEY MAY RELAX, BUT NO ONE LEAVES THE BUILDING.

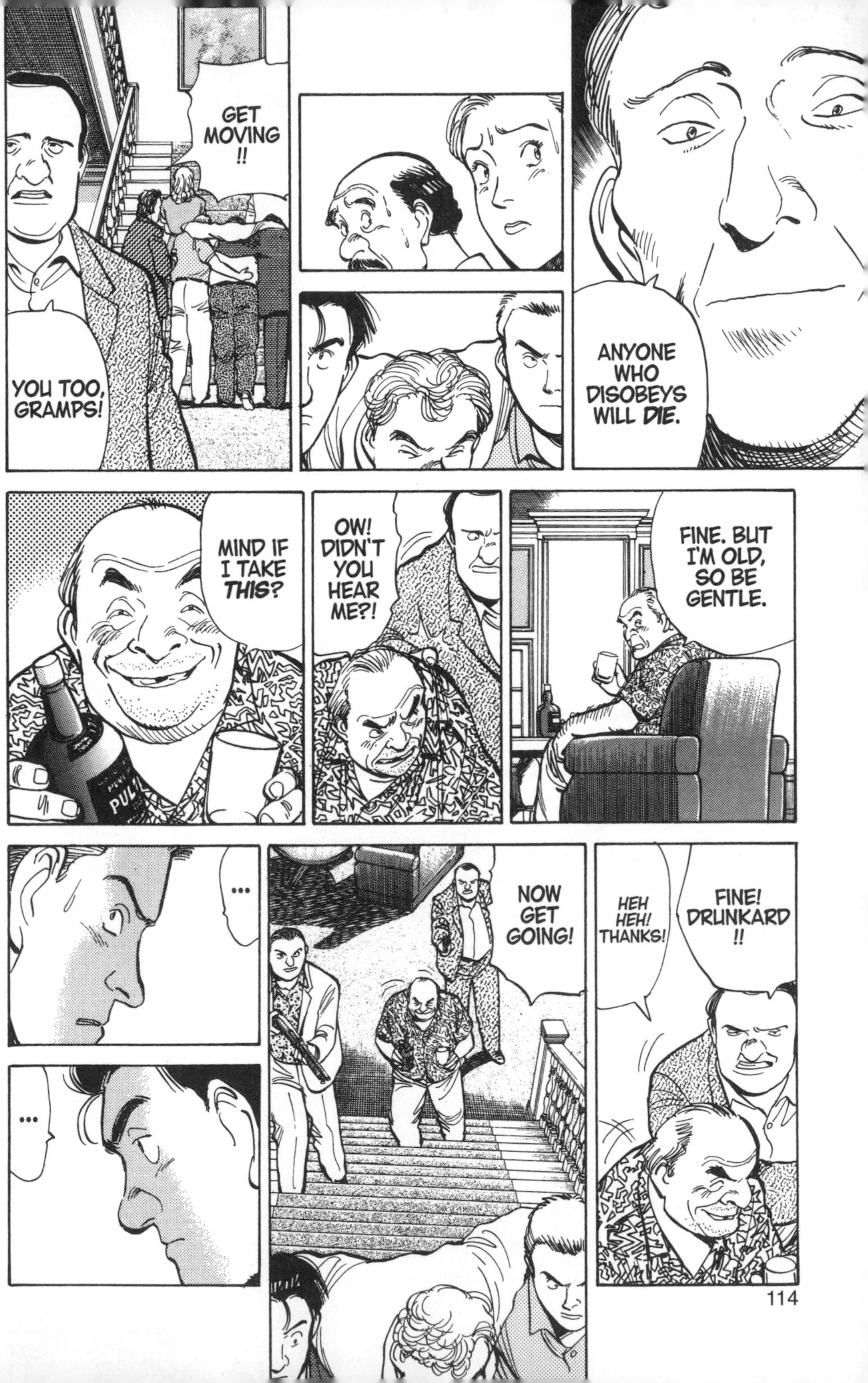
ANYONE WHO DISOBEYS WILL DIE.
GET MOVING !!
YOU TOO, GRAMPS!
FINE. BUT I'M OLD, SO BE GENTLE.
OW! DIDN'T YOU HEAR ME?!
MIND IF I TAKE THIS?
FINE! DRUNKARD !!
HEH HEH! THANKS!
NOW GET GOING!
...
...

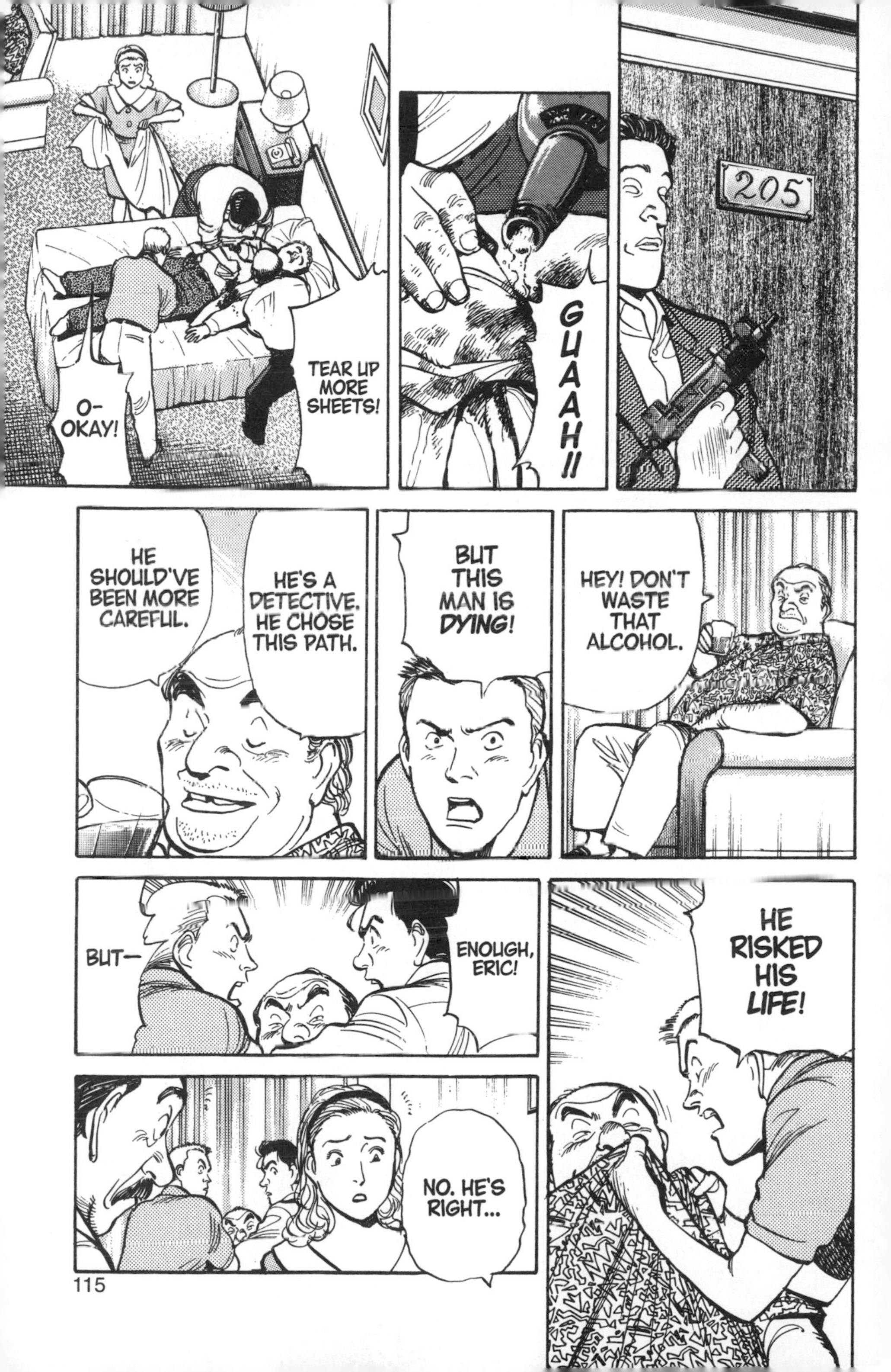
205
GUAAAH!!
TEAR UP MORE SHEETS!
O-OKAY!
HEY! DON'T WASTE THAT ALCOHOL.
BUT THIS MAN IS *DYING*!
HE'S A DETECTIVE. HE CHOSE THIS PATH.
HE SHOULD'VE BEEN MORE CAREFUL.
HE RISKED HIS *LIFE*!
ENOUGH, ERIC!
BUT—
NO. HE'S RIGHT...

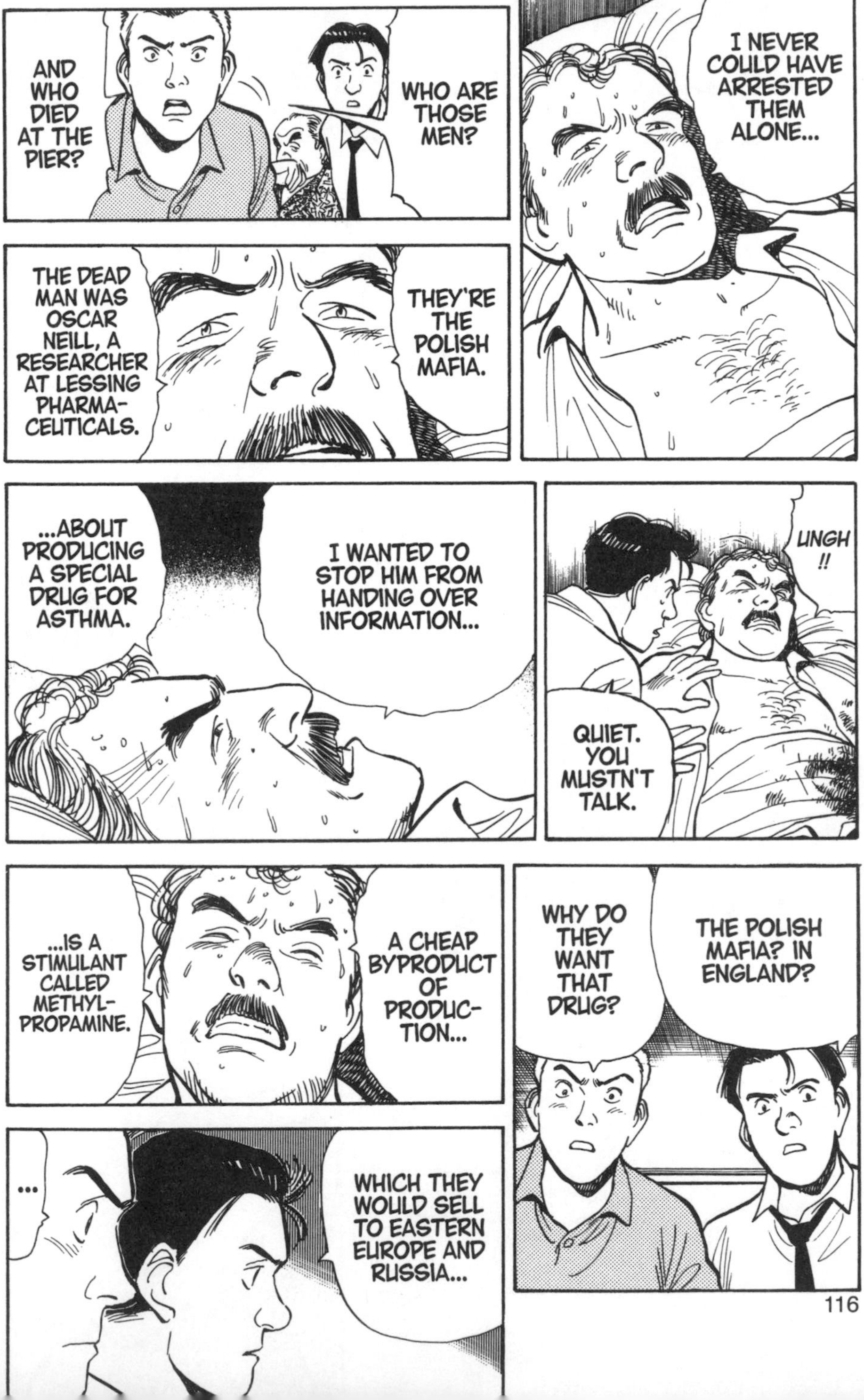
I NEVER COULD HAVE ARRESTED THEM ALONE...
WHO ARE THOSE MEN?
AND WHO DIED AT THE PIER?
THEY'RE THE POLISH MAFIA.
THE DEAD MAN WAS OSCAR NEILL, A RESEARCHER AT LESSING PHARMA-CEUTICALS.
UNGH !!
QUIET. YOU MUSTN'T TALK.
I WANTED TO STOP HIM FROM HANDING OVER INFORMATION...
...ABOUT PRODUCING A SPECIAL DRUG FOR ASTHMA.
THE POLISH MAFIA? IN ENGLAND?
WHY DO THEY WANT THAT DRUG?
A CHEAP BYPRODUCT OF PRODUC-TION...
...IS A STIMULANT CALLED METHYL-PROPAMINE.
WHICH THEY WOULD SELL TO EASTERN EUROPE AND RUSSIA...
...

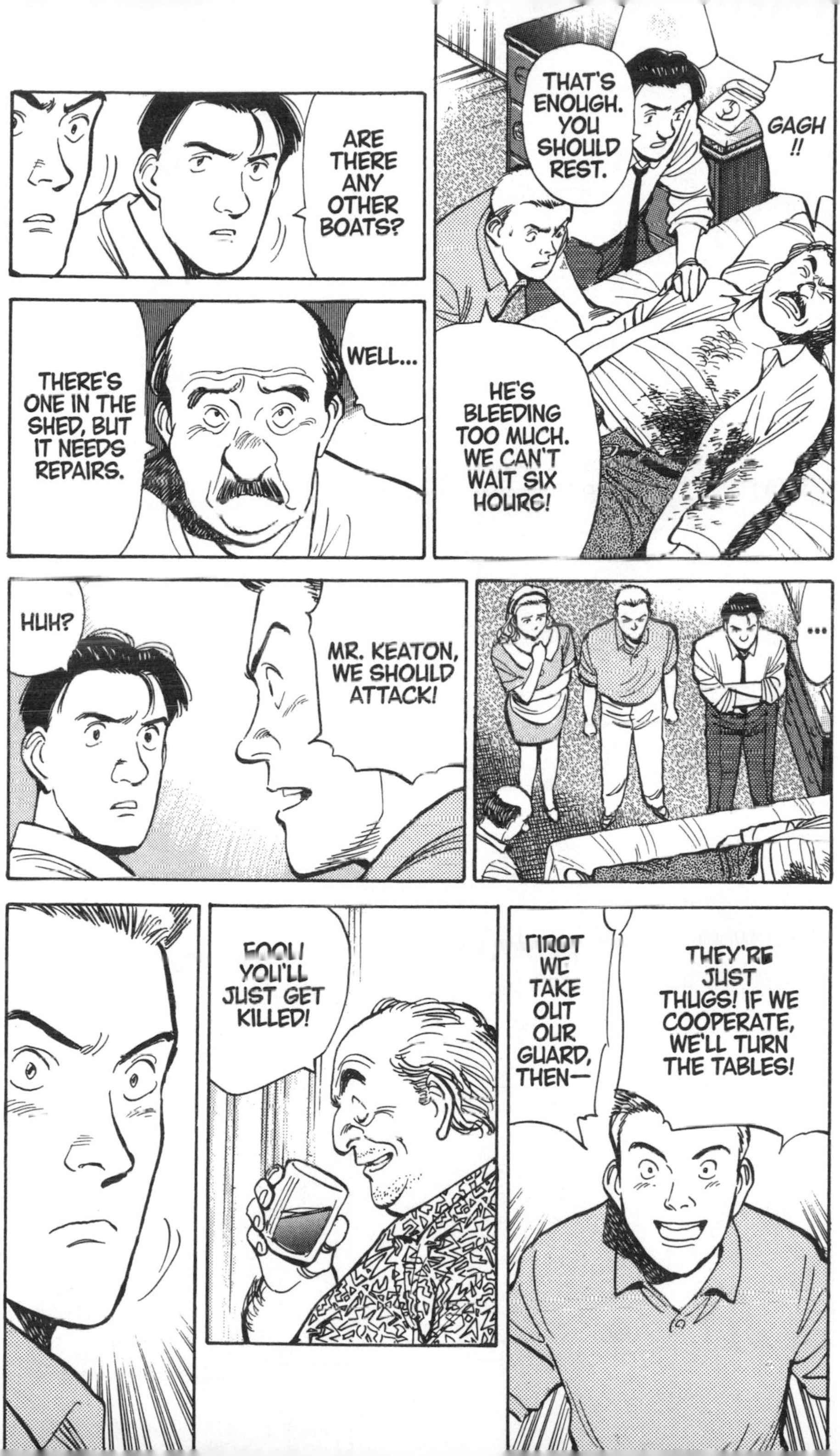
GAGH !!
THAT'S ENOUGH. YOU SHOULD REST.
HE'S BLEEDING TOO MUCH. WE CAN'T WAIT SIX HOURS!
ARE THERE ANY OTHER BOATS?
WELL...
THERE'S ONE IN THE SHED, BUT IT NEEDS REPAIRS.
...
MR. KEATON, WE SHOULD ATTACK!
HUH?
THEY'RE JUST THUGS! IF WE COOPERATE, WE'LL TURN THE TABLES!
FIRST WE TAKE OUT OUR GUARD, THEN—
FOOL! YOU'LL JUST GET KILLED!

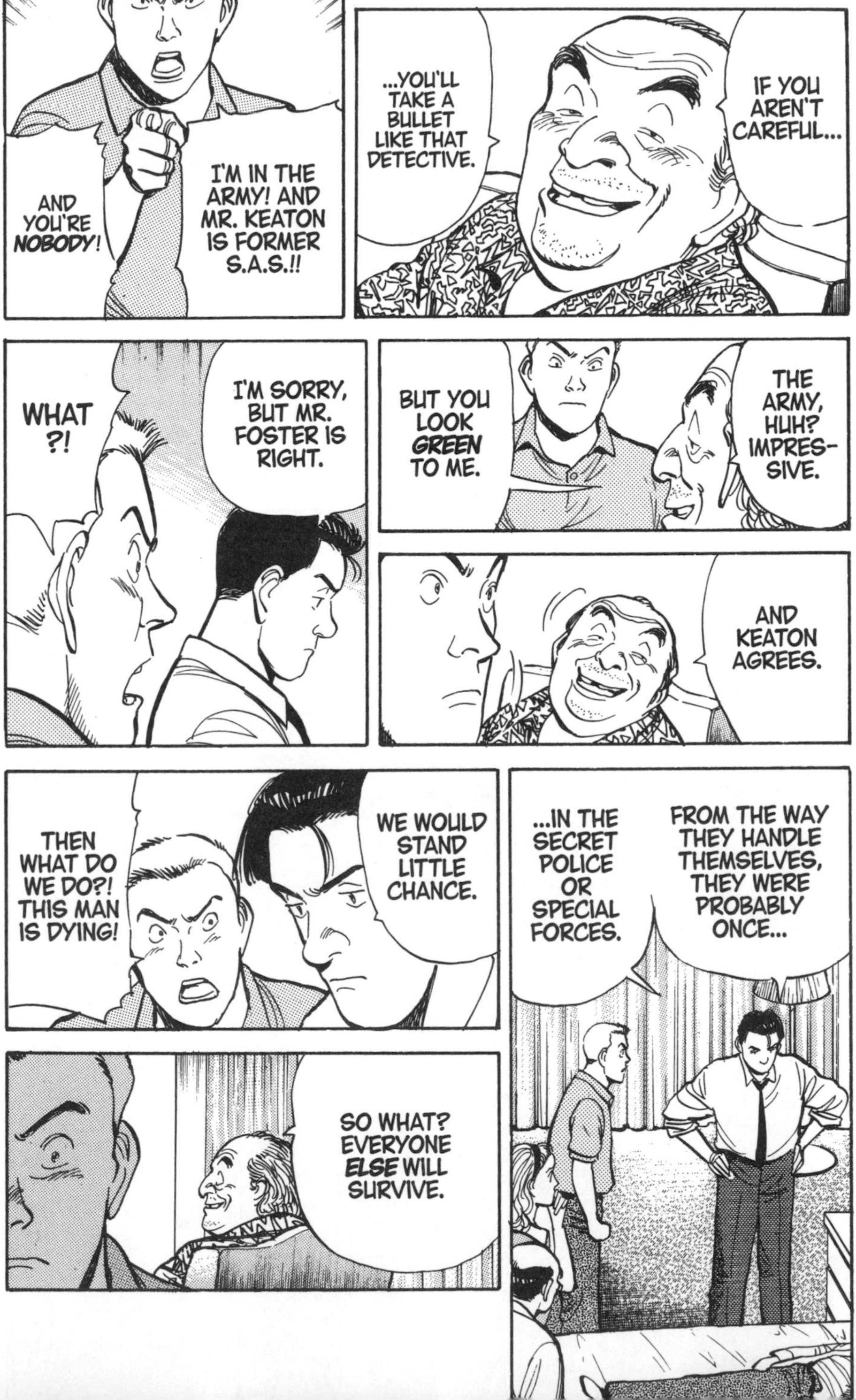
IF YOU AREN'T CAREFUL...
...YOU'LL TAKE A BULLET LIKE THAT DETECTIVE.
I'M IN THE ARMY! AND MR. KEATON IS FORMER S.A.S.!!
AND YOU'RE *NOBODY*!
THE ARMY, HUH? IMPRES-SIVE.
BUT YOU LOOK *GREEN* TO ME.
AND KEATON AGREES.
I'M SORRY, BUT MR. FOSTER IS RIGHT.
WHAT ?!
FROM THE WAY THEY HANDLE THEMSELVES, THEY WERE PROBABLY ONCE...
...IN THE SECRET POLICE OR SPECIAL FORCES.
WE WOULD STAND LITTLE CHANCE.
THEN WHAT DO WE DO?! THIS MAN IS DYING!
SO WHAT? EVERYONE *ELSE* WILL SURVIVE.

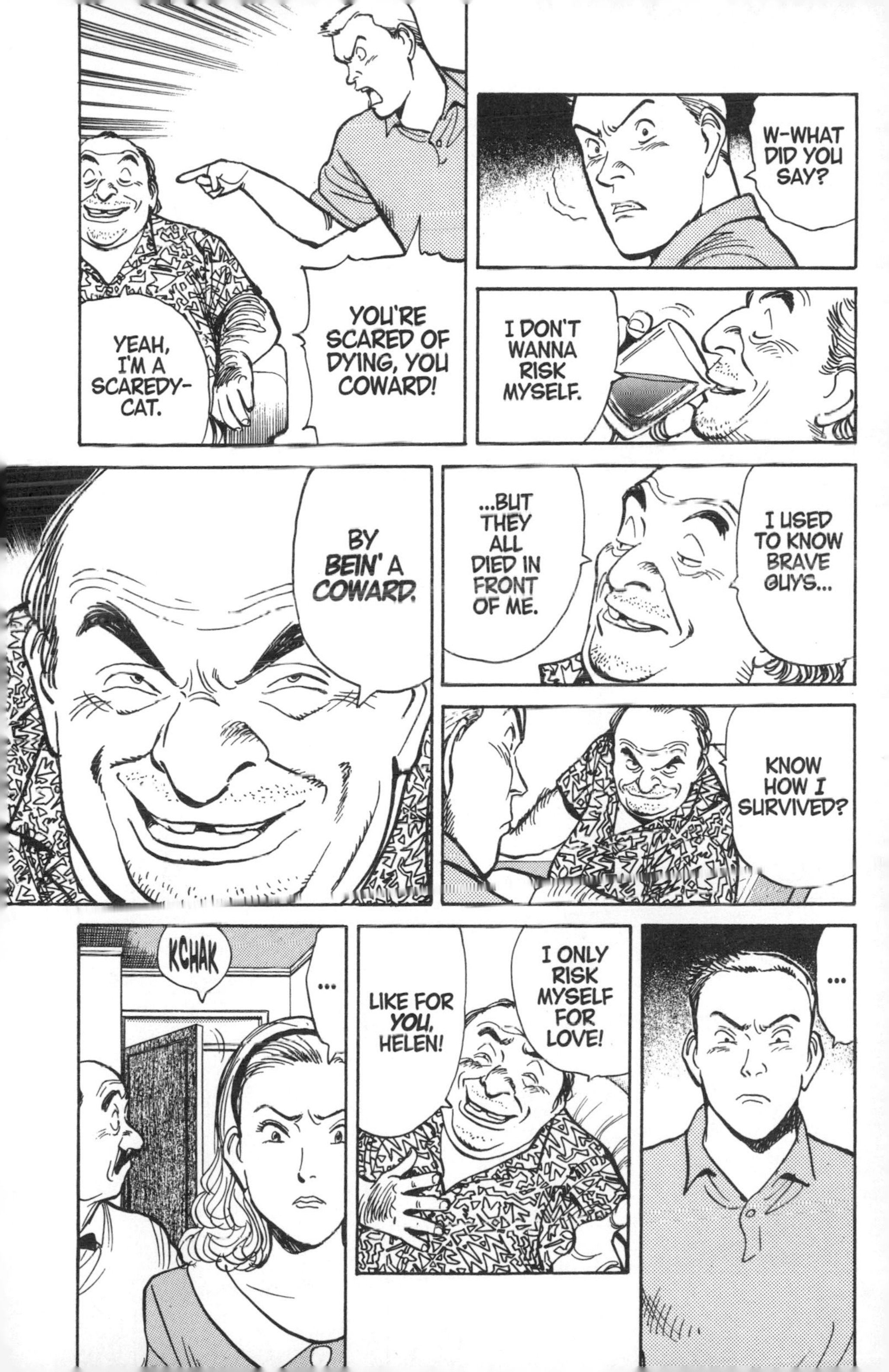
W-WHAT DID YOU SAY?
I DON'T WANNA RISK MYSELF.
YOU'RE SCARED OF DYING, YOU COWARD!
YEAH, I'M A SCAREDY-CAT.
I USED TO KNOW BRAVE GUYS...
...BUT THEY ALL DIED IN FRONT OF ME.
KNOW HOW I SURVIVED?
BY BEIN' A COWARD.
...
I ONLY RISK MYSELF FOR LOVE!
LIKE FOR YOU, HELEN!
KCHAK
...

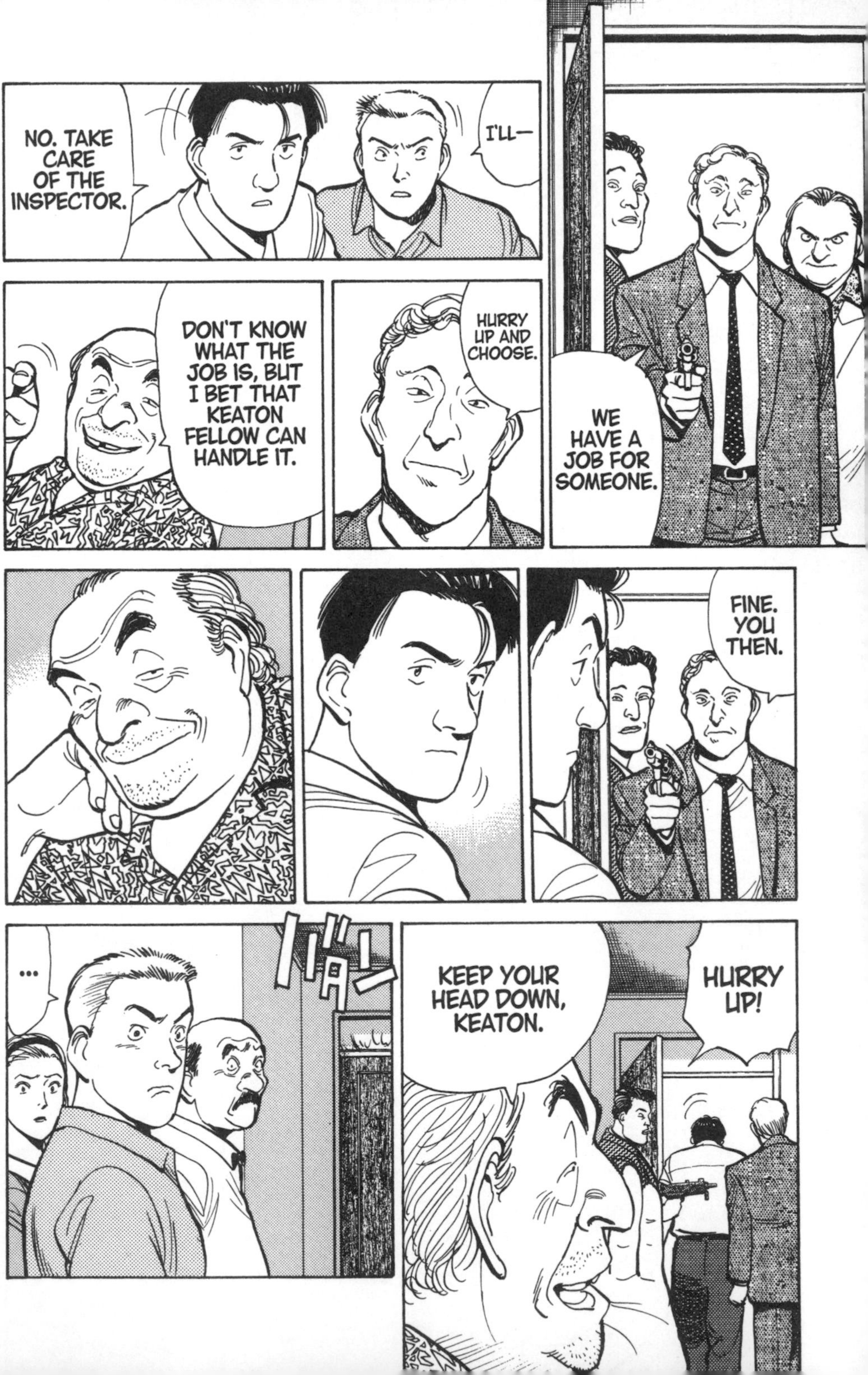
WE HAVE A JOB FOR SOMEONE.
I'LL—
NO. TAKE CARE OF THE INSPECTOR.
HURRY UP AND CHOOSE.
DON'T KNOW WHAT THE JOB IS, BUT I BET THAT KEATON FELLOW CAN HANDLE IT.
FINE. YOU THEN.
HURRY UP!
KEEP YOUR HEAD DOWN, KEATON.
...

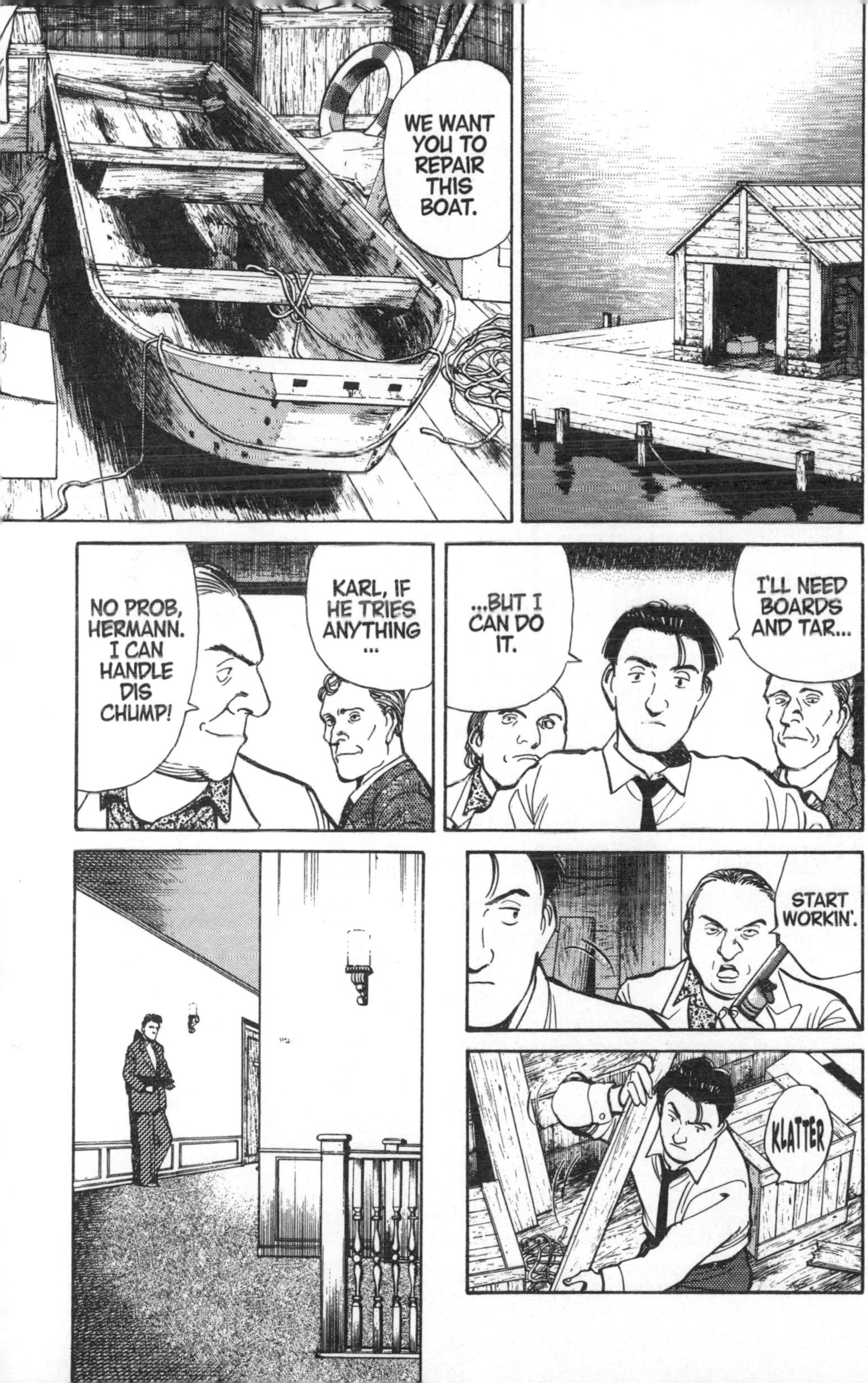
WE WANT YOU TO REPAIR THIS BOAT.
I'LL NEED BOARDS AND TAR...
...BUT I CAN DO IT.
KARL, IF HE TRIES ANYTHING ...
NO PROB, HERMANN. I CAN HANDLE DIS CHUMP!
START WORKIN'.
KLATTER

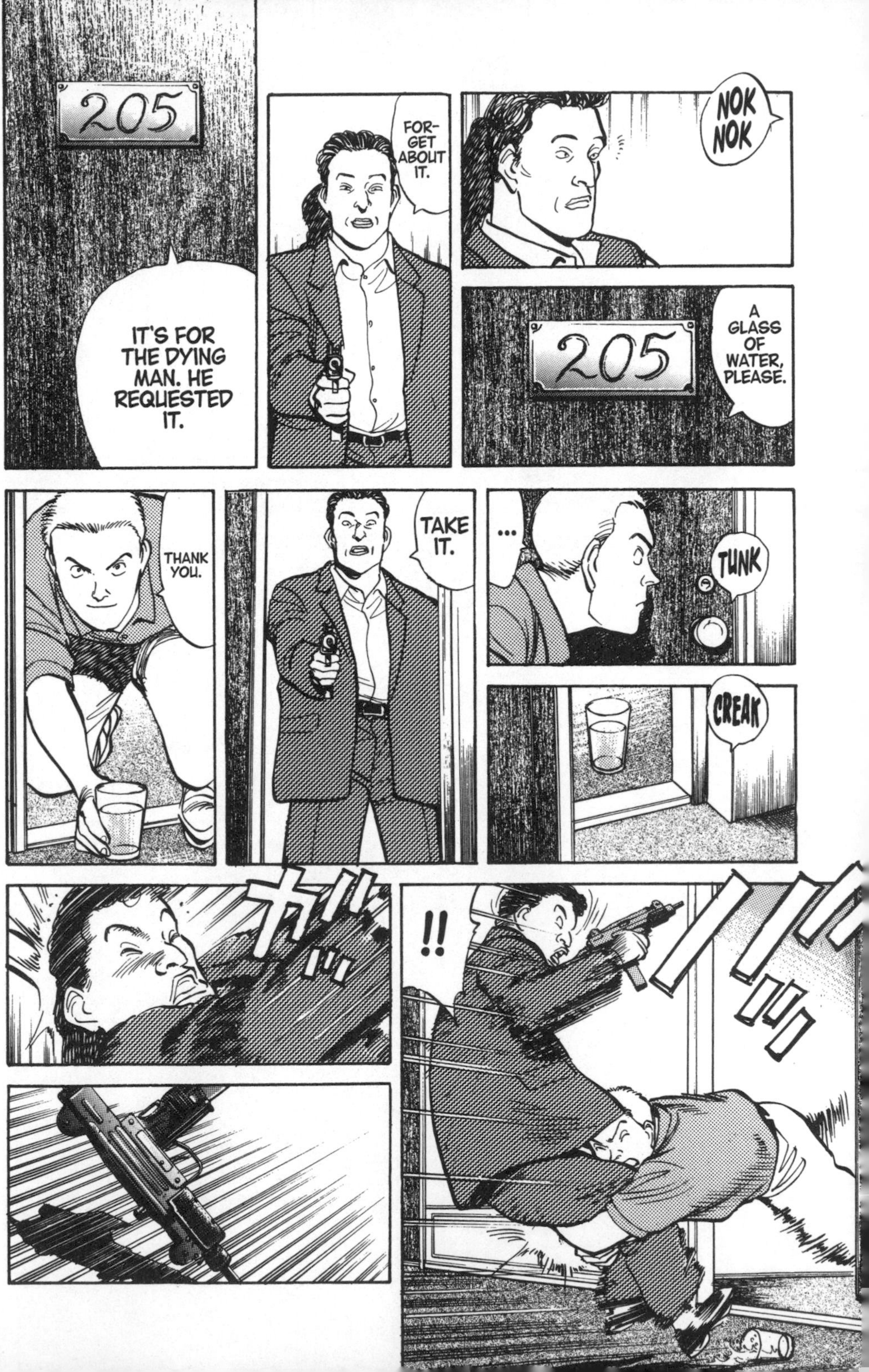
NOK NOK
205
A GLASS OF WATER, PLEASE.
FOR-GET ABOUT IT.
205
IT'S FOR THE DYING MAN. HE REQUESTED IT.
TUNK
...
CREAK
TAKE IT.
THANK YOU.
!!

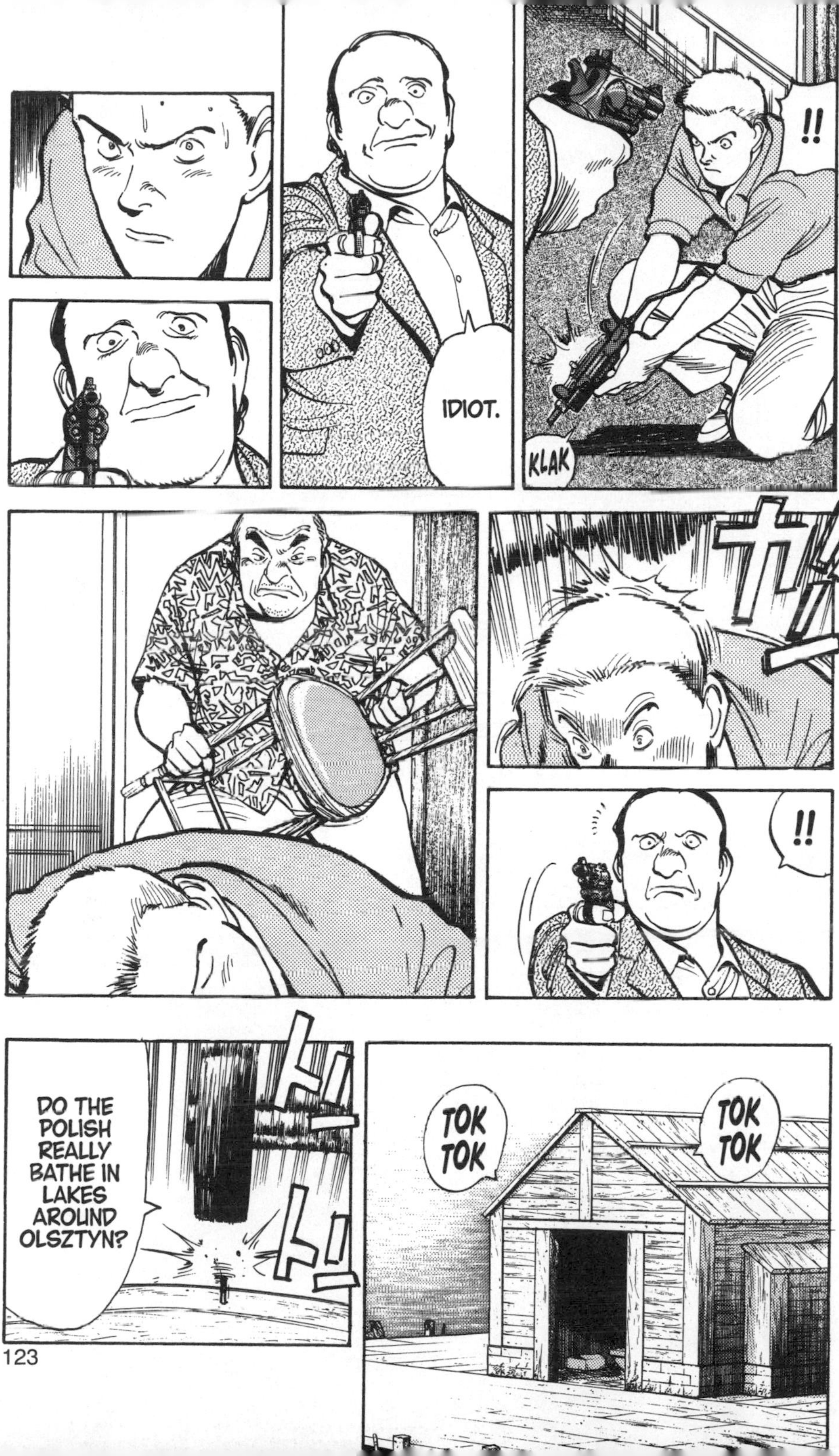
!!
KLAK
IDIOT.
!!
TOK TOK
TOK TOK
DO THE POLISH REALLY BATHE IN LAKES AROUND OLSZTYN?

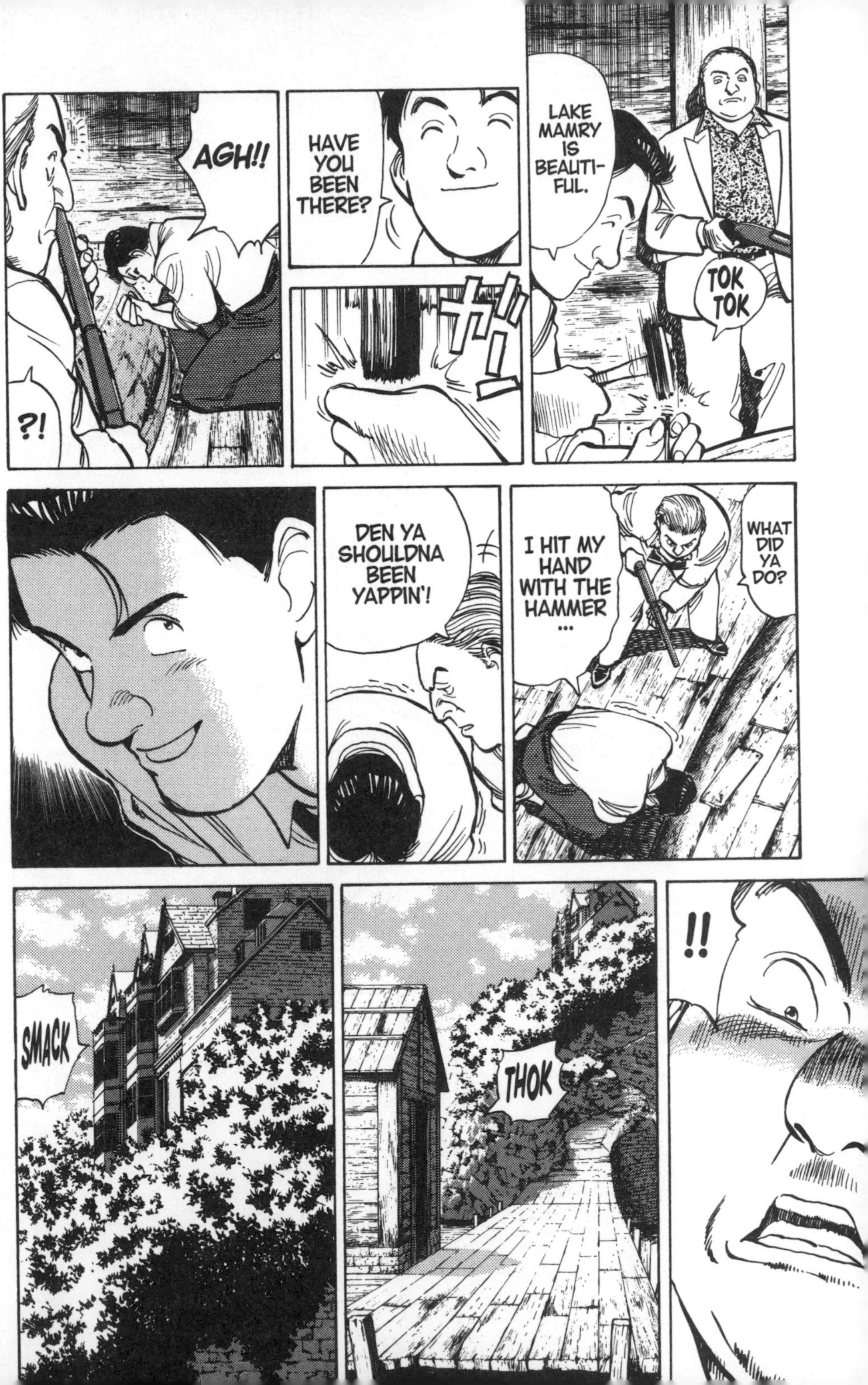
TOK TOK
LAKE MAMRY IS BEAUTI-FUL.
HAVE YOU BEEN THERE?
AGH!!
?!
WHAT DID YA DO?
I HIT MY HAND WITH THE HAMMER...
DEN YA SHOULDNA BEEN YAPPIN'!
!!
THOK
SMACK

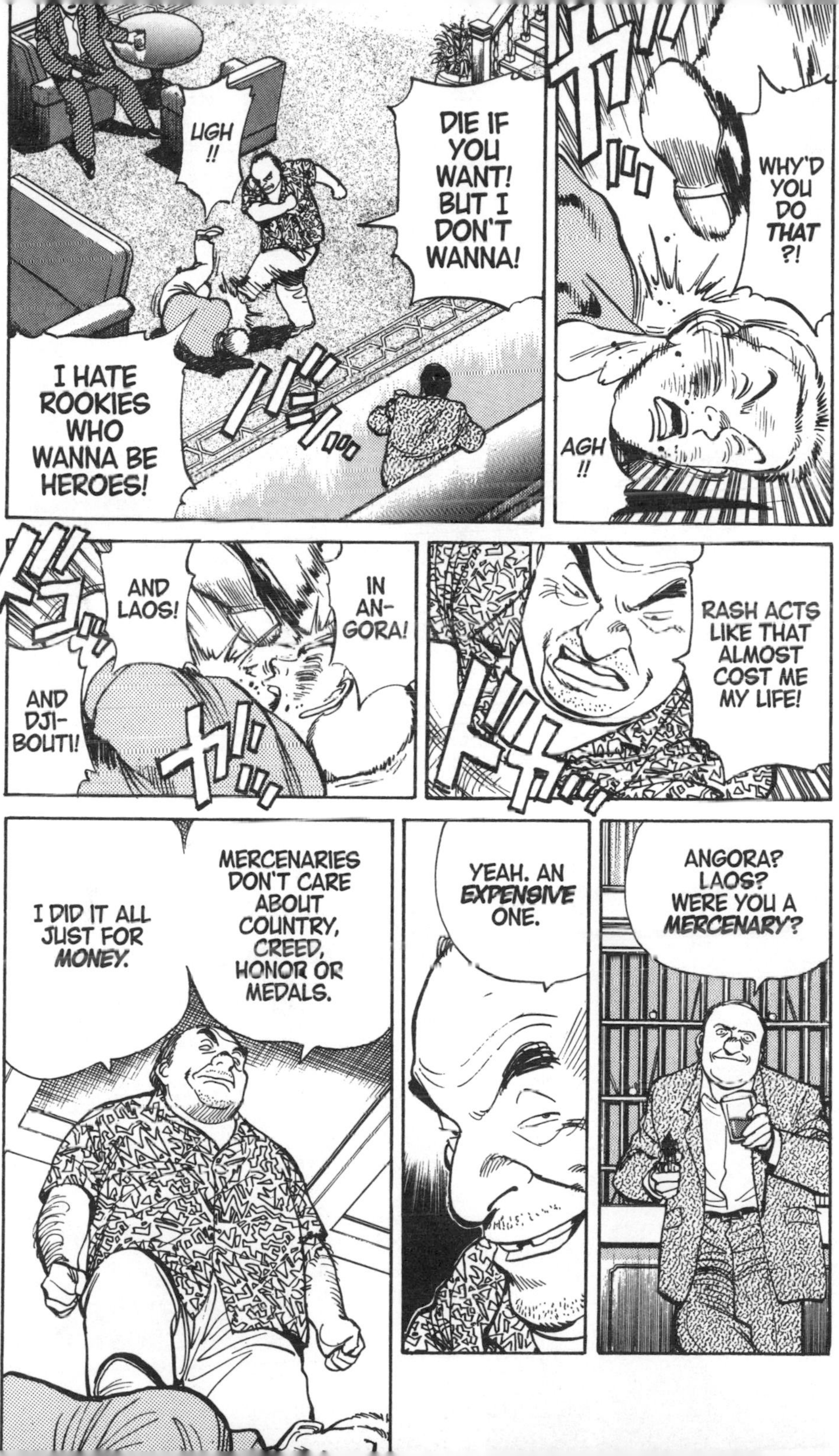
WHY'D YOU DO THAT?!
AGH!!
DIE IF YOU WANT! BUT I DON'T WANNA!
UGH!!
I HATE ROOKIES WHO WANNA BE HEROES!
RASH ACTS LIKE THAT ALMOST COST ME MY LIFE!
IN AN-GORA!
AND LAOS!
AND DJI-BOUTI!
ANGORA? LAOS? WERE YOU A MERCENARY?
YEAH. AN EXPENSIVE ONE.
MERCENARIES DON'T CARE ABOUT COUNTRY, CREED, HONOR OR MEDALS.
I DID IT ALL JUST FOR MONEY.

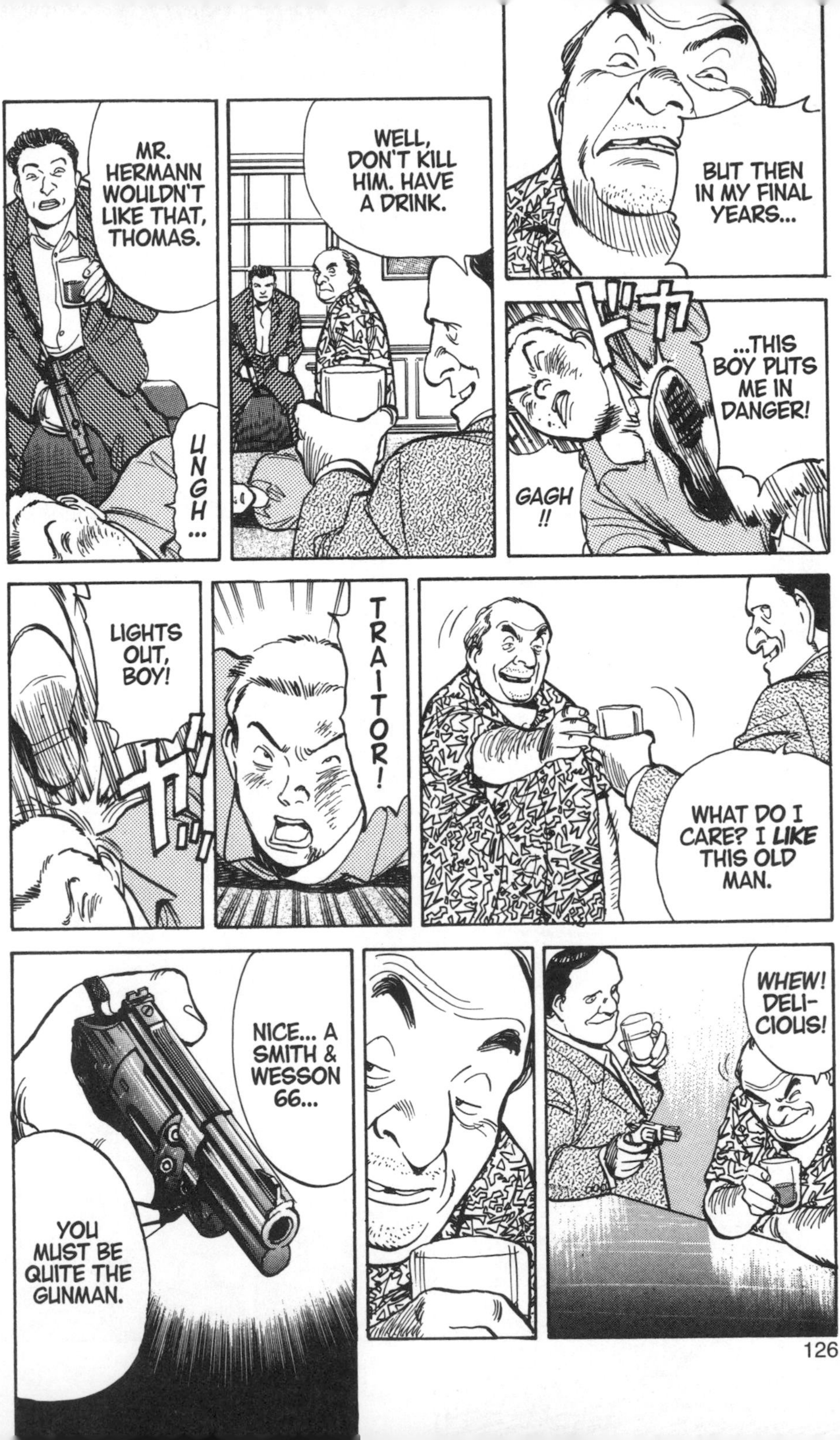
BUT THEN IN MY FINAL YEARS...
...THIS BOY PUTS ME IN DANGER!
GAGH !!
WELL, DON'T KILL HIM. HAVE A DRINK.
MR. HERMANN WOULDN'T LIKE THAT, THOMAS.
UNGH...
WHAT DO I CARE? I LIKE THIS OLD MAN.
TRAITOR!
LIGHTS OUT, BOY!
WHEW! DELI-CIOUS!
NICE... A SMITH & WESSON 66...
YOU MUST BE QUITE THE GUNMAN.

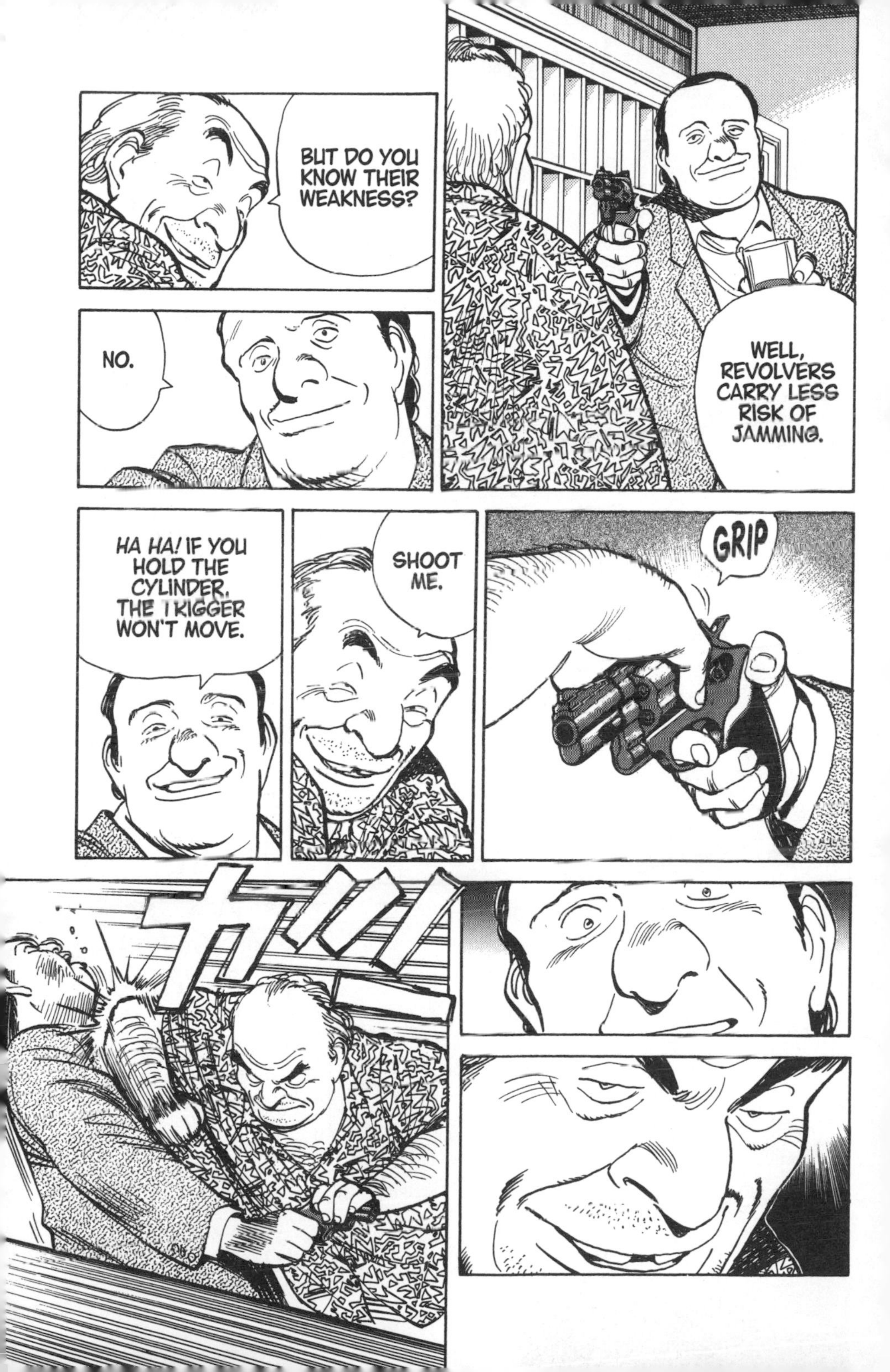
WELL, REVOLVERS CARRY LESS RISK OF JAMMING.
BUT DO YOU KNOW THEIR WEAKNESS?
NO.
GRIP
SHOOT ME.
HA HA! IF YOU HOLD THE CYLINDER, THE TRIGGER WON'T MOVE.

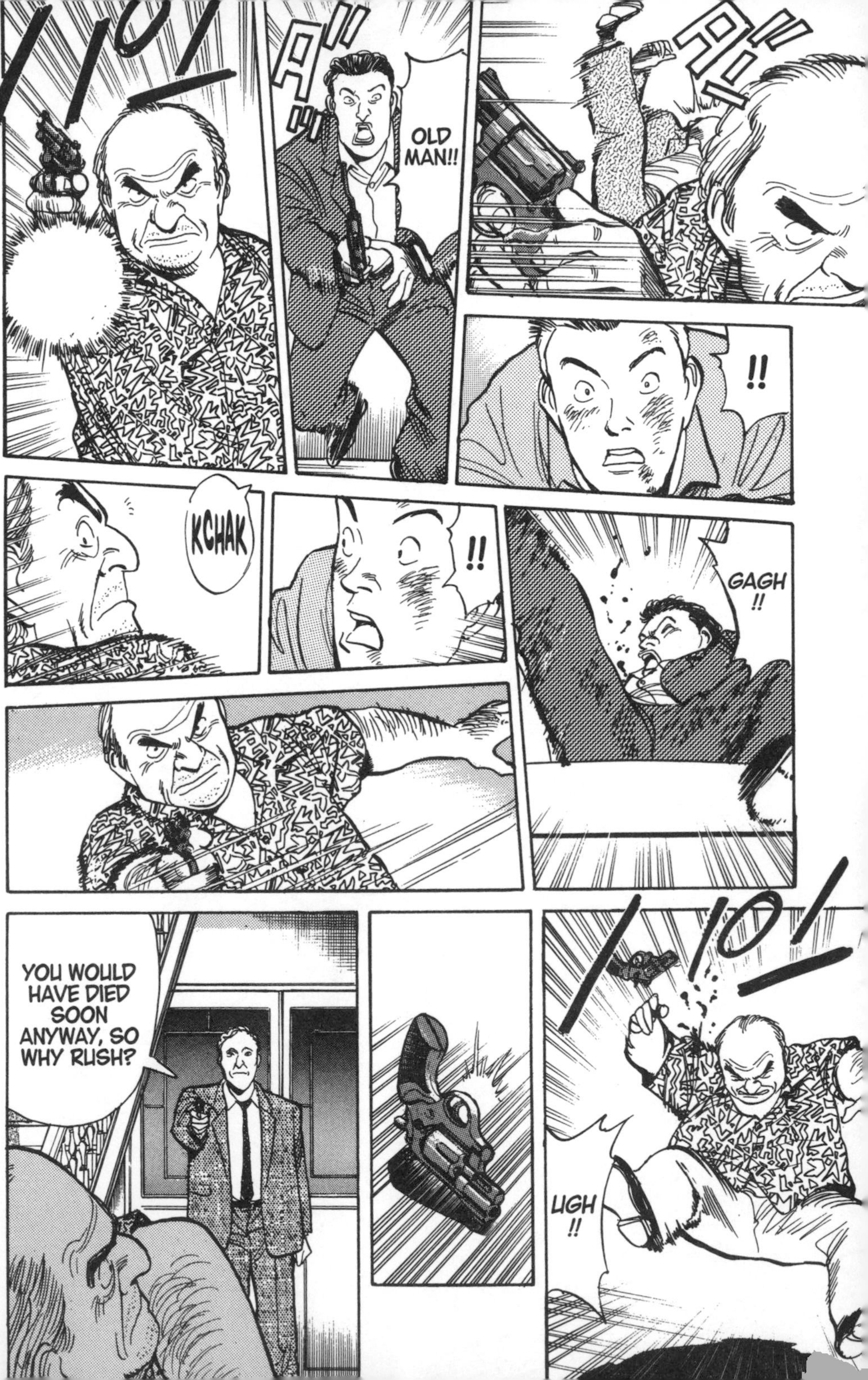
OLD MAN!!
!!
GAGH !!
!!
KCHAK
UGH !!
YOU WOULD HAVE DIED SOON ANYWAY, SO WHY RUSH?

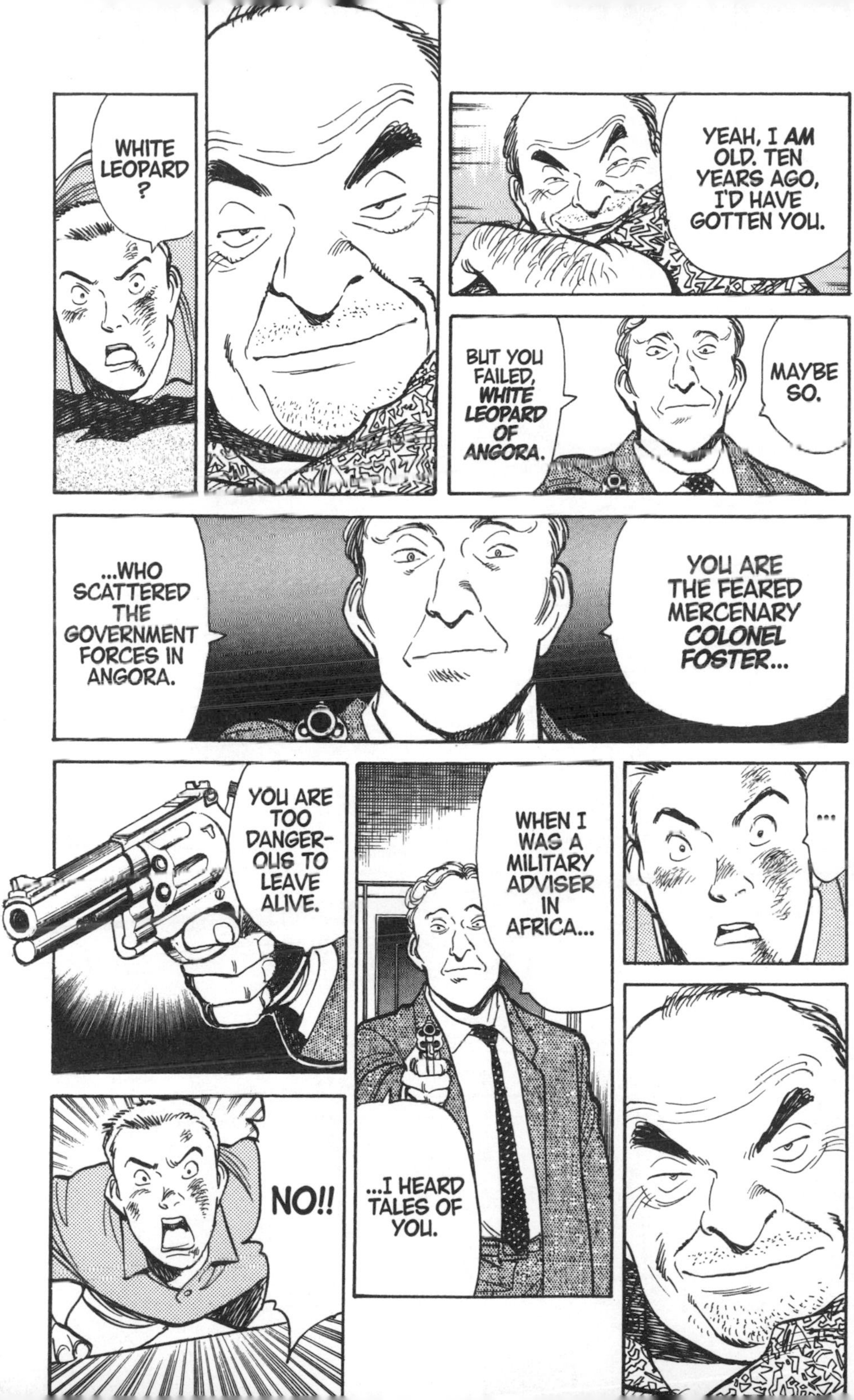
YEAH, I AM OLD. TEN YEARS AGO, I'D HAVE GOTTEN YOU.
BUT YOU FAILED, WHITE LEOPARD OF ANGORA.
MAYBE SO.
WHITE LEOPARD ?
YOU ARE THE FEARED MERCENARY COLONEL FOSTER...
...WHO SCATTERED THE GOVERNMENT FORCES IN ANGORA.
...
WHEN I WAS A MILITARY ADVISER IN AFRICA...
...I HEARD TALES OF YOU.
YOU ARE TOO DANGER-OUS TO LEAVE ALIVE.
NO!!

IT WAS MY MISTAKE, ERIC.
BUT YOU DID ALL THAT TO SAVE ME!
...
NAH. I HATE ROOKIES...
...SO I'D NEVER DO THAT.
...
THIS WAS FOR MYSELF. NOW I CAN DIE...
...AND PUT AN END TO MY BAD LUCK.
ARE YOU READY, OLD-TIMER?
YEAH. BUT I'VE GOT ONE LAST REQUEST.
WHICH IS?
LET ME HAVE A FINAL DRINK.

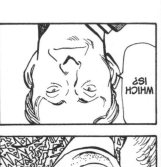

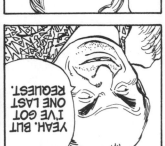

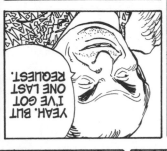

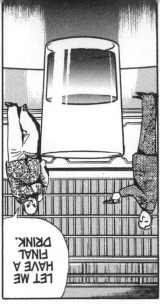

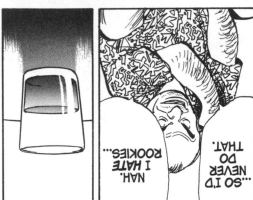

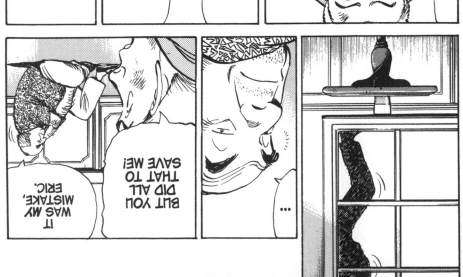

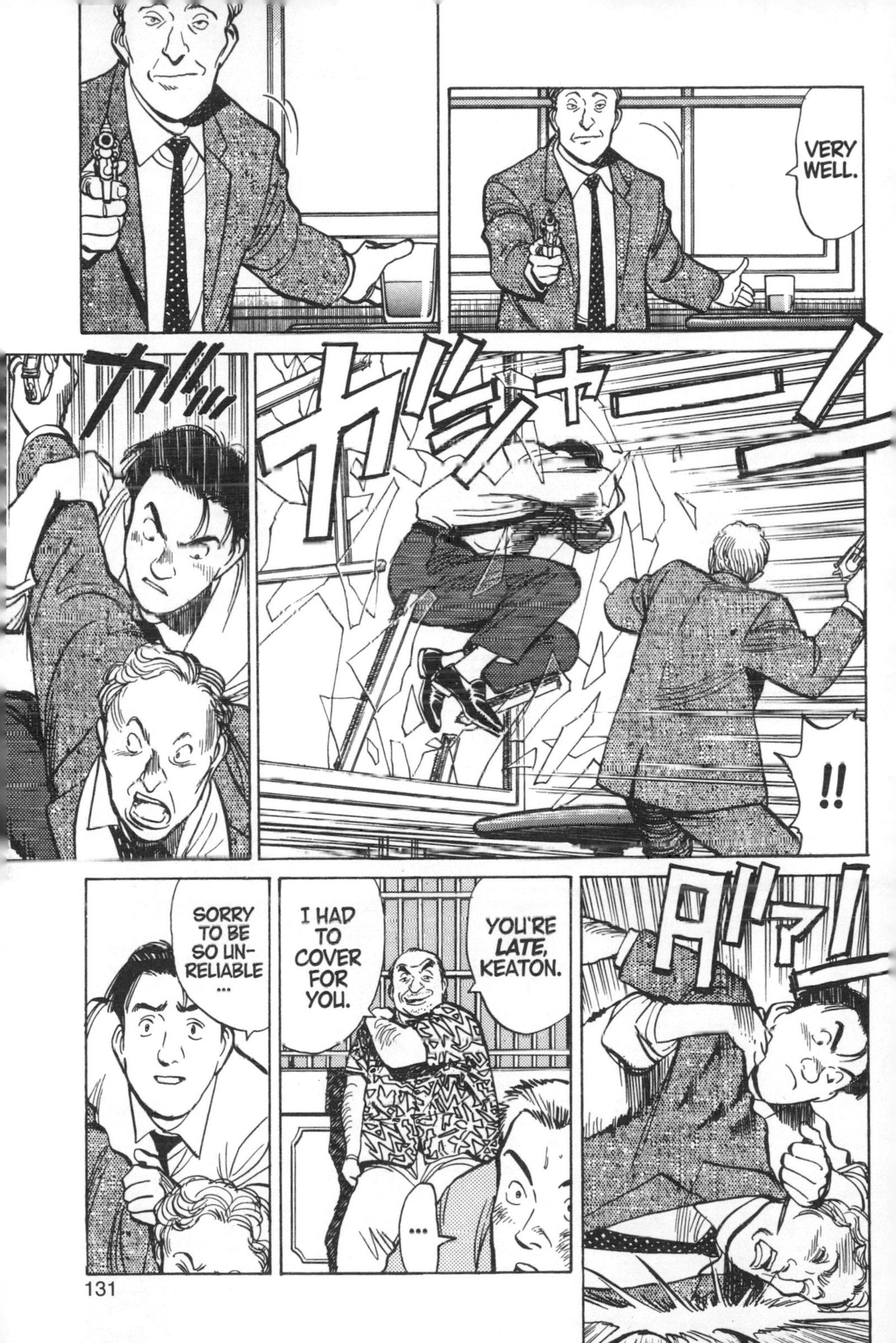
VERY WELL.
ガシャー!
!!
ガッ
ダァ!
YOU'RE LATE, KEATON.
I HAD TO COVER FOR YOU.
...
SORRY TO BE SO UN-RELIABLE ...

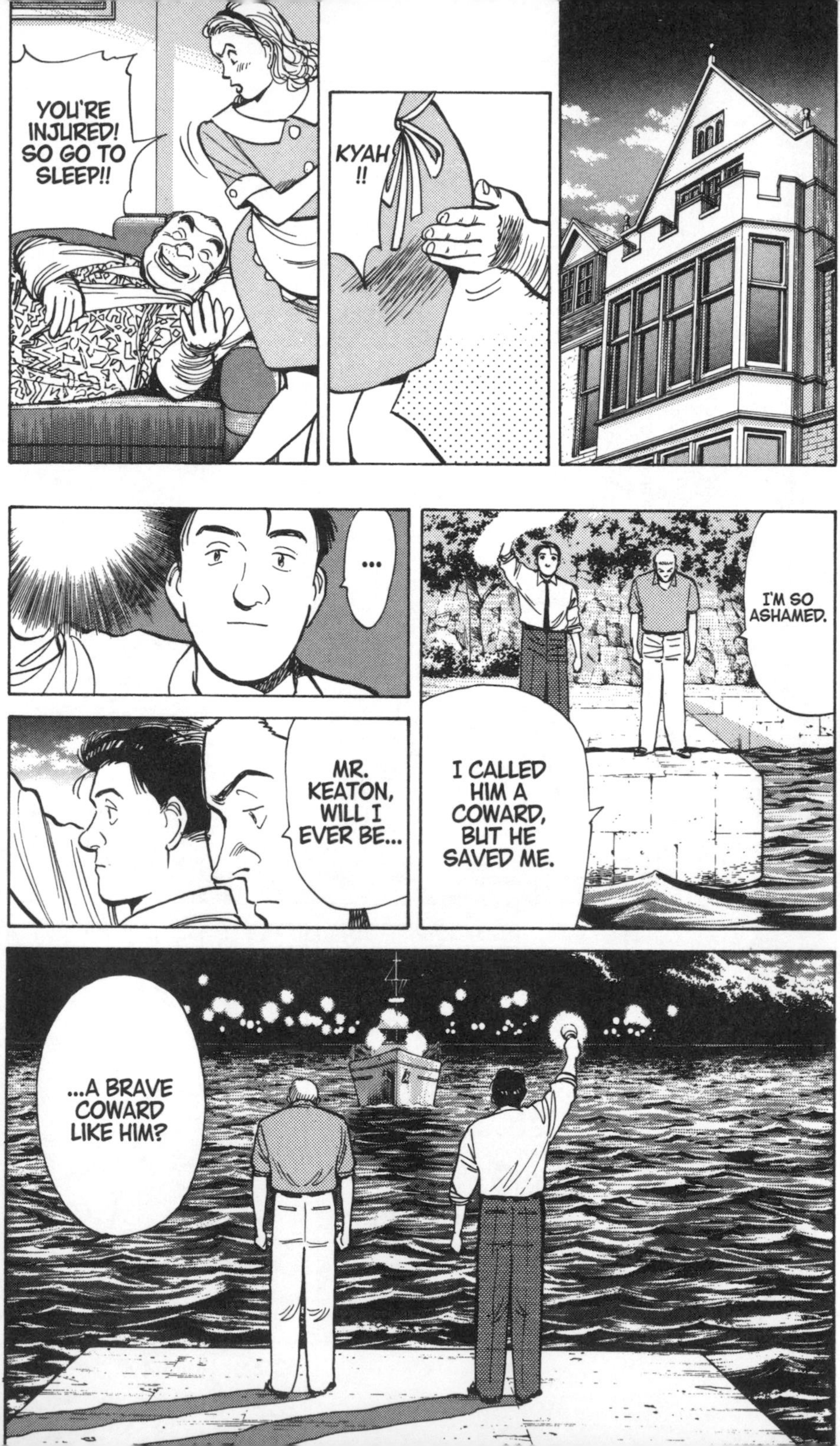
KYAH !!
YOU'RE INJURED! SO GO TO SLEEP!!
I'M SO ASHAMED.
I CALLED HIM A COWARD, BUT HE SAVED ME.
...
MR. KEATON, WILL I EVER BE...
...A BRAVE COWARD LIKE HIM?

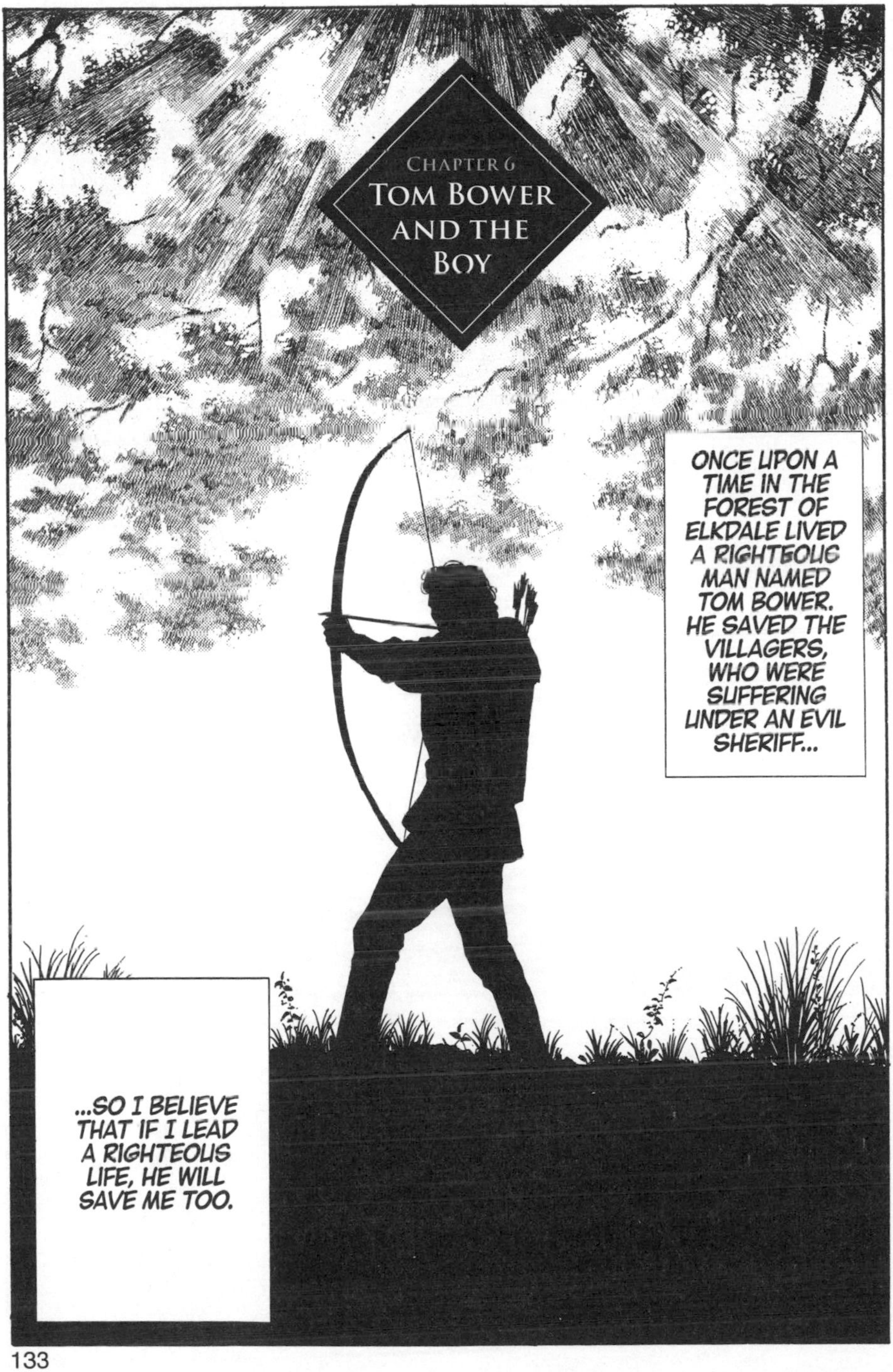
CHAPTER 6
TOM BOWER AND THE BOY
ONCE UPON A TIME IN THE FOREST OF ELKDALE LIVED A RIGHTEOUS MAN NAMED TOM BOWER. HE SAVED THE VILLAGERS, WHO WERE SUFFERING UNDER AN EVIL SHERIFF...
...SO I BELIEVE THAT IF I LEAD A RIGHTEOUS LIFE, HE WILL SAVE ME TOO.

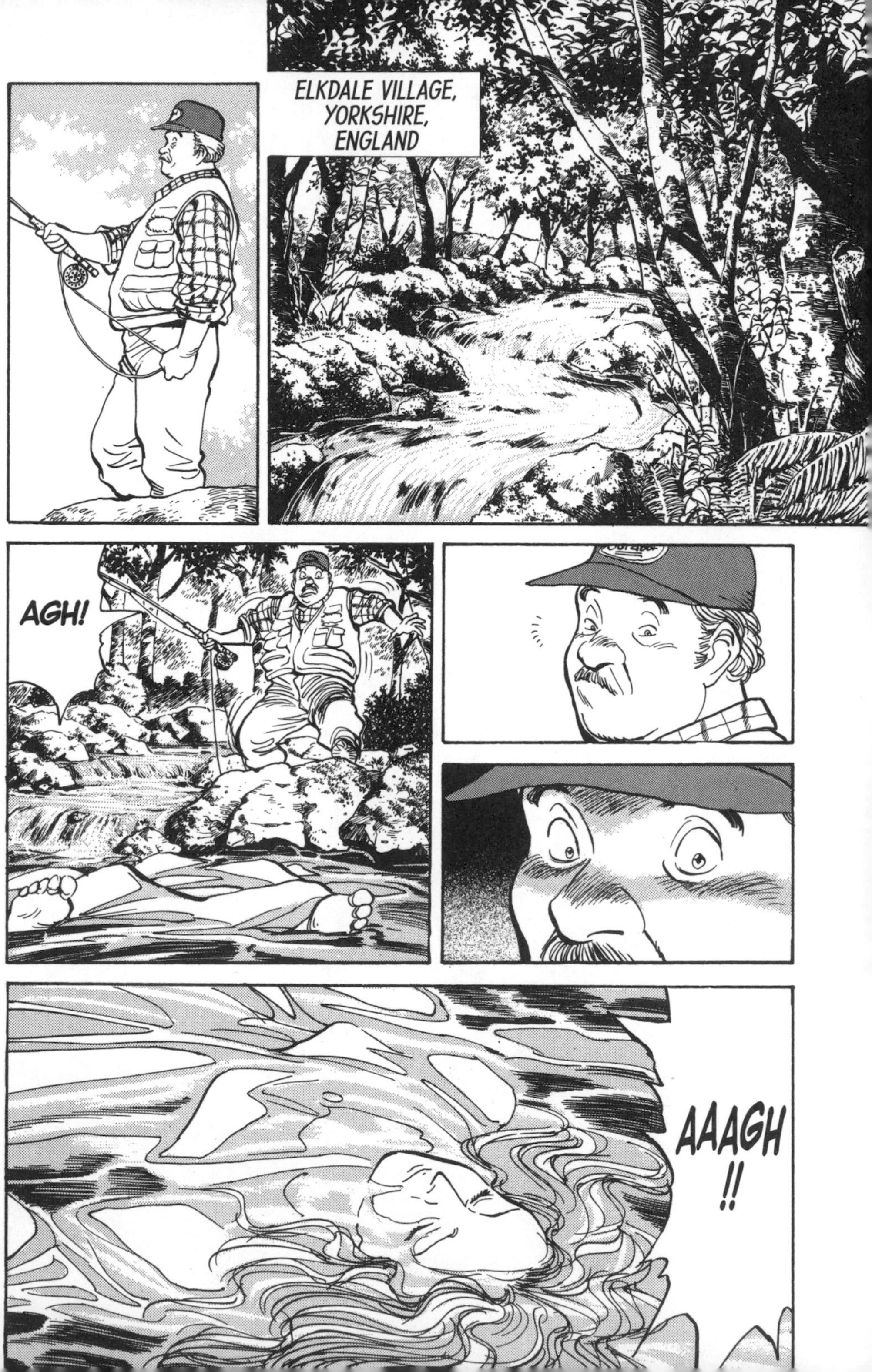
ELKDALE VILLAGE, YORKSHIRE, ENGLAND
AGH!
AAAGH!!

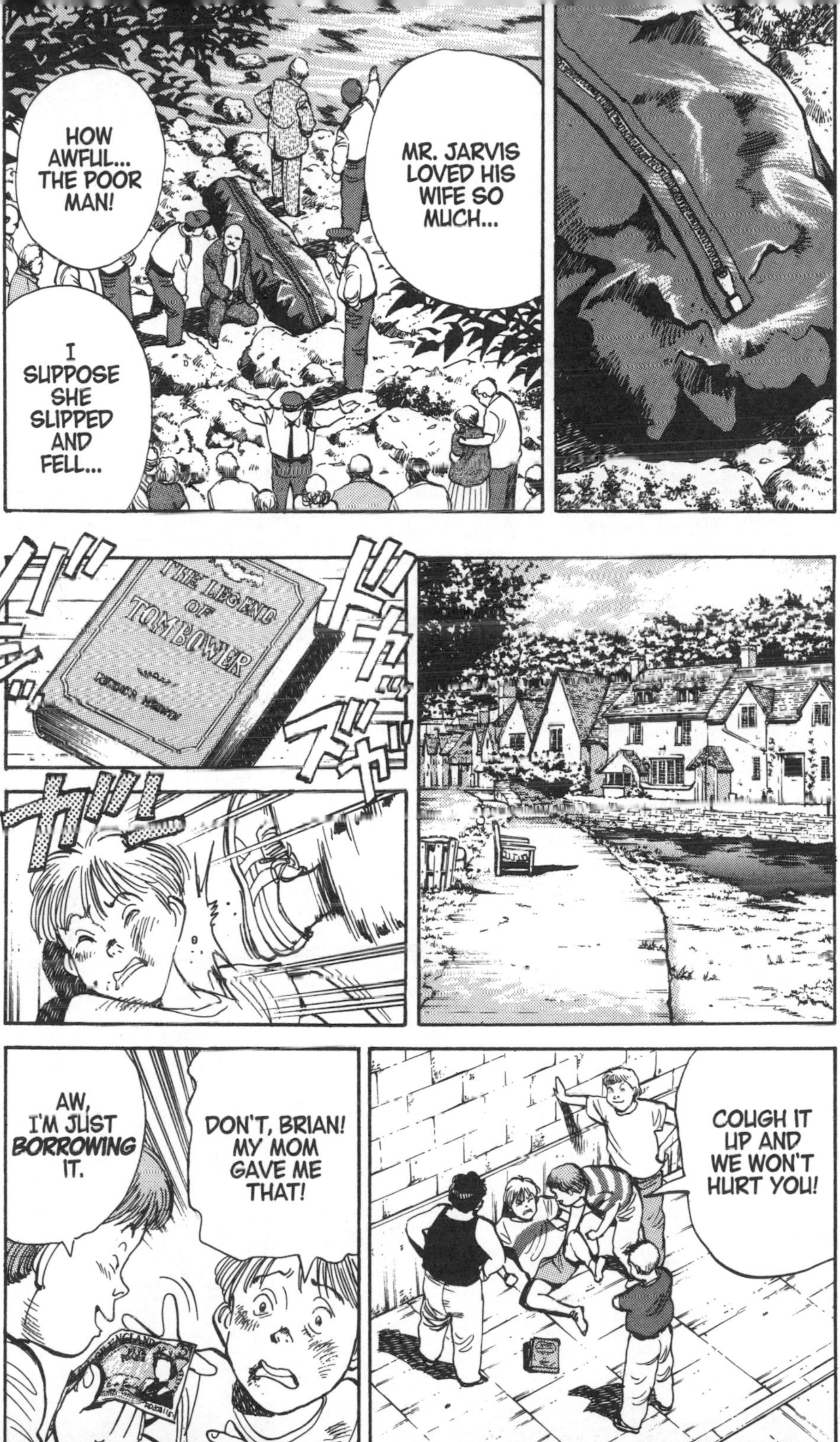
MR. JARVIS LOVED HIS WIFE SO MUCH...
HOW AWFUL... THE POOR MAN!
I SUPPOSE SHE SLIPPED AND FELL...
THE LEGEND OF TOMBOWER
COUGH IT UP AND WE WON'T HURT YOU!
DON'T, BRIAN! MY MOM GAVE ME THAT!
AW, I'M JUST BORROWING IT.

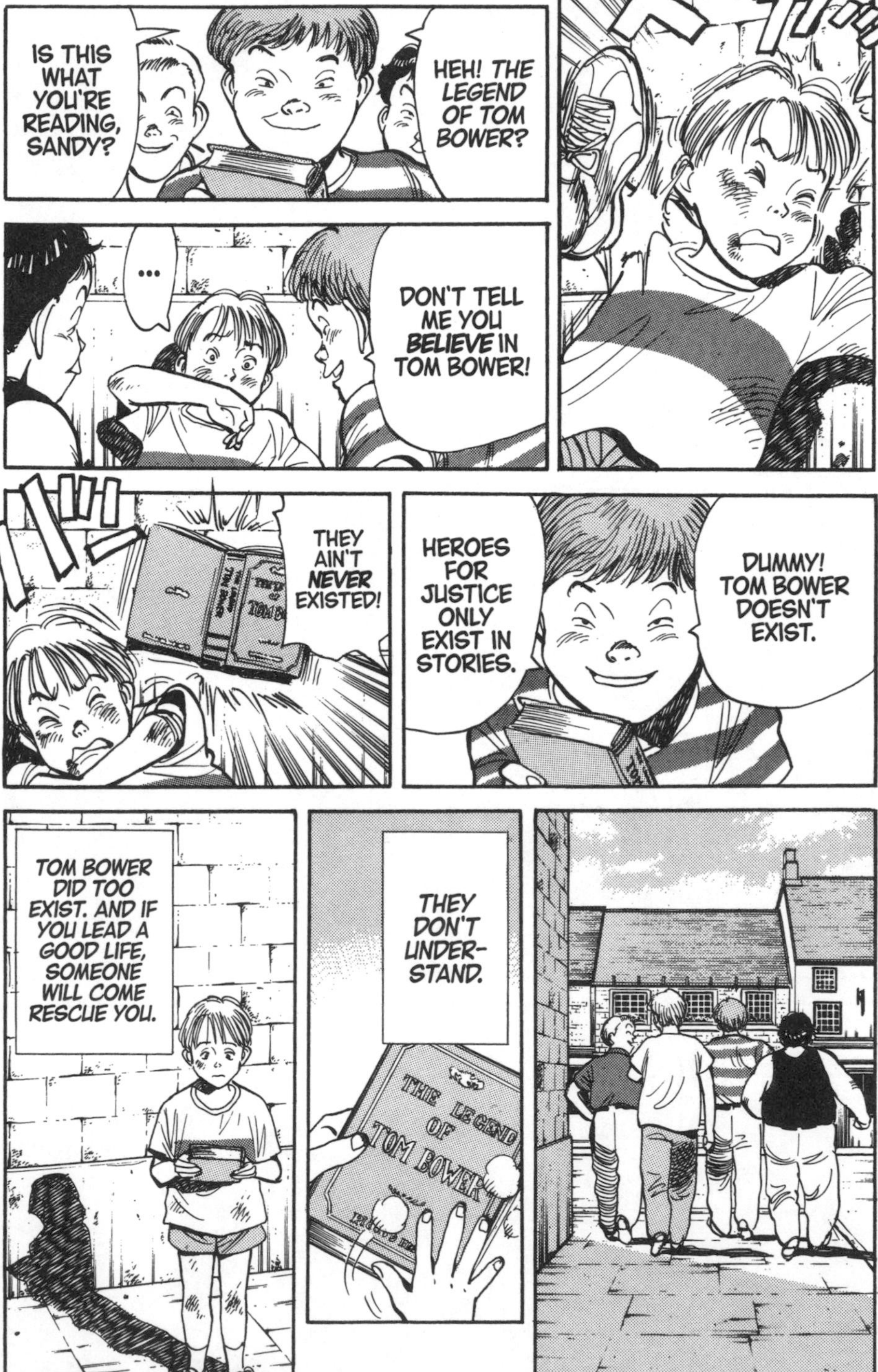
HEH! THE LEGEND OF TOM BOWER?
IS THIS WHAT YOU'RE READING, SANDY?
DON'T TELL ME YOU BELIEVE IN TOM BOWER!
...
DUMMY! TOM BOWER DOESN'T EXIST.
HEROES FOR JUSTICE ONLY EXIST IN STORIES.
THEY AIN'T NEVER EXISTED!
THE LEGEND OF TOM BOWER
THEY DON'T UNDER-STAND.
TOM BOWER DID TOO EXIST. AND IF YOU LEAD A GOOD LIFE, SOMEONE WILL COME RESCUE YOU.

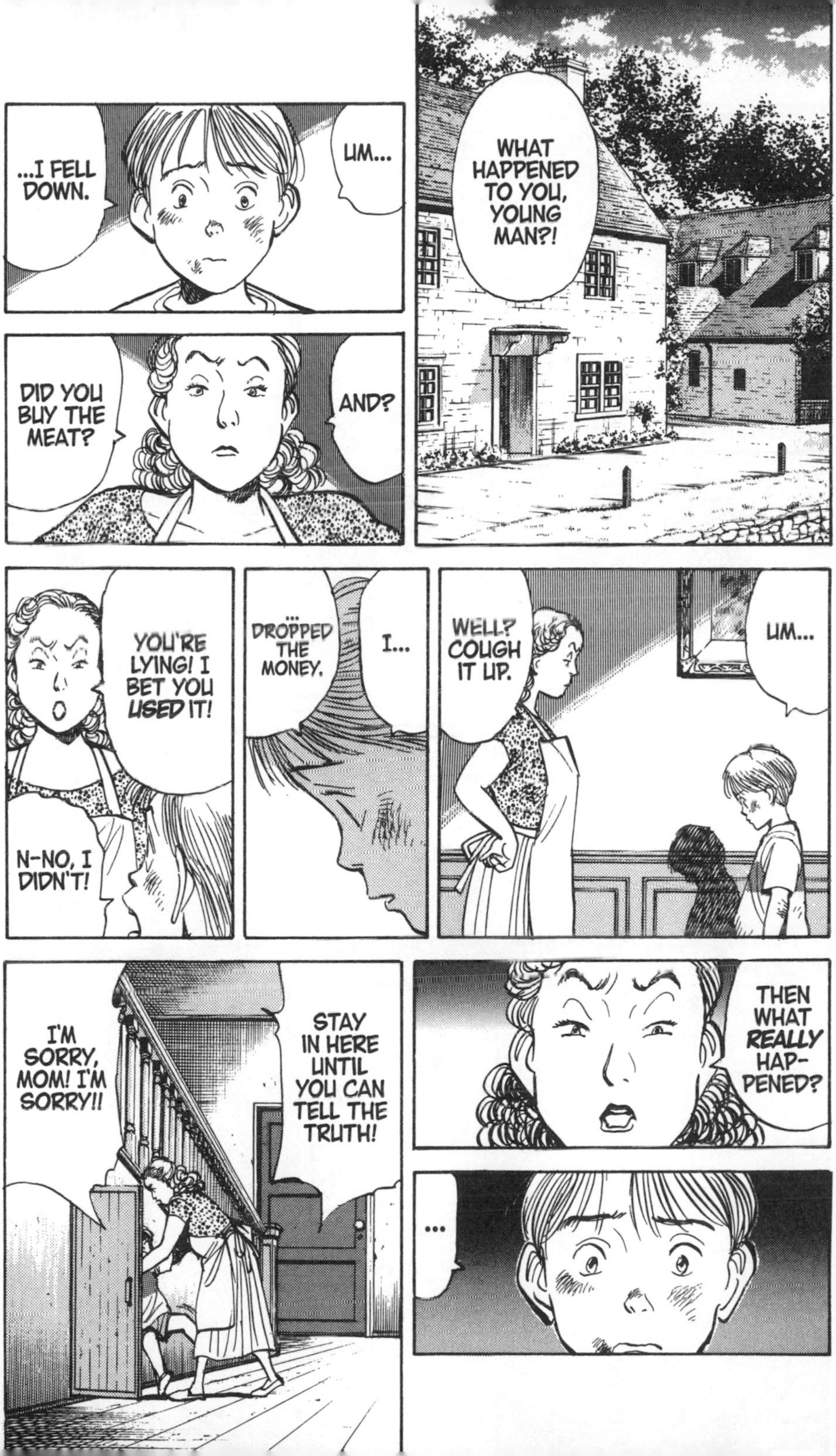
WHAT HAPPENED TO YOU, YOUNG MAN?!
UM...
...I FELL DOWN.
AND?
DID YOU BUY THE MEAT?
UM...
WELL? COUGH IT UP.
I...
...DROPPED THE MONEY.
YOU'RE LYING! I BET YOU USED IT!
N-NO, I DIDN'T!
THEN WHAT REALLY HAP-PENED?
...
STAY IN HERE UNTIL YOU CAN TELL THE TRUTH!
I'M SORRY, MOM! I'M SORRY!!

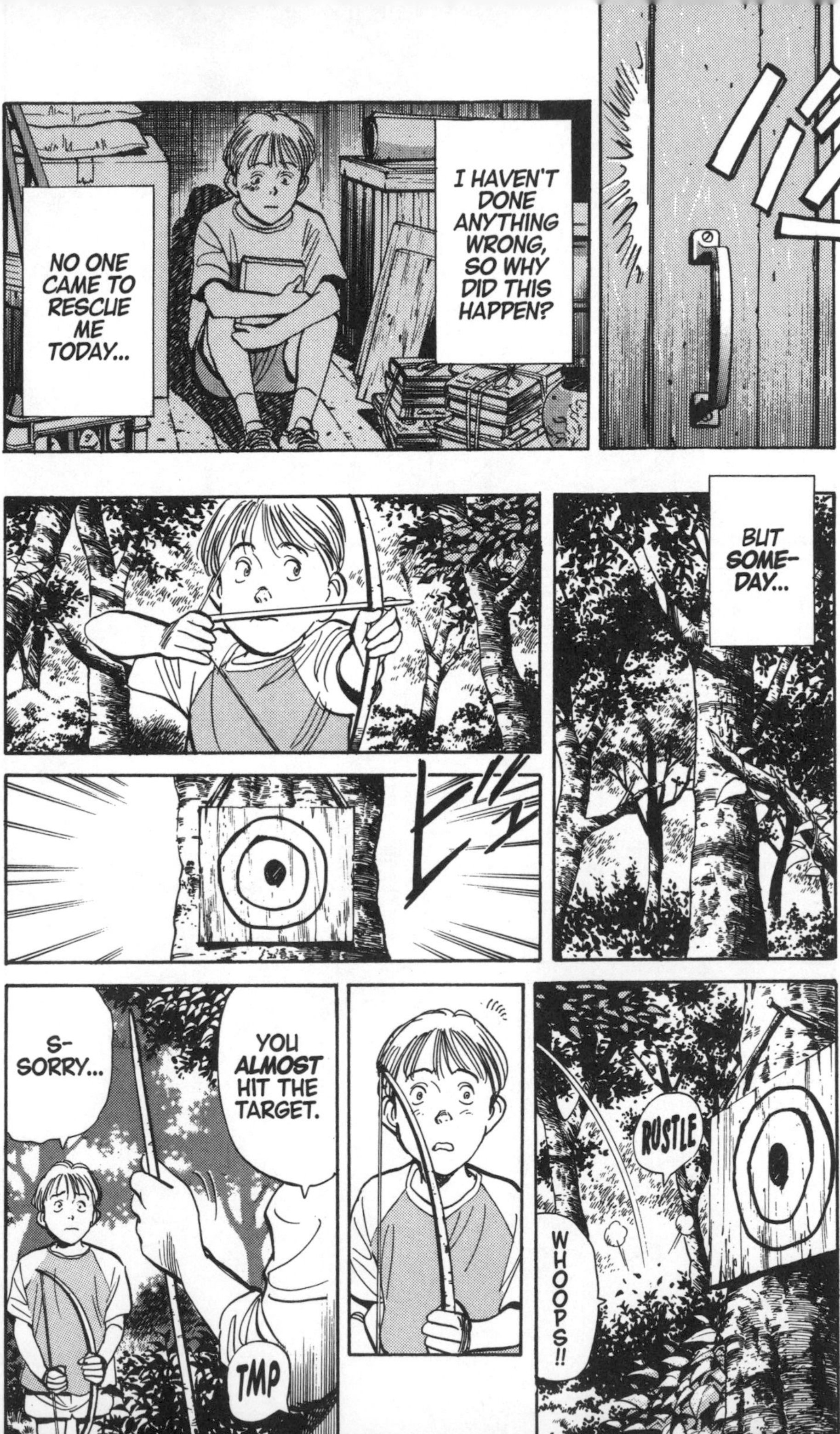
I HAVEN'T DONE ANYTHING WRONG, SO WHY DID THIS HAPPEN?
NO ONE CAME TO RESCUE ME TODAY...
BUT SOME-DAY...
RUSTLE
WHOOPS!!
YOU ALMOST HIT THE TARGET.
TMP
S-SORRY...

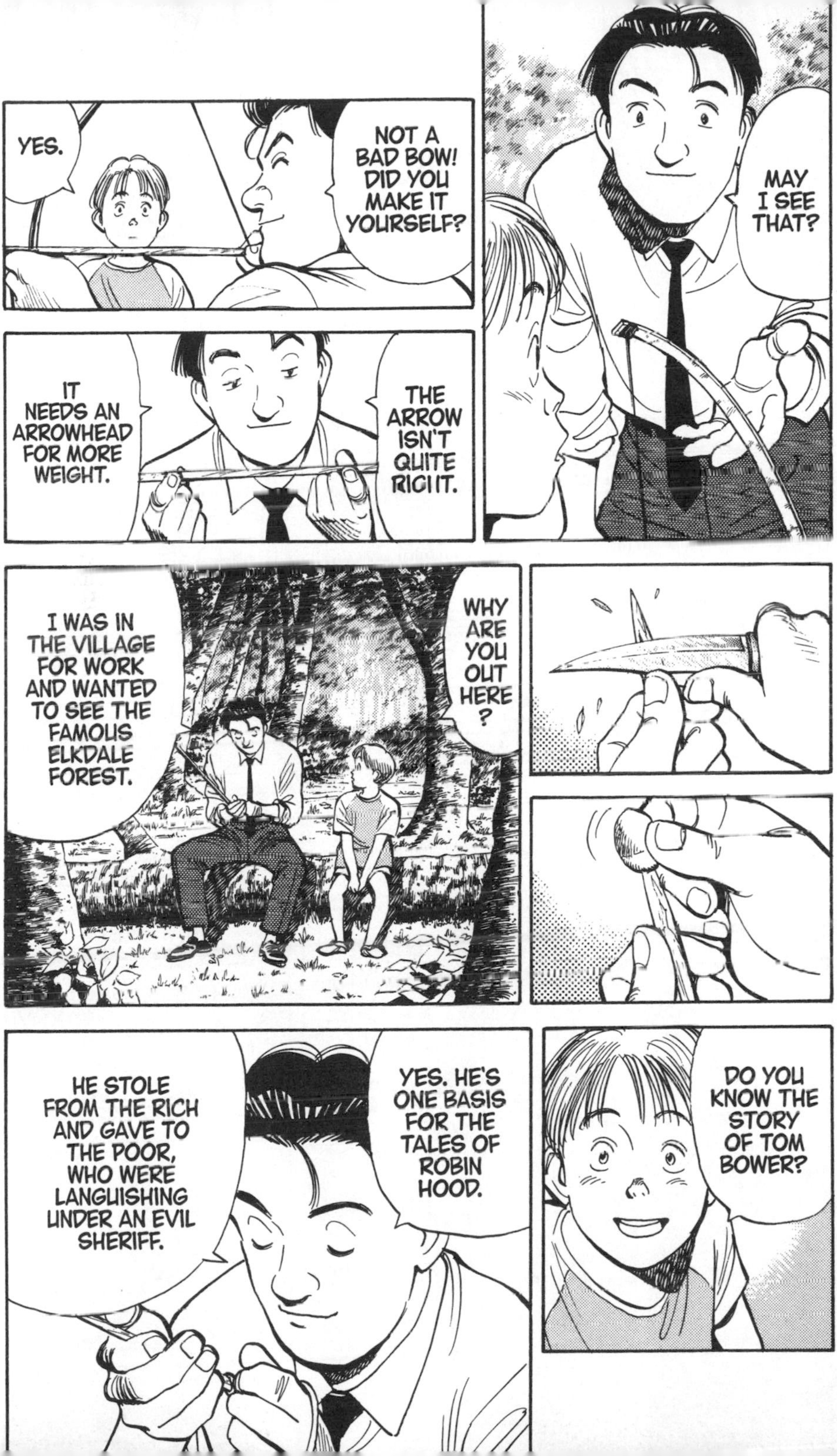
MAY I SEE THAT?
NOT A BAD BOW! DID YOU MAKE IT YOURSELF?
YES.
THE ARROW ISN'T QUITE RIGHT.
IT NEEDS AN ARROWHEAD FOR MORE WEIGHT.
WHY ARE YOU OUT HERE?
I WAS IN THE VILLAGE FOR WORK AND WANTED TO SEE THE FAMOUS ELKDALE FOREST.
DO YOU KNOW THE STORY OF TOM BOWER?
YES. HE'S ONE BASIS FOR THE TALES OF ROBIN HOOD.
HE STOLE FROM THE RICH AND GAVE TO THE POOR, WHO WERE LANGUISHING UNDER AN EVIL SHERIFF.

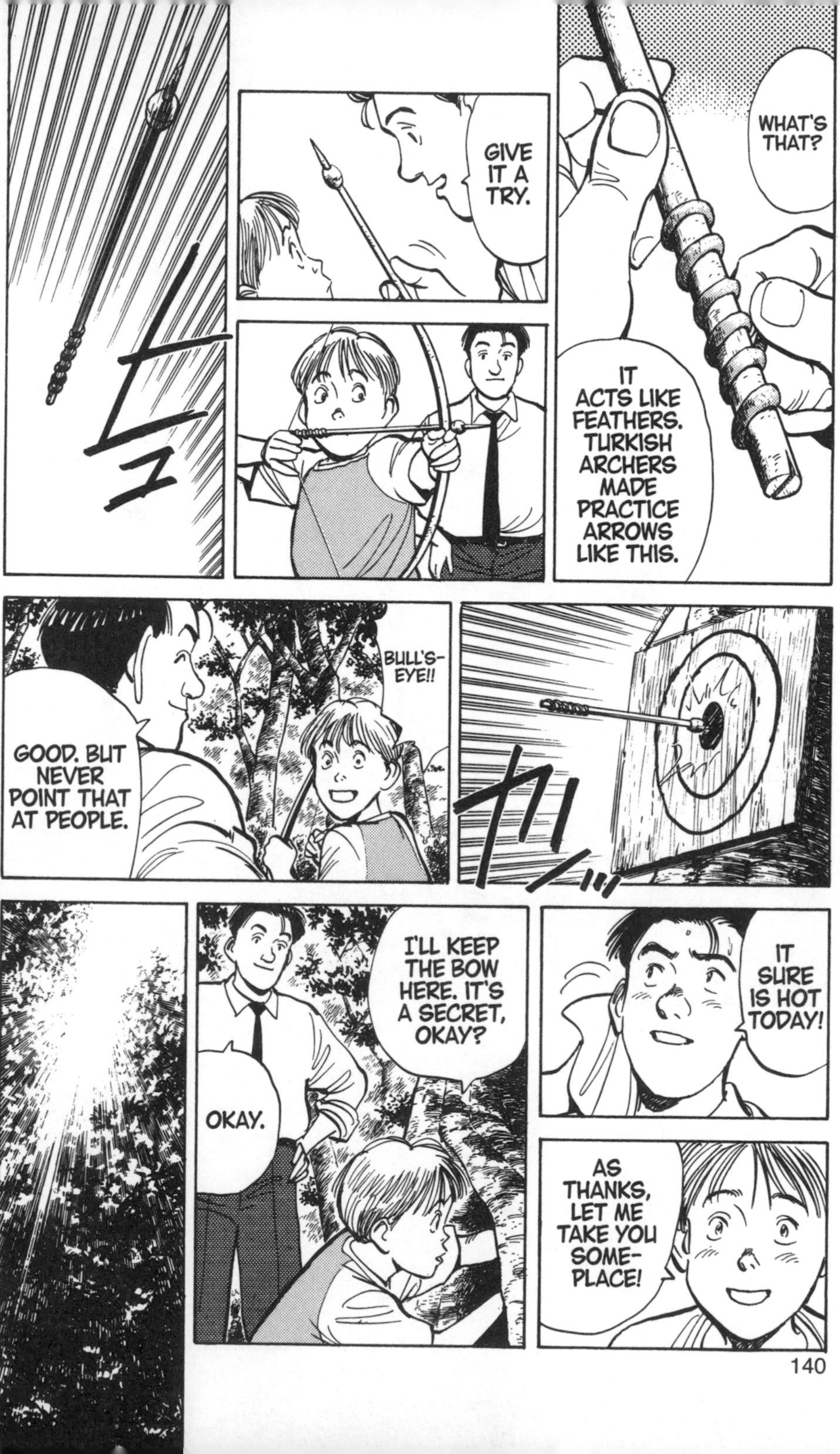
WHAT'S THAT?
IT ACTS LIKE FEATHERS. TURKISH ARCHERS MADE PRACTICE ARROWS LIKE THIS.
GIVE IT A TRY.
BULL'S-EYE!!
GOOD. BUT NEVER POINT THAT AT PEOPLE.
IT SURE IS HOT TODAY!
AS THANKS, LET ME TAKE YOU SOME-PLACE!
I'LL KEEP THE BOW HERE. IT'S A SECRET, OKAY?
OKAY.

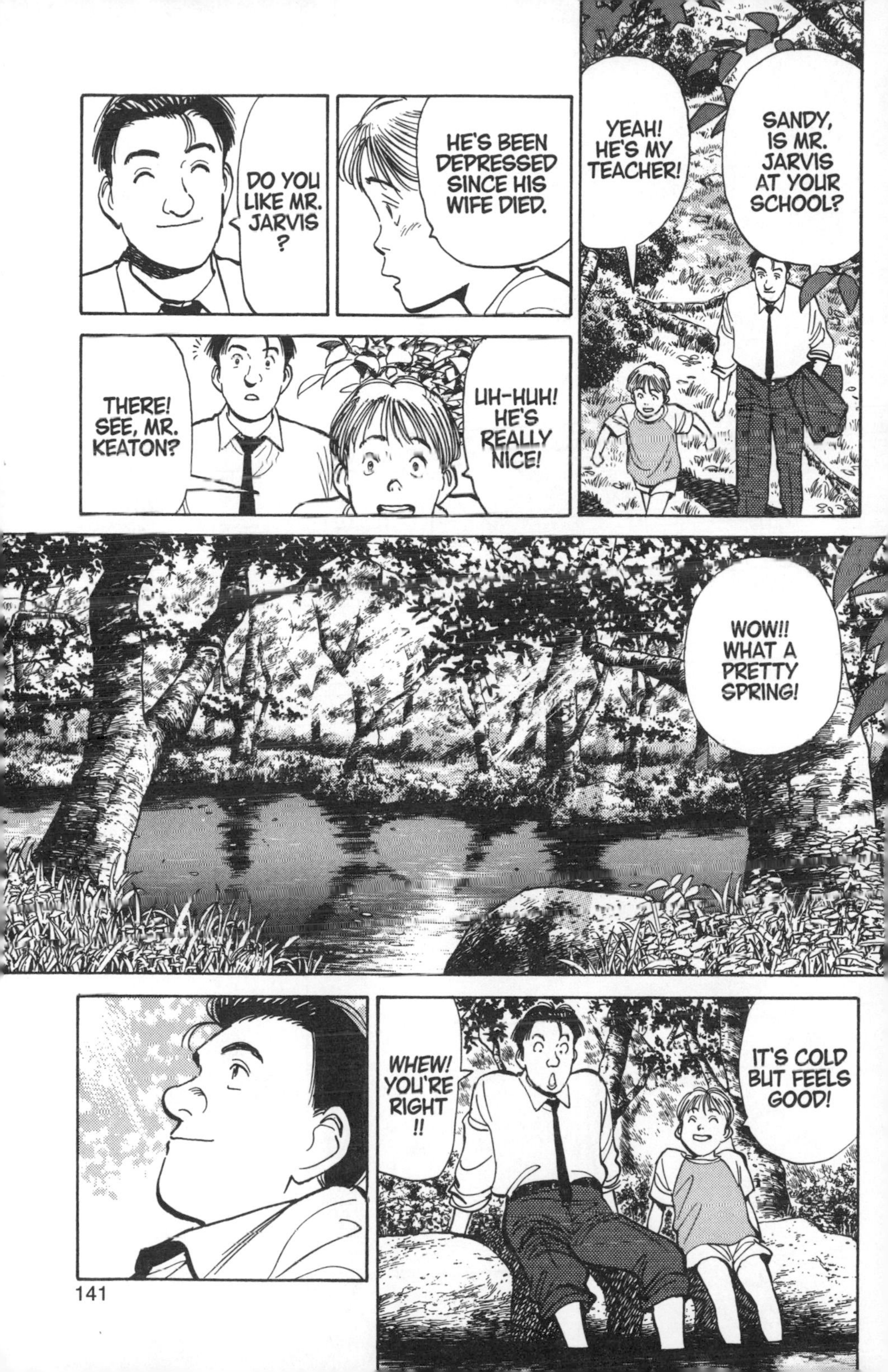
SANDY, IS MR. JARVIS AT YOUR SCHOOL?
YEAH! HE'S MY TEACHER!
HE'S BEEN DEPRESSED SINCE HIS WIFE DIED.
DO YOU LIKE MR. JARVIS ?
UH-HUH! HE'S REALLY NICE!
THERE! SEE, MR. KEATON?
WOW!! WHAT A PRETTY SPRING!
IT'S COLD BUT FEELS GOOD!
WHEW! YOU'RE RIGHT !!

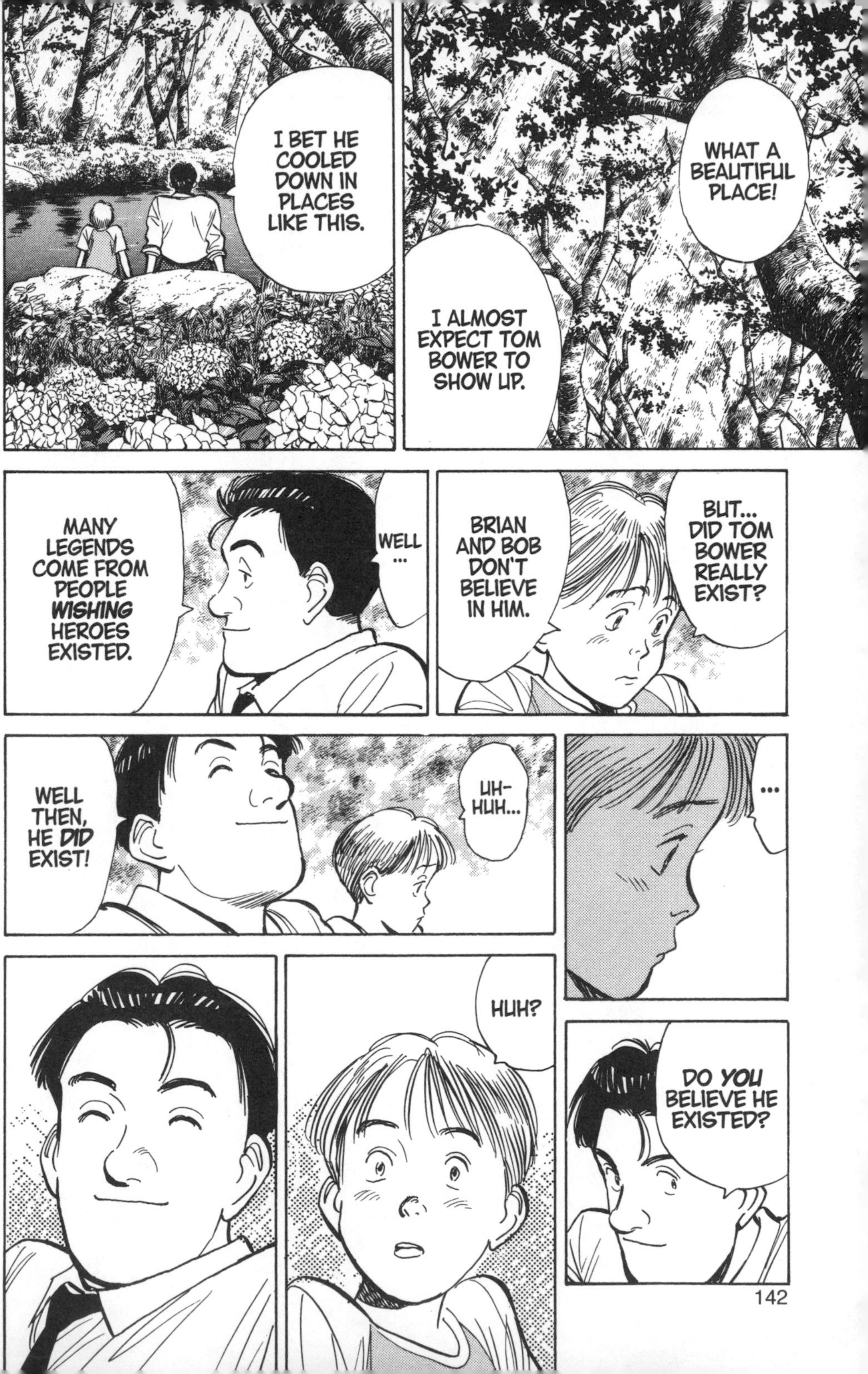
WHAT A BEAUTIFUL PLACE!
I ALMOST EXPECT TOM BOWER TO SHOW UP.
I BET HE COOLED DOWN IN PLACES LIKE THIS.
BUT... DID TOM BOWER REALLY EXIST?
BRIAN AND BOB DON'T BELIEVE IN HIM.
WELL ...
MANY LEGENDS COME FROM PEOPLE *WISHING* HEROES EXISTED.
WELL THEN, HE *DID* EXIST!
UH-HUH...
...
DO *YOU* BELIEVE HE EXISTED?
HUH?

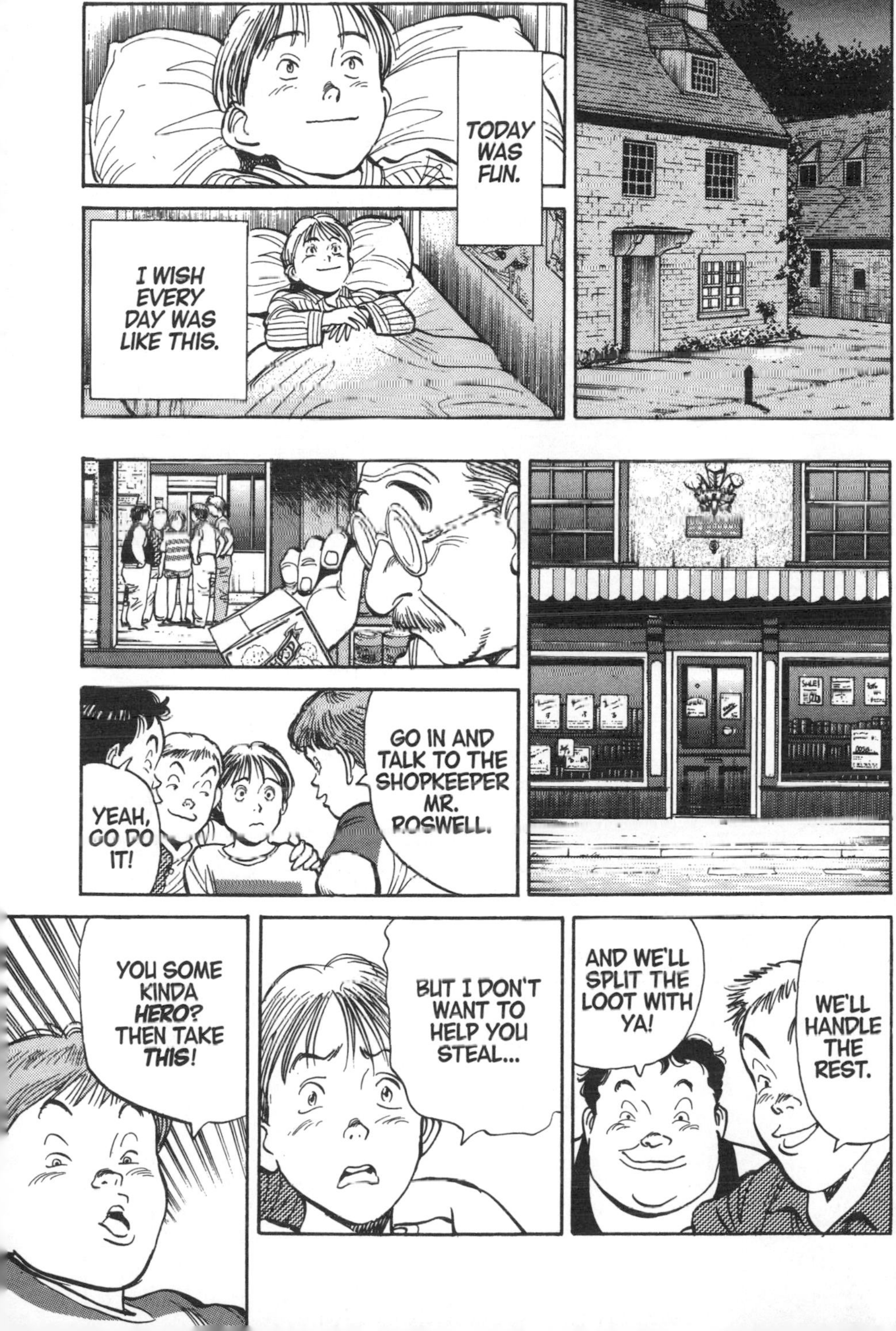
TODAY WAS FUN.
I WISH EVERY DAY WAS LIKE THIS.
GO IN AND TALK TO THE SHOPKEEPER MR. ROSWELL.
YEAH, GO DO IT!
WE'LL HANDLE THE REST.
AND WE'LL SPLIT THE LOOT WITH YA!
BUT I DON'T WANT TO HELP YOU STEAL...
YOU SOME KINDA HERO? THEN TAKE THIS!

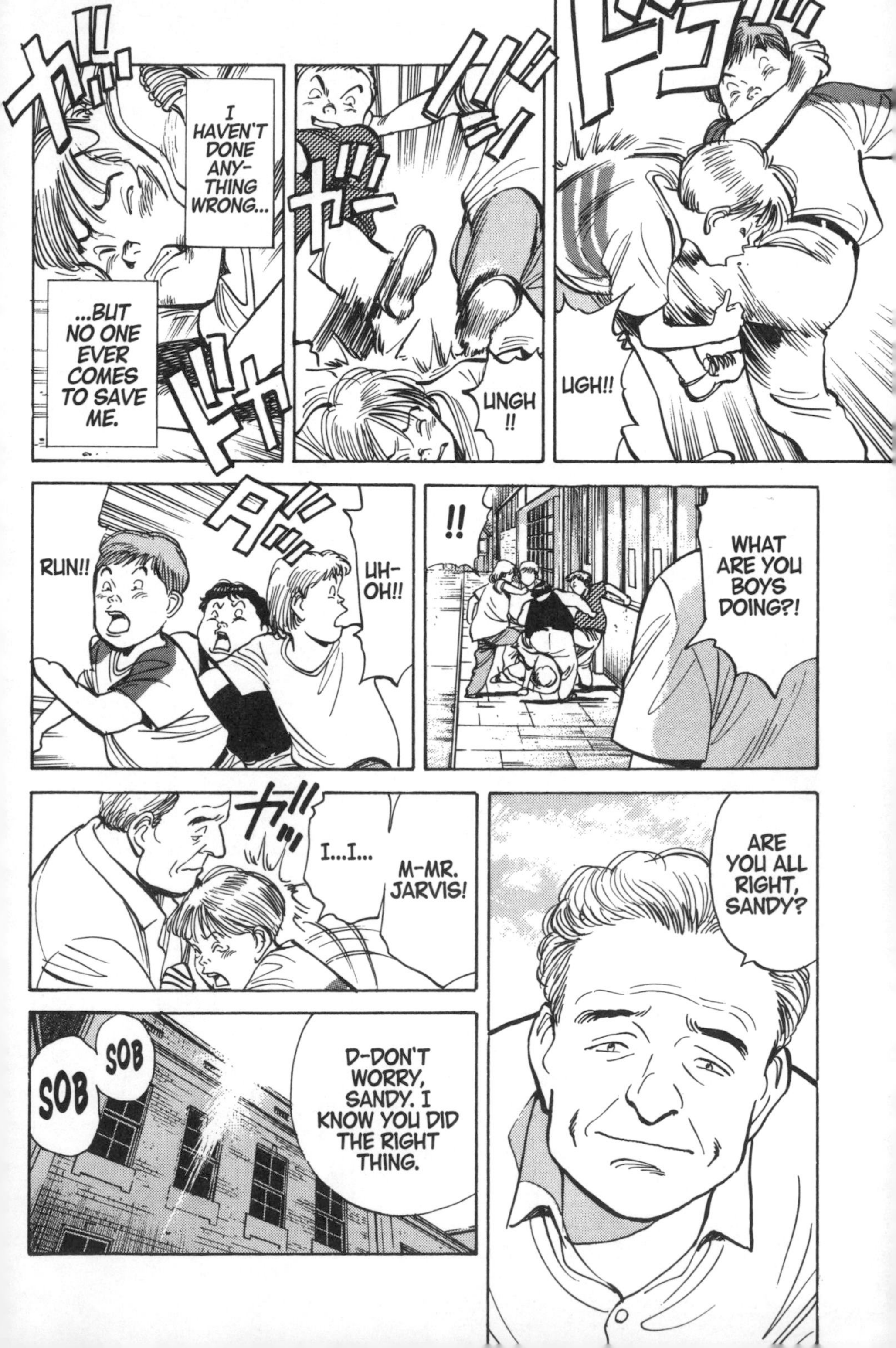

UGH!!
UNGH !!
I HAVEN'T DONE ANY-THING WRONG...
...BUT NO ONE EVER COMES TO SAVE ME.
!!
WHAT ARE YOU BOYS DOING?!
UH-OH!!
RUN!!
ARE YOU ALL RIGHT, SANDY?
M-MR. JARVIS!
I...I...
D-DON'T WORRY, SANDY. I KNOW YOU DID THE RIGHT THING.
SOB
SOB

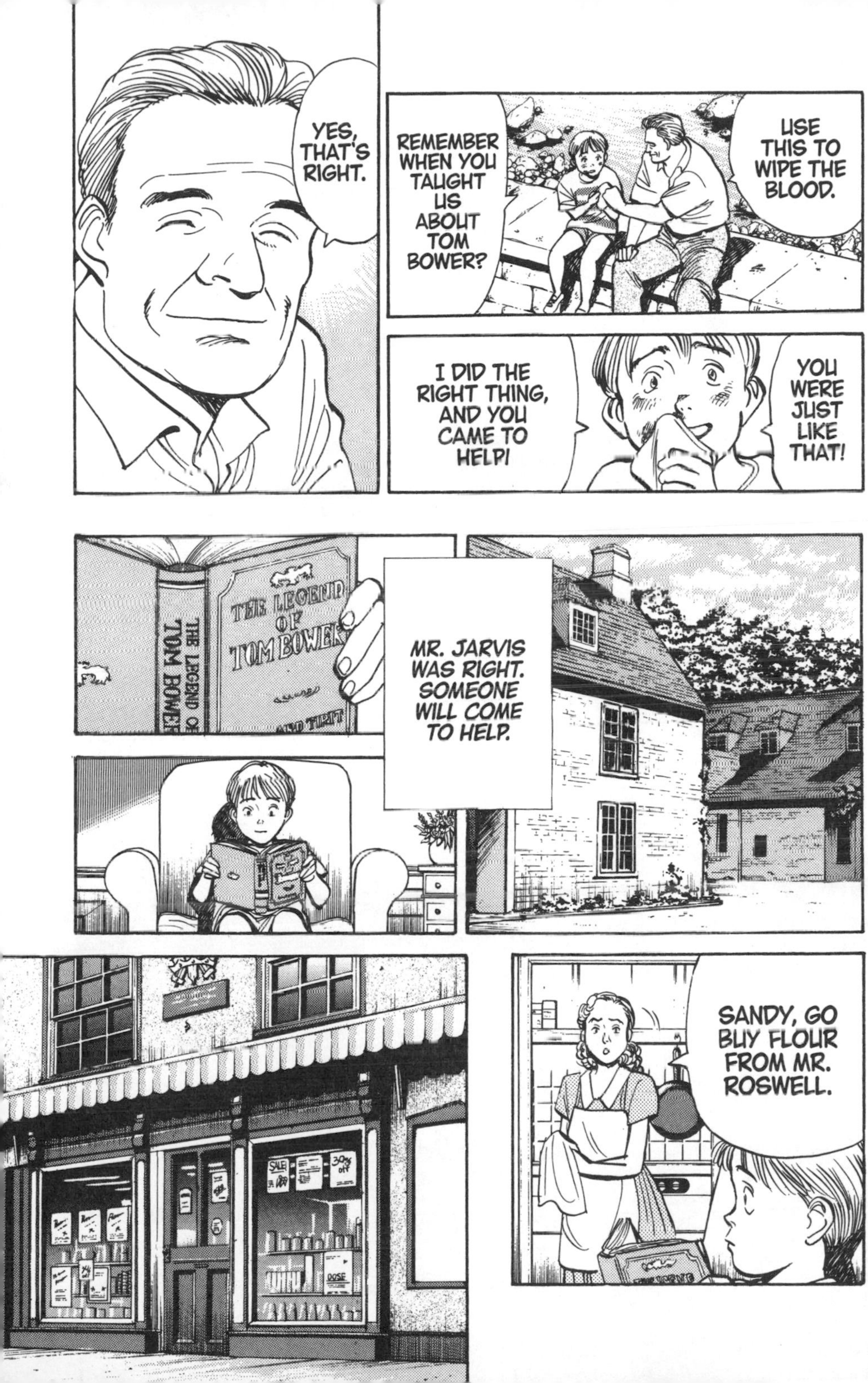
USE THIS TO WIPE THE BLOOD.
REMEMBER WHEN YOU TAUGHT US ABOUT TOM BOWER?
YOU WERE JUST LIKE THAT!
I DID THE RIGHT THING, AND YOU CAME TO HELP!
YES, THAT'S RIGHT.
MR. JARVIS WAS RIGHT. SOMEONE WILL COME TO HELP.
THE LEGEND OF TOM BOWER
THE LEGEND OF TOM BOWER
SANDY, GO BUY FLOUR FROM MR. ROSWELL.
SALE
30% off
DOSE

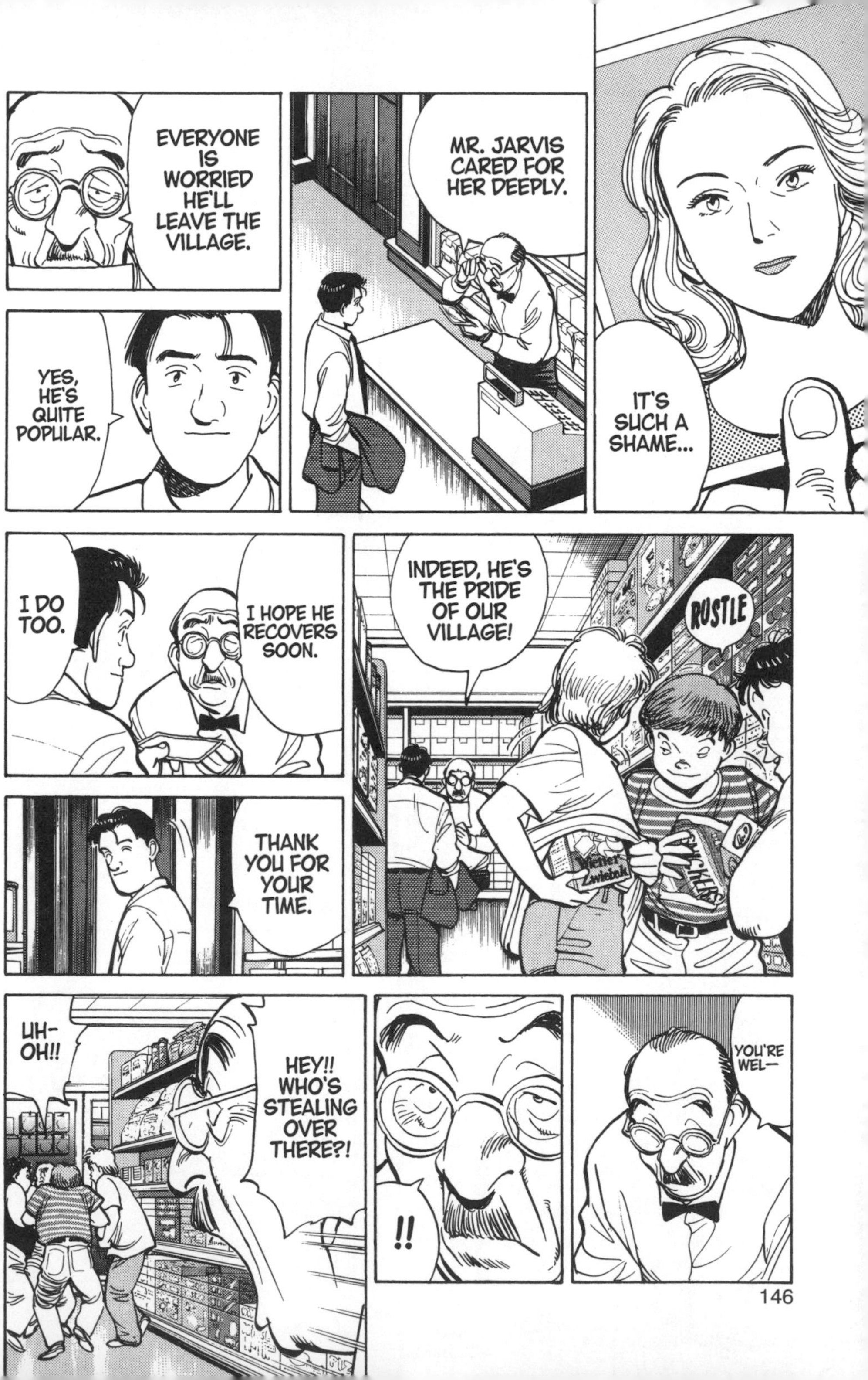
IT'S SUCH A SHAME...
MR. JARVIS CARED FOR HER DEEPLY.
EVERYONE IS WORRIED HE'LL LEAVE THE VILLAGE.
YES, HE'S QUITE POPULAR.
INDEED, HE'S THE PRIDE OF OUR VILLAGE!
RUSTLE
I HOPE HE RECOVERS SOON.
I DO TOO.
THANK YOU FOR YOUR TIME.
YOU'RE WEL—
!!
HEY!! WHO'S STEALING OVER THERE?!
UH-OH!!

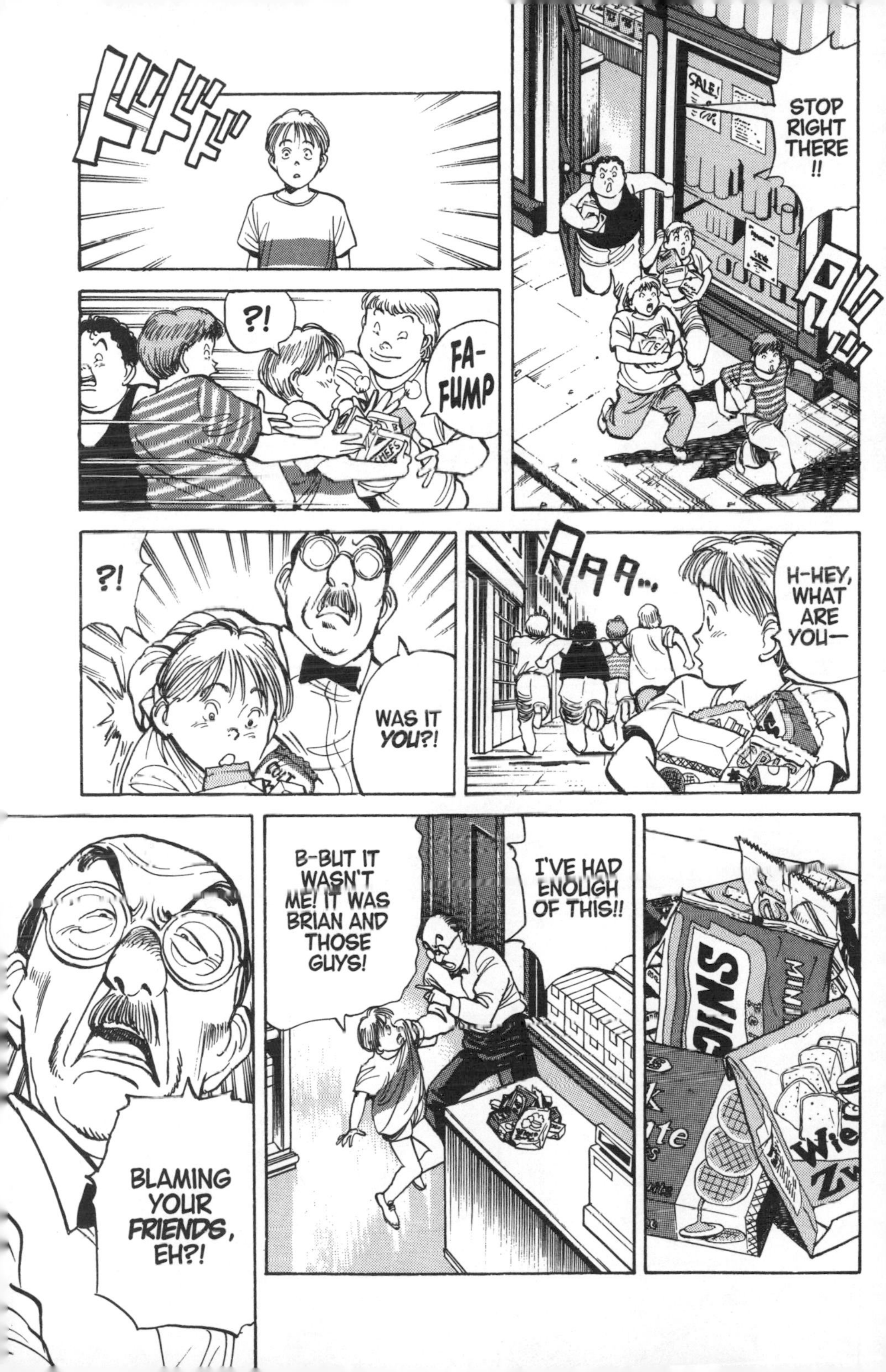
STOP RIGHT THERE !!
FA-FUMP
?!
H-HEY, WHAT ARE YOU—
?!
WAS IT YOU?!
I'VE HAD ENOUGH OF THIS!!
B-BUT IT WASN'T ME! IT WAS BRIAN AND THOSE GUYS!
BLAMING YOUR FRIENDS, EH?!

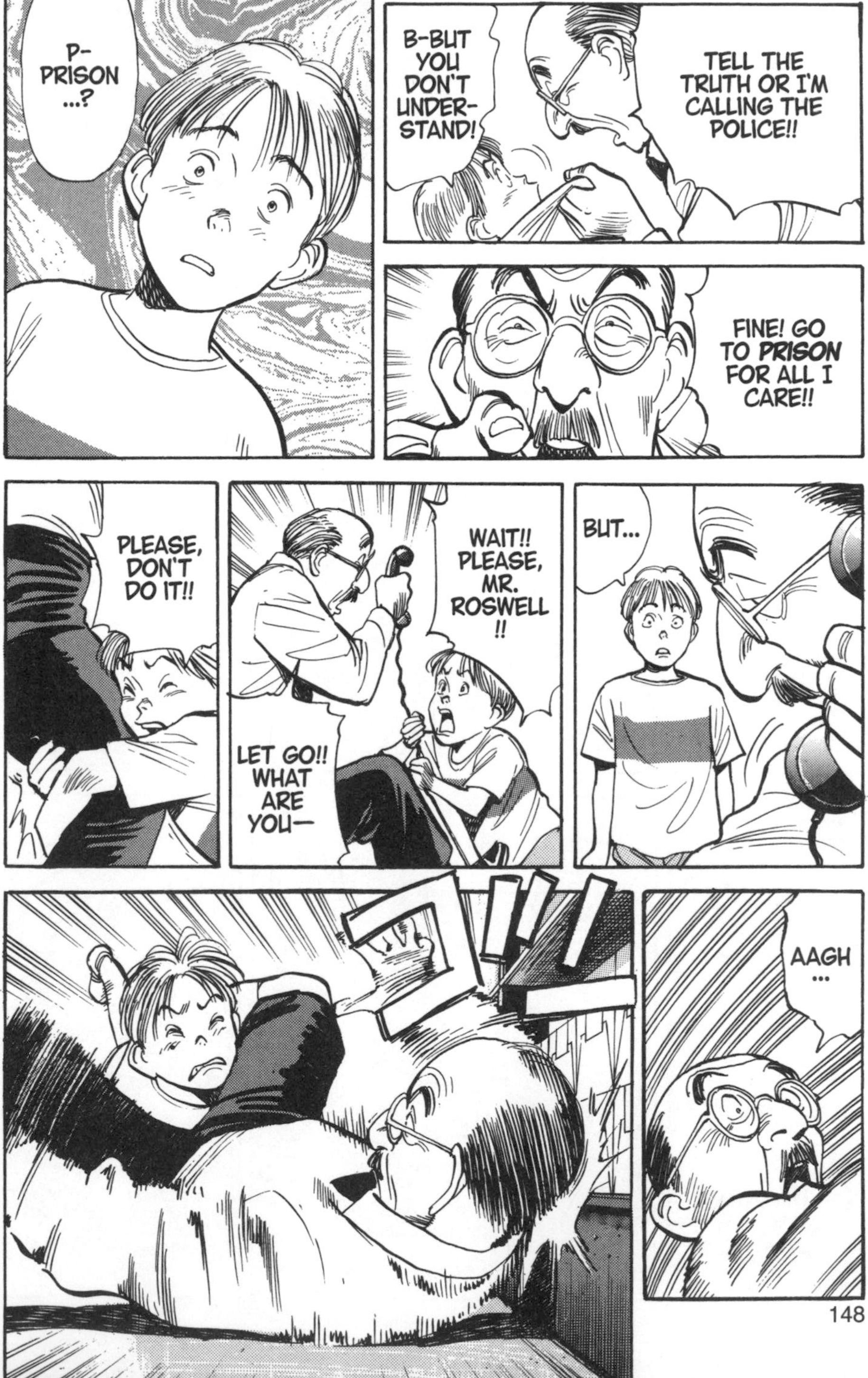
TELL THE TRUTH OR I'M CALLING THE POLICE!!
B-BUT YOU DON'T UNDER-STAND!
FINE! GO TO **PRISON** FOR ALL I CARE!!
P-PRISON ...?
BUT...
WAIT!! PLEASE, MR. ROSWELL !!
LET GO!! WHAT ARE YOU—
PLEASE, DON'T DO IT!!
AAGH ...

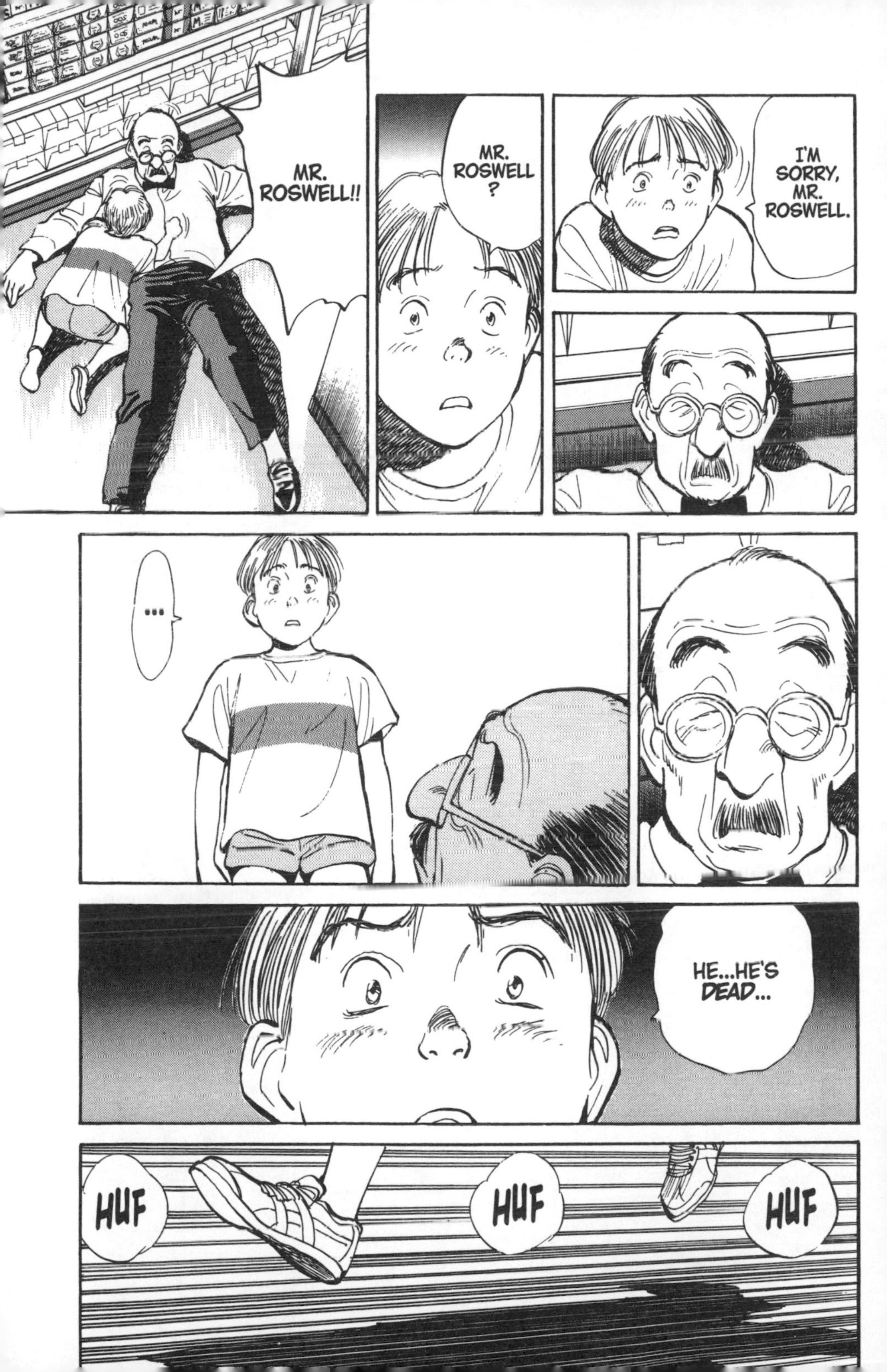
I'M SORRY, MR. ROSWELL.
MR. ROSWELL?
MR. ROSWELL!!
...
HE...HE'S DEAD...
HUF
HUF
HUF

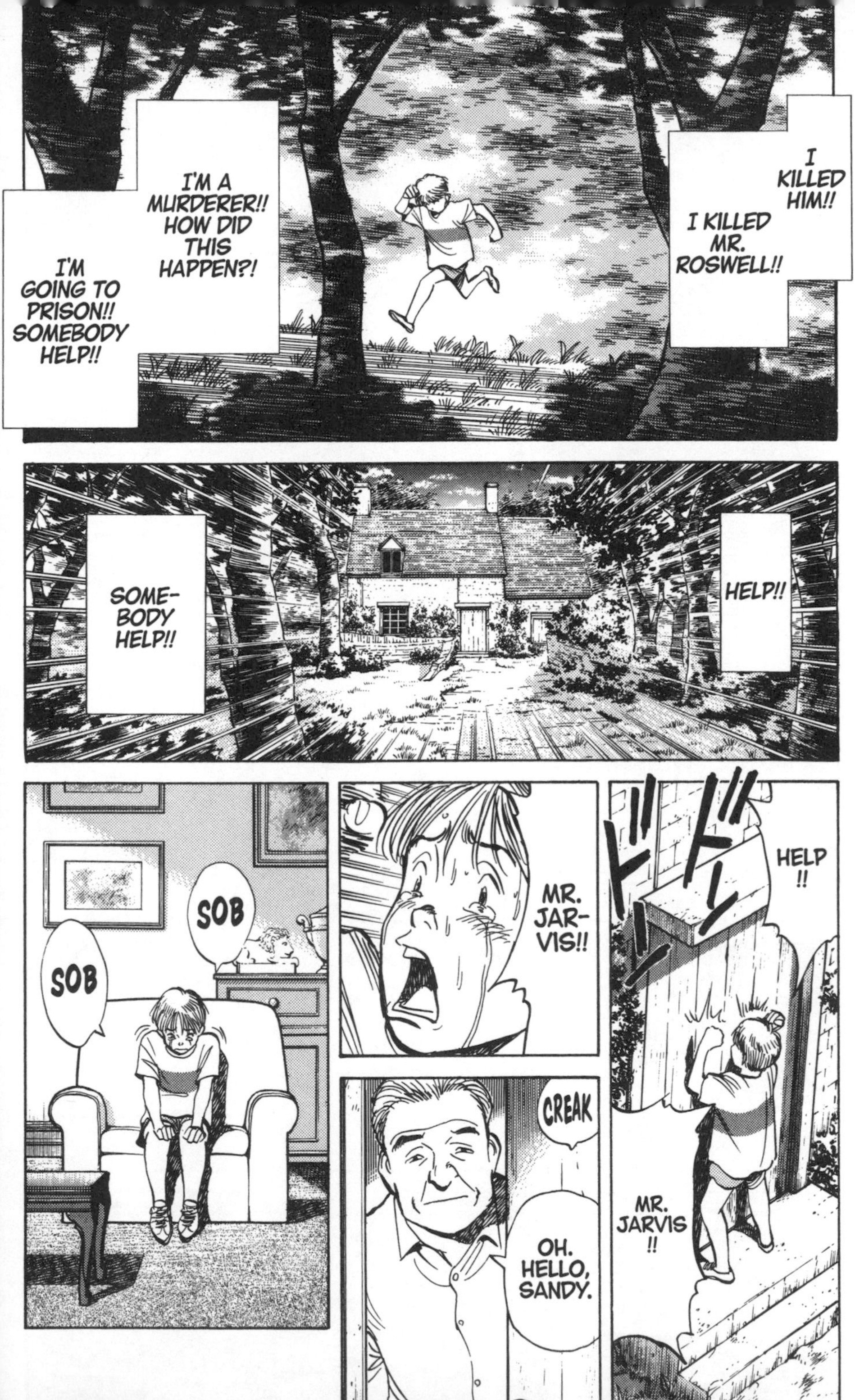
I KILLED HIM!!
I KILLED MR. ROSWELL!!
I'M A MURDERER!! HOW DID THIS HAPPEN?!
I'M GOING TO PRISON!! SOMEBODY HELP!!
HELP!!
SOME-BODY HELP!!
HELP !!
MR. JARVIS !!
MR. JAR-VIS!!
CREAK
OH. HELLO, SANDY.
SOB
SOB

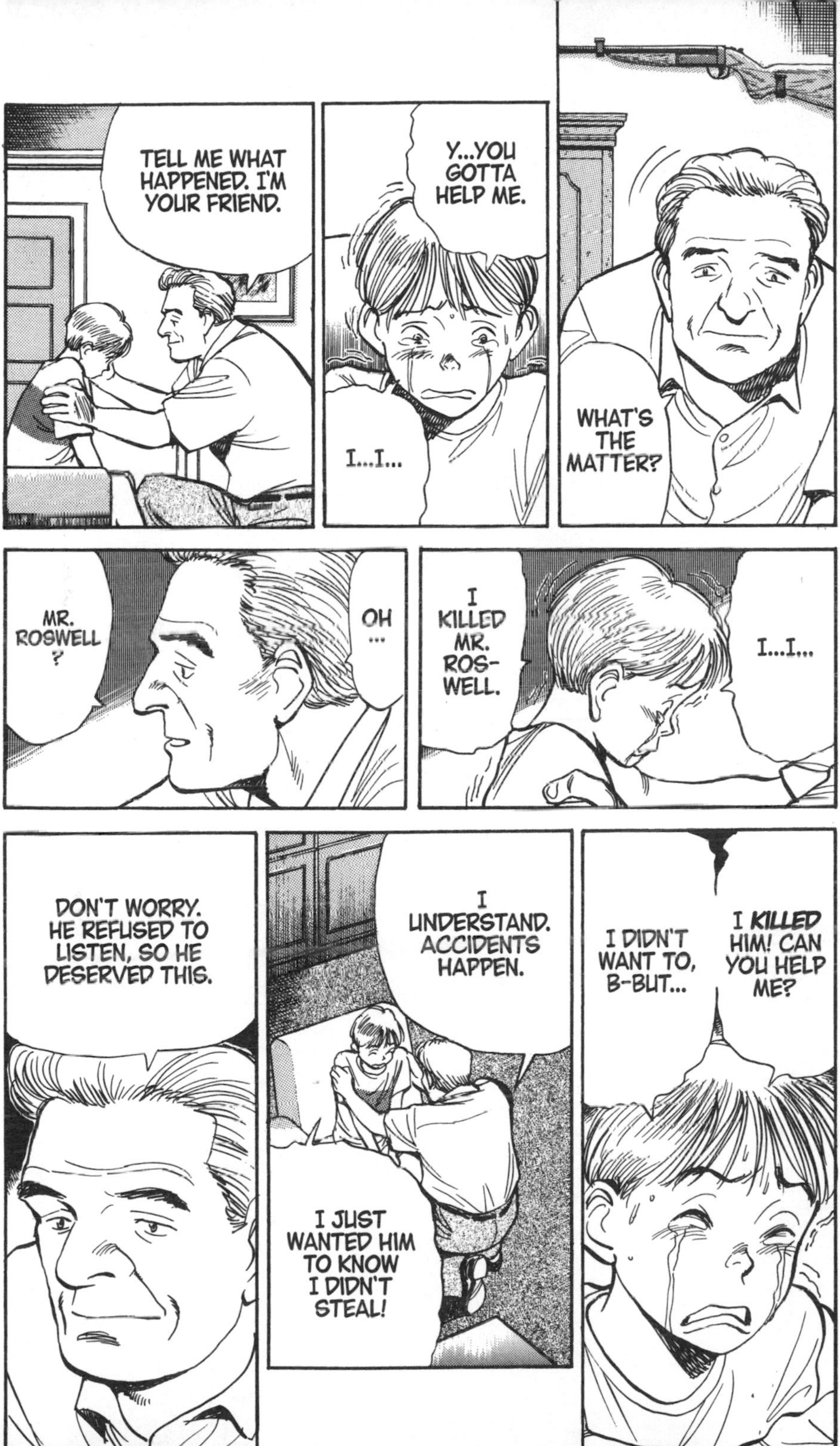
WHAT'S THE MATTER?
Y...YOU GOTTA HELP ME.
I...I...
TELL ME WHAT HAPPENED. I'M YOUR FRIEND.
I...I...
I KILLED MR. ROSWELL.
OH ...
MR. ROSWELL ?
I **KILLED** HIM! CAN YOU HELP ME?
I DIDN'T WANT TO, B-BUT...
I UNDERSTAND. ACCIDENTS HAPPEN.
I JUST WANTED HIM TO KNOW I DIDN'T STEAL!
DON'T WORRY. HE REFUSED TO LISTEN, SO HE DESERVED THIS.

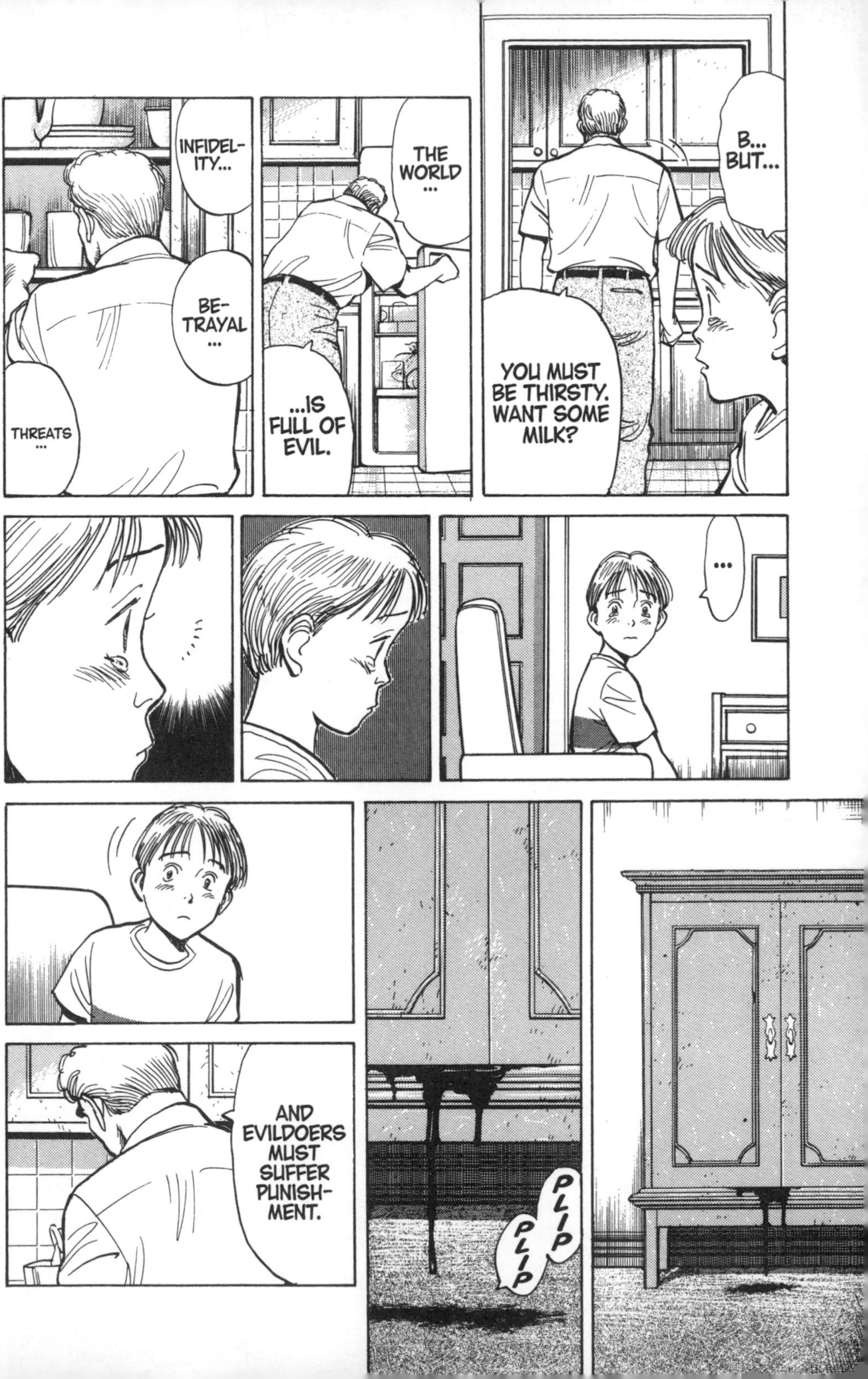
B... BUT...
YOU MUST BE THIRSTY. WANT SOME MILK?
THE WORLD ...
...IS FULL OF EVIL.
INFIDELITY...
BE-TRAYAL ...
THREATS ...
...
PLIP PLIP
AND EVILDOERS MUST SUFFER PUNISH-MENT.

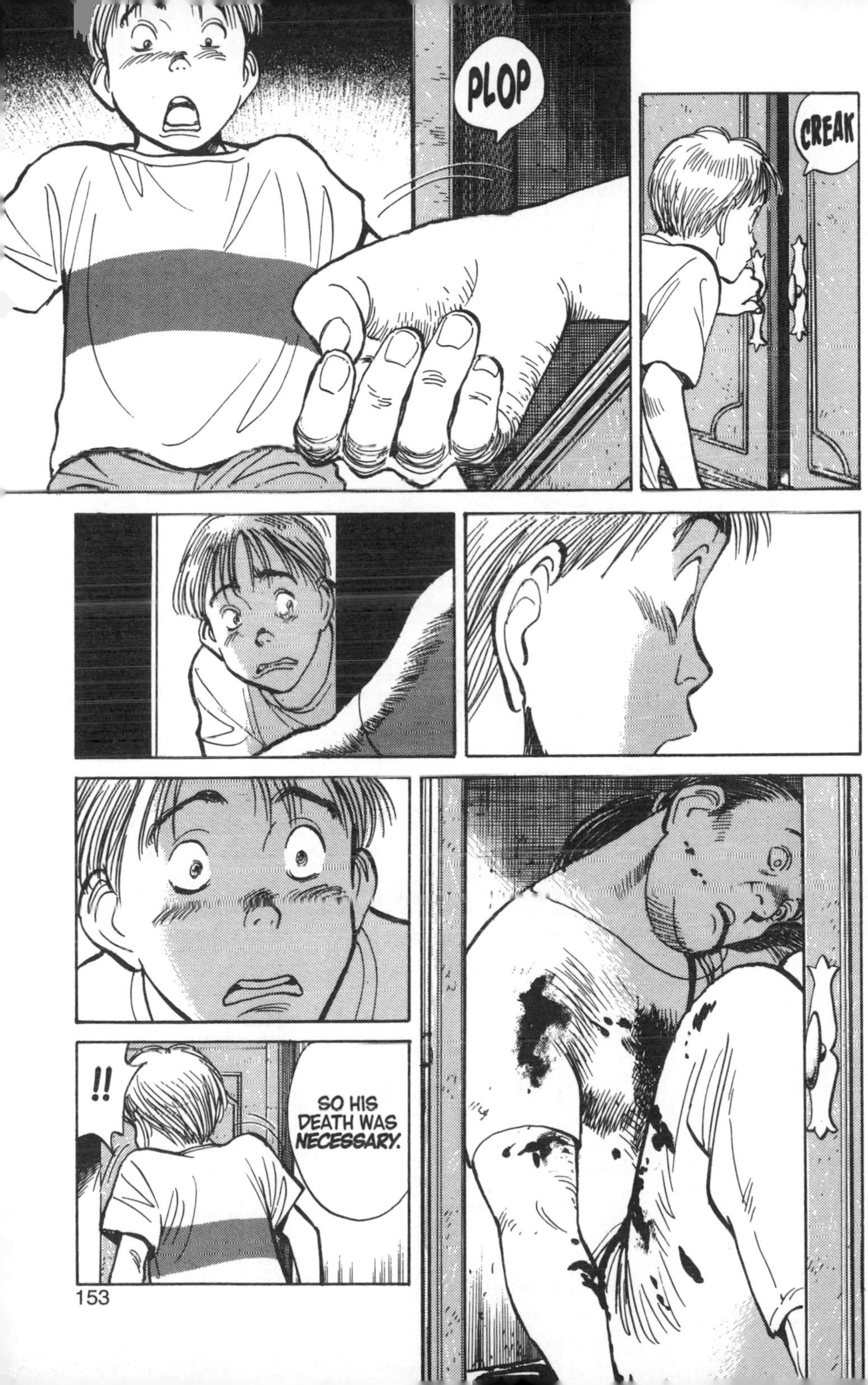
CREAK
PLOP
SO HIS DEATH WAS NECESSARY.
!!

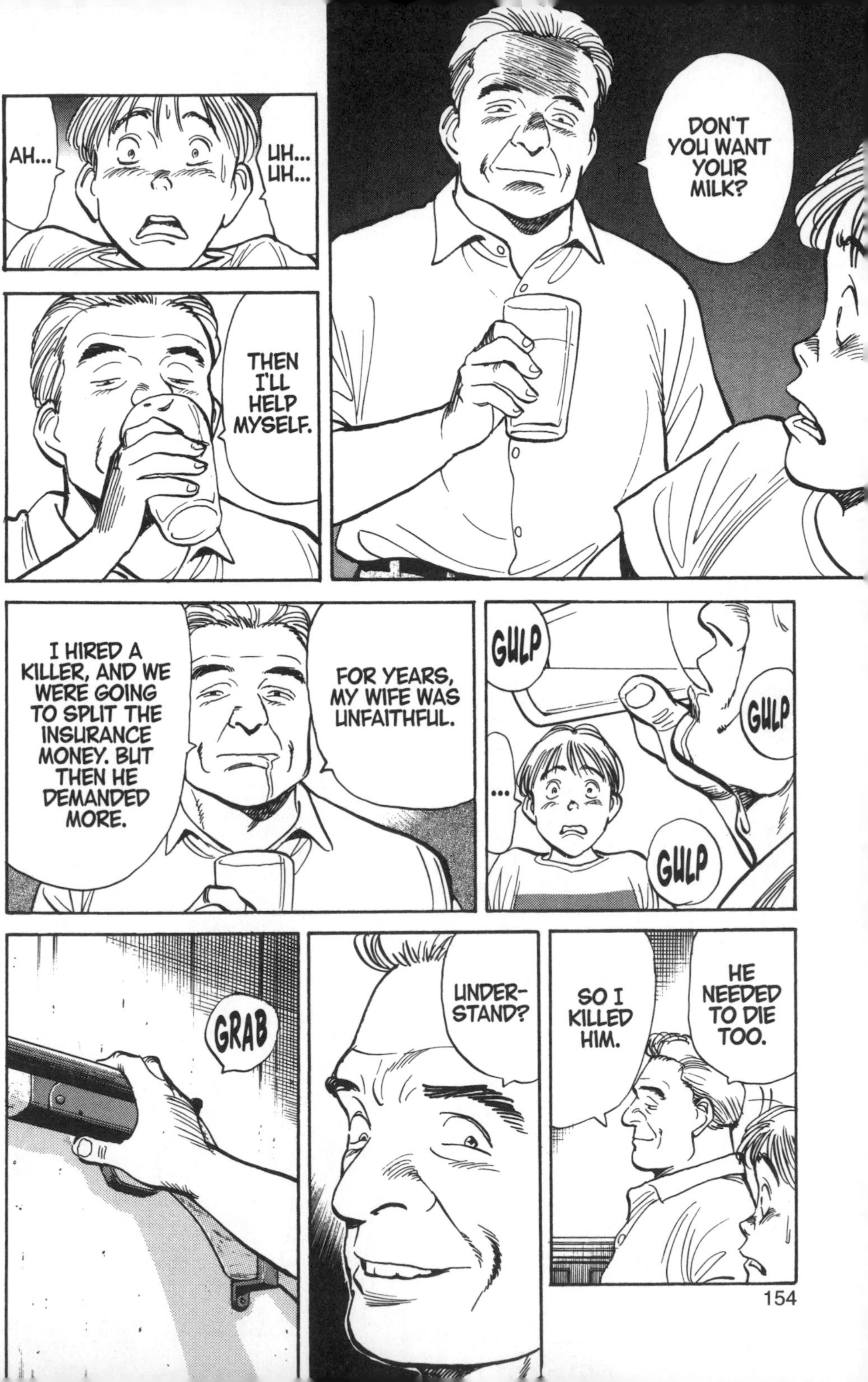
DON'T YOU WANT YOUR MILK?
UH... UH...
AH...
THEN I'LL HELP MYSELF.
GULP
GULP
...
GULP
FOR YEARS, MY WIFE WAS UNFAITHFUL.
I HIRED A KILLER, AND WE WERE GOING TO SPLIT THE INSURANCE MONEY. BUT THEN HE DEMANDED MORE.
HE NEEDED TO DIE TOO.
SO I KILLED HIM.
UNDER-STAND?
GRAB

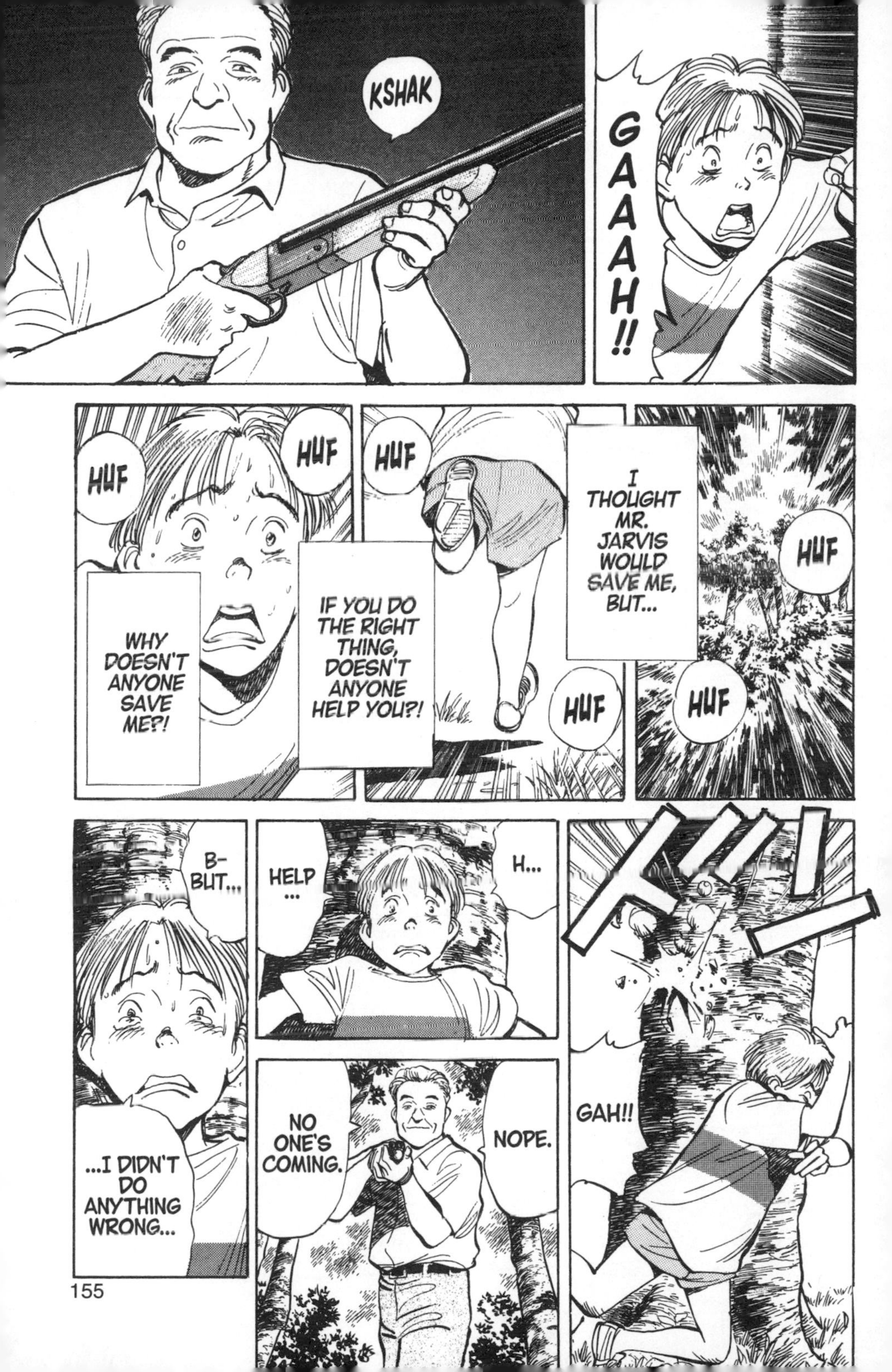
GAAAH!!
KSHAK
HUF
I THOUGHT MR. JARVIS WOULD SAVE ME, BUT...
HUF
HUF
IF YOU DO THE RIGHT THING, DOESN'T ANYONE HELP YOU?!
HUF
HUF
HUF
WHY DOESN'T ANYONE SAVE ME?!
GAH!!
H...
HELP ...
NOPE.
NO ONE'S COMING.
B-BUT...
...I DIDN'T DO ANYTHING WRONG...

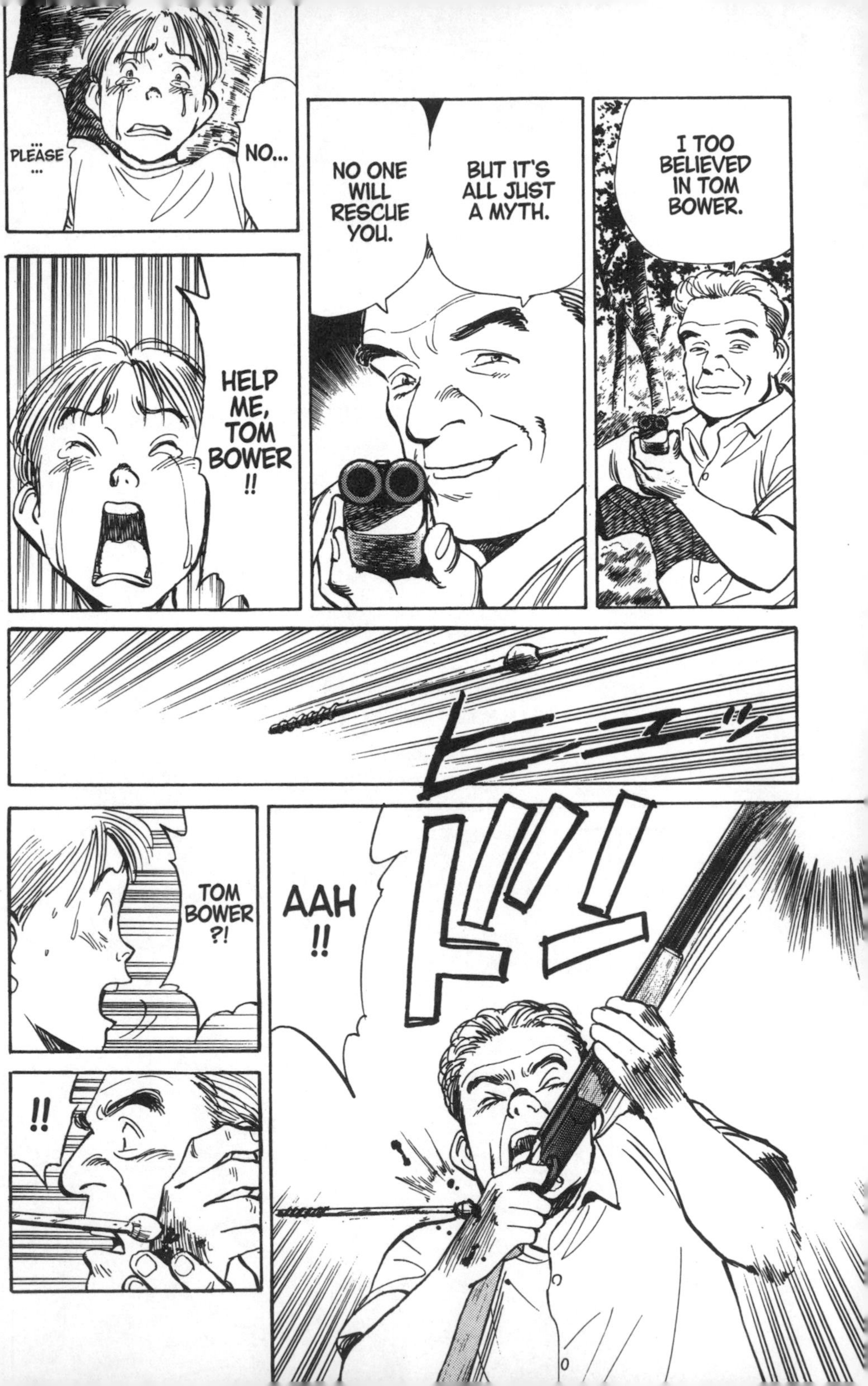
I TOO BELIEVED IN TOM BOWER.
BUT IT'S ALL JUST A MYTH.
NO ONE WILL RESCUE YOU.
NO...
... PLEASE ...
HELP ME, TOM BOWER !!
ヒューッ
ドン
AAH !!
TOM BOWER ?!
!!

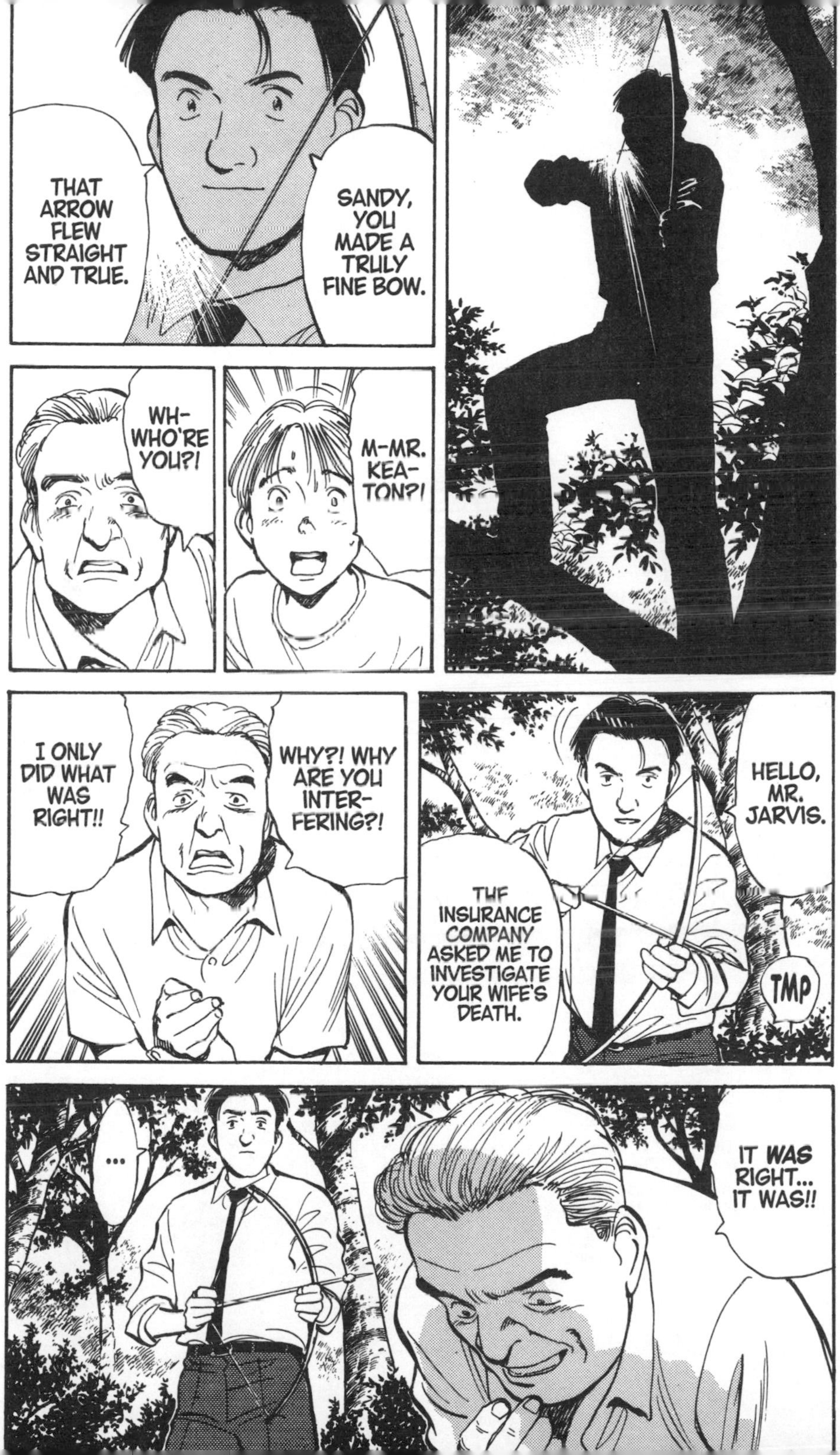
SANDY, YOU MADE A TRULY FINE BOW.
THAT ARROW FLEW STRAIGHT AND TRUE.
M-MR. KEA-TON?!
WH-WHO'RE YOU?!
HELLO, MR. JARVIS.
THE INSURANCE COMPANY ASKED ME TO INVESTIGATE YOUR WIFE'S DEATH.
TMP
WHY?! WHY ARE YOU INTER-FERING?!
I ONLY DID WHAT WAS RIGHT!!
IT WAS RIGHT... IT WAS!!
...

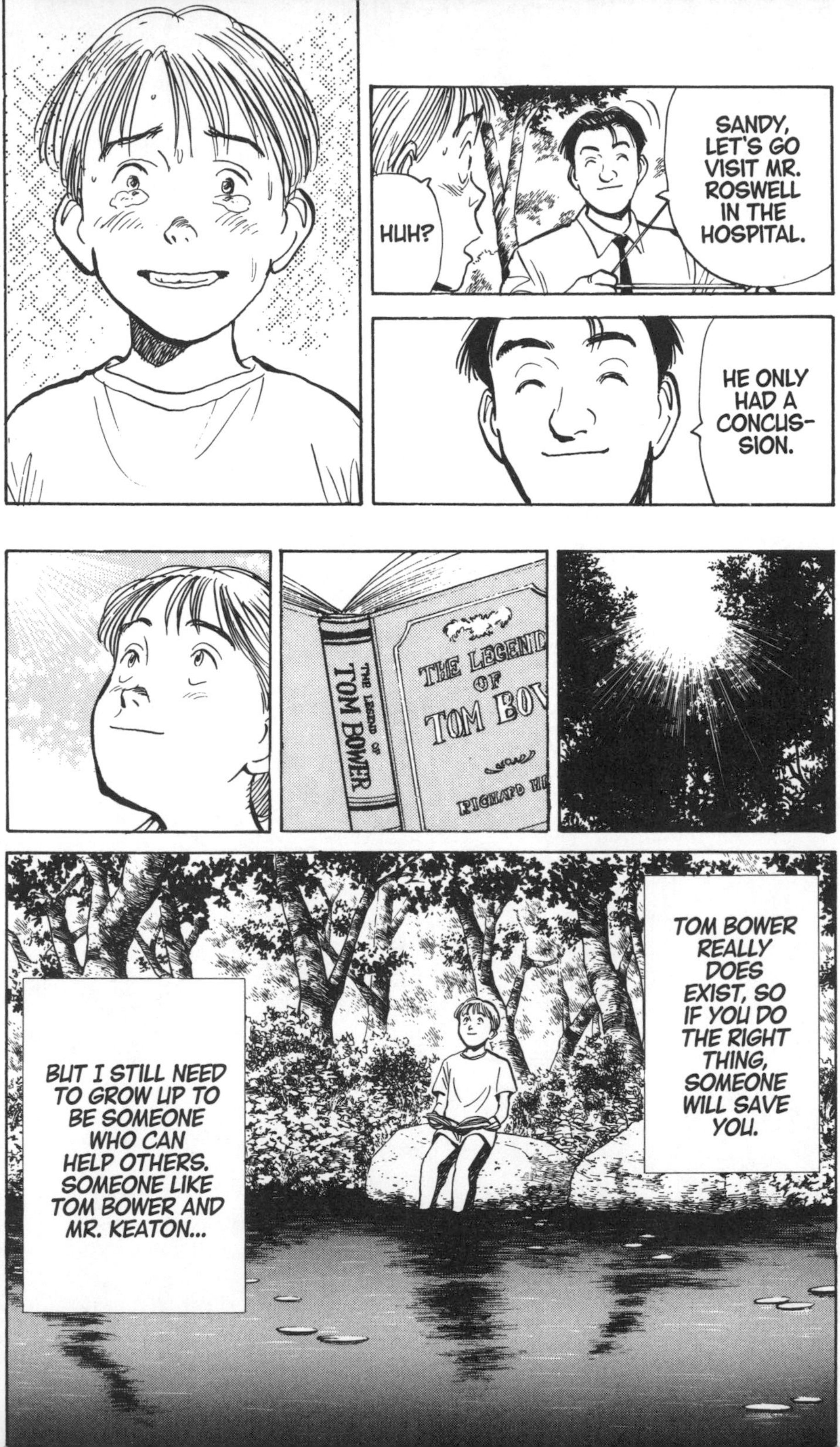
SANDY, LET'S GO VISIT MR. ROSWELL IN THE HOSPITAL.
HUH?
HE ONLY HAD A CONCUS-SION.
THE LEGEND OF TOM BOWER
TOM BOWER REALLY DOES EXIST, SO IF YOU DO THE RIGHT THING, SOMEONE WILL SAVE YOU.
BUT I STILL NEED TO GROW UP TO BE SOMEONE WHO CAN HELP OTHERS. SOMEONE LIKE TOM BOWER AND MR. KEATON...

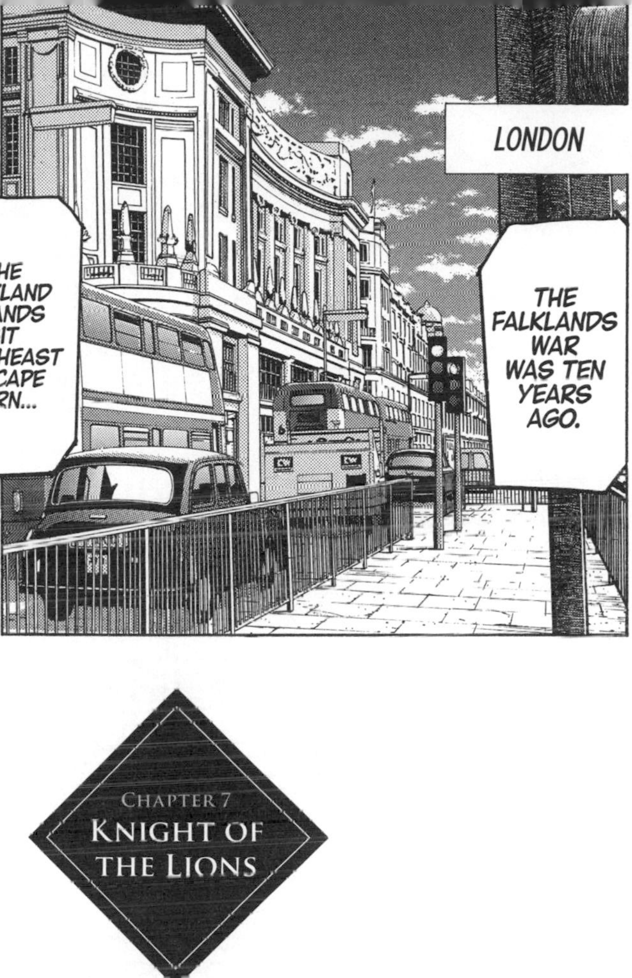
LONDON
THE FALKLANDS WAR WAS TEN YEARS AGO.

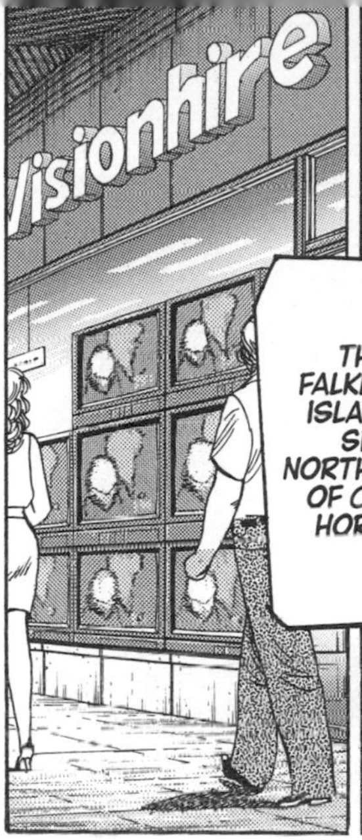
Visionhire
THE FALKLAND ISLANDS SIT NORTHEAST OF CAPE HORN...

CHAPTER 7
KNIGHT OF THE LIONS

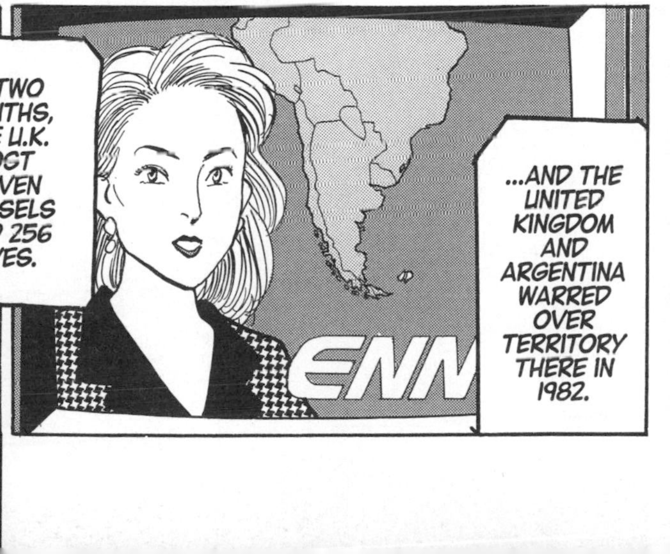
...AND THE UNITED KINGDOM AND ARGENTINA WARRED OVER TERRITORY THERE IN 1982.
IN TWO MONTHS, THE U.K. LOST SEVEN VESSELS AND 256 LIVES.
ENN

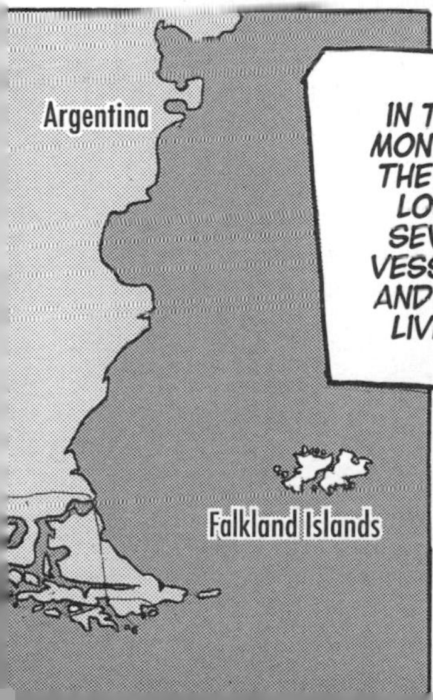
Argentina
Falkland Islands

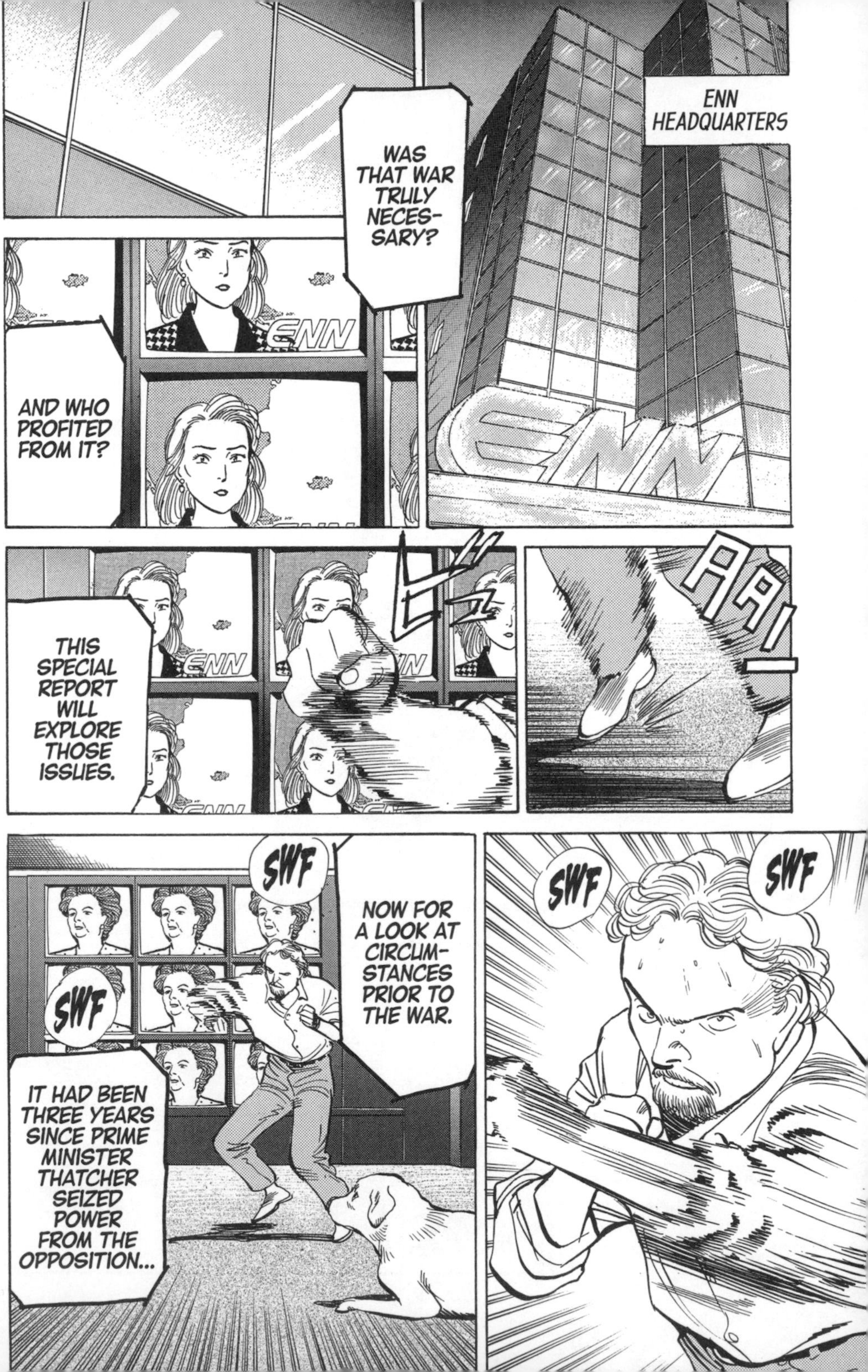
ENN HEADQUARTERS
WAS THAT WAR TRULY NECES-SARY?
AND WHO PROFITED FROM IT?
AAI
THIS SPECIAL REPORT WILL EXPLORE THOSE ISSUES.
SWF
SWF
SWF
NOW FOR A LOOK AT CIRCUM-STANCES PRIOR TO THE WAR.
SWF
IT HAD BEEN THREE YEARS SINCE PRIME MINISTER THATCHER SEIZED POWER FROM THE OPPOSITION...

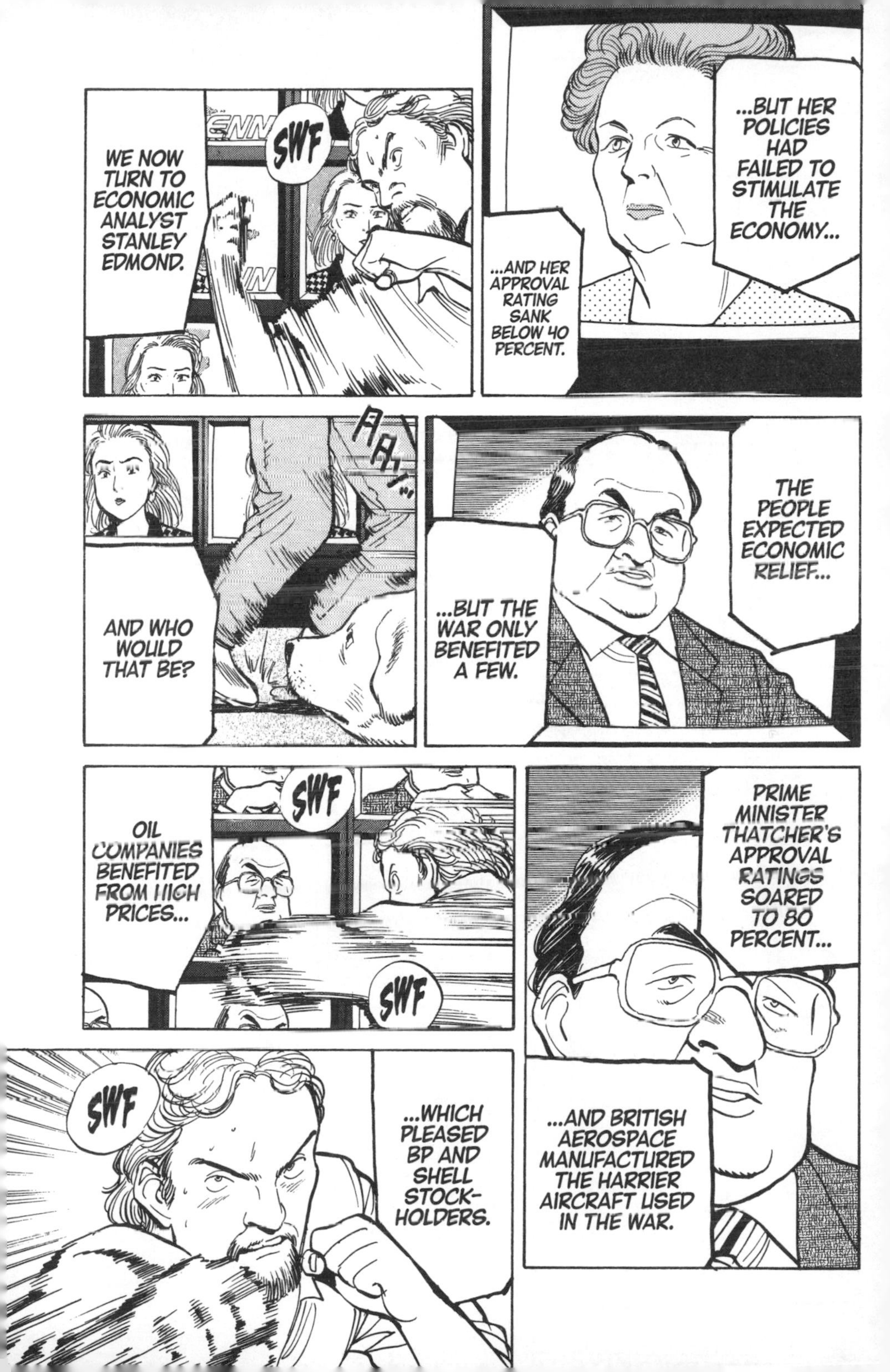
...BUT HER POLICIES HAD FAILED TO STIMULATE THE ECONOMY...
...AND HER APPROVAL RATING SANK BELOW 40 PERCENT.
WE NOW TURN TO ECONOMIC ANALYST STANLEY EDMOND.
SWF
THE PEOPLE EXPECTED ECONOMIC RELIEF...
...BUT THE WAR ONLY BENEFITED A FEW.
AAA!...
AND WHO WOULD THAT BE?
PRIME MINISTER THATCHER'S APPROVAL RATINGS SOARED TO 80 PERCENT...
...AND BRITISH AEROSPACE MANUFACTURED THE HARRIER AIRCRAFT USED IN THE WAR.
SWF
OIL COMPANIES BENEFITED FROM HIGH PRICES...
SWF
SWF
...WHICH PLEASED BP AND SHELL STOCK-HOLDERS.

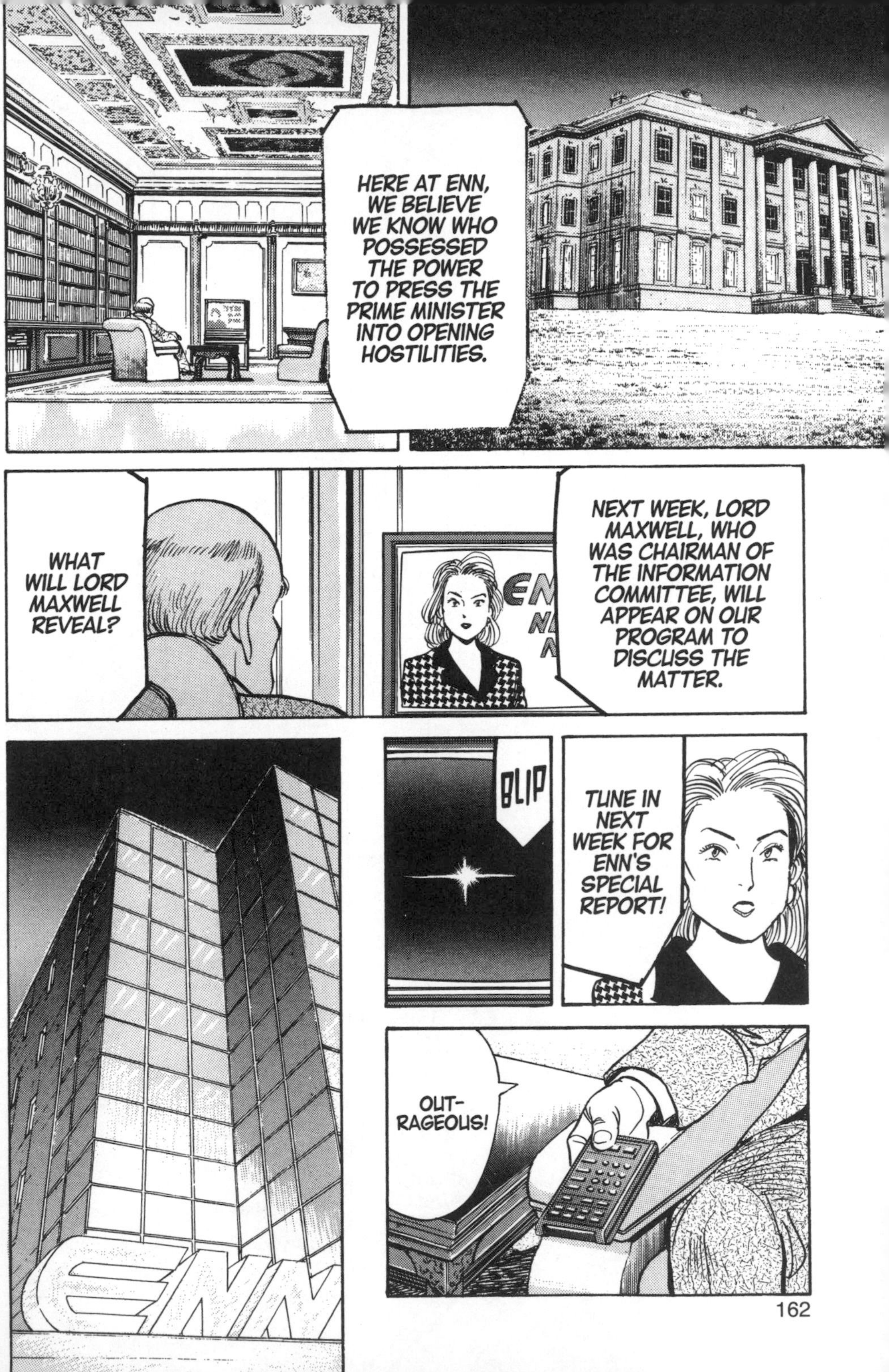
HERE AT ENN, WE BELIEVE WE KNOW WHO POSSESSED THE POWER TO PRESS THE PRIME MINISTER INTO OPENING HOSTILITIES.
NEXT WEEK, LORD MAXWELL, WHO WAS CHAIRMAN OF THE INFORMATION COMMITTEE, WILL APPEAR ON OUR PROGRAM TO DISCUSS THE MATTER.
WHAT WILL LORD MAXWELL REVEAL?
TUNE IN NEXT WEEK FOR ENN'S SPECIAL REPORT!
BLIP
OUT-RAGEOUS!

IT'S ALMOST TIME, LOUIS.
THIS IS THE BEGINNING!
PRESI-DENT LESTER?
WHY THE LONG FACE, MORRIS?
WE JUST THREW DOWN THE GAUNTLET!
I HATE TO TELL YOU THIS...
...BUT LORD MAXWELL IS DEAD.
WHAT...?

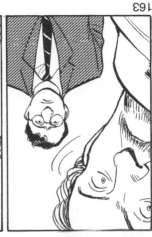

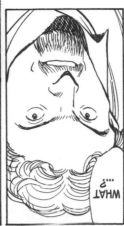

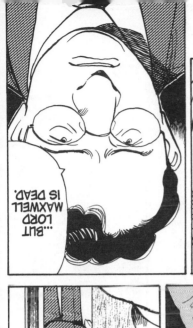

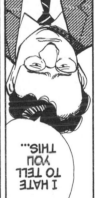

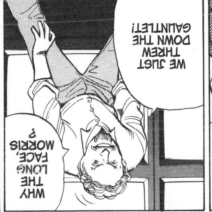

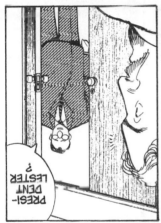

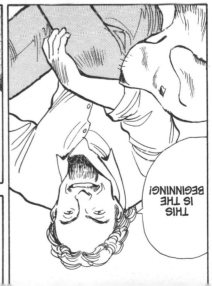

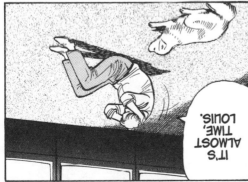

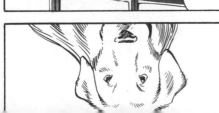

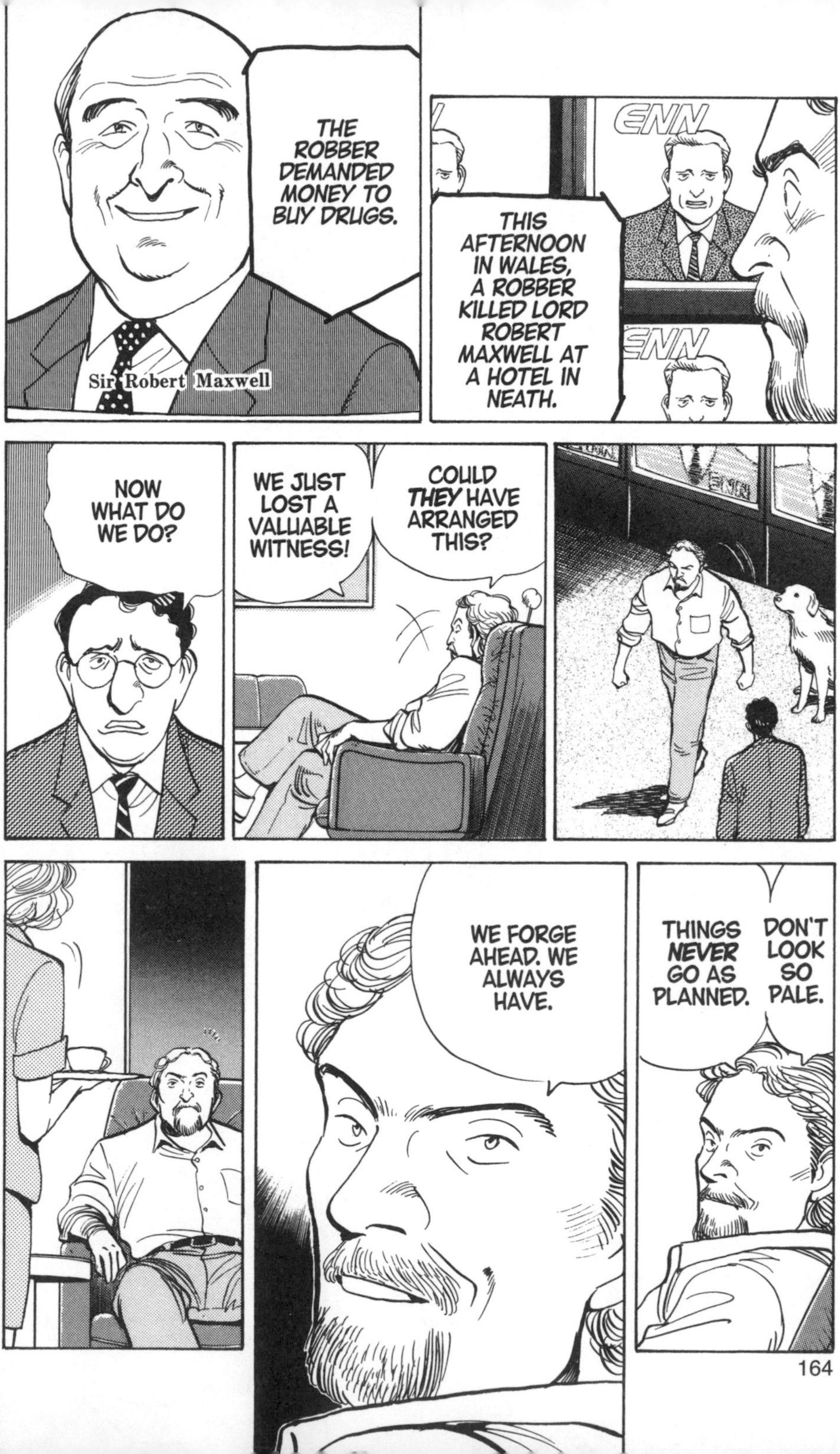
ENN
THIS AFTERNOON IN WALES, A ROBBER KILLED LORD ROBERT MAXWELL AT A HOTEL IN NEATH.
ENN
THE ROBBER DEMANDED MONEY TO BUY DRUGS.
Sir Robert Maxwell
COULD *THEY* HAVE ARRANGED THIS?
WE JUST LOST A VALLIABLE WITNESS!
NOW WHAT DO WE DO?
DON'T LOOK SO PALE.
THINGS *NEVER* GO AS PLANNED.
WE FORGE AHEAD. WE ALWAYS HAVE.

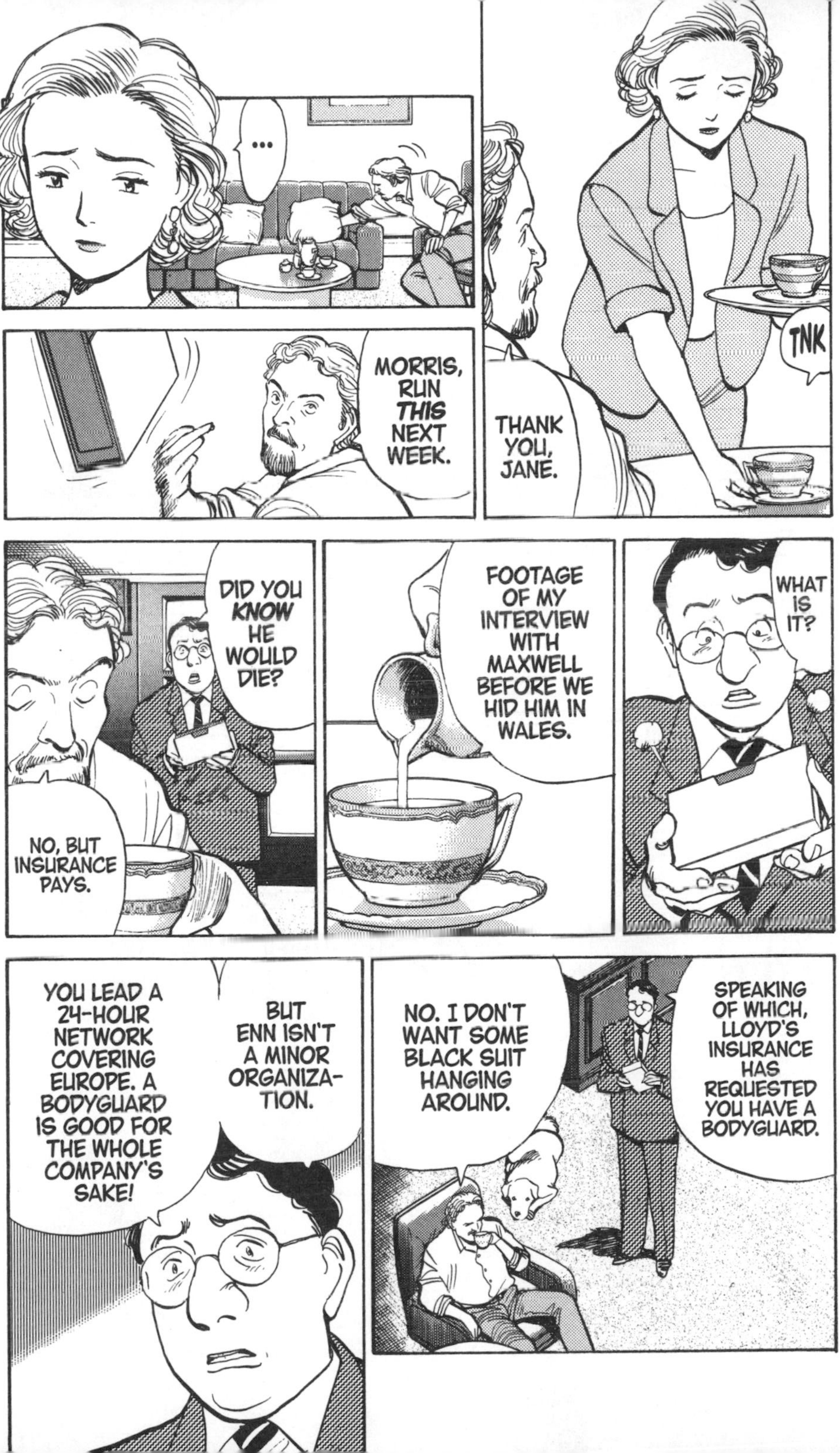

TNK
THANK YOU, JANE.
...
MORRIS, RUN *THIS* NEXT WEEK.
WHAT IS IT?
FOOTAGE OF MY INTERVIEW WITH MAXWELL BEFORE WE HID HIM IN WALES.
DID YOU *KNOW* HE WOULD DIE?
NO, BUT INSURANCE PAYS.
SPEAKING OF WHICH, LLOYD'S INSURANCE HAS REQUESTED YOU HAVE A BODYGUARD.
NO. I DON'T WANT SOME BLACK SUIT HANGING AROUND.
BUT ENN ISN'T A MINOR ORGANIZA-TION.
YOU LEAD A 24-HOUR NETWORK COVERING EUROPE. A BODYGUARD IS GOOD FOR THE WHOLE COMPANY'S SAKE!

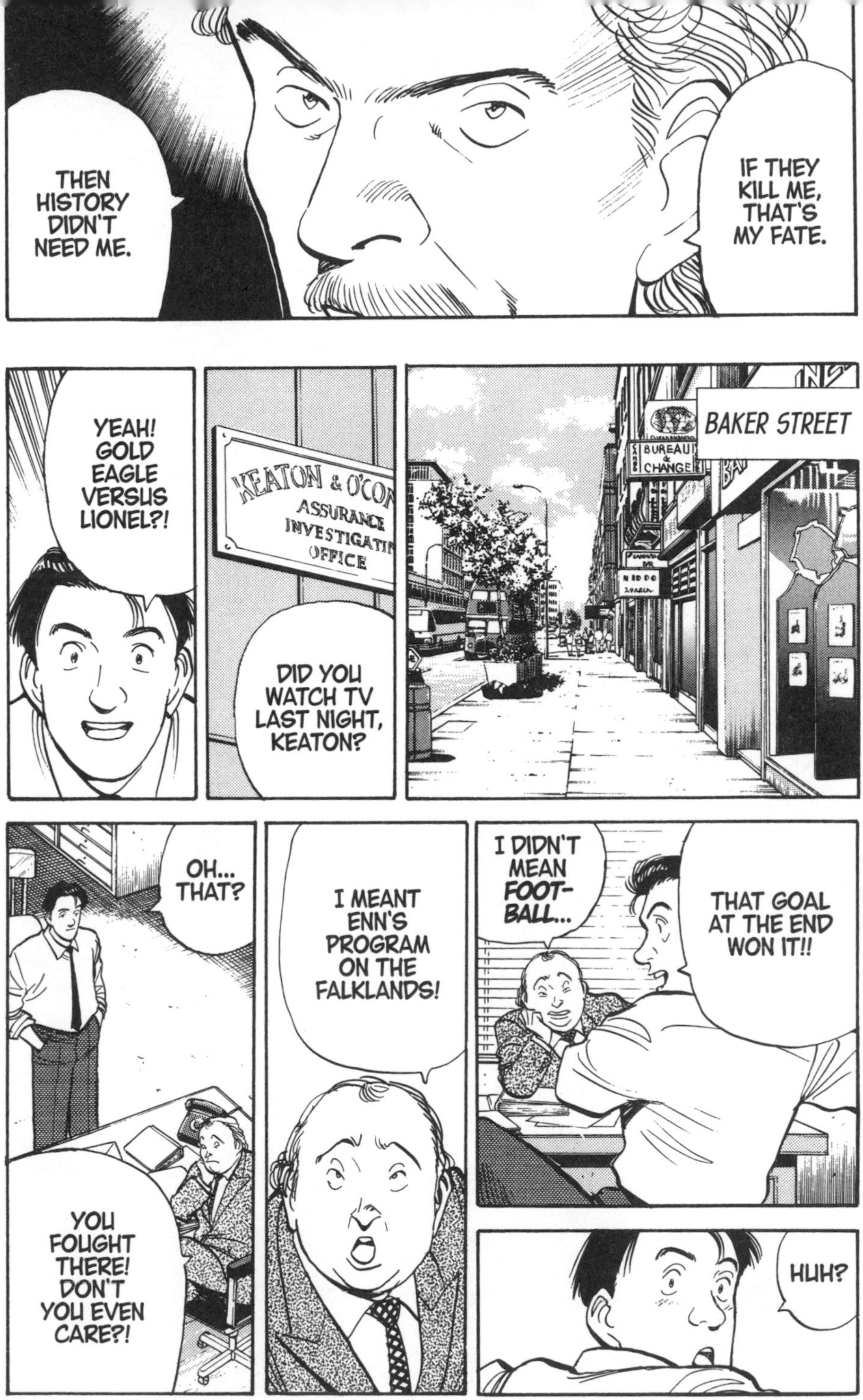
IF THEY KILL ME, THAT'S MY FATE.
THEN HISTORY DIDN'T NEED ME.
BAKER STREET
BUREAU & CHANGE
KEATON & O'CON
ASSURANCE INVESTIGATI
OFFICE
DID YOU WATCH TV LAST NIGHT, KEATON?
YEAH! GOLD EAGLE VERSUS LIONEL?!
THAT GOAL AT THE END WON IT!!
I DIDN'T MEAN FOOT-BALL...
HUH?
I MEANT ENN'S PROGRAM ON THE FALKLANDS!
OH... THAT?
YOU FOUGHT THERE! DON'T YOU EVEN CARE?!

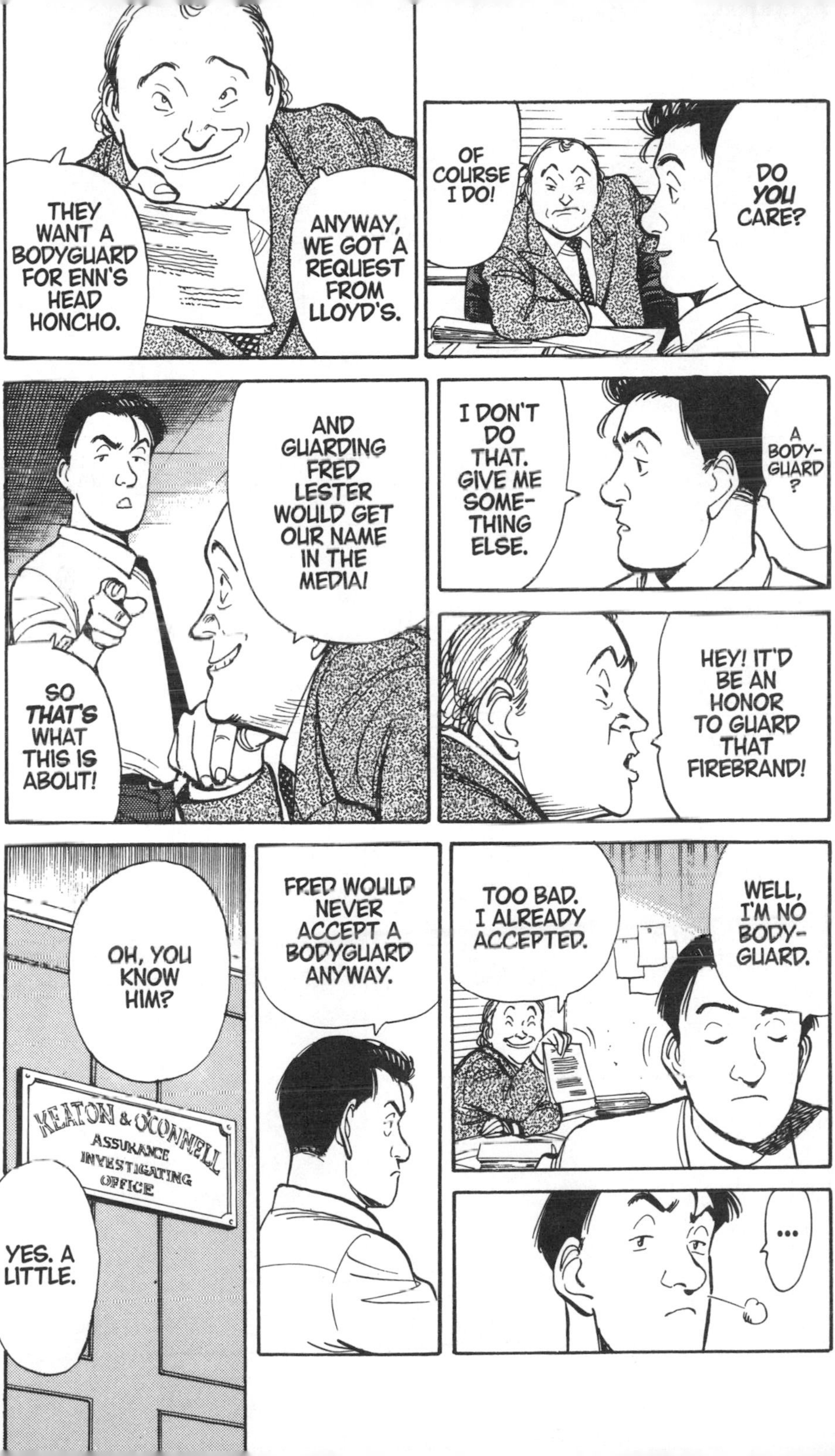
DO YOU CARE?
OF COURSE I DO!
ANYWAY, WE GOT A REQUEST FROM LLOYD'S.
THEY WANT A BODYGUARD FOR ENN'S HEAD HONCHO.
A BODY-GUARD?
I DON'T DO THAT. GIVE ME SOME-THING ELSE.
HEY! IT'D BE AN HONOR TO GUARD THAT FIREBRAND!
AND GUARDING FRED LESTER WOULD GET OUR NAME IN THE MEDIA!
SO THAT'S WHAT THIS IS ABOUT!
WELL, I'M NO BODY-GUARD.
TOO BAD. I ALREADY ACCEPTED.
...
FRED WOULD NEVER ACCEPT A BODYGUARD ANYWAY.
OH, YOU KNOW HIM?
KEATON & O'CONNELL
ASSURANCE INVESTIGATING OFFICE
YES. A LITTLE.

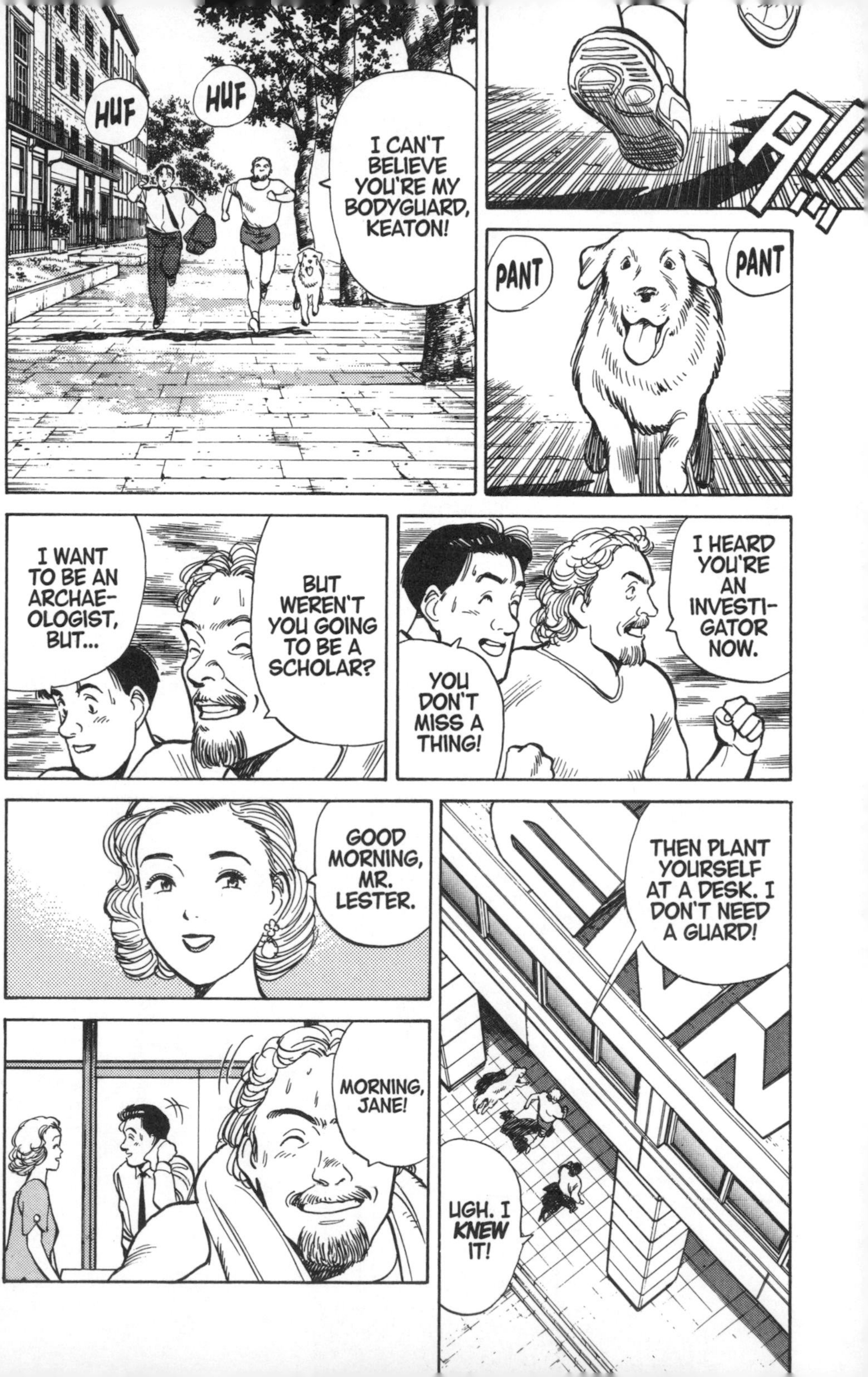
PANT
PANT
HUF
HUF
I CAN'T BELIEVE YOU'RE MY BODYGUARD, KEATON!
I HEARD YOU'RE AN INVESTI-GATOR NOW.
YOU DON'T MISS A THING!
BUT WEREN'T YOU GOING TO BE A SCHOLAR?
I WANT TO BE AN ARCHAE-OLOGIST, BUT...
THEN PLANT YOURSELF AT A DESK. I DON'T NEED A GUARD!
UGH. I KNEW IT!
GOOD MORNING, MR. LESTER.
MORNING, JANE!

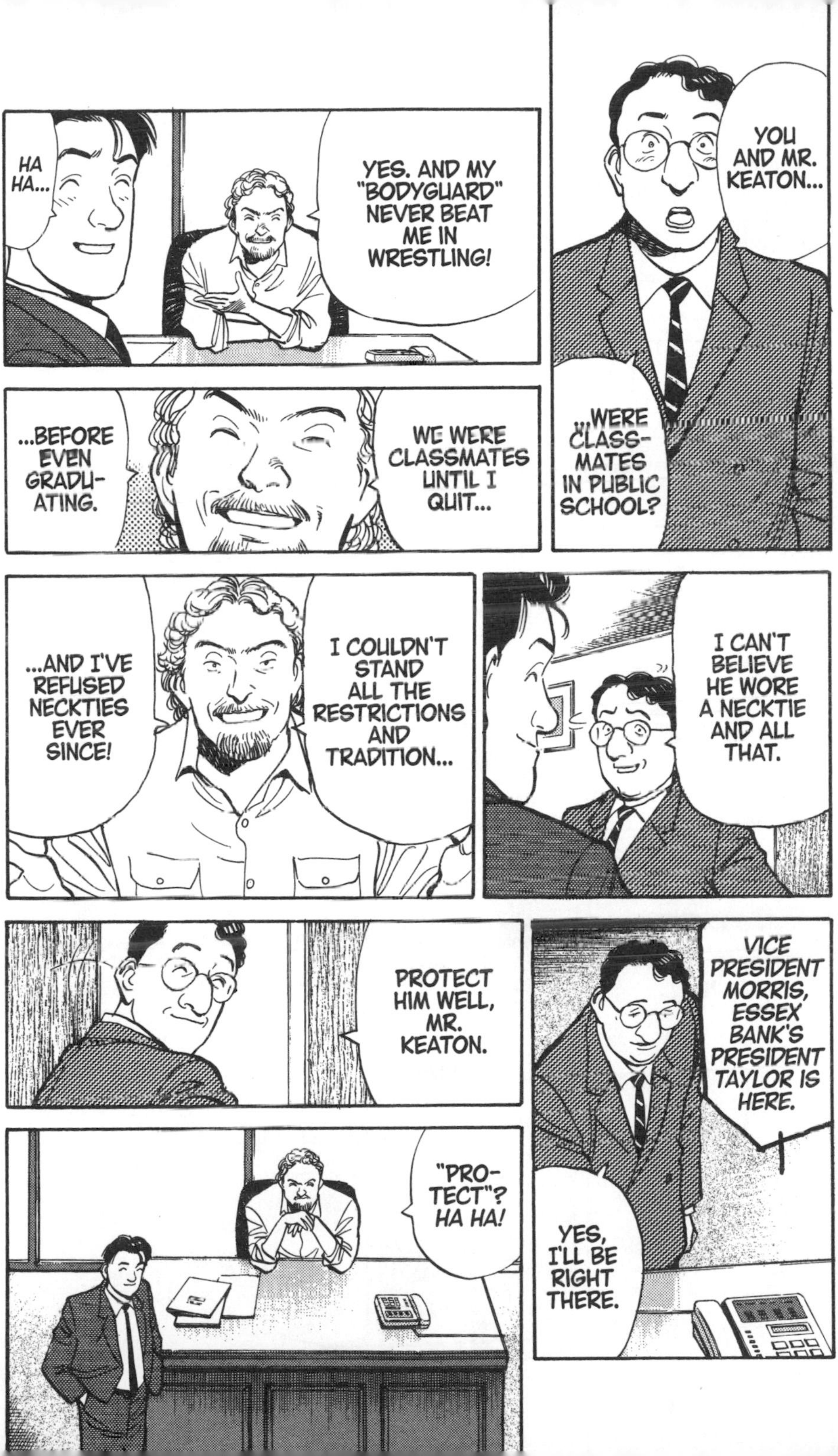
YOU AND MR. KEATON...
...WERE CLASS-MATES IN PUBLIC SCHOOL?
YES. AND MY "BODYGUARD" NEVER BEAT ME IN WRESTLING!
HA HA...
WE WERE CLASSMATES UNTIL I QUIT...
...BEFORE EVEN GRADU-ATING.
I CAN'T BELIEVE HE WORE A NECKTIE AND ALL THAT.
I COULDN'T STAND ALL THE RESTRICTIONS AND TRADITION...
...AND I'VE REFUSED NECKTIES EVER SINCE!
VICE PRESIDENT MORRIS, ESSEX BANK'S PRESIDENT TAYLOR IS HERE.
YES, I'LL BE RIGHT THERE.
PROTECT HIM WELL, MR. KEATON.
"PRO-TECT"? HA HA!

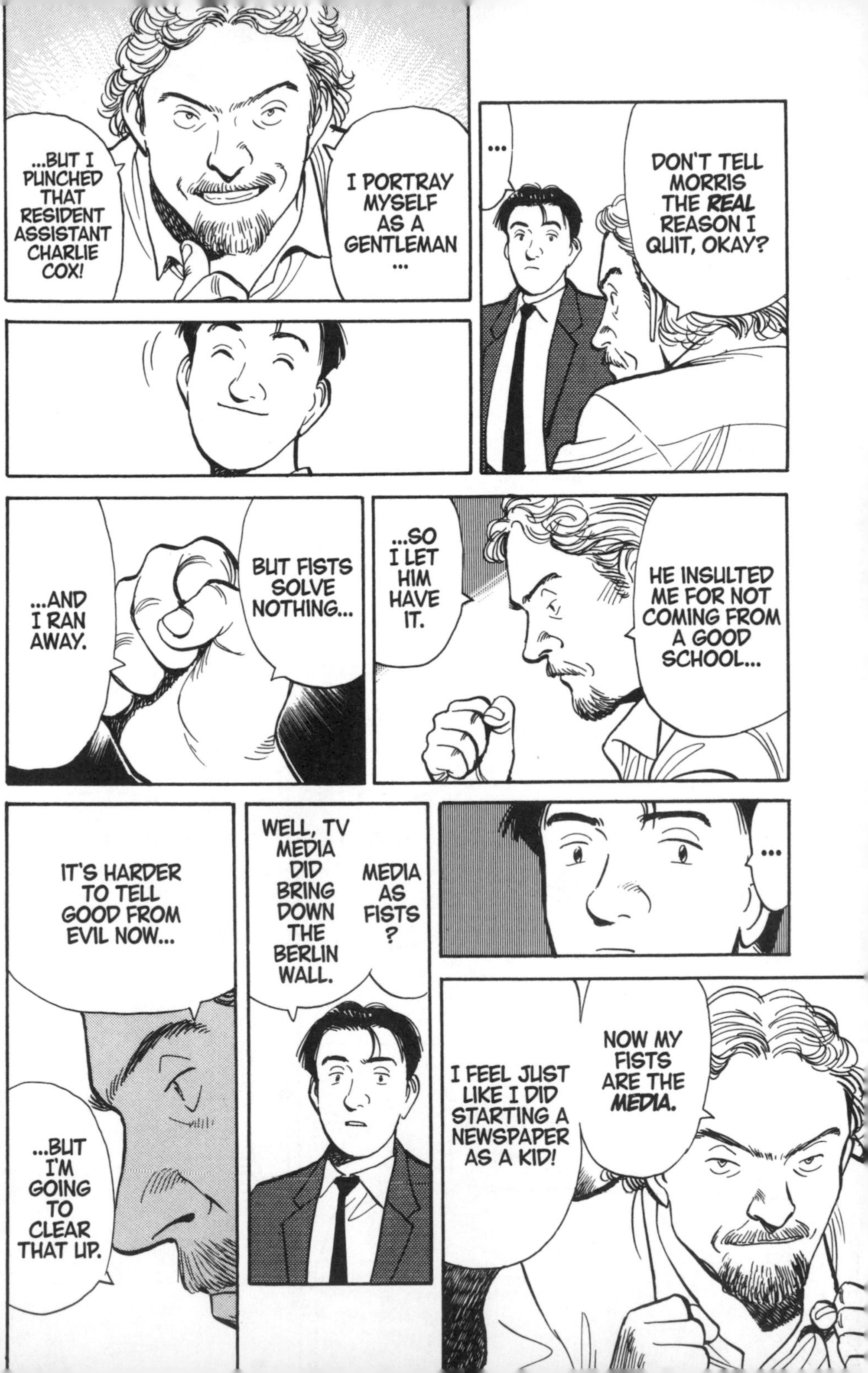
DON'T TELL MORRIS THE REAL REASON I QUIT, OKAY?
...
I PORTRAY MYSELF AS A GENTLEMAN ...
...BUT I PUNCHED THAT RESIDENT ASSISTANT CHARLIE COX!
HE INSULTED ME FOR NOT COMING FROM A GOOD SCHOOL...
...SO I LET HIM HAVE IT.
BUT FISTS SOLVE NOTHING...
...AND I RAN AWAY.
...
NOW MY FISTS ARE THE MEDIA.
I FEEL JUST LIKE I DID STARTING A NEWSPAPER AS A KID!
MEDIA AS FISTS?
WELL, TV MEDIA DID BRING DOWN THE BERLIN WALL.
IT'S HARDER TO TELL GOOD FROM EVIL NOW...
...BUT I'M GOING TO CLEAR THAT UP.

BY USING THE MEDIA LIKE FISTS!
...
WHENEVER I DEFIED THE OLDER STUDENTS, YOU COMPARED ME TO DON QUIXOTE.
OH... DID I?
I AM A BIT LIKE DON QUIXOTE ...
...AND I TAKE IT AS A COMPLI-MENT.
BUT I HAVE TO KEEP FIGHTING!
I UNDERSTAND WHY YOU'RE PRODUCING THIS SPECIAL REPORT...
YEAH, BUT I'M USED TO TROUBLE.
BE MY FRIEND INSTEAD OF MY GUARD, ALL RIGHT?
NOK NOK
...BUT OTHERS WON'T BE SO PLEASED.
MR. LESTER, YOU SHOULD TALK TO MR. TAYLOR.

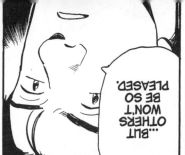

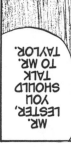

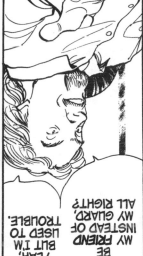

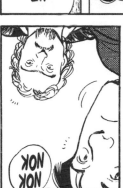

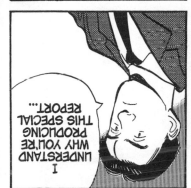

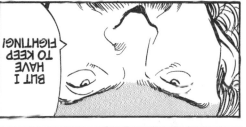

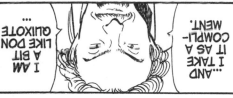

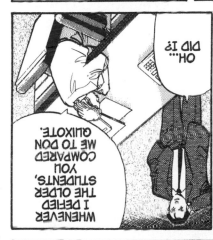

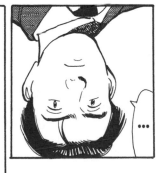

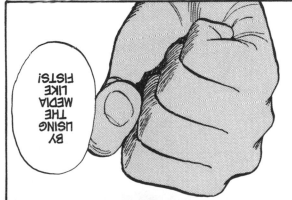

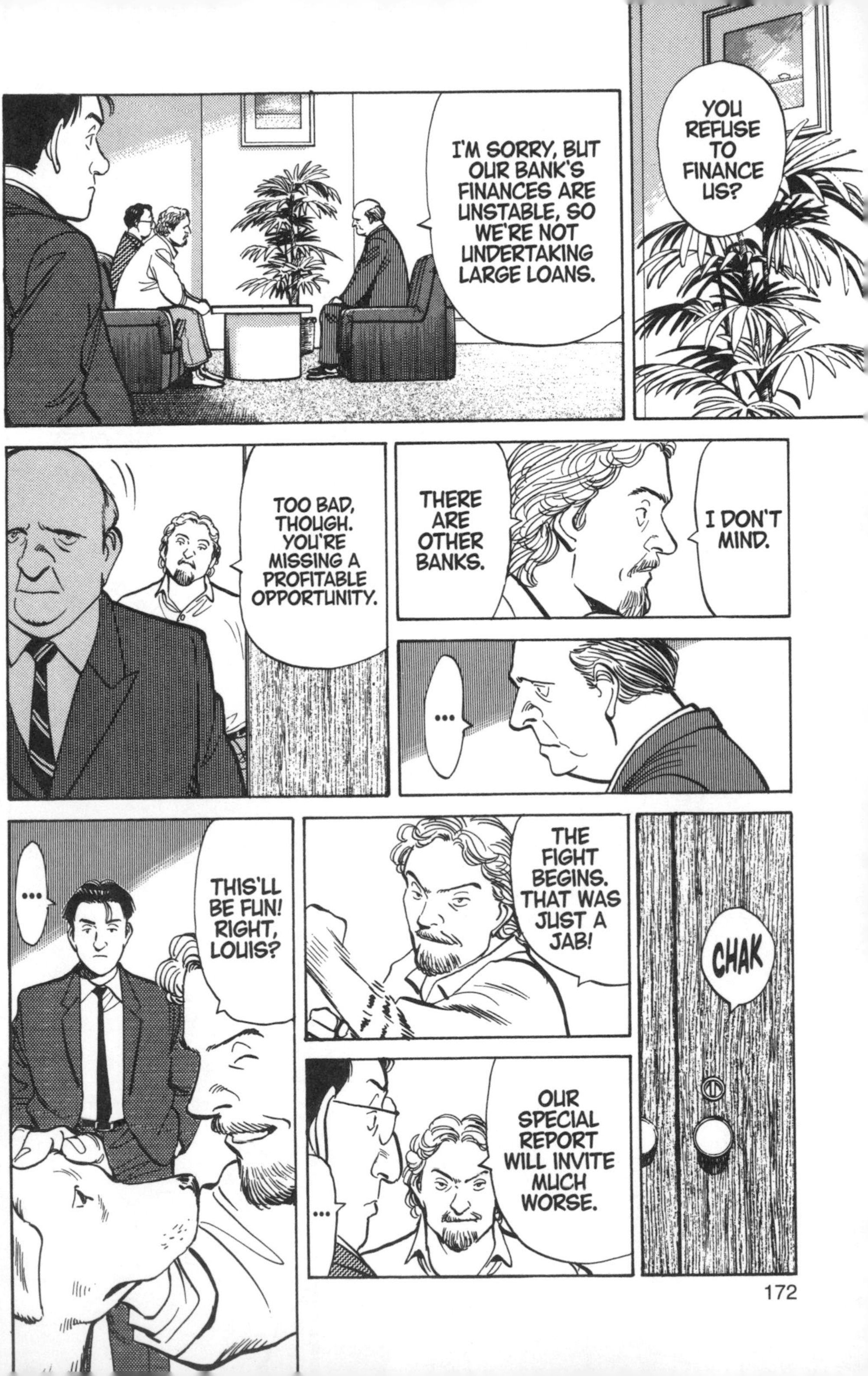
YOU REFUSE TO FINANCE US?
I'M SORRY, BUT OUR BANK'S FINANCES ARE UNSTABLE, SO WE'RE NOT UNDERTAKING LARGE LOANS.
I DON'T MIND.
THERE ARE OTHER BANKS.
...
TOO BAD, THOUGH. YOU'RE MISSING A PROFITABLE OPPORTUNITY.
CHAK
THE FIGHT BEGINS. THAT WAS JUST A JAB!
OUR SPECIAL REPORT WILL INVITE MUCH WORSE.
...
THIS'LL BE FUN! RIGHT, LOUIS?
...

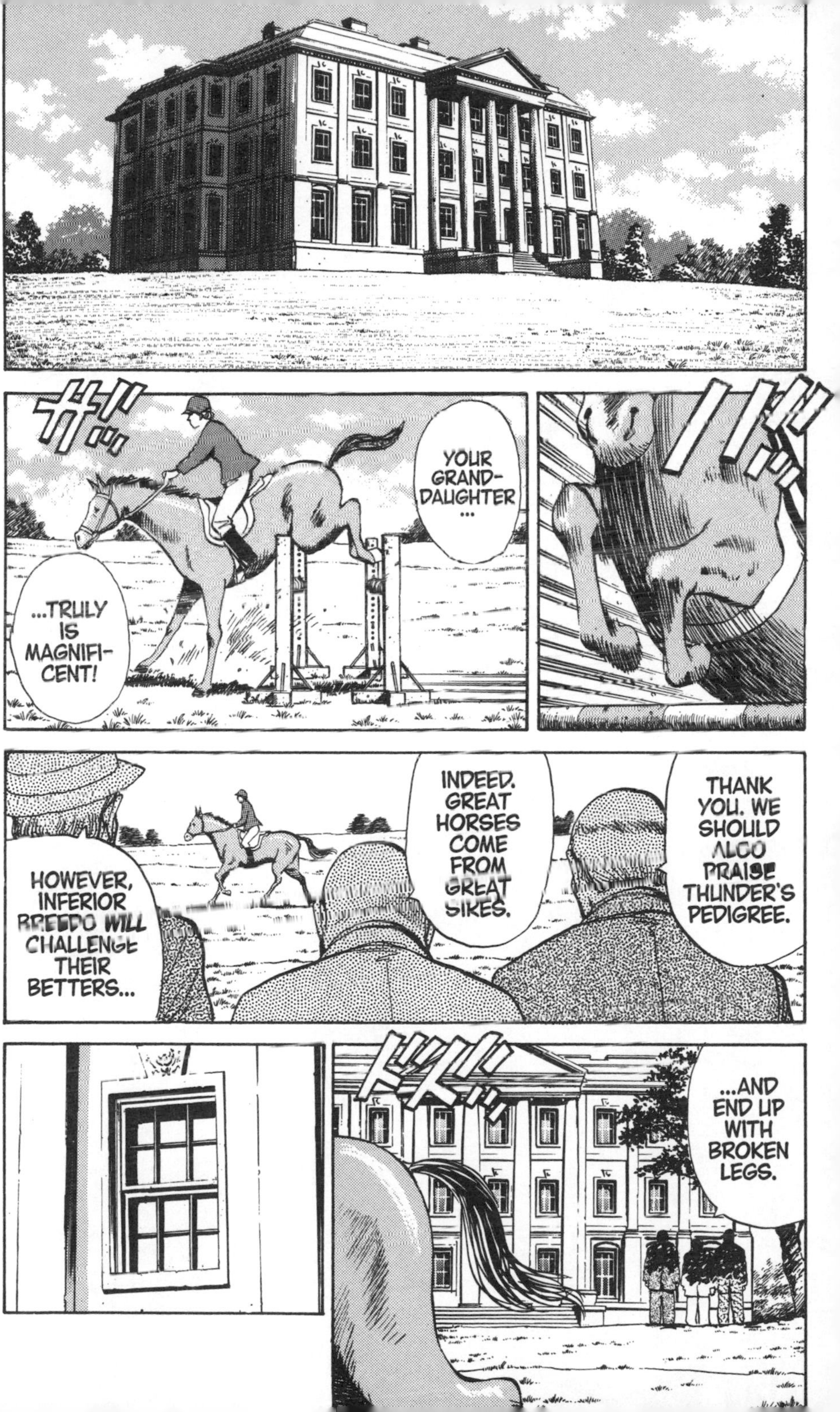
YOUR GRAND-DAUGHTER...
...TRULY IS MAGNIFI-CENT!
THANK YOU. WE SHOULD ALSO PRAISE THUNDER'S PEDIGREE.
INDEED. GREAT HORSES COME FROM GREAT SIRES.
HOWEVER, INFERIOR BREEDS WILL CHALLENGE THEIR BETTERS...
...AND END UP WITH BROKEN LEGS.

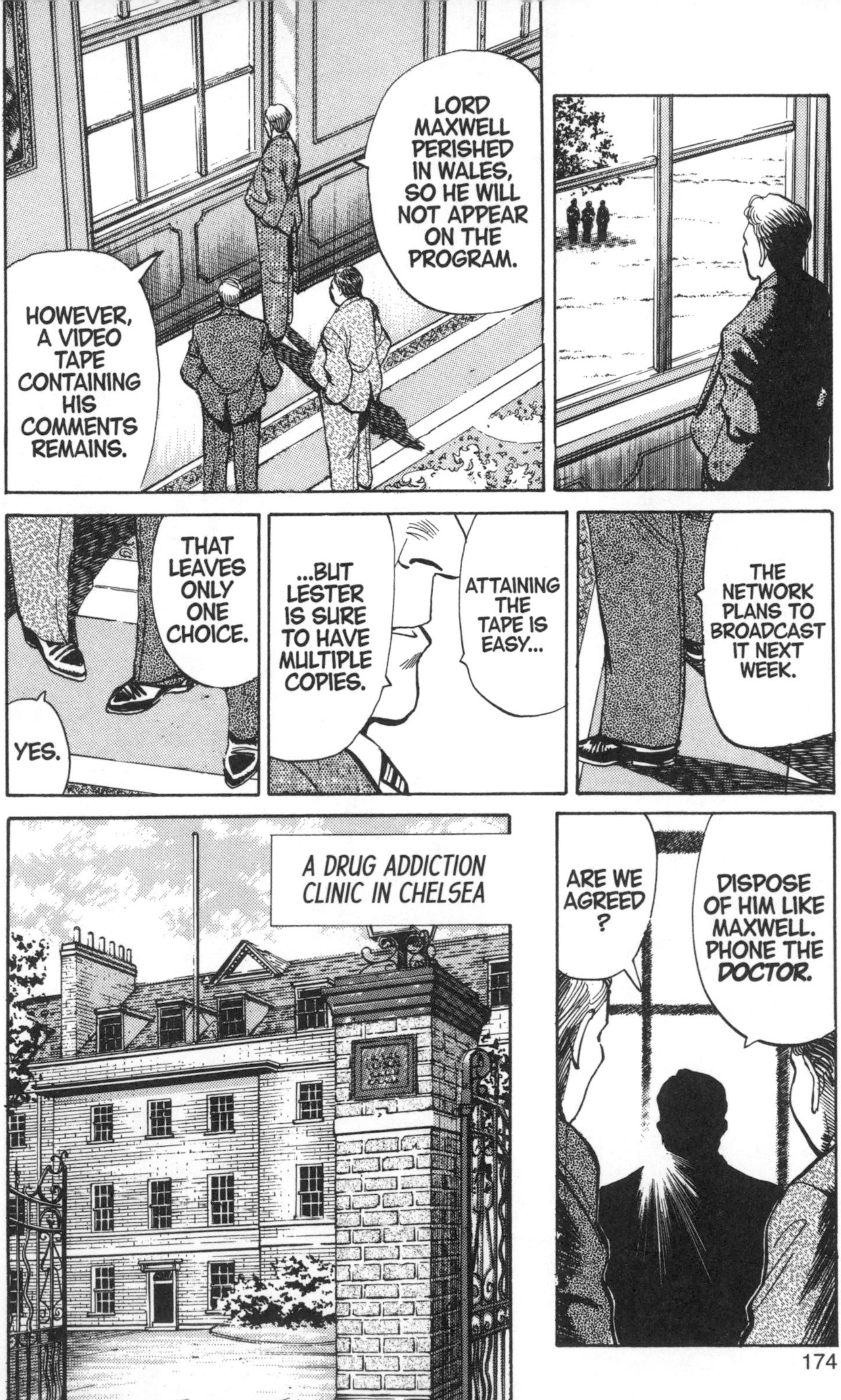
LORD MAXWELL PERISHED IN WALES, SO HE WILL NOT APPEAR ON THE PROGRAM.
HOWEVER, A VIDEO TAPE CONTAINING HIS COMMENTS REMAINS.
THE NETWORK PLANS TO BROADCAST IT NEXT WEEK.
ATTAINING THE TAPE IS EASY...
...BUT LESTER IS SURE TO HAVE MULTIPLE COPIES.
THAT LEAVES ONLY ONE CHOICE.
YES.
DISPOSE OF HIM LIKE MAXWELL. PHONE THE *DOCTOR.*
ARE WE AGREED?
A DRUG ADDICTION CLINIC IN CHELSEA

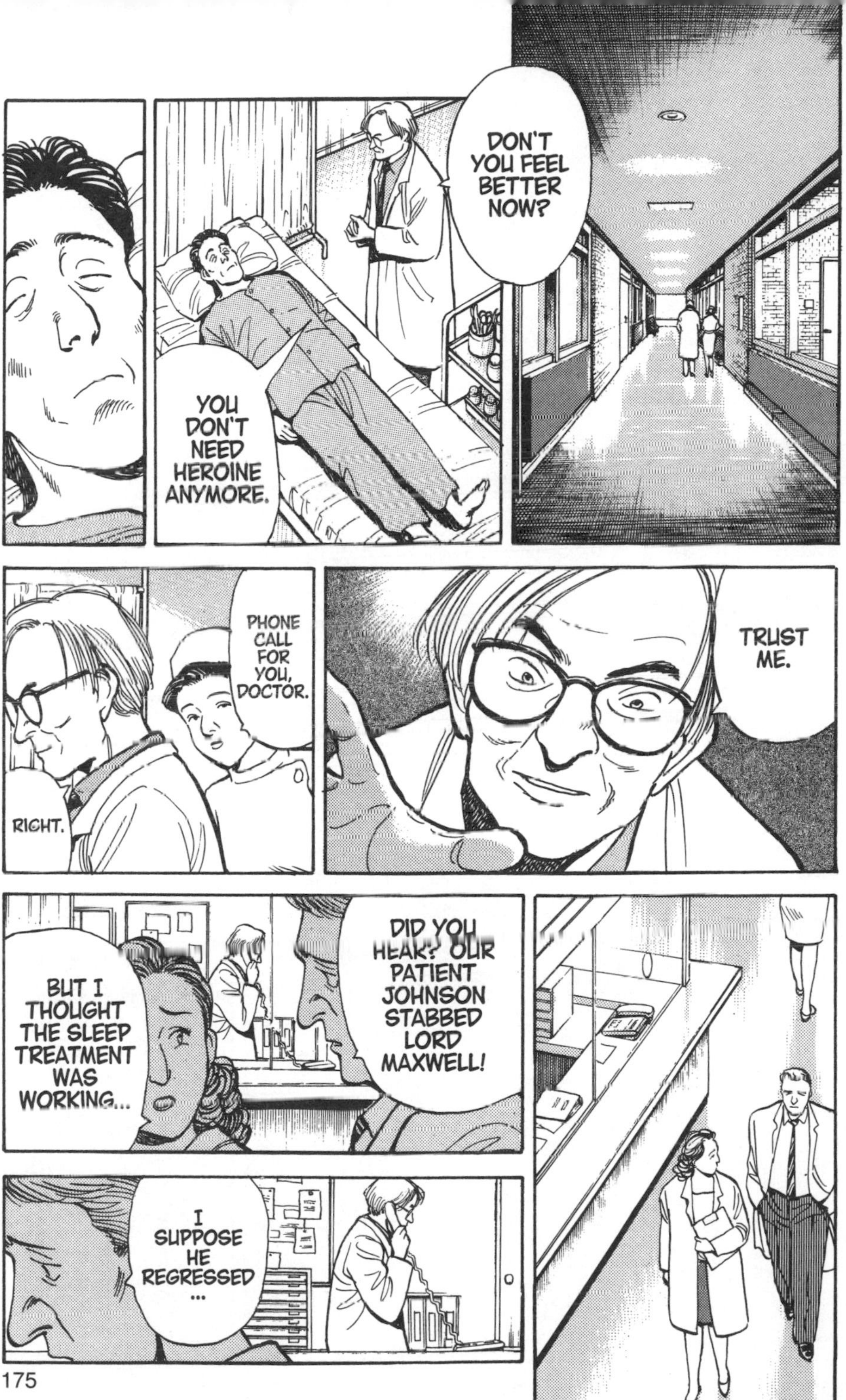
DON'T YOU FEEL BETTER NOW?
YOU DON'T NEED HEROINE ANYMORE.
TRUST ME.
PHONE CALL FOR YOU, DOCTOR.
RIGHT.
DID YOU HEAR? OUR PATIENT JOHNSON STABBED LORD MAXWELL!
BUT I THOUGHT THE SLEEP TREATMENT WAS WORKING...
I SUPPOSE HE REGRESSED ...

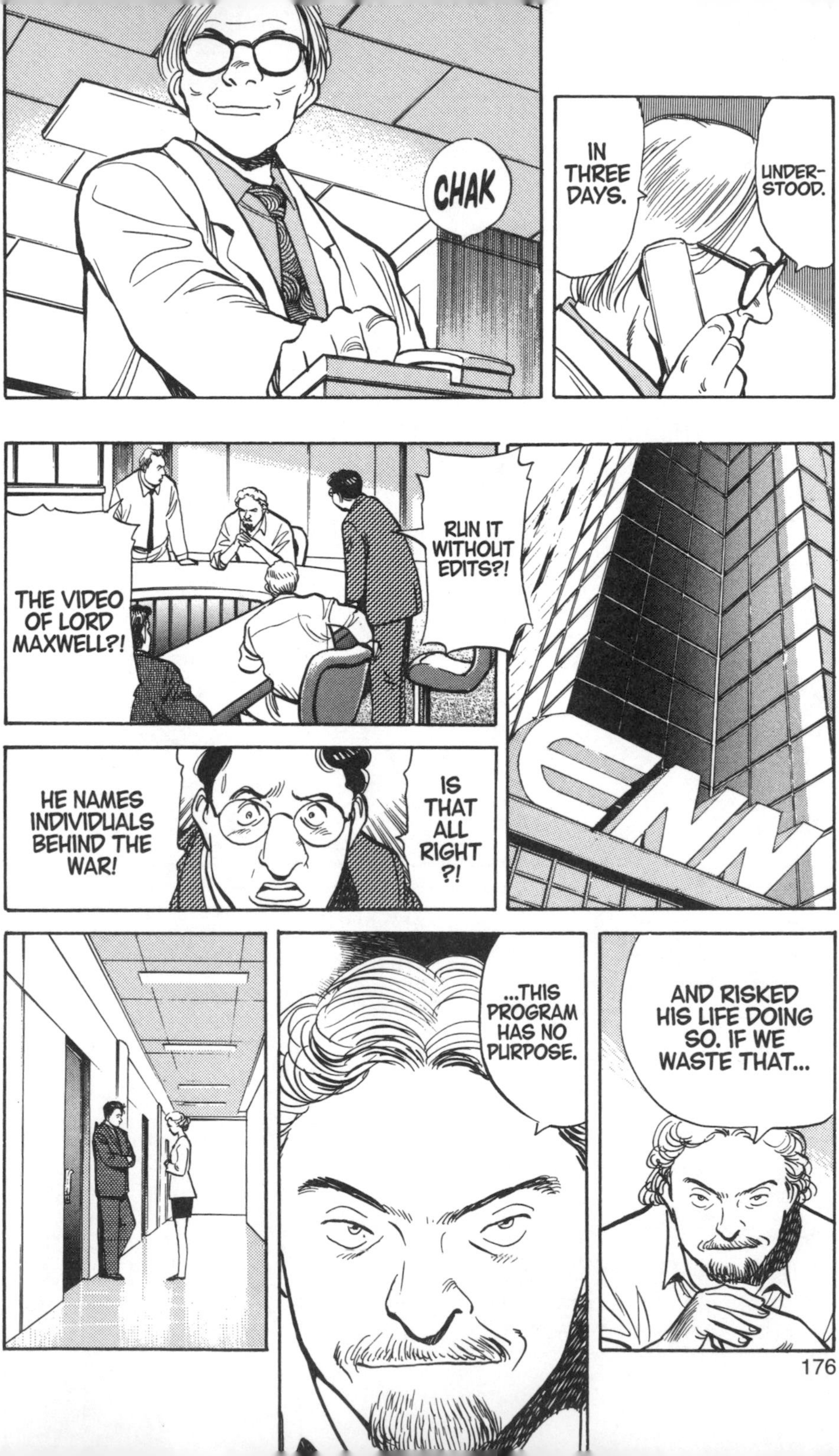
UNDER-STOOD.
IN THREE DAYS.
CHAK
RUN IT WITHOUT EDITS?!
THE VIDEO OF LORD MAXWELL?!
IS THAT ALL RIGHT?!
HE NAMES INDIVIDUALS BEHIND THE WAR!
AND RISKED HIS LIFE DOING SO. IF WE WASTE THAT...
...THIS PROGRAM HAS NO PURPOSE.

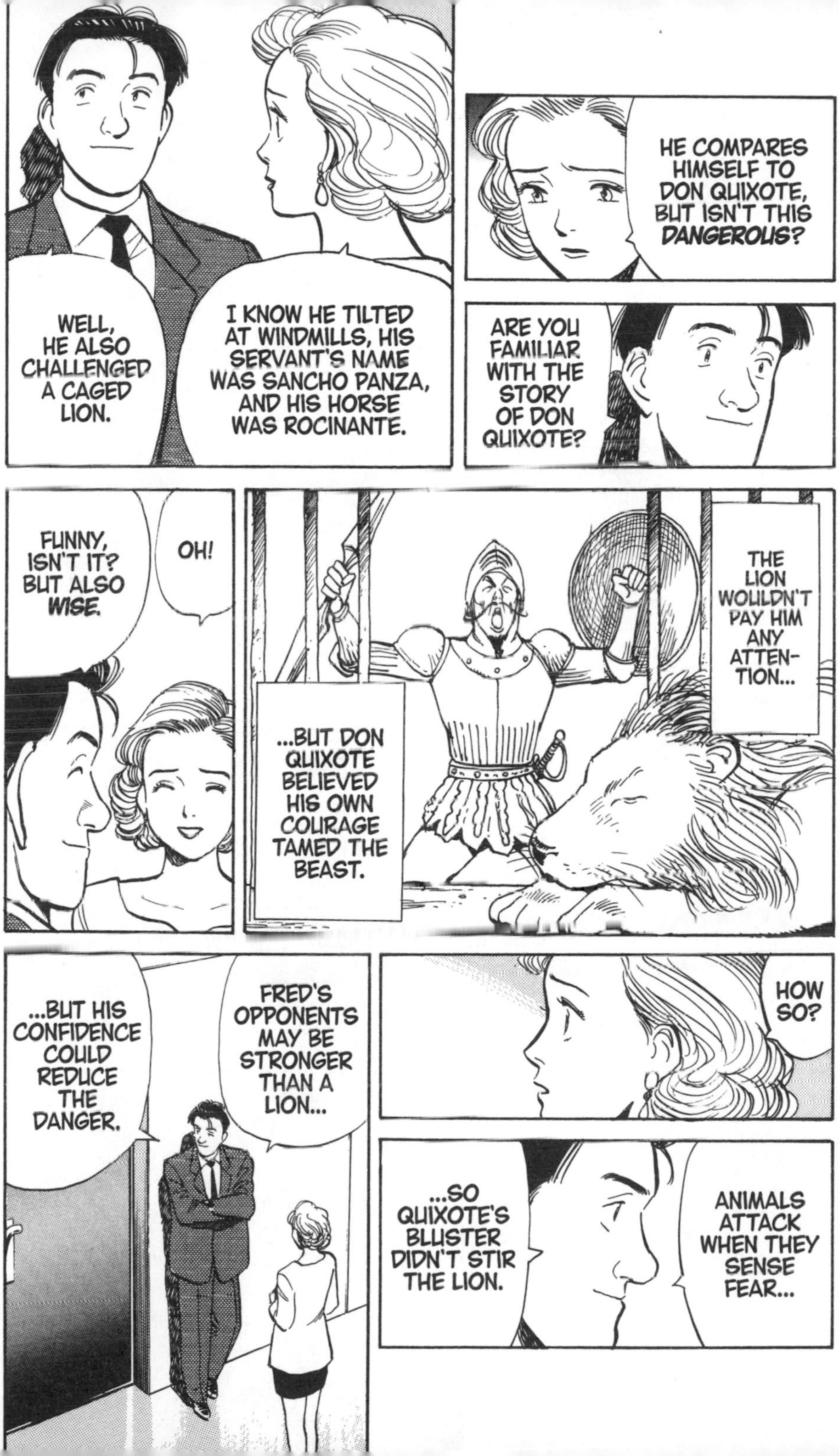
HE COMPARES HIMSELF TO DON QUIXOTE, BUT ISN'T THIS DANGEROUS?
ARE YOU FAMILIAR WITH THE STORY OF DON QUIXOTE?
I KNOW HE TILTED AT WINDMILLS, HIS SERVANT'S NAME WAS SANCHO PANZA, AND HIS HORSE WAS ROCINANTE.
WELL, HE ALSO CHALLENGED A CAGED LION.
THE LION WOULDN'T PAY HIM ANY ATTEN-TION...
...BUT DON QUIXOTE BELIEVED HIS OWN COURAGE TAMED THE BEAST.
OH!
FUNNY, ISN'T IT? BUT ALSO WISE.
HOW SO?
ANIMALS ATTACK WHEN THEY SENSE FEAR...
...SO QUIXOTE'S BLUSTER DIDN'T STIR THE LION.
FRED'S OPPONENTS MAY BE STRONGER THAN A LION...
...BUT HIS CONFIDENCE COULD REDUCE THE DANGER.

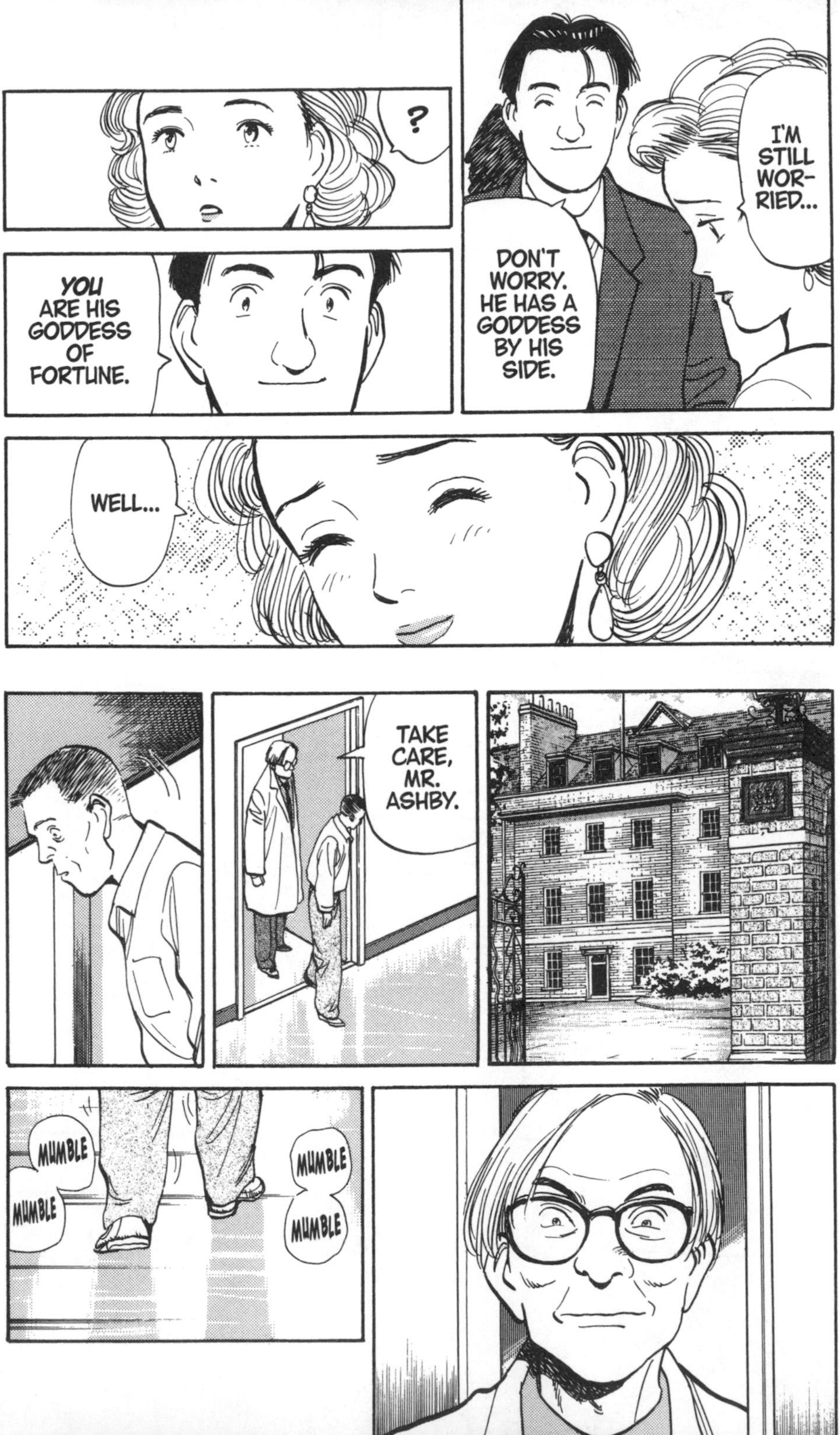
I'M STILL WORRIED...
DON'T WORRY. HE HAS A GODDESS BY HIS SIDE.
?
YOU ARE HIS GODDESS OF FORTUNE.
WELL...
TAKE CARE, MR. ASHBY.
MUMBLE
MUMBLE
MUMBLE
MUMBLE

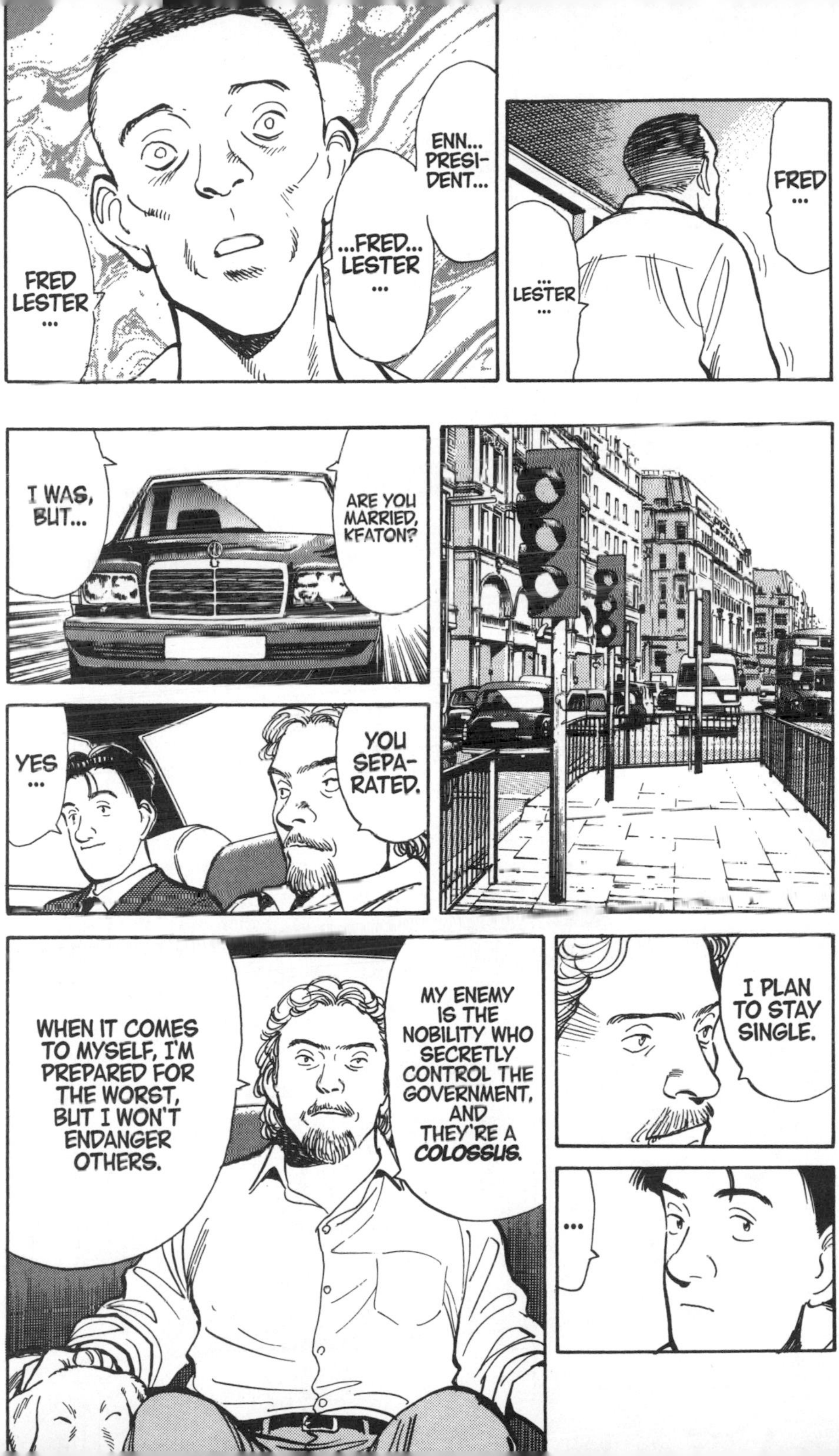
FRED ...
... LESTER ...
ENN... PRESIDENT...
...FRED... LESTER ...
FRED LESTER ...
ARE YOU MARRIED, KFATON?
I WAS, BUT...
YOU SEPARATED.
YES ...
I PLAN TO STAY SINGLE.
...
MY ENEMY IS THE NOBILITY WHO SECRETLY CONTROL THE GOVERNMENT, AND THEY'RE A *COLOSSUS*.
WHEN IT COMES TO MYSELF, I'M PREPARED FOR THE WORST, BUT I WON'T ENDANGER OTHERS.

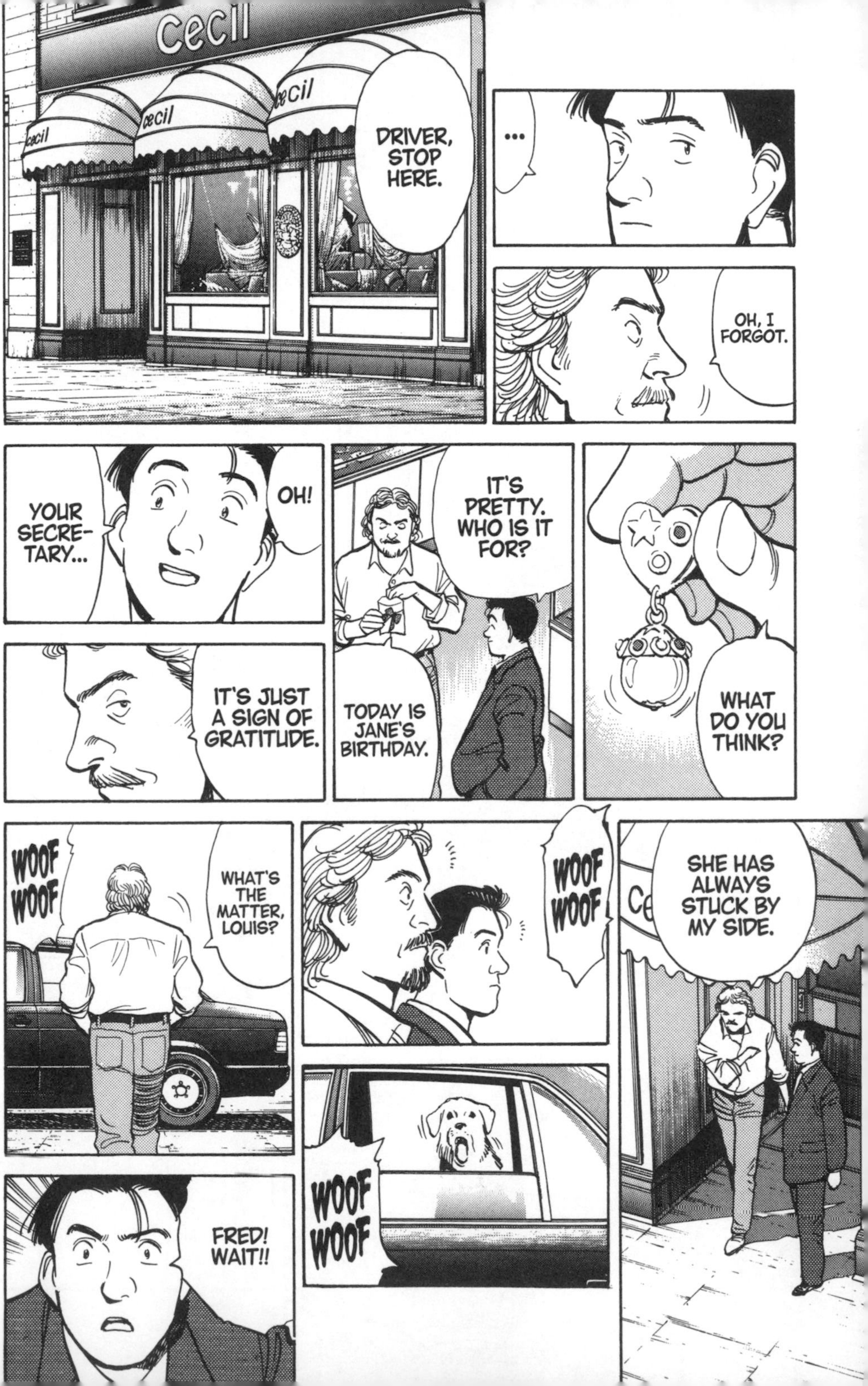
...
OH, I FORGOT.
DRIVER, STOP HERE.
cecil
cecil
cecil
cecil
WHAT DO YOU THINK?
IT'S PRETTY. WHO IS IT FOR?
TODAY IS JANE'S BIRTHDAY.
OH!
YOUR SECRETARY...
IT'S JUST A SIGN OF GRATITUDE.
SHE HAS ALWAYS STUCK BY MY SIDE.
WOOF WOOF
WOOF WOOF
WHAT'S THE MATTER, LOUIS?
WOOF WOOF
FRED! WAIT!!

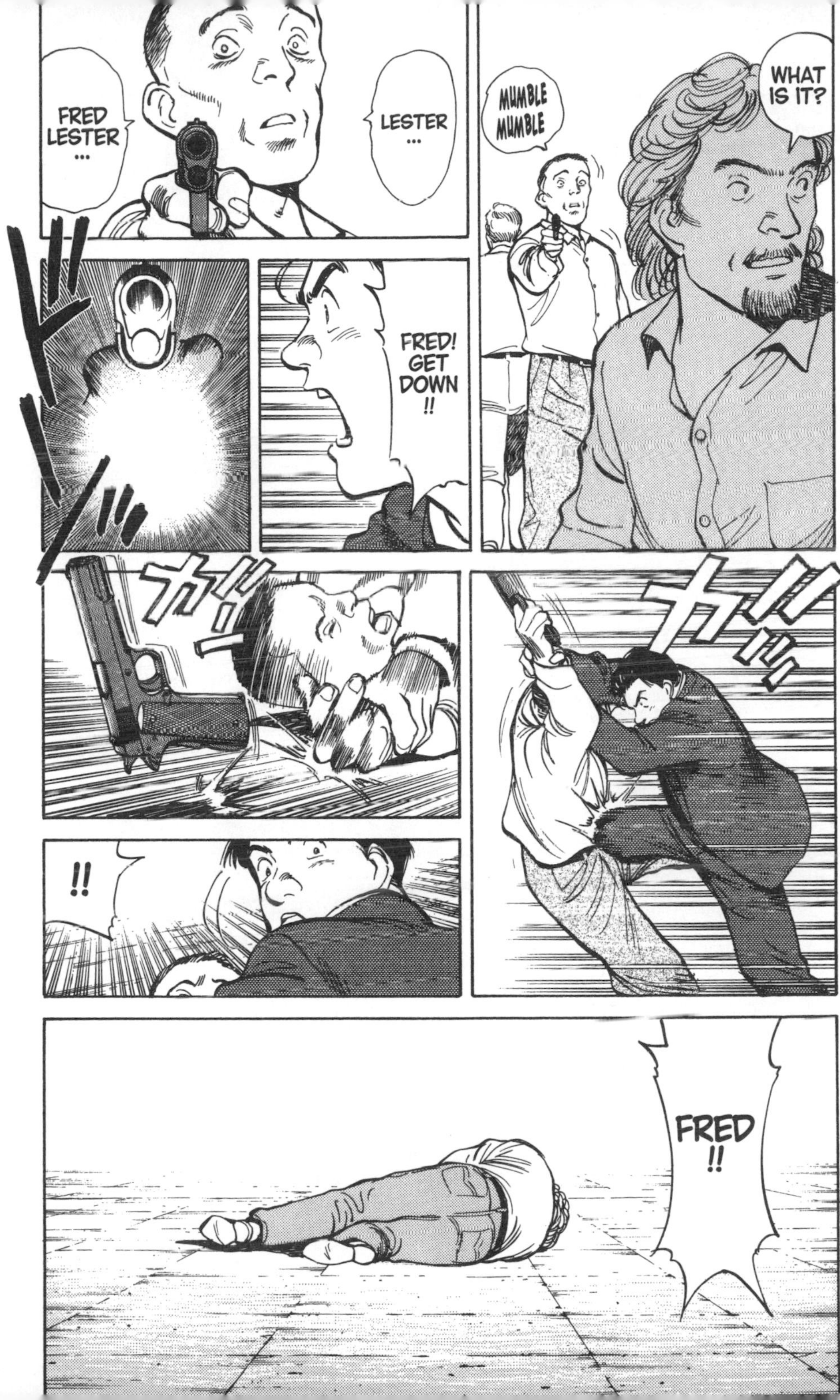
WHAT IS IT?
MUMBLE MUMBLE
LESTER ...
FRED LESTER ...
FRED! GET DOWN !!
!!
FRED !!

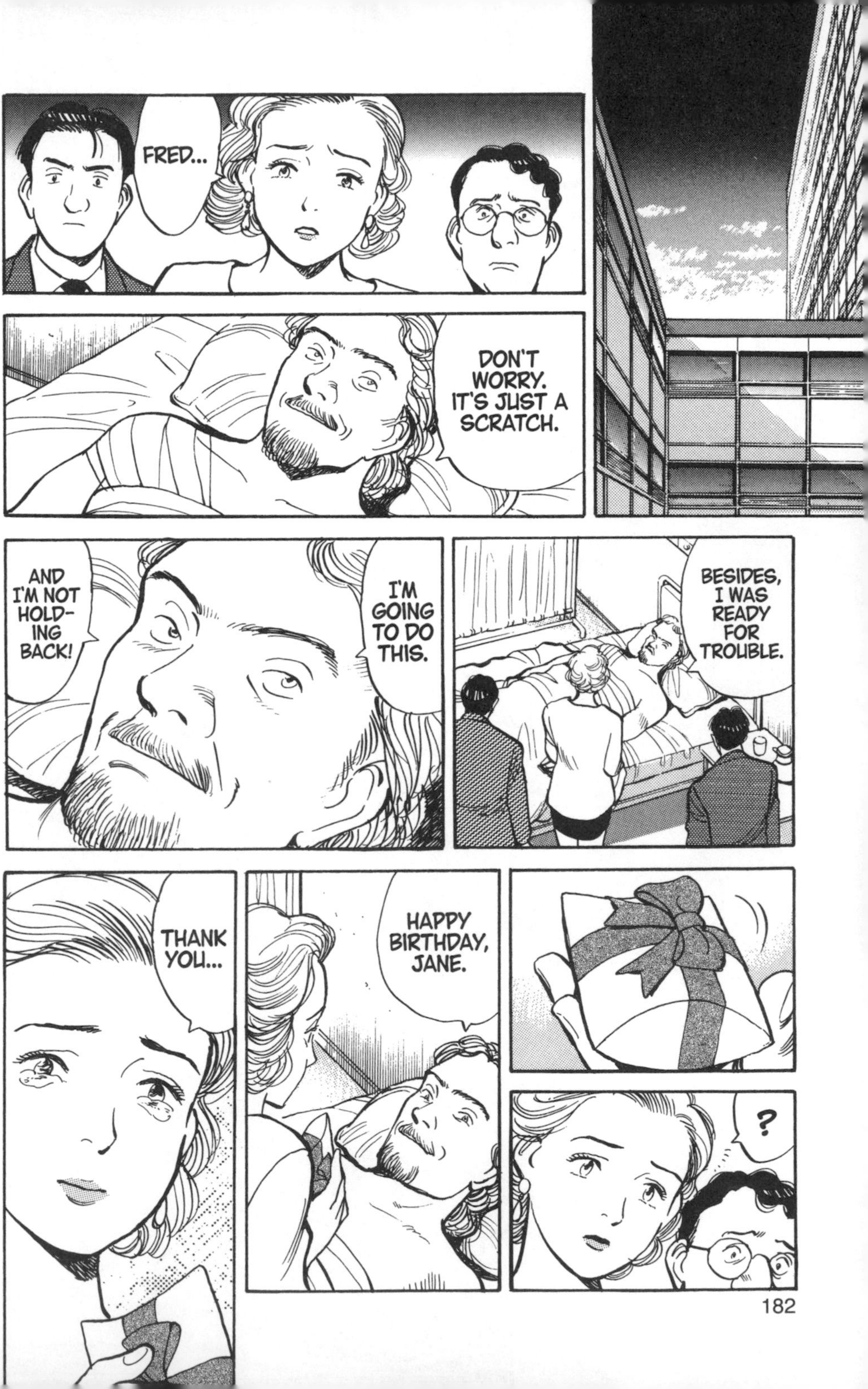
FRED...
DON'T WORRY. IT'S JUST A SCRATCH.
BESIDES, I WAS READY FOR TROUBLE.
I'M GOING TO DO THIS.
AND I'M NOT HOLD-ING BACK!
?
HAPPY BIRTHDAY, JANE.
THANK YOU...

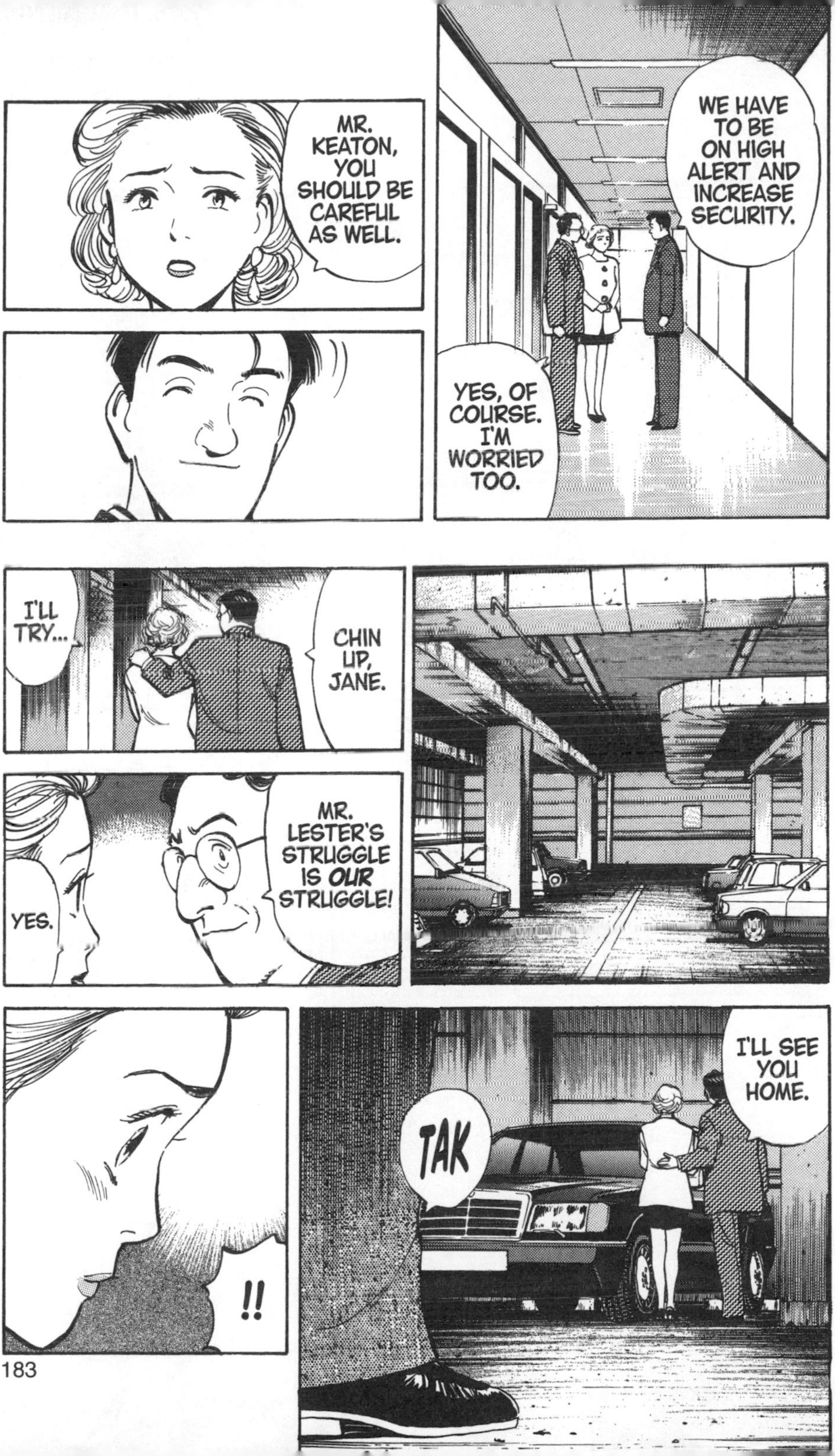
WE HAVE TO BE ON HIGH ALERT AND INCREASE SECURITY.
YES, OF COURSE. I'M WORRIED TOO.
MR. KEATON, YOU SHOULD BE CAREFUL AS WELL.
CHIN UP, JANE.
I'LL TRY...
MR. LESTER'S STRUGGLE IS OUR STRUGGLE!
YES.
I'LL SEE YOU HOME.
TAK
!!

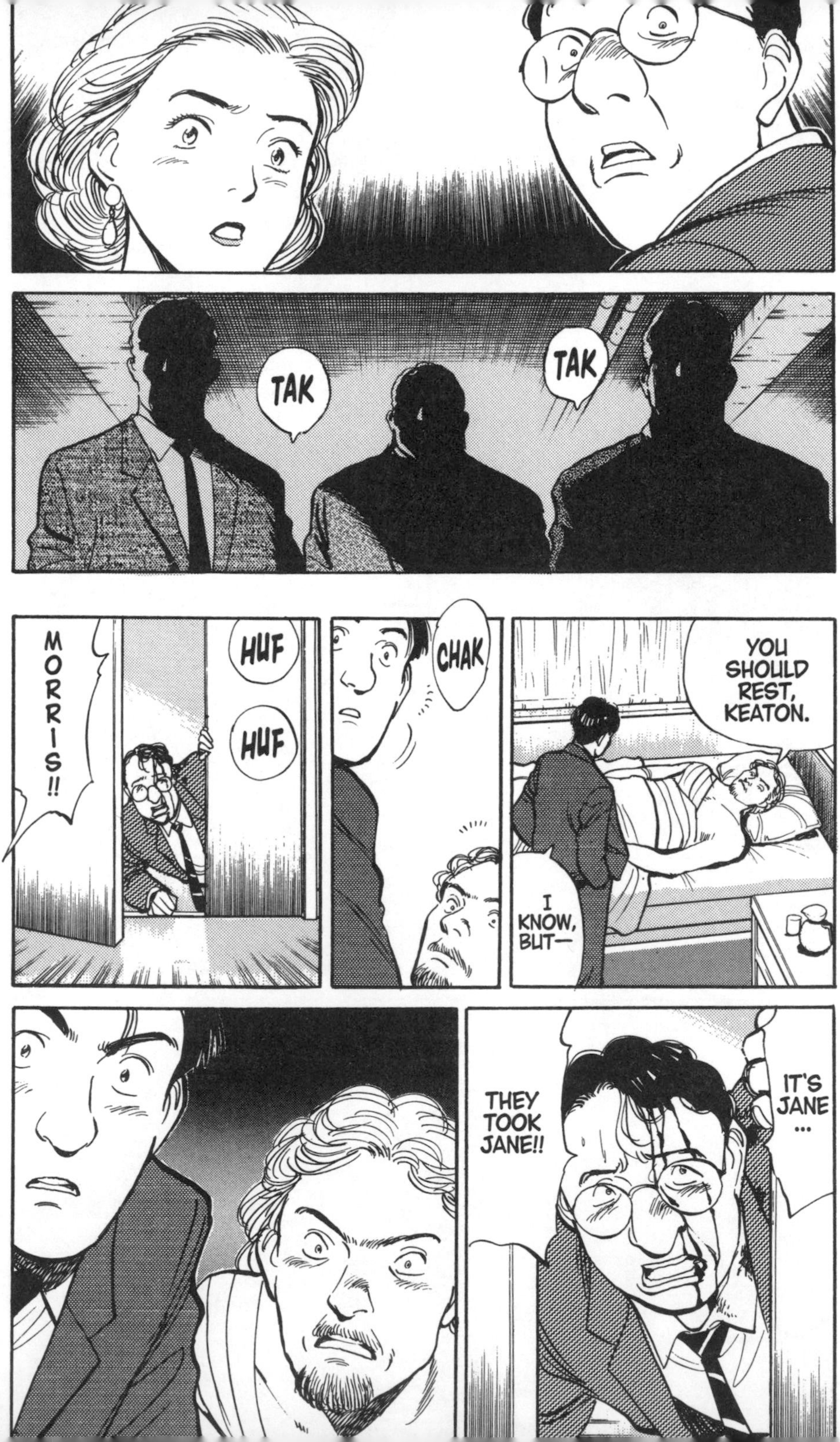
TAK
TAK
YOU SHOULD REST, KEATON.
I KNOW, BUT—
CHAK
HUF
HUF
MORRIS!!
IT'S JANE ...
THEY TOOK JANE!!

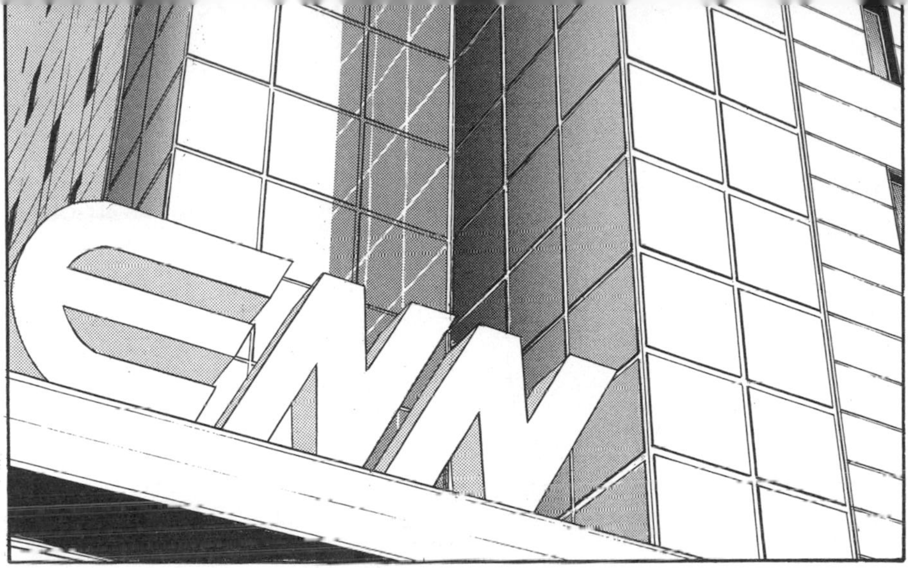
CNN

Chapter 8

Knight of the White Moon

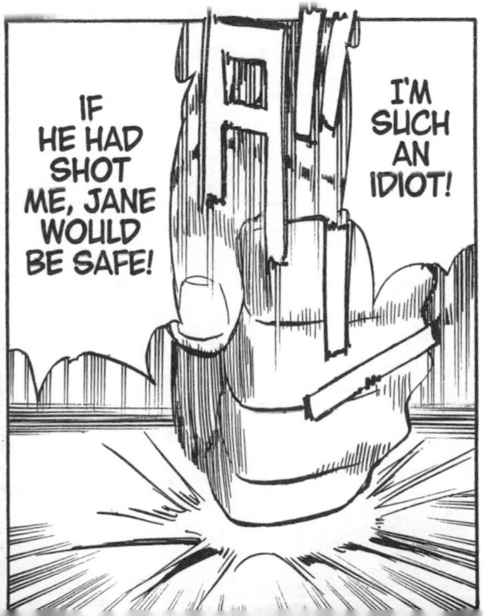
I'M SUCH AN IDIOT!
IF HE HAD SHOT ME, JANE WOULD BE SAFE!

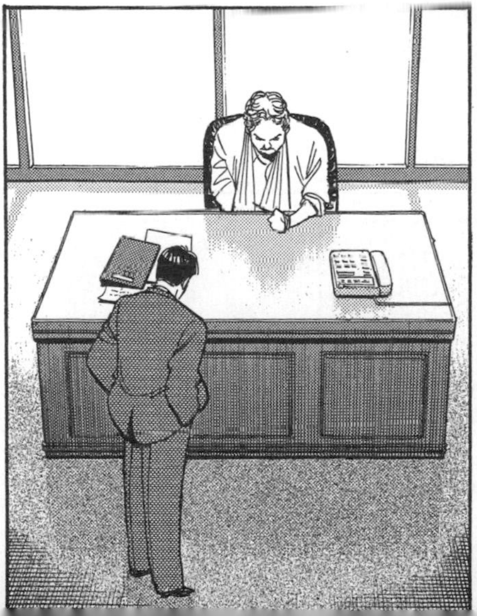

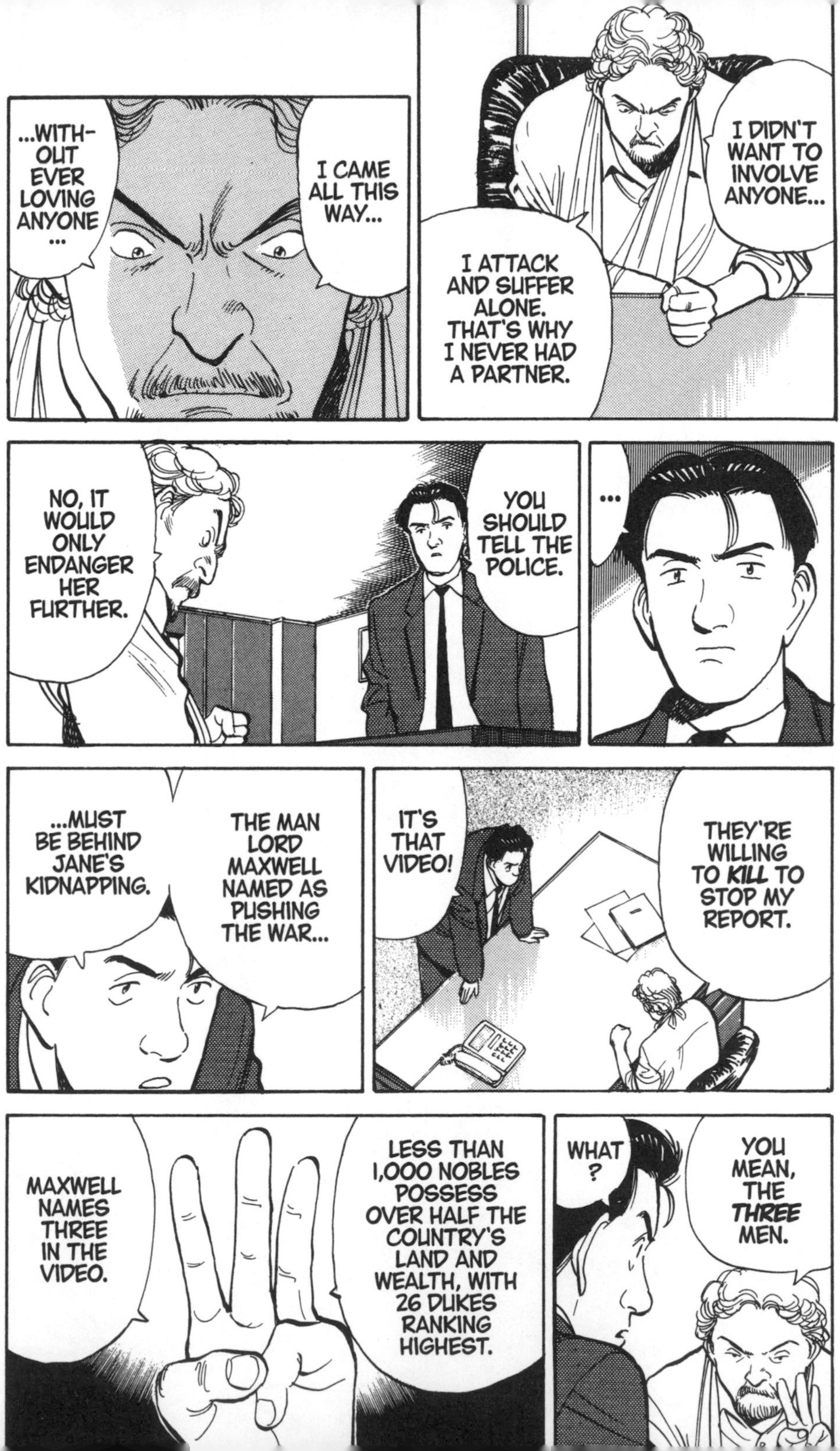
I DIDN'T WANT TO INVOLVE ANYONE...
I ATTACK AND SUFFER ALONE. THAT'S WHY I NEVER HAD A PARTNER.
I CAME ALL THIS WAY...
...WITH-OUT EVER LOVING ANYONE ...
...
YOU SHOULD TELL THE POLICE.
NO, IT WOULD ONLY ENDANGER HER FURTHER.
THEY'RE WILLING TO **KILL** TO STOP MY REPORT.
IT'S THAT VIDEO!
THE MAN LORD MAXWELL NAMED AS PUSHING THE WAR...
...MUST BE BEHIND JANE'S KIDNAPPING.
YOU MEAN, THE ***THREE*** MEN.
WHAT ?
LESS THAN 1,000 NOBLES POSSESS OVER HALF THE COUNTRY'S LAND AND WEALTH, WITH 26 DUKES RANKING HIGHEST.
MAXWELL NAMES THREE IN THE VIDEO.

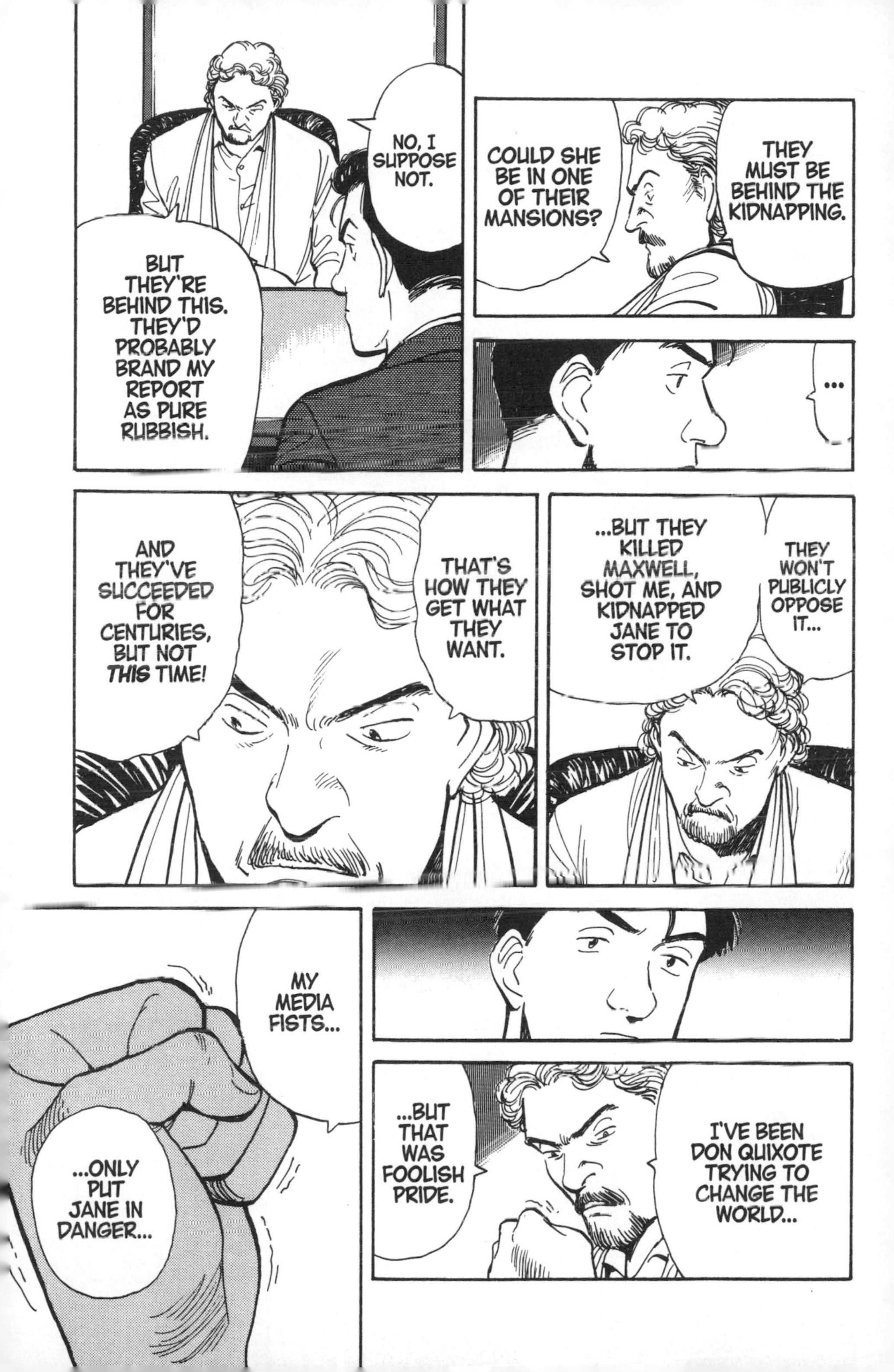
They must be behind the kidnapping.
Could she be in one of their mansions?
...
No, I suppose not.
But they're behind this. They'd probably brand my report as pure rubbish.
They won't publicly oppose it...
...but they killed Maxwell, shot me, and kidnapped Jane to stop it.
That's how they get what they want.
And they've succeeded for centuries, but not *this* time!
I've been Don Quixote trying to change the world...
...but that was foolish pride.
My media fists...
...only put Jane in danger...

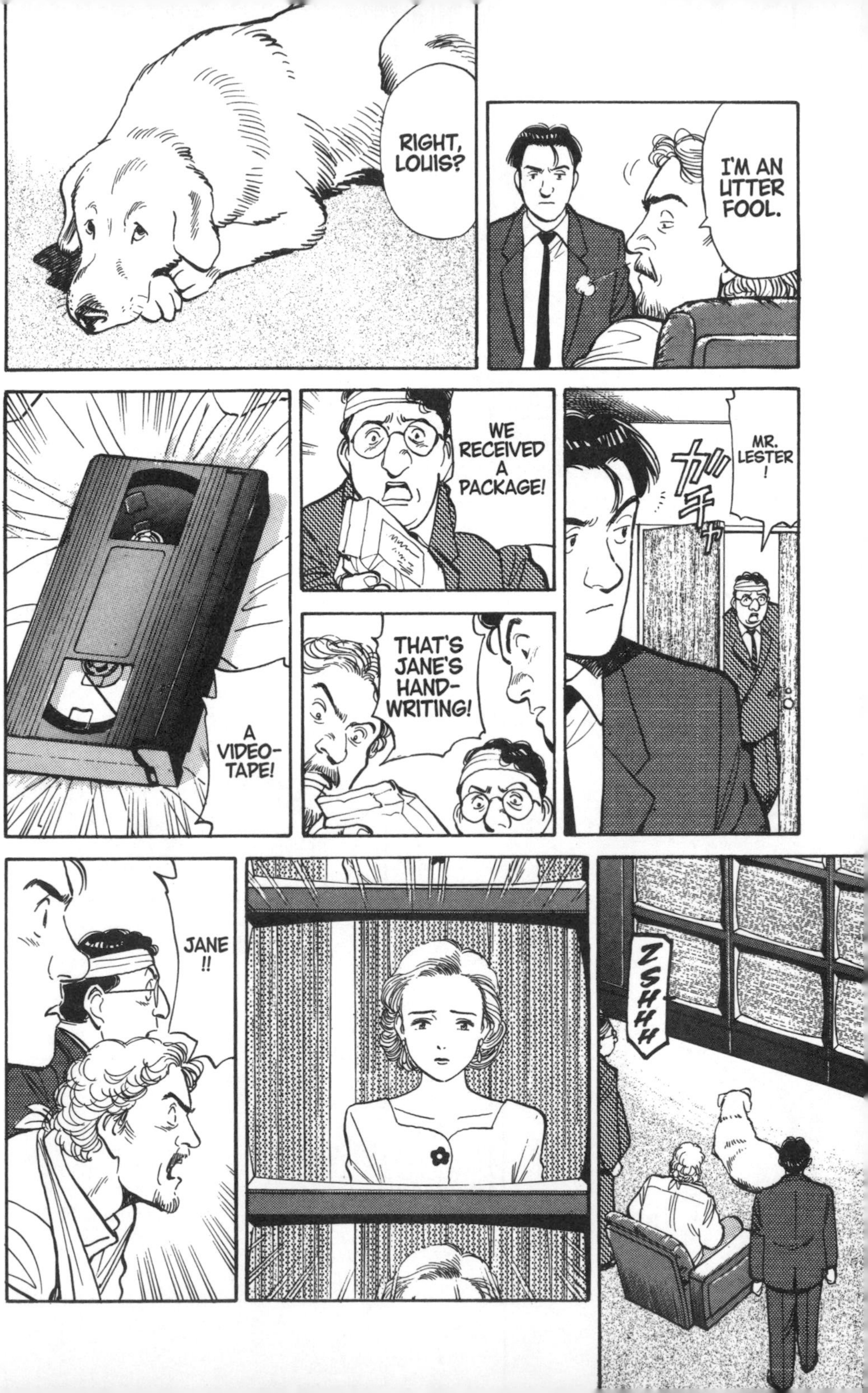
I'M AN UTTER FOOL.
RIGHT, LOUIS?
MR. LESTER!
WE RECEIVED A PACKAGE!
THAT'S JANE'S HAND-WRITING!
A VIDEO-TAPE!
ZSHHH
JANE!!

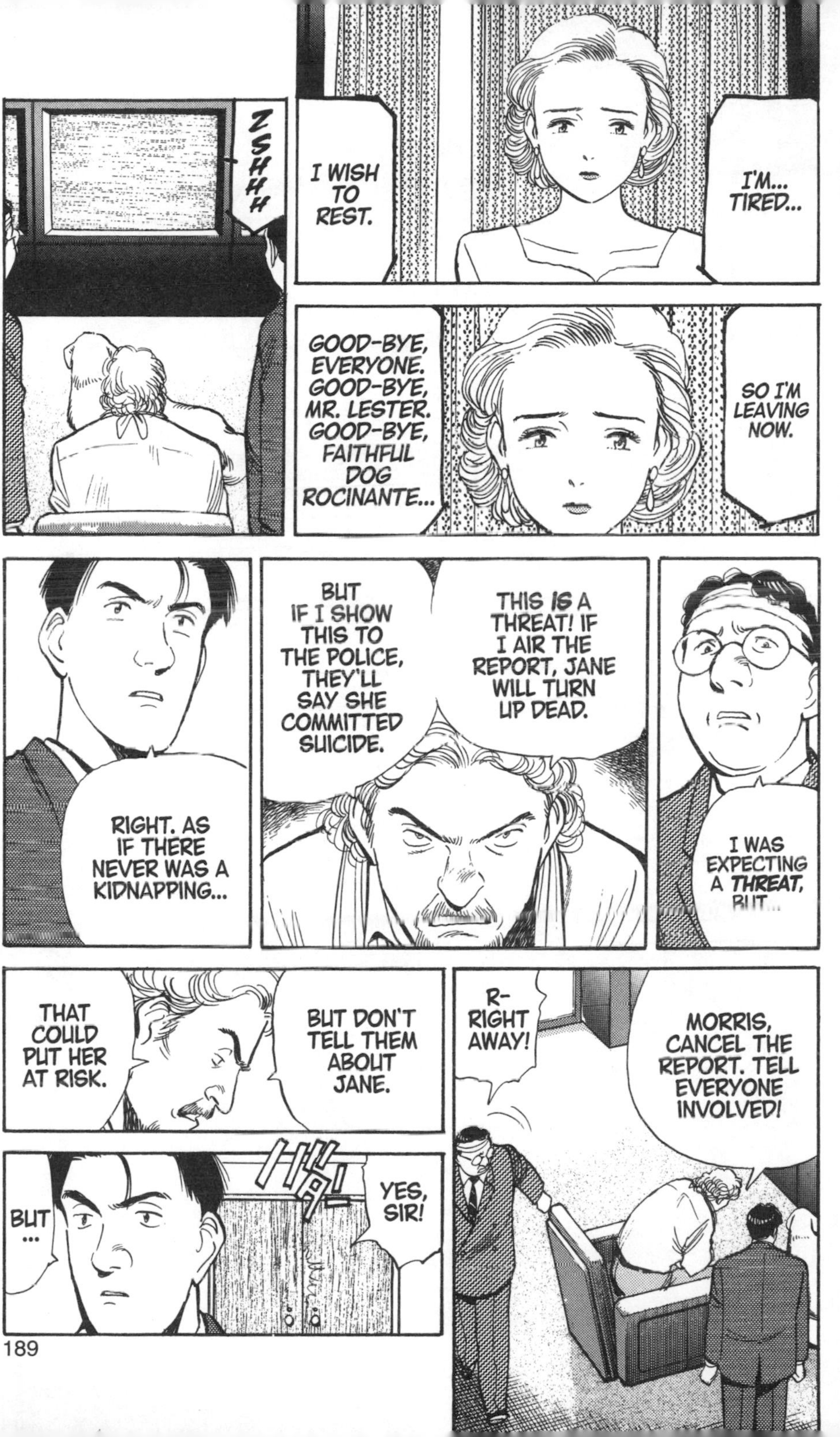
I'M... TIRED...
I WISH TO REST.
ZSHHH
SO I'M LEAVING NOW.
GOOD-BYE, EVERYONE. GOOD-BYE, MR. LESTER. GOOD-BYE, FAITHFUL DOG ROCINANTE...
I WAS EXPECTING A THREAT, BUT...
THIS IS A THREAT! IF I AIR THE REPORT, JANE WILL TURN UP DEAD.
BUT IF I SHOW THIS TO THE POLICE, THEY'LL SAY SHE COMMITTED SUICIDE.
RIGHT. AS IF THERE NEVER WAS A KIDNAPPING...
MORRIS, CANCEL THE REPORT. TELL EVERYONE INVOLVED!
R-RIGHT AWAY!
BUT DON'T TELL THEM ABOUT JANE.
THAT COULD PUT HER AT RISK.
YES, SIR!
BUT ...

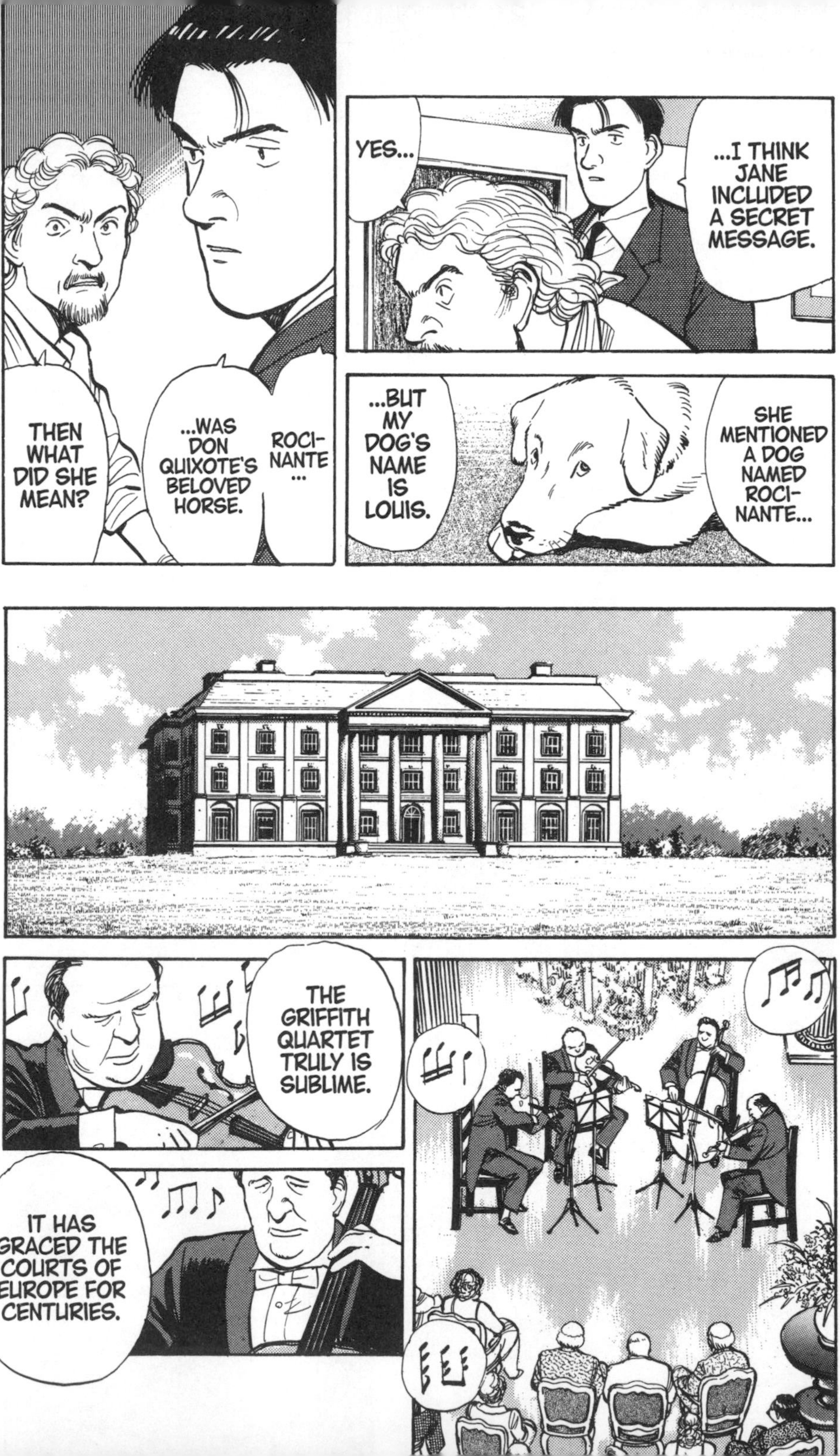
...I THINK JANE INCLUDED A SECRET MESSAGE.
YES...
SHE MENTIONED A DOG NAMED ROCI-NANTE...
...BUT MY DOG'S NAME IS LOUIS.
ROCI-NANTE ...
...WAS DON QUIXOTE'S BELOVED HORSE.
THEN WHAT DID SHE MEAN?
THE GRIFFITH QUARTET TRULY IS SUBLIME.
IT HAS GRACED THE COURTS OF EUROPE FOR CENTURIES.

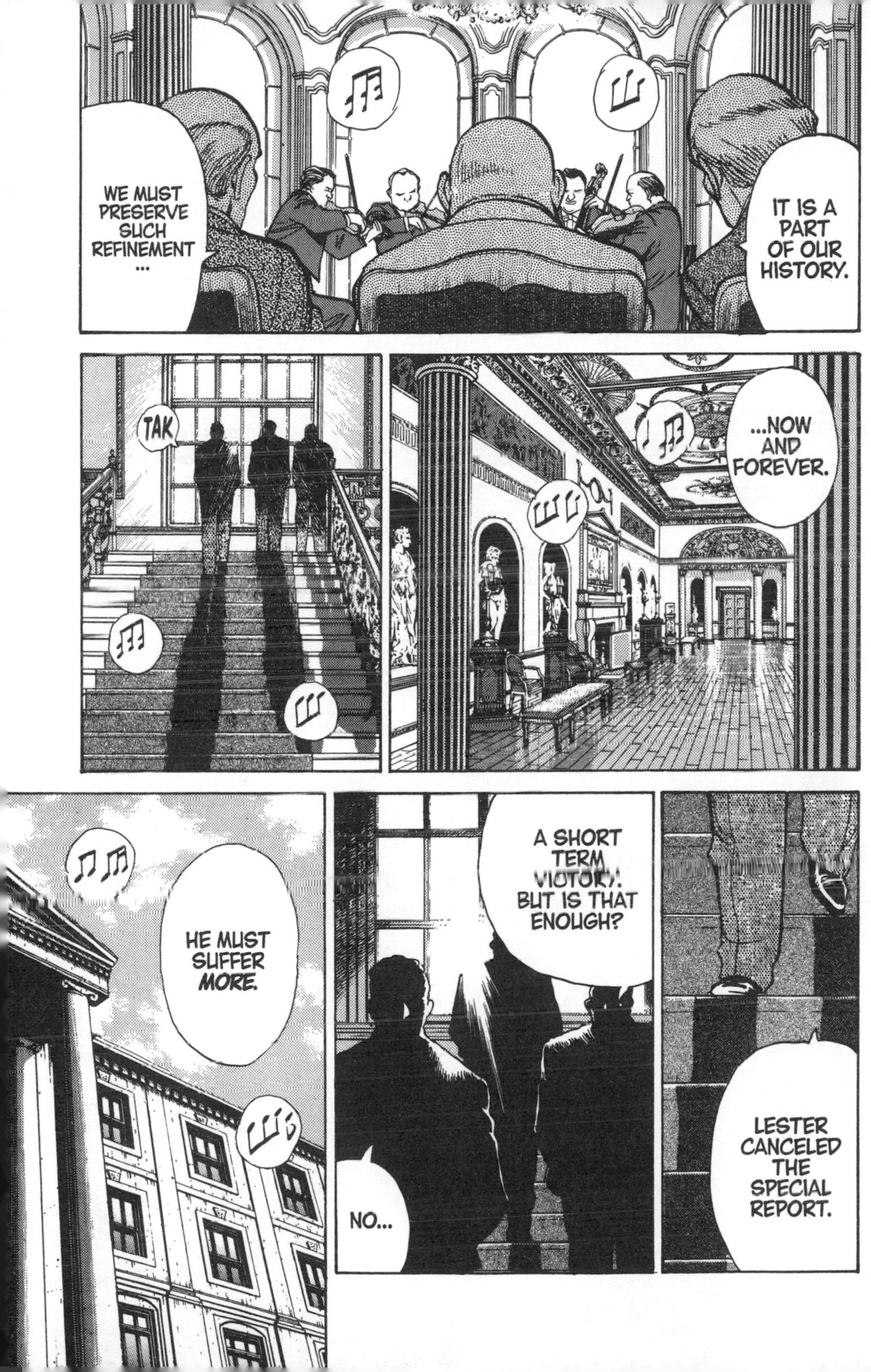
IT IS A PART OF OUR HISTORY.
WE MUST PRESERVE SUCH REFINEMENT ...
...NOW AND FOREVER.
TAK
LESTER CANCELED THE SPECIAL REPORT.
A SHORT TERM VICTORY. BUT IS THAT ENOUGH?
NO...
HE MUST SUFFER MORE.

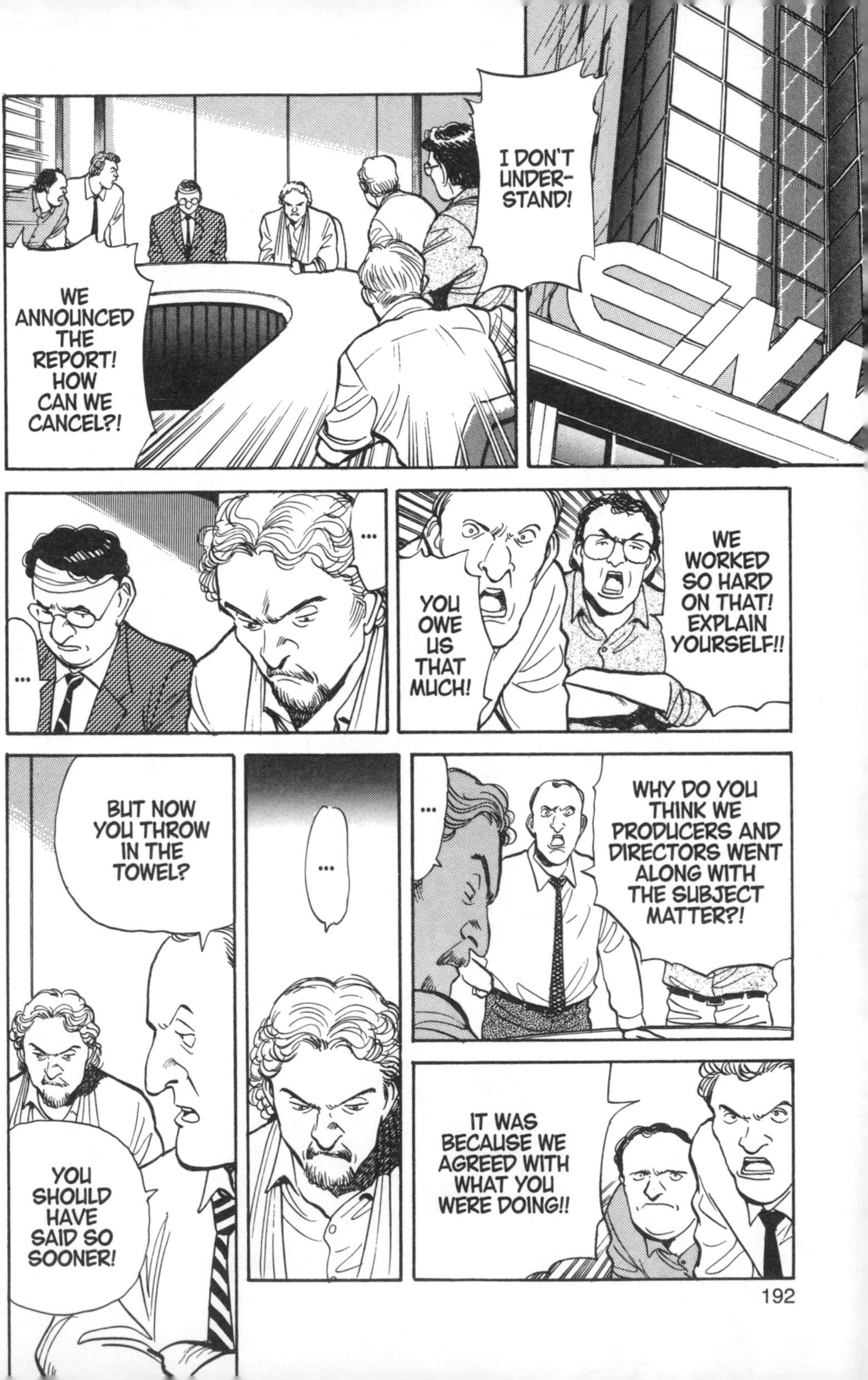
I DON'T UNDER-STAND!
WE ANNOUNCED THE REPORT! HOW CAN WE CANCEL?!
WE WORKED SO HARD ON THAT! EXPLAIN YOURSELF!!
YOU OWE US THAT MUCH!
...
...
WHY DO YOU THINK WE PRODUCERS AND DIRECTORS WENT ALONG WITH THE SUBJECT MATTER?!
...
IT WAS BECAUSE WE AGREED WITH WHAT YOU WERE DOING!!
...
BUT NOW YOU THROW IN THE TOWEL?
YOU SHOULD HAVE SAID SO SOONER!

FORGET IT. LET'S GO.
SOME-TIMES ACHIEVING YOUR GOALS REQUIRES COMPRO-MISE.
ISN'T THAT RIGHT, MR. LES-TER?
BIP
GOOD-BYE, FAITHFUL DOG ROCI-NANTE...
ZSHH
"I KNOW HE TILTED AT WINDMILLS, HIS SERVANT'S NAME WAS SANCHO PANZA, AND HIS HORSE WAS ROCINANTE."
...

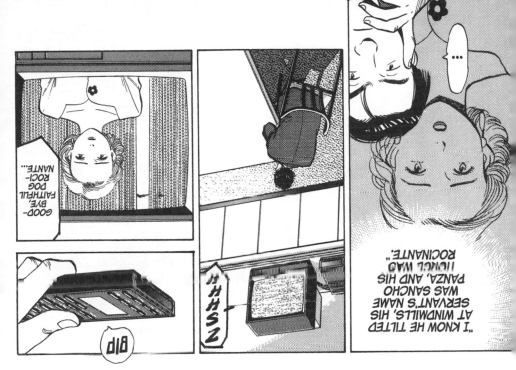

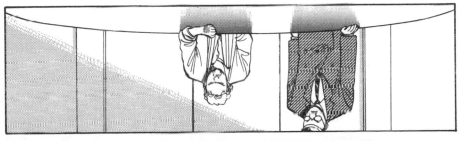

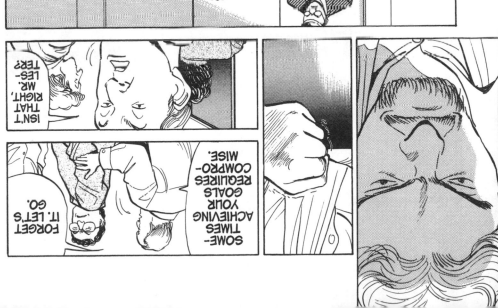

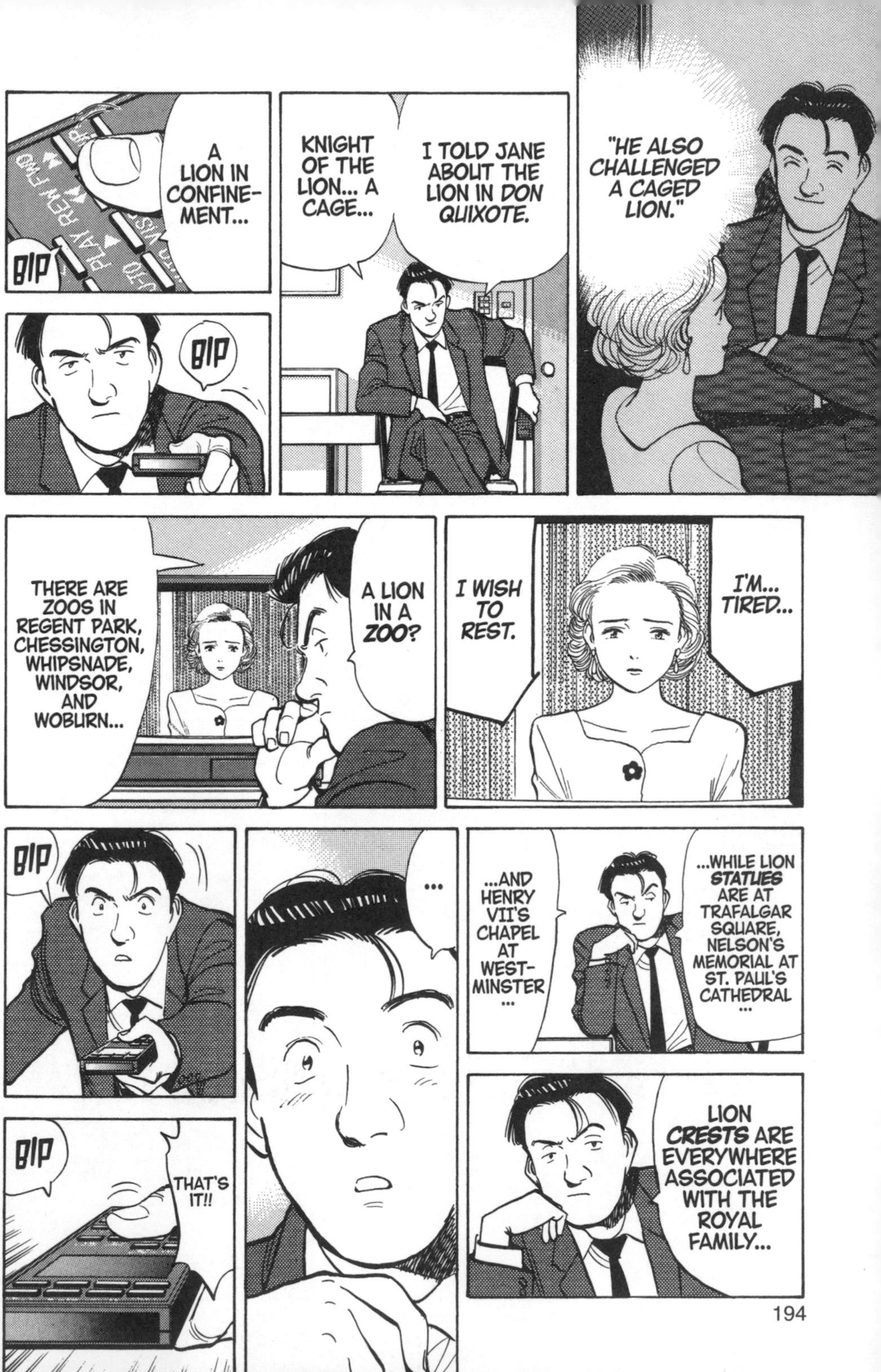
"HE ALSO CHALLENGED A CAGED LION."
I TOLD JANE ABOUT THE LION IN DON QUIXOTE.
KNIGHT OF THE LION... A CAGE...
A LION IN CONFINEMENT...
BIP
PLAY REW FWD
BIP
I'M... TIRED...
I WISH TO REST.
A LION IN A ZOO?
THERE ARE ZOOS IN REGENT PARK, CHESSINGTON, WHIPSNADE, WINDSOR, AND WOBURN...
...WHILE LION STATUES ARE AT TRAFALGAR SQUARE, NELSON'S MEMORIAL AT ST. PAUL'S CATHEDRAL...
...AND HENRY VII'S CHAPEL AT WEST-MINSTER...
LION CRESTS ARE EVERYWHERE ASSOCIATED WITH THE ROYAL FAMILY...
...
BIP
BIP
THAT'S IT!!

I WISH TO REST.
SO I'M LEAVING NOW.
GOOD-BYE, EVERY-ONE.
THAT BLACK MASS OUTSIDE THE CURTAINS...
BIRDS!!
PIGEONS? CROWS?
IN THE NEXT FRAME, THEY RISE...
...WITHOUT BEATING THEIR WINGS!!
THEY'RE HOVERING ON THE WIND!!

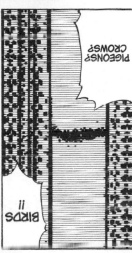

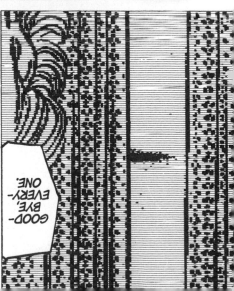

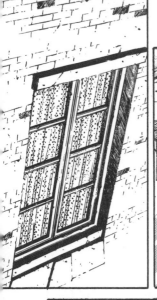

HELLO, DANIEL? I'M AT LION DOCK.

AWFULLY DREARY FOR A DATE, NO?

I'M WORKING, AND I HAVE A FAVOR TO ASK....

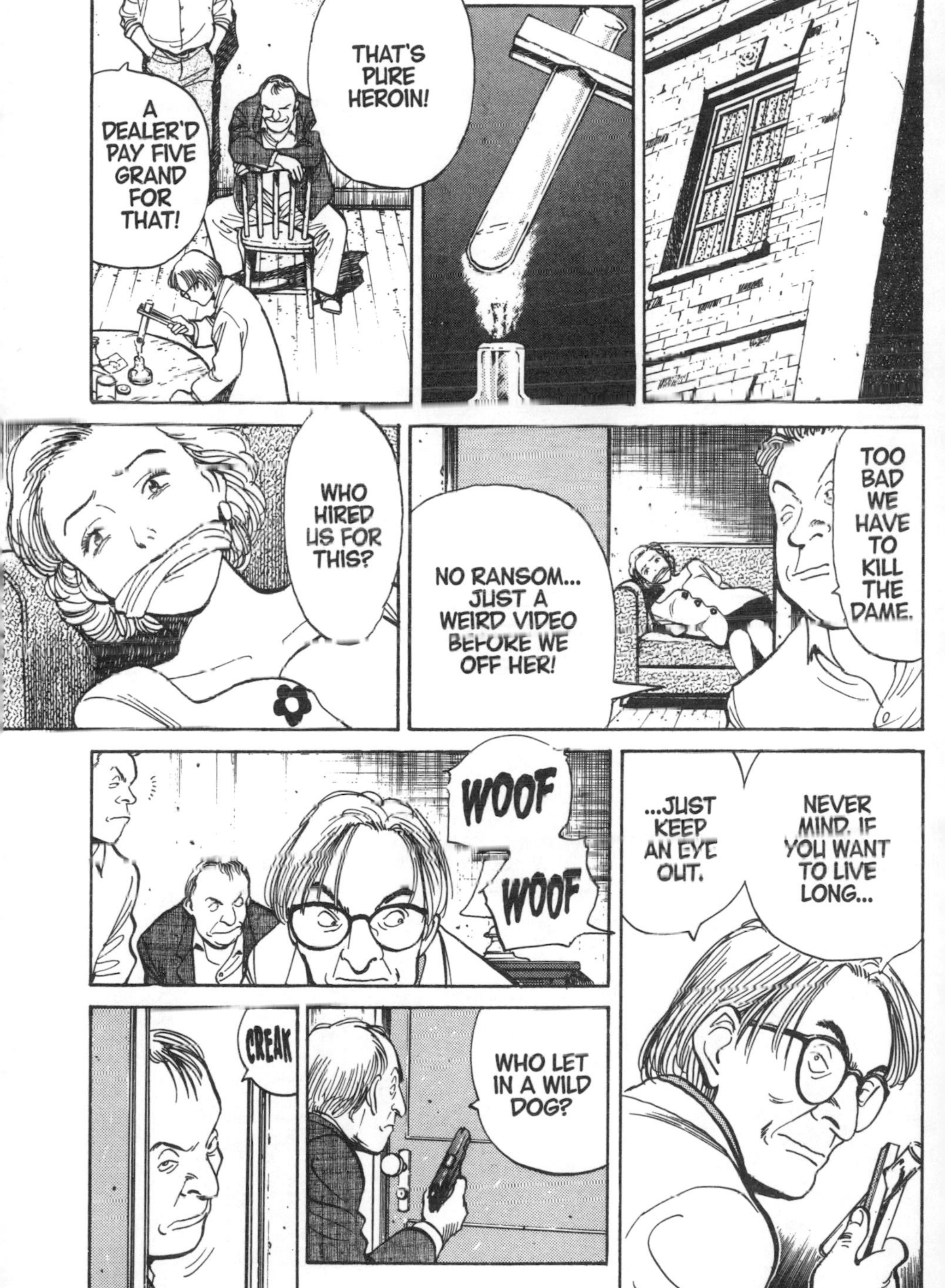
THAT'S PURE HEROIN!
A DEALER'D PAY FIVE GRAND FOR THAT!
TOO BAD WE HAVE TO KILL THE DAME.
NO RANSOM... JUST A WEIRD VIDEO BEFORE WE OFF HER!
WHO HIRED US FOR THIS?
NEVER MIND, IF YOU WANT TO LIVE LONG...
...JUST KEEP AN EYE OUT.
WOOF
WOOF
WHO LET IN A WILD DOG?
CREAK

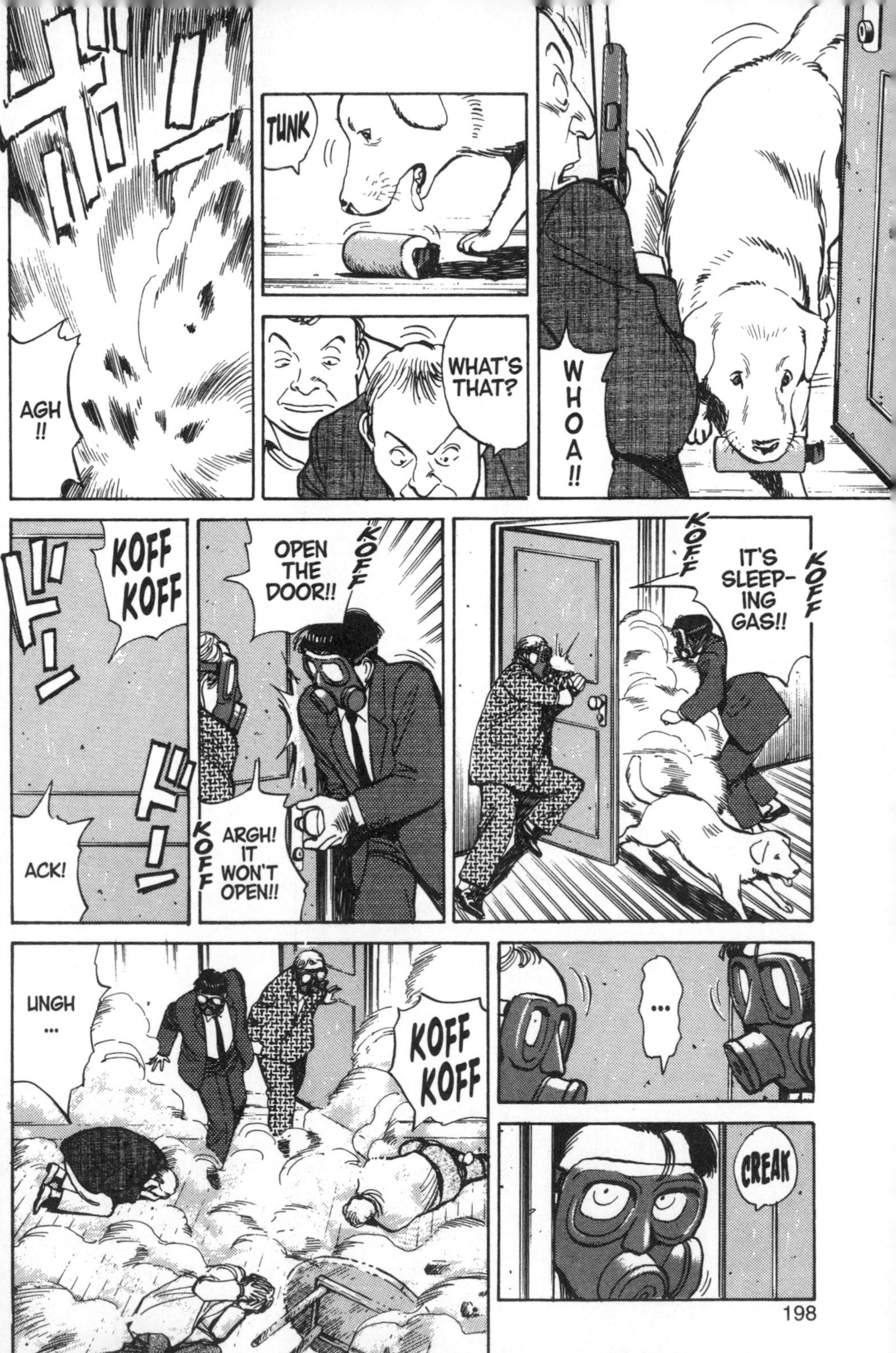
WHOA!!
TUNK
WHAT'S THAT?
AGH!!
KOFF
IT'S SLEEPING GAS!!
KOFF
KOFF
OPEN THE DOOR!!
ARGH! IT WON'T OPEN!!
KOFF
KOFF KOFF
ACK!
...
CREAK
KOFF KOFF
UNGH ...

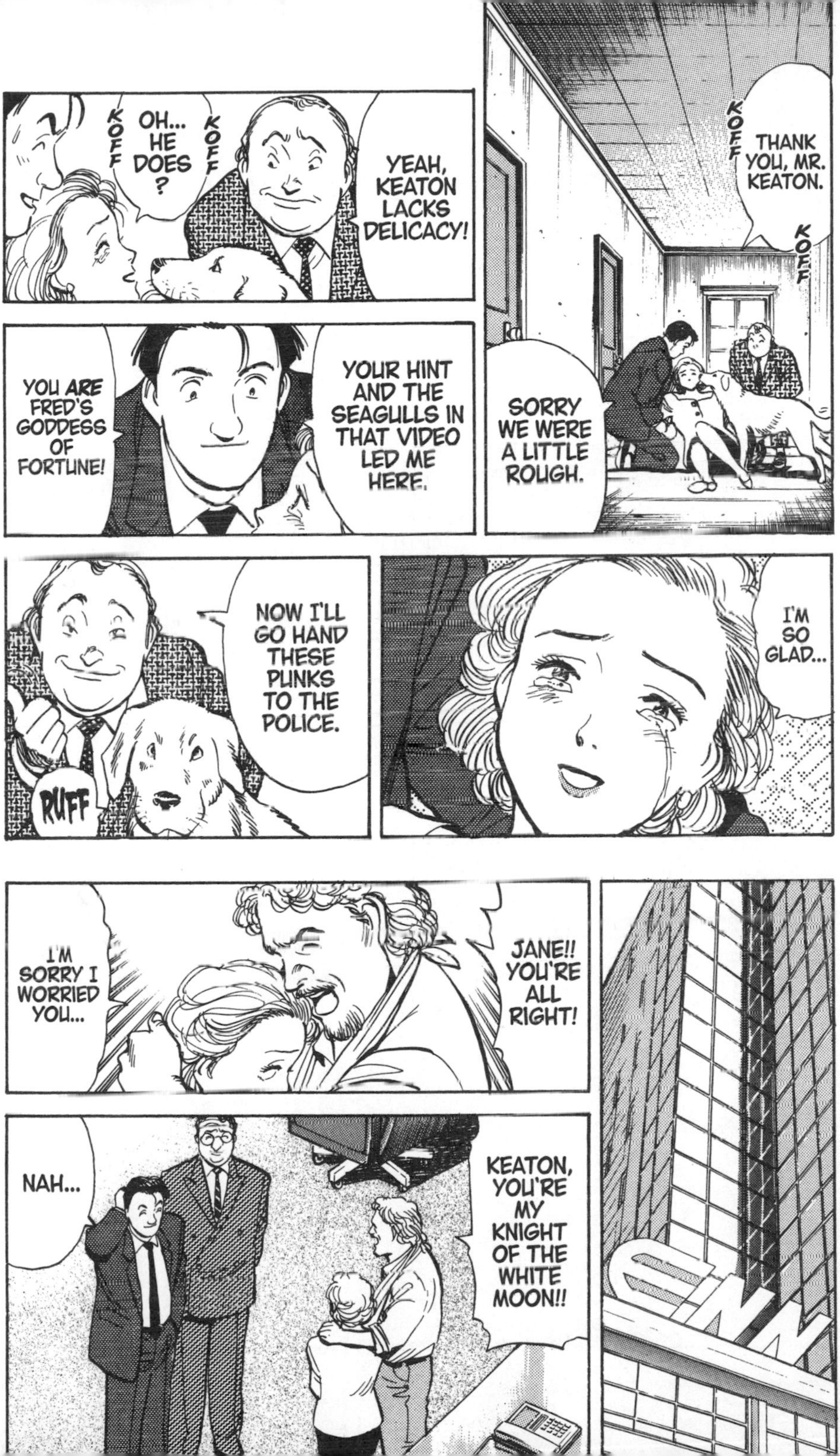
THANK YOU, MR. KEATON.
KOFF
KOFF
SORRY WE WERE A LITTLE ROUGH.
YEAH, KEATON LACKS DELICACY!
KOFF
OH... HE DOES?
KOFF
YOUR HINT AND THE SEAGULLS IN THAT VIDEO LED ME HERE.
YOU ARE FRED'S GODDESS OF FORTUNE!
I'M SO GLAD...
NOW I'LL GO HAND THESE PUNKS TO THE POLICE.
RUFF
CNN
JANE!! YOU'RE ALL RIGHT!
I'M SORRY I WORRIED YOU...
KEATON, YOU'RE MY KNIGHT OF THE WHITE MOON!!
NAH...

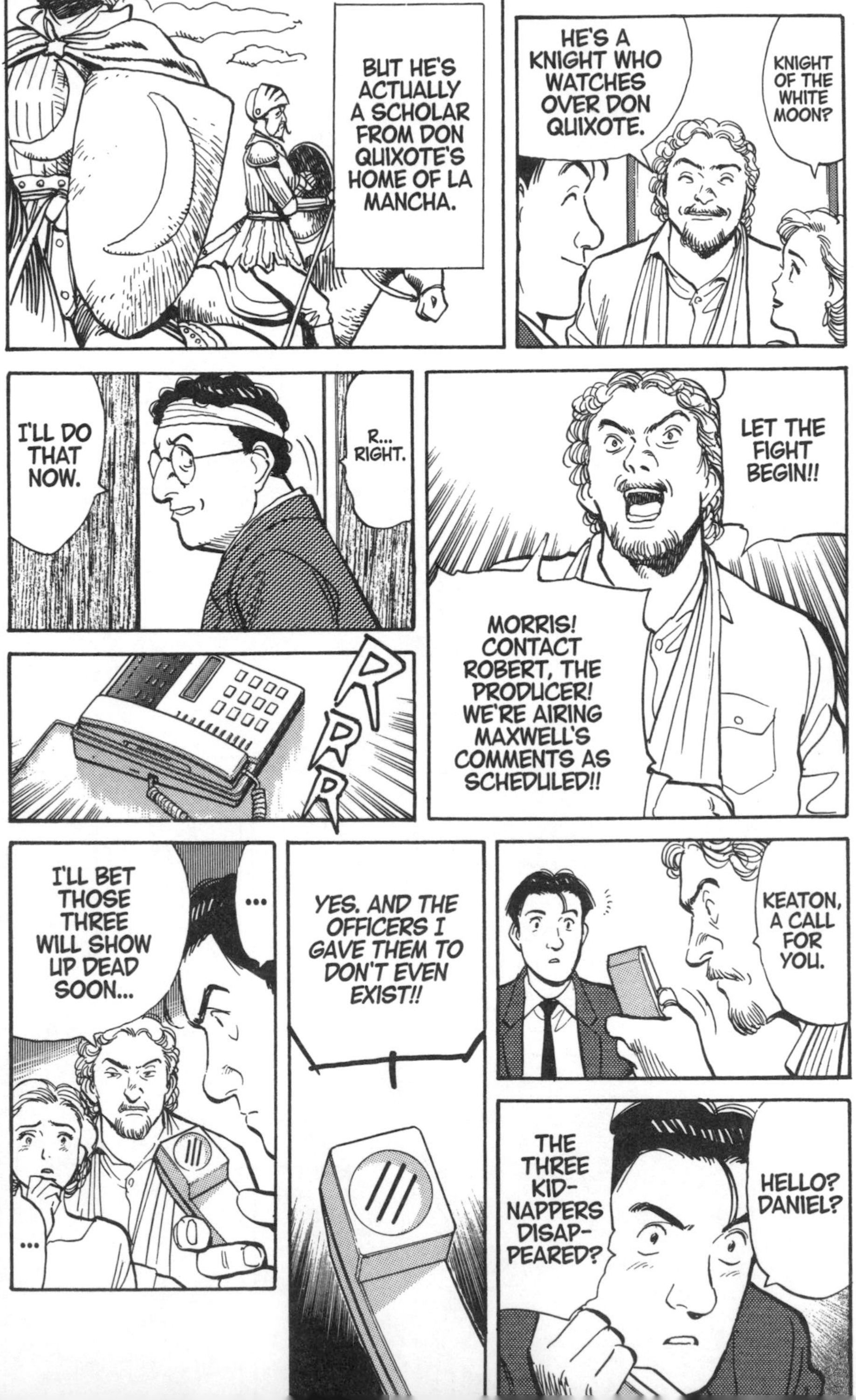
KNIGHT OF THE WHITE MOON?
HE'S A KNIGHT WHO WATCHES OVER DON QUIXOTE.
BUT HE'S ACTUALLY A SCHOLAR FROM DON QUIXOTE'S HOME OF LA MANCHA.
LET THE FIGHT BEGIN!!
MORRIS! CONTACT ROBERT, THE PRODUCER! WE'RE AIRING MAXWELL'S COMMENTS AS SCHEDULED!!
R... RIGHT.
I'LL DO THAT NOW.
RRR
KEATON, A CALL FOR YOU.
HELLO? DANIEL?
THE THREE KID-NAPPERS DISAP-PEARED?
YES. AND THE OFFICERS I GAVE THEM TO DON'T EVEN EXIST!!
...
I'LL BET THOSE THREE WILL SHOW UP DEAD SOON...
...

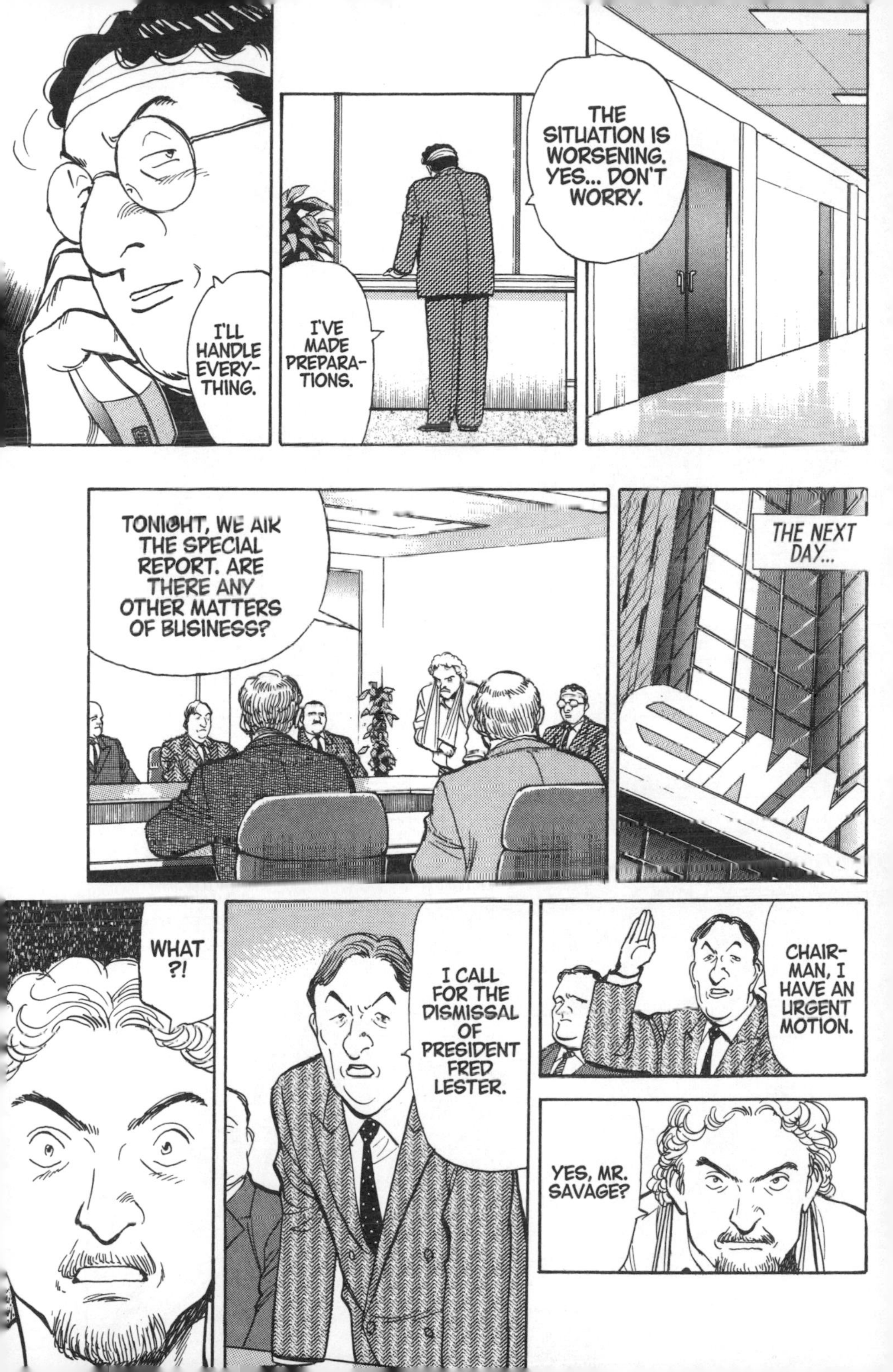
THE SITUATION IS WORSENING. YES... DON'T WORRY.
I'VE MADE PREPARA-TIONS.
I'LL HANDLE EVERY-THING.
THE NEXT DAY...
TONIGHT, WE AIR THE SPECIAL REPORT. ARE THERE ANY OTHER MATTERS OF BUSINESS?
CHAIR-MAN, I HAVE AN URGENT MOTION.
YES, MR. SAVAGE?
I CALL FOR THE DISMISSAL OF PRESIDENT FRED LESTER.
WHAT ?!

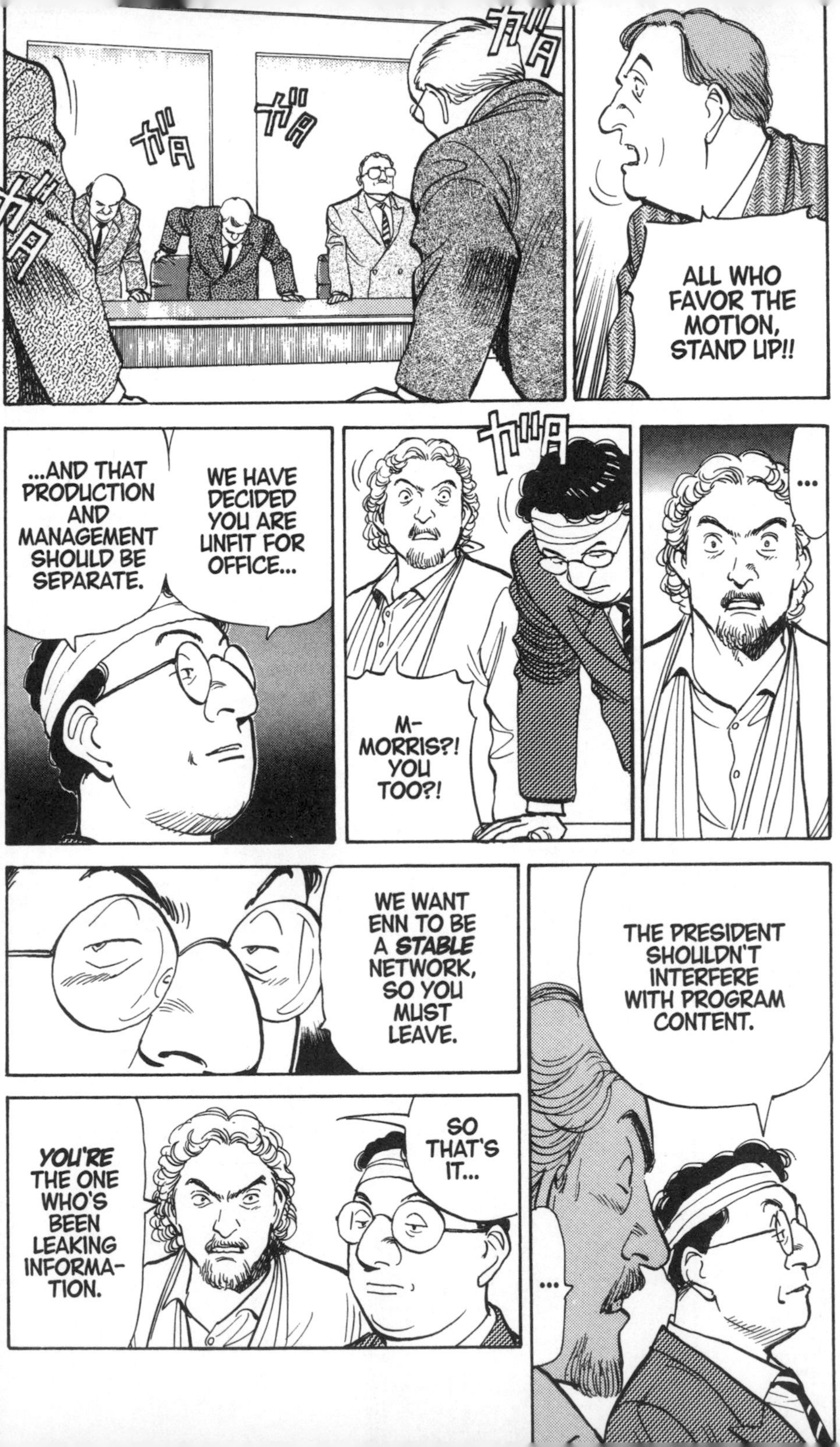
ALL WHO FAVOR THE MOTION, STAND UP!!
...
M-MORRIS?! YOU TOO?!
WE HAVE DECIDED YOU ARE UNFIT FOR OFFICE...
...AND THAT PRODUCTION AND MANAGEMENT SHOULD BE SEPARATE.
THE PRESIDENT SHOULDN'T INTERFERE WITH PROGRAM CONTENT.
...
WE WANT ENN TO BE A *STABLE* NETWORK, SO YOU MUST LEAVE.
SO THAT'S IT...
YOU'RE THE ONE WHO'S BEEN LEAKING INFORMATION.

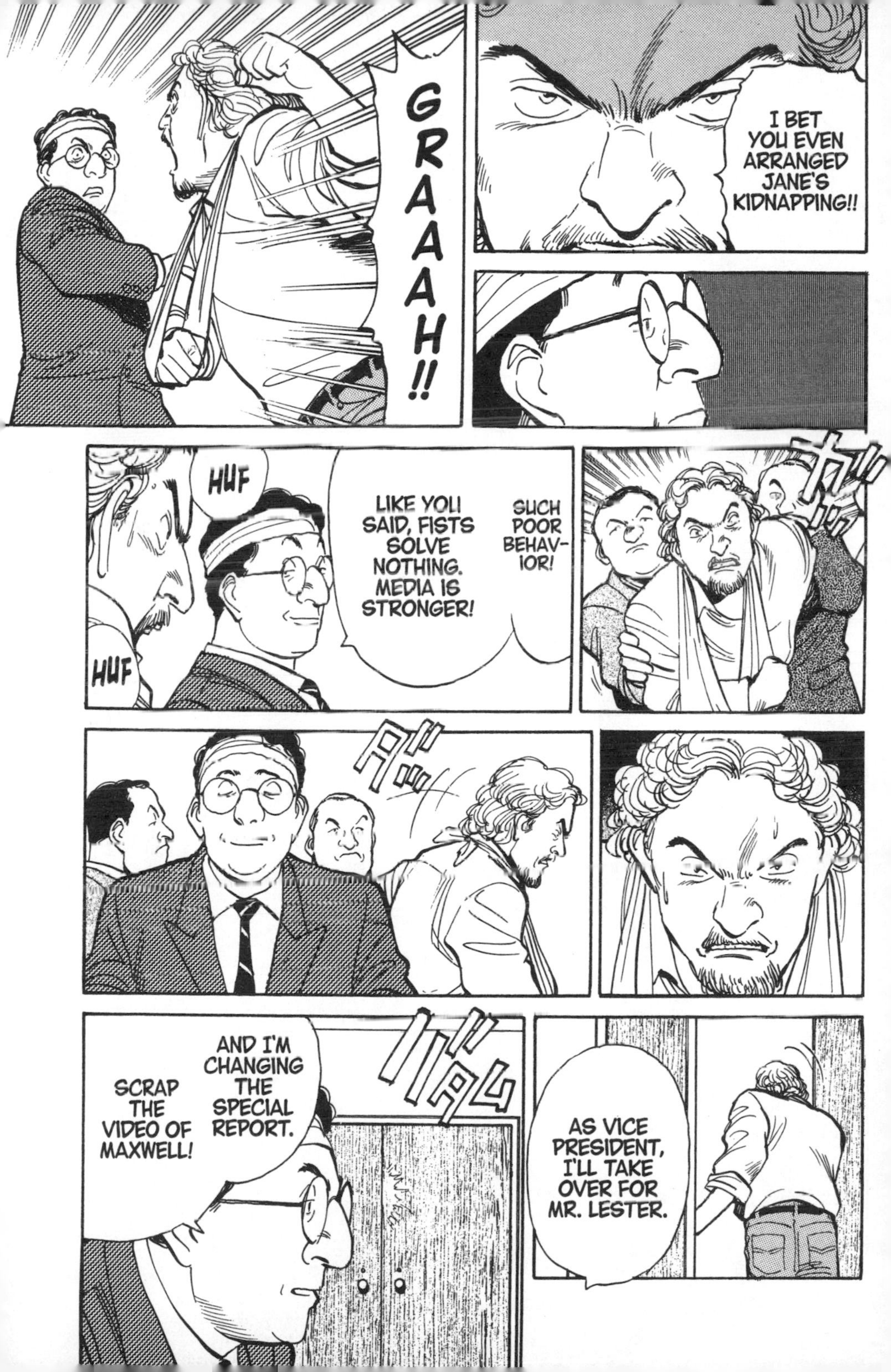
I BET YOU EVEN ARRANGED JANE'S KIDNAPPING!!
GRAAAAH!!
SUCH POOR BEHAVIOR!
LIKE YOU SAID, FISTS SOLVE NOTHING. MEDIA IS STRONGER!
HUF
HUF
AS VICE PRESIDENT, I'LL TAKE OVER FOR MR. LESTER.
AND I'M CHANGING THE SPECIAL REPORT.
SCRAP THE VIDEO OF MAXWELL!

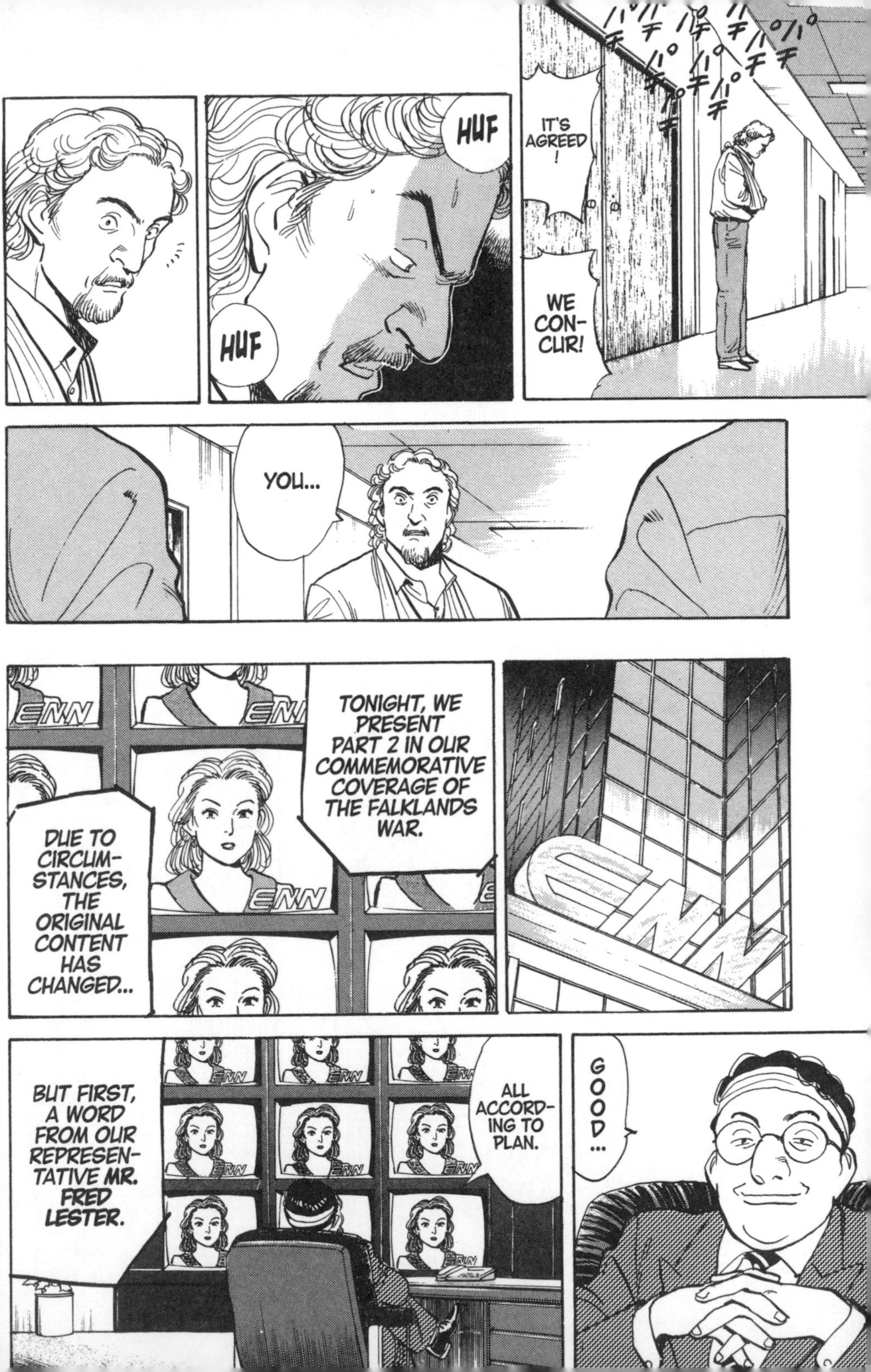
IT'S AGREED!
WE CONCUR!
HUF
HUF
YOU...
TONIGHT, WE PRESENT PART 2 IN OUR COMMEMORATIVE COVERAGE OF THE FALKLANDS WAR.
DUE TO CIRCUMSTANCES, THE ORIGINAL CONTENT HAS CHANGED...
GOOD...
ALL ACCORDING TO PLAN.
BUT FIRST, A WORD FROM OUR REPRESENTATIVE MR. FRED LESTER.

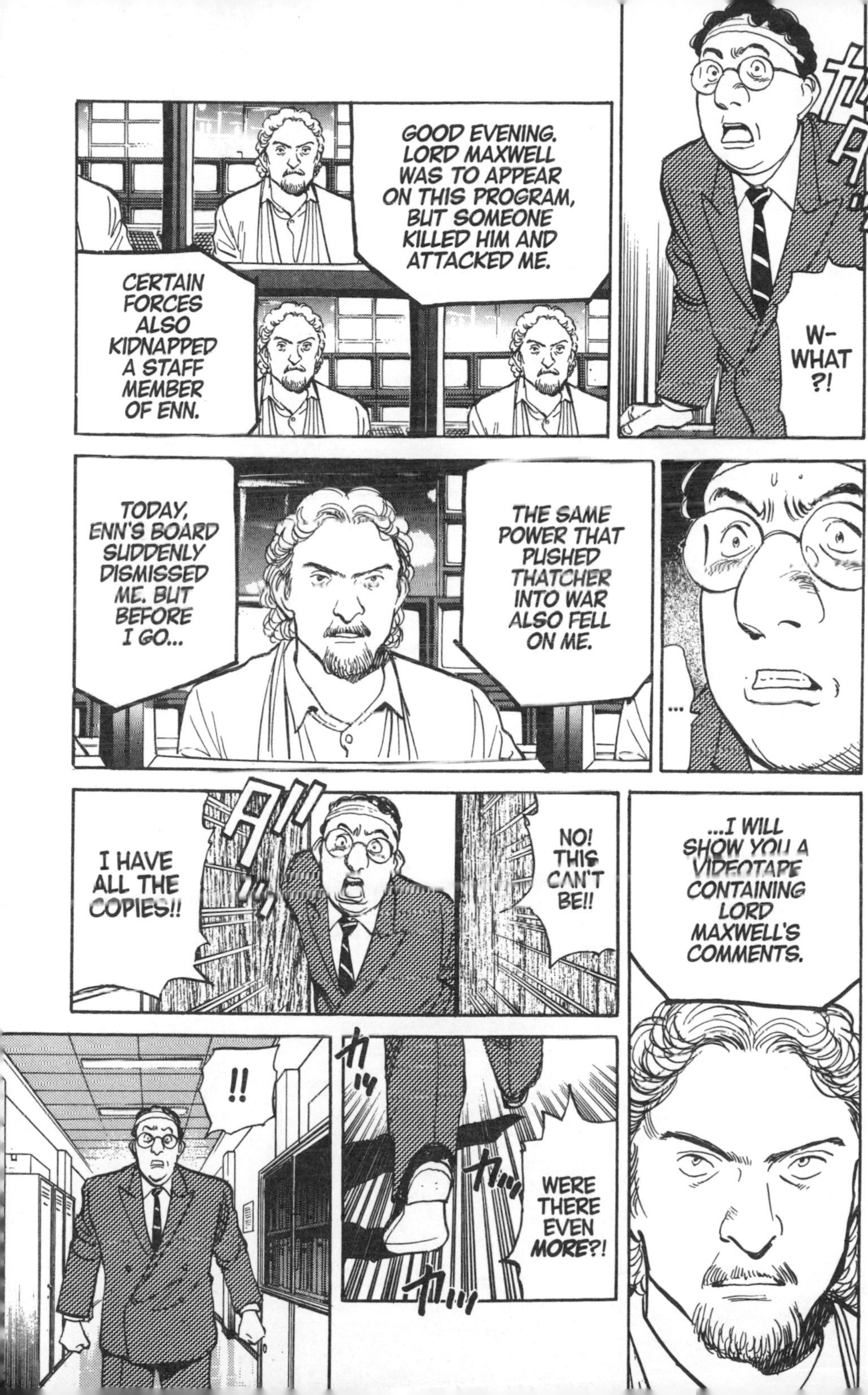
W-
WHAT
?!
GOOD EVENING. LORD MAXWELL WAS TO APPEAR ON THIS PROGRAM, BUT SOMEONE KILLED HIM AND ATTACKED ME.
CERTAIN FORCES ALSO KIDNAPPED A STAFF MEMBER OF ENN.
...
THE SAME POWER THAT PUSHED THATCHER INTO WAR ALSO FELL ON ME.
TODAY, ENN'S BOARD SUDDENLY DISMISSED ME. BUT BEFORE I GO...
...I WILL SHOW YOU A VIDEOTAPE CONTAINING LORD MAXWELL'S COMMENTS.
NO! THIS CAN'T BE!!
I HAVE ALL THE COPIES!!
WERE THERE EVEN MORE?!
!!

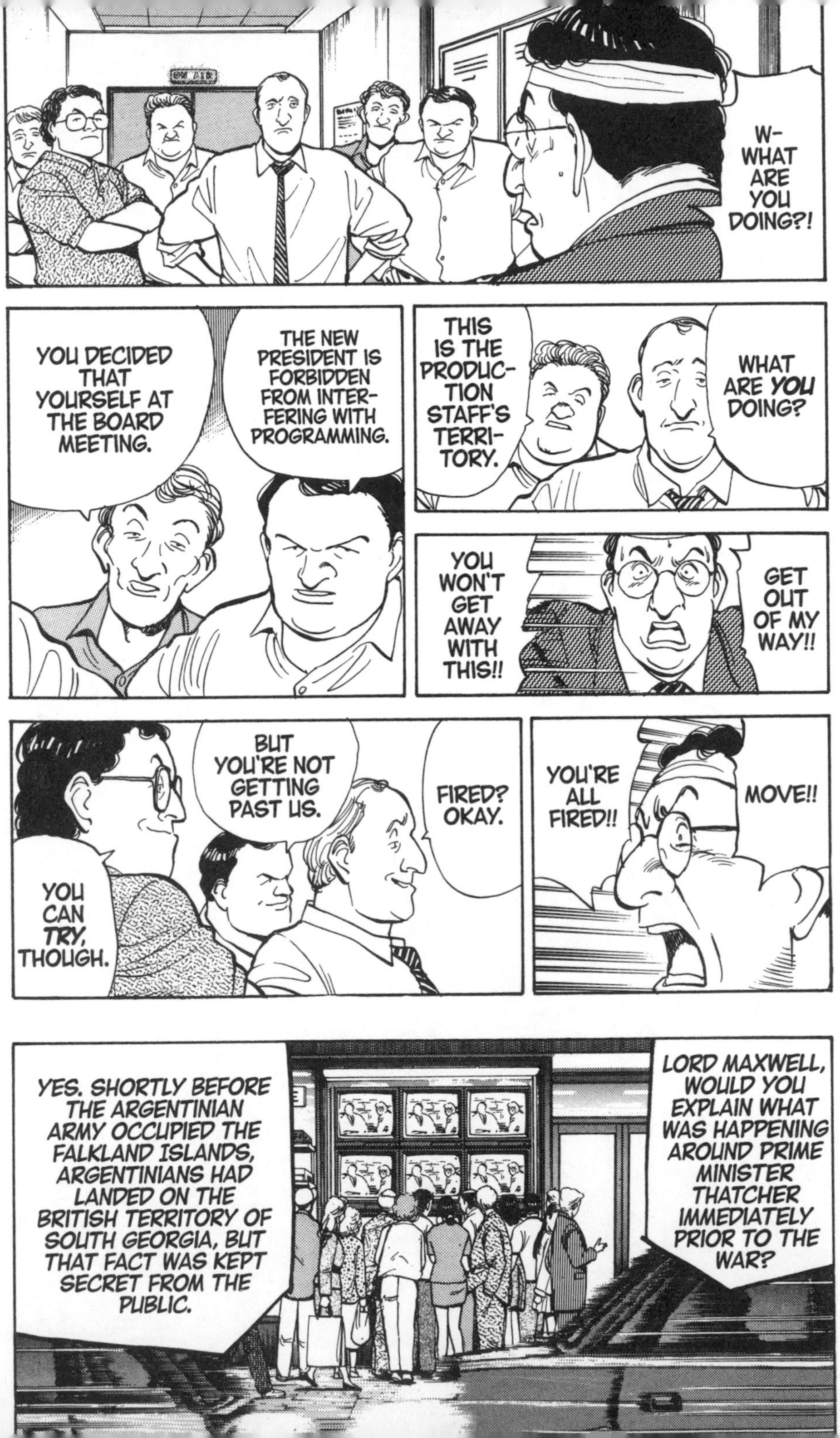
W-WHAT ARE YOU DOING?!
ON AIR
WHAT ARE YOU DOING?
THIS IS THE PRODUCTION STAFF'S TERRITORY.
GET OUT OF MY WAY!!
YOU WON'T GET AWAY WITH THIS!!
THE NEW PRESIDENT IS FORBIDDEN FROM INTERFERING WITH PROGRAMMING.
YOU DECIDED THAT YOURSELF AT THE BOARD MEETING.
MOVE!!
YOU'RE ALL FIRED!!
FIRED? OKAY.
BUT YOU'RE NOT GETTING PAST US.
YOU CAN TRY, THOUGH.
LORD MAXWELL, WOULD YOU EXPLAIN WHAT WAS HAPPENING AROUND PRIME MINISTER THATCHER IMMEDIATELY PRIOR TO THE WAR?
YES. SHORTLY BEFORE THE ARGENTINIAN ARMY OCCUPIED THE FALKLAND ISLANDS, ARGENTINIANS HAD LANDED ON THE BRITISH TERRITORY OF SOUTH GEORGIA, BUT THAT FACT WAS KEPT SECRET FROM THE PUBLIC.

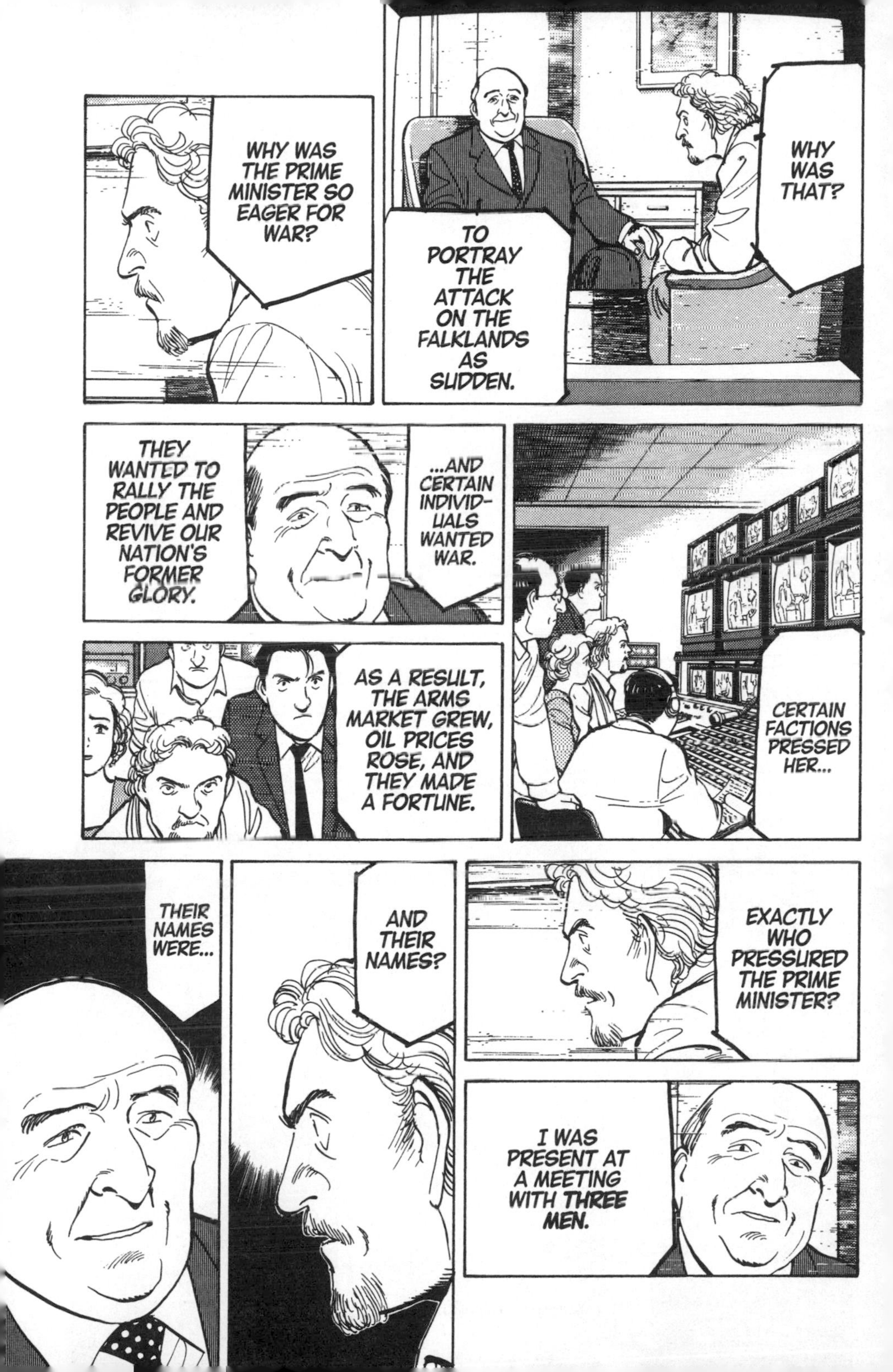
WHY WAS THAT?
TO PORTRAY THE ATTACK ON THE FALKLANDS AS SUDDEN.
WHY WAS THE PRIME MINISTER SO EAGER FOR WAR?
CERTAIN FACTIONS PRESSED HER...
...AND CERTAIN INDIVID-UALS WANTED WAR.
THEY WANTED TO RALLY THE PEOPLE AND REVIVE OUR NATION'S FORMER GLORY.
AS A RESULT, THE ARMS MARKET GREW, OIL PRICES ROSE, AND THEY MADE A FORTUNE.
EXACTLY WHO PRESSURED THE PRIME MINISTER?
I WAS PRESENT AT A MEETING WITH THREE MEN.
AND THEIR NAMES?
THEIR NAMES WERE...

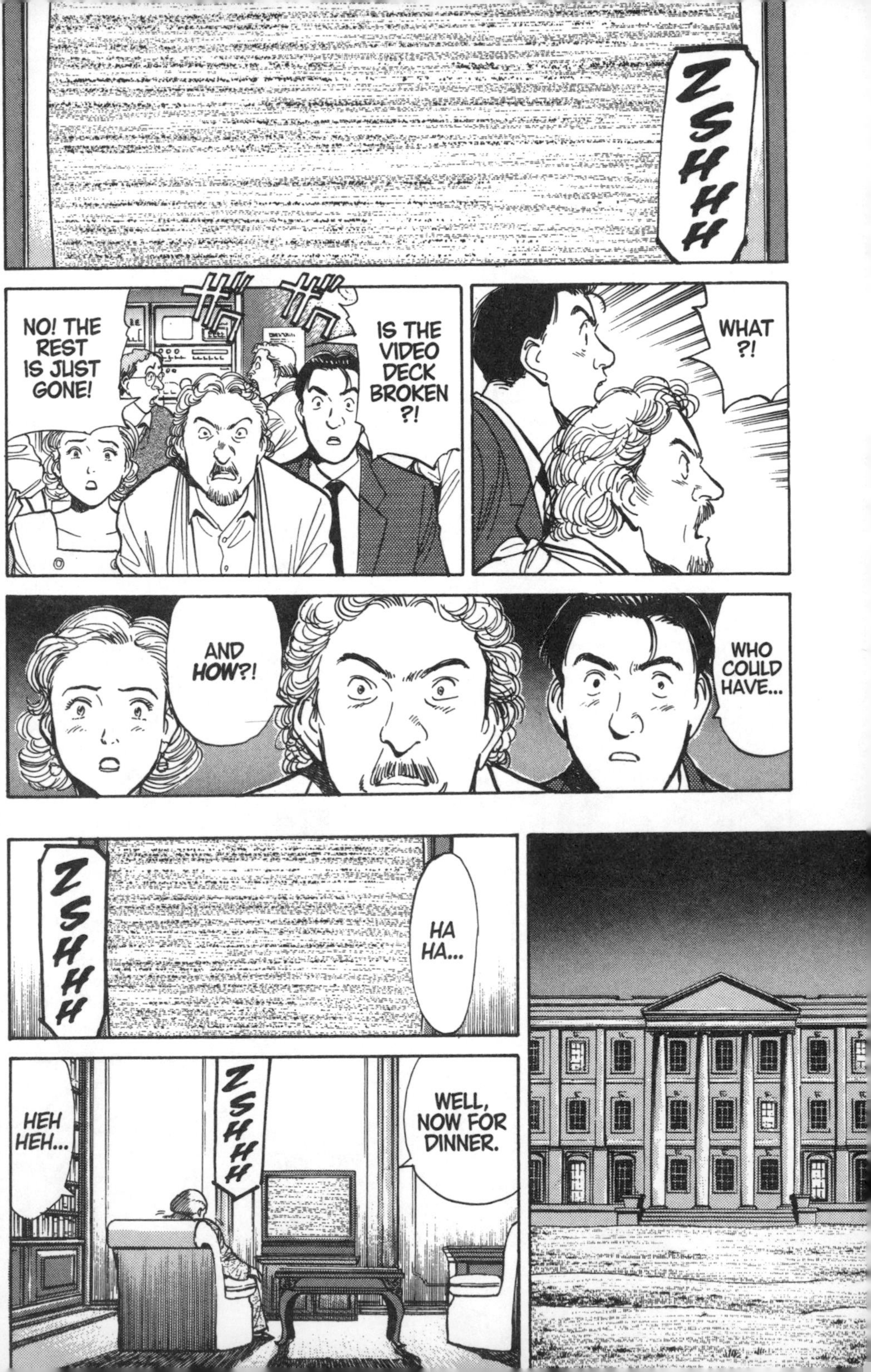
ZSHHH
WHAT?!
IS THE VIDEO DECK BROKEN?!
NO! THE REST IS JUST GONE!
WHO COULD HAVE...
AND HOW?!
HA HA...
ZSHHH
WELL, NOW FOR DINNER.
ZSHHH
HEH HEH...

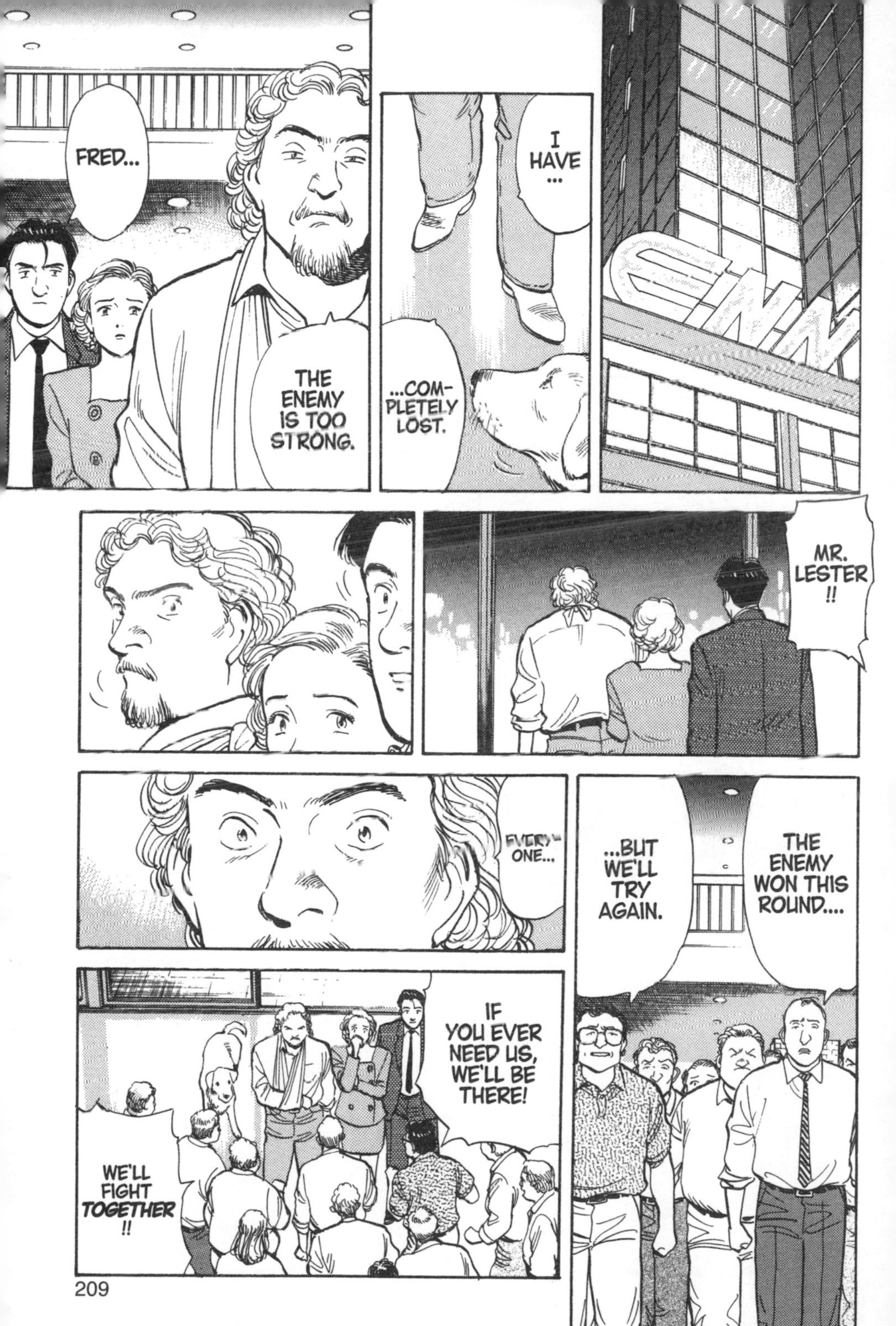
I HAVE ...
...COM-PLETELY LOST.
THE ENEMY IS TOO STRONG.
FRED...
MR. LESTER !!
THE ENEMY WON THIS ROUND....
...BUT WE'LL TRY AGAIN.
EVERY-ONE...
IF YOU EVER NEED US, WE'LL BE THERE!
WE'LL FIGHT TOGETHER !!

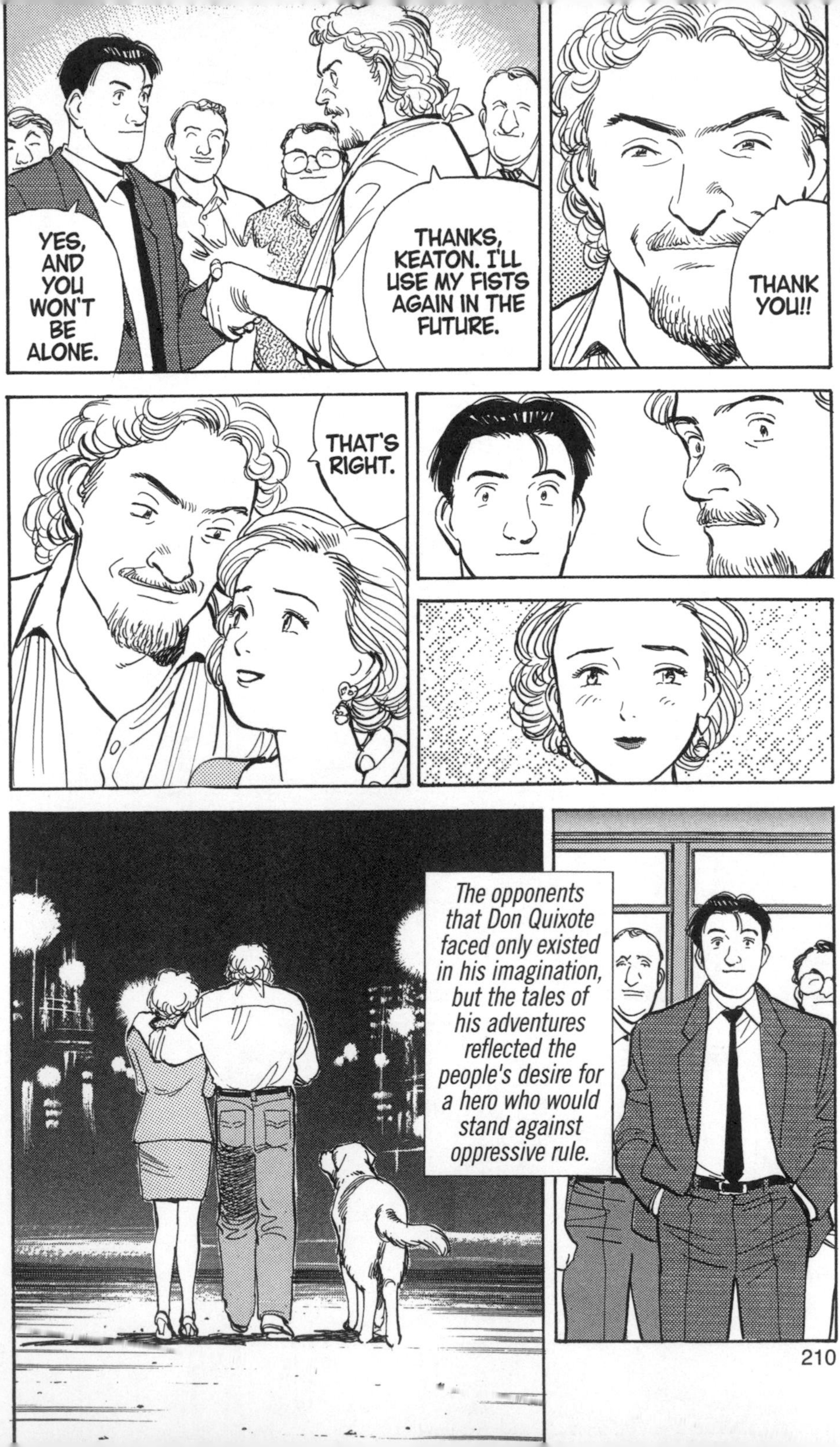
THANK YOU!!
THANKS, KEATON. I'LL USE MY FISTS AGAIN IN THE FUTURE.
YES, AND YOU WON'T BE ALONE.
THAT'S RIGHT.
The opponents that Don Quixote faced only existed in his imagination, but the tales of his adventures reflected the people's desire for a hero who would stand against oppressive rule.

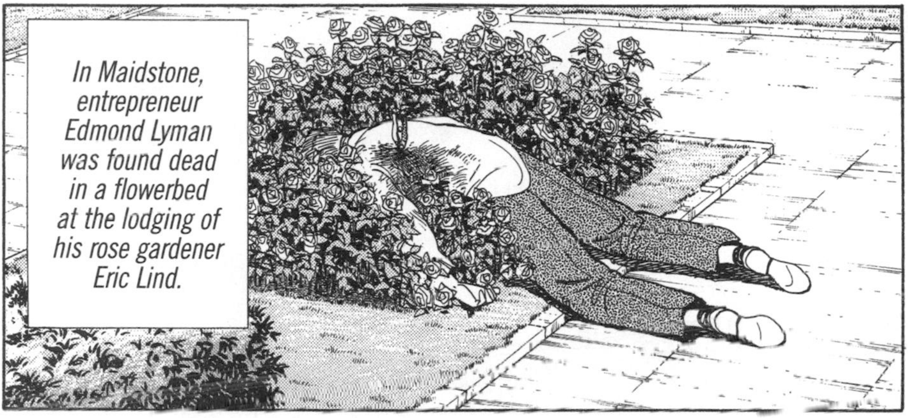
In Maidstone, entrepreneur Edmond Lyman was found dead in a flowerbed at the lodging of his rose gardener Eric Lind.

Chapter 9
House of Roses

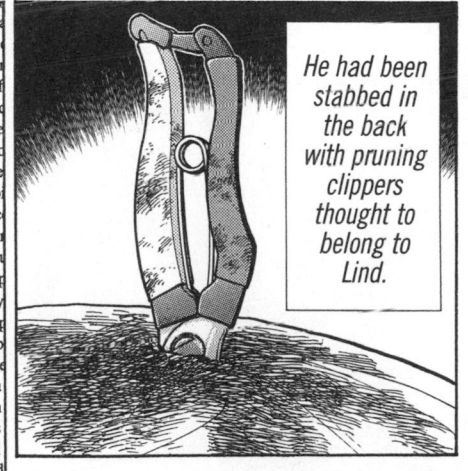

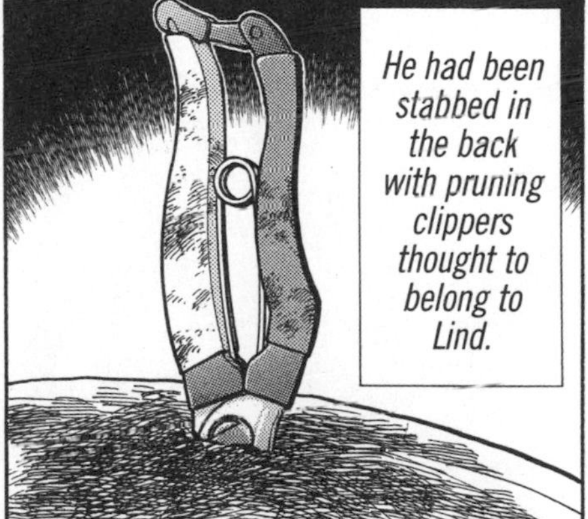
He had been stabbed in the back with pruning clippers thought to belong to Lind.

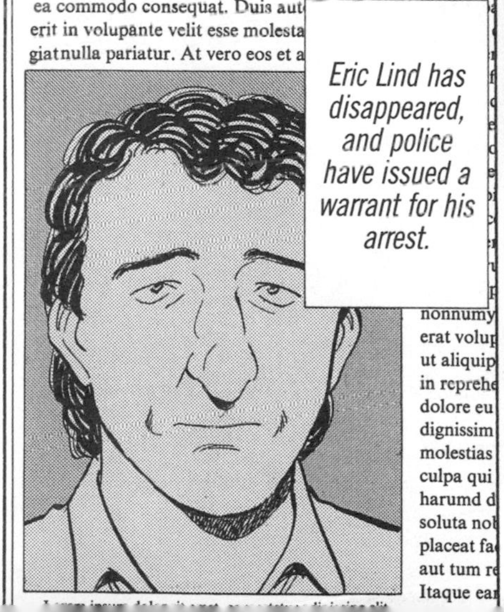
Eric Lind has disappeared, and police have issued a warrant for his arrest.

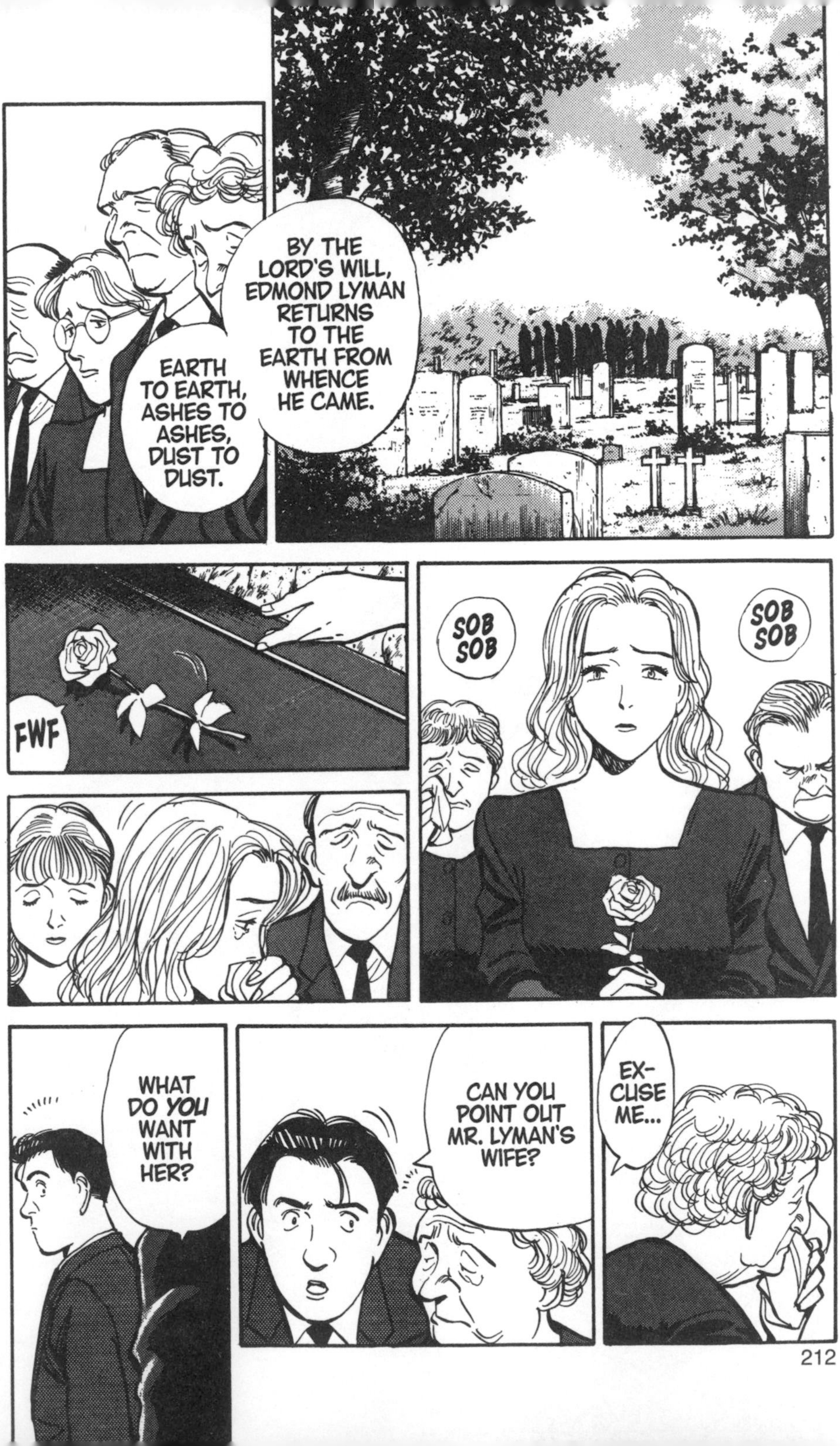
BY THE LORD'S WILL, EDMOND LYMAN RETURNS TO THE EARTH FROM WHENCE HE CAME.
EARTH TO EARTH, ASHES TO ASHES, DUST TO DUST.
SOB SOB
SOB SOB
FWF
EX-CUSE ME...
CAN YOU POINT OUT MR. LYMAN'S WIFE?
WHAT DO YOU WANT WITH HER?

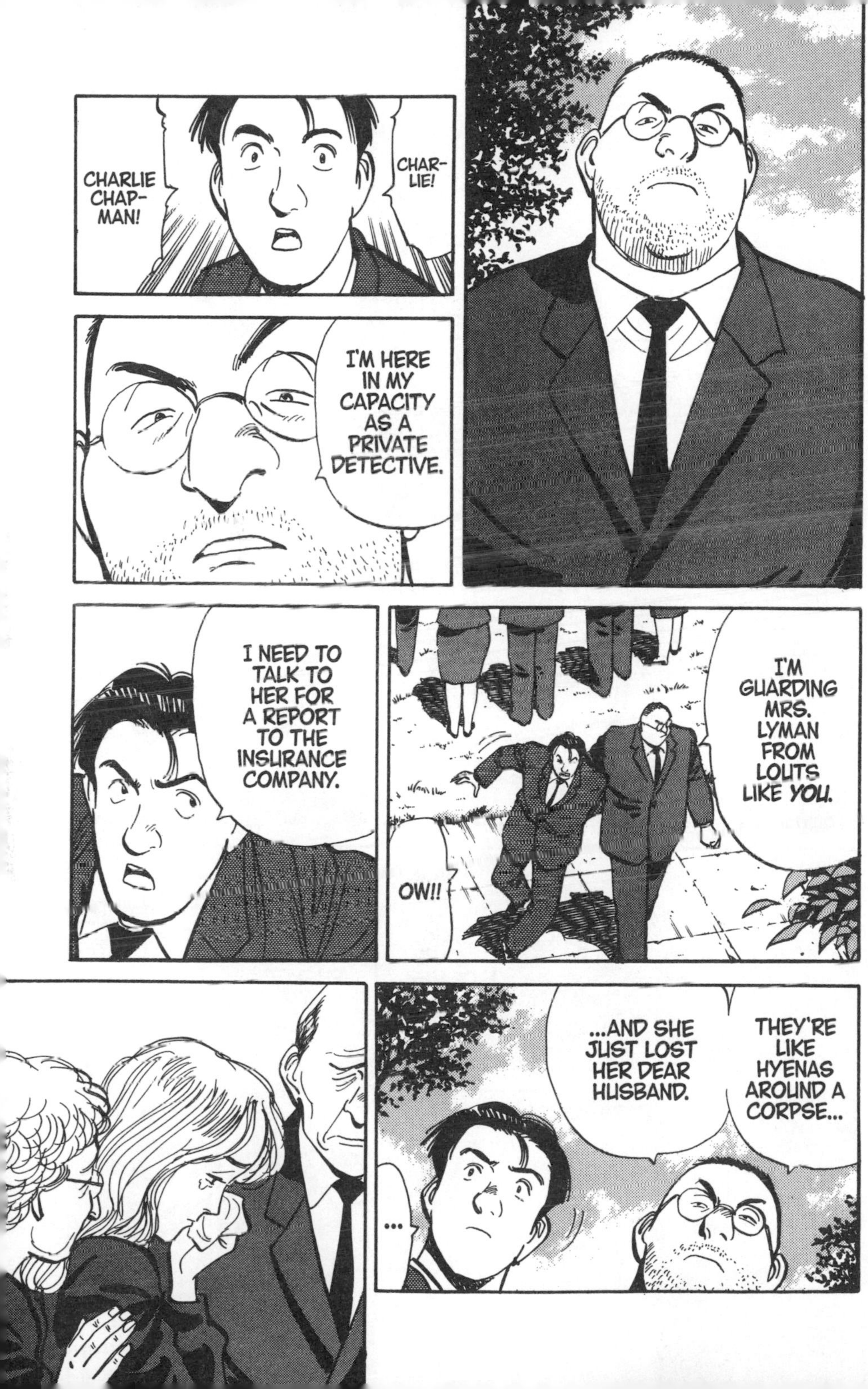
CHAR-LIE!
CHARLIE CHAP-MAN!
I'M HERE IN MY CAPACITY AS A PRIVATE DETECTIVE.
I'M GUARDING MRS. LYMAN FROM LOUTS LIKE YOU.
OW!!
I NEED TO TALK TO HER FOR A REPORT TO THE INSURANCE COMPANY.
THEY'RE LIKE HYENAS AROUND A CORPSE...
...AND SHE JUST LOST HER DEAR HUSBAND.
...

I WON'T LET ANYONE HURT HER, NOT EVEN YOU.
WHAT WAS THAT LOOK FOR?!
OH, NOTHING ...
YOU ALWAYS RUIN THINGS, SO GET LOST.
BUT—
I SAID GET LOST!
IF YOU BOTHER MRS. LYMAN, YOU'LL REGRET IT!
THANK YOU. I'LL TAKE CARE OF HER.
...

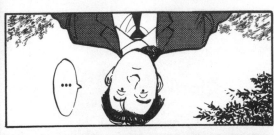

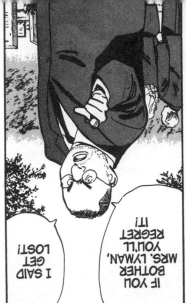

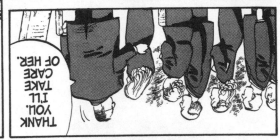

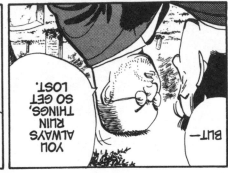

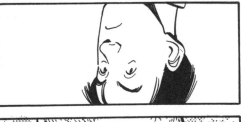

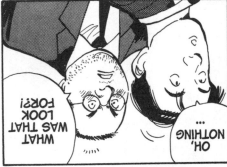

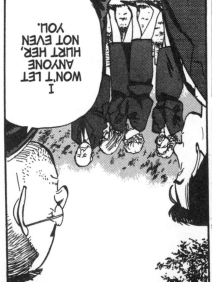

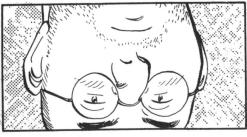

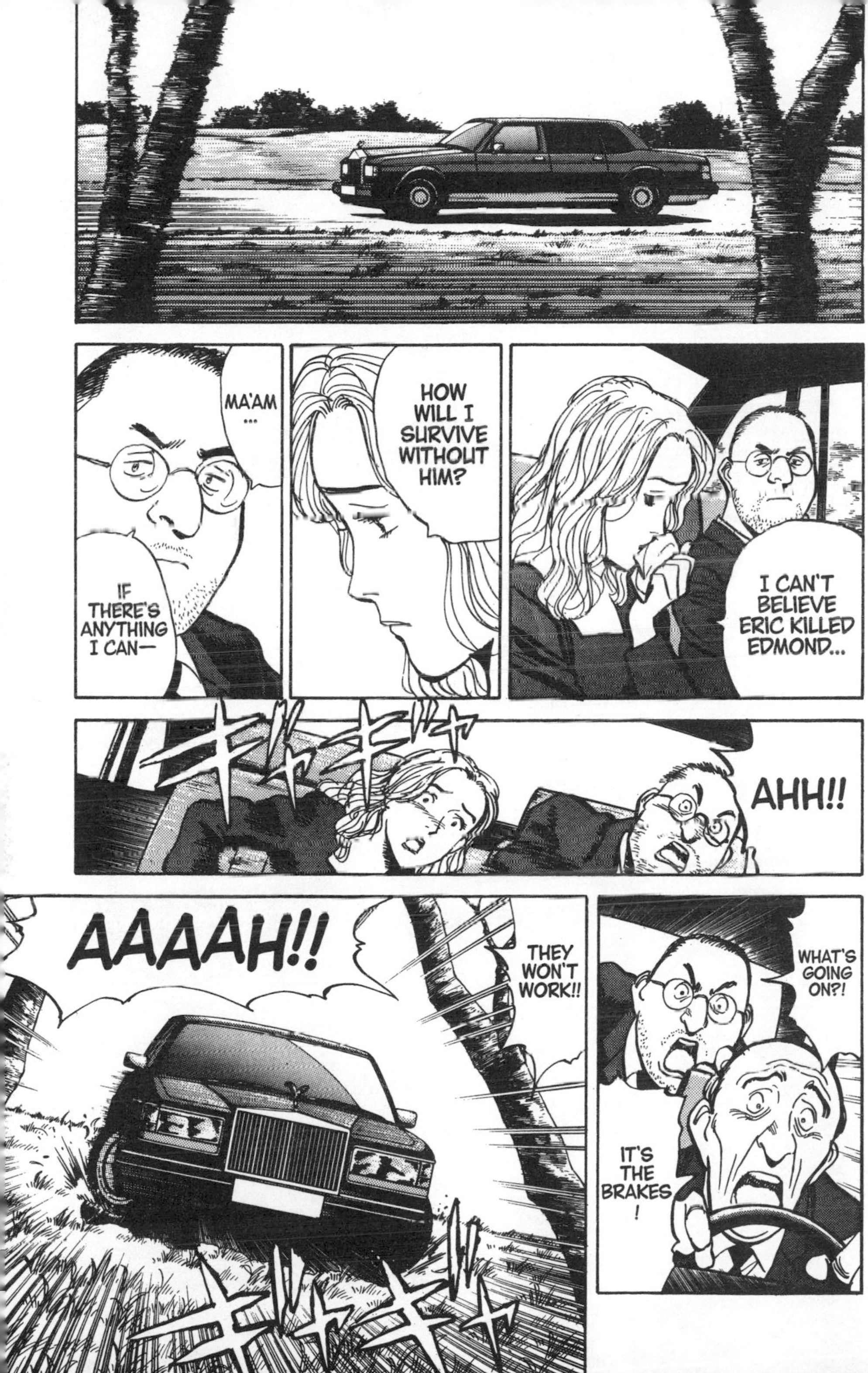
I CAN'T BELIEVE ERIC KILLED EDMOND...
HOW WILL I SURVIVE WITHOUT HIM?
MA'AM...
IF THERE'S ANYTHING I CAN—
AHH!!
WHAT'S GOING ON?!
IT'S THE BRAKES!
THEY WON'T WORK!!
AAAAH!!

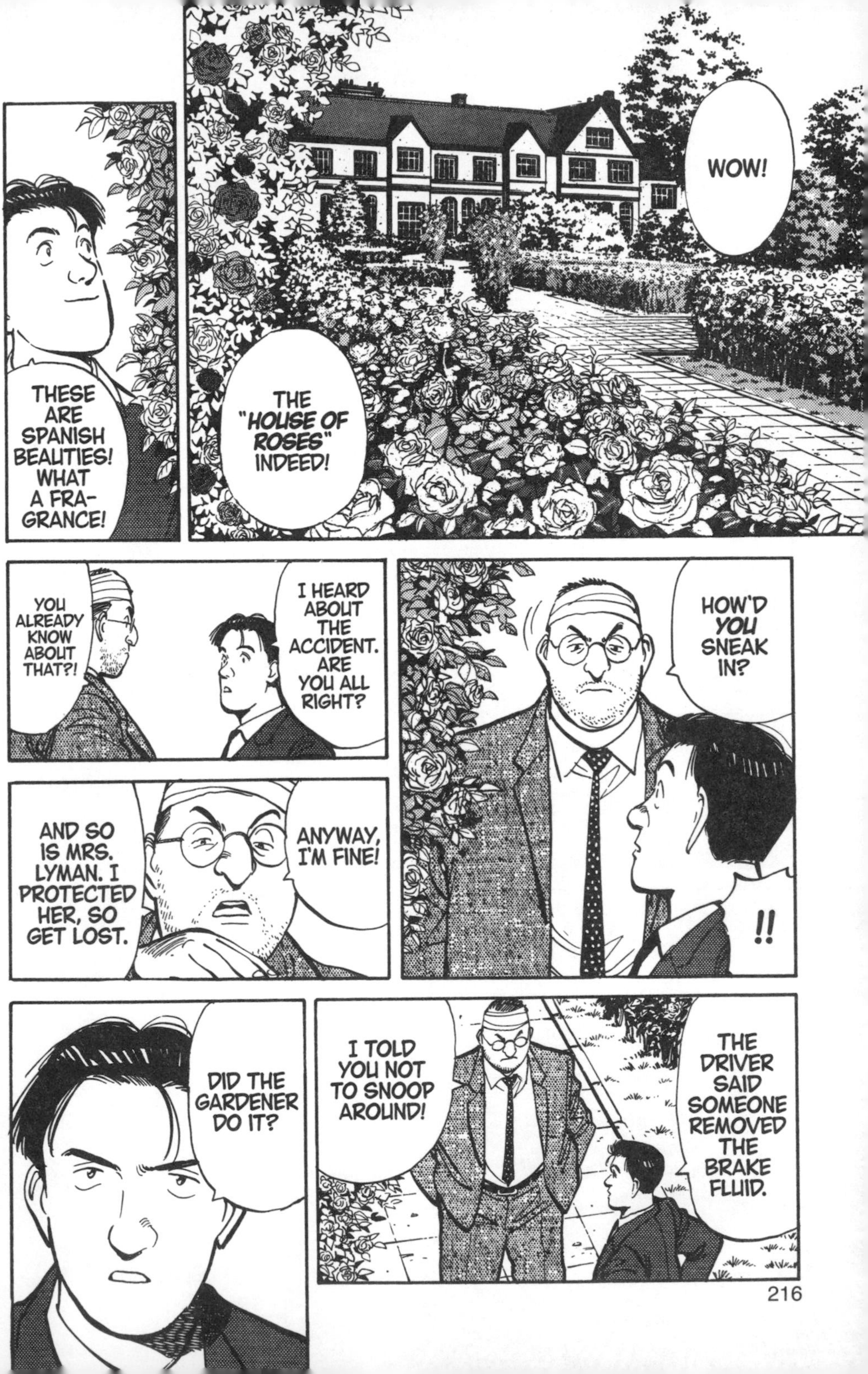
WOW!
THE "HOUSE OF ROSES" INDEED!
THESE ARE SPANISH BEAUTIES! WHAT A FRA-GRANCE!
HOW'D YOU SNEAK IN?
!!
I HEARD ABOUT THE ACCIDENT. ARE YOU ALL RIGHT?
YOU ALREADY KNOW ABOUT THAT?!
ANYWAY, I'M FINE!
AND SO IS MRS. LYMAN. I PROTECTED HER, SO GET LOST.
THE DRIVER SAID SOMEONE REMOVED THE BRAKE FLUID.
I TOLD YOU NOT TO SNOOP AROUND!
DID THE GARDENER DO IT?

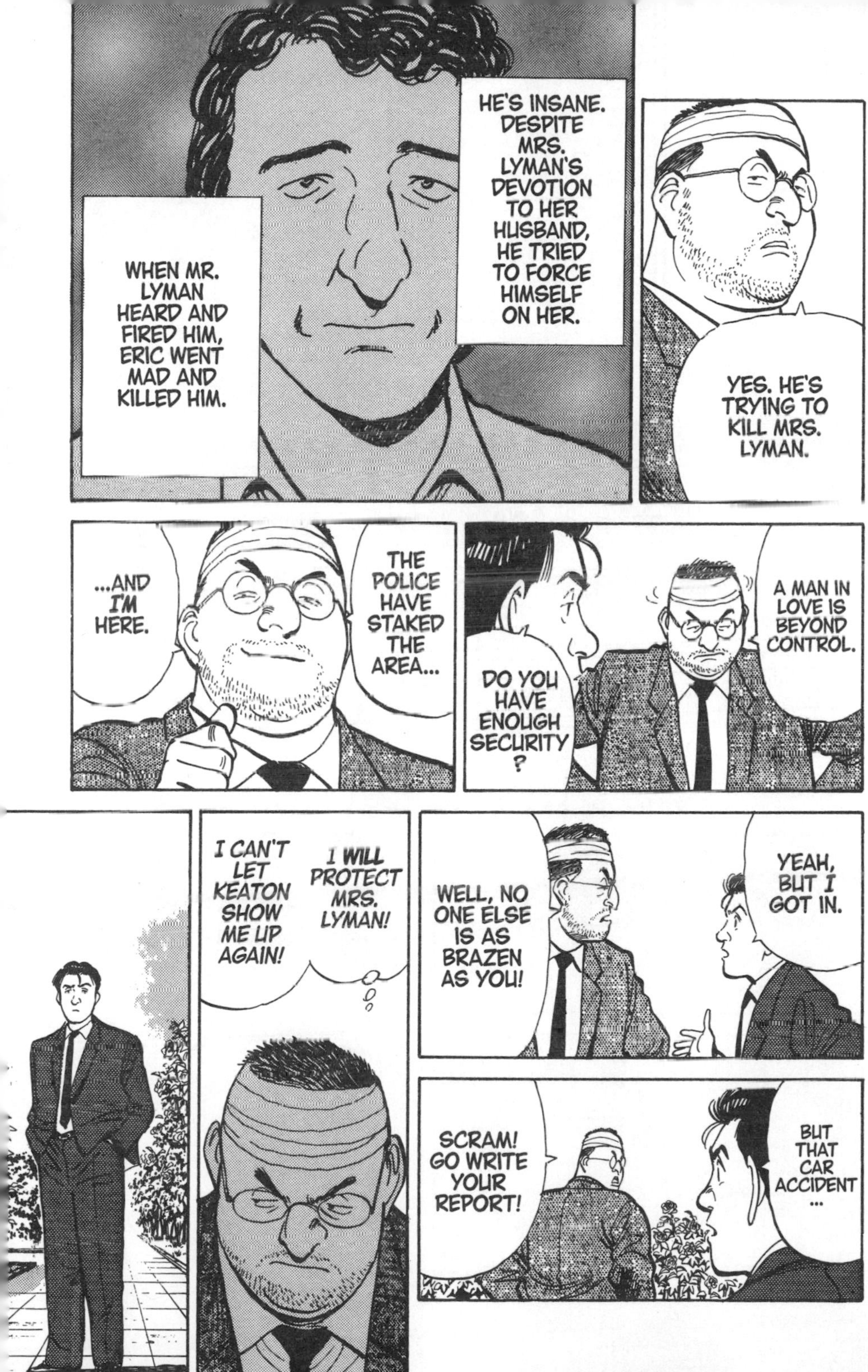
YES. HE'S TRYING TO KILL MRS. LYMAN.
HE'S INSANE. DESPITE MRS. LYMAN'S DEVOTION TO HER HUSBAND, HE TRIED TO FORCE HIMSELF ON HER.
WHEN MR. LYMAN HEARD AND FIRED HIM, ERIC WENT MAD AND KILLED HIM.
A MAN IN LOVE IS BEYOND CONTROL.
DO YOU HAVE ENOUGH SECURITY ?
THE POLICE HAVE STAKED THE AREA...
...AND I'M HERE.
YEAH, BUT I GOT IN.
WELL, NO ONE ELSE IS AS BRAZEN AS YOU!
BUT THAT CAR ACCIDENT ...
SCRAM! GO WRITE YOUR REPORT!
I WILL PROTECT MRS. LYMAN!
I CAN'T LET KEATON SHOW ME UP AGAIN!

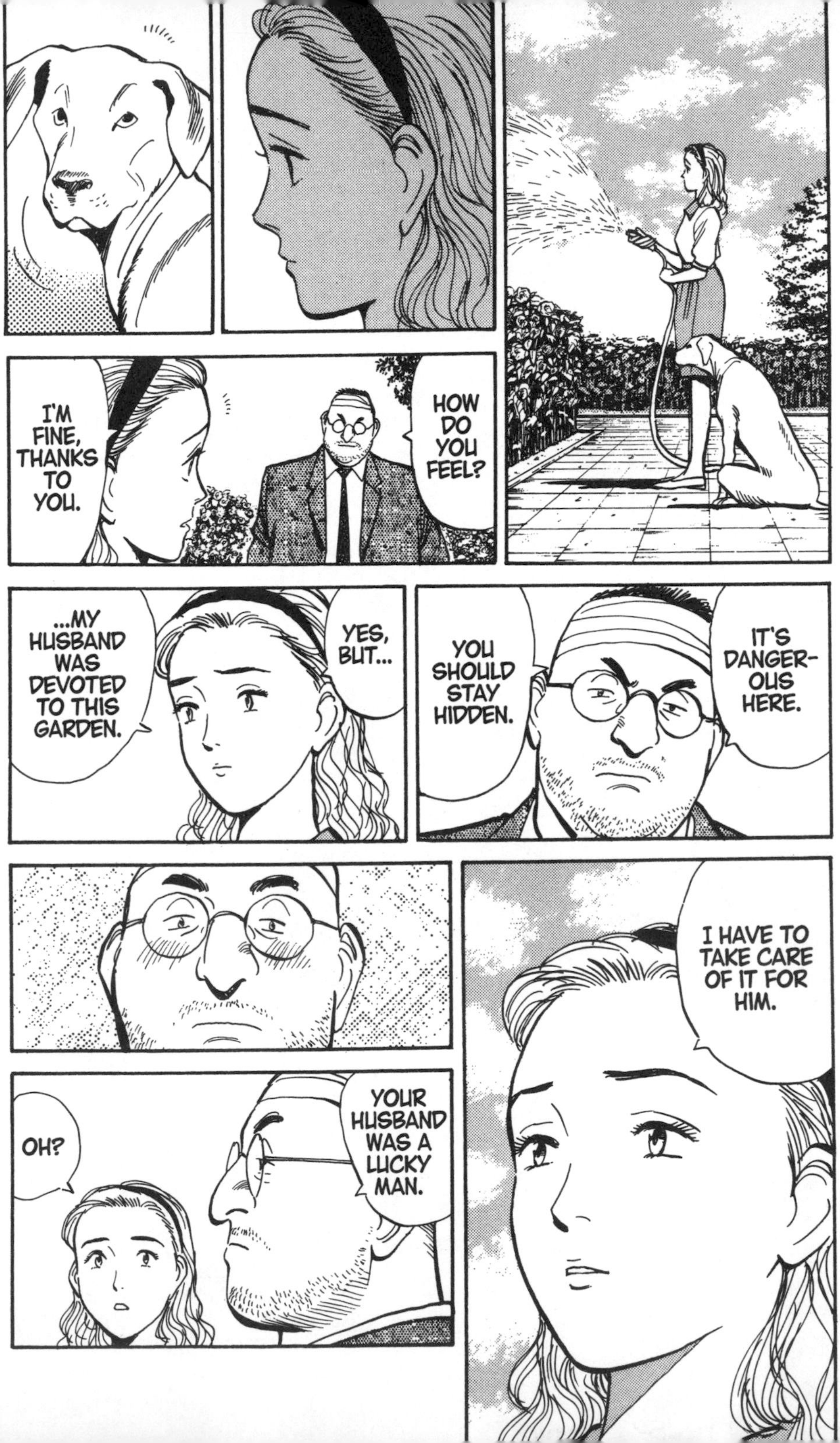

HOW DO YOU FEEL?
I'M FINE, THANKS TO YOU.
IT'S DANGER-OUS HERE.
YOU SHOULD STAY HIDDEN.
YES, BUT...
...MY HUSBAND WAS DEVOTED TO THIS GARDEN.
I HAVE TO TAKE CARE OF IT FOR HIM.
YOUR HUSBAND WAS A LUCKY MAN.
OH?

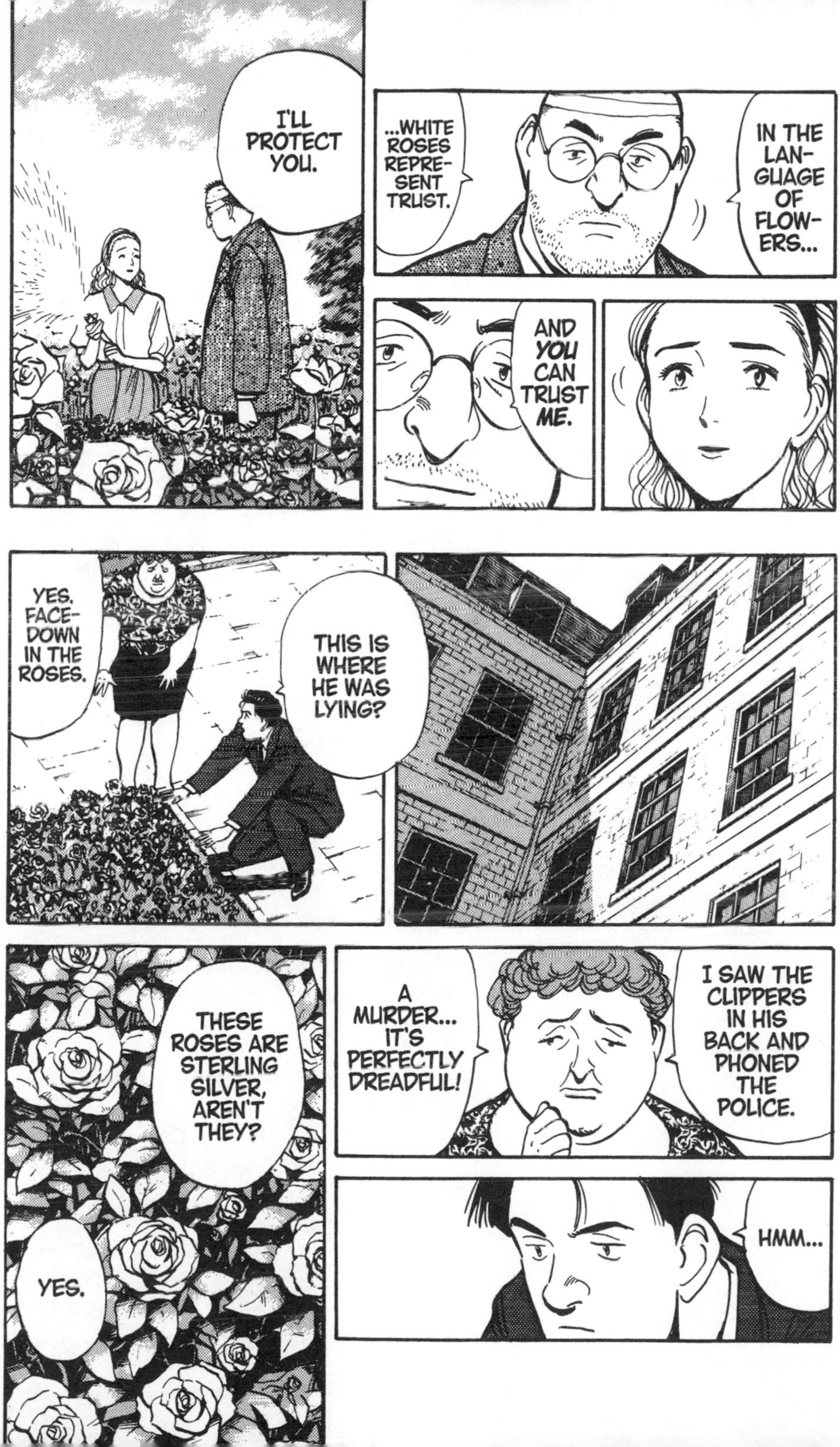

IN THE LAN-GUAGE OF FLOW-ERS...
...WHITE ROSES REPRE-SENT TRUST.
AND YOU CAN TRUST ME.
I'LL PROTECT YOU.
THIS IS WHERE HE WAS LYING?
YES. FACE-DOWN IN THE ROSES.
I SAW THE CLIPPERS IN HIS BACK AND PHONED THE POLICE.
A MURDER... IT'S PERFECTLY DREADFUL!
HMM...
THESE ROSES ARE STERLING SILVER, AREN'T THEY?
YES.

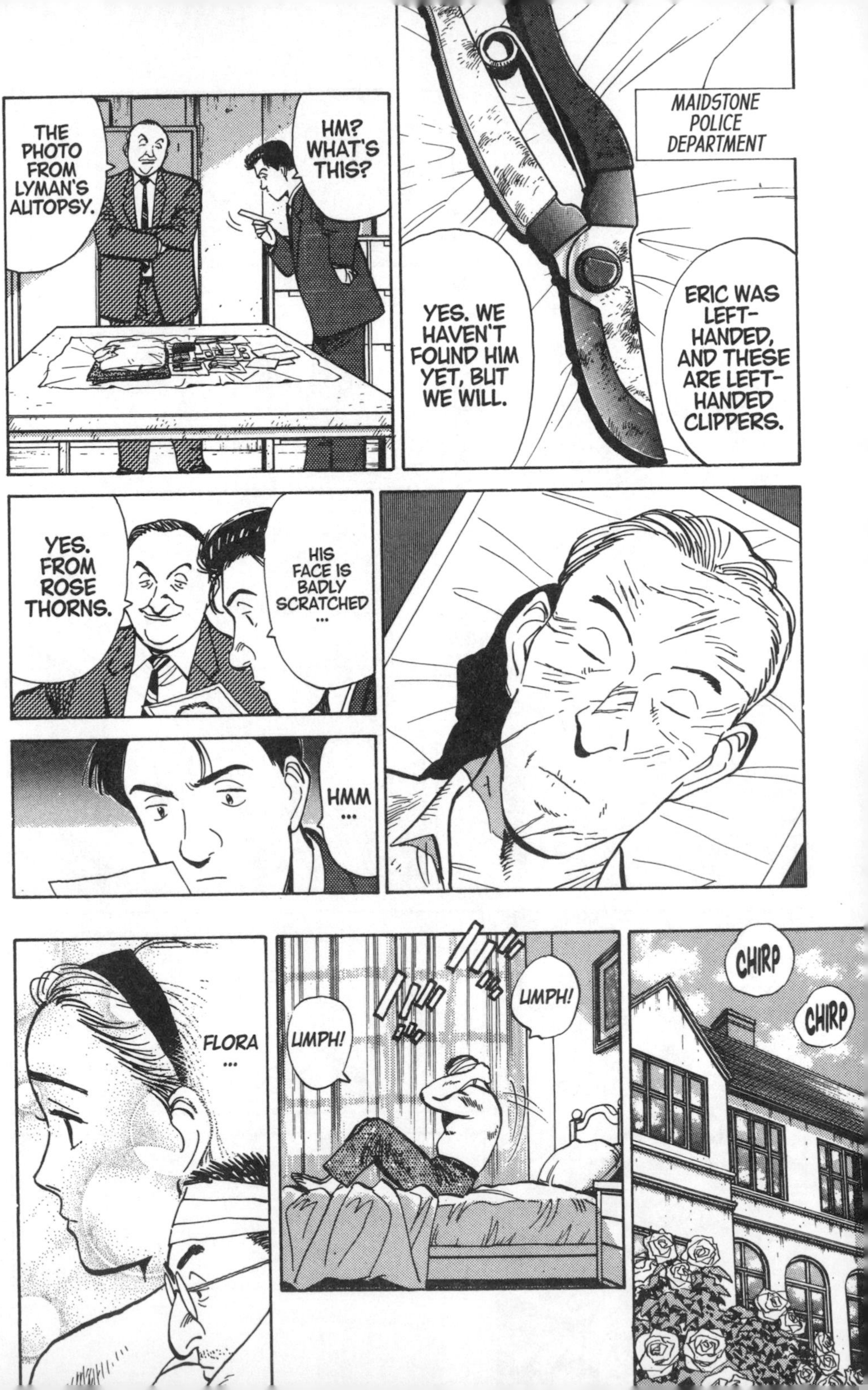
MAIDSTONE POLICE DEPARTMENT
ERIC WAS LEFT-HANDED, AND THESE ARE LEFT-HANDED CLIPPERS.
YES. WE HAVEN'T FOUND HIM YET, BUT WE WILL.
HM? WHAT'S THIS?
THE PHOTO FROM LYMAN'S AUTOPSY.
HIS FACE IS BADLY SCRATCHED ...
YES. FROM ROSE THORNS.
HMM ...
CHIRP
CHIRP
UMPH!
UMPH!
FLORA ...

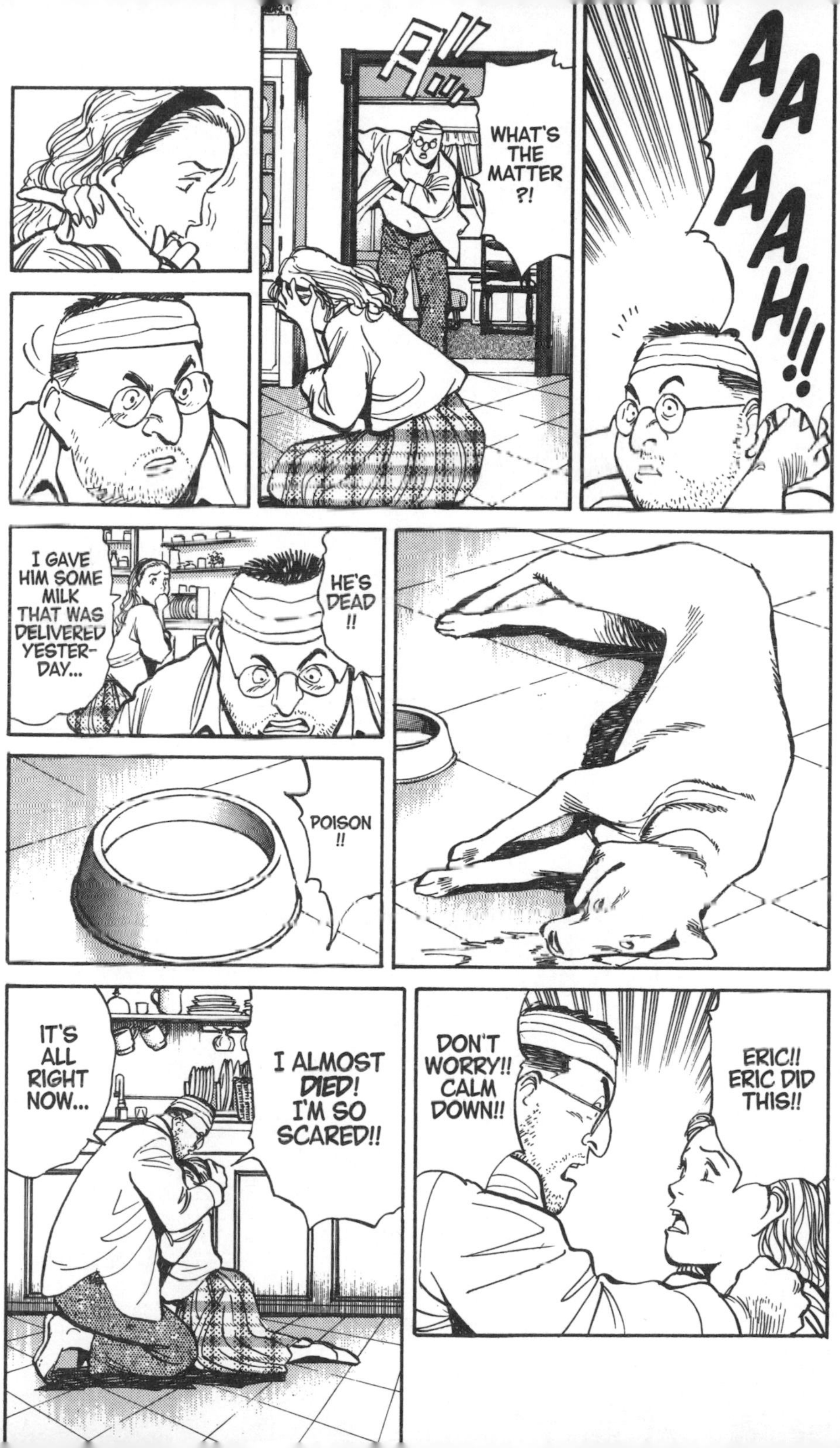
AAAAH!!
WHAT'S THE MATTER ?!
HE'S DEAD !!
I GAVE HIM SOME MILK THAT WAS DELIVERED YESTER-DAY...
POISON !!
ERIC!! ERIC DID THIS!!
DON'T WORRY!! CALM DOWN!!
I ALMOST DIED! I'M SO SCARED!!
IT'S ALL RIGHT NOW...

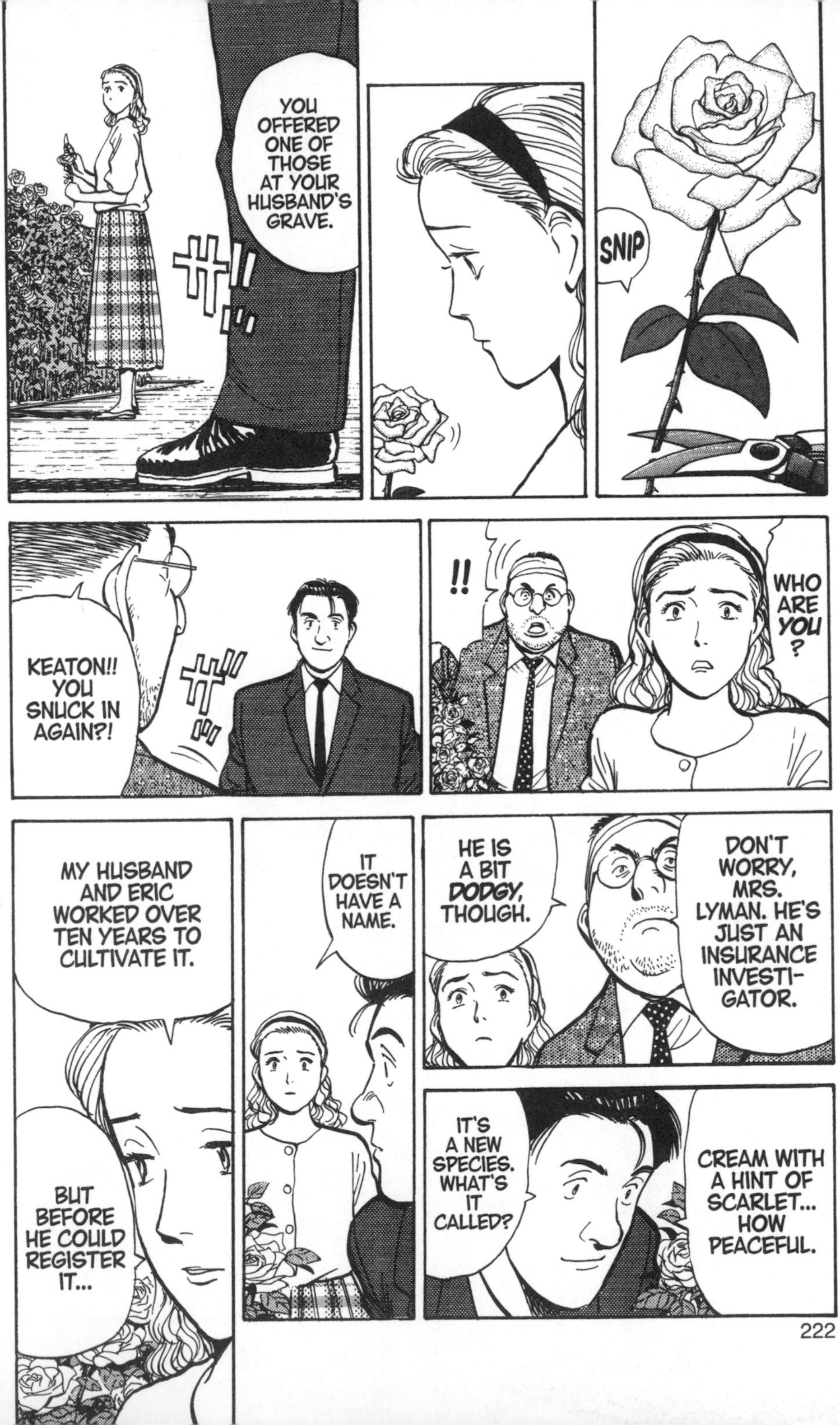
SNIP
YOU OFFERED ONE OF THOSE AT YOUR HUSBAND'S GRAVE.
WHO ARE YOU?
!!
KEATON!! YOU SNUCK IN AGAIN?!
DON'T WORRY, MRS. LYMAN. HE'S JUST AN INSURANCE INVESTI-GATOR.
HE IS A BIT DODGY, THOUGH.
CREAM WITH A HINT OF SCARLET... HOW PEACEFUL.
IT'S A NEW SPECIES. WHAT'S IT CALLED?
IT DOESN'T HAVE A NAME.
MY HUSBAND AND ERIC WORKED OVER TEN YEARS TO CULTIVATE IT.
BUT BEFORE HE COULD REGISTER IT...

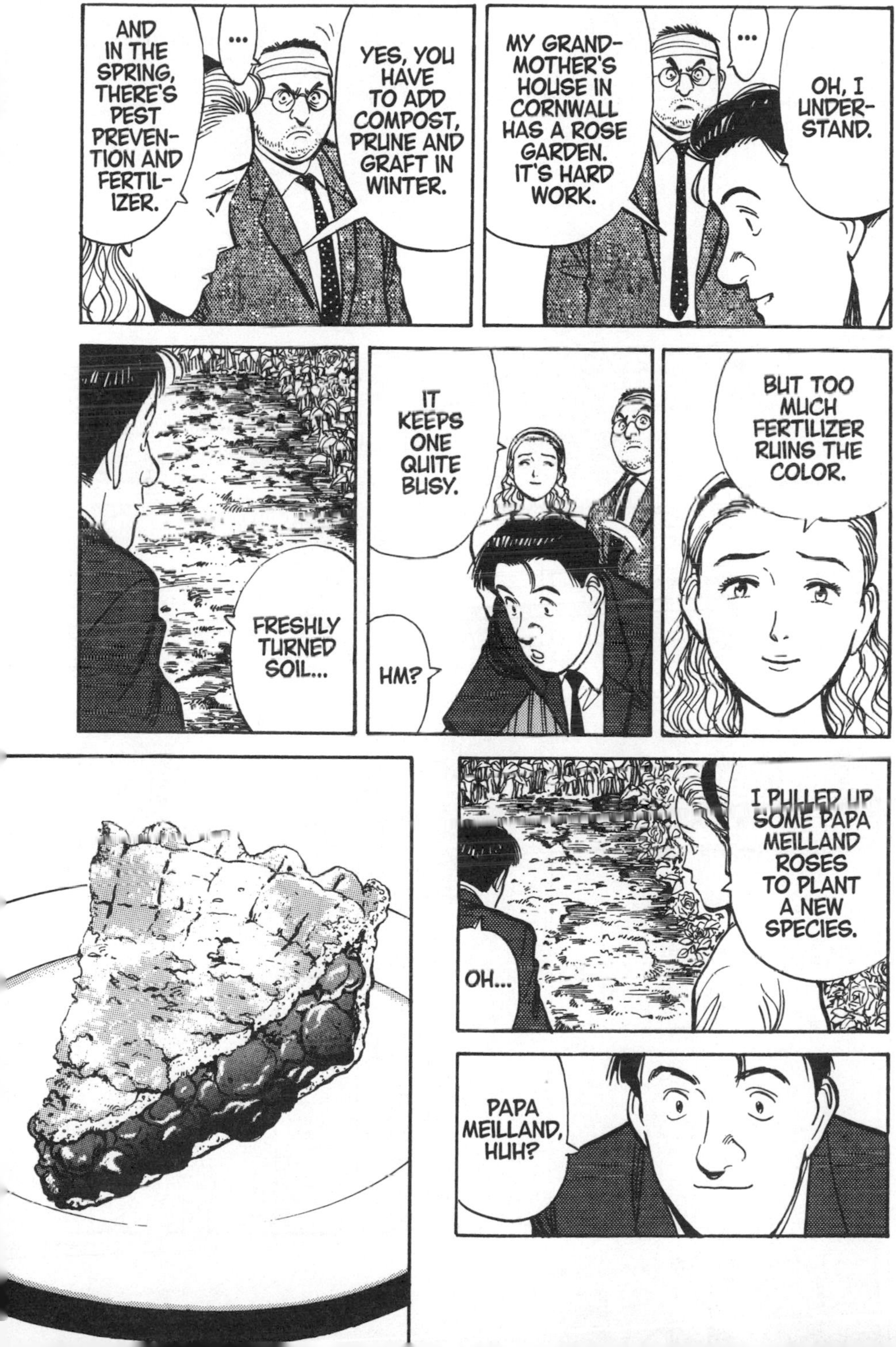
OH, I UNDER-STAND.
...
MY GRAND-MOTHER'S HOUSE IN CORNWALL HAS A ROSE GARDEN. IT'S HARD WORK.
YES, YOU HAVE TO ADD COMPOST, PRUNE AND GRAFT IN WINTER.
...
AND IN THE SPRING, THERE'S PEST PREVEN-TION AND FERTIL-IZER.
BUT TOO MUCH FERTILIZER RUINS THE COLOR.
IT KEEPS ONE QUITE BUSY.
HM?
FRESHLY TURNED SOIL...
I PULLED UP SOME PAPA MEILLAND ROSES TO PLANT A NEW SPECIES.
OH...
PAPA MEILLAND, HUH?

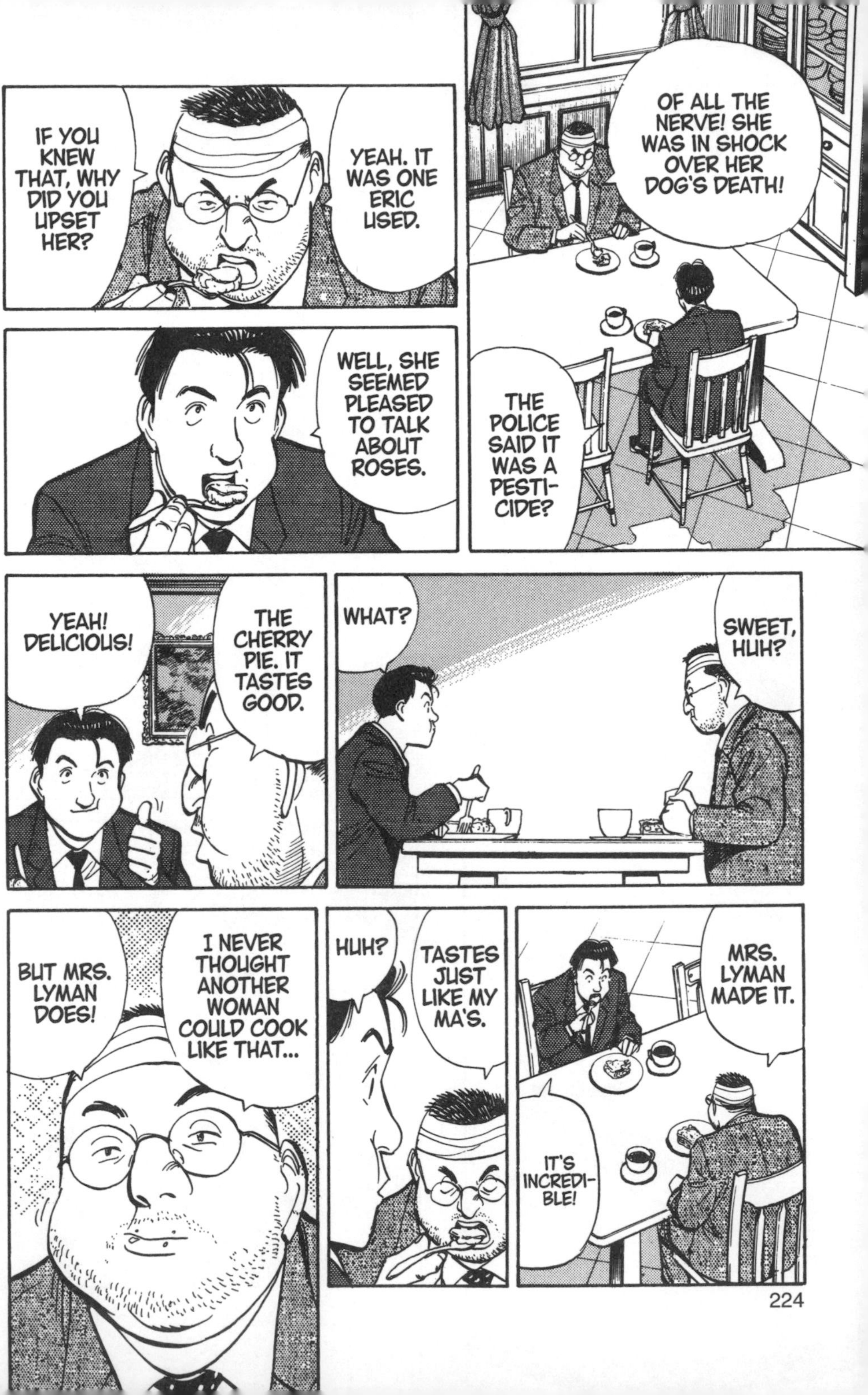
OF ALL THE NERVE! SHE WAS IN SHOCK OVER HER DOG'S DEATH!
THE POLICE SAID IT WAS A PESTICIDE?
YEAH. IT WAS ONE ERIC USED.
IF YOU KNEW THAT, WHY DID YOU UPSET HER?
WELL, SHE SEEMED PLEASED TO TALK ABOUT ROSES.
SWEET, HUH?
WHAT?
THE CHERRY PIE. IT TASTES GOOD.
YEAH! DELICIOUS!
MRS. LYMAN MADE IT.
IT'S INCREDIBLE!
TASTES JUST LIKE MY MA'S.
HUH?
I NEVER THOUGHT ANOTHER WOMAN COULD COOK LIKE THAT...
BUT MRS. LYMAN DOES!

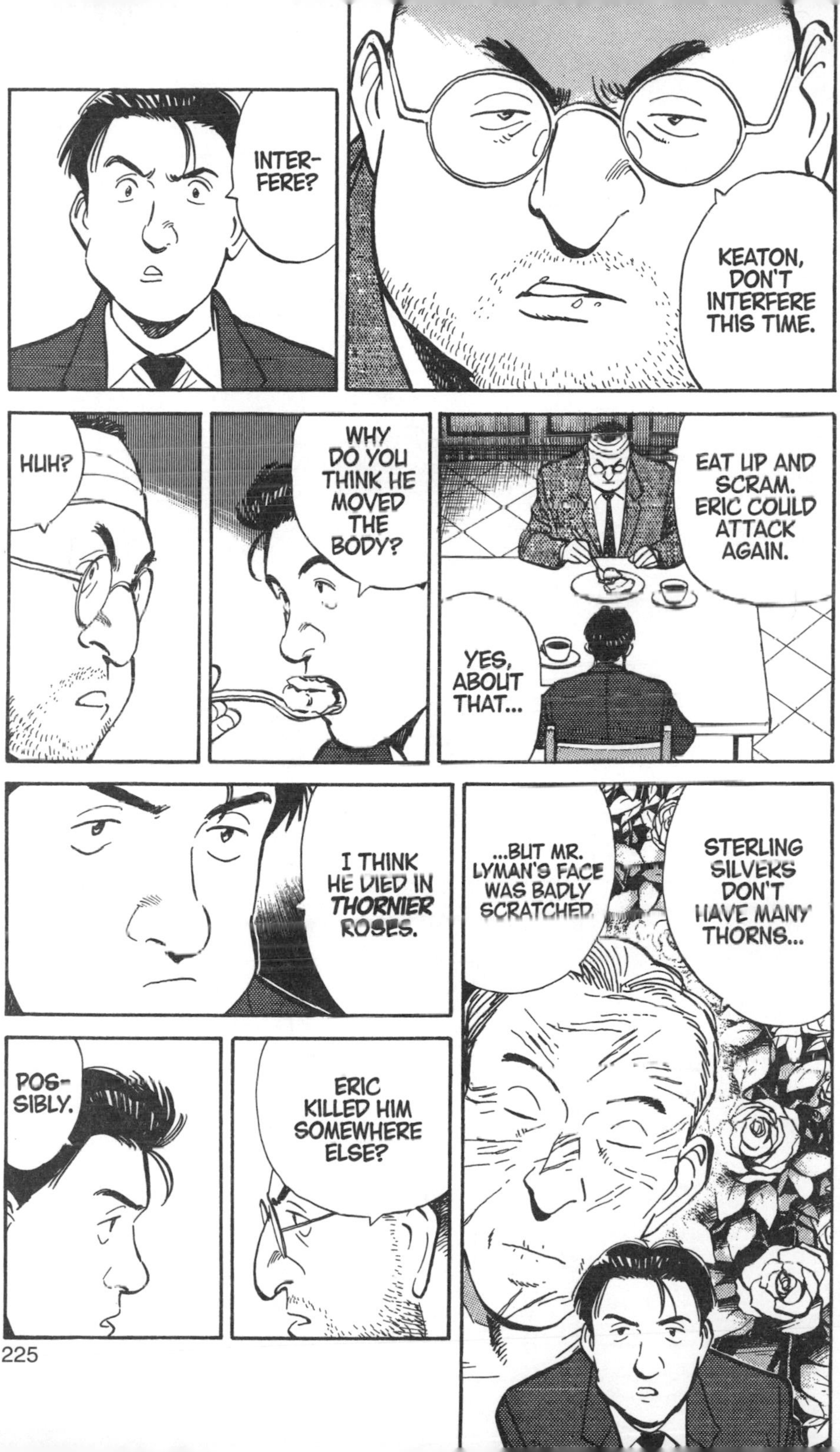
KEATON, DON'T INTERFERE THIS TIME.
INTER-FERE?
EAT UP AND SCRAM. ERIC COULD ATTACK AGAIN.
YES, ABOUT THAT...
WHY DO YOU THINK HE MOVED THE BODY?
HUH?
STERLING SILVERS DON'T HAVE MANY THORNS...
...BUT MR. LYMAN'S FACE WAS BADLY SCRATCHED.
I THINK HE DIED IN *THORNIER* ROSES.
ERIC KILLED HIM SOMEWHERE ELSE?
POS-SIBLY.

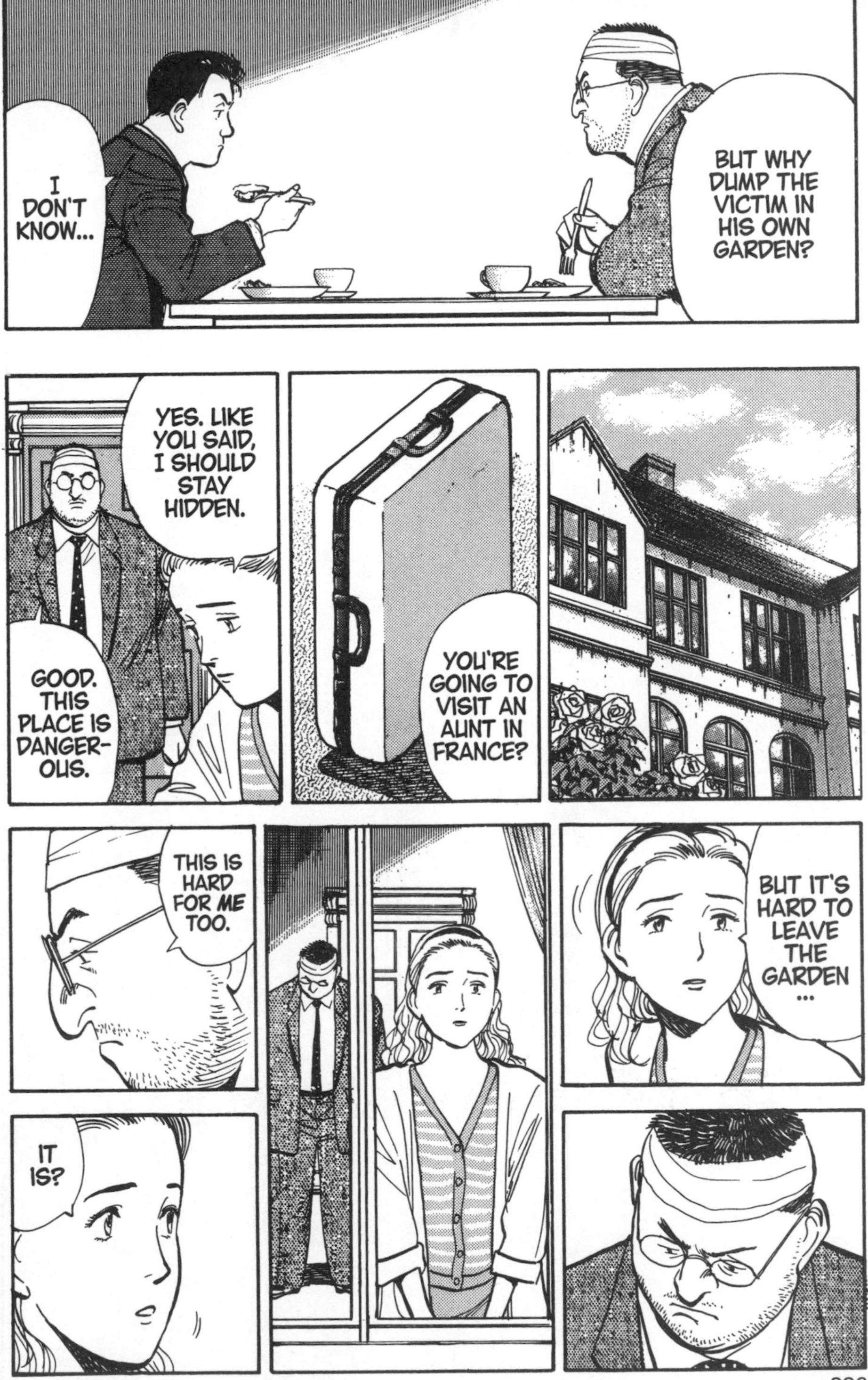
BUT WHY DUMP THE VICTIM IN HIS OWN GARDEN?
I DON'T KNOW...
YOU'RE GOING TO VISIT AN AUNT IN FRANCE?
YES. LIKE YOU SAID, I SHOULD STAY HIDDEN.
GOOD. THIS PLACE IS DANGER-OUS.
BUT IT'S HARD TO LEAVE THE GARDEN...
THIS IS HARD FOR ME TOO.
IT IS?

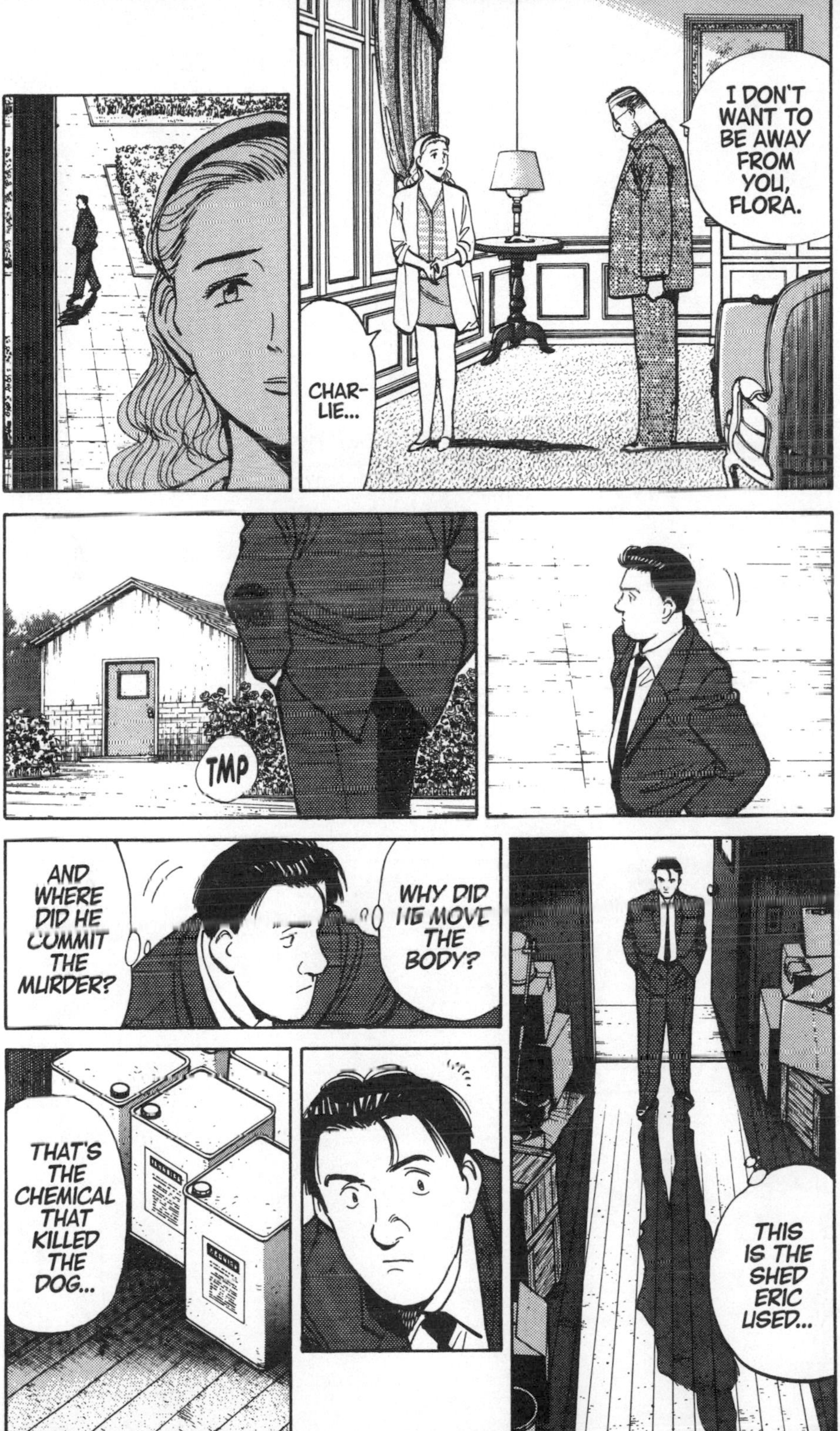
I DON'T WANT TO BE AWAY FROM YOU, FLORA.
CHAR-LIE...
TMP
THIS IS THE SHED ERIC USED...
WHY DID HE MOVE THE BODY?
AND WHERE DID HE COMMIT THE MURDER?
THAT'S THE CHEMICAL THAT KILLED THE DOG...

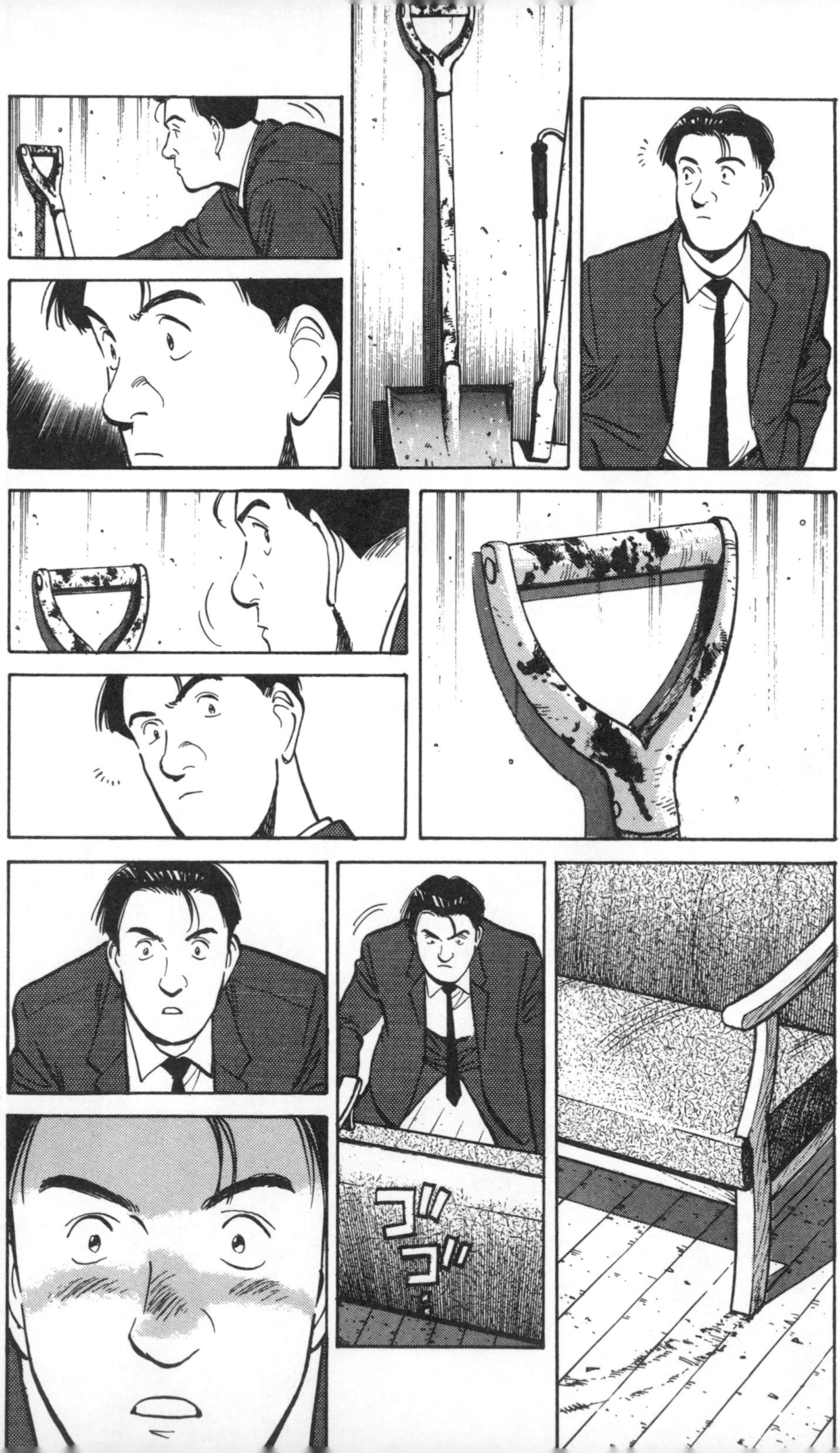
ゴゴ…

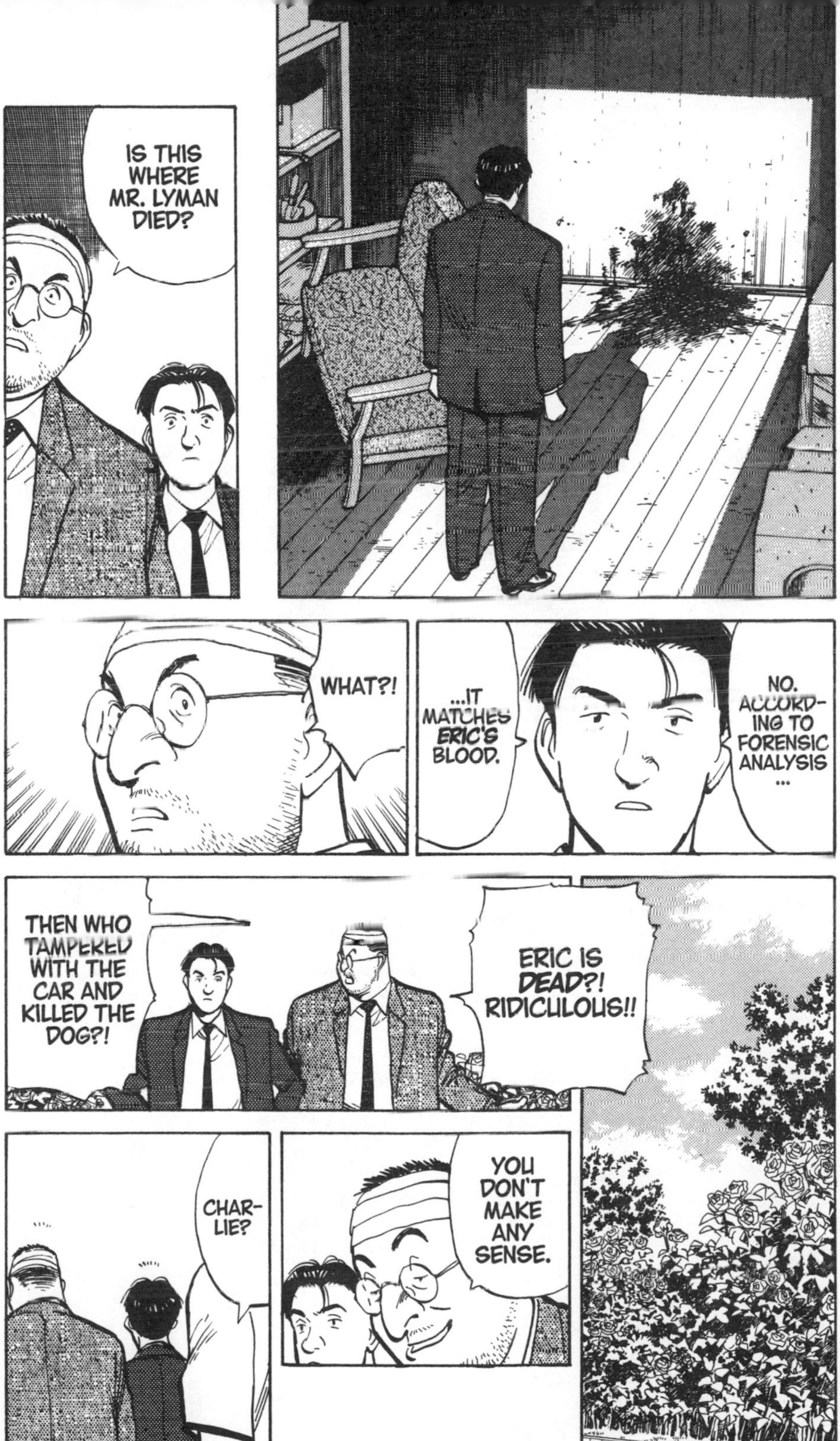
IS THIS WHERE MR. LYMAN DIED?
NO. ACCORDING TO FORENSIC ANALYSIS ...
...IT MATCHES ERIC'S BLOOD.
WHAT?!
ERIC IS DEAD?! RIDICULOUS!!
THEN WHO TAMPERED WITH THE CAR AND KILLED THE DOG?!
YOU DON'T MAKE ANY SENSE.
CHAR-LIE?

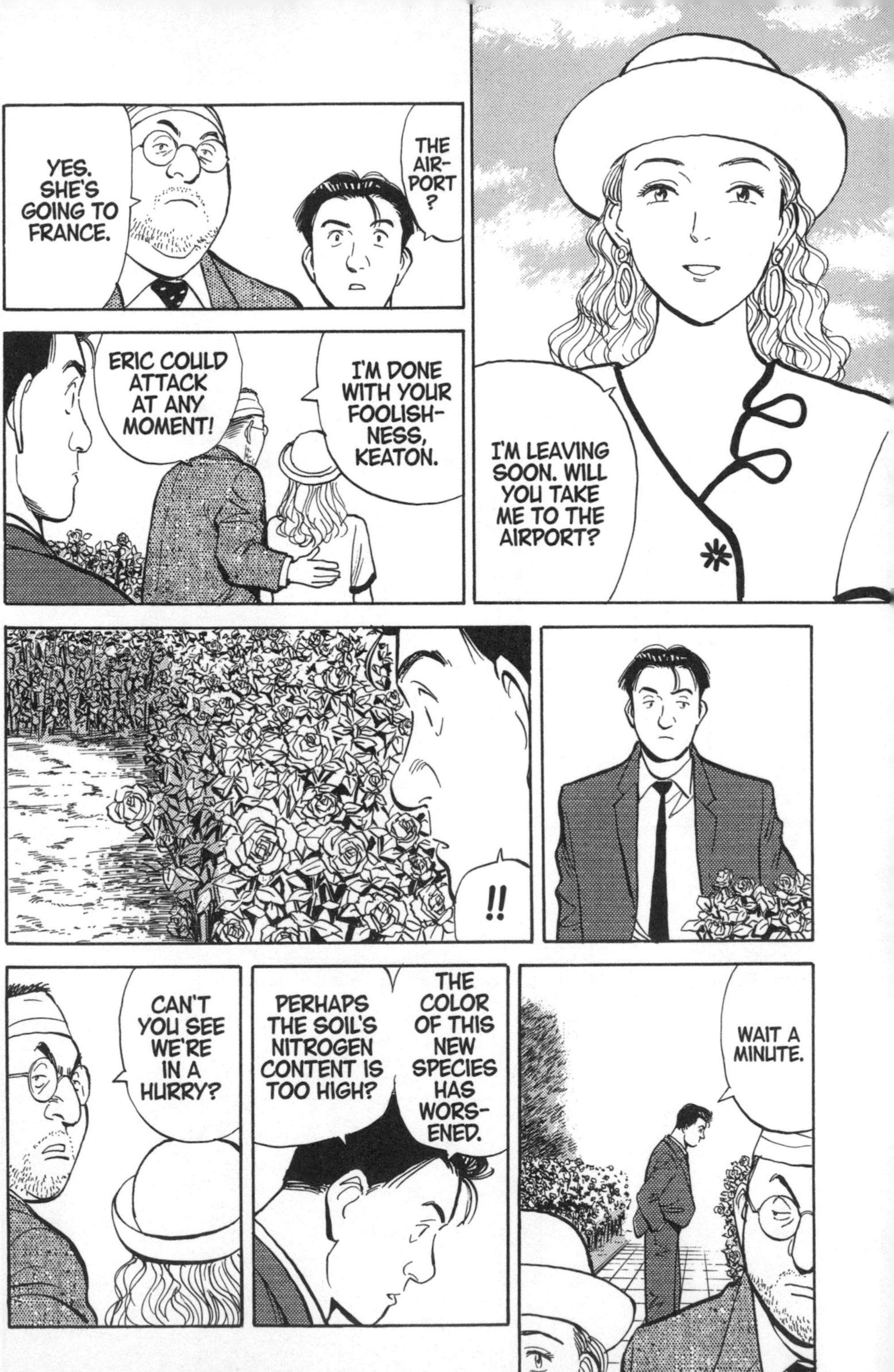
I'M LEAVING SOON. WILL YOU TAKE ME TO THE AIRPORT?
THE AIR-PORT ?
YES. SHE'S GOING TO FRANCE.
I'M DONE WITH YOUR FOOLISH-NESS, KEATON.
ERIC COULD ATTACK AT ANY MOMENT!
!!
WAIT A MINUTE.
THE COLOR OF THIS NEW SPECIES HAS WORS-ENED.
PERHAPS THE SOIL'S NITROGEN CONTENT IS TOO HIGH?
CAN'T YOU SEE WE'RE IN A HURRY?

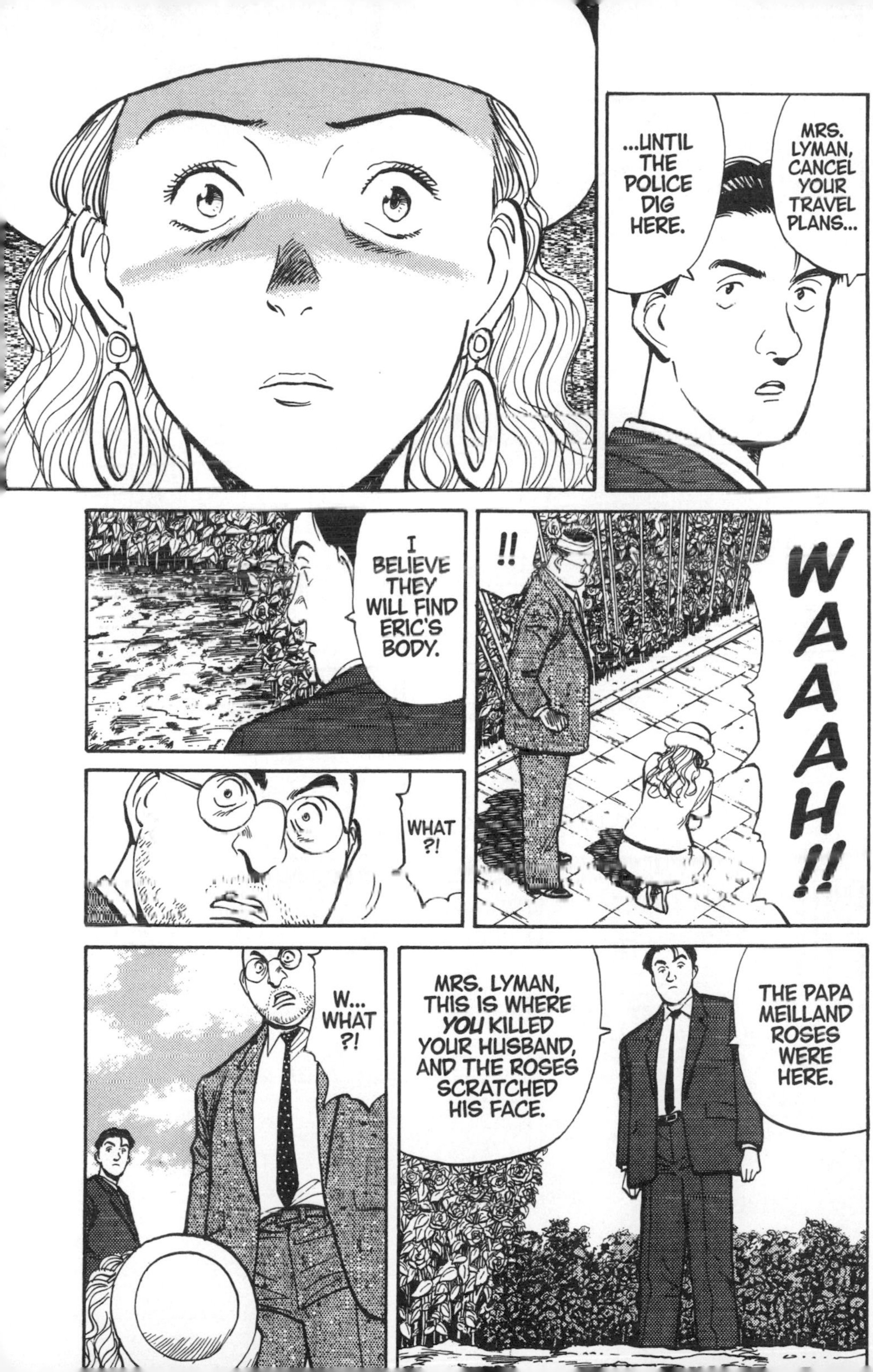
MRS. LYMAN, CANCEL YOUR TRAVEL PLANS...
...UNTIL THE POLICE DIG HERE.
WAAAH!!
!!
I BELIEVE THEY WILL FIND ERIC'S BODY.
WHAT ?!
THE PAPA MEILLAND ROSES WERE HERE.
MRS. LYMAN, THIS IS WHERE *YOU* KILLED YOUR HUSBAND, AND THE ROSES SCRATCHED HIS FACE.
W... WHAT ?!

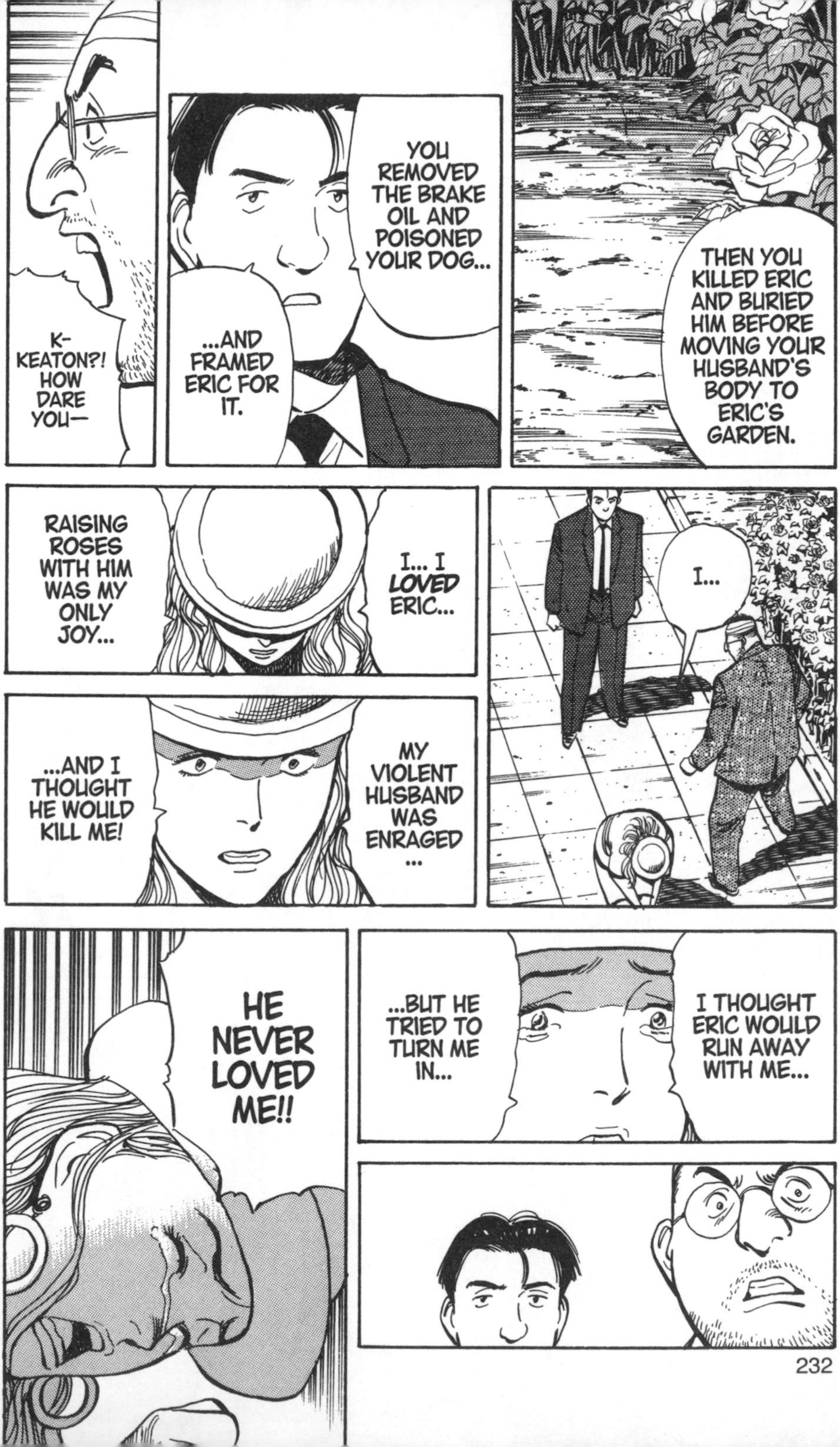
THEN YOU KILLED ERIC AND BURIED HIM BEFORE MOVING YOUR HUSBAND'S BODY TO ERIC'S GARDEN.
YOU REMOVED THE BRAKE OIL AND POISONED YOUR DOG...
...AND FRAMED ERIC FOR IT.
K-KEATON?! HOW DARE YOU—
I...
I... I *LOVED* ERIC...
RAISING ROSES WITH HIM WAS MY ONLY JOY...
MY VIOLENT HUSBAND WAS ENRAGED...
...AND I THOUGHT HE WOULD KILL ME!
I THOUGHT ERIC WOULD RUN AWAY WITH ME...
...BUT HE TRIED TO TURN ME IN...
HE NEVER LOVED ME!!

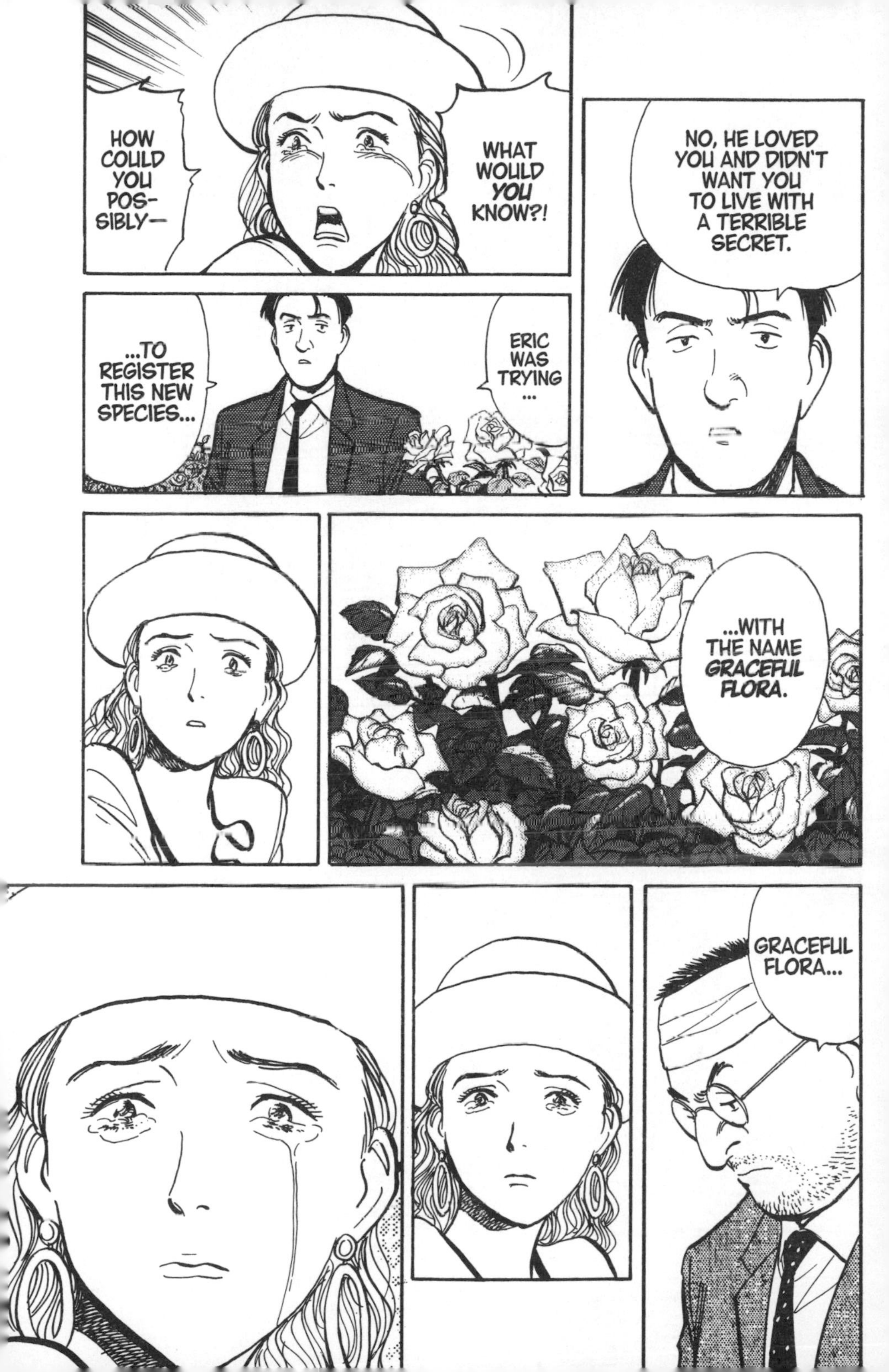
NO, HE LOVED YOU AND DIDN'T WANT YOU TO LIVE WITH A TERRIBLE SECRET.
WHAT WOULD YOU KNOW?!
HOW COULD YOU POS-SIBLY—
ERIC WAS TRYING ...
...TO REGISTER THIS NEW SPECIES...
...WITH THE NAME GRACEFUL FLORA.
GRACEFUL FLORA...

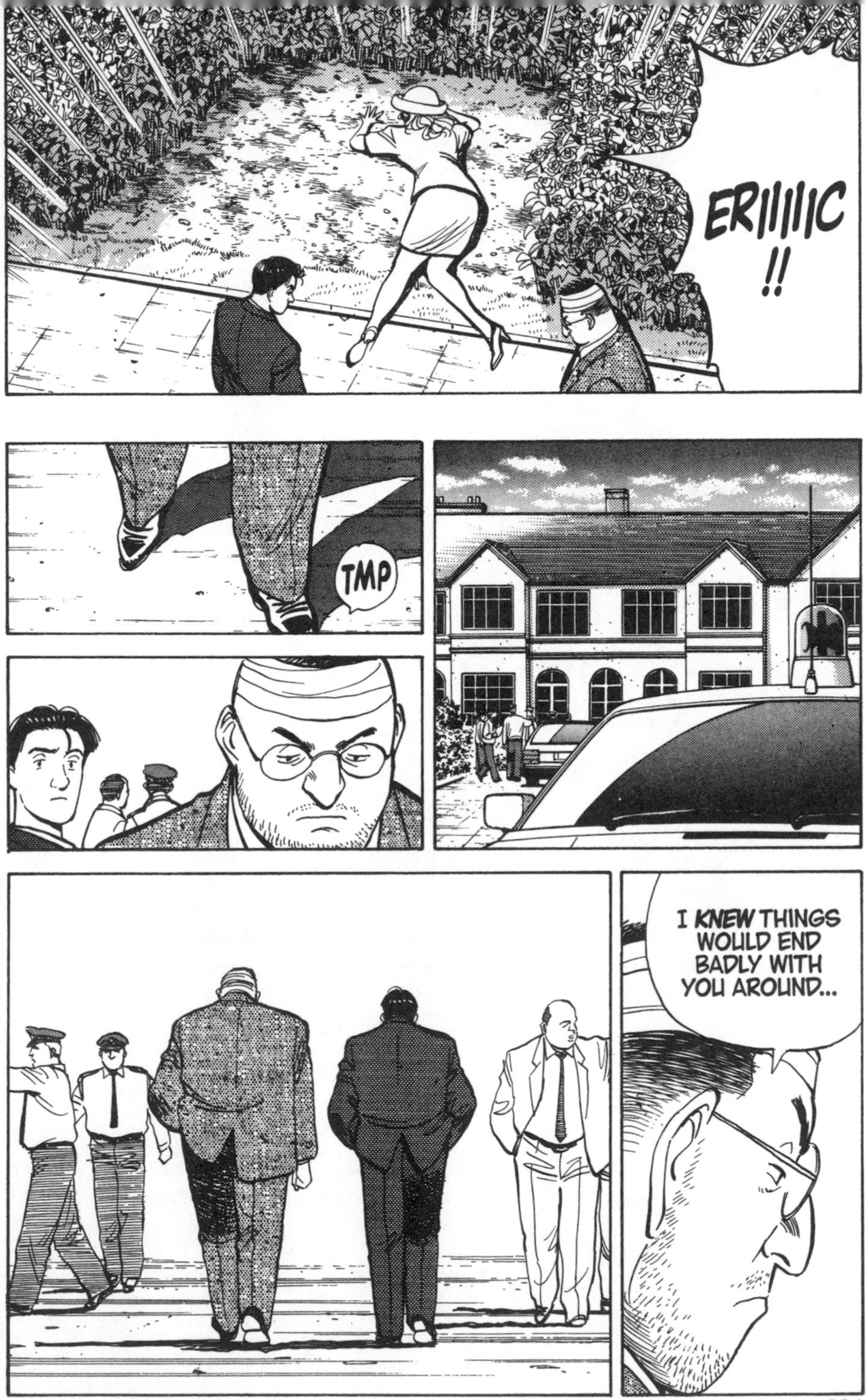
ERIIIIIC!!
TMP
I KNEW THINGS WOULD END BADLY WITH YOU AROUND...

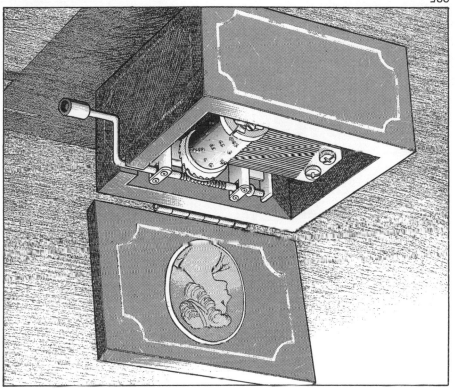

CHAPTER 10
THE HEART'S
WALLS

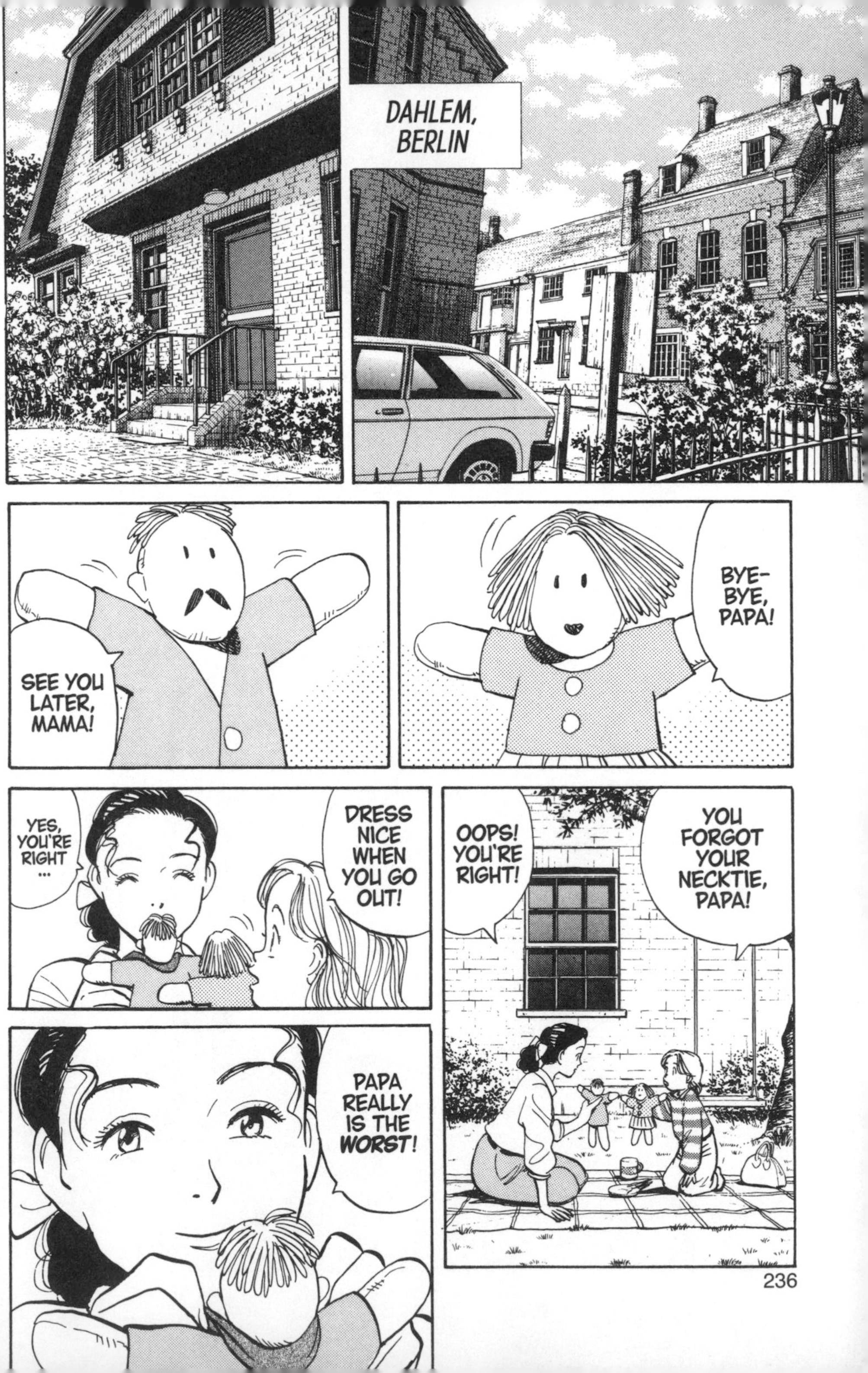
DAHLEM, BERLIN
BYE-BYE, PAPA!
SEE YOU LATER, MAMA!
YOU FORGOT YOUR NECKTIE, PAPA!
OOPS! YOU'RE RIGHT!
DRESS NICE WHEN YOU GO OUT!
YES, YOU'RE RIGHT ...
PAPA REALLY IS THE WORST!

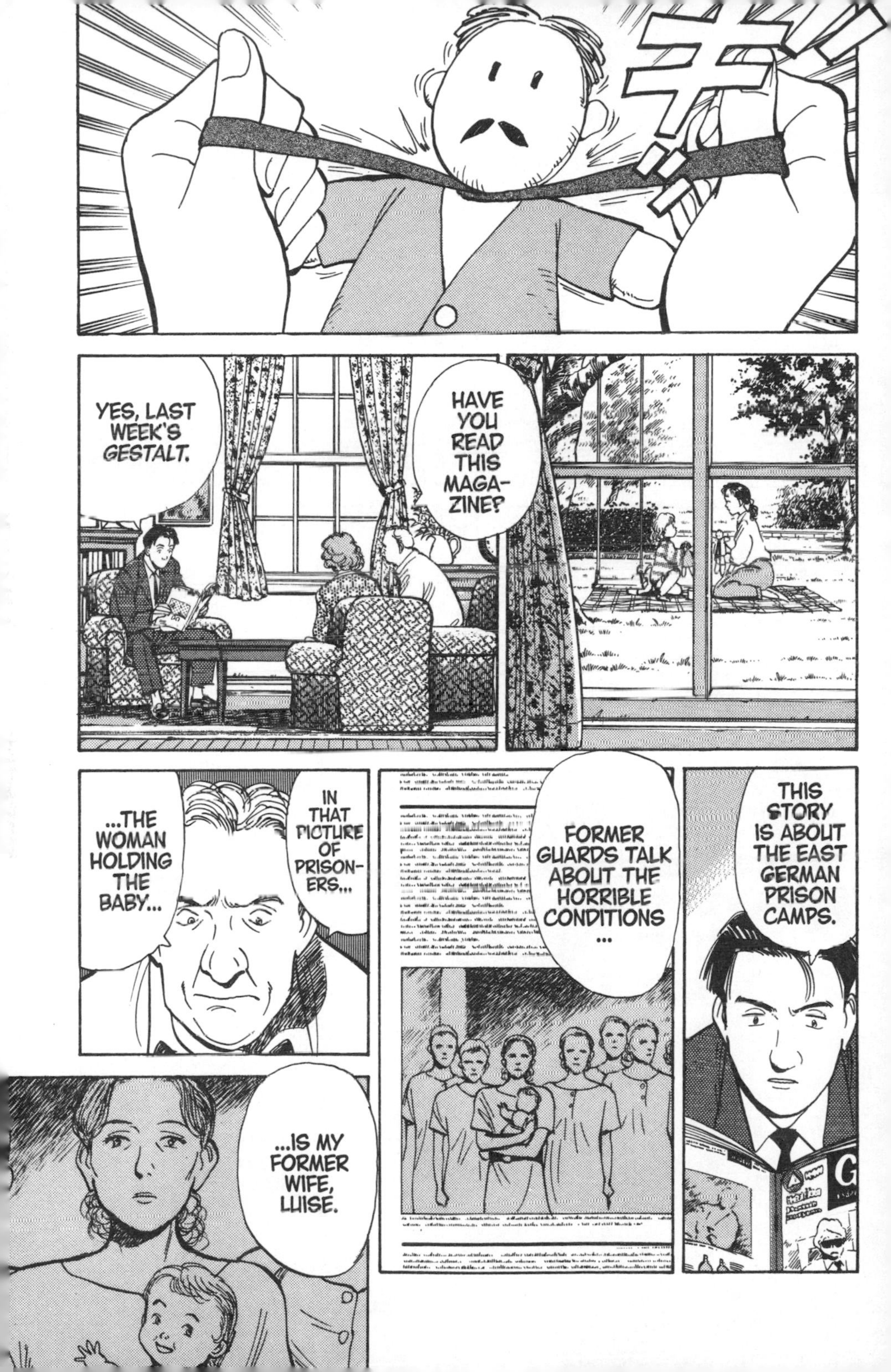
HAVE YOU READ THIS MAGAZINE?
YES, LAST WEEK'S GESTALT.
THIS STORY IS ABOUT THE EAST GERMAN PRISON CAMPS.
FORMER GUARDS TALK ABOUT THE HORRIBLE CONDITIONS ...
IN THAT PICTURE OF PRISONERS...
...THE WOMAN HOLDING THE BABY...
...IS MY FORMER WIFE, LUISE.

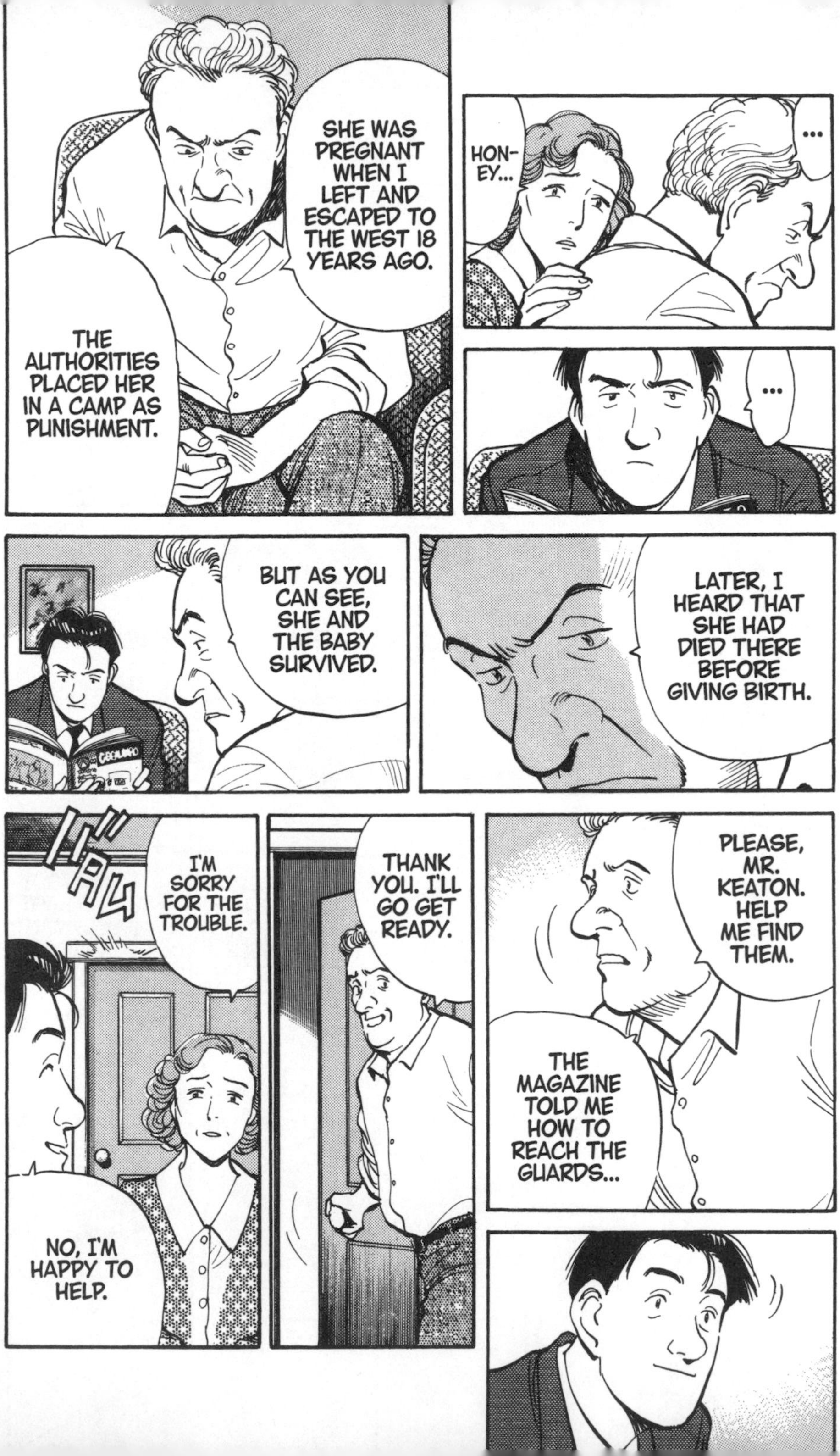

HON-
EY...
...
...
SHE WAS PREGNANT WHEN I LEFT AND ESCAPED TO THE WEST 18 YEARS AGO.
THE AUTHORITIES PLACED HER IN A CAMP AS PUNISHMENT.
LATER, I HEARD THAT SHE HAD DIED THERE BEFORE GIVING BIRTH.
BUT AS YOU CAN SEE, SHE AND THE BABY SURVIVED.
PLEASE, MR. KEATON. HELP ME FIND THEM.
THE MAGAZINE TOLD ME HOW TO REACH THE GUARDS...
THANK YOU. I'LL GO GET READY.
I'M SORRY FOR THE TROUBLE.
NO, I'M HAPPY TO HELP.

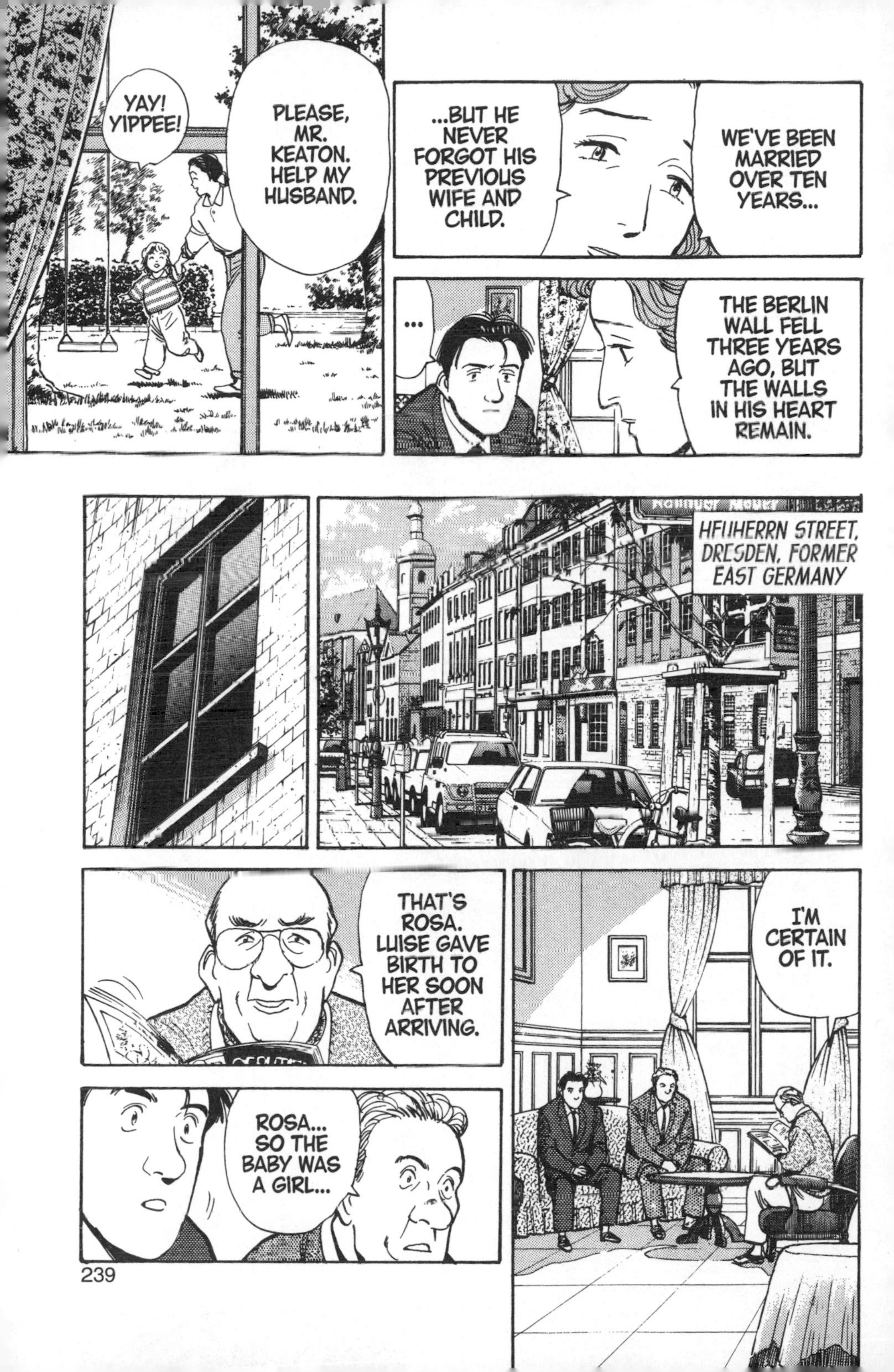
WE'VE BEEN MARRIED OVER TEN YEARS...
...BUT HE NEVER FORGOT HIS PREVIOUS WIFE AND CHILD.
THE BERLIN WALL FELL THREE YEARS AGO, BUT THE WALLS IN HIS HEART REMAIN.
...
PLEASE, MR. KEATON. HELP MY HUSBAND.
YAY! YIPPEE!
HFUHERRN STREET, DRESDEN, FORMER EAST GERMANY
I'M CERTAIN OF IT.
THAT'S ROSA. LUISE GAVE BIRTH TO HER SOON AFTER ARRIVING.
ROSA... SO THE BABY WAS A GIRL...

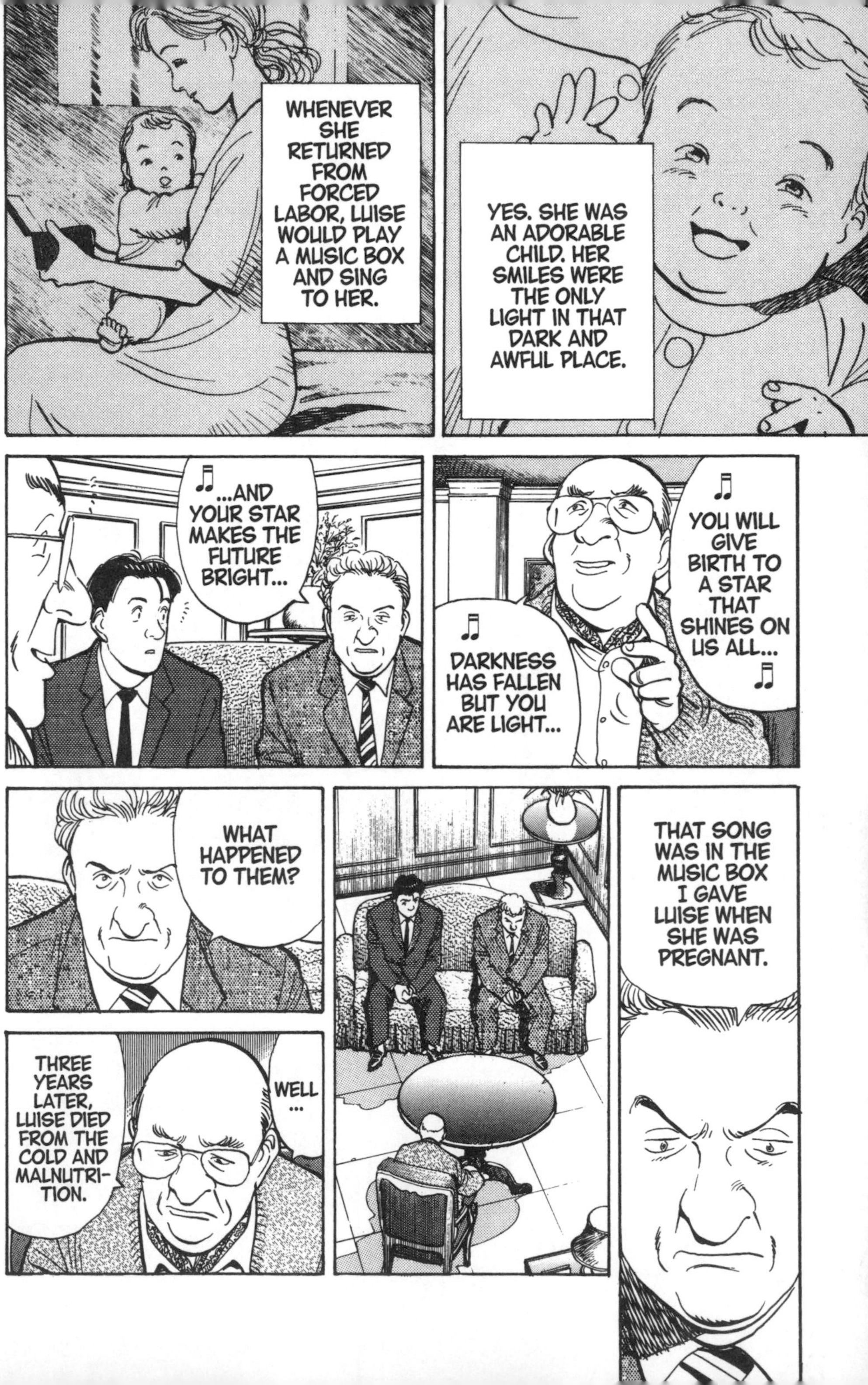
YES. SHE WAS AN ADORABLE CHILD. HER SMILES WERE THE ONLY LIGHT IN THAT DARK AND AWFUL PLACE.
WHENEVER SHE RETURNED FROM FORCED LABOR, LUISE WOULD PLAY A MUSIC BOX AND SING TO HER.
♫ YOU WILL GIVE BIRTH TO A STAR THAT SHINES ON US ALL... ♫
♫ DARKNESS HAS FALLEN BUT YOU ARE LIGHT...
♫ ...AND YOUR STAR MAKES THE FUTURE BRIGHT...
THAT SONG WAS IN THE MUSIC BOX I GAVE LUISE WHEN SHE WAS PREGNANT.
WHAT HAPPENED TO THEM?
WELL ...
THREE YEARS LATER, LUISE DIED FROM THE COLD AND MALNUTRI-TION.

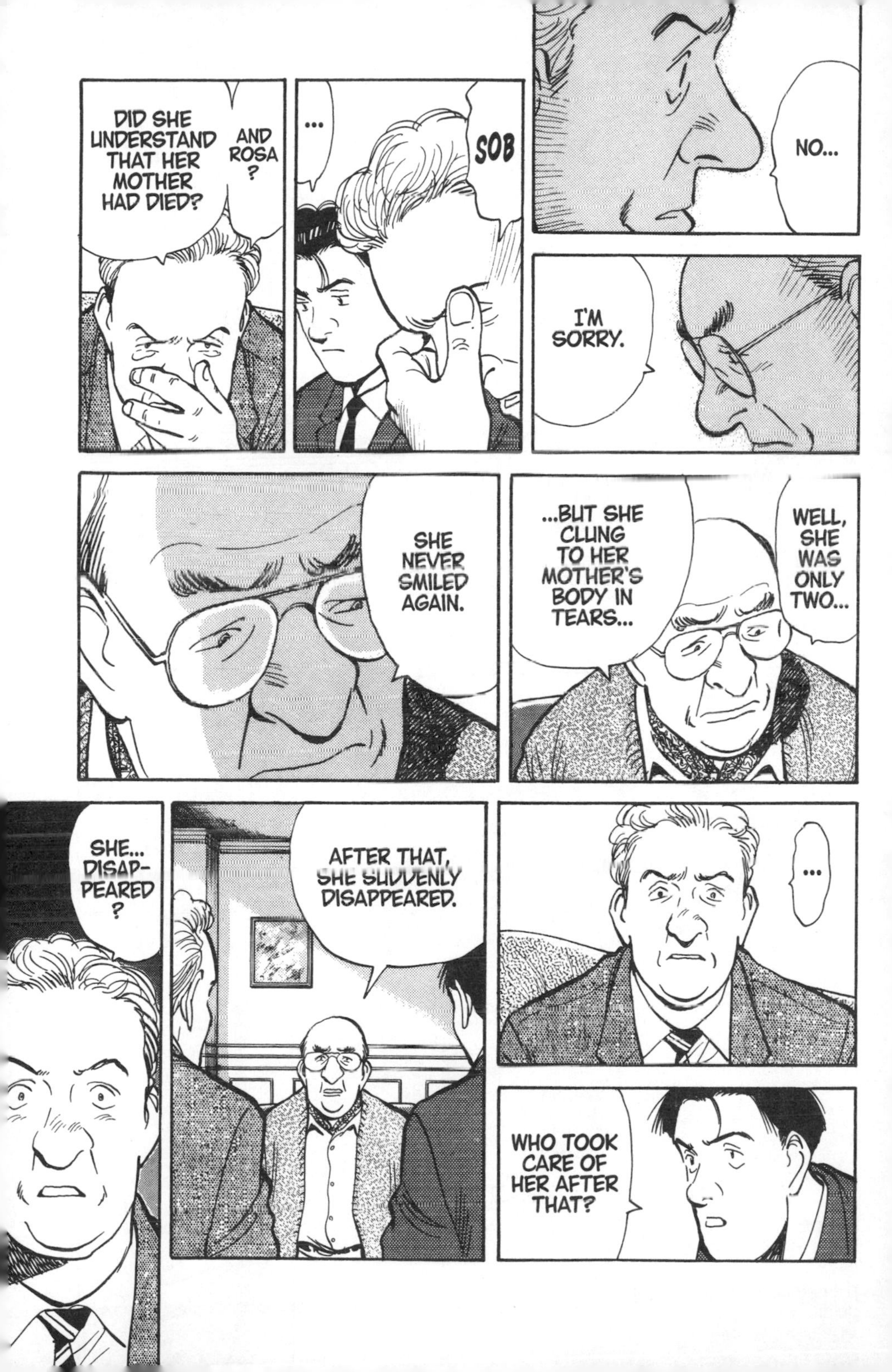
NO...
I'M SORRY.
SOB
...
AND ROSA?
DID SHE UNDERSTAND THAT HER MOTHER HAD DIED?
WELL, SHE WAS ONLY TWO...
...BUT SHE CLUNG TO HER MOTHER'S BODY IN TEARS...
SHE NEVER SMILED AGAIN.
...
WHO TOOK CARE OF HER AFTER THAT?
AFTER THAT, SHE SUDDENLY DISAPPEARED.
SHE... DISAPPEARED?

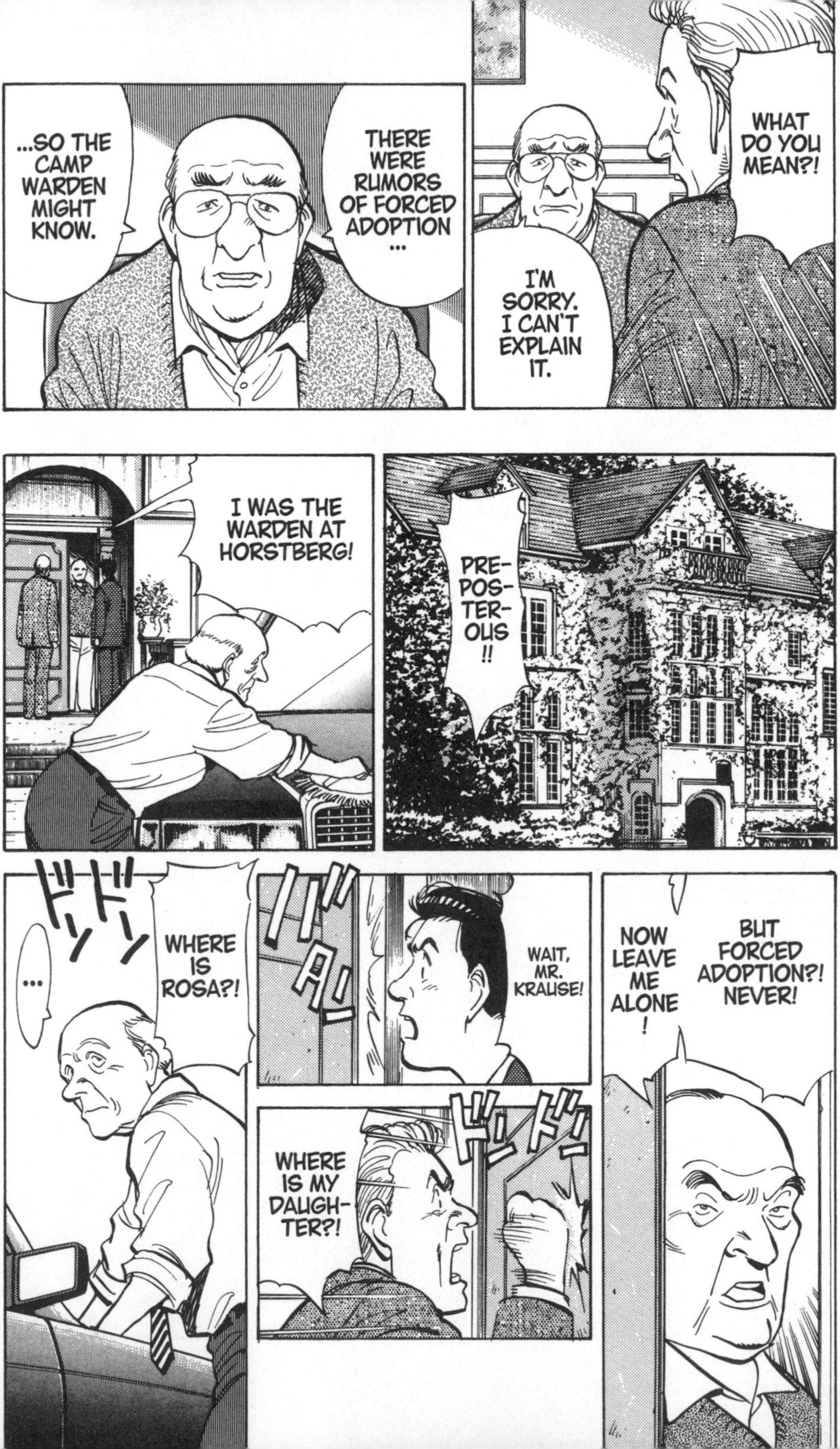
WHAT DO YOU MEAN?!
I'M SORRY. I CAN'T EXPLAIN IT.
THERE WERE RUMORS OF FORCED ADOPTION ...
...SO THE CAMP WARDEN MIGHT KNOW.
PRE-POS-TER-OUS !!
I WAS THE WARDEN AT HORSTBERG!
BUT FORCED ADOPTION?! NEVER!
NOW LEAVE ME ALONE !
WAIT, MR. KRAUSE!
WHERE IS MY DAUGH-TER?!
WHERE IS ROSA?!
...

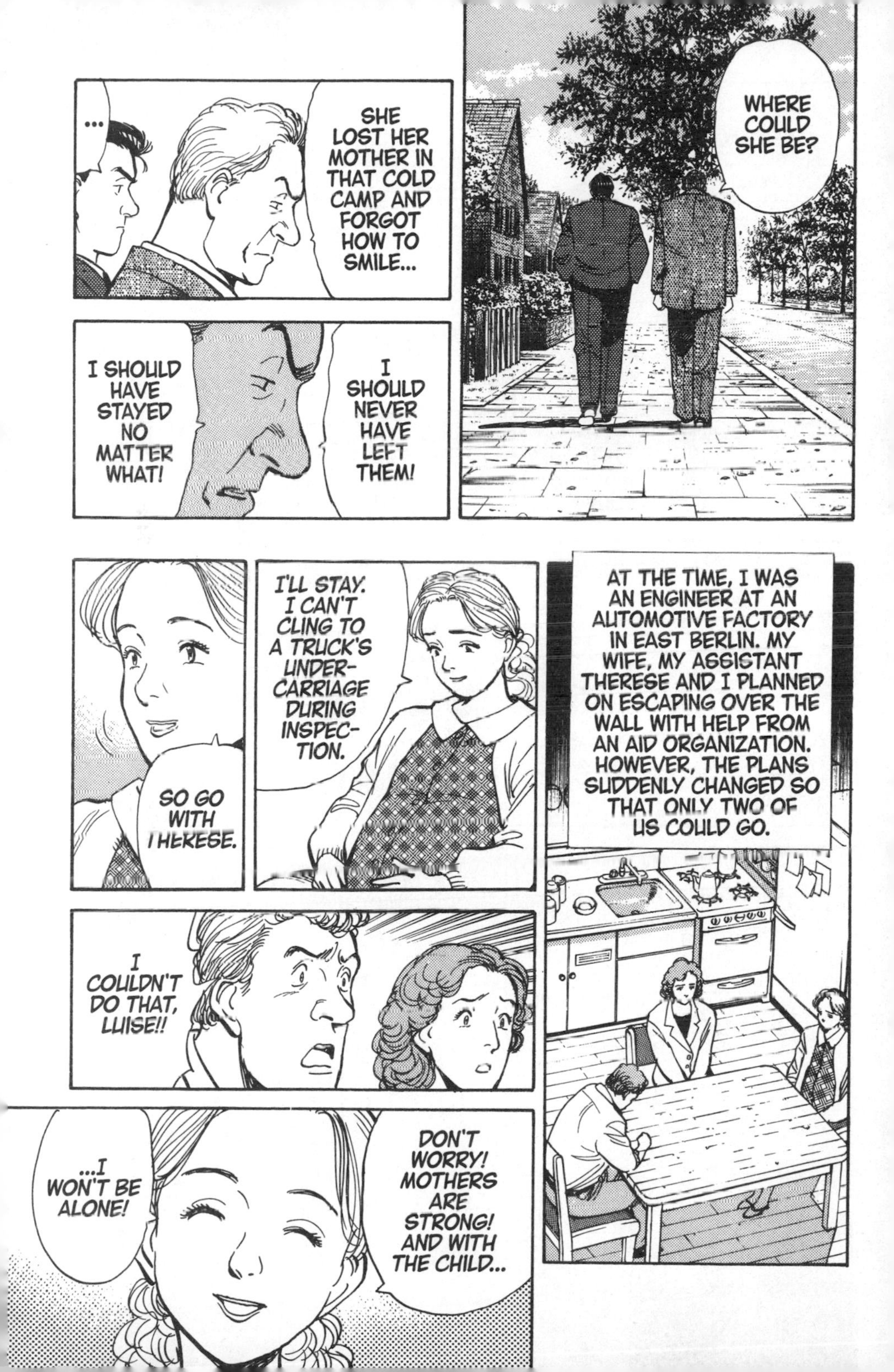
WHERE COULD SHE BE?
SHE LOST HER MOTHER IN THAT COLD CAMP AND FORGOT HOW TO SMILE...
...
I SHOULD NEVER HAVE LEFT THEM!
I SHOULD HAVE STAYED NO MATTER WHAT!
AT THE TIME, I WAS AN ENGINEER AT AN AUTOMOTIVE FACTORY IN EAST BERLIN. MY WIFE, MY ASSISTANT THERESE AND I PLANNED ON ESCAPING OVER THE WALL WITH HELP FROM AN AID ORGANIZATION. HOWEVER, THE PLANS SUDDENLY CHANGED SO THAT ONLY TWO OF US COULD GO.
I'LL STAY. I CAN'T CLING TO A TRUCK'S UNDER-CARRIAGE DURING INSPEC-TION.
SO GO WITH THERESE.
I COULDN'T DO THAT, LUISE!!
DON'T WORRY! MOTHERS ARE STRONG! AND WITH THE CHILD...
...I WON'T BE ALONE!

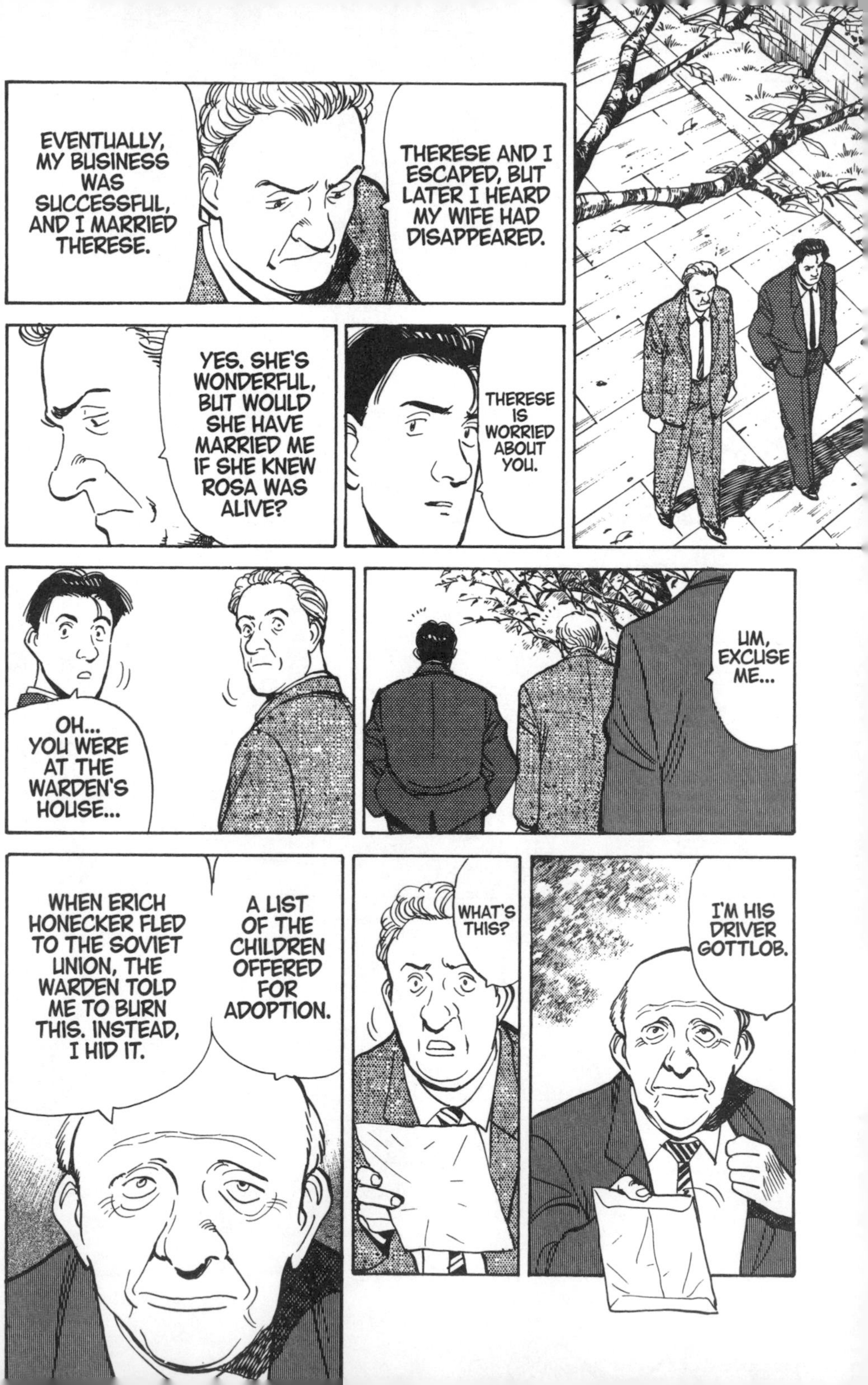
EVENTUALLY, MY BUSINESS WAS SUCCESSFUL, AND I MARRIED THERESE.
THERESE AND I ESCAPED, BUT LATER I HEARD MY WIFE HAD DISAPPEARED.
THERESE IS WORRIED ABOUT YOU.
YES. SHE'S WONDERFUL, BUT WOULD SHE HAVE MARRIED ME IF SHE KNEW ROSA WAS ALIVE?
UM, EXCUSE ME...
OH... YOU WERE AT THE WARDEN'S HOUSE...
I'M HIS DRIVER GOTTLOB.
WHAT'S THIS?
WHEN ERICH HONECKER FLED TO THE SOVIET UNION, THE WARDEN TOLD ME TO BURN THIS. INSTEAD, I HID IT.
A LIST OF THE CHILDREN OFFERED FOR ADOPTION.

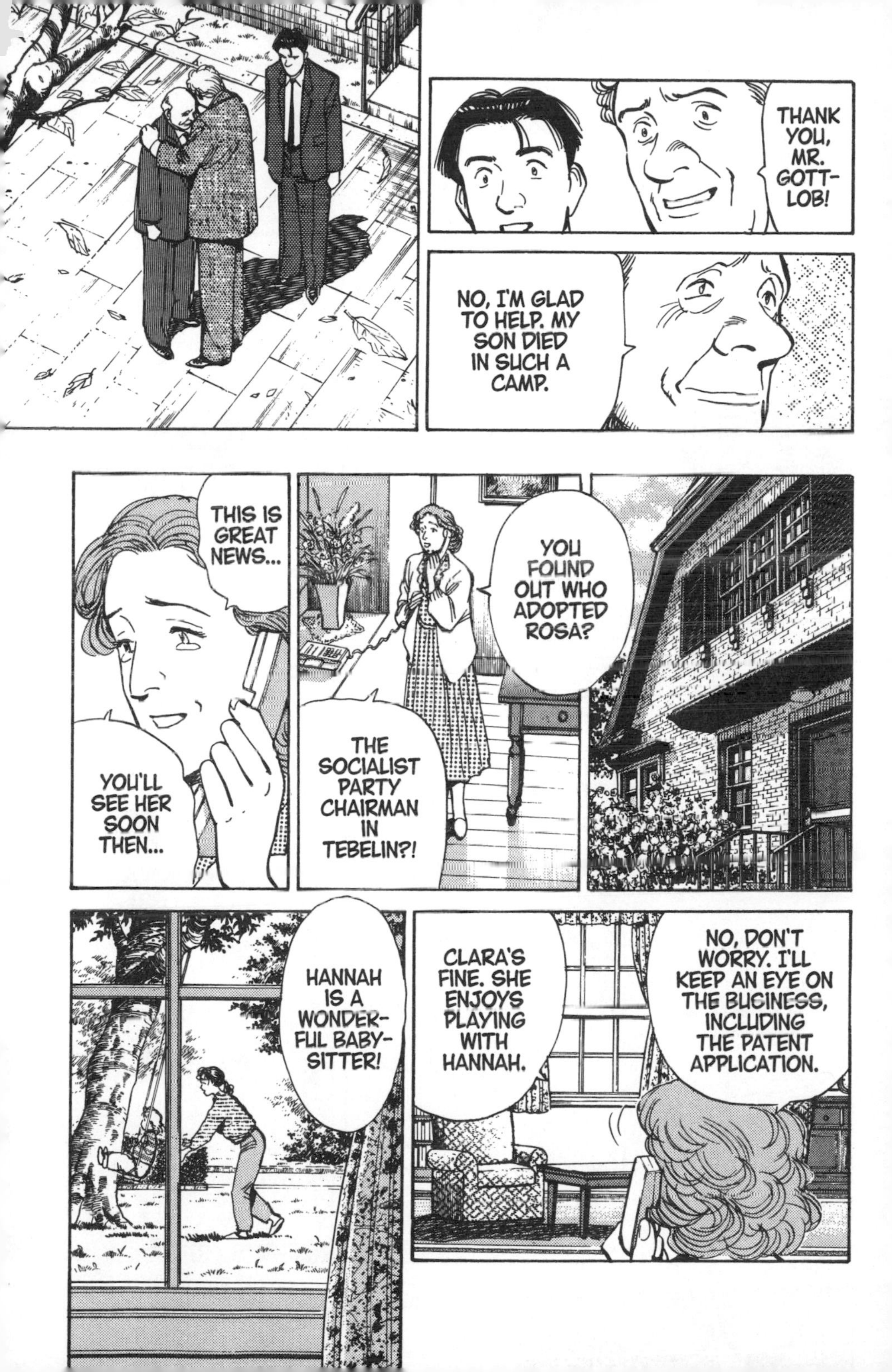
THANK YOU, MR. GOTT-LOB!
NO, I'M GLAD TO HELP. MY SON DIED IN SUCH A CAMP.
YOU FOUND OUT WHO ADOPTED ROSA?
THE SOCIALIST PARTY CHAIRMAN IN TEBELIN?!
THIS IS GREAT NEWS...
YOU'LL SEE HER SOON THEN...
NO, DON'T WORRY. I'LL KEEP AN EYE ON THE BUSINESS, INCLUDING THE PATENT APPLICATION.
CLARA'S FINE. SHE ENJOYS PLAYING WITH HANNAH.
HANNAH IS A WONDER-FUL BABY-SITTER!

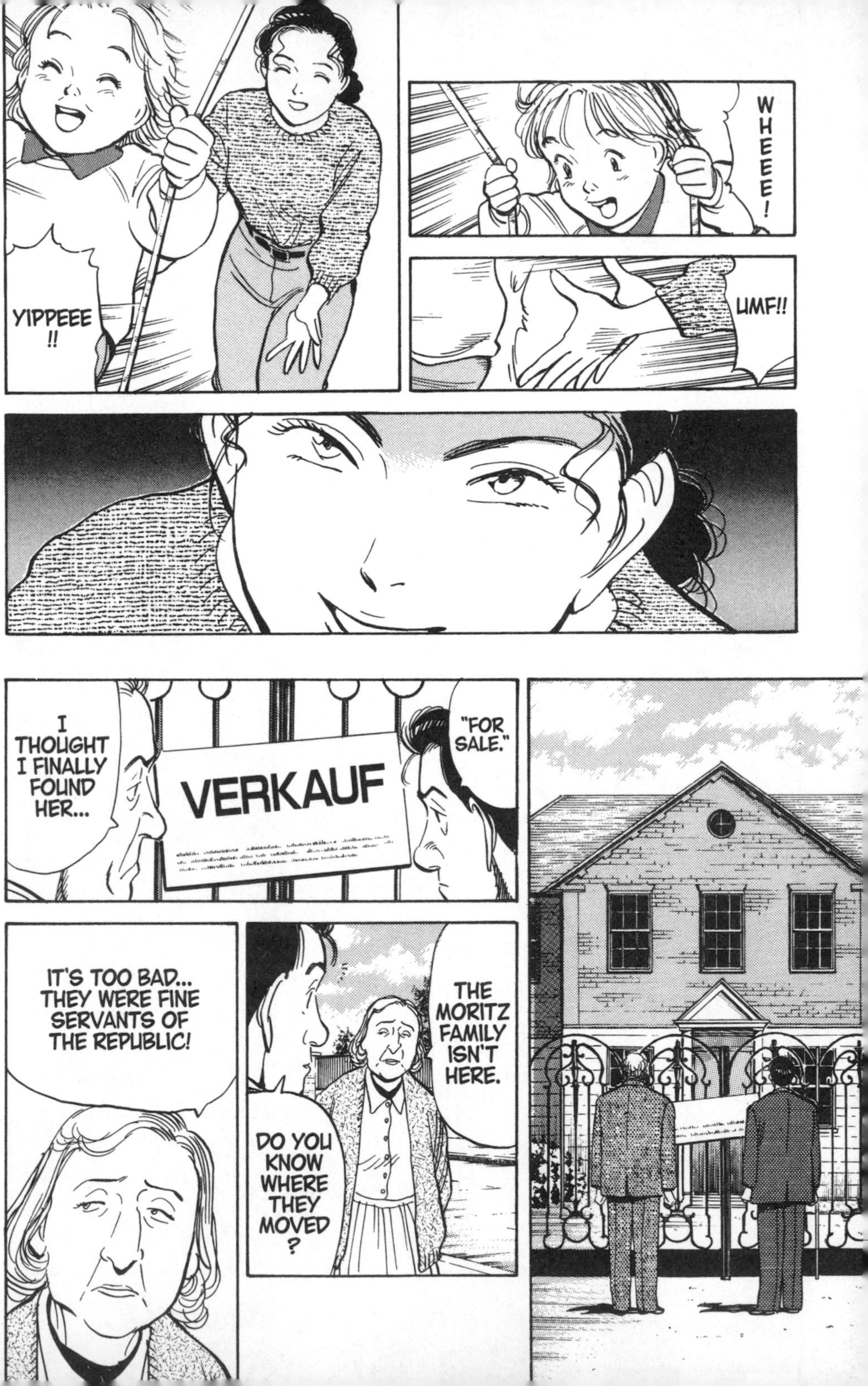
WHEEE!
UMF!!
YIPPEEE !!
"FOR SALE."
VERKAUF
I THOUGHT I FINALLY FOUND HER...
THE MORITZ FAMILY ISN'T HERE.
DO YOU KNOW WHERE THEY MOVED ?
IT'S TOO BAD... THEY WERE FINE SERVANTS OF THE REPUBLIC!

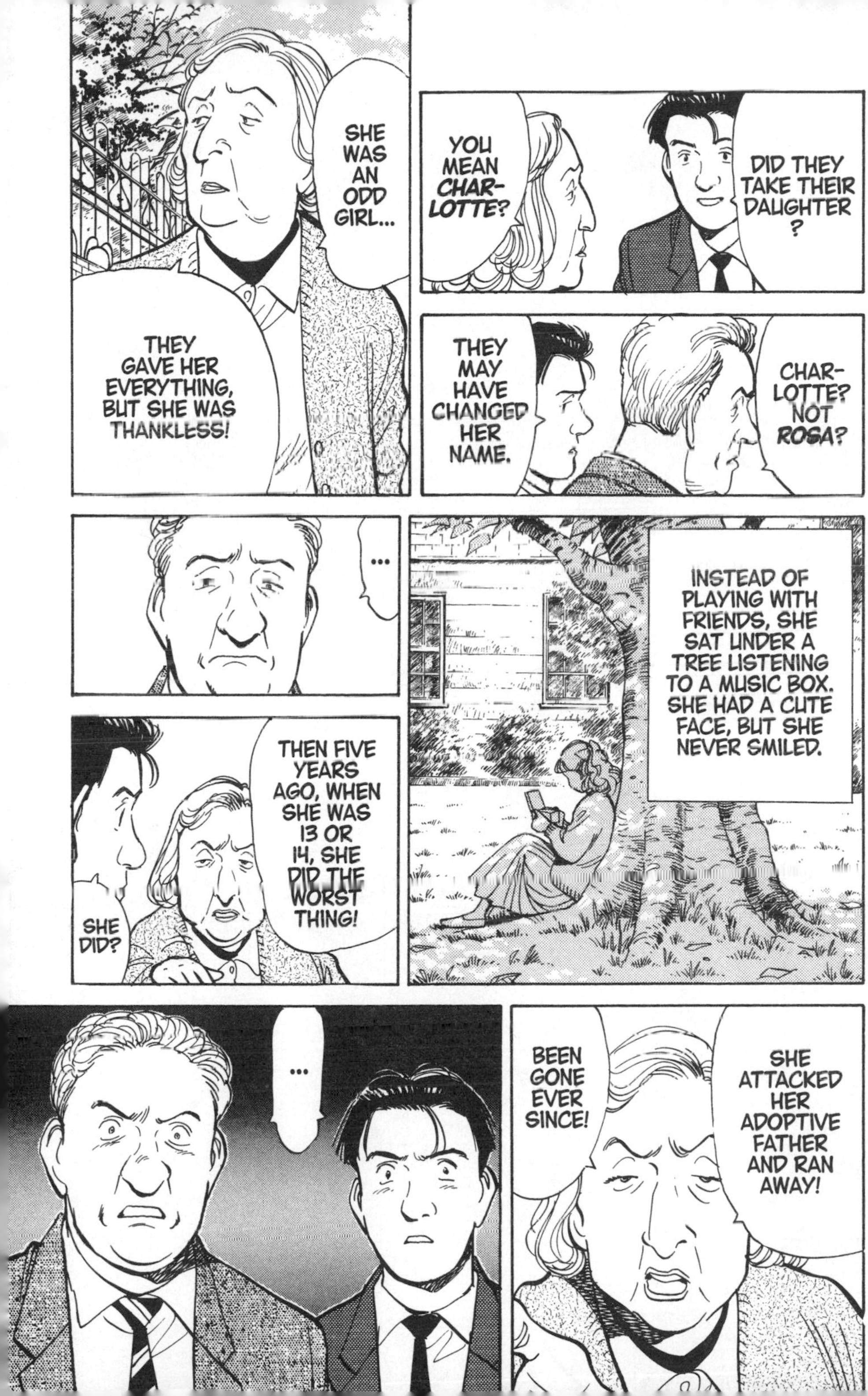
DID THEY TAKE THEIR DAUGHTER ?
YOU MEAN CHAR-LOTTE?
CHAR-LOTTE? NOT ROSA?
THEY MAY HAVE CHANGED HER NAME.
SHE WAS AN ODD GIRL...
THEY GAVE HER EVERYTHING, BUT SHE WAS THANKLESS!
INSTEAD OF PLAYING WITH FRIENDS, SHE SAT UNDER A TREE LISTENING TO A MUSIC BOX. SHE HAD A CUTE FACE, BUT SHE NEVER SMILED.
...
THEN FIVE YEARS AGO, WHEN SHE WAS 13 OR 14, SHE DID THE WORST THING!
SHE DID?
SHE ATTACKED HER ADOPTIVE FATHER AND RAN AWAY!
BEEN GONE EVER SINCE!
...

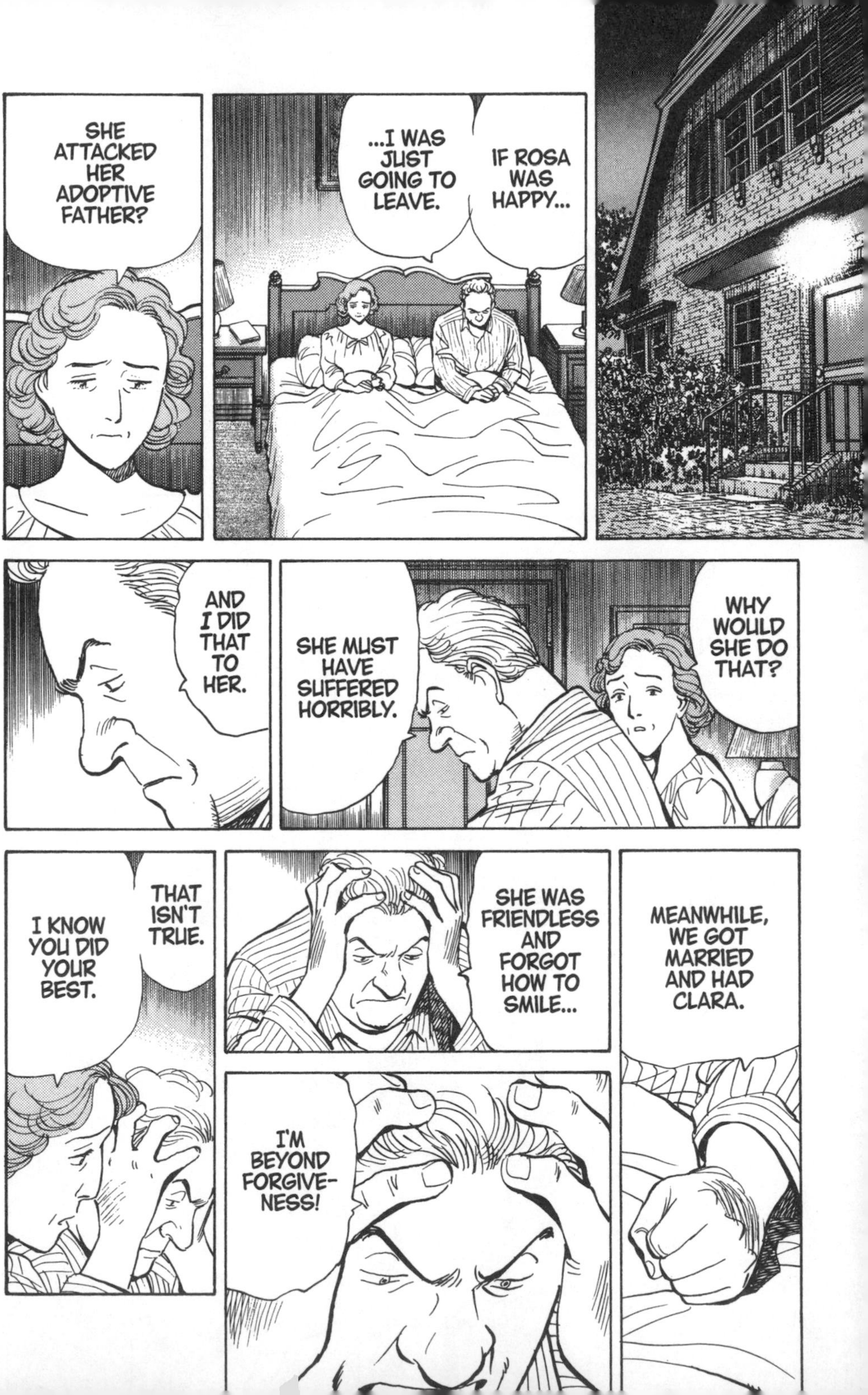
IF ROSA WAS HAPPY...
...I WAS JUST GOING TO LEAVE.
SHE ATTACKED HER ADOPTIVE FATHER?
WHY WOULD SHE DO THAT?
SHE MUST HAVE SUFFERED HORRIBLY.
AND I DID THAT TO HER.
MEANWHILE, WE GOT MARRIED AND HAD CLARA.
SHE WAS FRIENDLESS AND FORGOT HOW TO SMILE...
I'M BEYOND FORGIVE-NESS!
THAT ISN'T TRUE.
I KNOW YOU DID YOUR BEST.

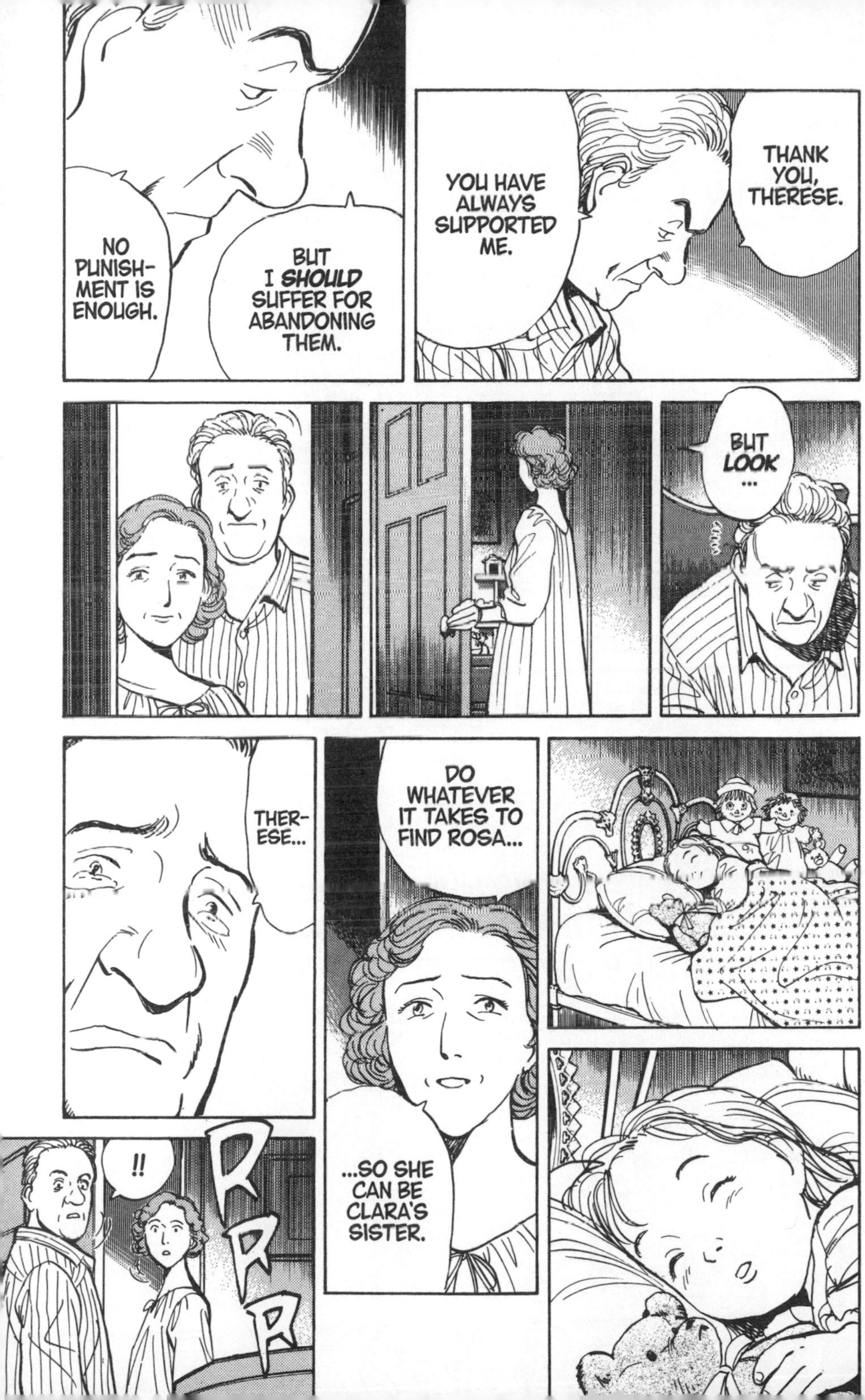
THANK YOU, THERESE.
YOU HAVE ALWAYS SUPPORTED ME.
BUT I **SHOULD** SUFFER FOR ABANDONING THEM.
NO PUNISHMENT IS ENOUGH.
BUT **LOOK** ...
DO WHATEVER IT TAKES TO FIND ROSA...
...SO SHE CAN BE CLARA'S SISTER.
THERESE...
!!
RRR

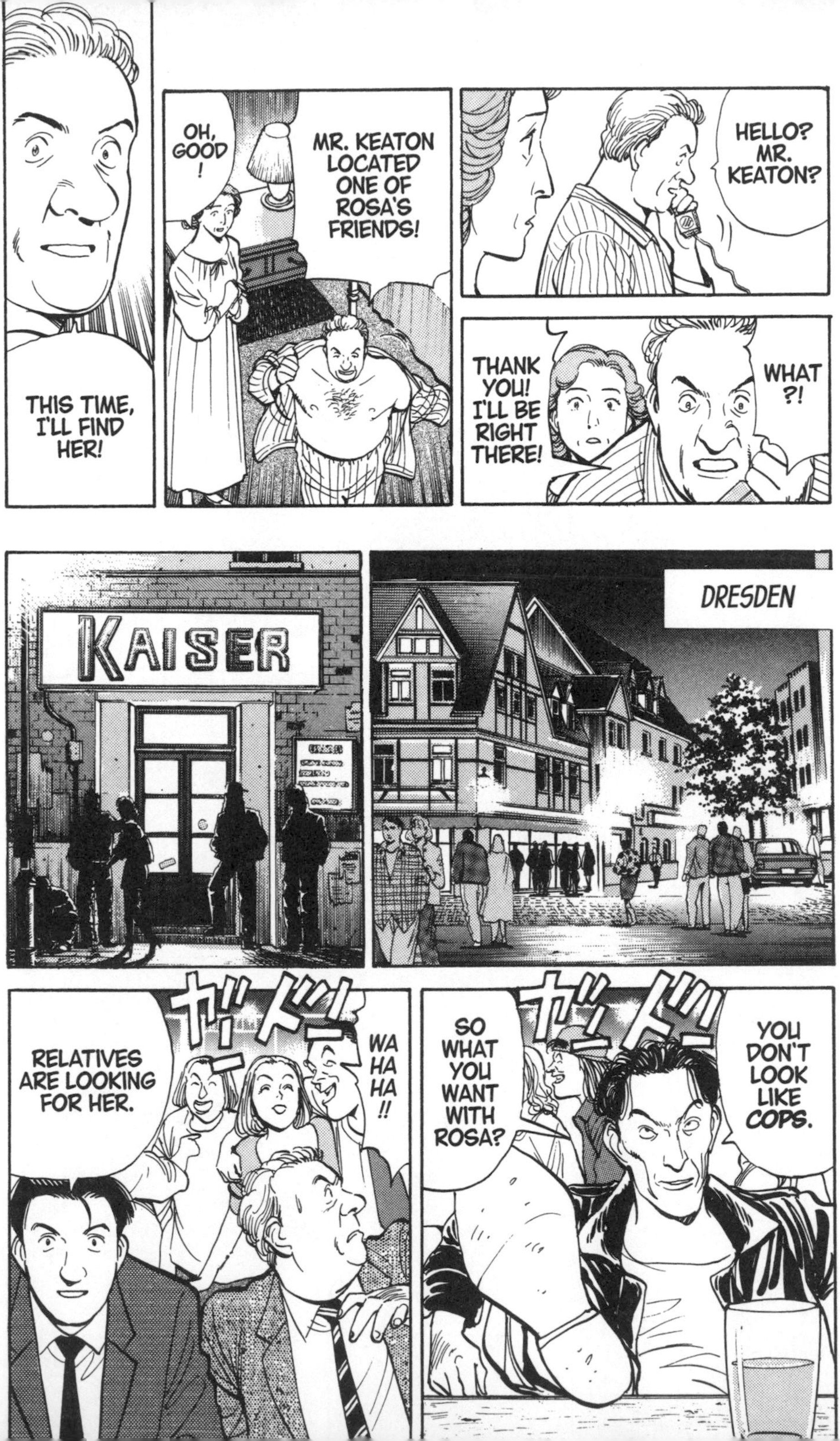
HELLO? MR. KEATON?
WHAT ?!
THANK YOU! I'LL BE RIGHT THERE!
OH, GOOD !
MR. KEATON LOCATED ONE OF ROSA'S FRIENDS!
THIS TIME, I'LL FIND HER!
DRESDEN
KAISER
YOU DON'T LOOK LIKE COPS.
SO WHAT YOU WANT WITH ROSA?
WA HA HA !!
RELATIVES ARE LOOKING FOR HER.

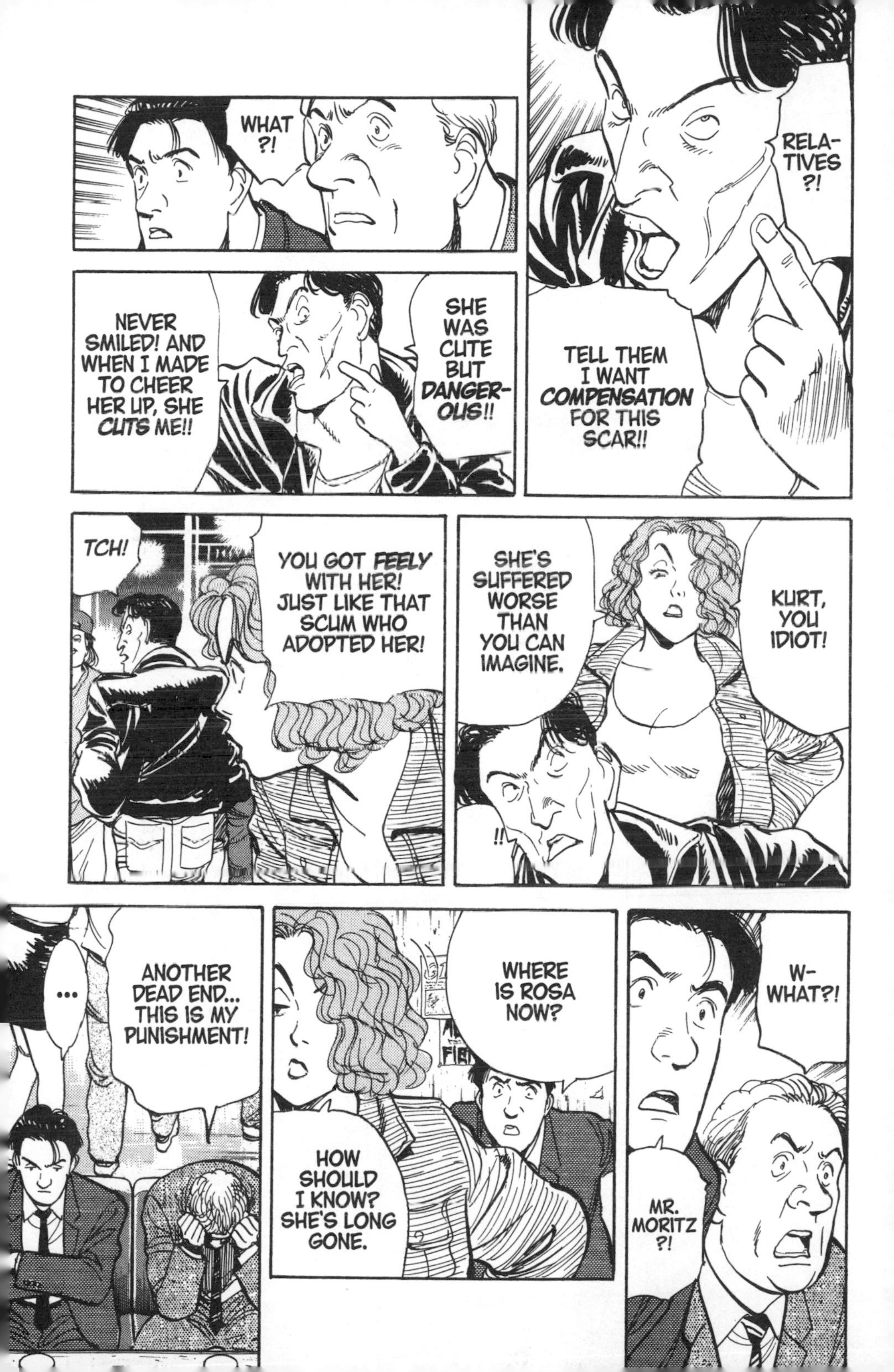
RELATIVES?!
TELL THEM I WANT COMPENSATION FOR THIS SCAR!!
WHAT?!
SHE WAS CUTE BUT DANGEROUS!!
NEVER SMILED! AND WHEN I MADE TO CHEER HER UP, SHE CUTS ME!!
KURT, YOU IDIOT!
SHE'S SUFFERED WORSE THAN YOU CAN IMAGINE.
!!
YOU GOT FEELY WITH HER! JUST LIKE THAT SCUM WHO ADOPTED HER!
TCH!
W-WHAT?!
MR. MORITZ?!
WHERE IS ROSA NOW?
HOW SHOULD I KNOW? SHE'S LONG GONE.
ANOTHER DEAD END... THIS IS MY PUNISHMENT!
...

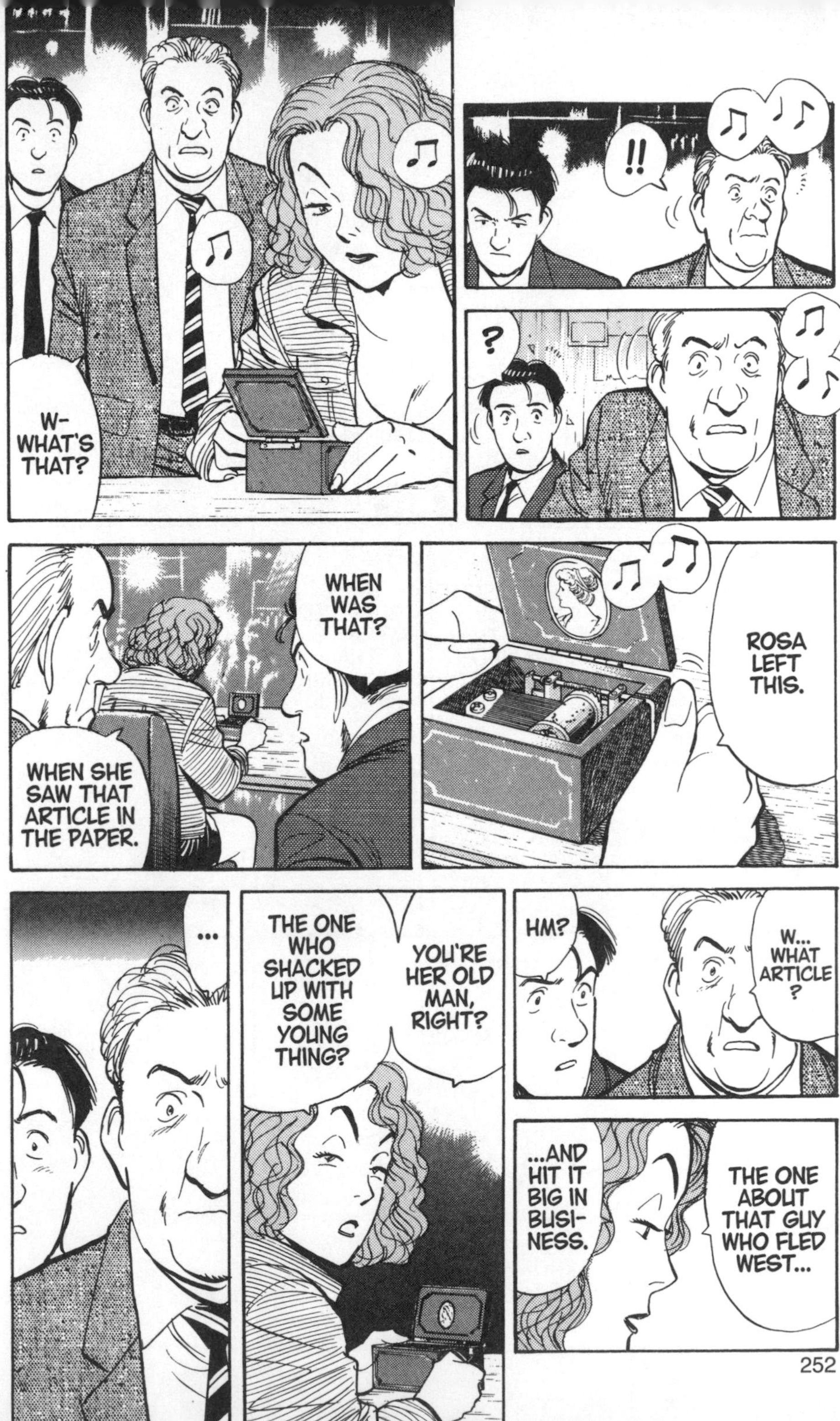
♫
!!
?
♫
♫
W-WHAT'S THAT?
♫
ROSA LEFT THIS.
WHEN WAS THAT?
WHEN SHE SAW THAT ARTICLE IN THE PAPER.
W... WHAT ARTICLE?
HM?
THE ONE ABOUT THAT GUY WHO FLED WEST...
...AND HIT IT BIG IN BUSI-NESS.
YOU'RE HER OLD MAN, RIGHT?
THE ONE WHO SHACKED UP WITH SOME YOUNG THING?
...

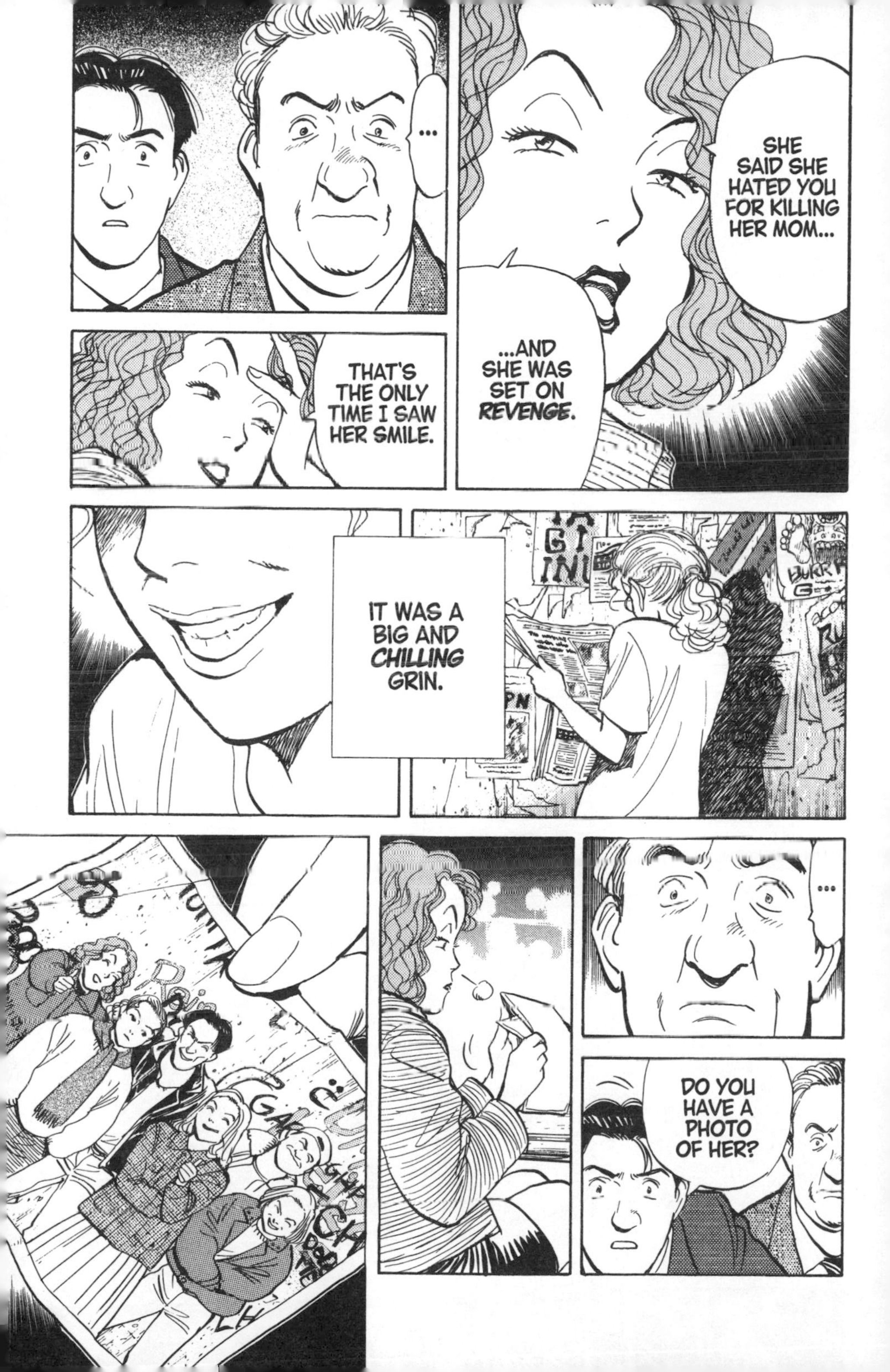
SHE SAID SHE HATED YOU FOR KILLING HER MOM...
...AND SHE WAS SET ON *REVENGE*.
...
THAT'S THE ONLY TIME I SAW HER SMILE.
IT WAS A BIG AND *CHILLING* GRIN.
...
DO YOU HAVE A PHOTO OF HER?

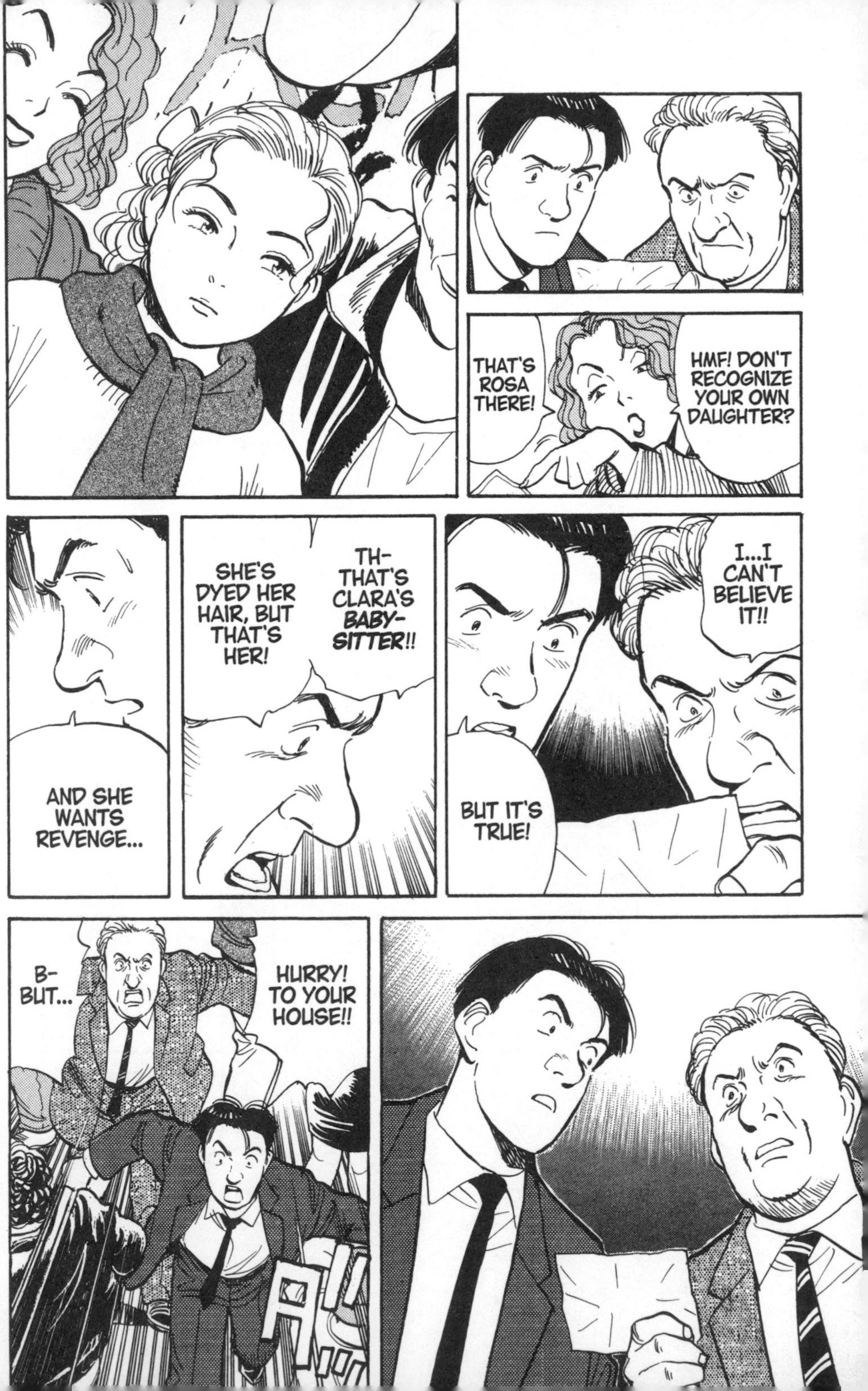
HMF! DON'T RECOGNIZE YOUR OWN DAUGHTER?
THAT'S ROSA THERE!
I...I CAN'T BELIEVE IT!!
BUT IT'S TRUE!
TH- THAT'S CLARA'S BABY-SITTER!!
SHE'S DYED HER HAIR, BUT THAT'S HER!
AND SHE WANTS REVENGE...
HURRY! TO YOUR HOUSE!!
B- BUT...

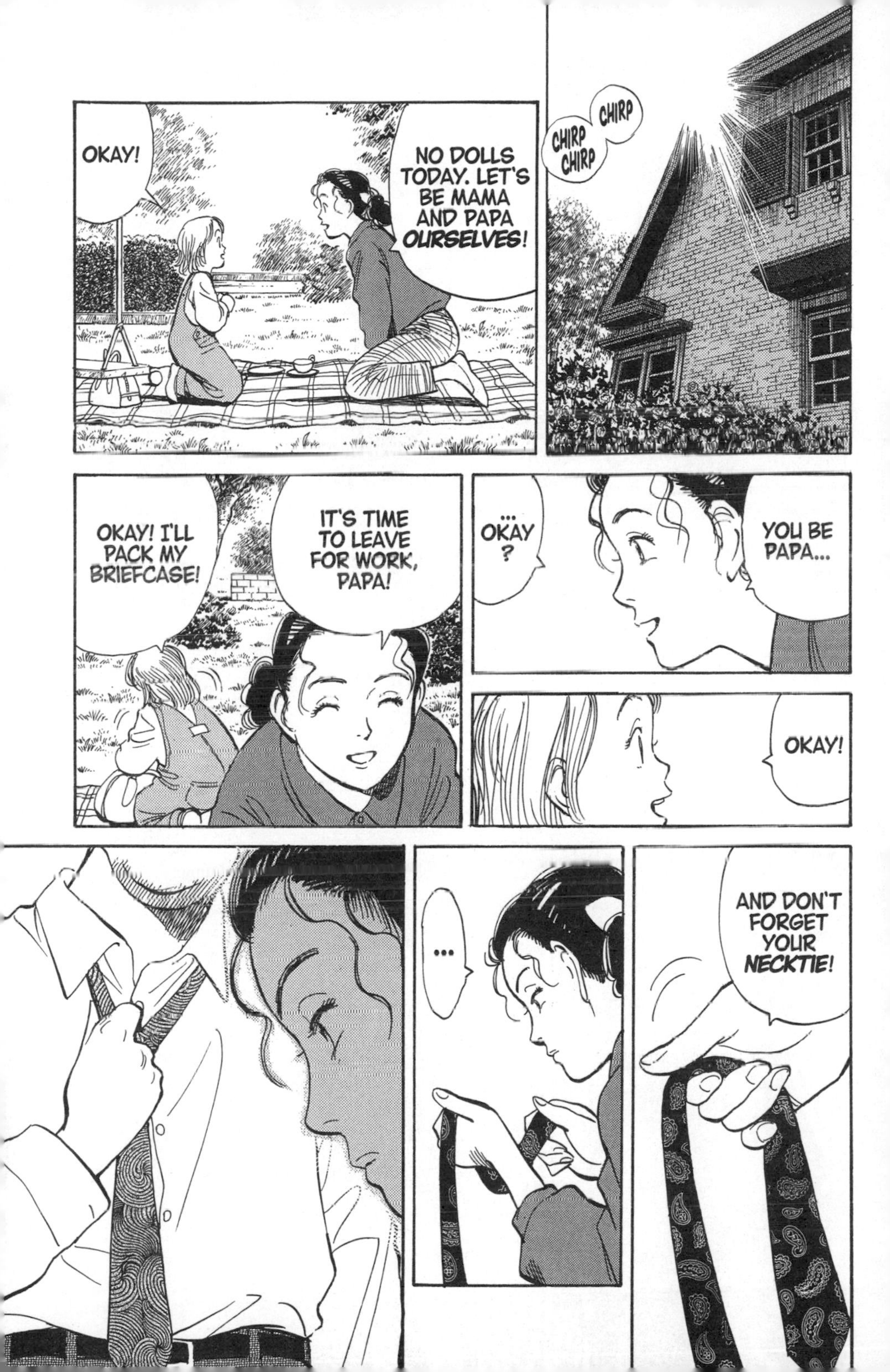
CHIRP
CHIRP CHIRP
NO DOLLS TODAY. LET'S BE MAMA AND PAPA OURSELVES!
OKAY!
YOU BE PAPA...
... OKAY ?
OKAY!
IT'S TIME TO LEAVE FOR WORK, PAPA!
OKAY! I'LL PACK MY BRIEFCASE!
AND DON'T FORGET YOUR NECKTIE!
...

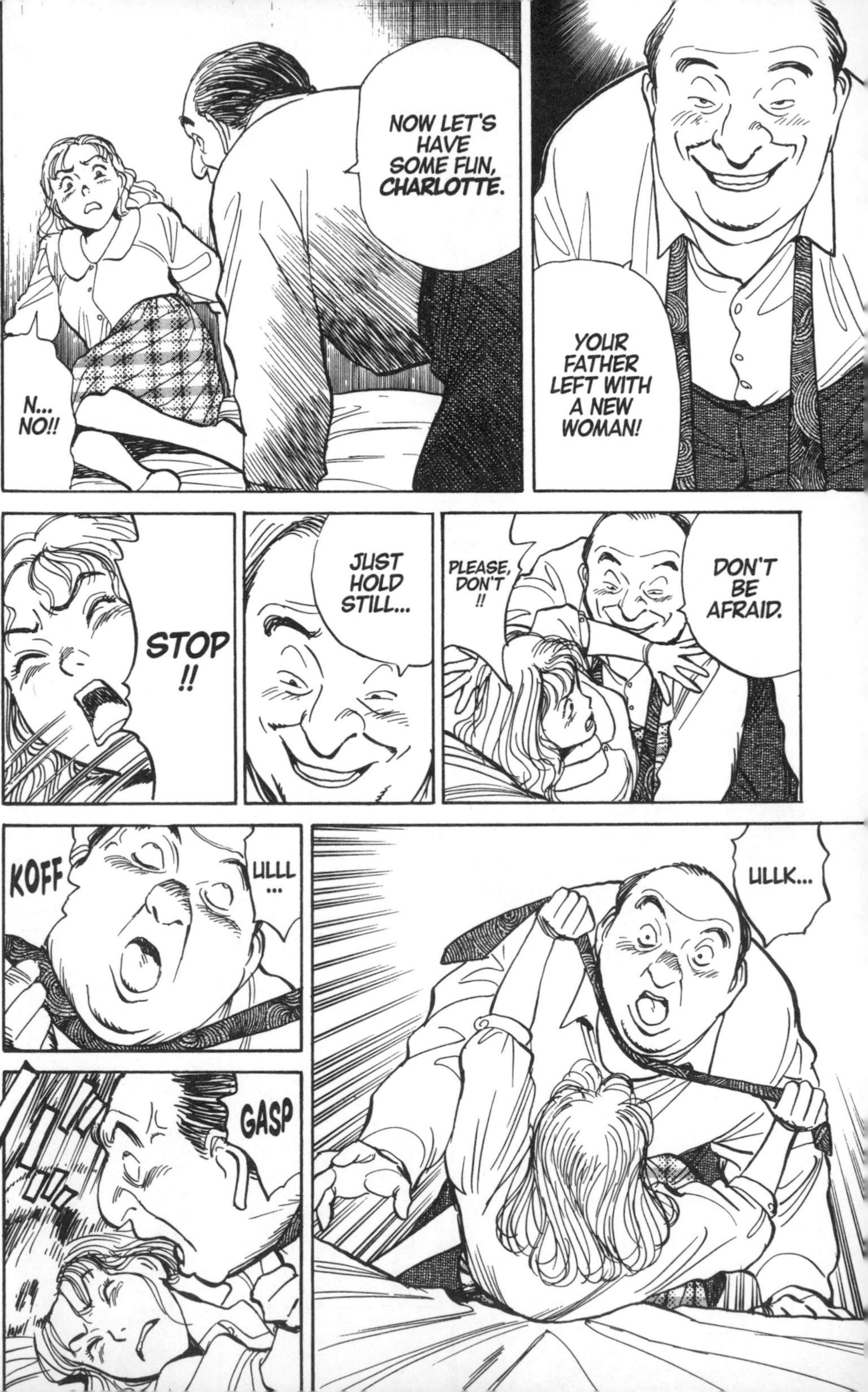
YOUR FATHER LEFT WITH A NEW WOMAN!
NOW LET'S HAVE SOME FUN, CHARLOTTE.
N... NO!!
DON'T BE AFRAID.
PLEASE, DON'T !!
JUST HOLD STILL...
STOP !!
ULLK...
ULLL ...
KOFF
GASP

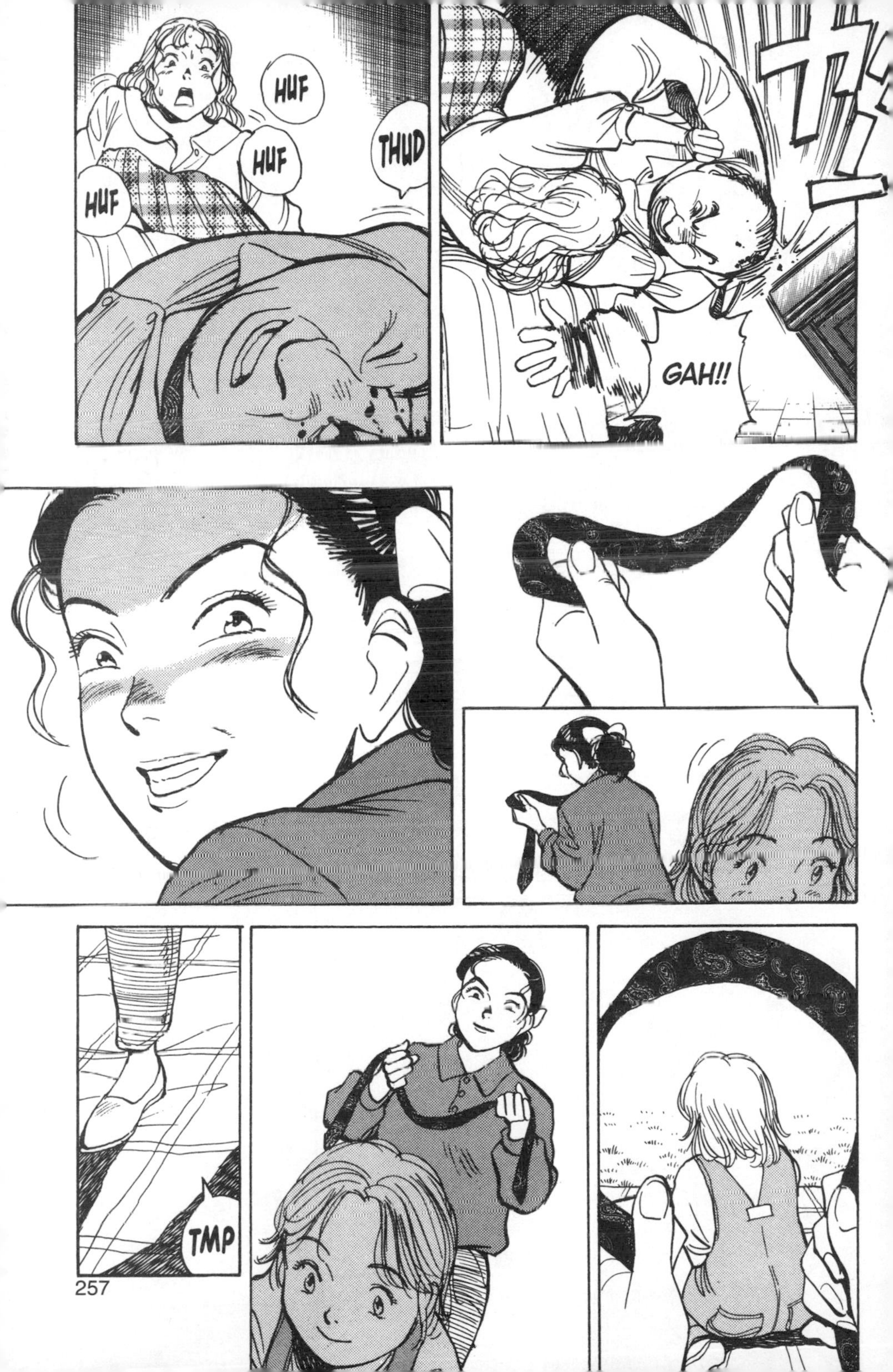
GAH!!
HUF
HUF
HUF
THUD
TMP

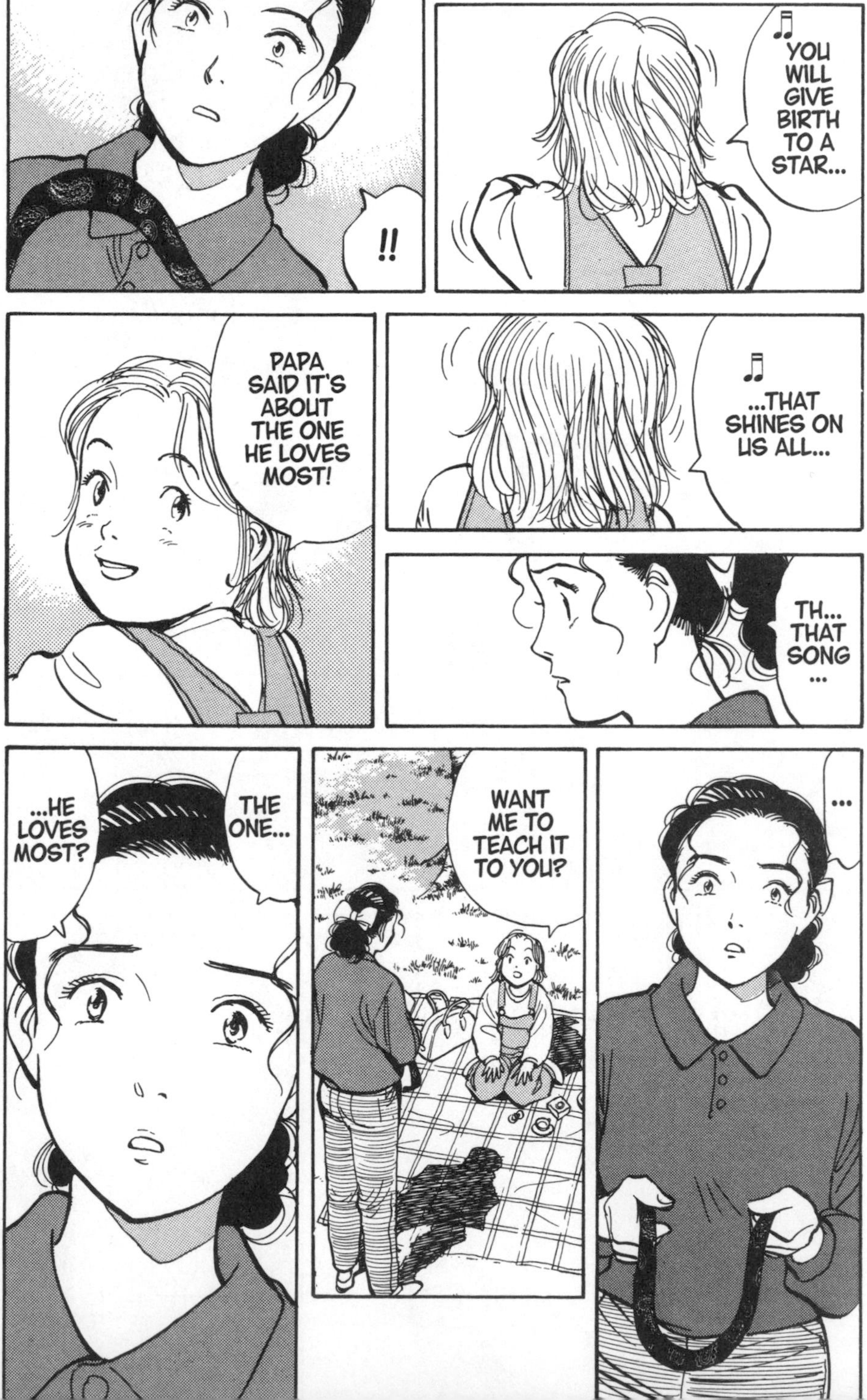
♬ YOU WILL GIVE BIRTH TO A STAR...
!!
♬ ...THAT SHINES ON US ALL...
TH... THAT SONG...
PAPA SAID IT'S ABOUT THE ONE HE LOVES MOST!
...
WANT ME TO TEACH IT TO YOU?
THE ONE...
...HE LOVES MOST?

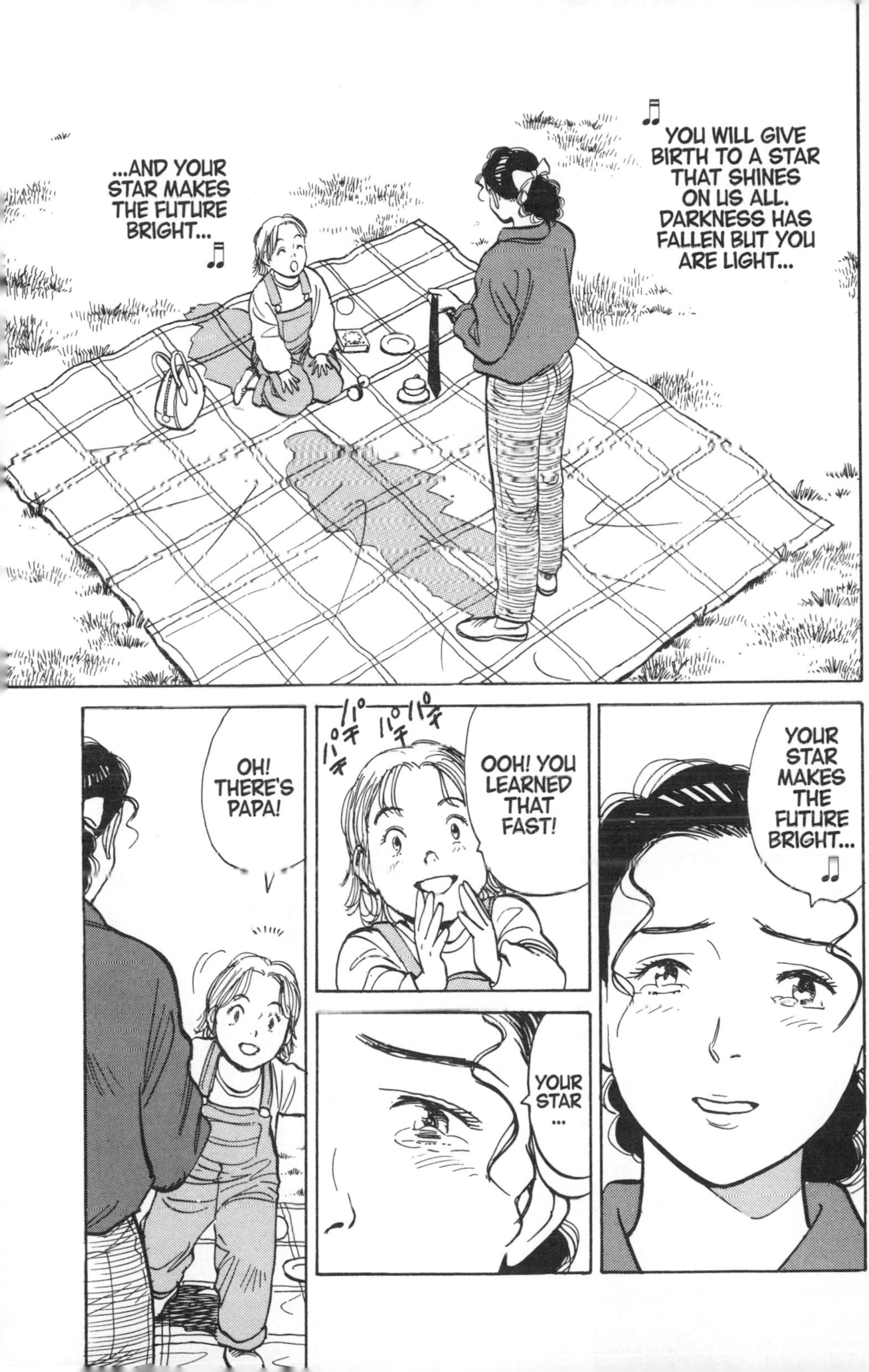
YOU WILL GIVE BIRTH TO A STAR THAT SHINES ON US ALL. DARKNESS HAS FALLEN BUT YOU ARE LIGHT...
...AND YOUR STAR MAKES THE FUTURE BRIGHT...
YOUR STAR MAKES THE FUTURE BRIGHT...
パチ パチ パチ
OOH! YOU LEARNED THAT FAST!
YOUR STAR ...
OH! THERE'S PAPA!

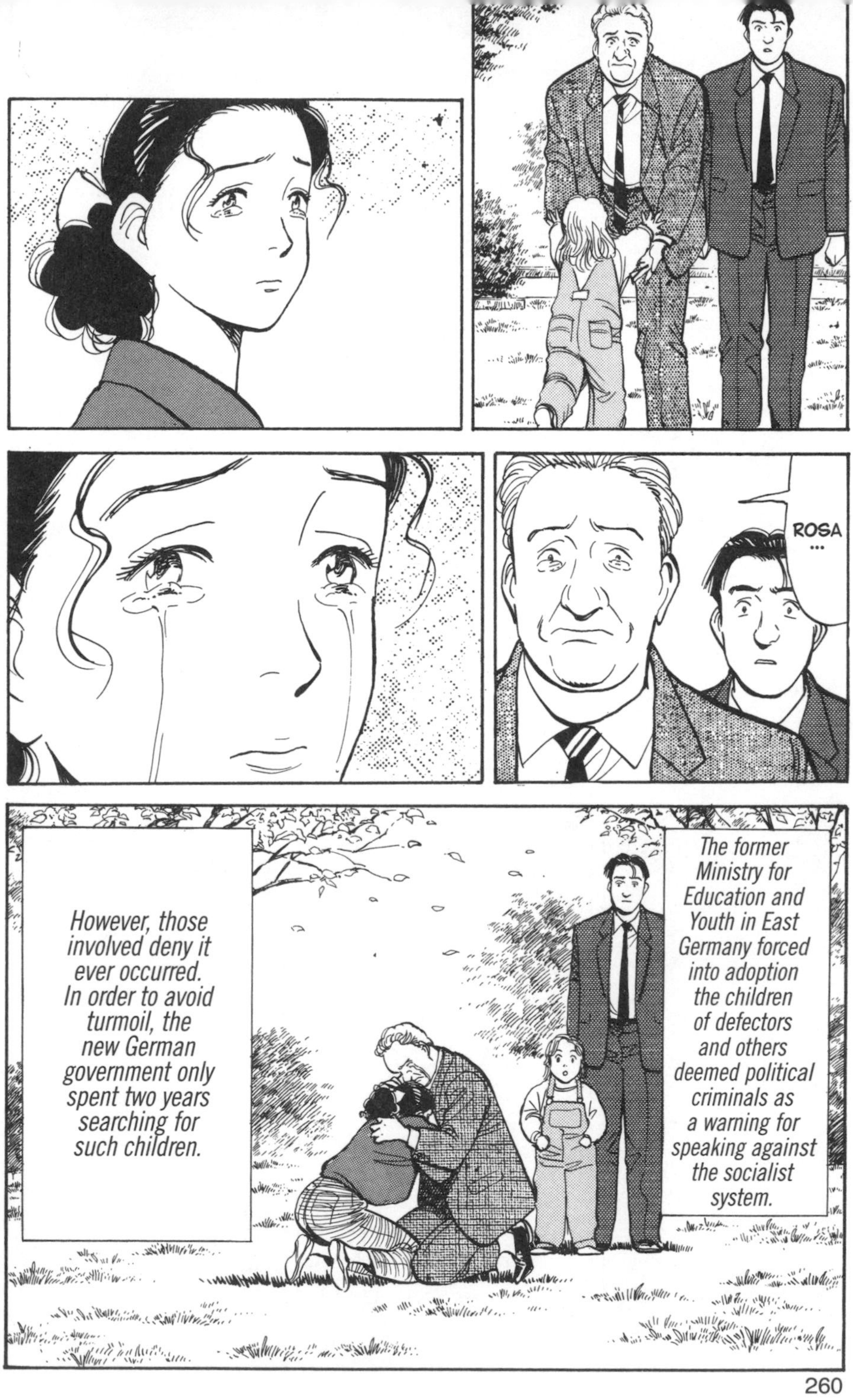
ROSA ...
The former Ministry for Education and Youth in East Germany forced into adoption the children of defectors and others deemed political criminals as a warning for speaking against the socialist system.
However, those involved deny it ever occurred. In order to avoid turmoil, the new German government only spent two years searching for such children.

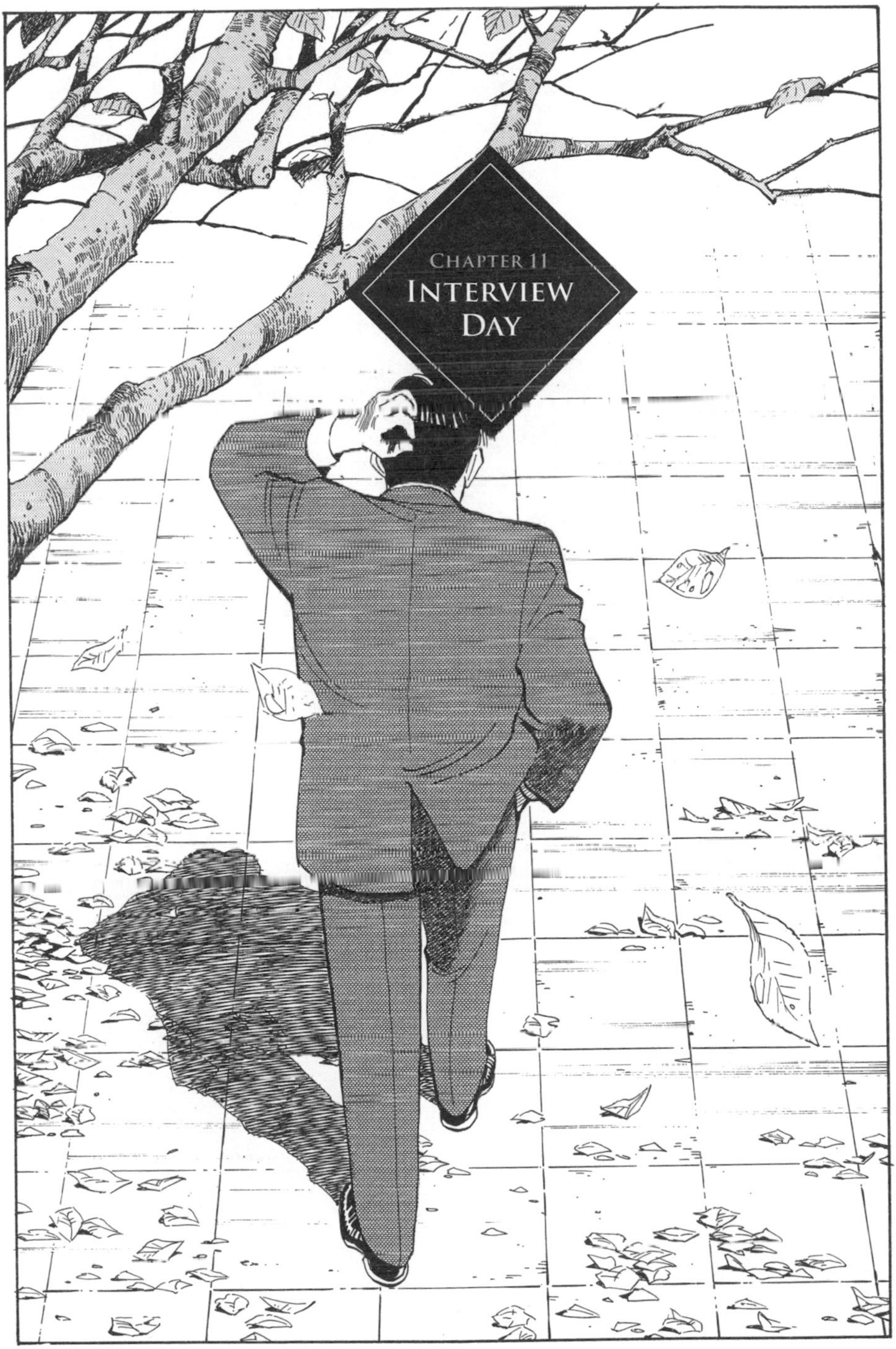
CHAPTER 11
INTERVIEW DAY

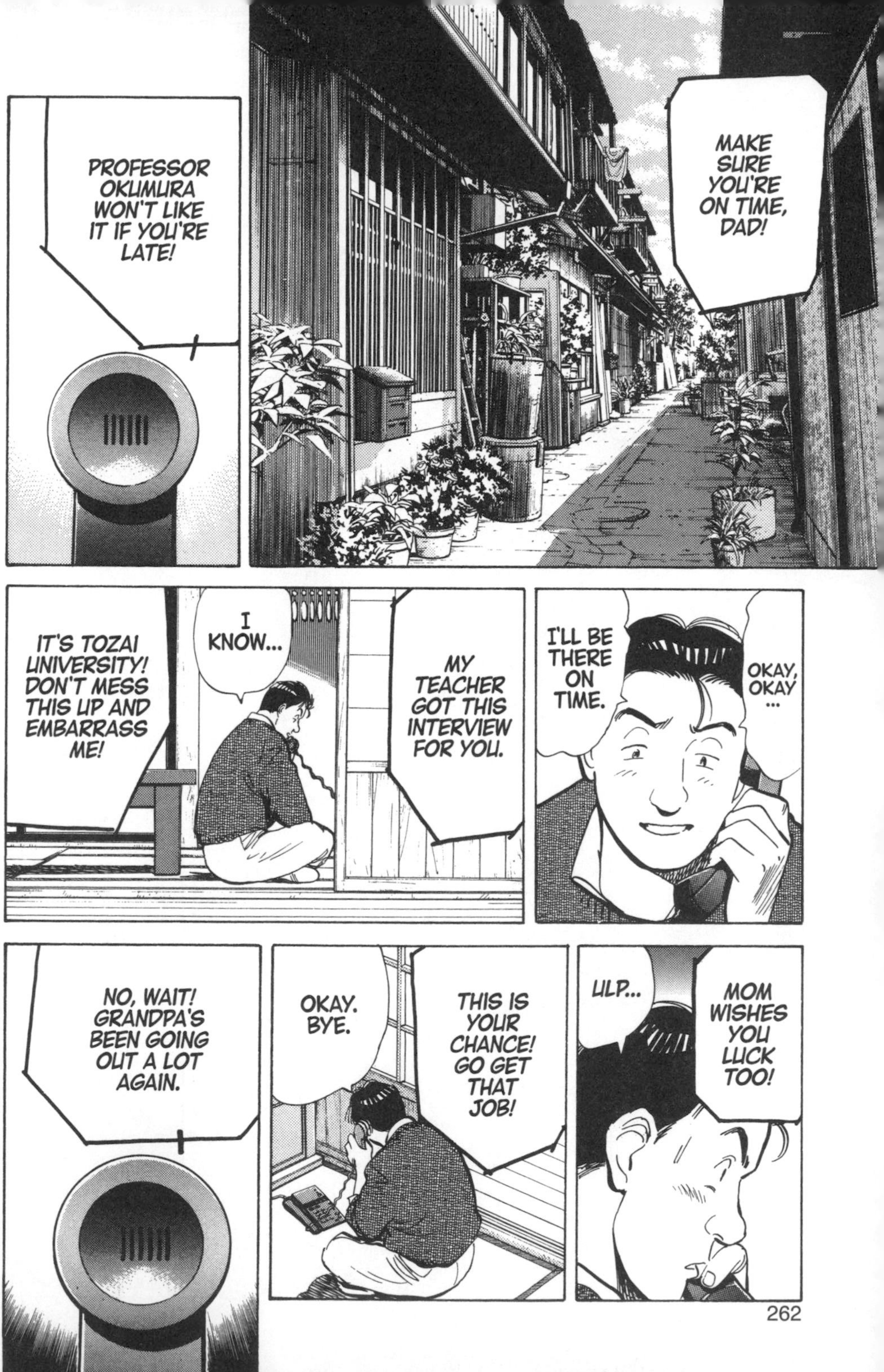
MAKE SURE YOU'RE ON TIME, DAD!
PROFESSOR OKUMURA WON'T LIKE IT IF YOU'RE LATE!
OKAY, OKAY ...
I'LL BE THERE ON TIME.
MY TEACHER GOT THIS INTERVIEW FOR YOU.
I KNOW...
IT'S TOZAI UNIVERSITY! DON'T MESS THIS UP AND EMBARRASS ME!
MOM WISHES YOU LUCK TOO!
ULP...
THIS IS YOUR CHANCE! GO GET THAT JOB!
OKAY. BYE.
NO, WAIT! GRANDPA'S BEEN GOING OUT A LOT AGAIN.

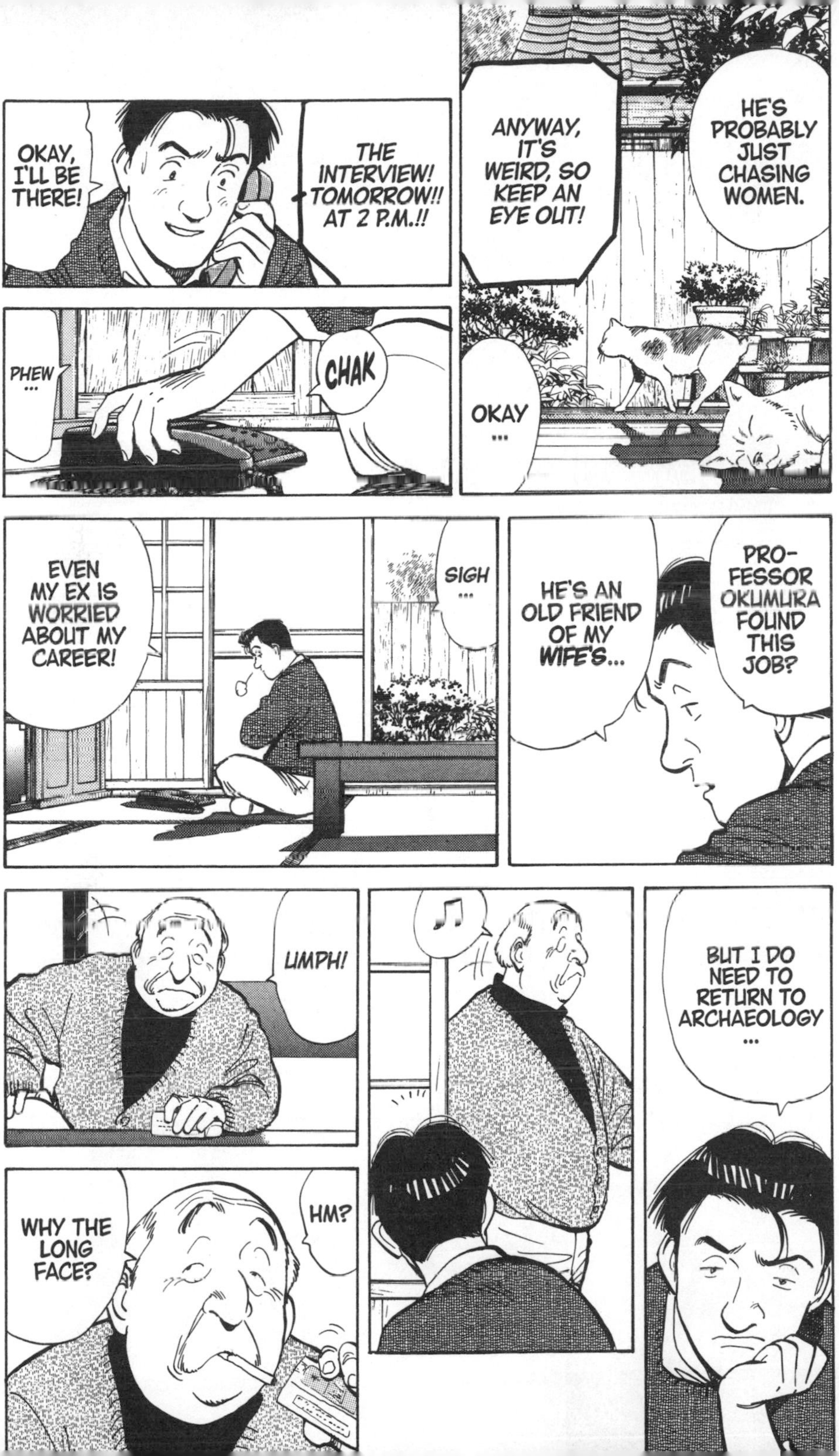
HE'S PROBABLY JUST CHASING WOMEN.
ANYWAY, IT'S WEIRD, SO KEEP AN EYE OUT!
OKAY ...
THE INTERVIEW! TOMORROW!! AT 2 P.M.!!
OKAY, I'LL BE THERE!
CHAK
PHEW ...
PRO-FESSOR OKUMURA FOUND THIS JOB?
HE'S AN OLD FRIEND OF MY WIFE'S...
SIGH ...
EVEN MY EX IS WORRIED ABOUT MY CAREER!
BUT I DO NEED TO RETURN TO ARCHAEOLOGY ...
♪
UMPH!
HM?
WHY THE LONG FACE?

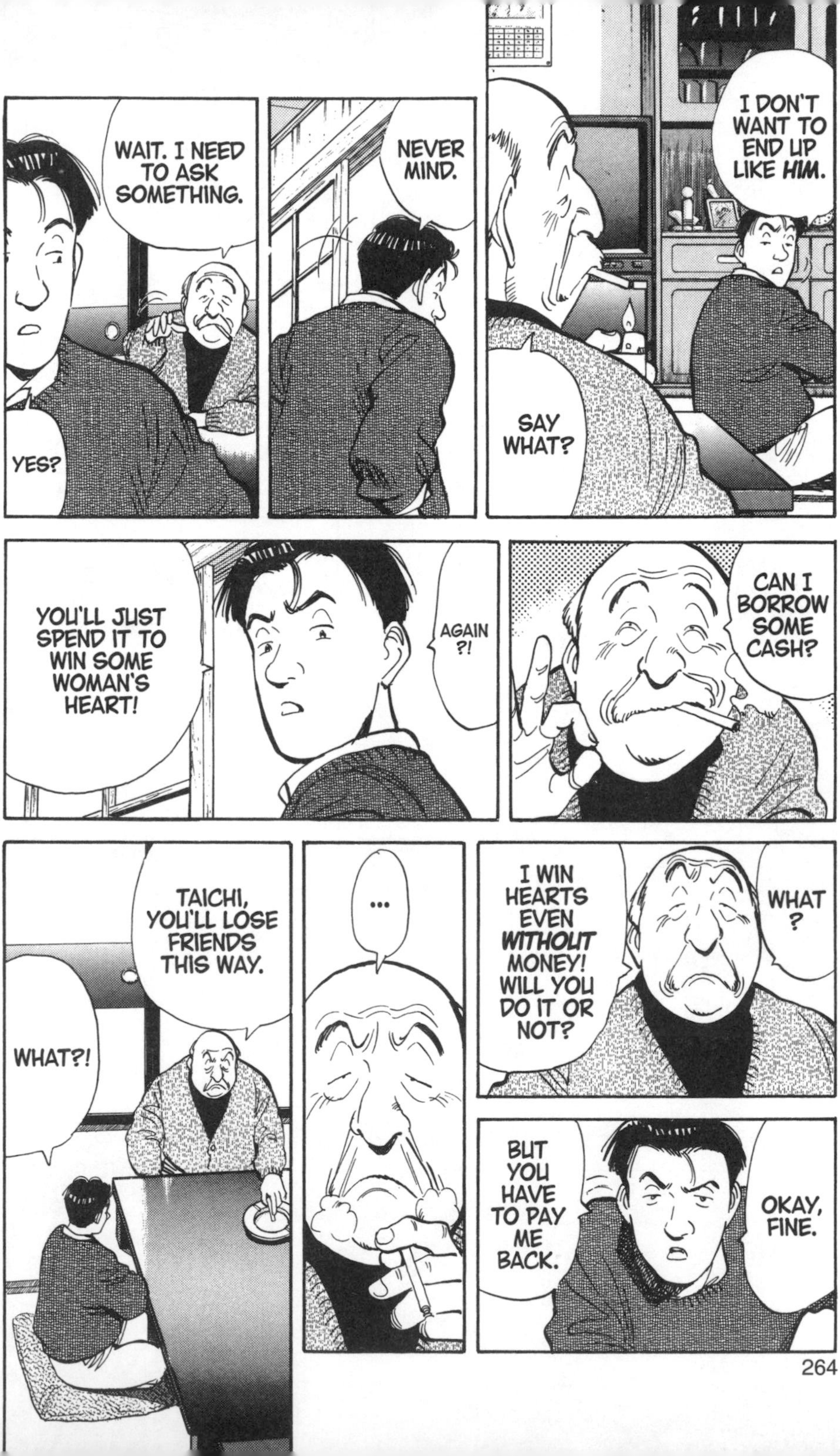
I DON'T WANT TO END UP LIKE *HIM*.
SAY WHAT?
NEVER MIND.
WAIT. I NEED TO ASK SOMETHING.
YES?
CAN I BORROW SOME CASH?
AGAIN ?!
YOU'LL JUST SPEND IT TO WIN SOME WOMAN'S HEART!
WHAT ?
I WIN HEARTS EVEN ***WITHOUT*** MONEY! WILL YOU DO IT OR NOT?
OKAY, FINE.
BUT YOU HAVE TO PAY ME BACK.
...
TAICHI, YOU'LL LOSE FRIENDS THIS WAY.
WHAT?!

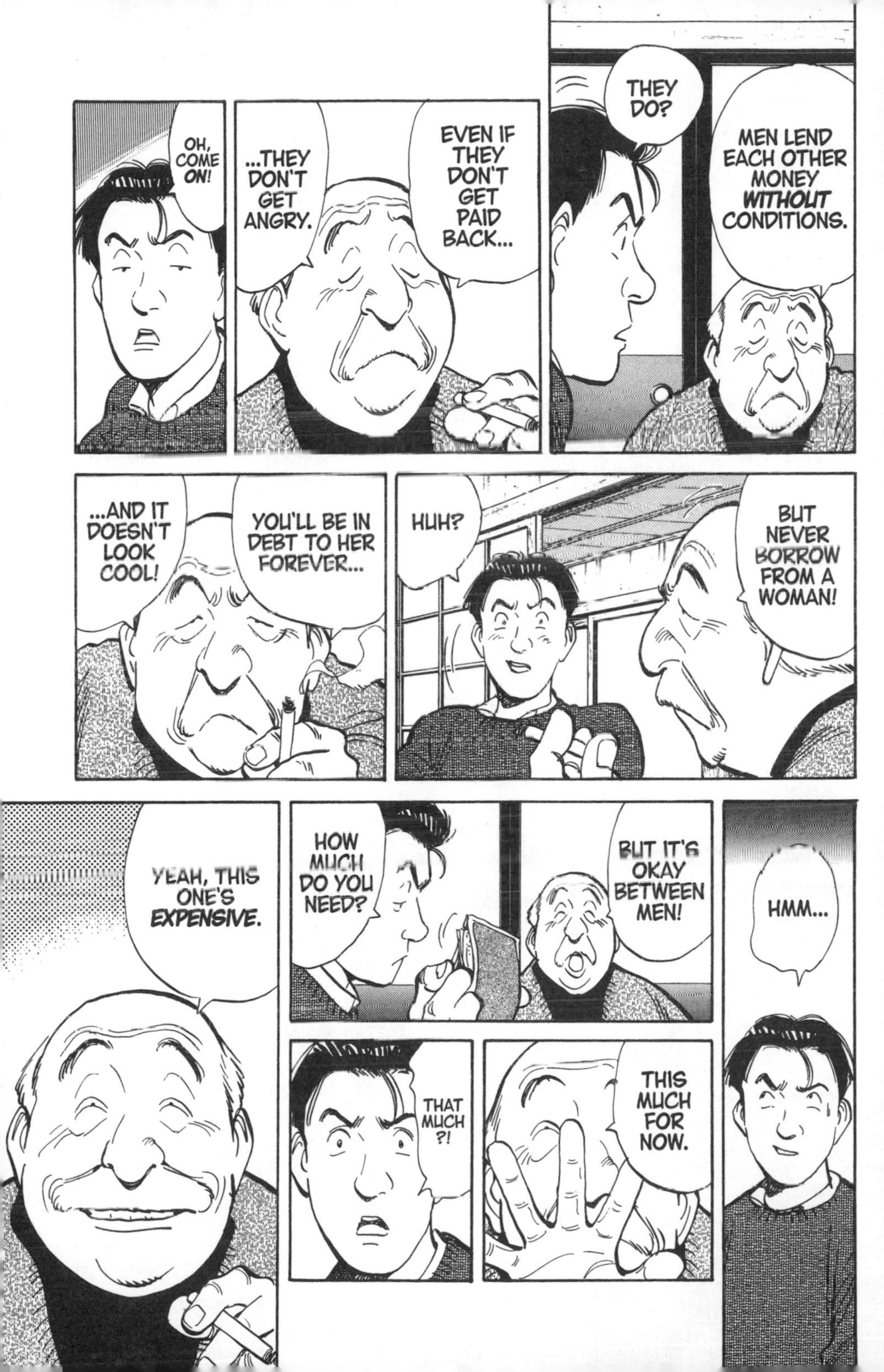
MEN LEND EACH OTHER MONEY *WITHOUT* CONDITIONS.
THEY DO?
EVEN IF THEY DON'T GET PAID BACK...
...THEY DON'T GET ANGRY.
OH, COME *ON*!
BUT NEVER BORROW FROM A WOMAN!
HUH?
YOU'LL BE IN DEBT TO HER FOREVER...
...AND IT DOESN'T LOOK COOL!
HMM...
BUT IT'S OKAY BETWEEN MEN!
HOW MUCH DO YOU NEED?
THIS MUCH FOR NOW.
THAT MUCH ?!
YEAH, THIS ONE'S *EXPENSIVE*.

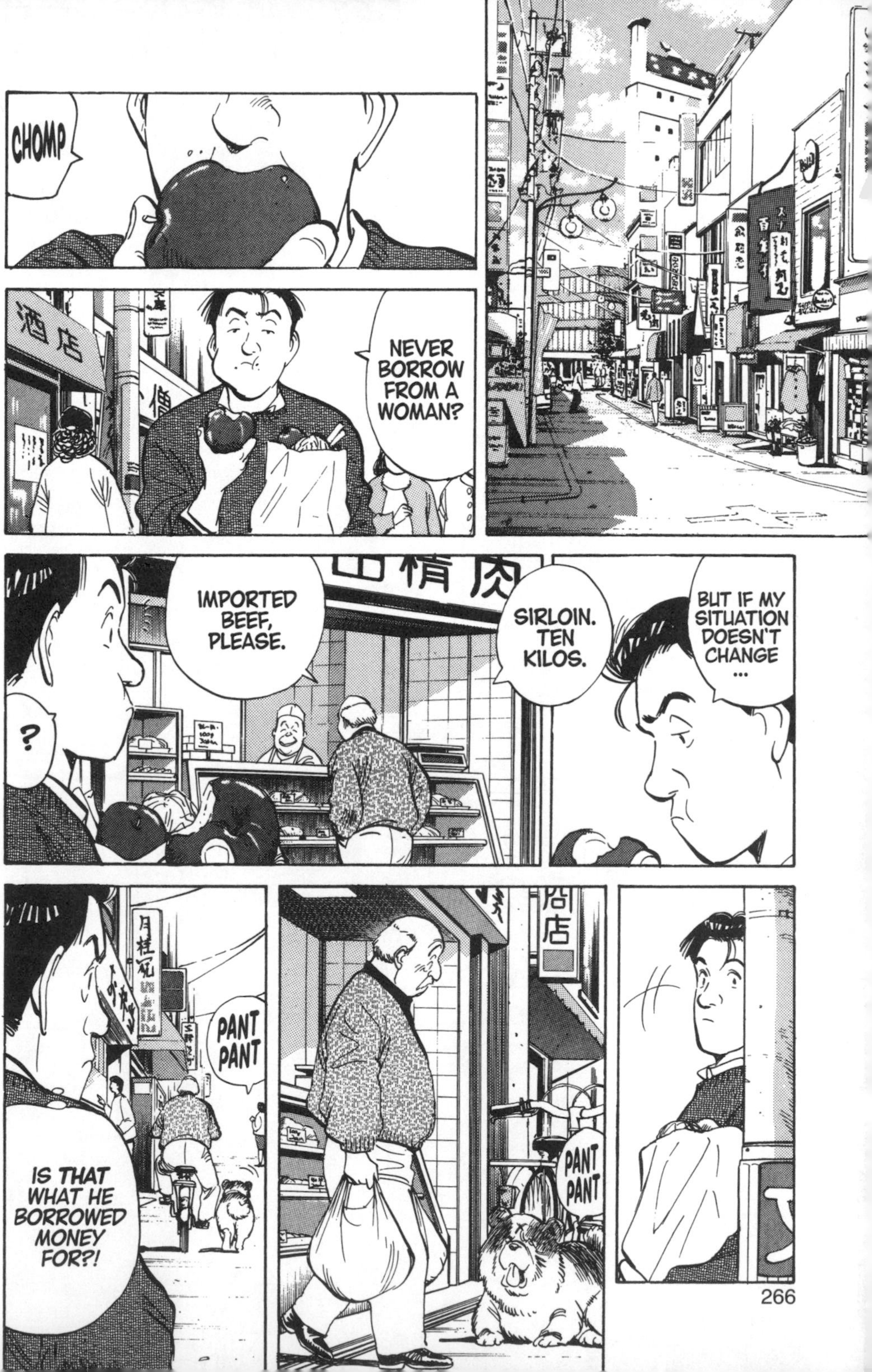
CHOMP
NEVER BORROW FROM A WOMAN?
BUT IF MY SITUATION DOESN'T CHANGE ...
SIRLOIN. TEN KILOS.
IMPORTED BEEF, PLEASE.
?
PANT PANT
PANT PANT
IS THAT WHAT HE BORROWED MONEY FOR?!

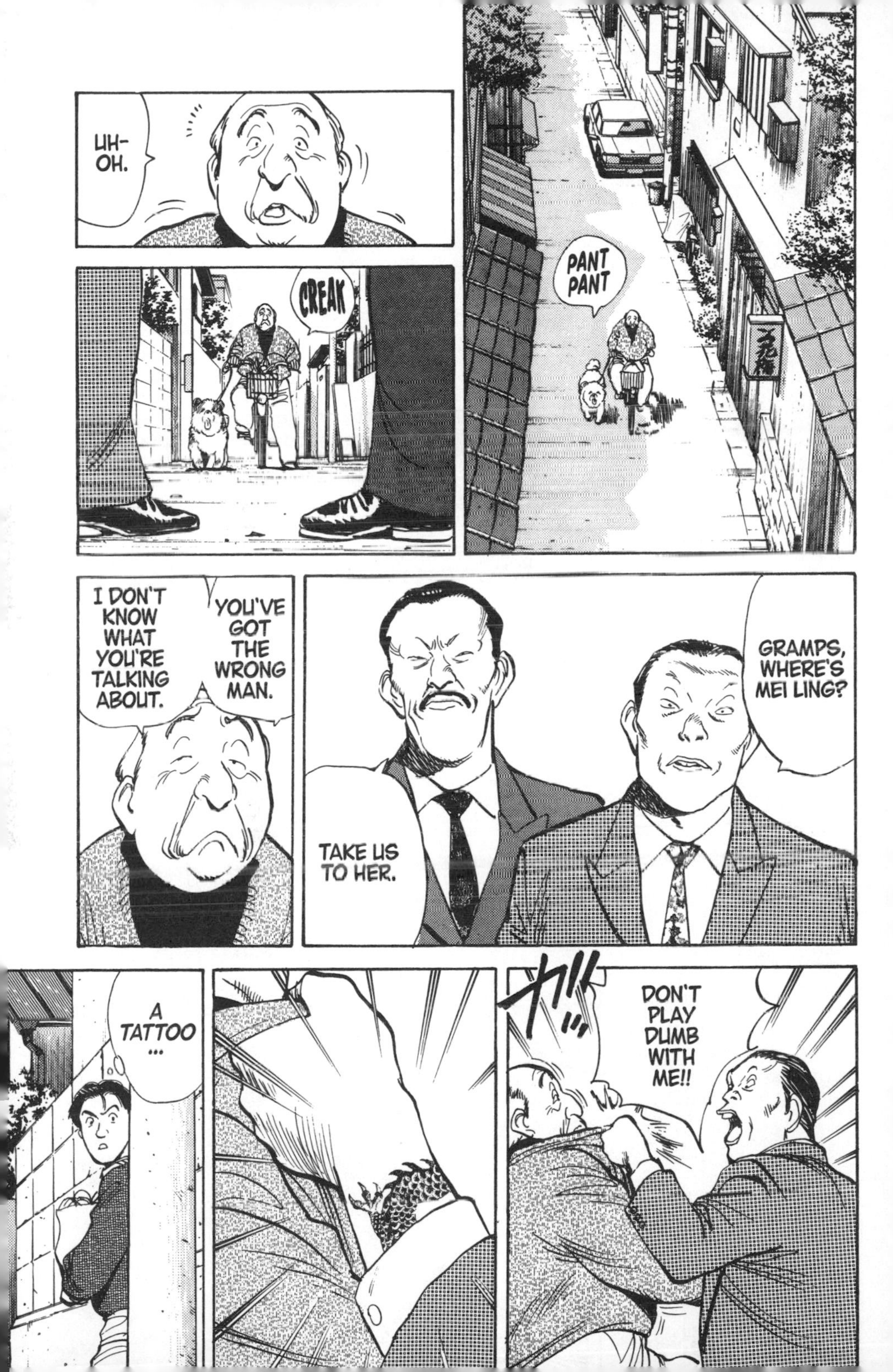
PANT PANT
UH-OH.
CREAK
GRAMPS, WHERE'S MEI LING?
TAKE US TO HER.
I DON'T KNOW WHAT YOU'RE TALKING ABOUT.
YOU'VE GOT THE WRONG MAN.
DON'T PLAY DUMB WITH ME!!
A TATTOO ...

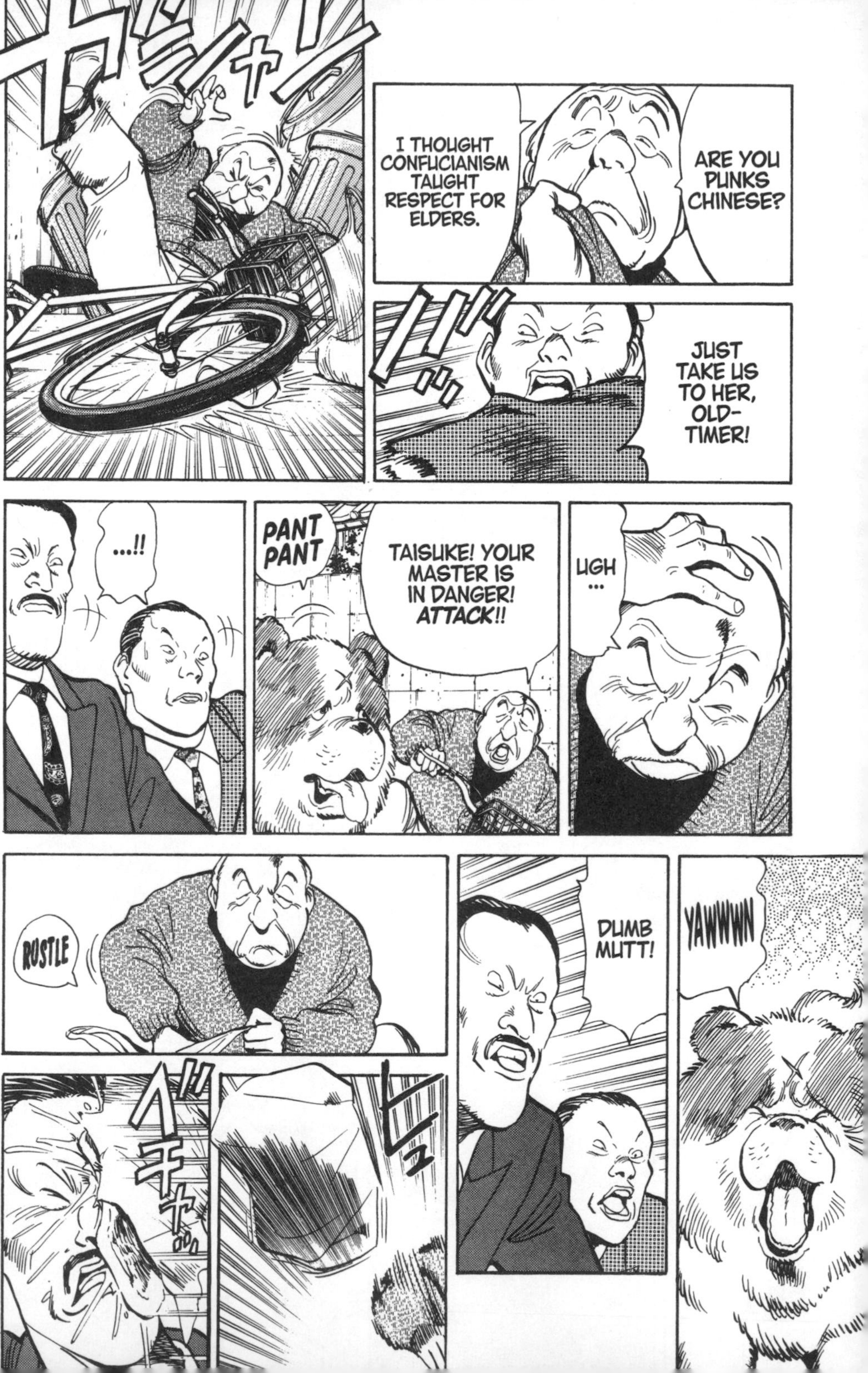
ARE YOU PUNKS CHINESE?
I THOUGHT CONFUCIANISM TAUGHT RESPECT FOR ELDERS.
JUST TAKE US TO HER, OLD-TIMER!
UGH ...
TAISUKE! YOUR MASTER IS IN DANGER! ATTACK!!
PANT PANT
...!!
YAWWWN
DUMB MUTT!
RUSTLE

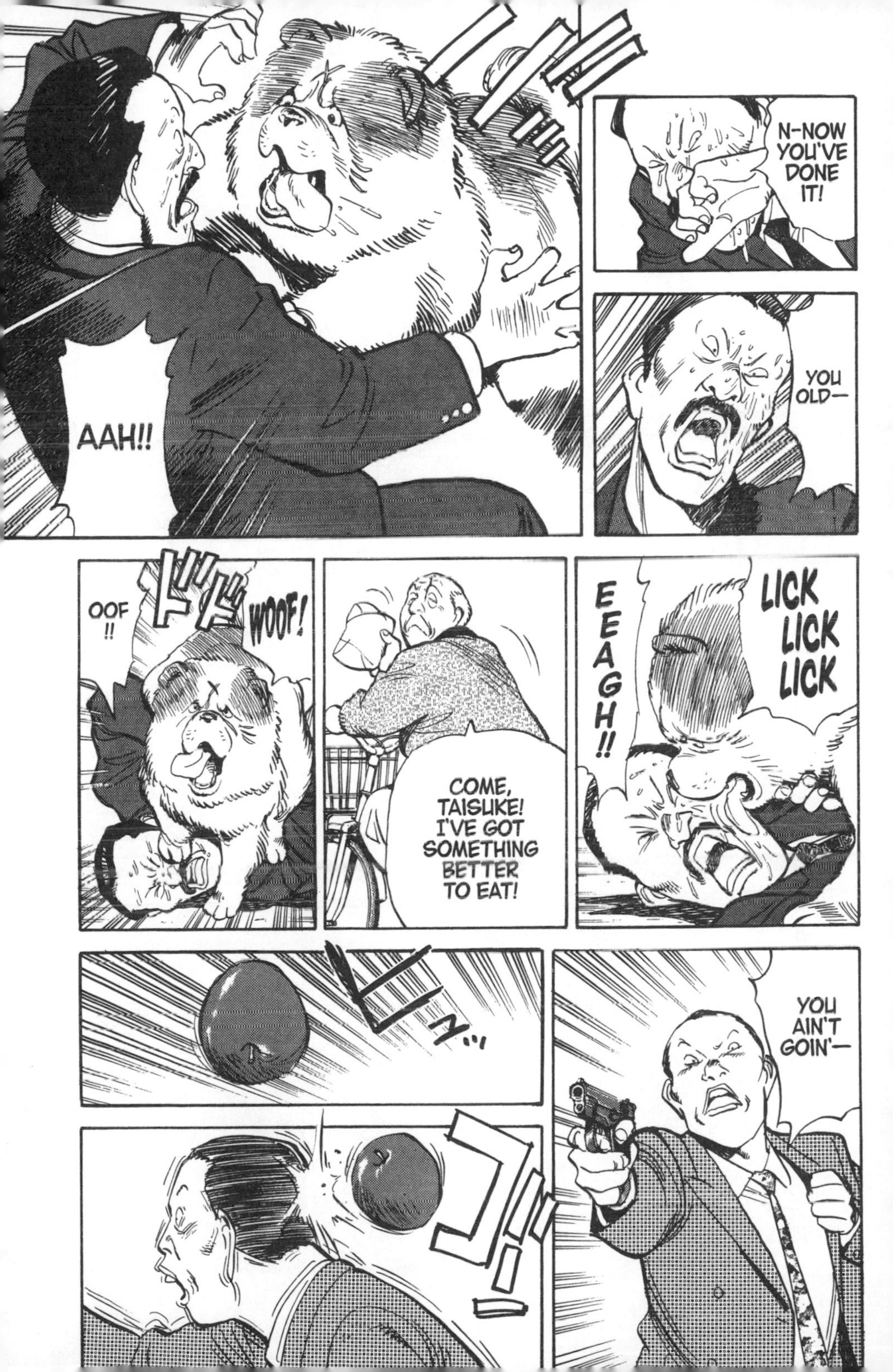
N-NOW YOU'VE DONE IT!
YOU OLD—
AAH!!
LICK LICK LICK
EEAGH!!
COME, TAISUKE! I'VE GOT SOMETHING BETTER TO EAT!
OOF !!
WOOF!
YOU AIN'T GOIN'—

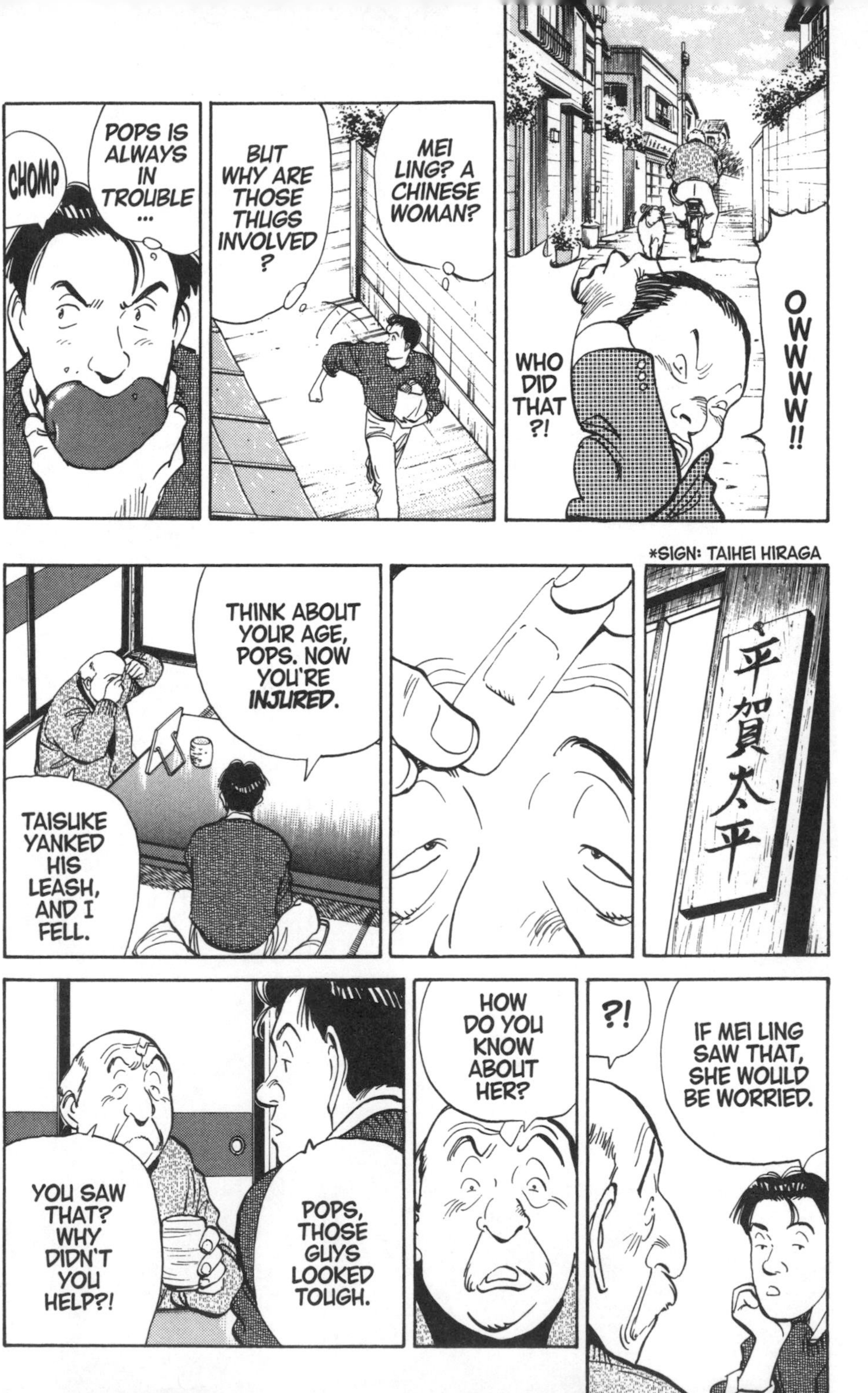
OWWWW!!
WHO DID THAT?!
MEI LING? A CHINESE WOMAN?
BUT WHY ARE THOSE THUGS INVOLVED?
POPS IS ALWAYS IN TROUBLE...
CHOMP
平賀太平
*SIGN: TAIHEI HIRAGA
THINK ABOUT YOUR AGE, POPS. NOW YOU'RE INJURED.
TAISUKE YANKED HIS LEASH, AND I FELL.
IF MEI LING SAW THAT, SHE WOULD BE WORRIED.
?!
HOW DO YOU KNOW ABOUT HER?
POPS, THOSE GUYS LOOKED TOUGH.
YOU SAW THAT? WHY DIDN'T YOU HELP?!

YOU WOULDN'T UNDER-STAND.
LOVE REQUIRES ENTERING THE TIGER'S DEN!
...
I'M OLD, BUT I'M ACTIVE! DANGER IS WORTH IT...
...FOR MEI LING AND PAI LI!!
MEI LING ...
...AND PAI LI?!
TWO WOMEN?!
GRIN
THE NEXT DAY...
チューン チューン
YAWN
POPS SAID I SHOULDN'T BORROW FROM WOMEN...
ANYWAY! THE INTERVIEW IS AT 2 P.M.!
FUMP BUMP

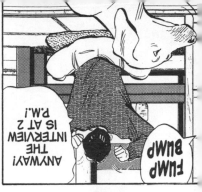

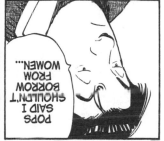

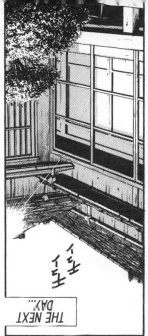

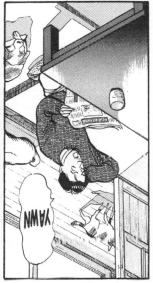

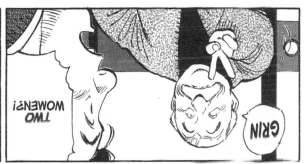

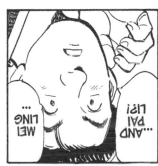

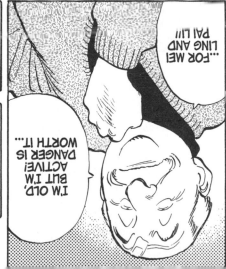

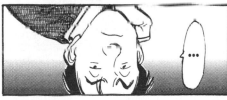

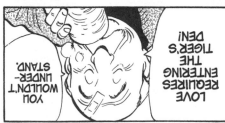

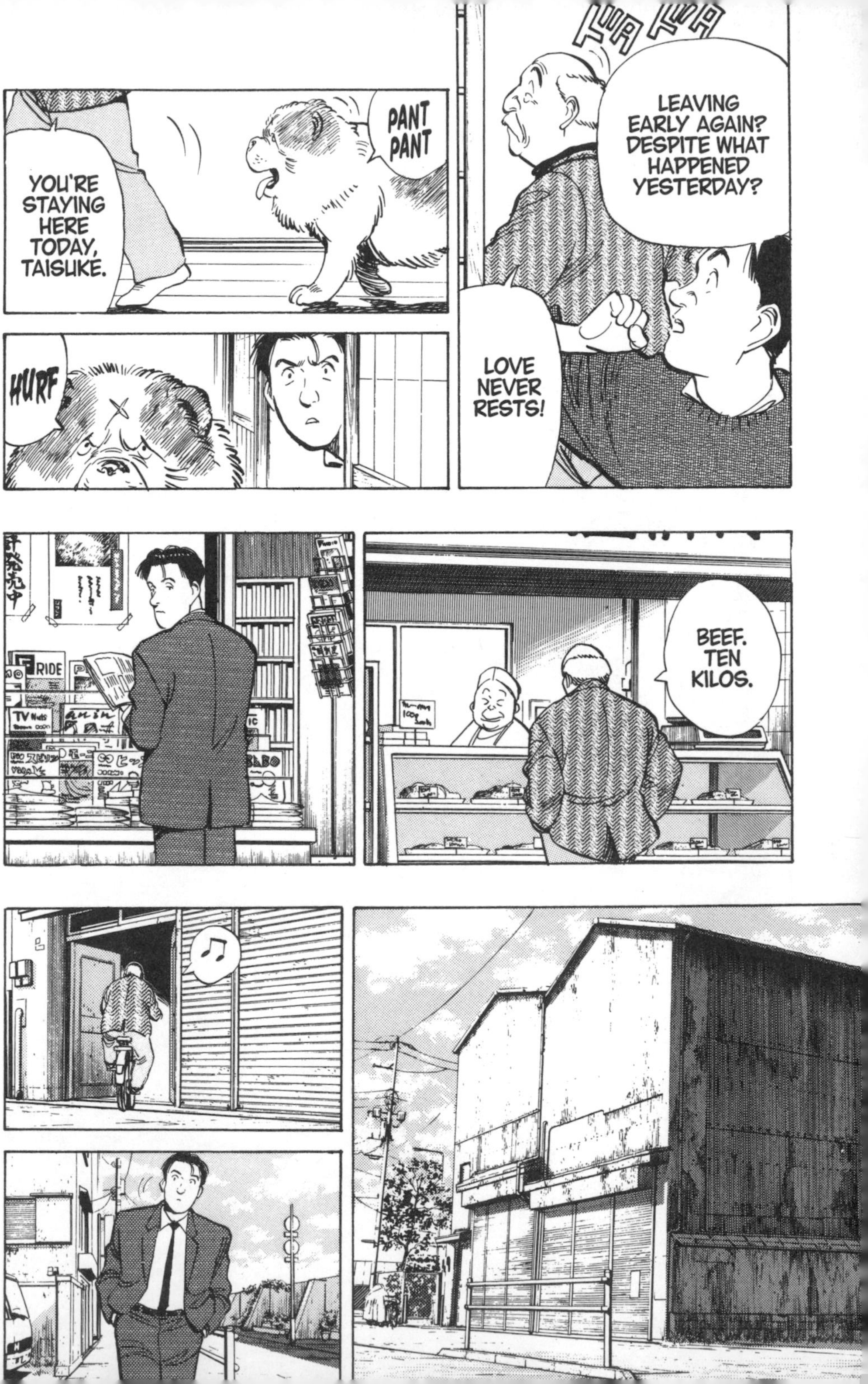
LEAVING EARLY AGAIN? DESPITE WHAT HAPPENED YESTERDAY?
LOVE NEVER RESTS!
PANT PANT
YOU'RE STAYING HERE TODAY, TAISUKE.
HURF
BEEF. TEN KILOS.

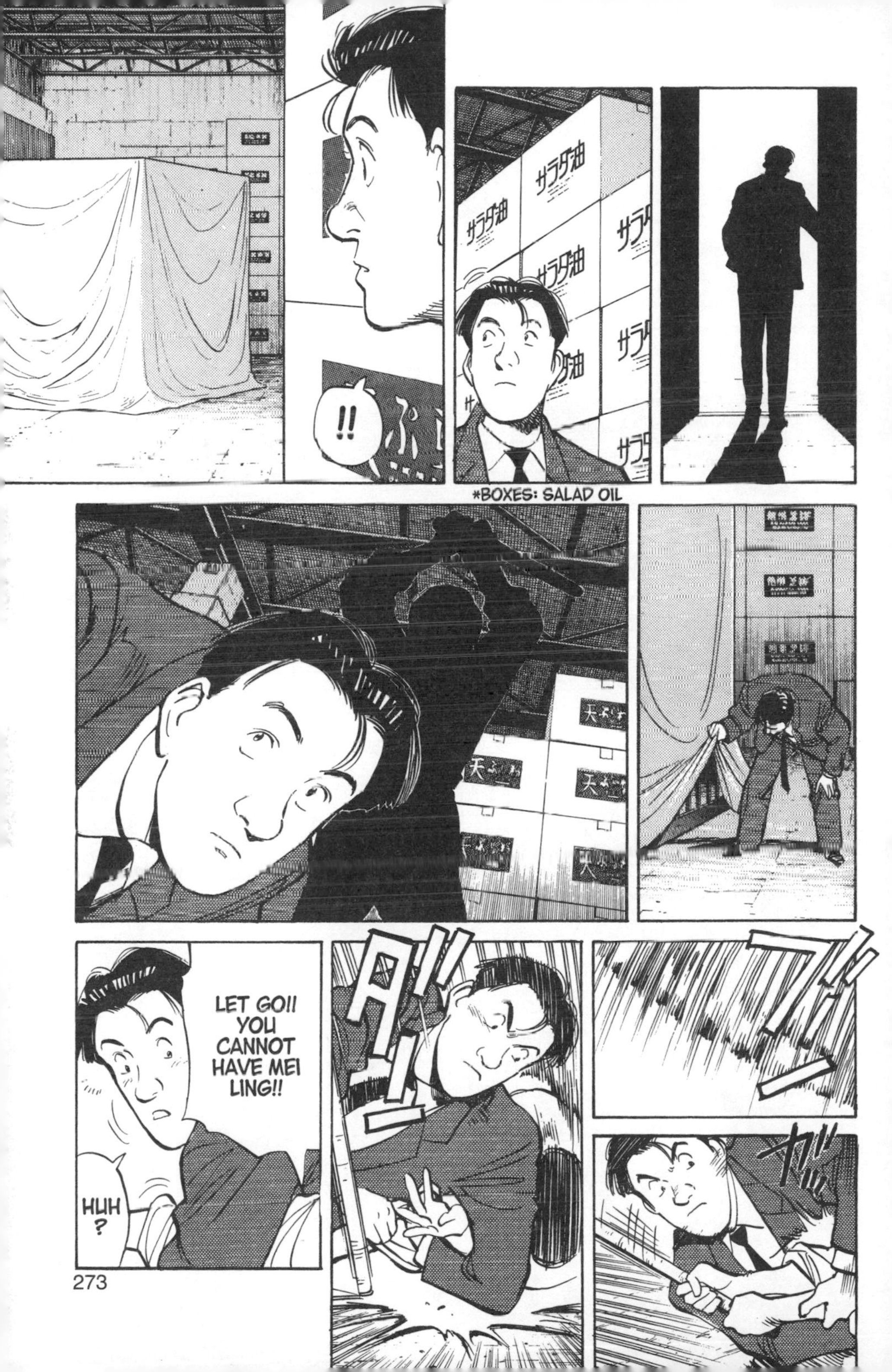
サラダ油
!!
*BOXES: SALAD OIL
LET GO!! YOU CANNOT HAVE MEI LING!!
HUH?

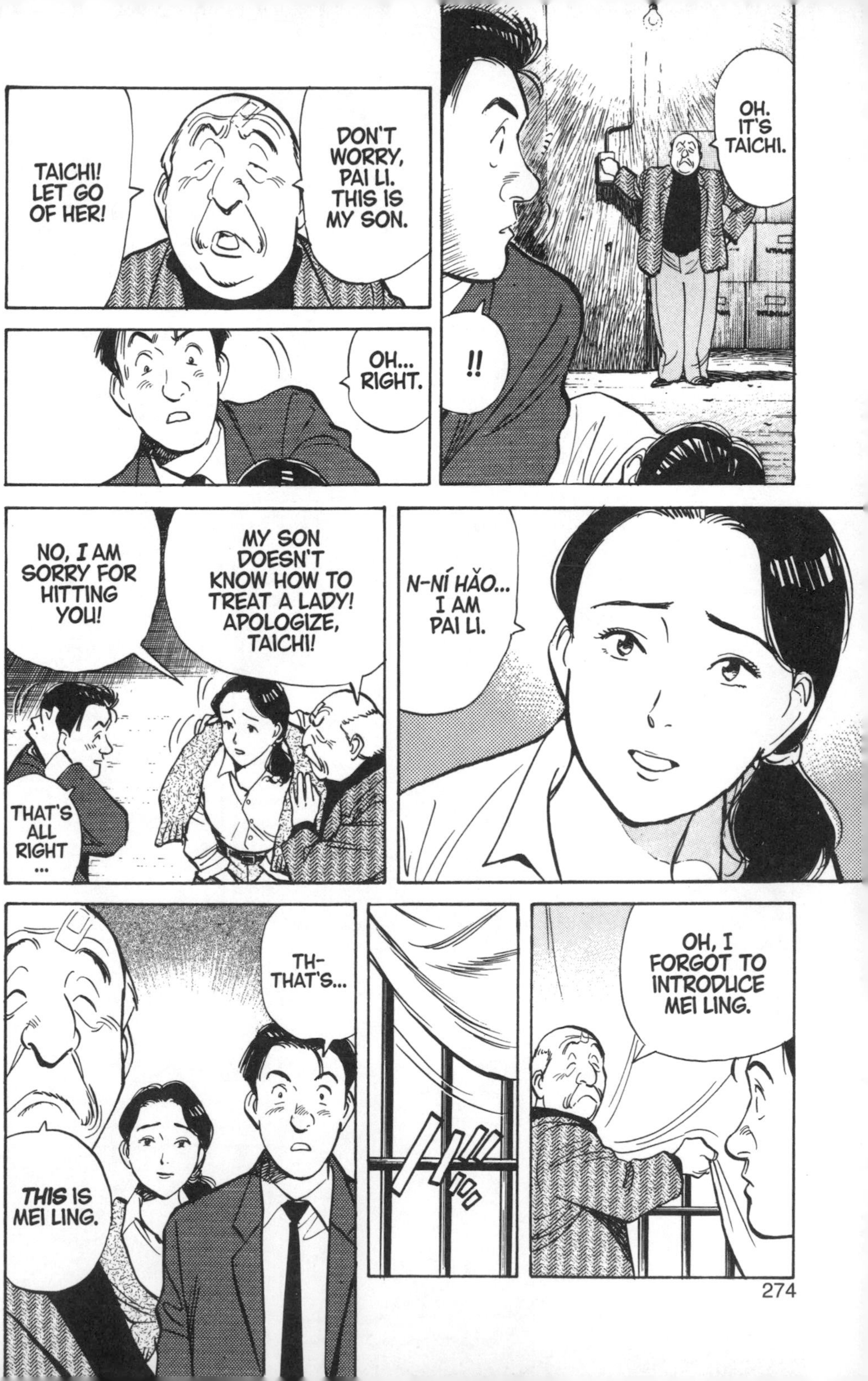
OH. IT'S TAICHI.
!!
DON'T WORRY, PAI LI. THIS IS MY SON.
TAICHI! LET GO OF HER!
OH... RIGHT.
N-NÍ HǍO... I AM PAI LI.
MY SON DOESN'T KNOW HOW TO TREAT A LADY! APOLOGIZE, TAICHI!
NO, I AM SORRY FOR HITTING YOU!
THAT'S ALL RIGHT ...
OH, I FORGOT TO INTRODUCE MEI LING.
TH- THAT'S...
THIS IS MEI LING.

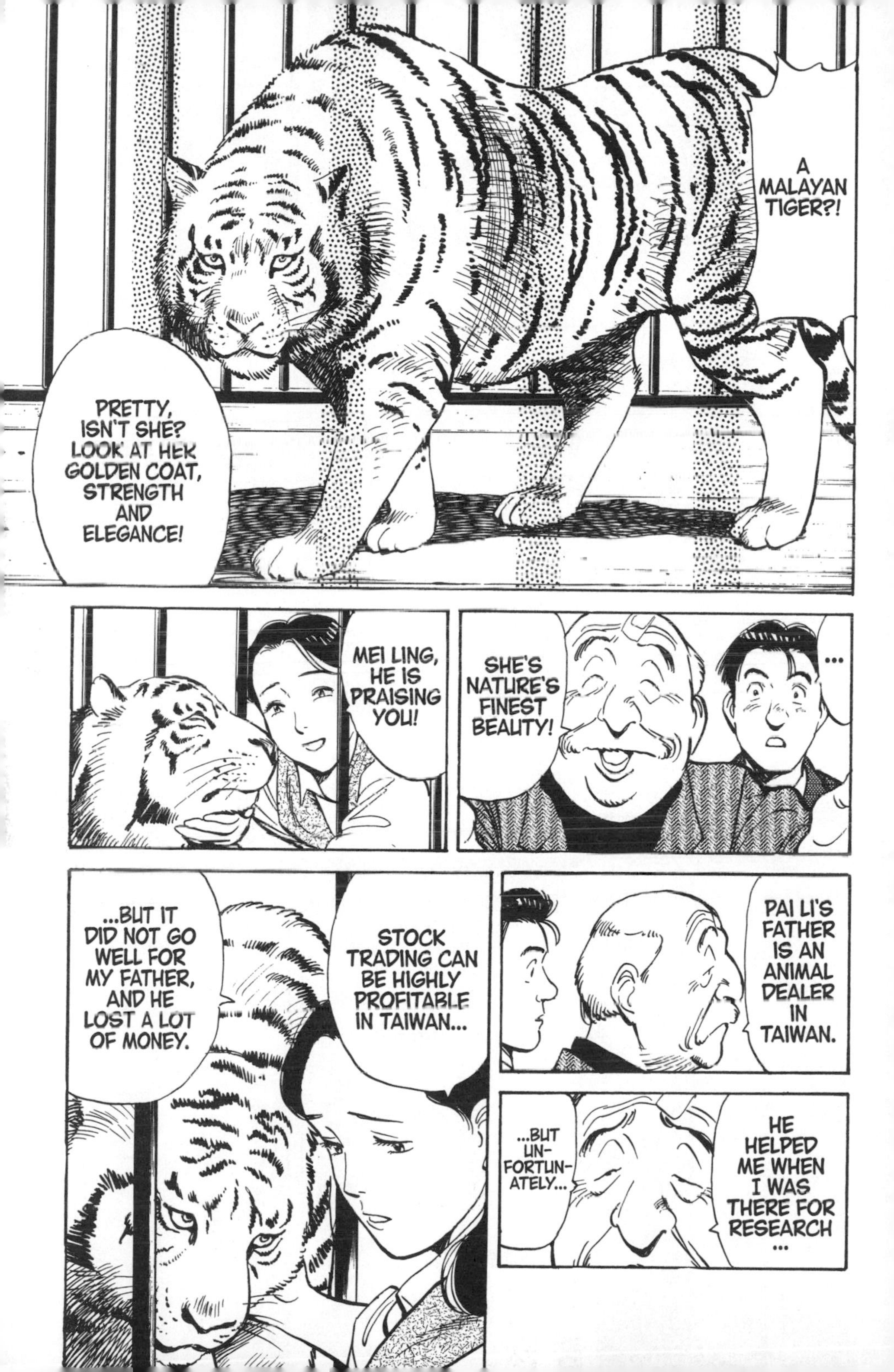
A MALAYAN TIGER?!
PRETTY, ISN'T SHE? LOOK AT HER GOLDEN COAT, STRENGTH AND ELEGANCE!
...
SHE'S NATURE'S FINEST BEAUTY!
MEI LING, HE IS PRAISING YOU!
PAI LI'S FATHER IS AN ANIMAL DEALER IN TAIWAN.
HE HELPED ME WHEN I WAS THERE FOR RESEARCH ...
...BUT UN-FORTUN-ATELY...
STOCK TRADING CAN BE HIGHLY PROFITABLE IN TAIWAN...
...BUT IT DID NOT GO WELL FOR MY FATHER, AND HE LOST A LOT OF MONEY.

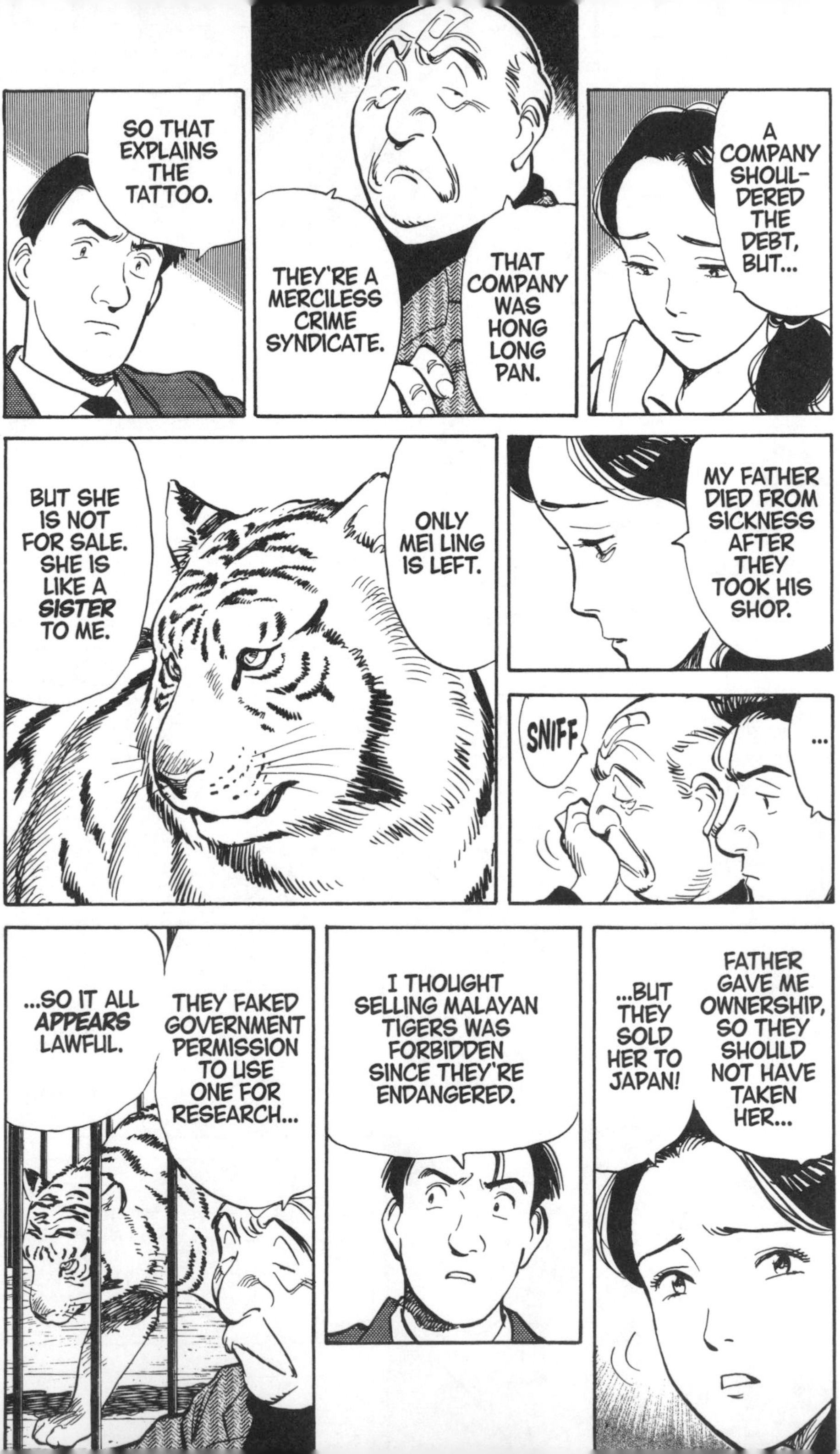
A COMPANY SHOULDERED THE DEBT, BUT...
THAT COMPANY WAS HONG LONG PAN.
THEY'RE A MERCILESS CRIME SYNDICATE.
SO THAT EXPLAINS THE TATTOO.
MY FATHER DIED FROM SICKNESS AFTER THEY TOOK HIS SHOP.
...
SNIFF
ONLY MEI LING IS LEFT.
BUT SHE IS NOT FOR SALE. SHE IS LIKE A **SISTER** TO ME.
FATHER GAVE ME OWNERSHIP, SO THEY SHOULD NOT HAVE TAKEN HER...
...BUT THEY SOLD HER TO JAPAN!
I THOUGHT SELLING MALAYAN TIGERS WAS FORBIDDEN SINCE THEY'RE ENDANGERED.
THEY FAKED GOVERNMENT PERMISSION TO USE ONE FOR RESEARCH...
...SO IT ALL **APPEARS** LAWFUL.

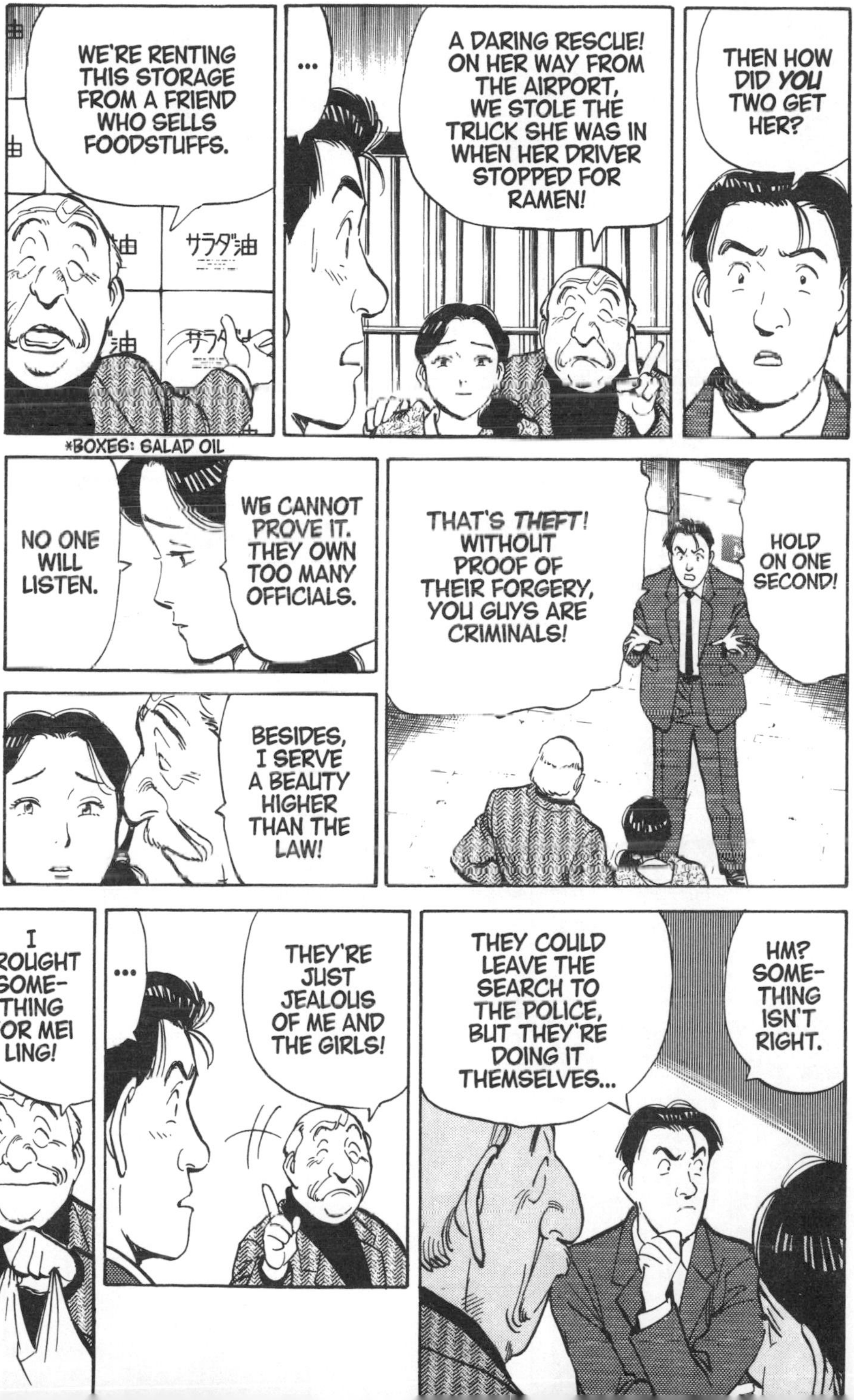
THEN HOW DID *YOU* TWO GET HER?
...
A DARING RESCUE! ON HER WAY FROM THE AIRPORT, WE STOLE THE TRUCK SHE WAS IN WHEN HER DRIVER STOPPED FOR RAMEN!
WE'RE RENTING THIS STORAGE FROM A FRIEND WHO SELLS FOODSTUFFS.
サラダ油
*BOXES: SALAD OIL
HOLD ON ONE SECOND!
THAT'S *THEFT*! WITHOUT PROOF OF THEIR FORGERY, YOU GUYS ARE CRIMINALS!
WE CANNOT PROVE IT. THEY OWN TOO MANY OFFICIALS.
NO ONE WILL LISTEN.
BESIDES, I SERVE A BEAUTY HIGHER THAN THE LAW!
HM? SOME-THING ISN'T RIGHT.
THEY COULD LEAVE THE SEARCH TO THE POLICE, BUT THEY'RE DOING IT THEMSELVES...
THEY'RE JUST JEALOUS OF ME AND THE GIRLS!
...
I BROUGHT SOME-THING FOR MEI LING!

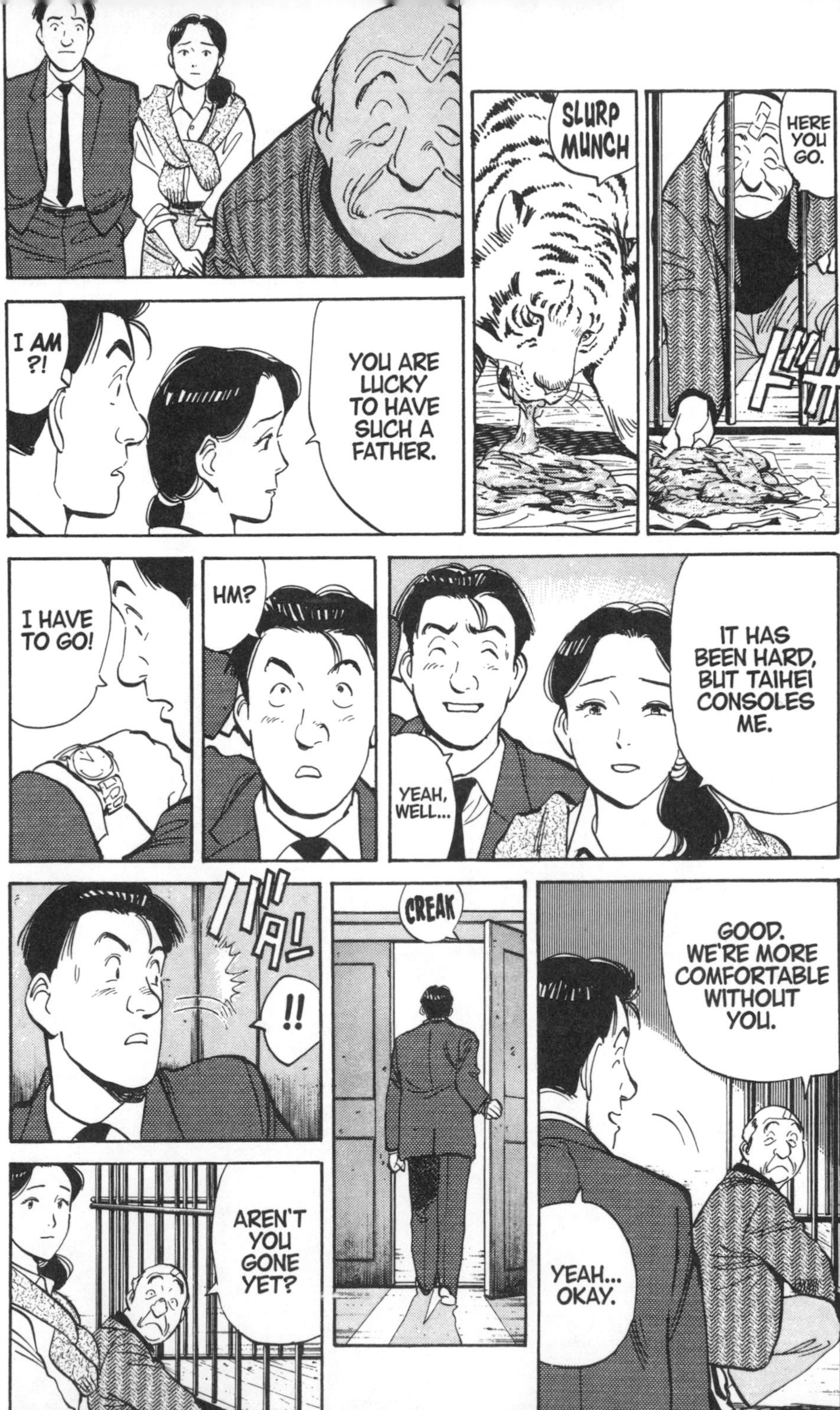
HERE YOU GO.
SLURP MUNCH
YOU ARE LUCKY TO HAVE SUCH A FATHER.
I AM ?!
IT HAS BEEN HARD, BUT TAIHEI CONSOLES ME.
YEAH, WELL...
HM?
I HAVE TO GO!
GOOD. WE'RE MORE COMFORTABLE WITHOUT YOU.
YEAH... OKAY.
CREAK
!!
AREN'T YOU GONE YET?

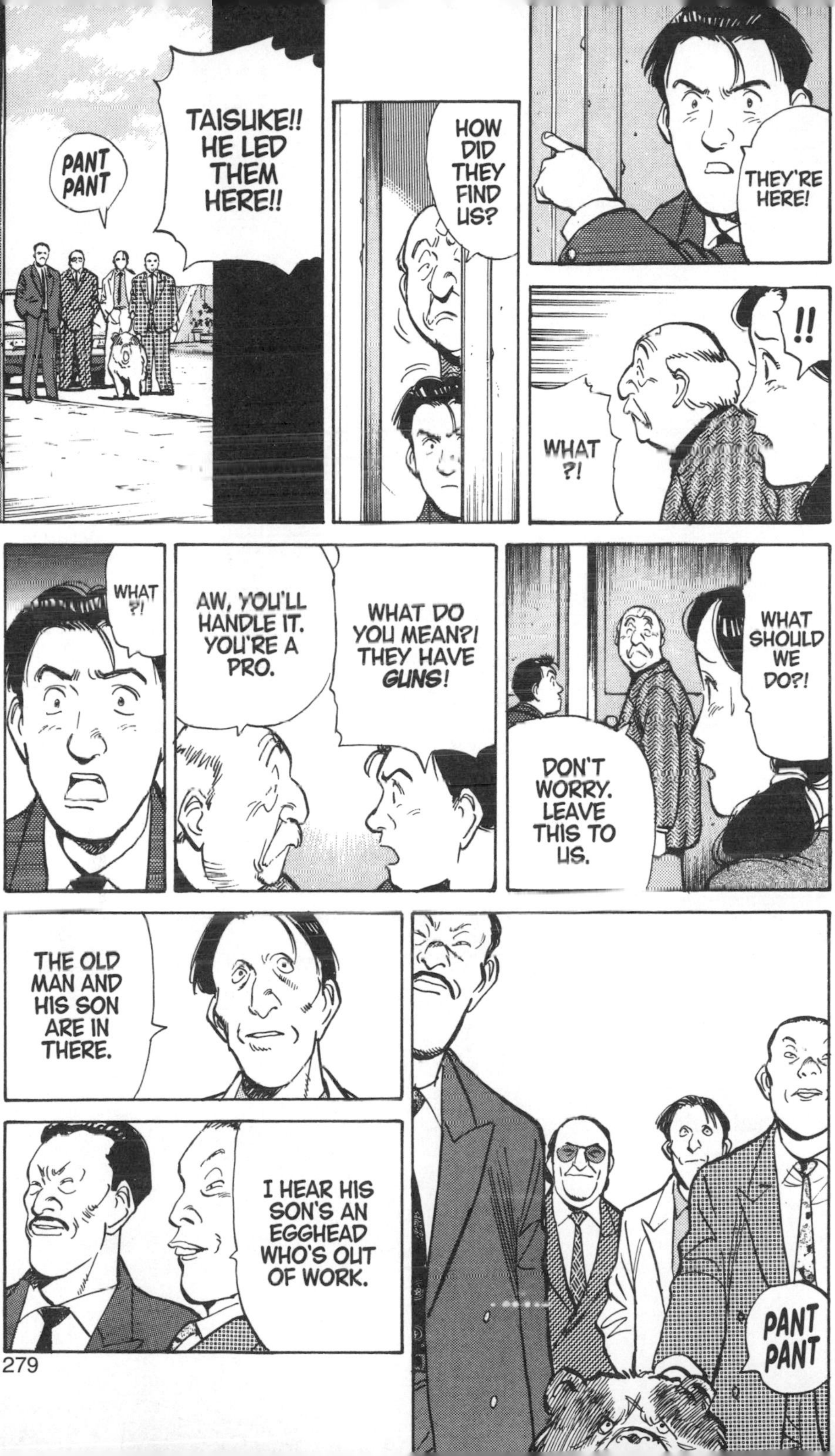
THEY'RE HERE!
!!
WHAT ?!
HOW DID THEY FIND US?
TAISUKE!! HE LED THEM HERE!!
PANT PANT
WHAT SHOULD WE DO?!
DON'T WORRY. LEAVE THIS TO US.
WHAT DO YOU MEAN?! THEY HAVE GUNS!
AW, YOU'LL HANDLE IT. YOU'RE A PRO.
WHAT ?!
PANT PANT
THE OLD MAN AND HIS SON ARE IN THERE.
I HEAR HIS SON'S AN EGGHEAD WHO'S OUT OF WORK.

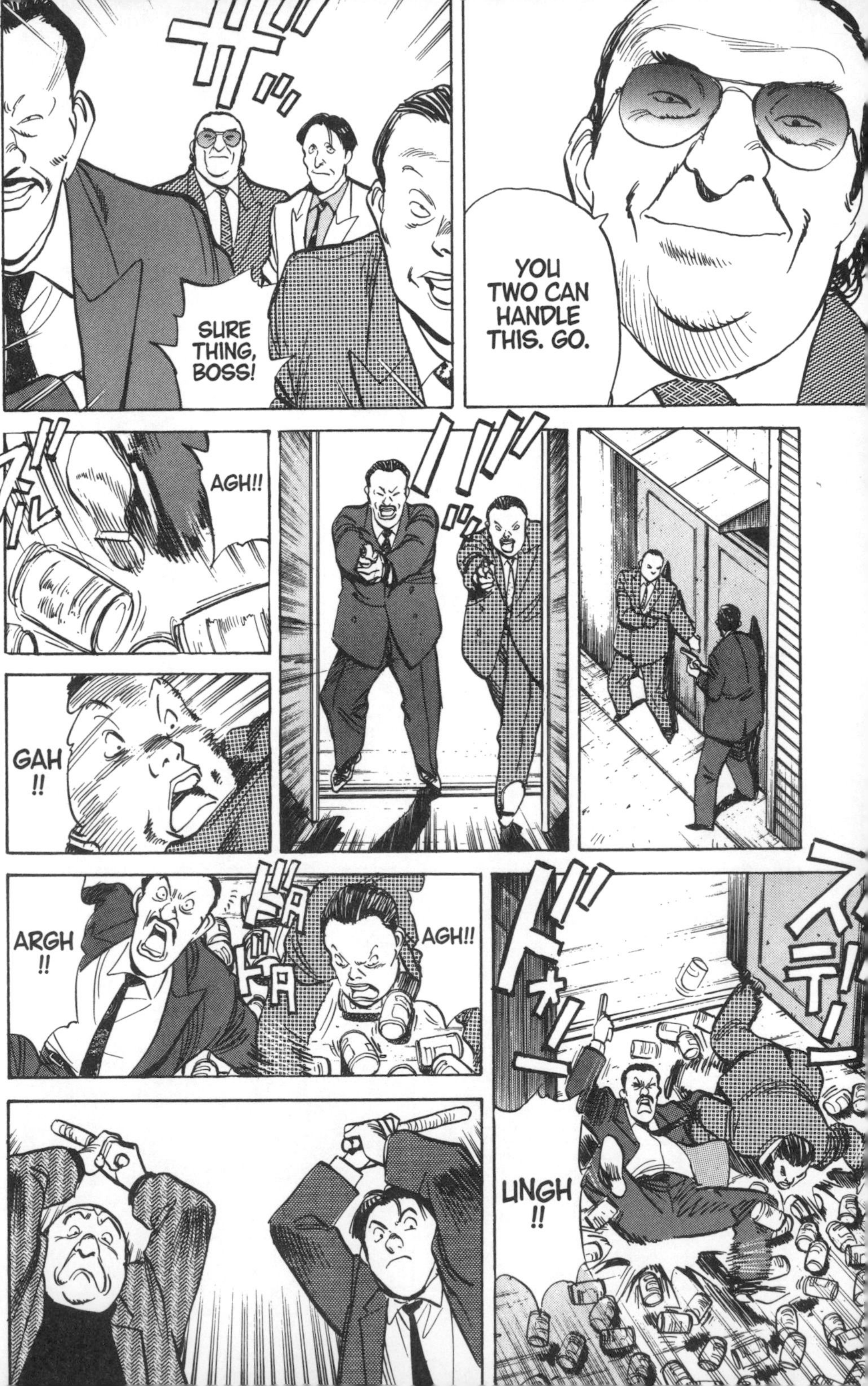
YOU TWO CAN HANDLE THIS. GO.
SURE THING, BOSS!
AGH!!
GAH !!
UNGH !!
AGH!!
ARGH !!

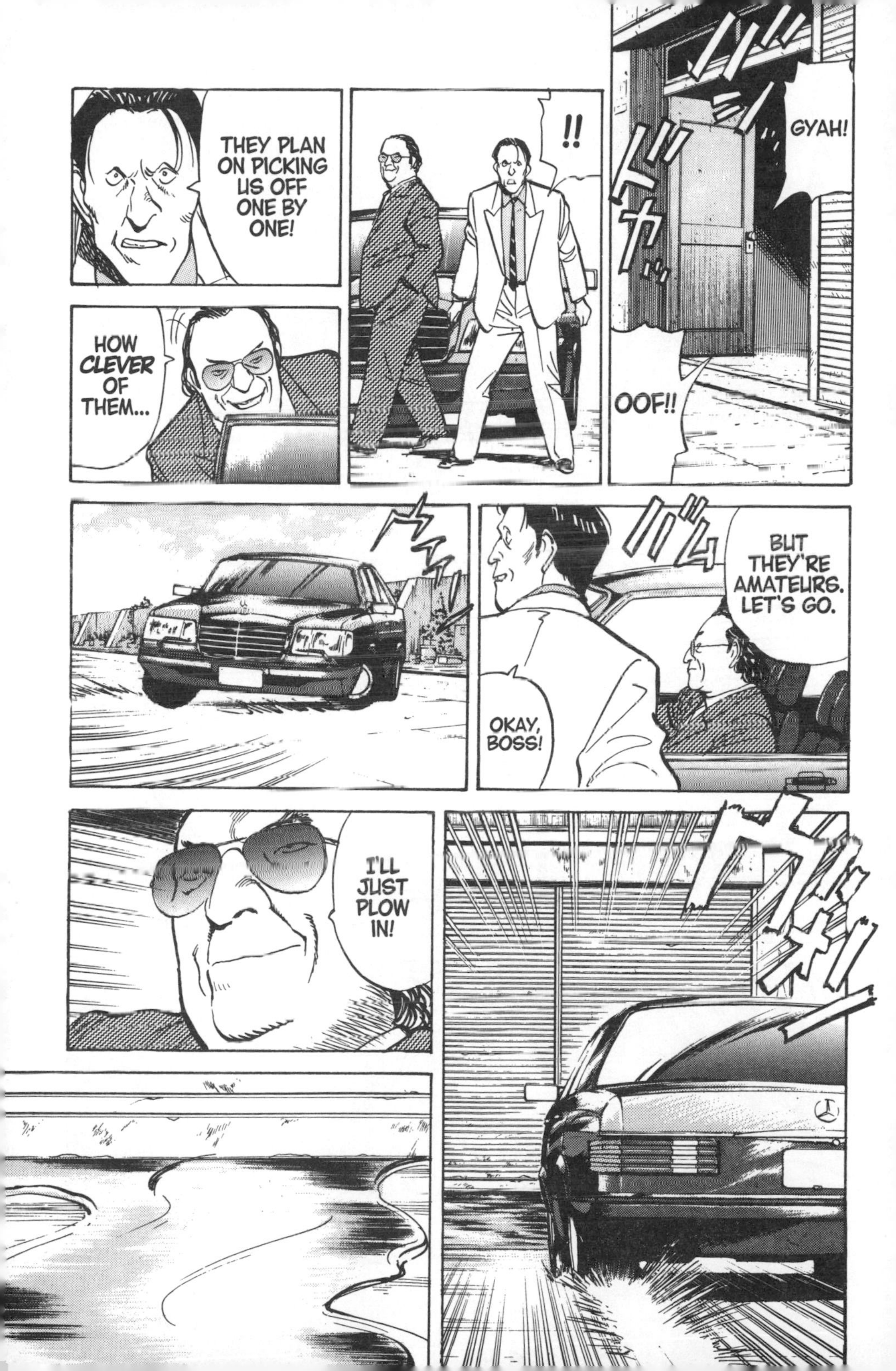
GYAH!
OOF!!
!!
THEY PLAN ON PICKING US OFF ONE BY ONE!
HOW CLEVER OF THEM...
BUT THEY'RE AMATEURS. LET'S GO.
OKAY, BOSS!
I'LL JUST PLOW IN!

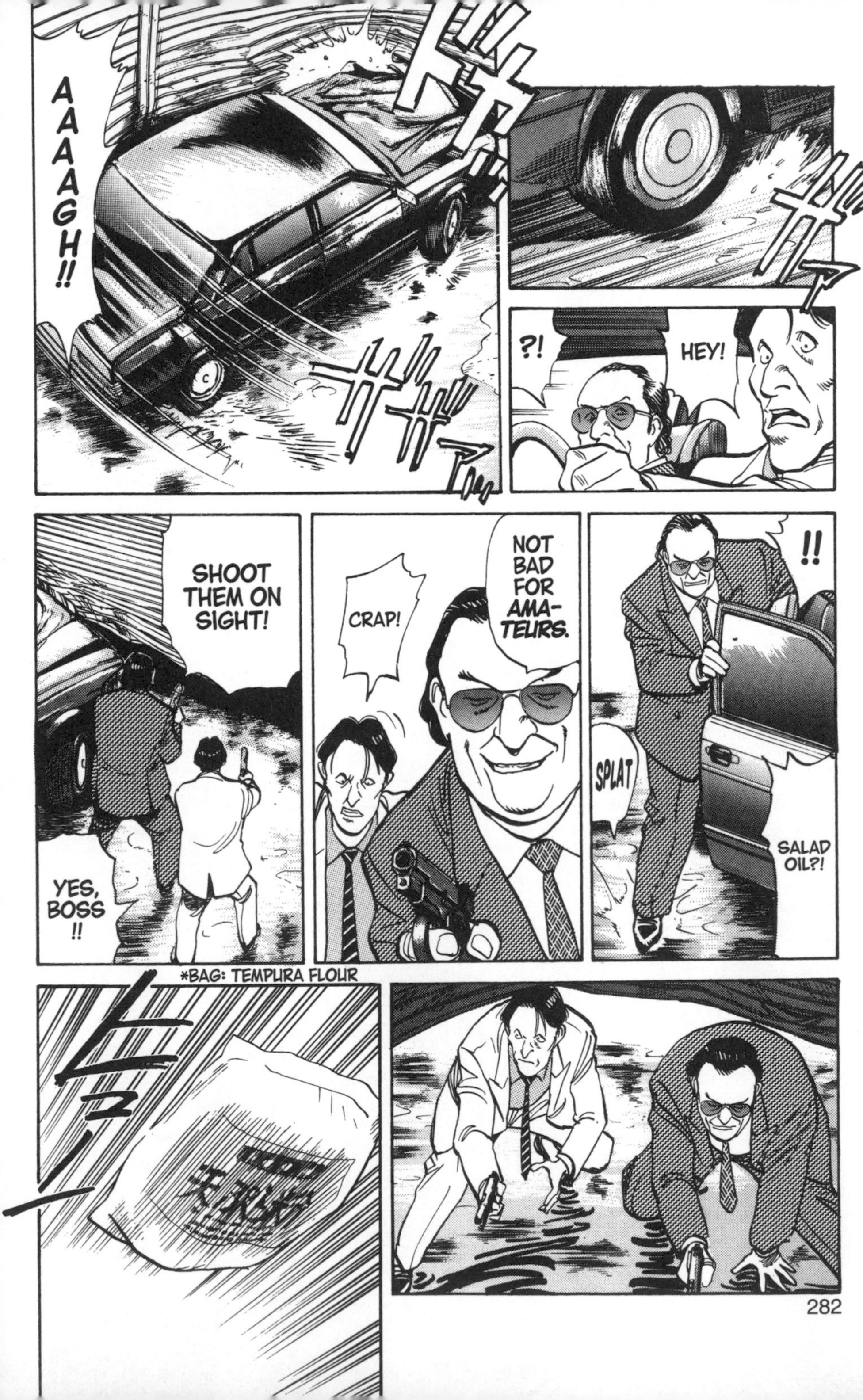
HEY!
?!
AAAAAGH!!
!!
SPLAT
SALAD OIL?!
NOT BAD FOR AMA-TEURS.
CRAP!
SHOOT THEM ON SIGHT!
YES, BOSS!!
*BAG: TEMPURA FLOUR

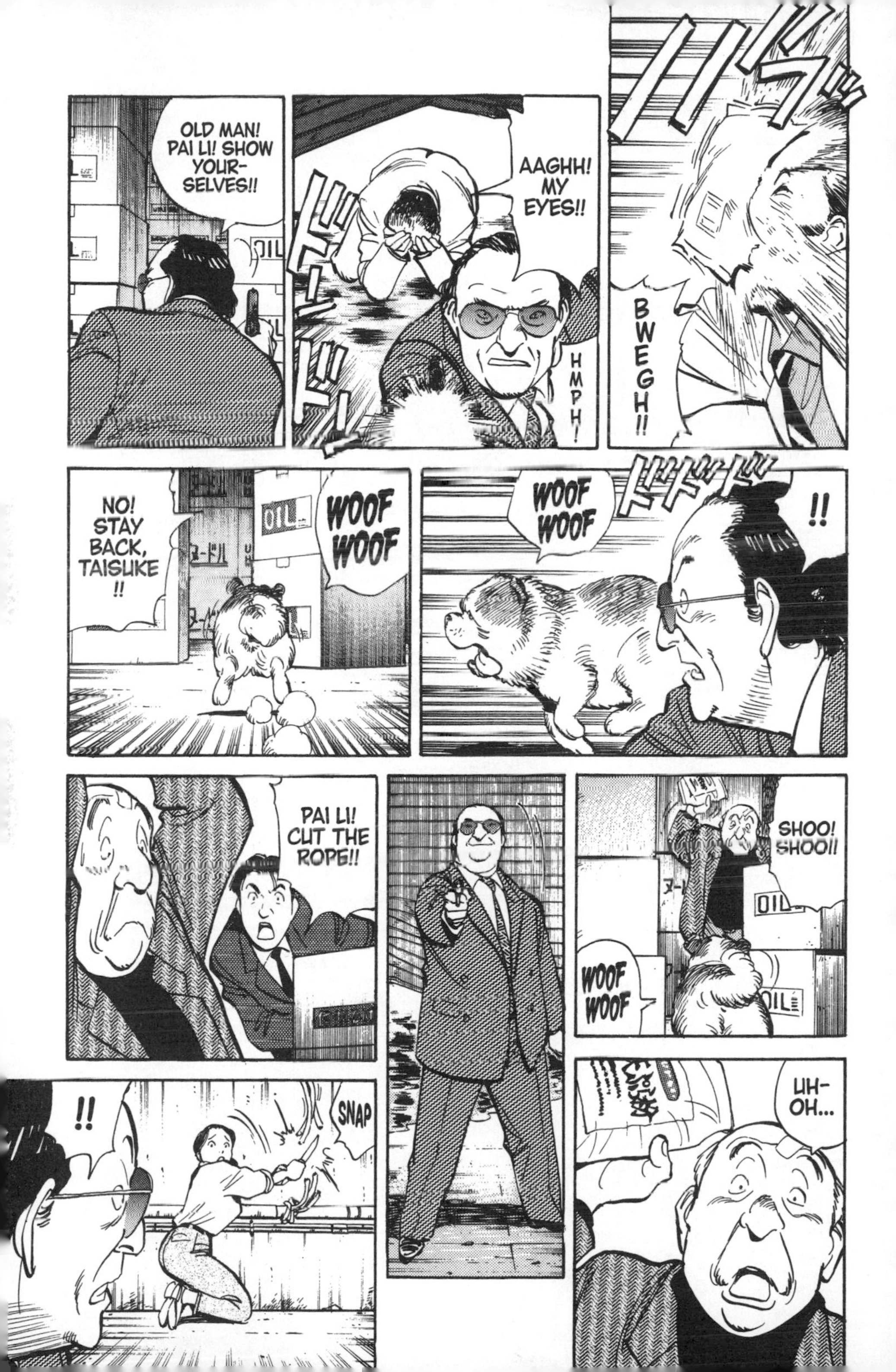
BWEGH!!
AAGHH! MY EYES!!
HMPH!
OLD MAN! PAI LI! SHOW YOUR-SELVES!!
!!
WOOF WOOF
WOOF WOOF
NO! STAY BACK, TAISUKE!!
SHOO! SHOO!!
WOOF WOOF
UH-OH...
PAI LI! CUT THE ROPE!!
SNAP
!!

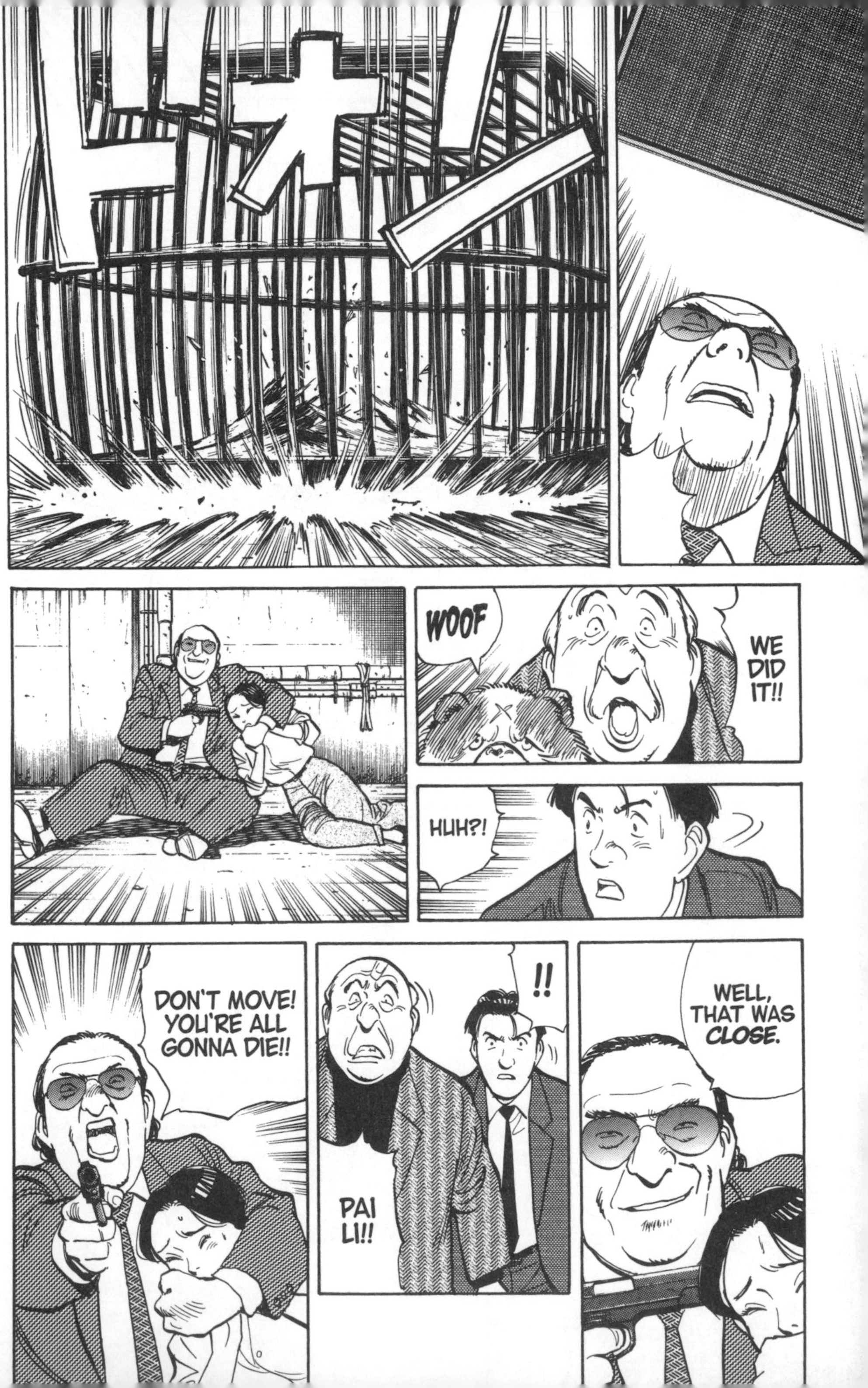
WE DID IT!!
WOOF
HUH?!
WELL, THAT WAS CLOSE.
!!
PAI LI!!
DON'T MOVE! YOU'RE ALL GONNA DIE!!

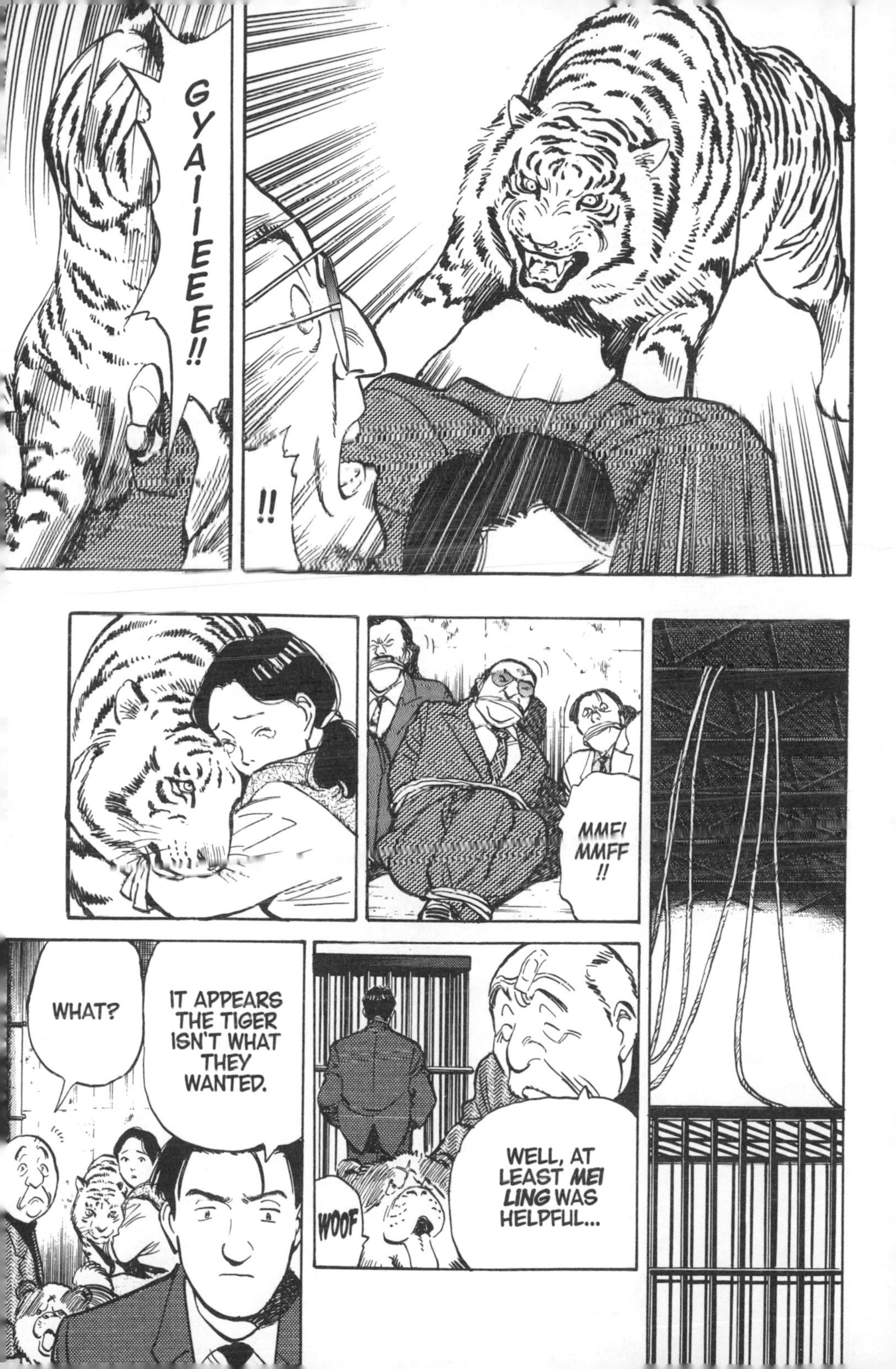
!!
GYAIIEEE!!
MMF! MMFF !!
WELL, AT LEAST *MEI LING* WAS HELPFUL...
WOOF
IT APPEARS THE TIGER ISN'T WHAT THEY WANTED.
WHAT?

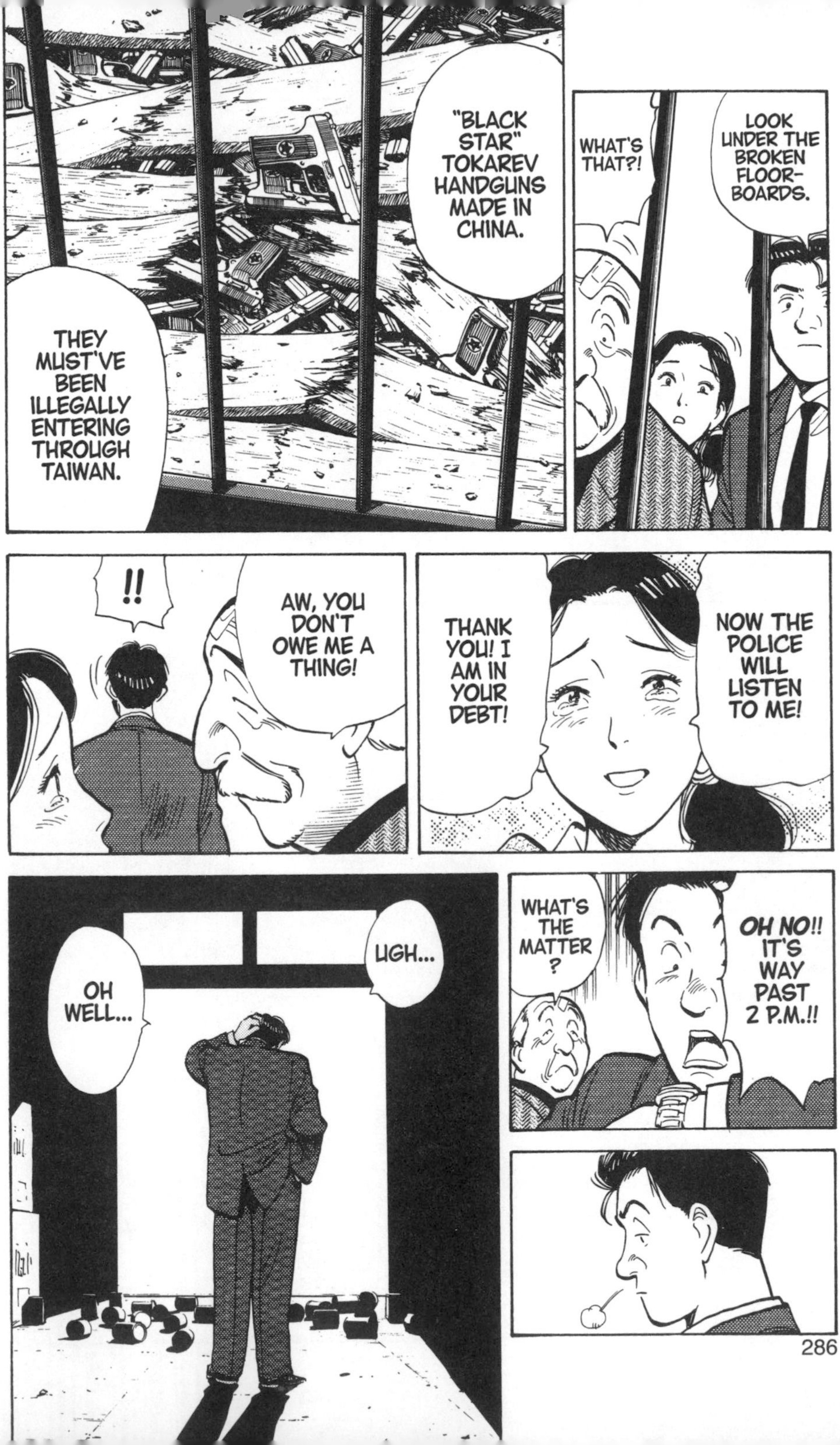
LOOK UNDER THE BROKEN FLOOR-BOARDS.
WHAT'S THAT?!
"BLACK STAR" TOKAREV HANDGUNS MADE IN CHINA.
THEY MUST'VE BEEN ILLEGALLY ENTERING THROUGH TAIWAN.
NOW THE POLICE WILL LISTEN TO ME!
THANK YOU! I AM IN YOUR DEBT!
AW, YOU DON'T OWE ME A THING!
!!
OH NO!! IT'S WAY PAST 2 P.M.!!
WHAT'S THE MATTER?
UGH...
OH WELL...

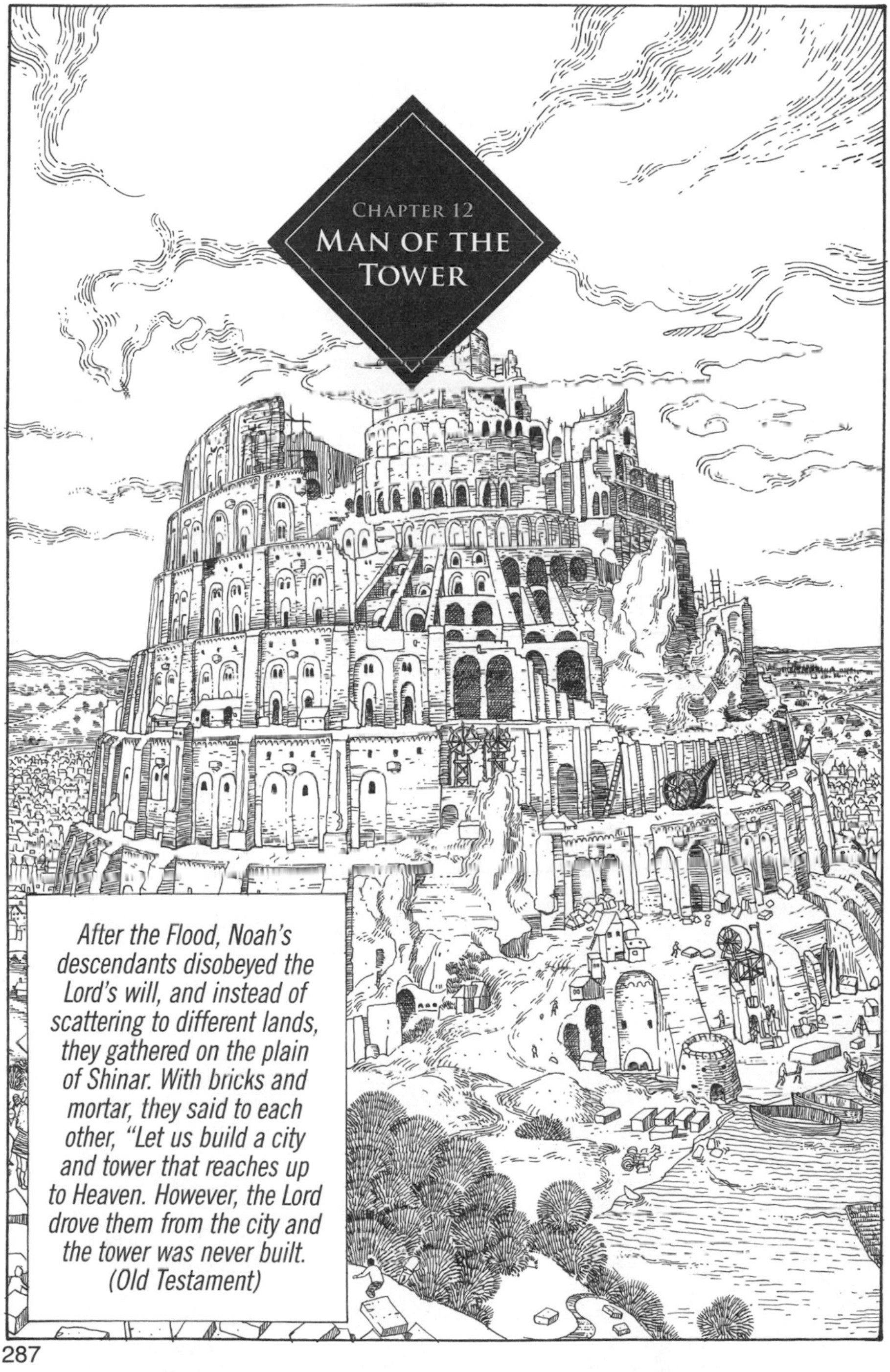
Chapter 12
Man of the Tower
After the Flood, Noah's descendants disobeyed the Lord's will, and instead of scattering to different lands, they gathered on the plain of Shinar. With bricks and mortar, they said to each other, "Let us build a city and tower that reaches up to Heaven. However, the Lord drove them from the city and the tower was never built. (Old Testament)

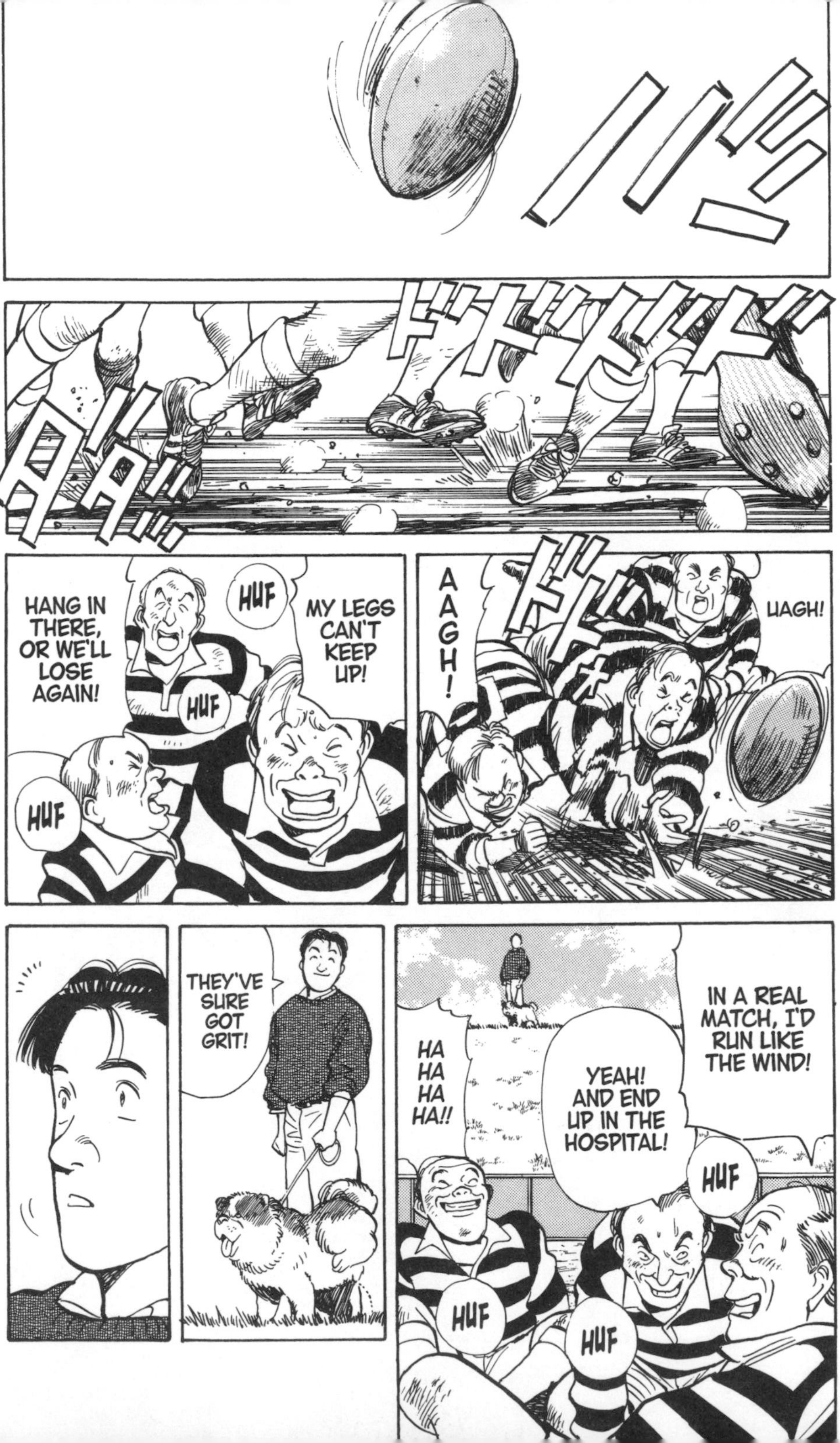
UAGH!
A A G H!
HANG IN THERE, OR WE'LL LOSE AGAIN!
HUF
MY LEGS CAN'T KEEP UP!
HUF
HUF
IN A REAL MATCH, I'D RUN LIKE THE WIND!
YEAH! AND END UP IN THE HOSPITAL!
HA HA HA HA!!
HUF
HUF
HUF
THEY'VE SURE GOT GRIT!

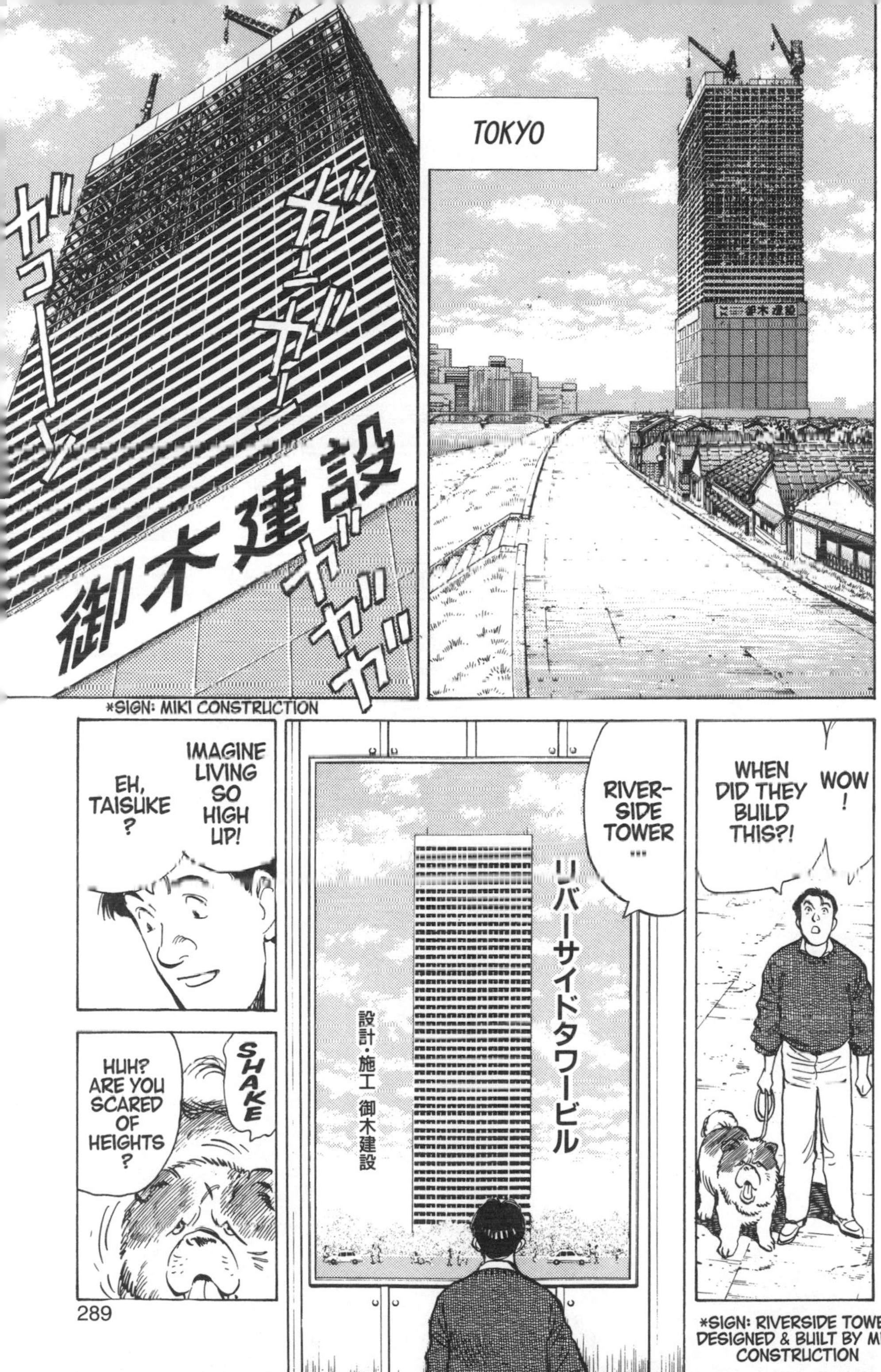
TOKYO
御木建設
御木建設
*SIGN: MIKI CONSTRUCTION
WOW!
WHEN DID THEY BUILD THIS?!
RIVER-SIDE TOWER ...
リバーサイドタワービル
設計・施工 御木建設
*SIGN: RIVERSIDE TOWER DESIGNED & BUILT BY MIKI CONSTRUCTION
IMAGINE LIVING SO HIGH UP!
EH, TAISUKE?
SHAKE
HUH? ARE YOU SCARED OF HEIGHTS?

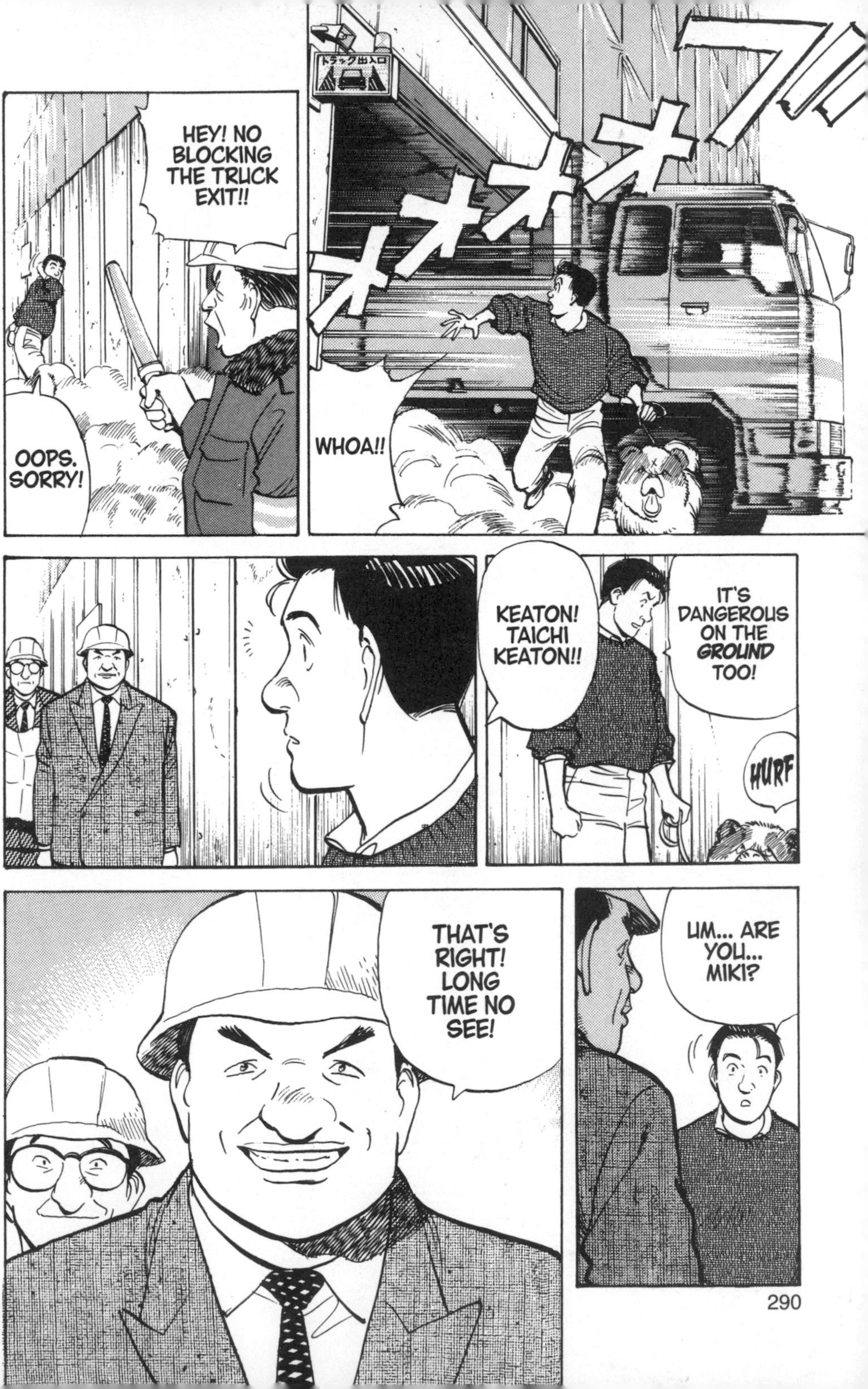
トラック出入口
WHOA!!
HEY! NO BLOCKING THE TRUCK EXIT!!
OOPS. SORRY!
IT'S DANGEROUS ON THE GROUND TOO!
HURF
KEATON! TAICHI KEATON!!
UM... ARE YOU... MIKI?
THAT'S RIGHT! LONG TIME NO SEE!

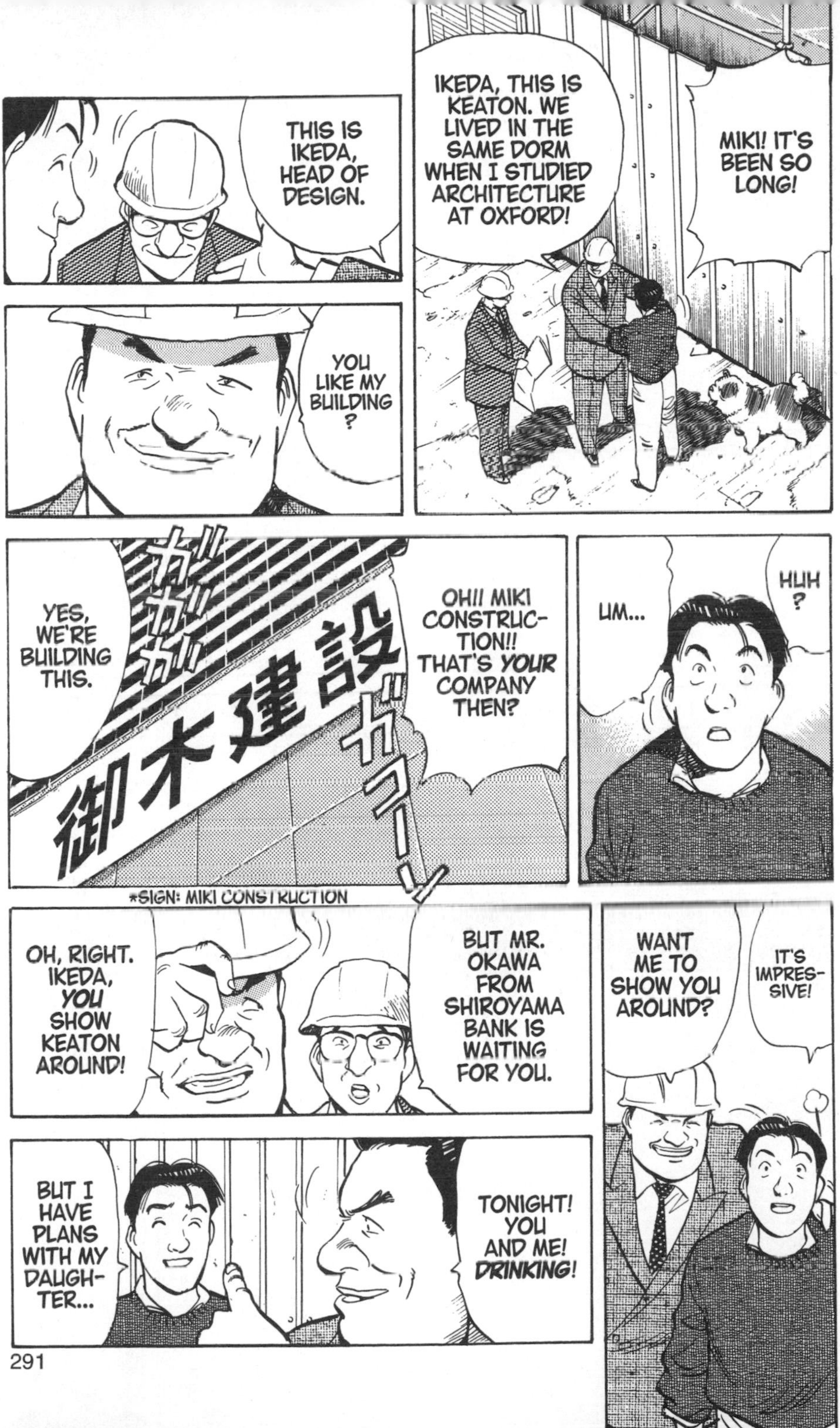
MIKI! IT'S BEEN SO LONG!
IKEDA, THIS IS KEATON. WE LIVED IN THE SAME DORM WHEN I STUDIED ARCHITECTURE AT OXFORD!
THIS IS IKEDA, HEAD OF DESIGN.
YOU LIKE MY BUILDING?
HUH?
UM...
OH!! MIKI CONSTRUCTION!! THAT'S *YOUR* COMPANY THEN?
YES, WE'RE BUILDING THIS.
ガガガ
御木建設
ガコーン
*SIGN: MIKI CONSTRUCTION
IT'S IMPRESSIVE!
WANT ME TO SHOW YOU AROUND?
BUT MR. OKAWA FROM SHIROYAMA BANK IS WAITING FOR YOU.
OH, RIGHT. IKEDA, *YOU* SHOW KEATON AROUND!
TONIGHT! YOU AND ME! *DRINKING*!
BUT I HAVE PLANS WITH MY DAUGHTER...

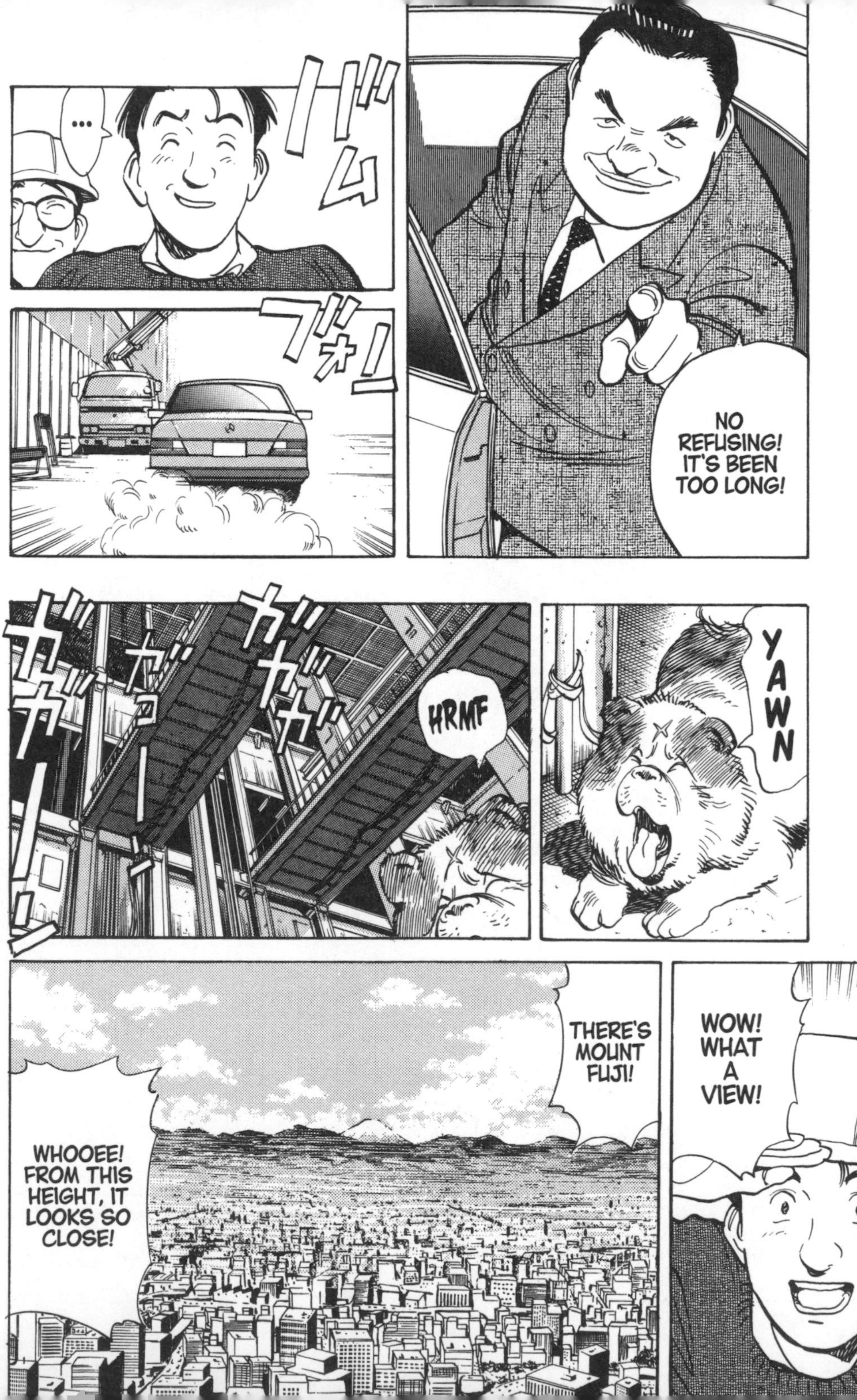
NO REFUSING! IT'S BEEN TOO LONG!
...
YAWN
HRMF
WOW! WHAT A VIEW!
THERE'S MOUNT FUJI!
WHOOEE! FROM THIS HEIGHT, IT LOOKS SO CLOSE!

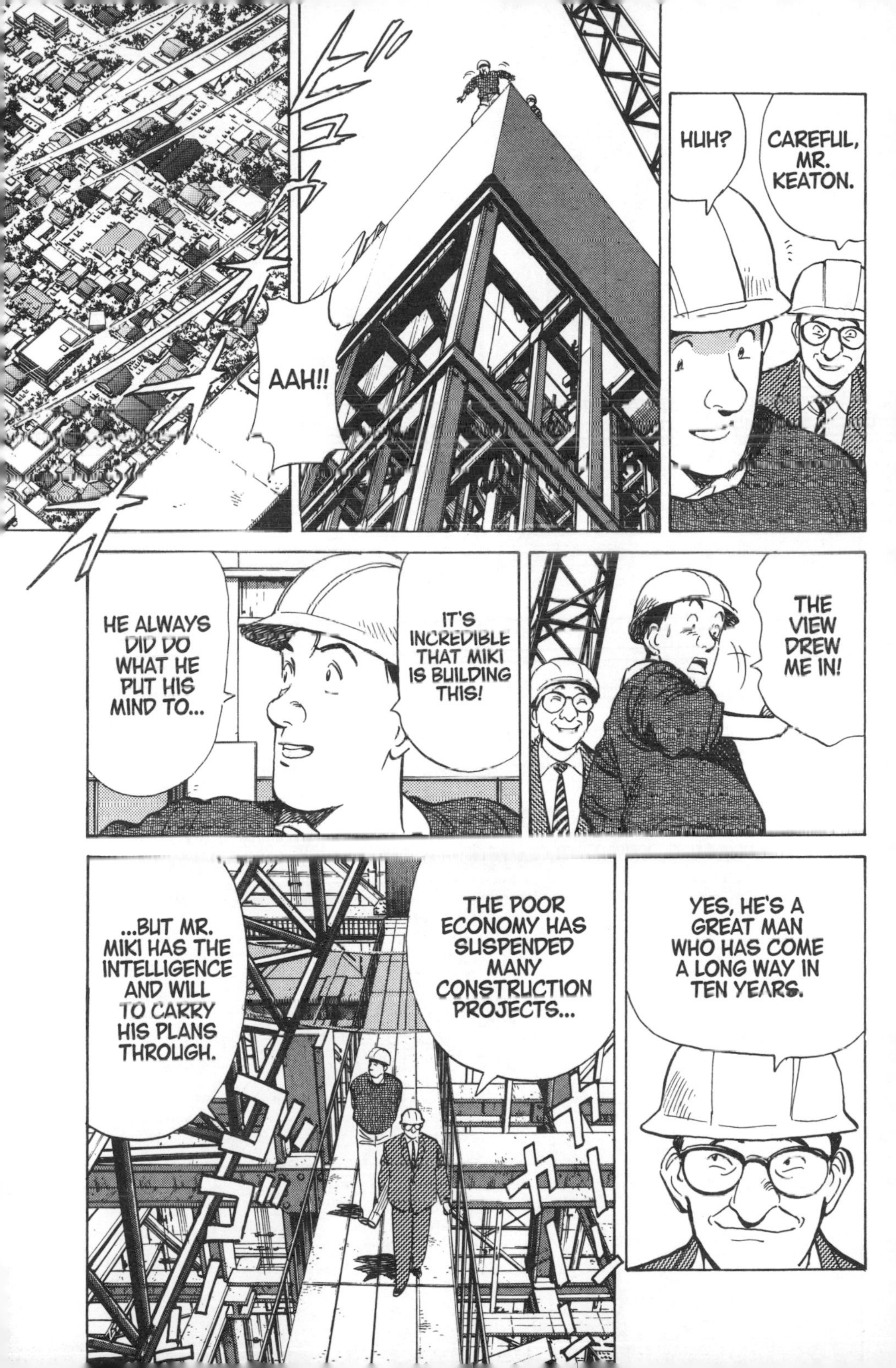
CAREFUL, MR. KEATON.
HUH?
AAH!!
THE VIEW DREW ME IN!
IT'S INCREDIBLE THAT MIKI IS BUILDING THIS!
HE ALWAYS DID DO WHAT HE PUT HIS MIND TO...
YES, HE'S A GREAT MAN WHO HAS COME A LONG WAY IN TEN YEARS.
THE POOR ECONOMY HAS SUSPENDED MANY CONSTRUCTION PROJECTS...
...BUT MR. MIKI HAS THE INTELLIGENCE AND WILL TO CARRY HIS PLANS THROUGH.

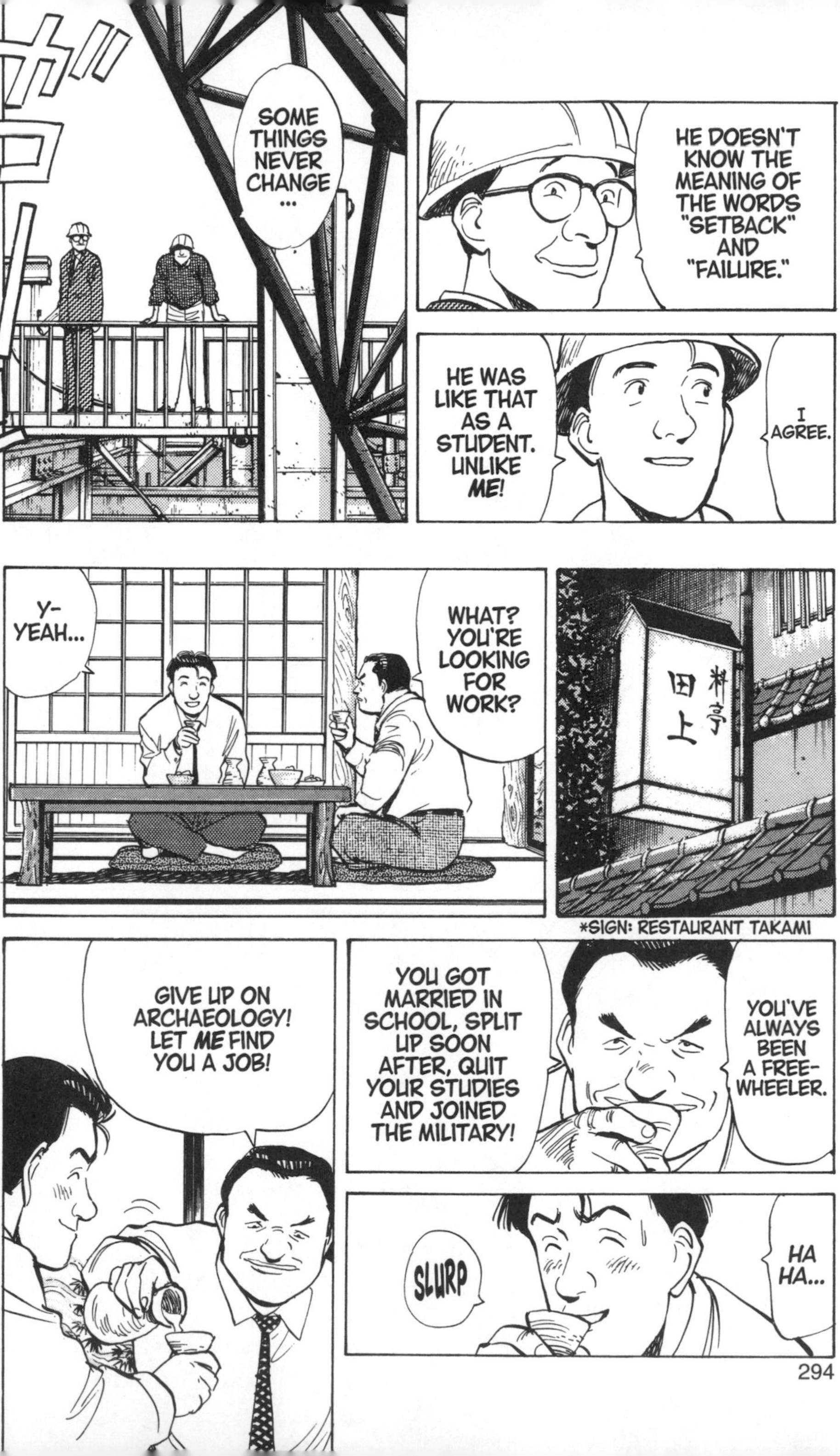
HE DOESN'T KNOW THE MEANING OF THE WORDS "SETBACK" AND "FAILURE."
HE WAS LIKE THAT AS A STUDENT. UNLIKE *ME*!
I AGREE.
SOME THINGS NEVER CHANGE...
ガコ
料亭
田上
*SIGN: RESTAURANT TAKAMI
WHAT? YOU'RE LOOKING FOR WORK?
Y-YEAH...
YOU GOT MARRIED IN SCHOOL, SPLIT UP SOON AFTER, QUIT YOUR STUDIES AND JOINED THE MILITARY!
YOU'VE ALWAYS BEEN A FREE-WHEELER.
SLURP
HA HA...
GIVE UP ON ARCHAEOLOGY! LET *ME* FIND YOU A JOB!

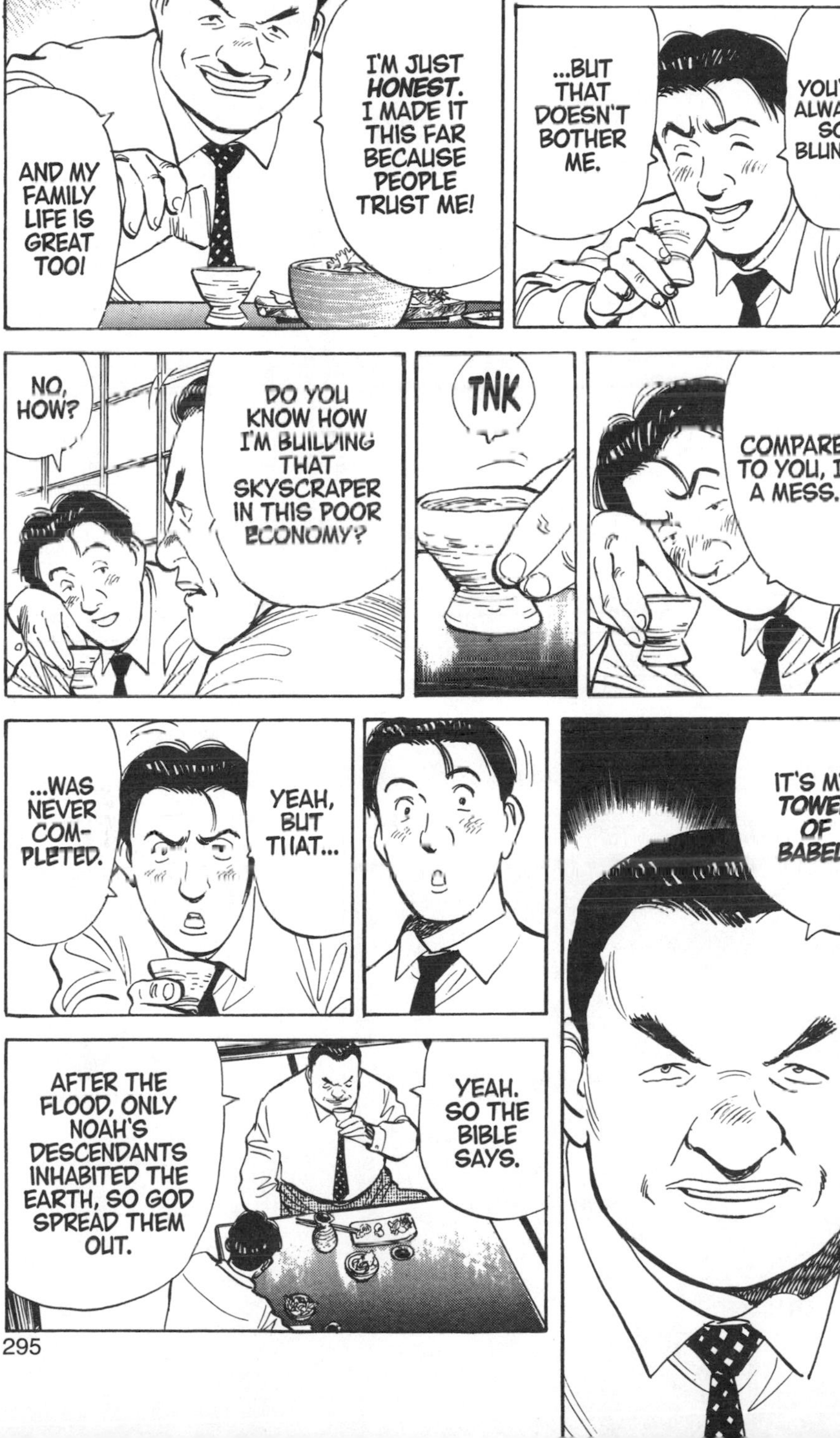
YOU'RE ALWAYS SO BLUNT...
...BUT THAT DOESN'T BOTHER ME.
I'M JUST HONEST. I MADE IT THIS FAR BECAUSE PEOPLE TRUST ME!
AND MY FAMILY LIFE IS GREAT TOO!
COMPARED TO YOU, I'M A MESS...
TNK
DO YOU KNOW HOW I'M BUILDING THAT SKYSCRAPER IN THIS POOR ECONOMY?
NO, HOW?
IT'S MY TOWER OF BABEL.
YEAH, BUT THAT...
...WAS NEVER COM-PLETED.
YEAH. SO THE BIBLE SAYS.
AFTER THE FLOOD, ONLY NOAH'S DESCENDANTS INHABITED THE EARTH, SO GOD SPREAD THEM OUT.

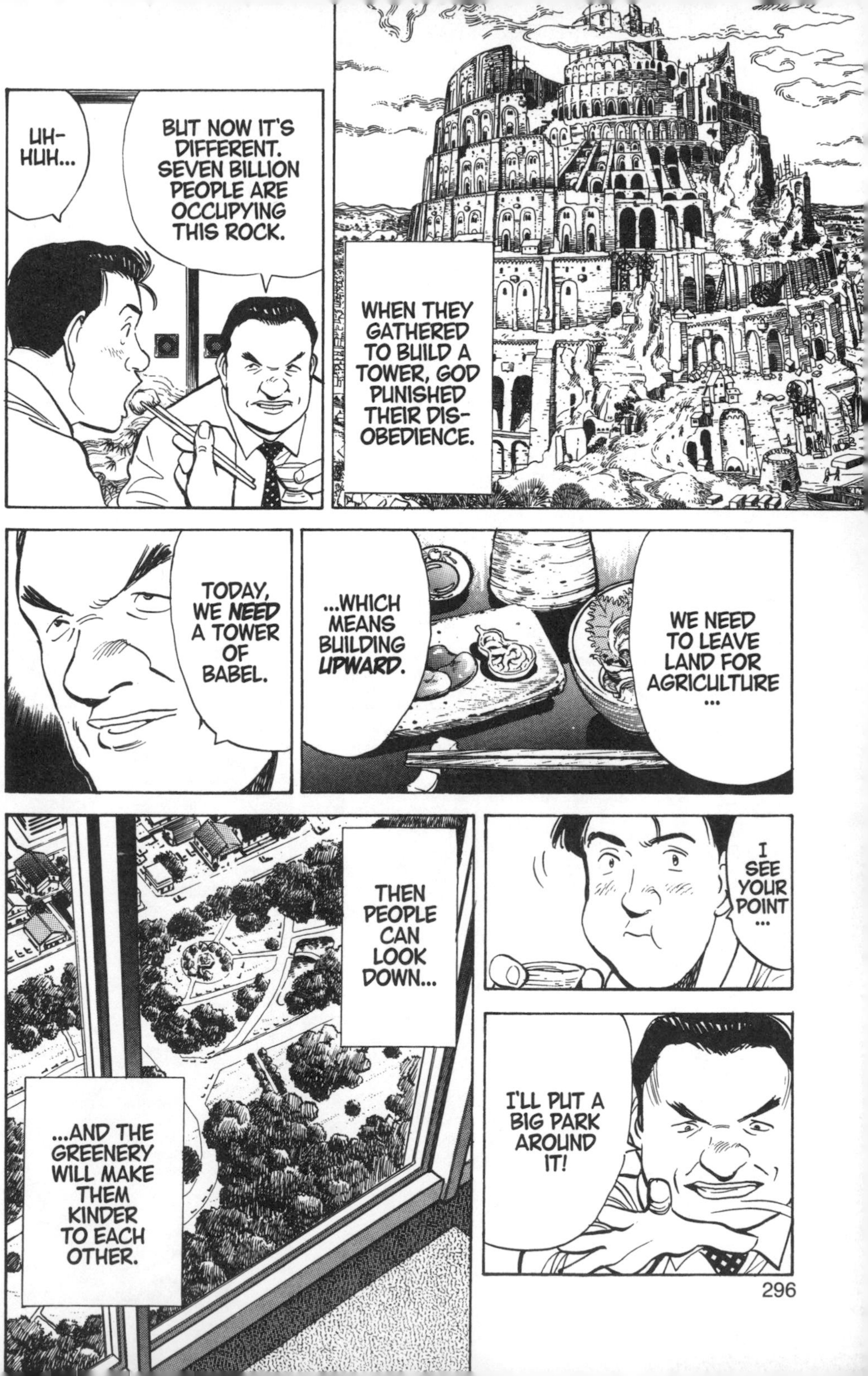
WHEN THEY GATHERED TO BUILD A TOWER, GOD PUNISHED THEIR DIS-OBEDIENCE.
BUT NOW IT'S DIFFERENT. SEVEN BILLION PEOPLE ARE OCCUPYING THIS ROCK.
UH-HUH...
WE NEED TO LEAVE LAND FOR AGRICULTURE ...
...WHICH MEANS BUILDING *UPWARD*.
TODAY, WE *NEED* A TOWER OF BABEL.
I SEE YOUR POINT ...
I'LL PUT A BIG PARK AROUND IT!
THEN PEOPLE CAN LOOK DOWN...
...AND THE GREENERY WILL MAKE THEM KINDER TO EACH OTHER.

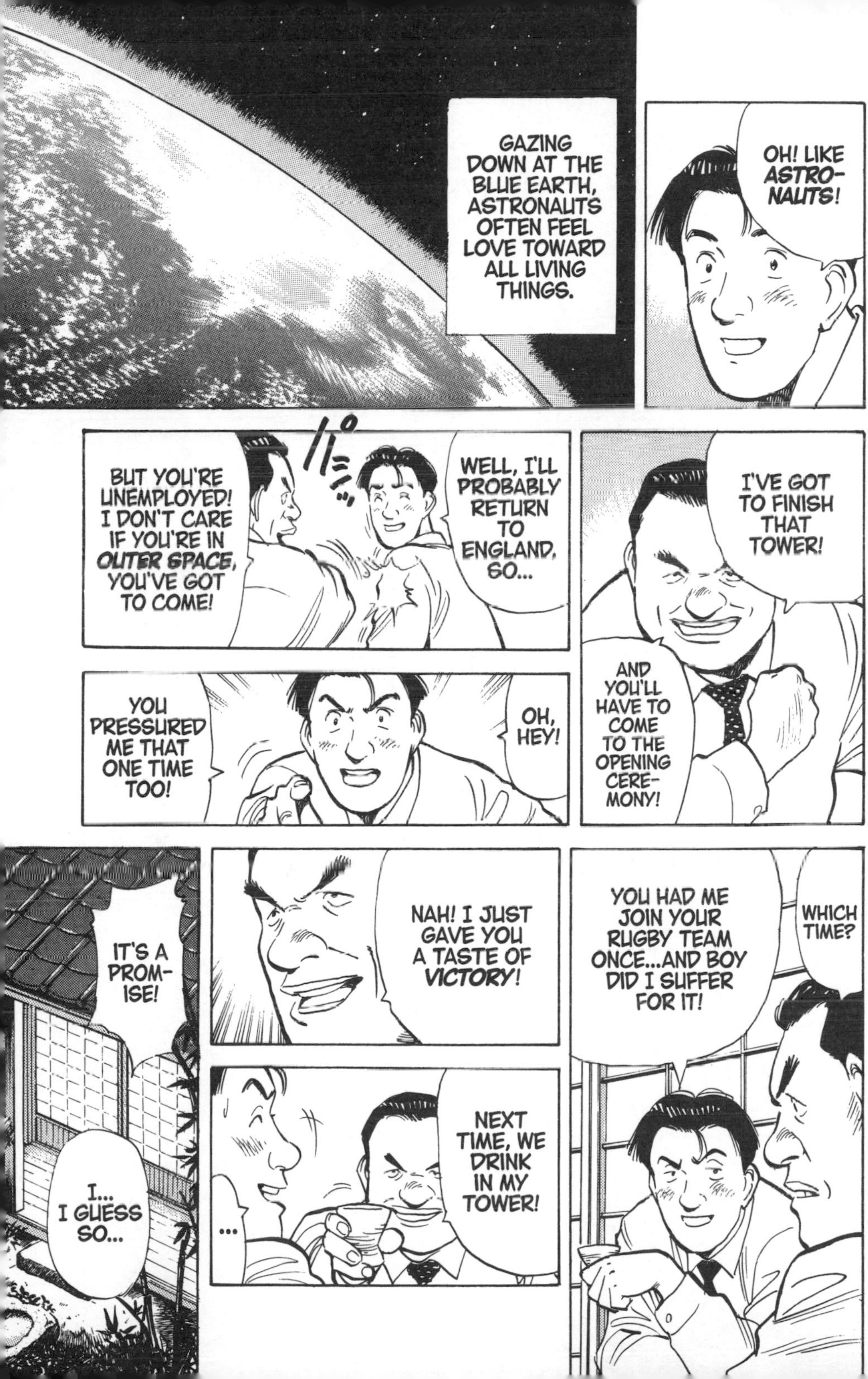
OH! LIKE ASTRO-NAUTS!
GAZING DOWN AT THE BLUE EARTH, ASTRONAUTS OFTEN FEEL LOVE TOWARD ALL LIVING THINGS.
I'VE GOT TO FINISH THAT TOWER!
AND YOU'LL HAVE TO COME TO THE OPENING CERE-MONY!
WELL, I'LL PROBABLY RETURN TO ENGLAND, SO...
BUT YOU'RE UNEMPLOYED! I DON'T CARE IF YOU'RE IN OUTER SPACE, YOU'VE GOT TO COME!
OH, HEY!
YOU PRESSURED ME THAT ONE TIME TOO!
WHICH TIME?
YOU HAD ME JOIN YOUR RUGBY TEAM ONCE...AND BOY DID I SUFFER FOR IT!
NAH! I JUST GAVE YOU A TASTE OF VICTORY!
NEXT TIME, WE DRINK IN MY TOWER!
...
IT'S A PROM-ISE!
I... I GUESS SO...

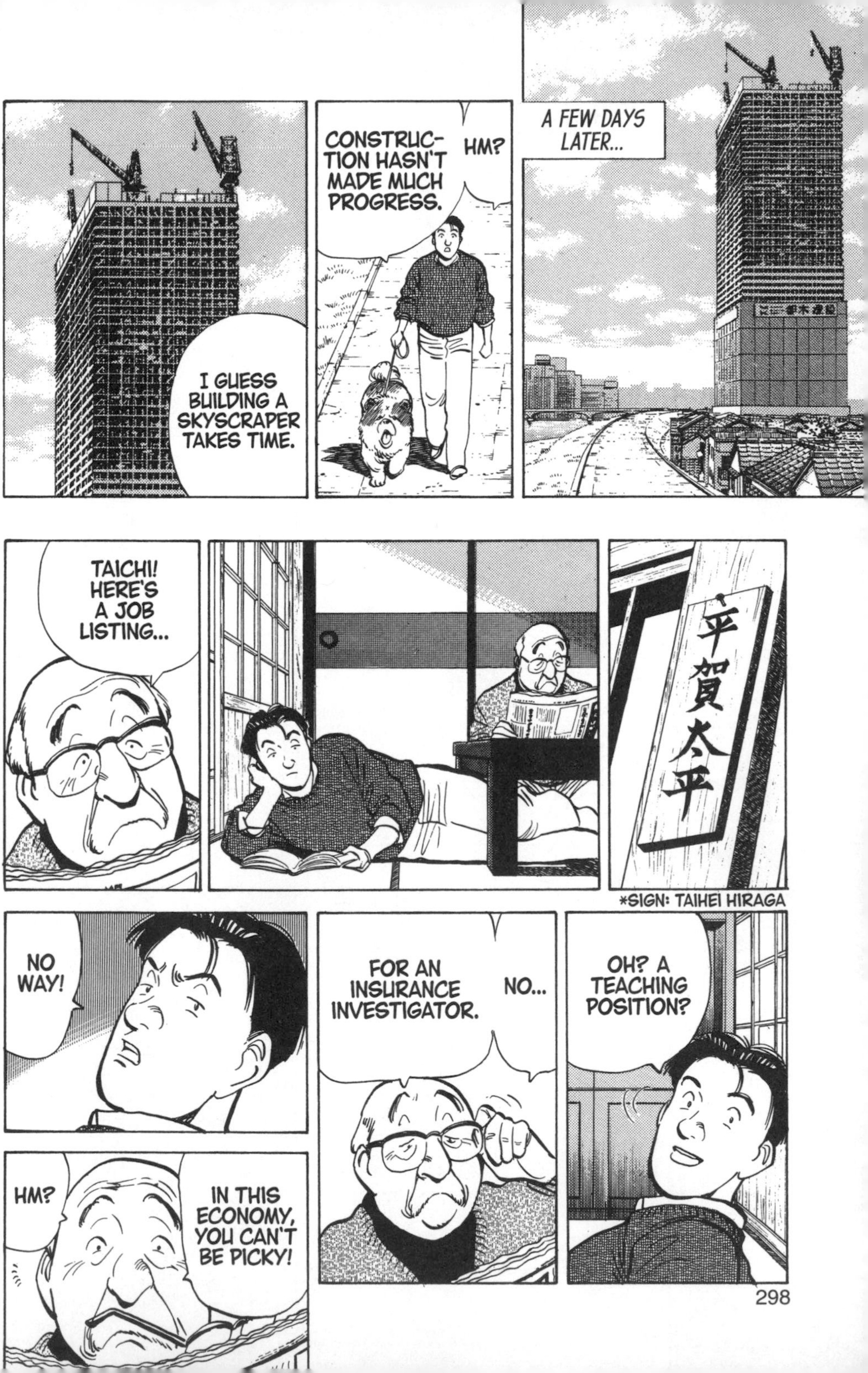
A FEW DAYS LATER...
CONSTRUCTION HASN'T MADE MUCH PROGRESS.
HM?
I GUESS BUILDING A SKYSCRAPER TAKES TIME.
平賀太平
*SIGN: TAIHEI HIRAGA
TAICHI! HERE'S A JOB LISTING...
OH? A TEACHING POSITION?
NO...
FOR AN INSURANCE INVESTIGATOR.
NO WAY!
IN THIS ECONOMY, YOU CAN'T BE PICKY!
HM?

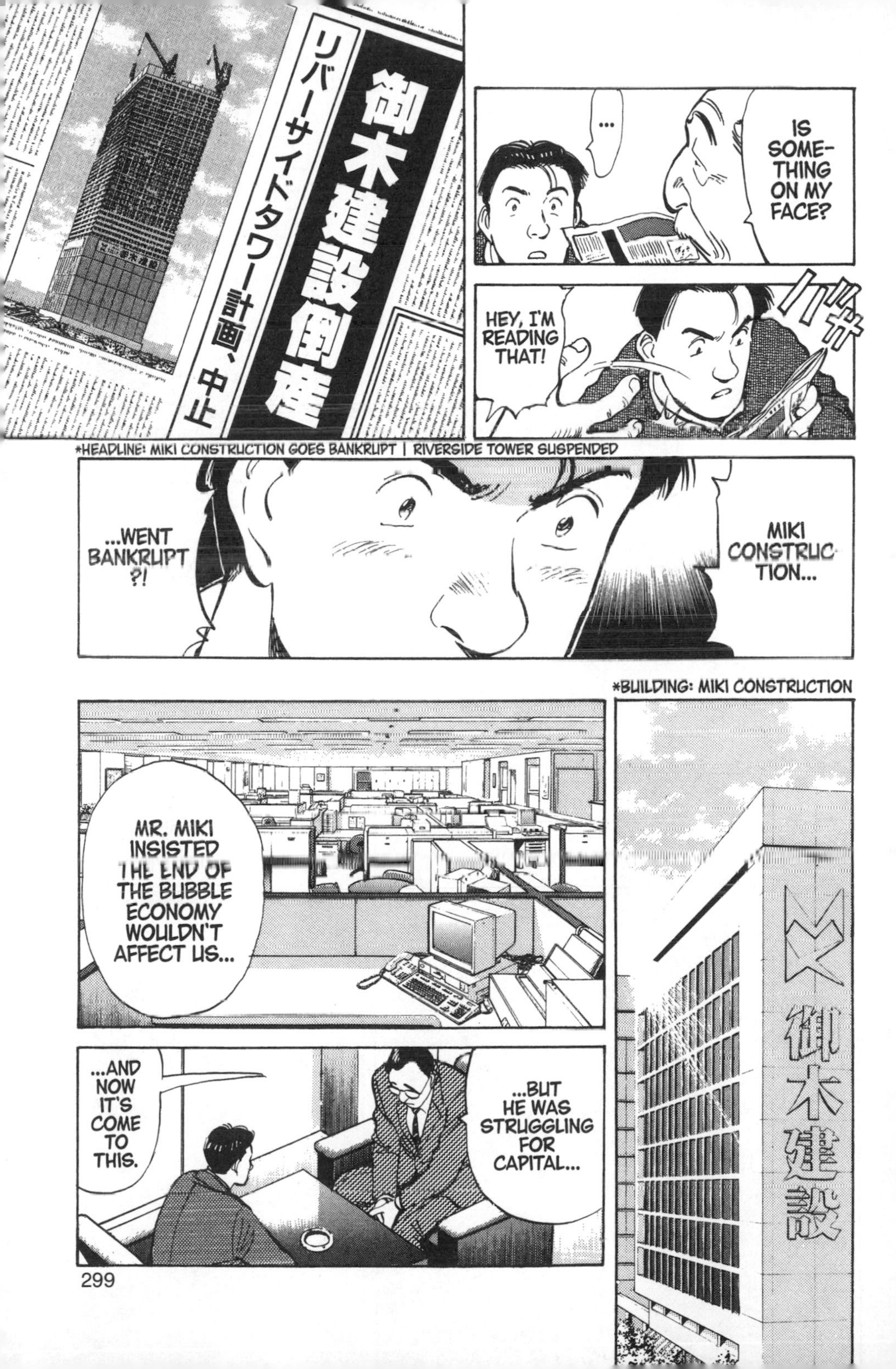
IS SOME-THING ON MY FACE?
...
HEY, I'M READING THAT!
ハッ
御木建設倒産
リバーサイドタワー計画、中止
*HEADLINE: MIKI CONSTRUCTION GOES BANKRUPT | RIVERSIDE TOWER SUSPENDED
MIKI CONSTRUC-TION...
...WENT BANKRUPT ?!
*BUILDING: MIKI CONSTRUCTION
御木建設
MR. MIKI INSISTED THE END OF THE BUBBLE ECONOMY WOULDN'T AFFECT US...
...BUT HE WAS STRUGGLING FOR CAPITAL...
...AND NOW IT'S COME TO THIS.

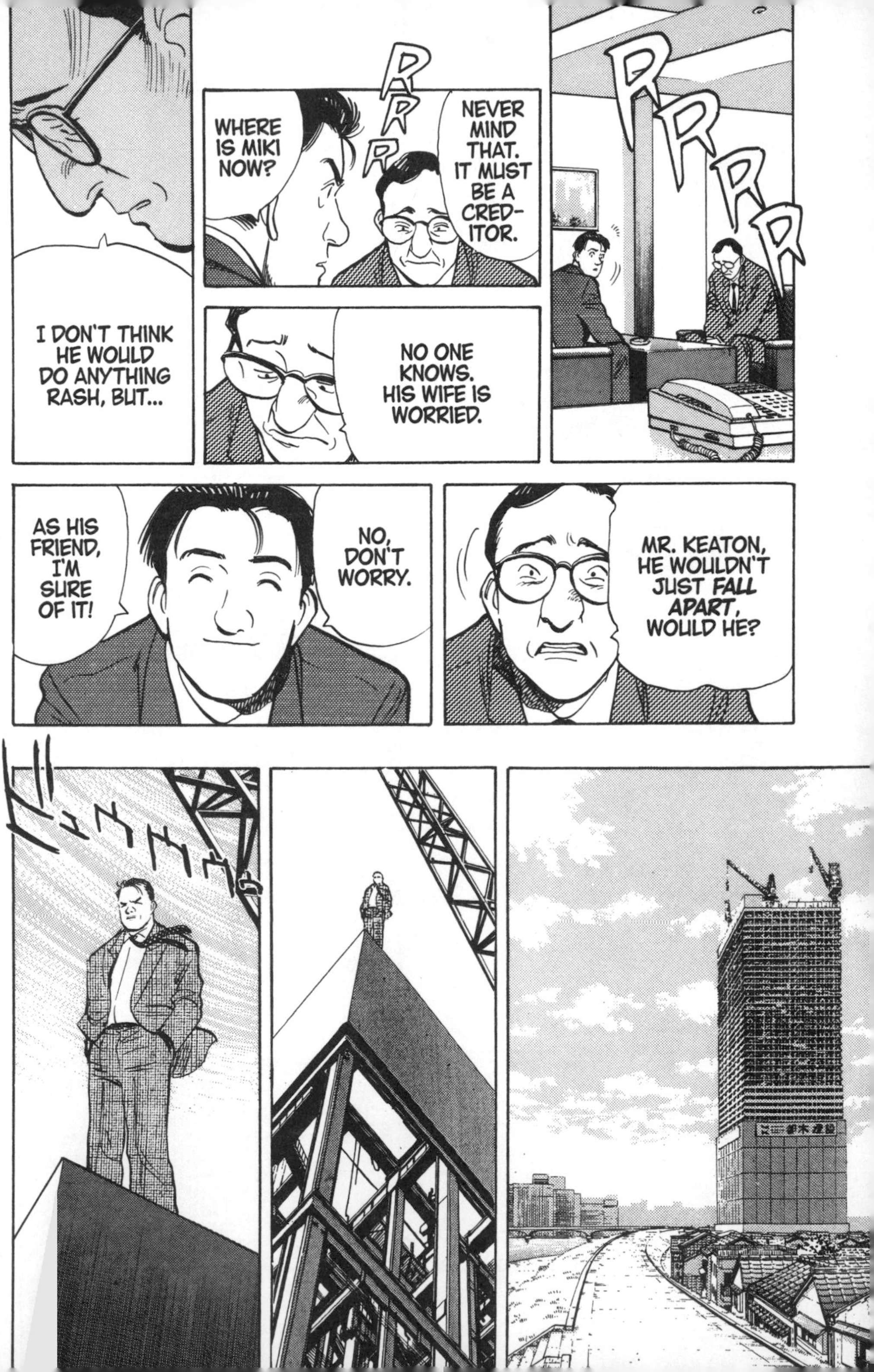
RRRR
NEVER MIND THAT. IT MUST BE A CRED-ITOR.
RRR
WHERE IS MIKI NOW?
NO ONE KNOWS. HIS WIFE IS WORRIED.
I DON'T THINK HE WOULD DO ANYTHING RASH, BUT...
MR. KEATON, HE WOULDN'T JUST *FALL APART*, WOULD HE?
NO, DON'T WORRY.
AS HIS FRIEND, I'M SURE OF IT!

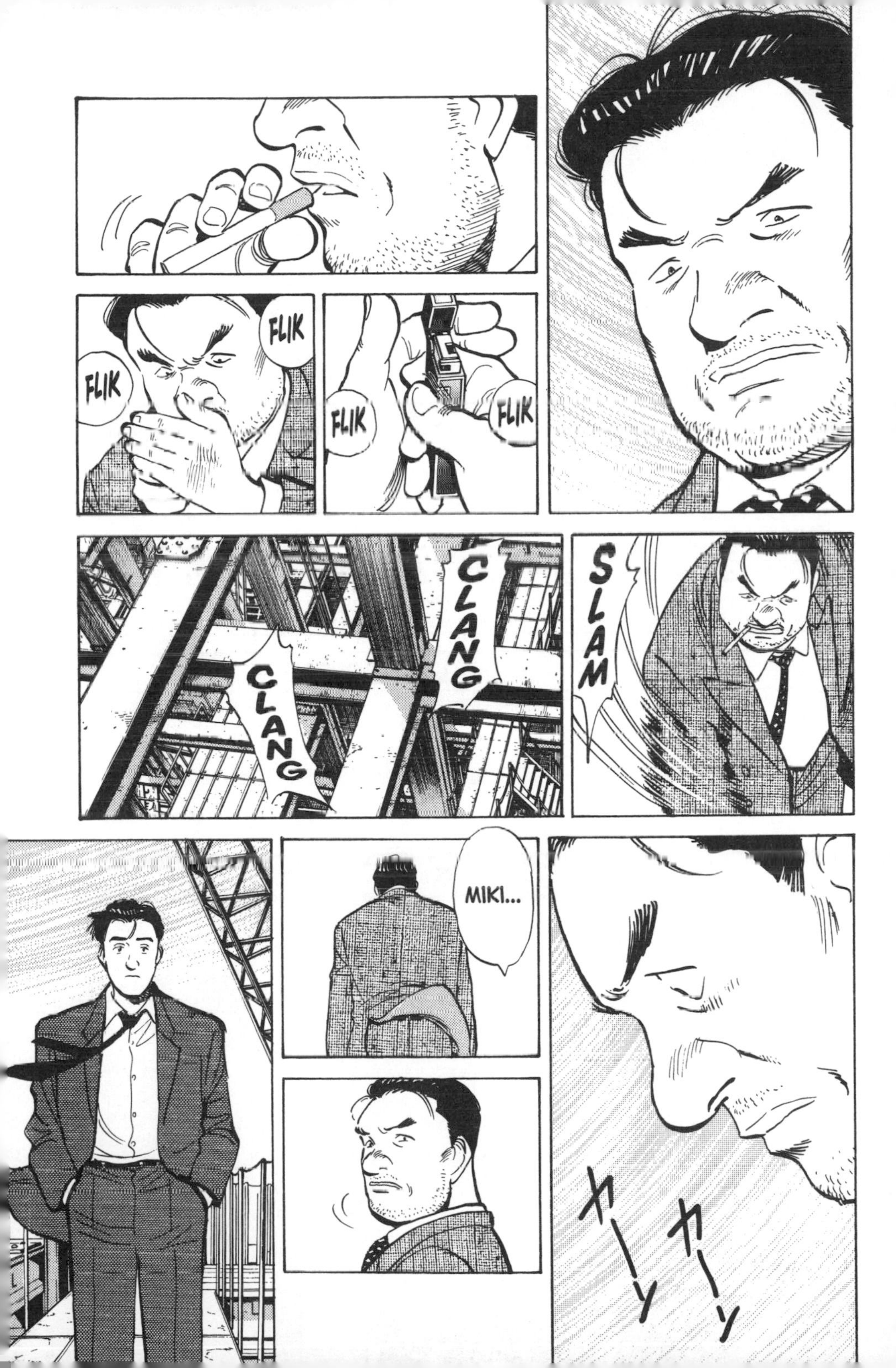
FLIK
FLIK
FLIK
FLIK
SLAM
CLANG
CLANG
MIKI...
カーン
カーン

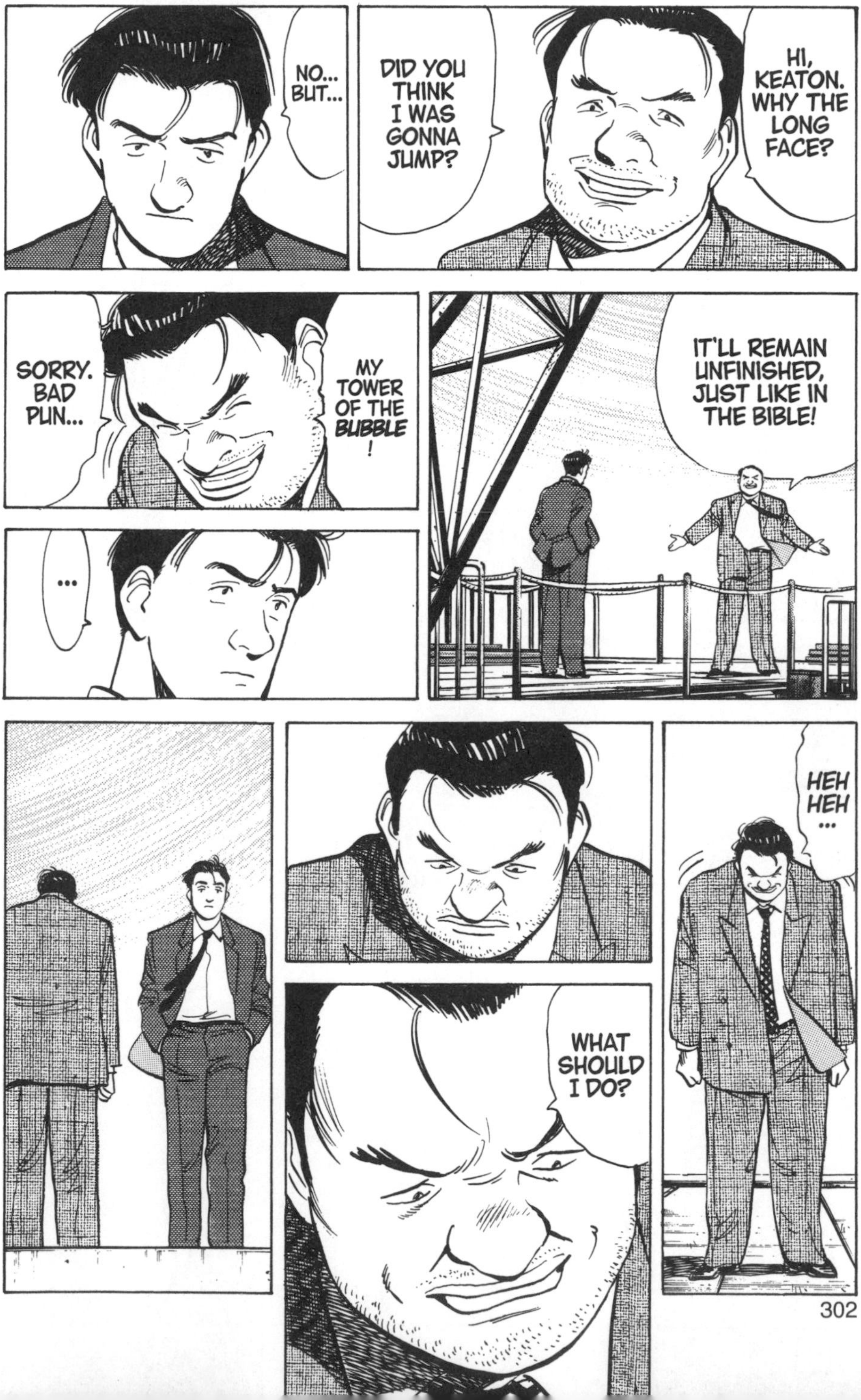
HI, KEATON. WHY THE LONG FACE?
DID YOU THINK I WAS GONNA JUMP?
NO... BUT...
IT'LL REMAIN UNFINISHED, JUST LIKE IN THE BIBLE!
MY TOWER OF THE *BUBBLE*!
SORRY. BAD PUN...
...
HEH HEH ...
WHAT SHOULD I DO?

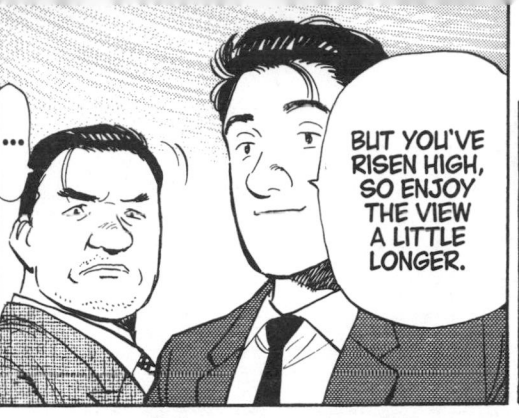

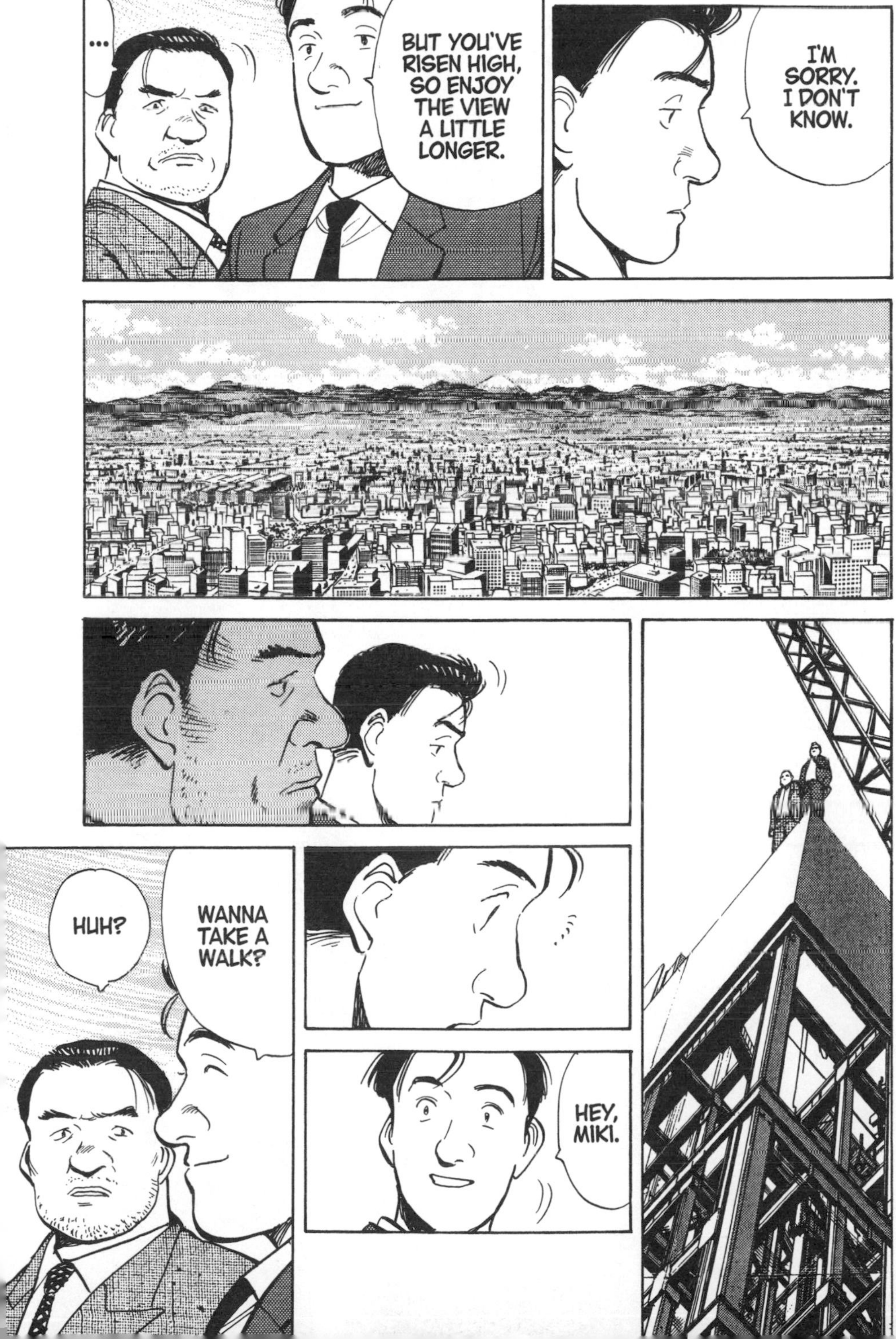
I'M SORRY. I DON'T KNOW.
BUT YOU'VE RISEN HIGH, SO ENJOY THE VIEW A LITTLE LONGER.
...
HEY, MIKI.
WANNA TAKE A WALK?
HUH?

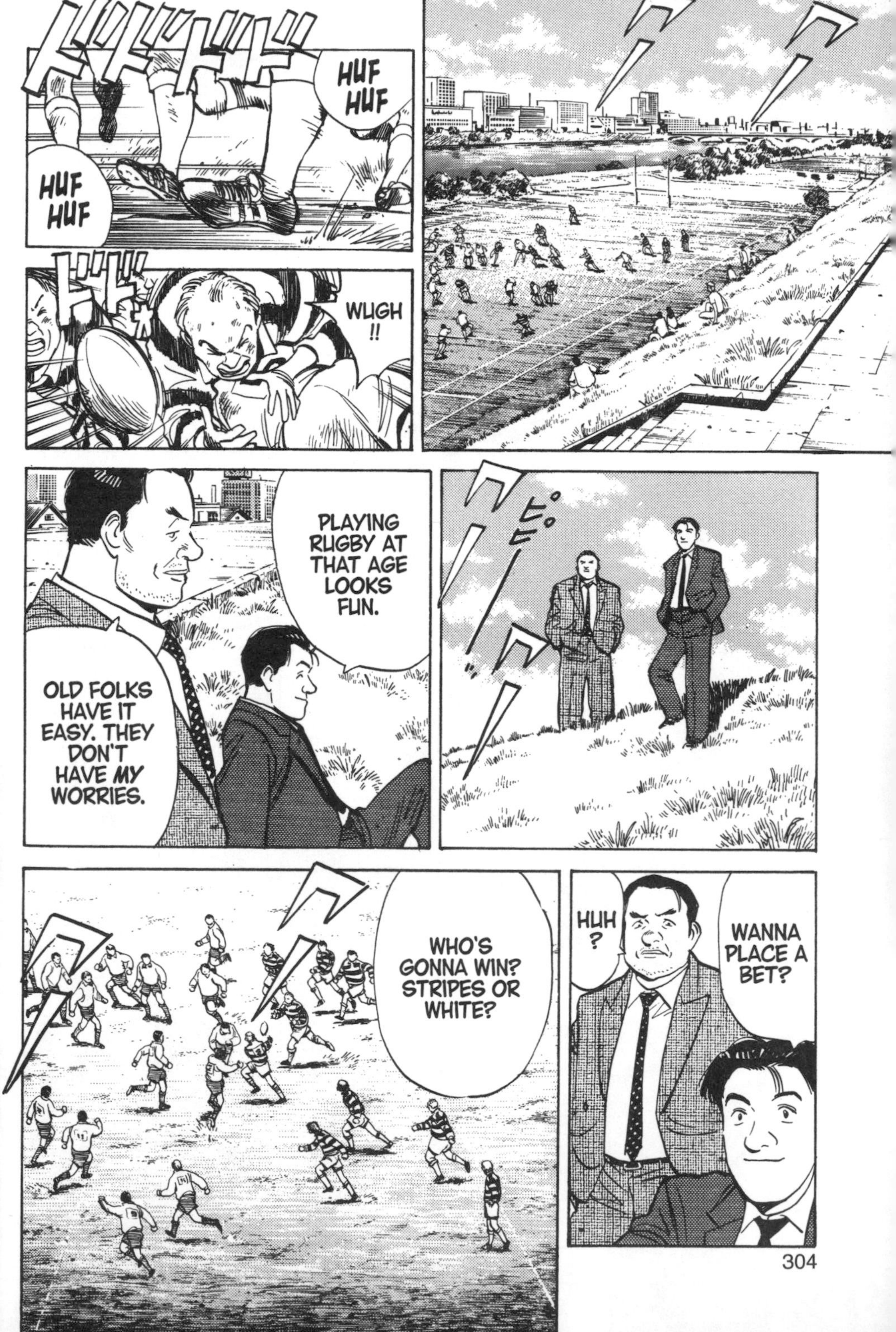
HUF HUF
HUF HUF
WUGH !!
PLAYING RUGBY AT THAT AGE LOOKS FUN.
OLD FOLKS HAVE IT EASY. THEY DON'T HAVE MY WORRIES.
WANNA PLACE A BET?
HUH ?
WHO'S GONNA WIN? STRIPES OR WHITE?

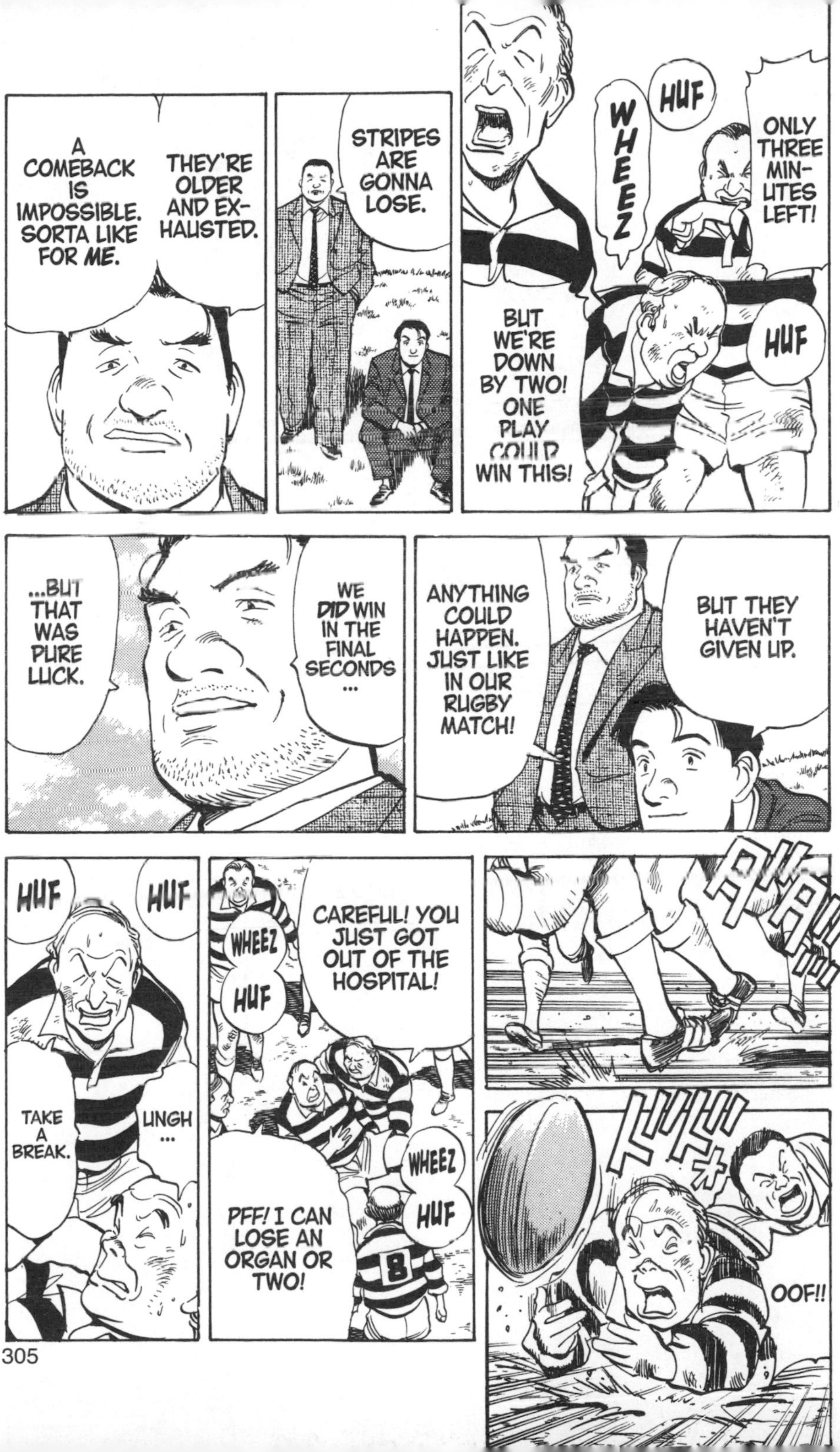
ONLY THREE MIN-UTES LEFT!
HUF
WHEEZ
HUF
BUT WE'RE DOWN BY TWO! ONE PLAY COULD WIN THIS!
STRIPES ARE GONNA LOSE.
THEY'RE OLDER AND EX-HAUSTED.
A COMEBACK IS IMPOSSIBLE. SORTA LIKE FOR ME.
BUT THEY HAVEN'T GIVEN UP.
ANYTHING COULD HAPPEN. JUST LIKE IN OUR RUGBY MATCH!
WE DID WIN IN THE FINAL SECONDS ...
...BUT THAT WAS PURE LUCK.
OOF!!
CAREFUL! YOU JUST GOT OUT OF THE HOSPITAL!
WHEEZ
HUF
WHEEZ
HUF
PFF! I CAN LOSE AN ORGAN OR TWO!
HUF
HUF
UNGH ...
TAKE A BREAK.

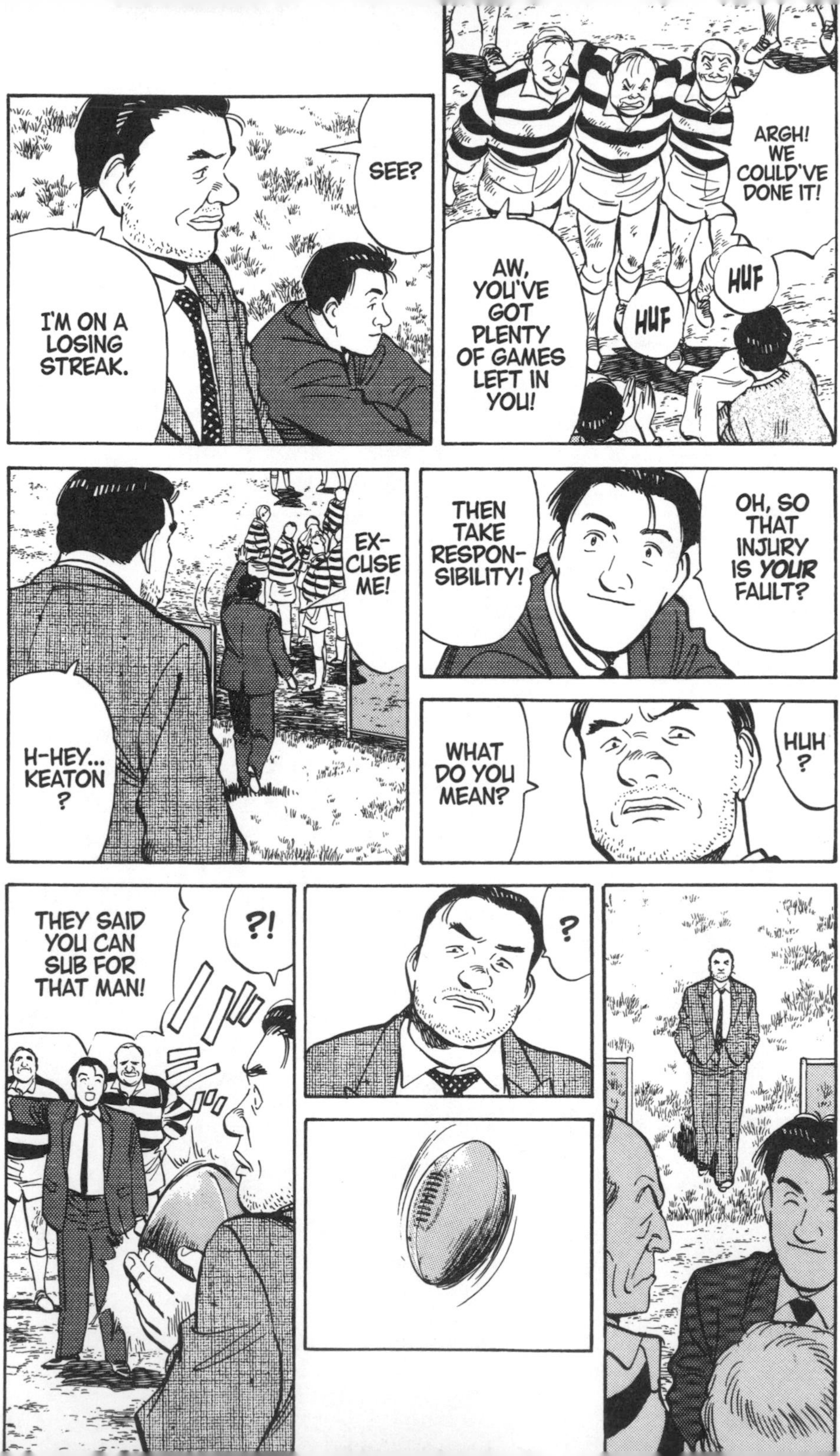
ARGH! WE COULD'VE DONE IT!
AW, YOU'VE GOT PLENTY OF GAMES LEFT IN YOU!
HUF
HUF
SEE?
I'M ON A LOSING STREAK.
OH, SO THAT INJURY IS *YOUR* FAULT?
THEN TAKE RESPONSIBILITY!
HUH?
WHAT DO YOU MEAN?
EX-CUSE ME!
H-HEY... KEATON?
?
?!
THEY SAID YOU CAN SUB FOR THAT MAN!

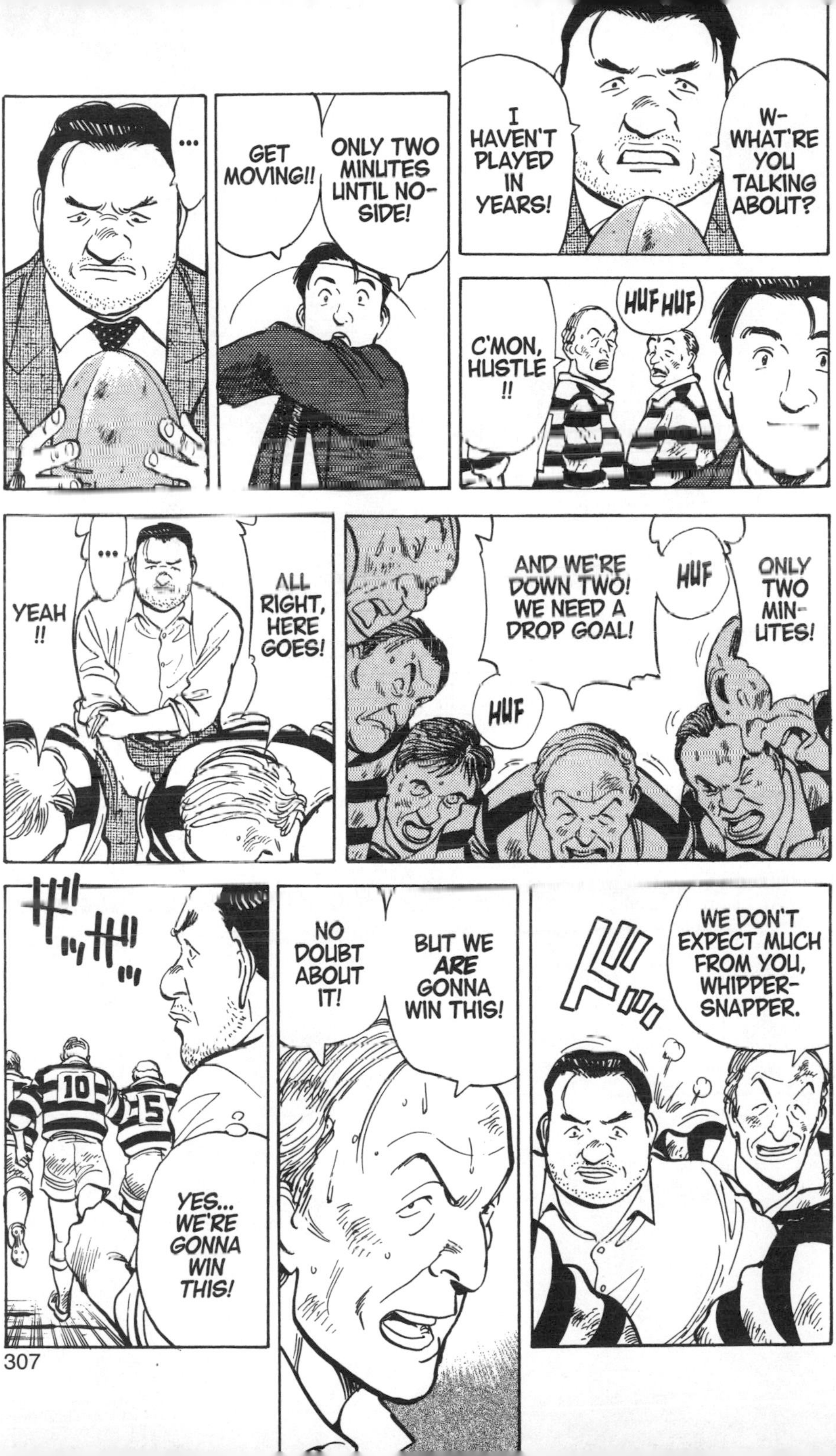
W-WHAT'RE YOU TALKING ABOUT?
I HAVEN'T PLAYED IN YEARS!
HUF HUF
C'MON, HUSTLE !!
ONLY TWO MINUTES UNTIL NO-SIDE!
GET MOVING!!
...
ONLY TWO MIN-UTES!
HUF
AND WE'RE DOWN TWO! WE NEED A DROP GOAL!
HUF
ALL RIGHT, HERE GOES!
...
YEAH !!
WE DON'T EXPECT MUCH FROM YOU, WHIPPER-SNAPPER.
BUT WE ARE GONNA WIN THIS!
NO DOUBT ABOUT IT!
YES... WE'RE GONNA WIN THIS!

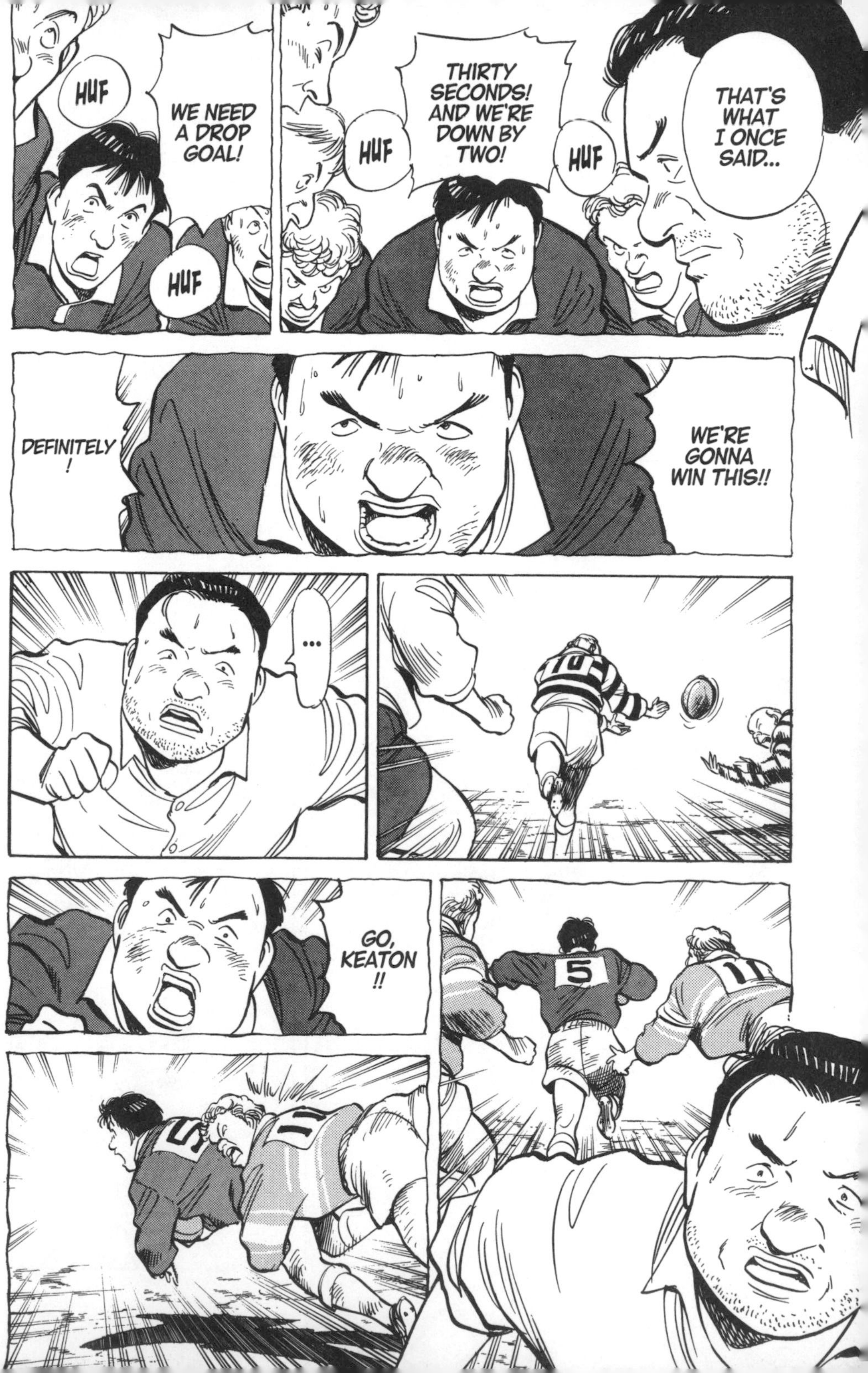
THAT'S WHAT I ONCE SAID...
HUF
THIRTY SECONDS! AND WE'RE DOWN BY TWO!
HUF
HUF
WE NEED A DROP GOAL!
HUF
WE'RE GONNA WIN THIS!!
DEFINITELY!
...
GO, KEATON!!

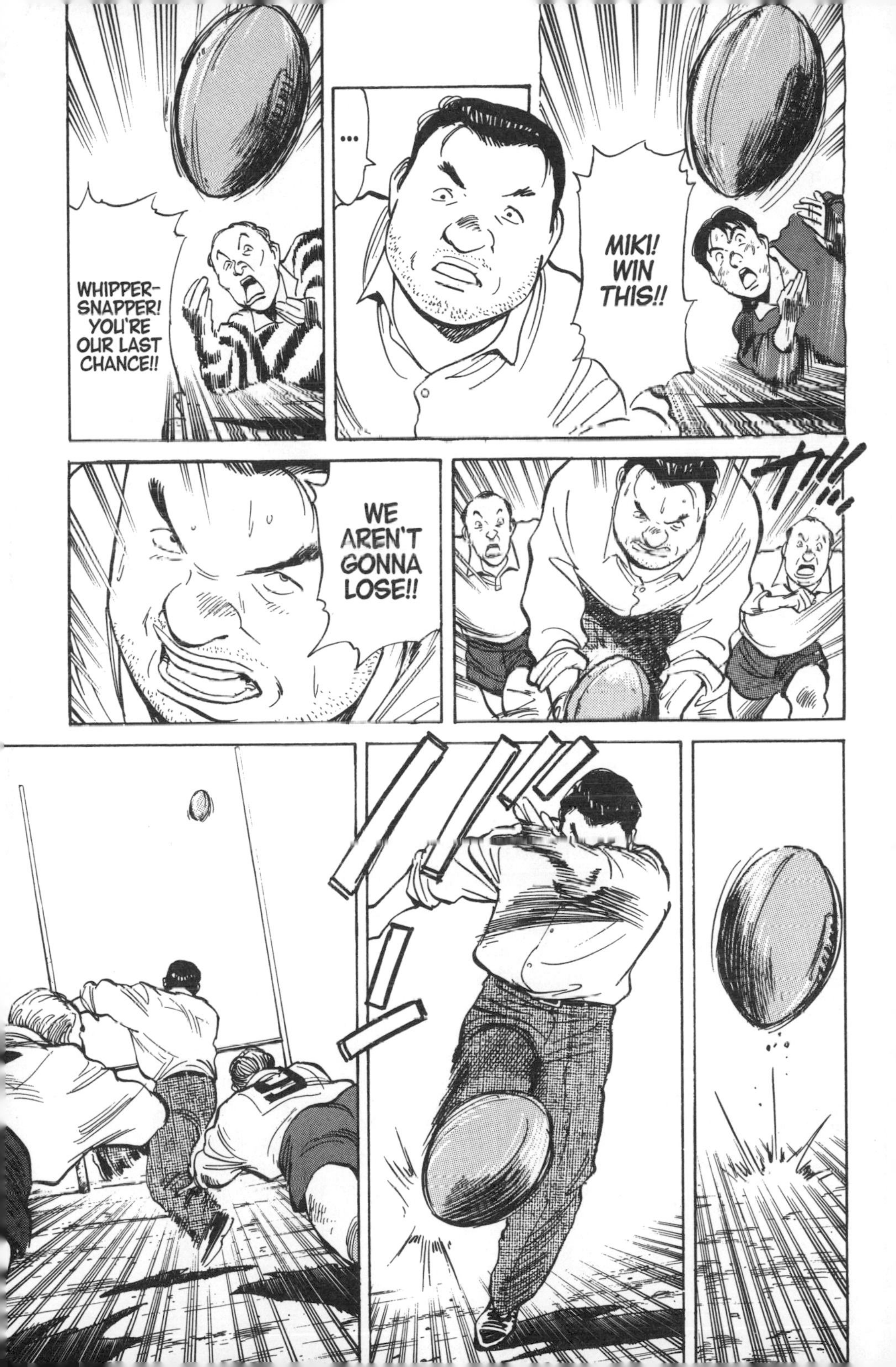
MIKI! WIN THIS!!
...
WHIPPER-SNAPPER! YOU'RE OUR LAST CHANCE!!
WE AREN'T GONNA LOSE!!

I GUESS TODAY... ISN'T LIKE BEFORE.

GO IN!!

MOM!

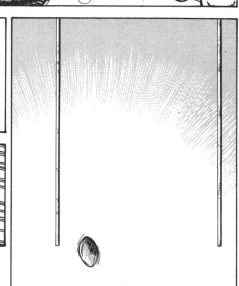

HE DID IT!!

HUF
HUF
NICE KICK!
EVEN IF IT WAS OUTSIDE THE BARS!
HUF
HUF
AW, DON'T LET LOSING GET YOU DOWN!
THE MORE YOU LOSE, THE SWEETER VICTORY TASTES!
WHIP-PER-SNAP-PER!
R-RIGHT...
GOOD GAME!
JOIN US AGAIN SOME-TIME!

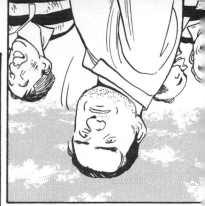

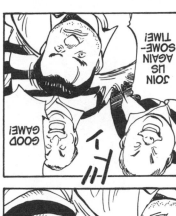

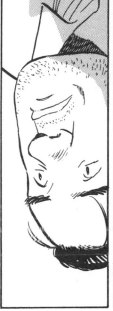

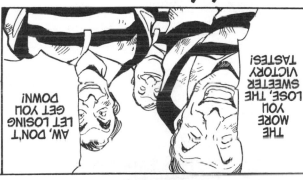

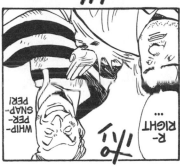

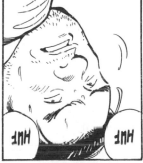

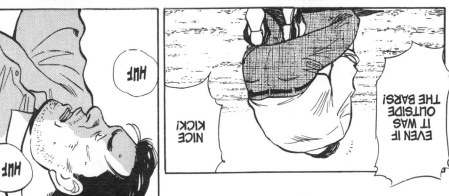

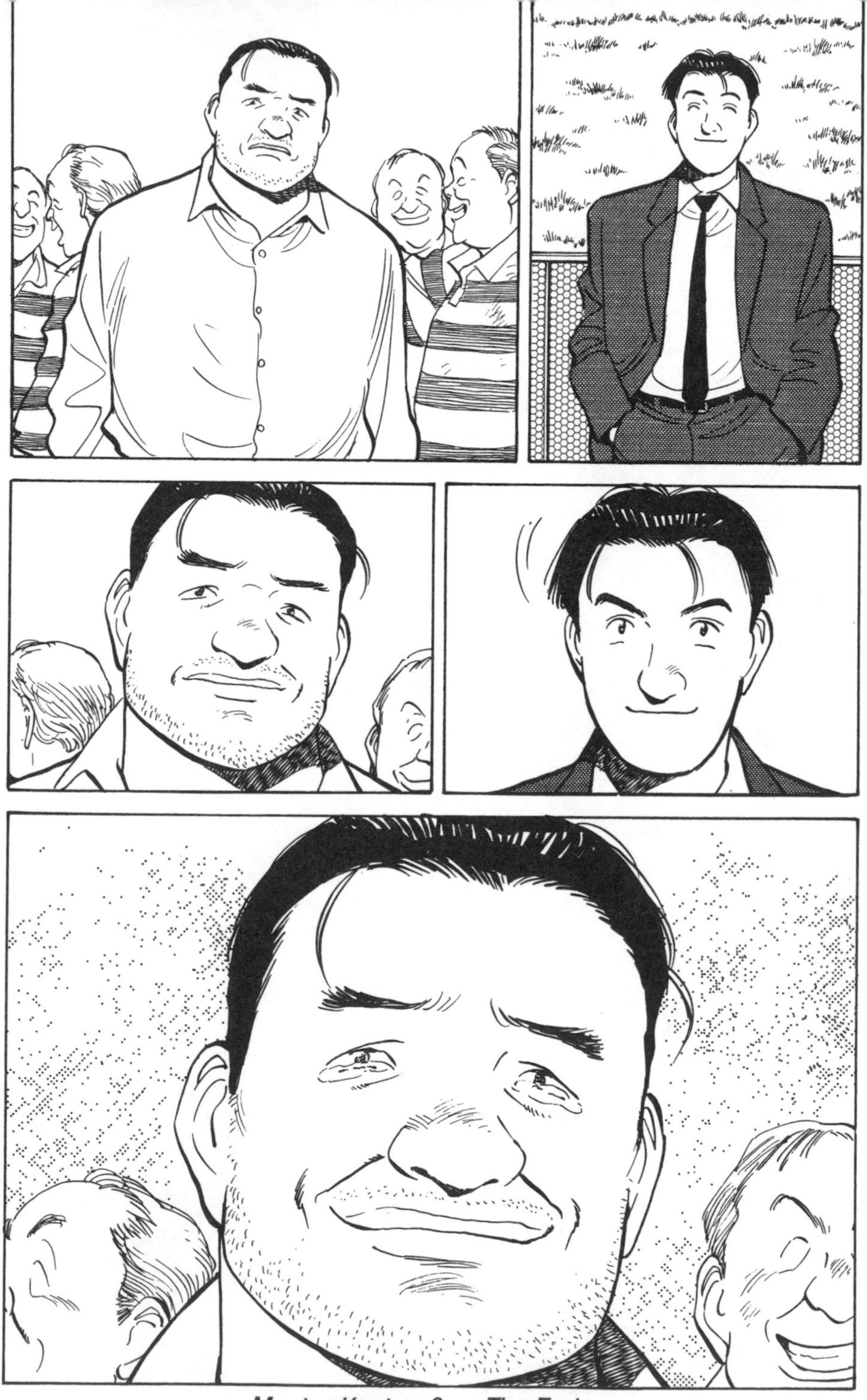

Master Keaton 9 —The End—

Sound Effects Glossary

The sound effects in *Master Keaton* have been preserved in their original Japanese format. To avoid additional lettering cluttering up the panels, a list of the sound effects (FX) is provided here. Each FX is listed by page and panel number. For example, "3.3" means the FX is on page 3, panel 3.

3.3 – vrrr (viiin: scooter moving)
3.7 – skiddd (gyagya: sliding)
4-5.5 – vrumm (dodododo: vehicle engine)
4-5.6 – revv (dorun: engine)
7.1 – vroom (dodododo: motorcycle roar)
7.2 – vroom (dododo: motorcycle roar)
7.4 – whoosh (buon: car zooming past)
7.5 – screech (gyagya: car braking)
8.4 – revv (dorun: engine revving)
8.5 – vroom (waun: motorcycle driving away)
8.6 – blam (don: gunshot)
8.7 – vroom (ooooo: motorcycle speeding away)
8.7 – blam blam (don don: gunshots)
10.4 – vroom put put (dorun do do: engine)
10.7 – vroom (dodododo: motorcycle roar)
11.1 – vroom (dodododo: motorcycle roar)
11.3 – vroom (dododododo: motorcycle roar)
12.8 – shatter (gashan: glass breaking)
13.1-2 – whsh (ba: ducking)
13.3 – tunk tunk (goton gatan: knocking over tables)
13.7 – blam blam (don don: gunshots)
13.8 – blam blam blam (don don don: gunshots)
14.1 – whok (bashi: hitting)
14.2 – tunk (dan: gun falling)
14.3 – kshak (ga: grabbing gun)
14.4 – fwip (ba: raising gun)
15.5 – psss (jojoo: urinating)
16.7 – revv (dorun: engine revving)
16.8 – vroom (dodododo: motorcycle roar)
17.6 – vroom (dodododo: motorcycle roar)
18.2 – vroom (dododododo: motorcycle roar)
19.5 – blam (don: gunshot)
19.6 – thud (dodada: falling)
21.1 – vroom (dodododo: motorcycle roar)
21.3 – revv (dorun: engine)
22.3 – blam (don: gunshot)
22.6 – shatter (gashan: mirror breaking)
22.10 – shup (za: crawling)
23.2 – kshak (gyakin: cocking)
24.1 – wham (gan: hitting)
24.4 – shwf shwf (ga ga: digging)
26.6 – kaboom (dogooon: explosion)
27.4-5 – flap flap flap flap flap flap flap flap flap (babababa babababababa: birds flying)
30.1 – blam (dokyuuuun: gunshot)
30.4 – stumble (gura: walking unsteadily)
30.5 – splash (basha: falling into water)
33.7 – rustle (basa: jostling newspaper)
50.3 – chak (batamu: door closing)
53.6 – tmp (za: footstep)
58.6 – rustle (zaza: movement in bushes)
60.1 – chatter chatter chatter chatter (zawa zawa zawa zawa: talking)
63.1 – flash (pika: lightning)
63.3 – rumble (gorogorogoro: thunder)
63.4 – tshhh (zaaa: rain)
69.3 – swoosh (zaza: something moving)
69.4 – swoosh (zaza: something moving)
73.2 – tmp (ta: footstep)
75.6 – chatter chatter (zawa zawa: talking)
75.8 – whsh (da: running)
76.3 – grp (ga: grabbing)
77.3 – vroom (buoon: vehicle driving off)
77.5 – swoosh (zaza: something moving)
77.6 – swoosh (zazaza: something moving)
77.8 – vroom (buoooo: vehicle moving)
78.3 – swoosh (za: something moving)
78.4 – whsh (ba: something moving)
78.5 – wham (gaan: landing on car)
78.6 – tmp (za: footstep)
79.4 – chatter chatter (zawa zawa: talking)
83.1 – hwish (byu: wind blowing)
92.3 – hwoo (byu: wind blowing)
93.4 – swish (hyu: paper airplane flying)
96.2 – shaa (zabaan: waves crashing)
96.5 – tik tok (kacchi kacchi: clock)
96.6 – tik tok (kacchi kacchi: clock)
96.7 – tik tok (kacchi kacchi: clock)
96.8 – tik tok (kacchi kacchi: clock)
97.1 – shaa (zabaan: waves crashing)
98.1 – krakk (ka: lightning)
98.2 – zshhh (zaaa: rain)
98.2 – rumble (gorogorogoro: thunder)
98.3-4 – zshhh (zaaa: rain)
99.8 – zshhh (zaaa: rain)
101.7 – bonk (kon: ball hitting)
102.6 – tmp (ta: footstep)
111.3 – blam blam (dokyuun dokyuun: gunshots)
111.5 – tmp (ba: running)
120.9 – chak (batan: door closing)
122.9 – whup (ba: tackling)
122.10 – thok (ga: hitting)
123.5 – whok (gan: hitting)
123.9 – tok tok (ton ton: hammering)
124.3 – wham (gan: hitting hand)
125.1 – whok (ga: kicking)
125.2 – wump (bashi: kicking)
125.3 – thok (doka: kicking)
125.4 – whok whok (doko ga: kicking)
126.2 – whok (doka: kicking)
126.7 – whok (ga: kicking)
127.9 – thok (gan: hitting)
128.1 – thud (dan: falling)
128.3 – whsh (da: moving quickly)
128.4 – blam (pan: gunshot)
128.9 – blam (pan: gunshot)
131.3 – krash (gashaan: window breaking)
131.4 – gwup (ga: grabbing)
131.5 – thwam (daan: tackling)
135.4 – whok thok smak (doka zuka bashi: beating up)
135.5 – stomp (gan: kicking)
136.1 – whok (doka: kicking)

136.5 – fwam (ban: throwing book)
138.1 – slam (ban: door closing)
138.5 – fshh (byu: arrow flying)
140.4 – thwip (byu: arrow flying)
140.5 – thok (kan: arrow hitting)
144.1 – whok (dogo: kicking)
144.2 – stomp whok (bashi gan: kicking)
144.3 – whok whok (ga doka: kicking)
144.5 – dash (da: running)
144.7 – bump (ga: colliding)
147.1 – dash (da: running)
147.2 – tromp (dododo: running)
147.4 – tromp (tatata: footsteps)
148.8 – wham (gon: hitting head)
150.3 – bam bam (don don: hitting the door)
155.6 – blam (don: gunshot)
156.5 – fshh (byu: arrow flying)
156.6 – blam (don: gunshot)
160.4 – ta-tmp (tatan: footsteps)
160.5 – fwsh (byu: moving fist quickly)
161.4 – ta-tmp (tatan: footsteps)
168.1 – tmp (da: running)
173.2 – hwsh (ba: horse jumping)
173.3 – clop (za: horse landing)
173.5 – trot (dodo: horse walking)
181.4 – blam (don: gunshot)
181.5 – wham (ga: kicking)
181.6 – ktak (gan: dropping gun)
185.2 – slam (dan: fist hitting desk)
188.3 – kchak (gacha: door opening)
189.9 – chak (batan: door closing)
195.8 – flap (ba: wings flapping)
198.4 – boom (bon: explosion)
198.7 – bam bam (don don: hitting the door)
200.5 – rrring (RRR: phone ringing)
202.2 – chak chak chak chak
(gata gata gata gata: standing up)
202.4 – chak (gata: standing up)
203.4 – grab (ga: restraining)
203.7 – stomp (da: walking away)
203.9 – slam (batamu: door closing)
204.1 – clap clap clap clap clap clap clap clap clap clap
(pachi pachi pachi pachi pachi pachi pachi pachi pachi pachi: clapping)
205.1 – chak (gata: standing up)
205.6 – whsh (da: moving quickly)
205.7 – tak tak tak (ka ka ka: footsteps)
208.3 – mrmr mrmr (zawa zawa: murmuring)
215.5 – screeech (gyagya: tires squealing)
215.7 – skiddd (gyagya: car swerving)
220.7 – wup wup (baba: sit-ups)
221.2 – dash (da: moving quickly)
222.3 – tmp (za: footstep)
222.5 – tmp (za: footstep)
228.9 – ktunk (gogo: moving chair)
237.1 – shwip (ki: tightening)
238.9 – chak (batamu: door shutting)
242.6 – slam (batan: door closing)
242.7 – bam bam (don don: hitting the door)
242.8 – bam bam (don don: hitting the door)
249.10 – rrring (RRR: phone ringing)
250.7 – clang bang (don gan: loud music)
250.8 – thrum hum (don gan: loud music)
254.8 – dash (da: running away)
256.8 – whsh (ba: moving away)
257.1 – wham (gan: hitting)
259.3 – clap clap clap clap
(pachi pachi pachi pachi: clapping)
267.6 – grp (ga: grabbing)
268.2 – fwsh (ba: throwing)
268.3 – thwud (gashaan: falling)
268.10 – hwoosh (hyu: throwing bag)
268.11 – splat (becha: bag hitting)
269.3 – swoof (ba: dog jumping)
269.6 – smush (dodo: dog walking)
269.8 – hwsh (hyu: apple flying)
269.9 – thonk (gon: hitting)
271.6 – chirp chirp (chun chun: birds singing)
272.1 – tmp tmp (dota dota: walking)
273.6 – bwsh (bun: swinging bat)
273.7 – gwup (ga: grabbing)
273.8 – thwam (dan: tackling)
274.7 – swuf (ba: removing cloth)
278.1 – shumf (dosa: setting down food)
278.10 – chak (batan: door closing)
280.2 – clomp (za: footsteps)
280.4 – whsh (ba: storming in)
280.5 – swup (zuru: slipping)
280.7 – thud fwam (zuden doon: falling)
280.8 – slip fumble (dota dota: struggling to rise)
281.1 – wham thok (bashi doka: fighting)
281.5 – tunk (bamu: car door closing)
281.6 – vroom (uiin: car speeding)
281.7 – vwoom (uon: car speeding)
282.1 – skidd (zaa: wheels spinning)
282.3 – wham (doka: crashing)
282.3 – swoosh (zazaa: sliding)
282.8 – hwoosh (hyun: bag flying)
283.1 – bomf (bafu: bag striking)
283.2 – blam blam (don don: gunshots)
283.4 – whoosh (dododo: dog running)
284.2 – klang (doon: cage falling)
288.1 – bomp (ban: ball bouncing)
288.2 – thadadum (dododo: footsteps)
288.2 – ta-tomp (dada: footsteps)
288.3 – thwomp (dodo: falling)
289.2 – kaklang vrrr babang
(gangan gagaga gakoon: construction)
290.1 – whooom (buoooo: truck speeding past)
291.5 – kaklang vrrr (gakoon gagaga: construction)
292.2 – tunk (bamu: car door closing)
292.3 – vroom (buon: car driving away)
292.5 – vrrr klang babang
(gagaga gakoon gagaan: construction)
293.2-3 – hwooo (byuooo: wind)
293.7 – tok tok gaklang
(kaan kaan gogoon: construction)
294.3 – klannnk (gakoon: construction)
297.4 – smack (pasha: hitting)
300.1 – rrring (RRRR: phone ringing)
300.2 – rrring (RRR: phone ringing)
300.9 – hwooo (byuuuu: wind)
301.7 – tink tonk (kaan kaan: lighter falling)
304.1 – raah raah (waa waa: cheers)
304.2 – tmp tmp tmp (dodododo: running)
304.3 – whomp (dodo: falling)
304.4 – raah raah (waa waa: cheers)
304.4 – fweet (pipii: whistle)

304.7 – raah raah (waa waa: cheers)
305.6 – tromp (dada: running)
305.7 – fwam (dodo: falling)
306.9 – fwup (pasha: catching)
307.7 – bwump (do: bumping)
307.9 – tmp tmp (za za: footsteps)
309.4 – shup (ga: catching)
309.7 – boomf (ban: kicking ball)
311.5 – smack (pon: hitting)
311.6 – bwump (don: bumping)
311.8 – ha ha ha (ha ha ha: laughing)

MASTER KEATON: THE PERFECT EDITION
Volume 9
VIZ Signature Edition

by NAOKI URASAWA
Story by HOKUSEI KATSUSHIKA, NAOKI URASAWA

Translation & English Adaptation/John Werry
Lettering/Steve Dutro
Cover & Interior Design/Yukiko Whitley
Editor/Amy Yu

MASTER KEATON Vol.9
by Naoki URASAWA, Hokusei KATSUSHIKA
© 1989 Naoki URASAWA/Studio Nuts, Hokusei KATSUSHIKA, Takashi NAGASAKI
All rights reserved.
Original Japanese edition published by SHOGAKUKAN.
English translation rights in the United States of America, Canada, the United Kingdom,
Ireland, Australia and New Zealand arranged with SHOGAKUKAN.
Original Art Direction by Kazuo UMINO
Original cover design by Mikiyo KOBAYASHI + Bay Bridge Studio

Printed in the U.S.A.

Published by VIZ Media, LLC
P.O. Box 77010
San Francisco, CA 94107

10 9 8 7 6 5 4 3 2 1
First printing, December 2016

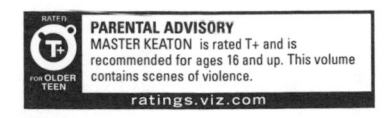

PARENTAL ADVISORY
MASTER KEATON is rated T+ and is
recommended for ages 16 and up. This volume
contains scenes of violence.
ratings.viz.com